Advanced Macroeconomics

To Rosie and Janet

Advanced Macroeconomics

A Primer

Patrick Minford

and

David Peel

Edward Elgar
Cheltenham, UK • Northampton, MA, USA

Published by
Edward Elgar Publishing Limited
Glensanda House
Montpellier Parade
Cheltenham
Glos GL50 1UA
UK

Edward Elgar Publishing, Inc.
136 West Street
Suite 202
Northampton
Massachusetts 01060
USA

A catalogue record for this book
is available from the British Library

Library of Congress Cataloguing in Publication Data
Minford, Patrick.
Advanced macroeconomics : a primer / Patrick Minford and D. Peel
p. cm.
Includes bibliographical references and index.
1. Macroeconomics. 2. Macroeconomics—Mathematical models. 3. Mathematical economics. 4. Rational expectations (Economic theory) 5. Economic policy. I. Peel, D. II. Title.

HB172.5 .M548 2002
339—dc21 2002021392

ISBN 1 84064 090 1 (cased)
1 84376 090 8 (paperback)

Printed and bound in Great Britain by MPG Books Ltd, Bodmin, Cornwall

Contents

Figures

Tables

Preface

The origin of this book lies in a book we wrote twenty years ago which aimed to explain the then new rational expectations revolution in macroeconomics. Since then macroeconomics has changed massively, adopting that revolution and building on it in a spectacular way. In this book we have attempted to take the story forwards to the present day and guide the student through what has become the conceptual and mathematical maze of modern macroeconomics. It is entitled 'Advanced Macroeconomics' because it is intended primarily for the postgraduate student — to guide this student from the beginning of the subject through to its most difficult reaches. But it is also 'a primer'; by this is meant, as when describing the grammar books of our schooldays, that it explains the basics of each topic but does not exhaustively go through the full gamut of models in each — rather it gives a grounding so that the student can then, fortified by the principles and a few examples, tackle more complex and detailed material in that area. What we have found from our experience of teaching the subject is that there is a gap in the textbook market between intermediate texts and texts that assume, like journal articles, already advanced knowledge. We have aimed this book at that gap.

It is our hope that parts of the book will also be useful for undergraduates, notably in their third year of economics. The chapters are organised in topics that are more or less self-contained, other than the requirement that the student has mastered the methods for solving rational expectations models set out in Chapter 2. Many of these topics are appropriate for teaching undergraduates who have done an intermediate course in macroeconomics. We ourselves have taught a fair amount of the material covered here in our third year macroeconomics courses.

A brief word on style: we follow the conventions of the Queen's English, in particular the use of the masculine as the default gender when both men and women are designated.

We gratefully acknowledge crucial help. Naveen Srinivasan has compiled a Manual of relevant exercises with worked answers: this can be downloaded from a link at www.patrickminford.com. James Davidson most kindly provided us with a template he developed for generating a book in Scientific Word. Bruce Webb generated the final LaTeX-typeset version, camera-ready, from our inelegant text and graphic inputs. We are particularly grateful to Sir Julian Hodge for his personal and financial support in setting up the Julian Hodge Institute of Applied Macroeconomics on whose resources we have extensively drawn.

Our students over many years have located errors in earlier editions and working versions of this book and also pointed out obscurities and gaps.

We thank them all, and last but not least our long-suffering wives to whom this book is dedicated.

Patrick Minford
David Peel

Part I

Models of the Economy

1

Macroeconomics: a succinct introduction

For many postgraduates macroeconomics is a totally new subject. For some undergraduates, it is useful to have a bird's eye view of the basics of the subject before plunging into more advanced material. This chapter therefore sketches in some basic elements of macroeconomics as a foundation for what follows. It takes nothing for granted except a knowledge of elementary microeconomics — essentially supply and demand. Macroeconomics is about the behaviour of whole economies but since these are made up of individuals and firms acting in the marketplace together with other institutions like governments that are responsible to individuals, it is natural to think of our understanding coming from microeconomics which analyses how people interact in a particular market and build up the whole economy from there. That is how the 'classical' economists — those who wrote before John Maynard Keynes — naturally analysed the economy. While their thinking was for a long time overlaid by the work of Keynes and his followers, in recent times it has once again become the core of our macroeconomic analysis; we shall begin with the early classical thinking, then sketch in the ideas of Keynes and of his later followers, before building up the modern macroeconomic theory that rests essentially on classical foundations with some extra elements drawn from Keynes' work. This approach, via a short history of macroeconomic thought, is the easiest way, experience shows, to reach an understanding of modern thought. (Students may like to consult a good intermediate textbook such as Parkin and Bade, *Modern Macroeconomics*, any edition, in conjunction with this chapter.)

THE CLASSICAL MODEL

The natural starting point for macroeconomics is the classical model, where it is assumed that prices and wages are flexible as in the familiar microeconomic model of a market with supply and demand. The difference from that model is that supply and demand are for the aggregate of all agents in the economy — it is assumed that one can meaningfully aggregate up or average the behaviour of all in this way; implicitly we assume that when income or activity is redistributed across people or firms the average is not much affected so that we can focus on the average forces affecting the economy rather than on their distribution across agents. Aggregate supply in this theory depends on technology, preferences and relative prices. Demand depends on the quantity of money and on incomes.

Supply

Figure 1.1 shows four quadrants, bottom left is the labour market, top left the production function, top right a 45° graph transferring output through to the bottom right, which is the supply curve between the price level and output.

The production function, PF, which can be thought of as the optimal behaviour of the average firm times the number of firms, takes capital as given and hence shows diminishing returns of output (Q) to increasing labour input (L). From it is derived the demand for labour, DD, where (for the average firm) the real wage equals the marginal product of labour, or equivalently the price = marginal cost, the first-order condition of a profit maximum. The supply of labour, SS, is shown with a flattish slope, indicating that the substitution effect of rising real wages, $\frac{W}{P}$, is substantially larger than the income effect; this could come about because either workers substitute effort across time or unemployment benefits are generous and long-lasting (as discussed below, respectively, in Chapters 3 and 9).

Two aggregate supply, AS, curves are shown. One is vertical, indicating that if all prices (P) rise the supply of and demand for labour will not change since wages (offered and demanded) will rise in proportion, and so with relative prices the same there is no inducement to alter offers. The second curve is upward sloping; the reason is that as prices rise people do not realise that all prices are rising (inflation). Workers in particular do not realise this and in this diagram are assumed to be slow therefore in raising their wages. Hence as prices rise wages lag behind and real wages fall to the right along the demand for labour curve (this

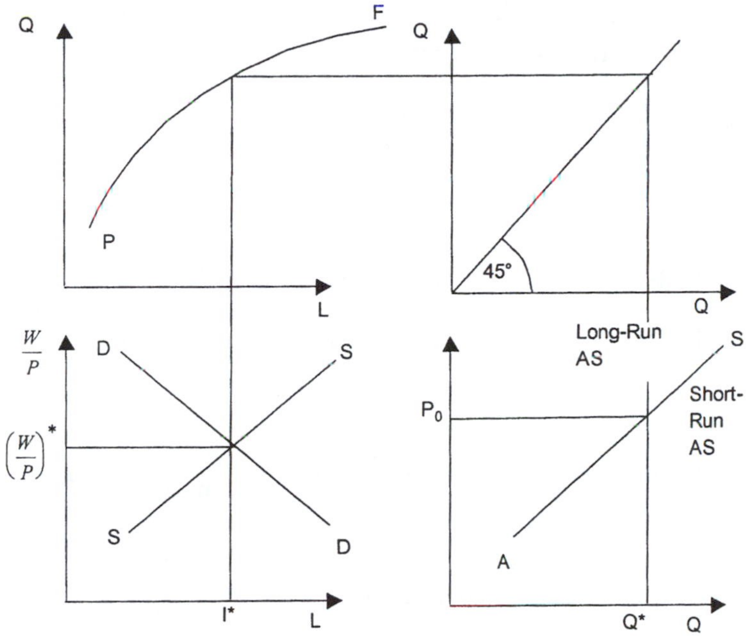

Figure 1.1: Aggregate Supply

can be thought of as a rightward shift of the labour supply curve). This generates more employment and more output (this is developed fully in Chapter 3, first section, 'The New Classical Phillips Curve').

Demand

We suppose for simplicity an economy where there is no alternative to using cash for paying workers and for buying goods. In this 'cash-in-advance' transactions technology, we also assume there is a payment period, one month for example. Then the economy 'turns money over' as illustrated in Figure 1.2).

At the end of the month workers are paid and spend their cash through the succeeding month. As cash moves from workers to firms the total holding of it remains constant — this is the demand for cash for transactions. If we measure money output, PQ, in a year or at an annual rate, it follows that cash required is equal to one month's output and so the demand for money, $M^D = (1/12) \times PQ$ (where 1/12 is the fraction of output required as money, K) or equivalently $M^D \times 12 = PQ$

(where 12 is the 'velocity', V, of money); respectively the Cambridge (UK) and the quantity theory ways of writing money demand.

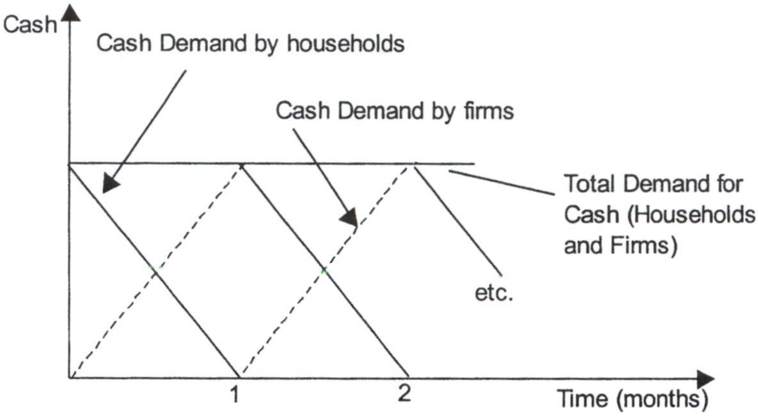

Figure 1.2: Transactions Demand for Money

Begin by supposing that the money supply M equals M^D, that is there is equilibrium in the money market. Under our assumptions this also implies that income equals spending (as in figure 1.2). Now suppose the government increases the money supply by 10 per cent (by printing more) and gives the extra money to workers at the end of the month. At existing $PQ(0)$ the workers plan normal spending of $PQ(0)$ which is their normal income and firms need to pay out only PQ(0) in wages; so neither workers or firms need to hold on to the extra money for future months. The workers will therefore spend the extra money on buying goods, driving up PQ along the AS curve. At this point $PQ(1)$ is higher; firms hold more money to pay for extra work. But when M returns to consumers, still $M^S > M^D$ and again $AD > PQ(1)$. Hence the process will repeat itself and PQ will rise again. Only when PQ has risen sufficiently for $M^S = M^D = \frac{PQ}{V}$ will we have $AD = PQ$. This is where $PQ = MV$. This is the 'aggregate demand' consistent with the stock of money (Figure 1.3).

In classical thinking prices and wages move rapidly to restore the economy to its potential, Q^*; hence interest rates move to ensure that saving equals investment — for example, if at Q^* people decide to save more this would mean more funds would be offered to investors in plant and machinery and interest rates (the cost of these 'loanable funds') would fall until the market for savings equilibrated with investments. So we can say that interest rates are not affected by the demand for or

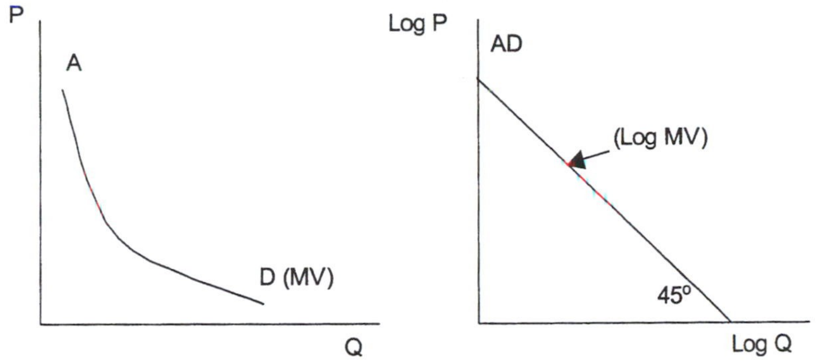

Figure 1.3: Aggregate Demand

supply of money, they are merely a (small) factor in determining the demand for money. Figure 1.4 illustrates the market for loanable funds.

Short- and long-run equilibrium in the classical system in response to a monetary expansion can be summarised by Figure 1.3. In the short run output rises because wages lag behind, but in the long run output is driven back to Q^* as wages rise in response to workers' realization that it is general prices that are rising.

To allow for the effect of government spending, G, and taxation, T, we simply note that $T - G$ is part of savings, viz. savings by government; while private savings are now $PQ - T - C$. So total savings are $T - G + PQ - T - C = PQ - G - C$. Hence for example a rise in government spending, taxes constant, would shift the SS curve in Figure 1.4 leftwards and raise interest rates; it would not raise output even in the short run. (It could do so indirectly via the effect of higher interest rates on the demand for money, a factor we introduce in the next section — by reducing this demand it would shift the aggregate demand curve outwards. However this effect is likely to be quite small, since the transactions demand for money is rather inelastic.)

Allowing money to respond to interest rates: the Wicksellian mechanism

We have assumed up to now that interest rates have a negligible effect on the demand for money, and that therefore we could treat the market for money and bonds as essentially unconnected. But this can only be a stringent simplifying assumption. In fact interest rates do affect the demand for money because people and firms can put their money into

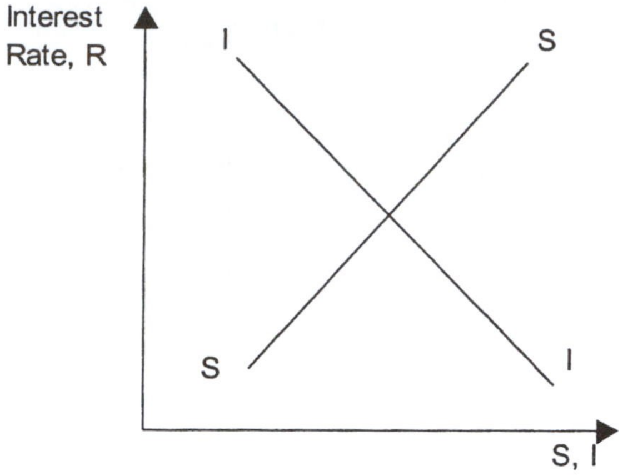

Figure 1.4: Supply and demand for loanable funds

deposits (short-term bonds or loans, in other words) as an alternative to continuously holding the money they will eventually need for transactions. Households can, for example, deposit half their month's wages for the first half of the month and then withdraw them half-way through the month in time to carry out the second half of the month's transactions; firms can in turn deposit their takings from the first half of the month and then withdraw them at the end of the month, just in time to pay the wages. This is illustrated in Figure 1.5. Clearly people decide whether to carry out this deposit strategy by weighing up the cost versus the benefit: the cost is making two trips to the bank or loan market (one to deposit, one to withdraw) per month; the benefit is the interest received. The higher the interest rate the more people may decide to deposit; for example, households could deposit three-quarters of their wages and then withdraw a quarter after week 1, a quarter after week 2, and the last quarter after week 3, while similarly firms could deposit all their first three weeks' takings and withdraw them at the end of the month — making four trips in all for both firms and households. We now find that the demand for money falls with higher interest rates, with the demand for deposits moving in the opposite direction — imagine Figure 1.5 with twice as frequent deposits and withdrawals, implying that the demand for money is half as much again as in the figure.

Now that we have linked the two markets the question arises: what happens when extra money is printed and, say, distributed to households in our previous experiment? Previously we said that households and

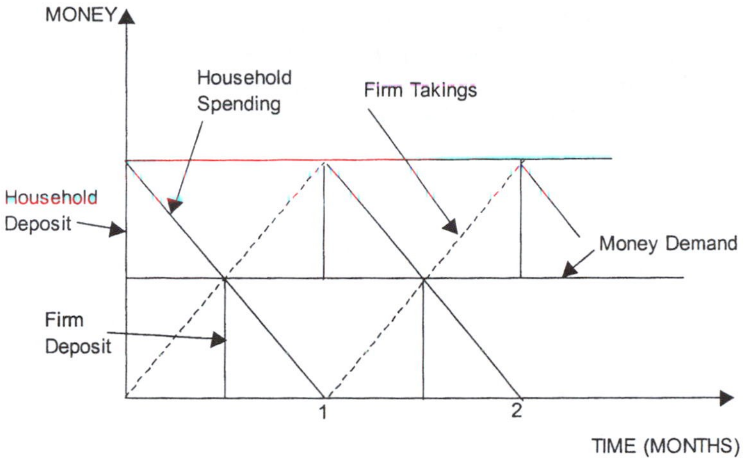

Figure 1.5: Money demand when money is deposited/withdrawn once per month

firms would spend any money surplus to their transactions needs. But now we would argue that they would put the extra money on deposit mainly, perhaps only spending a very small part of it; the reason would be that they would naturally wish to spread out the extra spending over a long period, given that they can now deposit it and obtain interest while waiting to spend it.

If they do this, then as the Swedish economist Knut Wicksell pointed out (Wicksell, 1970), in a way that foreshadowed Keynes' views of asset markets and demand, the depositing of the extra money would act indirectly to create excess demand by stimulating investment and reducing saving (stimulating consumption). Before the money injection, savings were equal to investment and hence demand for output was equal to supply of output: $S = I$ implies that $S = PQ - C - G = I$ so that $C + I + G = PQ$ that is demand equals output (as supplied along the AS curve). He thought of this situation as one where interest rates were at their 'natural' level: namely such as both to clear the loanable funds market and to set demand for output equal to supply of output.

But after the injection interest rates fall below this natural level, stimulating consumption and investment above these levels, and so creating excess demand. This would drive up prices or output in just the same way as we described before when we did not allow people to deposit their money. Aggregate demand would rise until the demand for money rose to the new level of money supply, at which point of course interest rates would return to their natural level as the injection of excess money into the loanable funds market would cease (see Figure 1.6). This mechanism of 'monetary transmission' via interest rates is close to what Keynes proposed and what we think today.

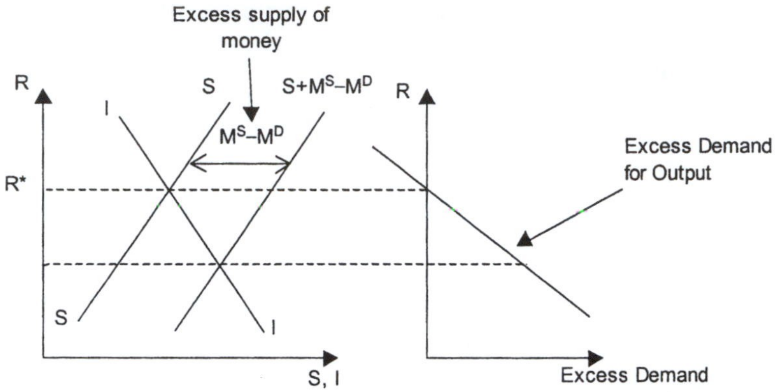

Figure 1.6: Wicksell's monetary transmission

We can think of the central bank carrying out monetary policy by 'open market operations' in the bond market which inject more or less money into the economy; for example, by buying bonds, the bank supplies extra loanable funds to the the bond market, shifting the SS curve rightwards by printing extra money. This drives down interest rates, creates a gap between investment and saving, that is, excess demand for output. In the following period the extra money has entered private sector holdings but being surplus to money demand is put back into the loanable funds market, keeping interest rates down until the excess demand has driven up PQ sufficiently to raise demand for money to equality with the extra supply.

We can also analyse what would happen if demand for money fell — say for the reason discussed above where people decide to take advantage of the interest rate opportunities from depositing (that is lending) their money. The surplus money would go into the loanable fund market like the extra money printed by the central bank just discussed; triggering the same process whereby PQ must rise until the available money supply is willingly held.

The algebra of the Classical system is:

Production function: $Q = f(L)$

Demand for Labour: $W/P = f'(L)$

Supply of Labour: $L = g(W/P^E) - P^E$ (the price level expected by workers) in the short run is assumed to lag behind the actual price level.

Aggregate Demand: $M.V(R) = PQ$ (this assumes that monetary disequilibrium has already been eliminated by the Wicksell process).

Loanable Funds: $S(R,\ PQ) = I(R)$

THE KEYNESIAN MODEL

The ideas of Keynes are best understood as a special case, or a degenerative distortion, of the classical model — created by assuming that wages and prices are inflexible. Nowadays we try to rationalise this assumption by referring to nominal wage contracts and 'menu costs' of raising prices. But neither Keynes nor his post-war followers did so: they simply pointed to the facts of wage and price rigidity and said that non-economic factors (such as conventions of fairness, policed by unions among others) could be responsible.

The simplest framework, which we will use here, assumes that both wages and prices are rigid — that is to say, are set by suppliers who thereby state their willingness to supply whatever is demanded at those rates. From time to time they may change them — in response to excess demand or supply, or to general inflation — but that does not alter the point that whatever they have set their supply is driven by the demand they face. It is natural to assume in the Keynesian model that wages are governed by bargaining between workers or unions and firms and that prices are set by firms operating in imperfect competition (where each firm has a different product and some short-run 'monopoly power' — that is a downward-sloping demand curve for its product). These assumptions imply price- and wage-setting behaviour (whereas perfect competition, for example, where wages and prices are given to the individual, would not).

With prices set in this way plainly demand sets output — in microeconomics we would say that the supply curve is horizontal. Keynes (and his co-workers, including Richard Kahn) evolved a theory of demand feedback which he called the 'multiplier'; the idea is illustrated on the 'Keynesian cross' diagram, Figure 1.7. Consumption, C, depends on income (= output); other demand is treated as exogenous — notably investment, I, which is mainly dependent on businessmen's optimism ('animal spirits'). Without government, aggregate demand, $AD = C+I$, therefore rises with income — the AD curve which slopes at an angle less than 45°. However, output is set by producers equal to demand; hence $Q = AD$ — the 45° line. Realistically Keynes thought of this output as responding with a lag to demand (initially orderbooks or inventories would respond). Output would go on moving until $Q = AD$, yet of course AD would respond (feedback) to changing Q. The two would settle down where the two curves intersected (Figure 1.7).

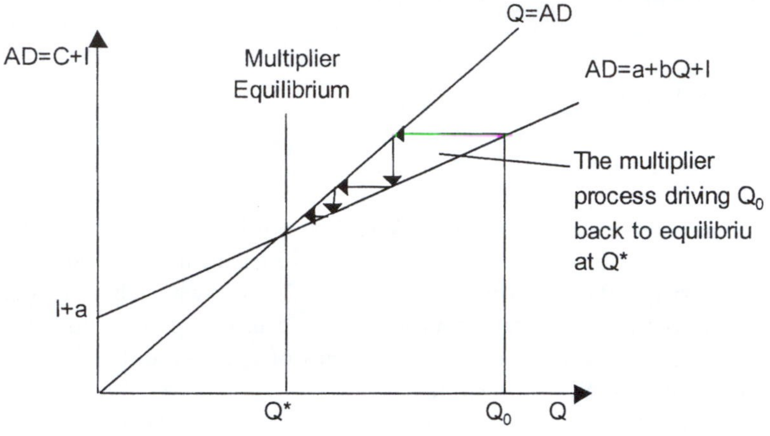

Figure 1.7: The Keynesian Cross

The algebra is:

$$C_t = a + bQ_t$$
$$AD_t = C_t + I$$
$$Q_t = AD_{t-1}$$

The equilibrium of this, where $AD = Q =$ constant, is found by setting Q and AD constant and solving the equations: $Q = (a+I)/(1-b)$. $1/(1-b)$ is the multiplier.

This set-up can be extended to allow for government: its spending, G, is exogenous and its taxation can be represented by a simple proportional tax rate, τ. This means that in Figure 1.7, I now becomes $I + G$ and that the slope of the AD curve is flatter because now extra income is partly taxed and does not have such a large effect on consumption. Algebraically:

$$\begin{aligned} C_t &= a + bQ_t[1-\tau] \\ AD_t &= C_t + I + G \\ Q_t &= AD_{t-1} \end{aligned}$$

The multiplier is now $1/[1 - b(1 - \tau)]$, smaller than before.

The IS curve

We now notice that when $Q = AD$ we also have savings (as planned — that is consistent with the consumption function above) equal to investment (as planned exogenously above) since it implies that $Q - C - G = I$. (Q is income, C is private consumption and G is government consumption; it is usual to include government investment in I.)

In passing, we should not be confused by the fact that in the short run savings can be unplanned (for example, when income rises it may take time to adjust spending) and also investment can be unplanned (for example, when demand falls inventories may increase as it takes time to adjust output; the rise in these inventories is included in actual investment). It is also a confusing fact that by the conventions of national accounting actual savings are always equal to actual investment because output minus actual spending = rise in inventories, DV by definition; therefore Q = actual consumption + G + investment in plant and machinery minus DV = actual $C + G +$ actual I. Hence $Q -$ actual $C - G =$ actual I. This, however, is an identity with no behavioural significance, unlike in the above paragraph.

In the Keynesian model planned savings = planned investment when output has settled down. Thus we would say that output is what drives them to equality, not interest rates as in the classical system. What then do interest rates do? According to Keynes they affect demand and so output — they merely change the output level at which savings are driven to equality with investment. (Unlike the classical system where output is driven to potential by supply via prices moving, and interest rates then drive savings to equality with investment.) Interest rates affect demand straightforwardly: as they rise consumption and investment fall because of the higher cost of borrowed funds and return to saving.

The result is a shift in the AD curve in the Keynesian cross diagram; we can plot the different Q equilibria as interest rates shift the curve. This is the IS curve, that is the curve showing how output changes with interest rates given that the goods (output) market is in equilibrium or equivalently that planned $S=$ planned I (Figure 1.8).

The LM curve

But how are interest rates determined? In the classical system by savings (supply of funds) and investment (demand for funds) clearing the market for loanable funds; but in Keynes' system savings and investment

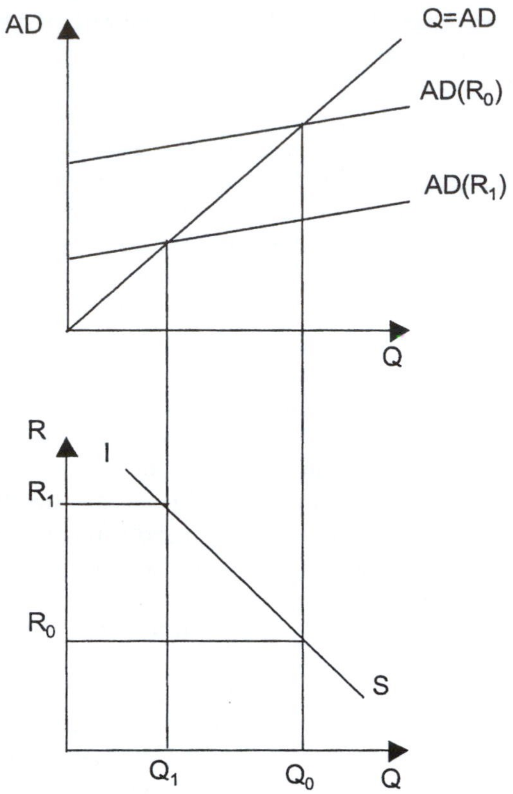

Figure 1.8: The *IS* curve

determine output (also affected by interest rates through their effect on savings and investment). But interest rates are not pinned down — the *IS* curve shows that instead they can vary, and as they do so output will also vary. So what pins them down?

In the classical world the market for money is cleared by income in the short run and then rather quickly by prices. This does not happen in Keynes' world. Prices are fixed or moving slowly in response to price setters' strategies. Output (income) is responding to aggregate demand which has nothing directly to do with the demand for money; it is certainly not moving to make demand for money equal to its supply. We must now ask what is happening in the money market.

Keynes took over the classical analysis of demand for money above but he also emphasised the alternatives to holding money (defined as non-interest-bearing cash): these were short-term or long-term 'bonds', that is loans. If we divide the world into private and public sectors, this meant that the private sector holding money (a liability of the government) could also hold public loans as an alternative. The commercial banks are assumed to be subject to government regulation (for example, by reserve ratios) and their deposits are usually treated as equivalent to cash; so cash and non-interest-bearing deposits are 'money'. Besides holding this money for transactions, private people and firms might hold it because they wanted to get out of bonds for speculative reasons: if interest rates were low (bond prices high), people would expect bond prices to fall back and so hold more cash and vice versa when interest rates were high (bond prices low). Private sector financial wealth in a closed economy is by definition equal to the value of public (and banking) sector liabilities, money, M and government bonds, B.

Holdings of equities are what firms issue to households as paper claims to the capital stock which of course households own; these equities have to be held by someone and so their price moves until they are willingly held by households. But note that as they are a liability of firms they cancel out within the private sector and hence do not constitute a financial asset for the private sector as a whole. So there is no way the private sector can move out of bonds and money into equities; all that would happen if they tried is that the equity price would go up to frustrate them. That equity price may have implications for the rest of the economy (for example, if it is high, it implies that expected returns on the capital stock are high and so investment is likely to increase); but as far as the market for bonds and money are concerned it has no implications of any importance as we shall see.

The total financial wealth of the private sector, consisting as we have seen of money and bonds, has therefore to be held either as money or bonds:

$$M + B = M^D + B^D$$

Hence when $M = M^D$, $B = B^D$. In other words the market for money is the mirror image of the market for bonds, as illustrated in Figure 1.9).

Hence interest rates are determined by the 'stock markets' in Keynes' model: specifically the markets for government stock (or equivalently the 'market for money'). Here we see that as output is driven higher or lower by the IS curve (the multiplier process) the demand for money moves higher or lower with it for transactions reasons; and this in turn drives interest rates higher or lower as the financial markets equilibrate. The

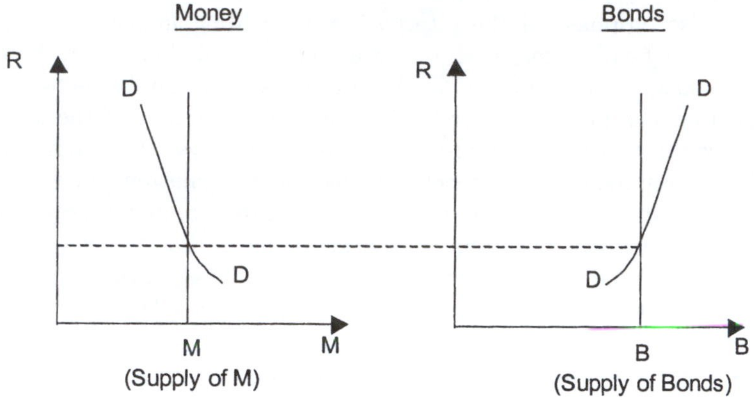

Figure 1.9: Demand for money and bonds

resulting relationship between output and interest rates is the LM curve (Figure 1.10).

So Keynes rearranged the relationships in the classical model, crucially allowing output to be driven far from potential because he cut off the equilibrating effect of flexible prices.

The algebra of the Keynesian model is:

$$(IS)Q = f(G, \tau)$$

determining Q

$$(LM)M = m(R, Q; P)$$

with P given; determining R.

THE PHILLIPS CURVE AND THE NEO-KEYNESIAN SYNTHESIS:

We now note that the Keynesian system has a hole — price determination. For a long time after the Second World War economists were not concerned because the assumption that prices moved slowly — at or close to zero inflation — stood up. But systematic policy stimulus keeping economies at low levels of unemployment produced inflationary behaviour that the Keynesian model could not account for. The first reaction of economists was to extend it to include a 'disequilibrium theory' of price change. The idea was simple: output was determined in the short

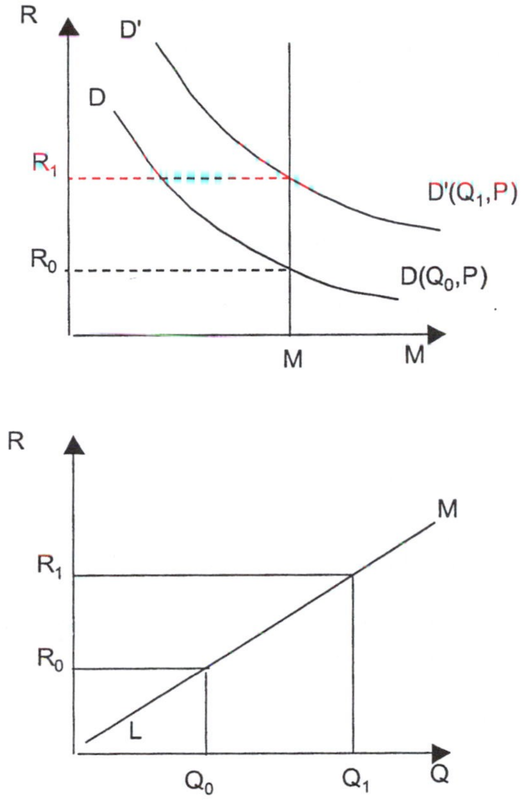

Figure 1.10: The *LM* curve

run by demand as in the Keynesian model but prices would be changed by price setters in response to the gap or disequilibrium between this and their supply as measured by output potential, the equilibrium produced by technology and preferences. Such a relationship was first estimated by A.W. Phillips (1958) for UK data on inflation and unemployment going back a century: hence the Phillips Curve. Since unemployment and output are closely related through the production function assuming some measure of the labour force given exogenously, the Phillips Curve can be drawn either with unemployment along the horizontal axis or with output along it but with a reversed slope.

This relationship worked well for the 1950s and 1960s but clearly broke down in the 1970s as rising inflation was associated with rising unemployment. The reason was suggested by Phelps (1970) and Friedman

(1968) independently: price setters were aiming to adjust relative prices in response to excess demand and so their actual price change would be equal to the response to excess demand, plus expected inflation — only then would relative prices rise by the response to excess demand. This expectations-augmented Phillips Curve is shown in Figure 1.11.

A further development was a theory of expectations formation rooted in rational calculation — 'adaptive expectations'. In parallel with the disregard of inflation had gone a casual attitude to expectations of inflation: it was typical to assume that expected inflation was equal to current inflation ('static' expectations); for some purposes this might be altered to 'extrapolative' expectations where the recent change would be extrapolated into the future. Both were arbitrary. Now economists such as Marc Nerlove (1958) and Phillip Cagan (1956) replaced them with the idea that expectations would be revised in response to past errors:

$$\dot{p}_t^e - \dot{p}_{t-1}^e = k[\dot{p}_t - \dot{p}_{t-1}^e]$$

where $\dot{p}_t^e$, $\dot{p}_t$ = expected and actual inflation. Under certain circumstances it is rational to adjust expectations in this manner — in particular, when people are ignorant about the model and the policy process it is a good approximation to a rational learning procedure.

Finally, in a world of inflationary expectations we must change the IS curve: demand now responds not to (nominal) interest rates but to real interest rates — that is interest rates minus the expected rate of inflation for the period of the loan. The reason is plain: consumers and firms borrowing to undertake purchases pay back their loans in money that is worth less by the rise in prices, hence the true expected annual cost to them of the loan is the rate of interest less the inflation rate they expect. (The same would apply if they were paying for their purchase by running down their savings — then it would be the real interest they expect to sacrifice on the savings deposit.)

We now have a model of the IS and LM curves to determine demand, output and interest rates in the short run; and a Phillips curve augmented by adaptive expectations (Figure 1.11) to determine output, inflation and interest rates in the long run, essentially as in the classical model. This neo-Keynesian synthesis between Keynesian and classical thinking dominated macreconomic thinking in the 1970s and 1980s and is still highly influential today. (For further reading about this model we recommend Laidler and Parkin (1975) and for mathematical back-up on solution methods a textbook on mathematics for economists, such as Chiang, 1984).

The model can be represented by five equations set out in Box 1.1; they are respectively the IS, LM and Phillips Curves, the adaptive expectations process, and the definition of the real interest rate. The equations are deliberately simplified to the maximum — especially, output and prices are all expressed as logs (hence the assumption is made that the relationships are linear, that is additive, in logs) and there are no lags except in expectations formation. Notice that in the IS curve real interest rates employ inflation expected for the coming period, $\dot{p}^e_{t+1}$, rather than inflation expected last period for this, p^e_t, which enters the Phillips Curve.

This model can of course be solved on a computer with numbers assigned to the parameters. But we would like to know its qualitative properties as well. There are two main ones: the nature of its equilibrium and its 'dynamic' properties (that is how it moves from one equilibrium to another when a shock occurs).

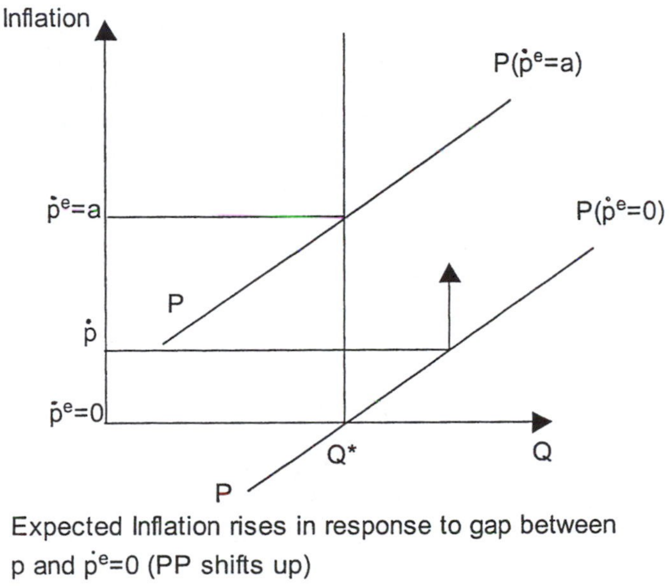

Figure 1.11: The expectations-augmented Phillips curve with adaptive expectations

Box 1.1 shows how the relevant inflation equilibrium — that is resting point — can be found for this model. Box 1.2 shows how the dynamic properties can be found.

Some notes on the equilibrium

Equilibrium is where the model economy comes to rest, that is, its endogenous variables attain a constant or steadily moving value. What this will be in detail depends on the motion of the exogenous variables (it is possible for a model not to have an equilibrium at all if these move in particular ways). In our case we will assume that $\bar{y}$ and $\bar{d}$ are both constant and that $\bar{m}_t$ is growing steadily; this will allow us to look and (as we shall see) find an equilibrium where inflation, expected inflation, interest rates (real and nominal) and output are all constant — and prices are growing steadily (in line with the constant inflation rate).

Box 1.1 shows the detailed steps. The meaning of these steps can be quickly explained. First, the Phillips Curve with adaptive expectations implies that the economy must be at $\bar{y}$, or on the 'long-run Phillips Curve' — by which is meant the relationship between inflation and output when expected inflation is equal to (has caught up with) actual inflation. This relationship can be understood by a policy experiment (a foolish one). Suppose the government decided to stimulate the economy and keep it above $\bar{y}$ permanently: inflation would rise initially along the short-run Phillips Curve, but then expected inflation would rise too, and inflation would rise further. It can easily be checked that inflation will rise indefinitely, hence the vertical curve in the long run — thus illustrating the point that for inflation to settle down, output cannot permanently exceed (or be less than) $\bar{y}$. This point is sometimes referred to as the accelerationist proposition. Figure 1.12.

Note that we still do not know where inflation will settle, only that output is at $\bar{y}$. So secondly we can enquire what inflation will be: this is given by the LM curve. If we ask what the implied rate of change of the variables in the LM curve must be in equilibrium, we can see that since neither interest rates nor output are changing then the rate of change of the money supply must be equal to that of prices, that is inflation equals the growth rate of money, the fundamental proposition of monetarists such as Milton Friedman, Karl Brunner and Allan Meltzer. This gives us the point on the long-run Phillips Curve where inflation will settle.

Given output at $\bar{y}$ we can establish what real interest rates will be from the IS curve: real interest rates must move to equate demand with the available supply — the 'crowding-out' principle (making space for any government demand pressure, $\bar{d}$, by reducing private demand). We can show this in the IS–LM diagram as follows: clearly in equilibrium the IS curve must be located so that output is $\bar{y}$ at the prevailing interest rates, the curve is shifted upwards by expected inflation and rightwards by $\bar{d}$, hence the point on this IS curve above $\bar{y}$ will be the implied nominal

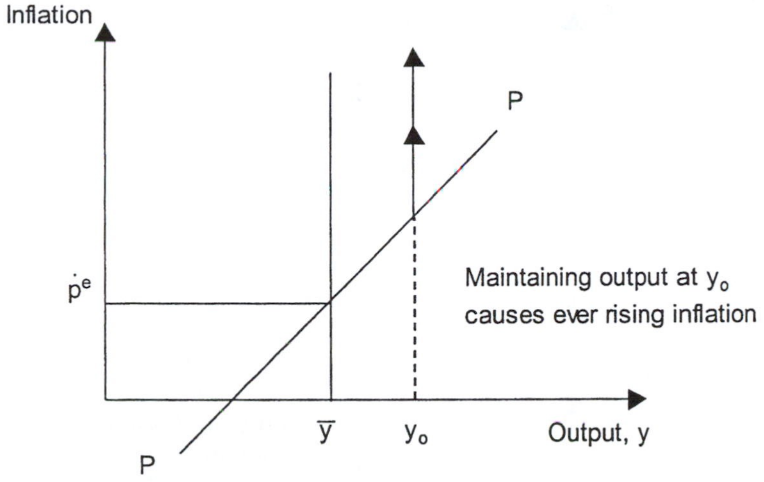

Figure 1.12: The accelerationist proposition

interest rate made up of inflation plus the necessary real interest rate — Figure 1.13.

This leaves us last with the price level. Diagrammatically we can see that the *LM* curve must intersect the *IS* curve at the point that lies above $\bar{y}$. We must shift the *LM* curve to this point: given that the money supply is on its steady growth path, the only way to do this is for prices to change. The *LM* curve is therefore solved for the price level.

Box 1.1

THE NEO-CLASSICAL/KEYNESIAN SYNTHESIS MODEL AND ITS EQUILIBRIUM

$$y_t = \bar{d} - \alpha r_t \text{ (IS)} \quad \text{(a)}$$
$$\overline{m}_t = p_t + \gamma y_t - \beta R_t \text{ (LM)} \quad \text{(b)}$$
$$\dot{p}_t = \dot{p}_t^e + \delta(y_t - \bar{y}) \text{ (Phillips curve, PP)} \quad \text{(c)}$$
$$\dot{p}_t^e = \lambda \dot{p}_{t-1} + (1-\lambda)\dot{p}_{t-1}^e \text{ (adaptive expectations, AE)} \quad \text{(d)}$$

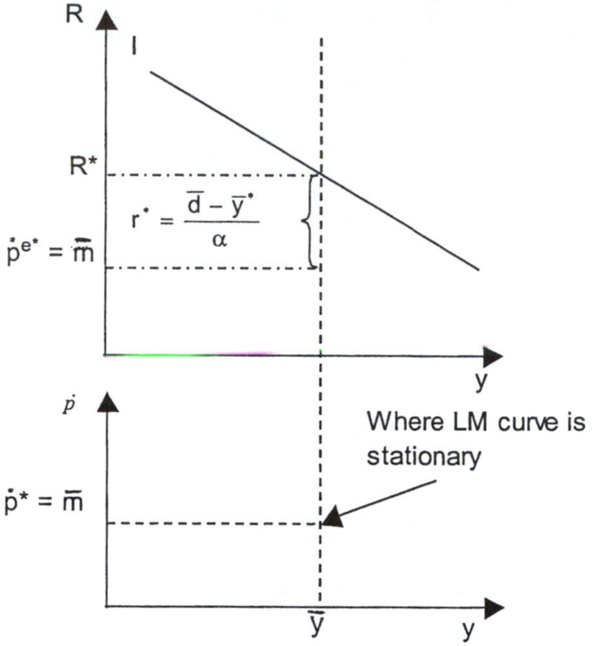

Figure 1.13: Inflation and interest rate equilibrium

$$R_t \quad = \quad r_t + \dot{p}^e_{t+1} \text{ real interest rate (RR)} \qquad \text{(e)}$$

Remembering that $\Delta \ln x_t = \frac{\Delta x_t}{x_t - x_{t-1}}$
y, p and m are respectively ln of real GDP, prices and money supply.
$\dot{x}_t = \Delta x_t = x_t - x_{t-1}$
$\dot{p}^e_t$ = inflation expected last period for this period
R_t = interest rate (fraction p.a.)
r_t = real (inflation-adjusted) interest rate (fraction p.a.)
The model's equilibrium
Suppose $\bar{d}$, $\bar{y}$ are constant; $\bar{m}_t$ is rising at a constant growth rate, $\Delta\bar{m}_t = \dot{\bar{m}}_t = \dot{\bar{m}}$. Then the model has an equilibrium where y_t, r_t, R_t, $\dot{p}_t$, $\dot{p}^e_t$ are all constant (and p_t is growing at a constant rate). Find it by setting all these variables to their constant values (for p_t at its equilibrium value along its constant-growth path) in the above equations, and then solving out for these values:

AE gives $0 = \Delta\dot{p}^{e*} = \lambda(\dot{p}^* - \dot{p}^{e*}) \Longrightarrow \dot{p}^* = \dot{p}^{e*}$
PP then gives $\dot{p}^* = \dot{p}^* + \delta(y^* - \overline{y}) \Longrightarrow y^* = \overline{y}$
IS then gives $r^* = \frac{\overline{d}-\overline{y}}{\alpha}$
RR gives $R^* = r^* + \dot{p}^*$
LM, differenced, gives $\Delta\bar{m} = \dot{p}^* + \gamma\Delta\overline{y} - \beta\Delta R^*$ so that as $\Delta\overline{y} = \Delta R^* = 0$ it follows that $\dot{p}^* = \Delta\overline{m}$
Finally solve for p^* from LM as

$$p_t^* = \overline{m}_t - \gamma\overline{y} + \beta[r^* + \dot{p}^*] = \overline{m}_t - \gamma\overline{y} + \beta[\frac{\overline{d} - \overline{y}}{\alpha} + \Delta\overline{m}]$$

This final step tells us an important feature of this model: that when the growth rate of the money supply rises the price level will rise by more than the money supply level — and vice versa when the money growth rate falls, prices fall by more than money supply. The reason for this is that the demand for money responds to interest rates: when money supply growth increases, interest rates rise and reduce money demand, so causing the excess money to be spent until prices have risen enough to restore the money demand to equality with money supply. This is sometimes referred to as 'price overshooting'. Consider, for example, a hyperinflation caused by a very large rise in money supply growth: this causes a 'flight from money' as above, which greatly adds to the inflationary pressure in the economy, driving prices to levels much higher than the rise in the money supply itself. The contrary holds when the hyperinflation is cured, say by a currency reform: then deflationary pressure sets in as people rush back into holding money, so cutting demand for goods — this implies that a currency reform should (oddly, it might seem) make liberal amounts of the new currency available in order to stave off a sharp deflation. Figure 1.14.

Notes on the dynamic properties

To understand the nature of the dynamic path we can conduct a policy experiment — a simple one-off money supply shock, for example — and examine how it affects the economy period by period, simply using the model's equations in a diagrammatic way. So in period 1 the LM curve shifts rightwards, triggering higher inflation; this raises expected inflation for the next period which shifts the IS curve upwards, giving us the period 1 effect marked as 1 in Figure 1.15. In period 2, the Phillips

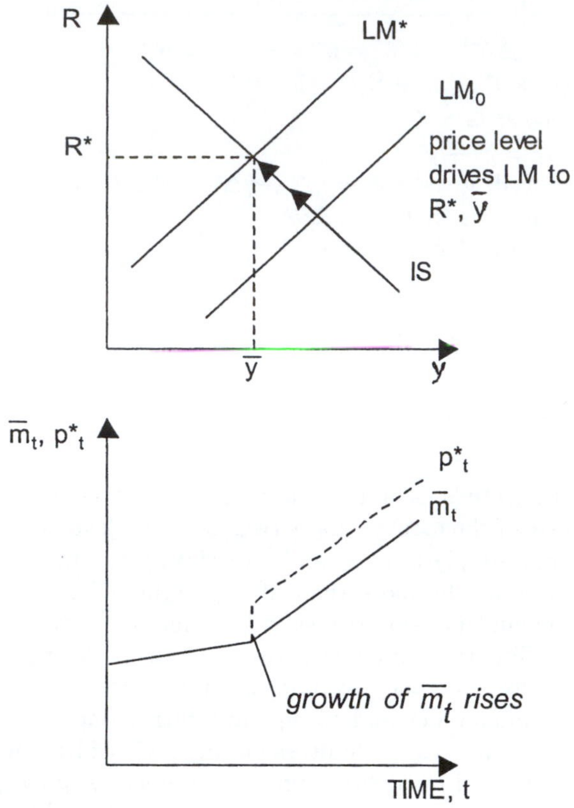

Figure 1.14: Price overshooting

curve shifts up with higher expected inflation; by now the LM curve is shifting back to the left as inflation exceeds the growth of money supply. The IS curve also continues shifting upwards with still higher expected inflation — giving us point 2 in Figure 1.15. It is easy to continue into further periods and show that the effects circle as shown. (This particular model in fact requires most unusual parameter values to behave in any other, non-circular, fashion, though it can do so.)

Figure 1.15 also illustrates that all the variables share the same motion. This follows from the simultaneity of the equations in the model — because all the variables react on one another they must obviously all move consistently, rather like the waves in a sea must all have the same sort of motion since they are all connected to one another. To discover

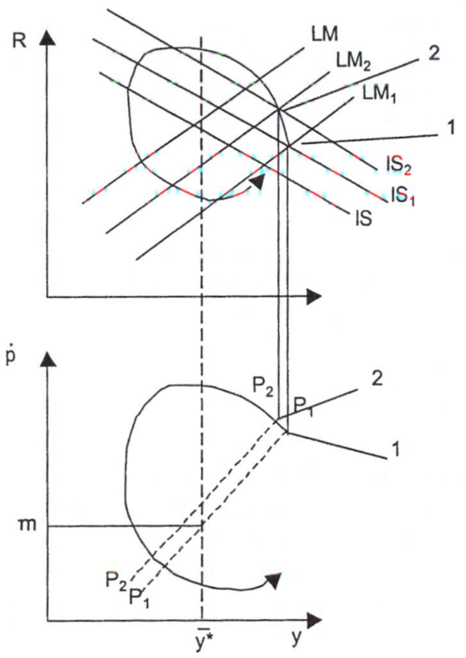

Figure 1.15: One-off rise in $\bar{m}_t$ — dynamics

the model's 'equation of motion' or 'characteristic equation', we follow a series of steps shown in the next box. What we are doing there is to reduce the model — by simple substitution — to a single equation in one variable (as deviations from its equilibrium value) and its lagged values: a difference equation (in this case 'homogeneous' because it equals zero, all the exogenous variables having been eliminated by expressing the endogenous variables in deviations from equilibrium). We can then readily show (see Box 1.2) that all the other variables have the same difference equation as the variable we have chosen.

Having obtained this equation we can then examine its behaviour, using the standard analysis of difference equations — see Chiang (1984) for example.

Comments on the model and its policy implications

The type of model we have been examining was the work-horse of macroeconomic modelling in the 1970s (clearly the versions used were often much more complicated, especially with the introduction of lags in the relationships). It has 'monetarist' properties as we have seen, in that inflation depends on money supply growth, and output equals its 'potential' or 'natural' level, in the long run. But it was also used by Keynesians, such as James Tobin, who stressed its short-run properties — such as taking a long time to get to long-run equilibrium and being prone to generate large business cycles. In a number of interchanges during the 1970s Keynesians and monetarists agreed to disagree about the likely size of different parameters in such a model and on appropriate policies but acknowledged that on the nature of the model itself they were essentially in agreement.

By the end of the 1970s the model was under serious challenge. At least as used by most forecasters it had failed to predict the serious inflation of the 1970s (associated with the tripling of the oil price in 1973) or the recession that went with it. The heart of the objection was the mechanism of adaptive expectations which gives the model its circular behaviour (as can readily be checked by reworking the model on the assumption that, for example, inflation expectations are determined by the growth of the money supply); the new 'rational expectations' school (discussed next) argued that people could do better. By 'adapting' they regularly made easily-preventable forecast errors: for example, if there were a one-off rise in the money supply of the sort we examined above, they would first underpredict, then overpredict, inflation and then repeat this cycle of errors indefinitely as the economy circled around its equilibrium inflation which of course remains precisely unchanged. Such expectations behaviour was unintelligent, irrational — hence unlikely — and a poor basis for predicting the behaviour of the economy, sensitive as this is to expectations.

Box 1.2

DYNAMIC PROPERTIES OF THE NEO-CLASSICAL/KEYNESIAN SYNTHESIS MODEL — REDUCING THE IS-LM-PHILLIPS CURVE MODEL TO CHARACTERISTIC EQUATION

1. Subtract equilibrium values from each equation, to write model in deviations from equilibrium e.g. IS curve:

$$\delta y_t = -\alpha r_t + \overline{d}$$

$$-y^* = +\alpha r^* - \overline{d}$$

implying $y_t - y^* = -\alpha(r_t - r^*)$

2. Model in deviation form becomes (all variables in deviations from equilibrium):

$$\begin{aligned} y_t &= -\alpha r_t \text{ (IS)} & \text{(a)} \\ 0 &= p_t + \gamma y_t - \beta R_t \text{ (LM)} & \text{(b)} \\ \dot{p}_t &= \dot{p}_t^e + \delta y_t \text{ (Phillips Curve)} & \text{(c)} \\ \dot{p}_t^e &= \lambda \dot{p}_{t-1} + (1-\lambda)\dot{p}_{t-1}^e \text{ (Adaptive expectations)} & \text{(d)} \\ R_t &= r_t + \dot{p}_{t+1}^e & \text{(e)} \end{aligned}$$

3. Derive Aggregate Demand function from (a), (b), (e). From (b) and (e).

$$r_t = +\frac{1}{\beta}p_t + \frac{\gamma}{\beta}y_t - \dot{p}_{t+1}^e$$

Substitute into (a) and collect terms, implying:

$$y_t = -\frac{\alpha}{\beta + \alpha\gamma}p_t + \frac{\alpha\beta}{\beta + \alpha\gamma}\dot{p}_{t+1}^e \text{ (AD curve)}$$

Write (c) as AS curve $y_t = \frac{1}{\delta}(\dot{p}_t - \dot{p}_t^e)$ and equate to AD

$$\Longrightarrow \frac{1}{\delta}(\dot{p}_t - \dot{p}_t^e) = -\frac{\alpha}{\beta + \alpha\gamma}p_t + \frac{\alpha\beta}{\beta + \alpha\gamma}\dot{p}_{t+1}^e$$

Now (Koyck transformation) subtract $(1-\lambda) \times$ lagged value from both sides. (Equivalently, use the lag operator, L, where $Lx_t = x_{t-1}$. So L is a symbol instructing us to lag a variable; it can be treated algebraically in the same way as a coefficient.
Rewrite $\dot{p}_t^e = \lambda L\dot{p}_t + (1-\lambda)L\dot{p}_t^e$ or $\dot{p}_t^e = \frac{\lambda L}{1-(1-\lambda)L}\dot{p}_t$. Now substitute this expression in the above equation and multiply through by $1 - (1-\lambda)L$.)
Through (d) this yields

$$\frac{1}{\delta}(\dot{p}_t - \dot{p}_{t-1}) = -\frac{\alpha}{\beta + \alpha\gamma}(p_t - [1-\lambda]p_{t-1}) + \frac{\alpha\beta}{\beta + \alpha\gamma}(\lambda\dot{p}_t)$$

Since $\dot{p}_t = p_t - p_{t-1}$, substitute all through for p_t, p_{t-1}, p_{t-2} in place of $\dot{p}_t$, $\dot{p}_{t-1}$ and collect terms to get:

$$p_t + ap_t + bp_{t-2} = 0$$

where

$$
\begin{aligned}
a &= \frac{-(1-\lambda+2s-r)}{1+s+r}; \\
b &= \frac{s}{1+s-r}; \\
s &= \frac{\beta+\alpha\gamma}{\alpha\delta}; \\
r &= \beta\lambda
\end{aligned}
$$

Notes on difference equations

Solutions to second order equation $x_t + ax_{t-1} + bx_{t-2} = 0$ is

$$x_t = A\lambda_1^t + B\lambda_2^t$$

where λ_1 and λ_2 are solutions of quadratic

$$\lambda^2 + a\lambda + b = 0, \lambda_1, \lambda_2 = \frac{-a \pm \sqrt{a^2-4b}}{2}$$

In case of complex roots (where $4b > a^2$), the solution can conveniently be written:

$$x_t = A\lambda^t \cos(\theta t - \varepsilon); \lambda = \sqrt{b}; \cos\theta = -\frac{a}{2\lambda}$$

The length of the cycle is $\frac{360°}{\theta}$.
The sufficient and necessary conditions for stability are:

$$
\begin{aligned}
1+a+b &> 0 \\
1-a+b &> 0 \\
1-b &> 0
\end{aligned}
$$

Against this critique, the model's users claimed that adaptive expectations were a reasonable approximation when, as was usually the case, people had poor knowledge either of the workings of the economy or the processes driving policy or both — a neat demonstration of this point was made by Benjamin Friedman (1979), no relative of Milton Friedman. Then adaptive expectations is close to an optimal learning procedure. True, if there were to be just one shock such as a money supply rise, then the model would break down as people would soon realise what had happened; but in practice a lot of shocks are continuously hitting the economy and so people cannot easily work out what is going on: the model would be a good approximation then.

If we accept for purposes of argument that the model does make sense in some such terms, what policy implications can we draw from it? We can identify three main issues:

1. Rules versus discretion in monetary policy.

Monetarists argued that the money supply should be kept to a steady growth rate as far as possible (rules) rather than being varied in response to the perceived state of the economy (discretion). The argument was based on the difficulty of knowing the parameters, or even the economy's actual state, accurately — the slogan used by Friedman was that 'the lags were long and variable'.

If one reacted excessively to the economy out of such ignorance, then the cycles one was trying to dampen would get worse, possibly much worse. One can examine this point by adding into the model a money supply response function, in place of the exogenous money supply we have assumed; this will change the dynamic properties of the model and depending on how well it is chosen, the model can become more or less cyclical. Monetarists argued that the prudent (risk-averse) government would prefer to avoid the chance of making things much worse to enjoying the possibility of making them much better — and so would opt for a rule.

Against this Keynesians argued that such fears were exaggerated — we did know enough from our improving econometrics to steer the economy along a less boom–bust course.

Clearly this argument was empirical; it could only be settled by seeing how well or badly discretionary policy did. The experience of the 1970s, when there was a strong boom in the early 1070s, followed by the oil crisis bust, then again followed by a sharp expansion leading to bad inflation — did not inspire confidence in the highly discretionary policies pursued in that era.

2. Gradualism

Friedman argued that when far away from the appropriate rule, policy should be shifted back in small repeated steps because a large shift would be highly destabilising for the economy. For example, faced with high inflation due to past excessive money supply growth, a government that suddenly cut money supply growth back to a much lower rate would precipitate first a huge recession, followed eventually by a large boom. This sequence would lead to the rejection of the policy. If, however, money supply growth is slowly cut, each step would induce a small recession but after a few steps this would come on top of revival from the first steps; while the economy would be making steady long-run progress back to low inflation, the side-effects in lost output and unemployment would be more tolerable politically.

This argument is obviously a strong one if this model is correct. However. it is not clear that even gradual steps would be easy to undertake politically because the length of time an economy would be suffering from (mild) recession would be very long. Since bad inflations have frequently been ended, this raises questions about the appropriateness of the model in examining the curing of inflation: the rational expectations school have argued that it is too pessimistic because governments can express the national willingness to cure inflation and this message can be understood by people in the economy — hence their inflation expectations will adjust rapidly downwards, and much less recession is required to reduce inflation therefore.

3. Indexation

Friedman argued that contracts (especially for wages — but also for government bonds) should be indexed to prices, for two reasons. First, this would reduce the economic damage in markets; there is a loss of consumer surplus due to taxes whose true rate is often raised by inflation — indexing the objects of taxation, levying the tax on the indexed rather than the nominal amount, would effectively lower the tax. Second, it would stabilise output around its natural or equilibrium level by speeding up the response of inflation to deviations from this level. In other words the Phillips Curve would shift more rapidly upwards in response to excess demand and drop more rapidly in response to excess supply. Friedman was most concerned in practice about curing inflation and so about the response under excess supply (brought about by cutting money supply growth). He saw indexation as a way to speed up the cutting of inflation without slump.

We can illustrate the point under the extreme case where indexation of wages is immediate and prices are a simple margin mark-up on wages adjusted for productivity: in this case the Phillips curve will become

$$\dot{p}_t = \dot{p}_t + q(y_t - \overline{y})$$

In other words expected inflation disappears from the equation (because wage bargainers do not need to forecast inflation any more), entirely replaced by actual inflation under indexation. It is easy to see that this gives us a vertical Phillips Curve — any excess supply raises inflation which then raises wages and so inflation ad infinitum. In this case, there is no need for gradualism; to cure high inflation, the government merely needs to cut money supply growth at once to its target inflation rate, and virtually overnight inflation will drop to it with a minimal cost in recession.

This seems an attractive argument; and yet of course indexation cannot in practice be so immediate. If so, it generates instead a Phillips Curve with lagged inflation on the right-hand side:

$$\dot{p}_t = \dot{p}_{t-1} + q(y_t - \overline{y})$$

for example, where the lag is one period. But as this example readily shows this may worsen the instability of the economy. In this particular case, the one-period lag is equivalent to adaptive expectations with an adaptive parameter of unity; this, as we saw in Box 1.2 above, may produce unstable behaviour. The cycle is faster but may be explosive.

Experience with indexation in the 1970s did indeed reveal that it increased the violence of the economy's responses to shocks — increasing inflation in the upswing and lowering it in the downswing. For example, the Heath government of the UK in 1970–74 indexed wages almost universally and presided as a result over an inflation explosion in response to a programme of policy stimulation. It was not clear from this experience that it was an advantage in counter-inflationary policy to have indexation in place. During the late 1980s when counter-inflationary policy became general in the Organization for Economic Cooperation and Development (OECD) several countries — including Italy and Belgium — abandoned indexation at the same time.

We now turn from this model to discuss rational expectations, the hypothesis which spearheaded the challenge to this way of understanding the economy.

Rational expectations: Introductory Ideas

Expectations are fundamental in economics. Every economic decision is about the future, given the existing situation. Even decisions apparently only involving the current situation such as choosing to buy apples rather than pears, implicitly involve a view of the future; in this case it is a view both about future income which underlies the budget one is prepared to allocate to apples and pears, and about future prices of apples and pears, which dictates whether it is worthwhile storing them in place of future purchases.

By definition the future is unknowable. Economics, the study of economic decision making, therefore is concerned with how people deal with the unknowable.

The Liverpool University economist, George Shackle, made this a constant theme of his work. In his view (fo example, Shackle, 1958) each individual constructs in his imagination different scenarios or possible outcomes following on different actions he is contemplating. He knows now the pleasure given by the consequences he imagines for each course of action. The course which gives him the most pleasure when its consequences are imagined spurs him to action. So Shackle envisages a hedonistic calculus of the imagination as the basis for economic choice.

For Shackle the pleasure involved in a course of action will depend not only on the 'expected pleasure' if the consequences anticipated were to occur, but also on the 'chances' of them occurring. A fine outcome will normally give less pleasure when imagined if it is fraught with uncertainty. But this will not always be true. For example, for some people the same outcome may seem the sweeter if it is accompanied by the challenge of possible failure. Too easy a victory may not inspire a sense of triumph at all and may not attract the decision taker.

Shackle therefore regards economic decisions as entirely subjective, because they are the product of the individual's imagination interacting with the known facts of the past and present.

Nor does he feel that we can predict how people will act except in matters where nature reproduces itself with regularity. For example, in inventory control where the product has a reliable distribution, the manager can and will stop production when a sample has a proportion of defective products higher than some percentage. In such cases Shackle says there is 'uncertainty'; the rules of probability can be applied by people and we can infer what they will do from a knowledge of their objectives and of the probability distributions.

For many decisions the major elements in the future outcome are not subject to reliable distributions. For example, what the voters of Warrington would do in July 1981, faced for the first time in Britain with a Social Democratic candidate, could not be described by a probability distribution. It was not a regular event. No sense could be given to 'the' probability distribution. Such elements Shackle terms sources of 'potential surprise'. In evaluating future outcomes with such elements, each person will make his individual assessment and we cannot say what he will do without a complete knowledge of his psychology, even if we have access to exactly the same facts as he has.

Shackle's perceptions appear to be quite devastating to the use of statistical models in economics (that is econometrics). For these models assert that economic behaviour is predictable and regular. Their implication is that economic agents take decisions about future outcomes which are predictable and subject to well-defined probability distributions. The models are supposed to be derived from assumptions about agents' preferences, technology and the probability distributions they face.

The keystone of econometrics is the implicit assertion that, in the mass, individual decisions exhibit regularity, even though each individual decision will be quite unpredictable. Suppose we could define the probability distribution of future outcomes. Then econometrics asserts that there is a 'typical' individual who, faced with this distribution, will decide in a certain way; we might in particular say that he 'maximizes an expected utility function', where the utility function is a mathematical representation of his preferences. Individuals, when aggregated in a large sample, will behave like many typical individuals.

This assertion is supported up to a point by the central limit theorem, according to which the distribution of the mean of a sample of n random variables each of variance σ^2 will have a variance equal to $\frac{\sigma^2}{n}$ and as the sample n gets larger will tend to normality regardless of the distributions of each variable in the sample (see, for example, Hoel, 1962, p. 145). But although the assertion is supported in this way, it is still required that an individual decision can be regarded as a random variable with a defined mean, generated by a systematic decision process. Shackle denies this, while econometrics asserts it. Furthermore, it was supposed in the above argument that the future outcomes had a probability distribution. But for this to be the case it is necessary that individuals do behave in the aggregate in the regular manner just described. For the distribution of future outcomes is the product of the interaction of individuals' behaviour — for example, the distribution of future prices and quantities for sugar results from the interaction of individuals' supplies and demands for sugar.

Thus the linchpin of the whole edifice of econometrics is the postulate of regularity in economic nature. That postulate in turn justifies the assumption that econometricians face regularities. Whether this postulate is 'true or false' can only be settled empirically, by evaluating the success and failure of econometrics in attempting to apply this basic assertion. But many economists regard it (as did Keynes — see, for example, Keynes, 1939) as an unfortunate development which has perverted policy on many important issues because of a false perception that numerical estimates of likely outcomes from different policies can be generated.

Some of the early hopes of econometricians were that econometrics would enable complex problems of decision making by governments, firms and individuals to be reduced to the mere application of known techniques to models of the relevant economic environment. But these hopes have been cruelly dashed. Nowhere has this been more so than in macroeconomics. Macroeconomic models of the Keynesian (and later neo-Keynesian synthesis) type were built in great profusion in the 1960s for most major countries and used, especially in Britain and the United States, as the basis for forecasting and policy. Crude forms of 'optimal control' were used by governments: typically governments made forecasts, using their models, of inflation and unemployment over some horizon and then varied policies to obtain better outcomes according to these models. By the mid-1970s disillusion with these methods was widespread, as the Western world grappled with a combination of high inflation and high unemployment which, in general, neither had been predicted by econometric models, nor had responded to policy in the manner predicted by these models.

The reaction to this disillusion has been varied, with the result that the consensus in macroeconomics that had appeared in the late 1960s had abruptly disappeared by the late 1970s, as we have seen in the previous section. To some this was a vindication of their scepticism about econometrics. Others, however, have searched for reformulations of the models which failed in the 1970s. Rational expectations has been one major result.

Rational expectations takes one step further the basic assertion of econometrics that individuals in the aggregate act in a regular manner as if each was a typical individual following a systematic decision process. The step is to assert that in this decision process the individual utilizes efficiently the information available to him in forming expectations about future outcomes.

By 'efficient utilization' is meant that the typical individual's perception of the probability distribution of future outcomes (his 'subjective distribution'), conditional on the available information, coincides with the actual probability distribution conditional on that information.

It cannot be stressed too heavily — since this is a source of repeated misunderstanding — that this is an assertion about the 'typical' individual; in other words, it is to be used operationally with reference to the aggregate behaviour of individuals. It cannot be falsified by examples of behaviour by any actual individual. Clearly particular individuals may behave in ways that exhibit no systematic rational behaviour or expectations formation according to normal criteria, and yet if the behaviour of other individuals, who contributed a dominant proportion of the variability in aggregate behaviour, were rational in this sense, this would be sufficient to generate aggregate behaviour that exhibited rationality.

A further point is that, like all assertions in econometrics, it is to be judged by statistical criteria which will be relative. Whether a relationship asserted to operate for the behaviour of a group 'exists' or not will depend upon how reliable it is statistically, relative to the uses to which it may be put. Such uses in turn may themselves evolve from the discovery of new relationships.

There is therefore no such thing as an objective criterion for judging whether an econometric assertion is valid. Rather there is a joint and interactive evolution of models and their uses. The 1970s crisis in macroeconomic policy and modelling described earlier arose because the uses to which models were being put required properties that those models turned out not to have. Therefore the question that the rational expectations research programme has to answer is: can models based on rational expectations be developed that are useful in application? If so, what are these uses, and how do they compare to the uses available for other modelling approaches?

The assertion (or 'hypothesis') of rational expectations in one sense vindicates Shackle's basic perception that expectations are at the centre of economic behaviour. For on this view behaviour reacts to expected future behaviour which in turn depends on current behaviour; the capacity therefore exists for changes in the environment to affect current behaviour sharply, as individuals react to their perceptions of the changed environment and its implications for the future. Expectations are therefore completely integrated into behaviour.

In previous theories of expectations, this integration was incomplete. Econometric models used 'proxies' for expectations of particular types of outcomes. These proxies were based on what had been found in the past to correlate well with behaviour in a way that could reasonably be attributed to the operation of expectations rather than actual events. Hence for any particular problem in hand a proxy would be sought *ad hoc* — the most satisfactory formulation on which we have dwelt was adaptive expectations. However it is obvious enough that if changes in the environment disturbed the previous relationship between the proxy's behaviour and expectations, this would affect behaviour in a way that would be inaccurately captured by the effect of changes in the proxy. Hence only under the restricted set of circumstances where the previous relationship is unaffected will the proxies be useful. Unfortunately, the restricted set excludes most of the policy experiments that are of interest to governments.

In another sense the rational expectations hypothesis conflicts with Shackle's vision in that it is an attempt to use econometrics to capture the integration of expectations into behaviour. As such, it could be rated as even more foolhardy than basic econometrics. For whereas in well-settled times, patterns of behaviour might conceivably evolve which could give rise to some econometric relationships, in times of change when expectations are being disturbed in an unfamiliar way, then surely to model the effect of the changes on expectations and on their interactions with behaviour must be a mad attempt. For there is the capacity for immense diversity of imagined outcomes from the changes taking place; the 'typically' imagined outcome will be a useless construct in this diversity, where different individuals will be behaving in unrelated and possibly conflicting ways.

This reaction correctly identifies the way in which rational expectations is a programme for pushing econometrics to the limits of its possibilities in the prediction of behaviour. At the same time the reaction correctly notes the ambition of this attempt. It is possible that the attempt is hopelessly over ambitious. If it is proved to be so, then at least the limits of econometrics will have been clearly defined. For it will be the case that econometric relationships can at best only be useful in the restricted circumstances where the environment shows considerable stability. This would imply that they could be used to forecast existing trends in an unchanged environment, but not to predict the effects of changes in the environment, especially policy changes. If this were so, then it would equally invalidate attempts to use econometric models to design 'optimal' policy rules. Hence the implications flowing from a proper exploration of the potentialities of rational expectations are substantial and important.

We wrote in our first edition: 'While our own view is that these potentialities are considerable, it will only be a decade or so before we will know with reasonable clarity just what can be delivered from this approach.' The view of the economics profession today, judging from the widespread application of rational expectations, is that much has been delivered from it that is useful; the hypothesis has evolved its own set of uses as well as revealing the limits of some traditional ones.

The early intellectual History of the Hypothesis — an Overview

As so often in economics, it turns out that early economists propounded ideas at different stages that bear a striking resemblance to the hypothesis. For example, Marshall (1887), in his evidence to a Royal Commission, argued that an increase in the supply of money would affect economic activity by lowering interest rates, increasing loans, expenditure and finally prices. However, he also added that if the increase in the supply of money was well known, then individuals would anticipate the consequent expansion in demand and the effect on prices would be much faster[1].

---

[1] This reference was pointed out to us by Richard Harrington.

Modigliani and Grunberg (1954) are credited by Robert Shiller (1978) with the earliest post-war promulgation of the ideas behind the hypothesis. However, it was one of Modigliani's collaborators, John Muth, who truly created the hypothesis (Muth, 1961) in the sense that he set it down in precise form and showed how it could be applied to specific problems.

Muth's article was written partly in order to defend the prevailing flagship of the 1960s in expectations modelling, adaptive expectations, according to which expectations of a variable are an exponentially weighted average of past values of this variable. It turns out that under certain circumstances this is the same as the rational expectation (see the appendix to chapter 2). These were the circumstances to which Muth seemed to draw attention. His other work published at the time was exclusively devoted to the use of exponentially weighted averages (Muth, 1960; Holt et al., 1960).

The use of a particular modelling technique depends as much on its perceived tractability by economists as on its inherent plausibility. It was in fact the best part of a decade before economists started to use Muth's concept in its own right in applied and theoretical work. Adaptive expectations seemed in the 1960s the best tool, partly perhaps because it was still new and relatively unexplored (it made its first journal appearance in Nerlove, 1958), partly because of its most convenient econometric transformation (due to Koyck, 1954) into a single lagged value of the dependent variable. By contrast, the techniques for using rational expectations (RE) were not widely available; the solution of models with RE presented difficulties, overcome by Muth in very simple models, but not readily dealt with in the larger models being developed in that decade. As we shall see, solution of larger models (and also estimation) required substantial computing power; and it may well be that the rapid quickening of interest in RE modelling from the mid-1970s has been due to the explosion in the capacity of the electronic computer.

The earliest published work in macroeconomics using Muth's concept seriously, if only to a limited extent, is that of Walters (1971) and Lucas (1972a). Walters showed that the effect of money on prices would be substantially quickened by RE. Lucas argued that under RE (unlike adaptive expectations) monetary expansion could not raise output permanently above the natural rate of average (the 'natural rate hypothesis'), although the responses of money to lagged output and prices (feedback responses) could affect the time-path of output in response to shocks. Note that neither author in these articles argued for the ineffectiveness of monetary policy feedback responses for influencing the time-path of output.

Another early paper was by Black (1973), who applied rational expectations to the foreign exchange market, an area which has seen many further and productive applications of the concept. Some of this subsequent work used Muth's original model in a partial equilibrium treatment of the market, treating macroeconomic variables exogenously (for example, Minford, 1978; Bell and Beenstock, 1980). Other work (for example, Frankel, 1979) has estimated reduced-form models of the exchange rate derived from monetary models with rational expectations. Shiller (1973) applied it to the term structure of interest rates; here too a separate but closely related body of work has been extremely fruitful.

This has taken the form of tests of the 'efficient market hypothesis'. This is a combination of the rational expectations hypothesis and some hypothesis about market behaviour, which thus makes it possible to test rational expectations through the behaviour of market prices. Eugene Fama (for example, 1970, 1976) and his collaborators at Chicago were prolific pioneers in this area, and covered not only financial markets but also a variety of commodity markets, with results which at the least substantially revised the popular notions of the early post-war period that markets were irrational and highly inefficient.

Work on general macroeconomic applications (that is to inflation and output) in the early 1970s was substantially that of Lucas (1972a, b) and Sargent and Wallace (1975). Lucas' concern was to develop the rationale for fluctuations in money supply to affect output; his problem being that if information on money is available, then movements in money should immediately be discounted in prices, as everyone seeks to maintain relative prices unchanged. He developed a theme due to Milton Friedman (1968) that individuals perceive economy-wide data such as money and the general price level with an information lag, and are forced to estimate whether the price changes they currently perceive at the market level are relative price changes or merely reflect general price movements (inflation). A positive relationship between output and money or price movements (a 'Phillips curve') can occur because of mistakes made by individuals in estimating current inflation; they supply more output mistakenly thinking that the relative price of their output has risen.

This 'surprise' supply function was an essential component of the small-scale macro models used by Sargent and Wallace to illustrate the potential implications for policy making of RE. They showed that in a 'Keynesian' model, if the Phillips curve (a standard Keynesian construct) is interpreted as a surprise supply function, then only monetary surprises can affect output; monetary plans, whatever they are, can only affect prices. Hence, in particular, sophisticated feedback rules (which, for example, raised money supply in response to a poor past output performance) would be ineffective in their output stabilization objective. However, Lucas and Sargent (1978) have pointed out that this work was not intended to imply that monetary policy was in general ineffective for output, merely that in a particular 'standard' model (which they did not in any case endorse) to which 'optimal' monetary control techniques were routinely applied, such techniques were in fact useless. The lesson they drew was cautionary: monetary policy rules should carefully allow for the reactions of private agents to the rules themselves.

Lucas (1975) and Sargent (1976a) proceeded in the later 1970s to develop an alternative to the standard model, the so-called 'equilibrium business cycle' model. In this model the information lag story is maintained, but all markets are treated as if they are auction markets in which all agents are atomistic competitive units. Households are consumers and suppliers of labour and, period by period, compute optimal intertemporal plans for consumption and work based on the price sequences they perceive themselves as facing. Firms, on the other side of the labour and goods markets from households, similarly compute (given their technology) optimal plans for hiring labour and producing goods based on the same price sequences. The price sequences that are perceived are the rational expectations equilibrium sequences that clear the markets today and are expected to clear them in the future. Because firms and households, once they have made a plan, incur 'sunk costs', there is an adjustment cost in changing plans as these past decisions are unwound. This imparts the correlation of prices and quantities over time that is a feature of business cycles. But the impulse to the cycle comes from shocks to the economy, whether from monetary policy, technological innovations or surprise shifts in household preferences.

Such a model is by no means mandatory in the rational expectations research programme. The 'surprise' supply function is hard to sustain when information about prices is as up to date as it is in the modern economy. Also, while the 'as if' assumption of auction markets and automatic agents may work well for economies with highly competitive structures, monopoly power, in labour markets particularly, is widespread in Western economies, markedly so in Europe, and could require explicit modelling. Furthermore, the role of long term contracts — in goods, labour and financial markets — may be inadequately captured by this 'as if' assumption; this assumption would imply that contracts were approximately 'fully contingent' (that is, such that prices and quantities altered in response to shocks in just the manner that optimal plans would call for if there were no contracts), yet this apparently is not generally the case, for reasons that are still not well understood but may well be entirely consistent with rationality. Later, 'menu costs' (the cost of changing prices, as on a printed menu) were introduced to justify the setting of prices in nominal contracts (Parkin, 1986; Rotemberg, 1983).

Work by Phelps and Taylor (1977) and Fischer (1977 a,b) took non-contingent contracts in goods and labour markets as given and set up simple models to explore the implications. The influential model of an 'overshooting' foreign exchange market in an open economy, by Dornbusch (1976), centred on the interaction of 'sticky' contracts in goods and labour markets with an auction foreign exchange market. The effect of changes in financial asset values due to the presence of financial contracts (such as long-term bonds) similarly played an important role in the models of Blanchard (1981) and Minford (1980). Integration of labour monopoly power into these models has been carried out by Minford (1983). These developments implied a model different in many aspects from the narrowly defined equilibrium model of Lucas and Sargent, although it should be stressed that a model with contracts and monopolies where agents have rational expectations could perhaps most naturally be described as an equilibrium model, in that contracts have been voluntarily entered into and monopolies have agency rights on behalf of their members (and if the state legitimizes a closed shop, their non-members too). The policy properties differ substantially; there is in general more scope for stabilization, although whether it would be beneficial is another matter, requiring careful welfare analysis (see Chapter 5).

There were yet other strands in the ongoing RE research programme. B. Friedman (1979) and Brunner et al. (1980) attempted to introduce the modelling of learning about the model, notably about the evolving 'permanent' elements in the model's structure. Research on learning and whether it converges to rational expectations equilibrium continued to be active (Frydman and Phelps, 1983), although tractability was (and remains) a problem.

Long and Plosser (1983) suggested that business cycles may be modelled without an appeal to information lags or the price supply function; they may stem from real shocks to consumer wealth which generate equilibrium cycles in consumption, production and relative prices. Correlations between money and output may be explainable by implication in terms of reverse causation (King and Plosser, 1981).

This 'real business cycle' approach has the attraction that it relies on fewer *ad hoc* institutional restrictions than the New Classical approach (where information on money and prices, though in principle available rapidly, is slow to arrive in practice) or the New Keynesian (where contracts have unexplained nominal rigidities). Kydland and Prescott (1982) showed that a model of this type, calibrated to US data from cross-section studies, could replicate the time-series properties of the US post-war economy.

An influential school led by Sims (1980) despaired of modelling the economy's structure, but was interested in time-series analysis for predictive purposes within stable structures using the vector autoregression, or VAR (the regression of a group of variables on the past of all members of the group). McNees (1986) and Litterman (1986) found that such VAR models could predict as well as the main US commercial forecasters; however, in the UK during the 1980s, VAR models were outperformed by the main forecasters (Holden and Broomhead, 1990). Finally, a large and growing theoretical literature deriving from the work of Lucas (1978) and Wallace (1980) explored the behaviour of artificial economies peopled by representative agents. These models give us insights into the role of money, taxes and government bonds in enabling exchanges between groups that may be separated by geography (as in Townsend's, 1980, tribes travelling in opposite directions along a turnpike) or time (as in Samuelson's, 1958, overlapping generations models, for example, Wallace, 1980).

In the rest of this book we develop these themes in macroeconomics — in its modern guise macroeconomics is based entirely on the idea that agents are rational. Hence rational expectations is central to the subject today.

2

Solving Rational Expectations Models

In Chapter 1 we defined the rational expectations hypothesis (REH) as the assumption that people's subjective probability distributions about future outcomes are the same as the actual probability distributions conditional on the information available to them. In practice we will be concerned with moments of these distributions, most frequently the mean, but also occasionally the variance, and very rarely the higher moments (the skewness and so on). When people talk about 'expectations' in popular discourse they mean some single number for the future outcome that is expected to occur; but a moment's thought shows at once that this is not a sensible definition of expectations. Since the future is governed by chance, this exact number will only occur by chance. A better definition would be that 'the expectation' is some summary measure of what may happen, that is, of the probability distribution. Such a summary measure would be, for the central tendency of the distribution, the mean (the first moment); and for the tendency for dispersion around the mean, the variance (the second moment). Then either implicitly or explicitly there would be an indication of the asymmetry of the distribution (its skewness or third moment), and its truncation at the tails (its kurtosis, or the fourth moment). These moments of a distribution over x_t are, respectively, Ex_t, $E(x_t - E\ x_t)^2$, $E(x_t - E\ x_t)^3$, $E(x_t - E\ x_t)^4$ and so on for higher moments. Hence 'expectations' are shorthand for some measure of a probability distribution; in practice we use the mean as the main summary measure, assuming that the other moments are known in some way — this implies that the main feature of the distribution that is changing over time is its mean.

The mathematical term for the mean of a distribution is its 'expected value', and it is usual for applied work on the REH to identify the 'expectation of x_{t+i} (x at time $t + i$)' with the mathematically expected value of x_{t+i}. In this book we shall use the notation $E_{t+j}x_{t+i}$ for expectations framed for the period $t+i$, on the basis of information generally available at time $t+j$; j, i can be positive or negative. E is the mathematical expectations operator, meaning 'mathematically expected value of'. Formally $E_{t+j}x_{t+i}$ is defined as $E(x_{t+i} \mid \Phi_{t+i})$ where Φ_{t+j} is the set of generally available information at time $t+j$. Of course, once x_{t+i} is part of the information set Φ_{t+j}, then $E_{t+j}x_{t+i} = x_{t+i}$ trivially.

If we wish to indicate that the information available to those framing expectations is restricted to a set θ_{t+j} at $t+j$, we shall write $E_{t+j}(x_{t+i} \mid \theta_{t+j})$, that is, the expectation of x at $t+i$ framed on the basis of information set θ available at $t+j$. It is natural to think of $E_{t+j}x_{t+i}$ as 'expectations formed at $t+j$ of x at $t+i$'; this will do for some purposes but it is not quite accurate. It is not in fact the date at which expectations are formed that matters but rather the date of the information set on the basis of which they are formed. Because of information lags, people may form expectations for this period on the basis of last period's information, and we would write this as $E_{t-1}x_t$.

Suppose for extreme simplicity that the model of x_t is:

$$x_{t+1} = x_t + \varepsilon_{t+1} \tag{1}$$

where ϵ_t is normally distributed with a mean of 0, a constant variance of σ^2, independence between successive values, and independence of all previous events; that is, $\varepsilon_t : N(0,\ \sigma^2)$, $E(\varepsilon_t + \varepsilon_{t+j}) = 0$ $(i \neq j)$ and $E\varepsilon_{t+i} \mid \Phi_{t+j} = 0$ $(i > j)$. Equation (1) states that x_t follows a 'random walk' (the change in x_t is random).

The expectation of x_t at t is x_t if we assume that people know x_t then. They cannot know ε_{t+1} because it has not yet occurred and as a random variable its expected value is zero. If we write Φ_t as the total information set at t, then:

$$E_t x_{t+1} = E(x_{t+1} \mid \Phi_t) = (x_t + \varepsilon_{t+1} \mid \Phi_t) = x_t + E(\varepsilon_{t+1} \mid \Phi_t) = x_t \tag{2}$$

$E_t x_{t+1}$ will be an unbiased predictor of x_{t+1}, that is, the mean (or expected value) of the prediction error $x_{t+1} - E_t x_{t+1}$ is zero. Thus:

$$E(x_{t+1} - E_t x_{t+1}) = E(x_t + \varepsilon_{t+1} - x_t) = E\varepsilon_{t+1} = 0 \tag{3}$$

$E_t x_{t+1}$ will also be the efficient predictor of x_{t+1}, that is, the variance of the predictor error is smaller than that of any other predictor. Thus:

$$\text{Variance } (x_{t+1} - E_t x_{t+1}) = E(x_{t+1} - E_t x_{t+1})^2 = E(\varepsilon_{t+1})^2 = \sigma^2 \tag{4}$$

This is the minimum variance possible in prediction of x_{t+1} because ε_{t+1} is distributed independently of previous events (the meaning of 'unpredictable'). Suppose we add any expression whatsoever, say βz_t, where z_t is a variable taken from Φ_t, to $E_t x_{t+1}$, making another predictor $\widehat{x}_{t+1}$:

$$\widehat{x}_{t+1} = x_t + \beta z_t \tag{5}$$

Then:

$$E(x_{t+1} - \widehat{x}_{t+1})^2 = E(\varepsilon_{t+1} - \beta z_t)^2 = \sigma^2 + \beta^2 E z_t^2 \tag{6}$$

The variance will be increased by the variance of the added expression, because this must be independent of ε_{t+1}.

The unbiasedness and efficiency of their forecasts are the two key properties of rational expectations forecasts that we will constantly return to in this book. However for the time being, in this chapter, we shall restrict ourselves to explaining how the rational expectation of variables determined in more complex models is to be found, and how those models are accordingly to be solved.

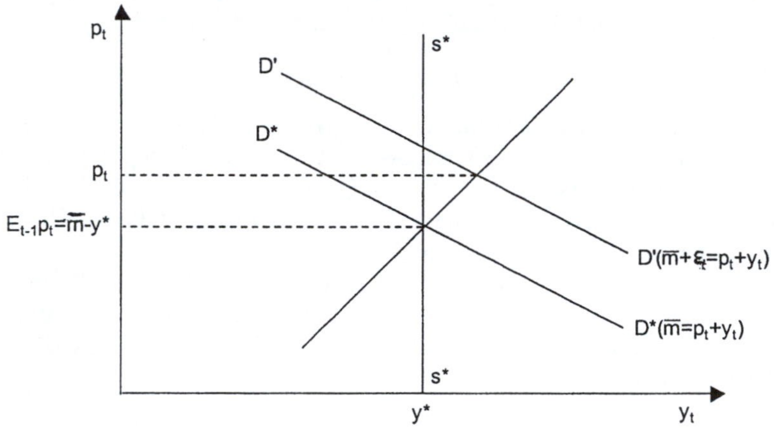

Figure 2.1: A simple macroeconomic model illustrated

THE BASIC METHOD

Now take a simple macro model (illustrated in Figure 2.1):

$$m_t = p_t + y_t \tag{7}$$

$$p_t = E_{t-1} p_t + \delta(y_t - y^*) \tag{8}$$

$$m_t = \overline{m} + \epsilon_t \tag{9}$$

where m, p, y are the logarithms of money supply, the price level, and output respectively; y^* is normal output, $\overline{m}$ is the monetary target (both are assumed to be known constants). Equation (7) is a simple money demand function with a zero interest elasticity and a unit income elasticity: in Figure 2.1 it is drawn as an aggregate demand curve with a slope of -1. Equation (9) is a money supply function in which the government aims for a monetary target with an error, ε_t, which has the properties of our previous ε in (2.1). As the error shocks the economy, aggregate demand shifts up and down around D^*D^*, its steady-state position set by $\overline{m}$. Equation (8) is a Phillips curve as can be seen by subtracting p_{t-1} from both sides; in this case it states that the rate of inflation equals last period's expectation of the inflation rate plus a function of 'excess demand'. We can think of the 'periods' as being 'quarters' and prices as being set, as quantities change, on the basis of last quarter's information about the general price level — hence we appeal to an information lag of one quarter and E_{t-1}refers to this quarter's expectation formed (the operative element) on the basis of last quarter's information. In Figure 2.1, equation (8) is drawn as the aggregate supply curve; rising output requires rising prices, given expected prices, because each producer wants his own relative price to be higher to compensate for the extra effort of higher supply. The vertical supply curve, S^*S^*, is the long-run Phillips curve, indicating that when producers know what the general price level is they will not be 'fooled' into supplying more output as it rises because they realize their own relative price is unchanged.

This model has three linear equations with three endogenous variables, two exogenous variables, $\overline{m}$ and ε_t, and an expectation variable, $E_{t-1}p_t$. Given the expectation, we can solve it normally, for example, by substitution. So substituting for $m_t$and p_t from (8) and (9) into (7) gives us:

$$\overline{m} + \varepsilon_t = E_{t-1}p_t + (1+\delta)y_t - \delta y^* \tag{10}$$

This corresponds to the intersection of the $D'D'$ and SS curves in Figure 2.1. But we now need to find $\mathrm{E}_{t-1}\mathrm{p}_t$, to get the full solution.

To do this, we write the model in expected form (i.e. taking expectations at $t-1$ throughout) as:

$$E_{t-1}m_t = E_{t-1}p_t + E_{t-1}y_t \tag{7^e}$$

$$E_{t-1}p_t = E_{t-1}p_t + \delta(E_{t-1}y_t - y^*) \tag{8^e}$$

$$E_{t-1}m_t = \overline{m} \tag{9^e}$$

Substituting $(8)^e$ and $(9)^e$into $(7)^e$ gives:

$$E_{t-1}p_t = \overline{m} - y^* \tag{11}$$

This is the intersection of the D^*D^* and S^*S^* curves in Figure 2.1. S^*S^* shows what producers will supply on the assumption that the prices they receive are those which they expect (this is an 'expected supply' curve); D^*D^* shows what output will be demanded at different prices on the assumption that the money supply is $\overline{m}$, as expected — (an 'expected demand' curve). Where these two curves intersect is accordingly expected output and prices.

Equation (11) is substituted into (10) to give the full meaning of the p_t, y_t intersection in figure 2.1:

$$y_t = y^* + \frac{1}{1+\delta}\varepsilon_t \tag{12}$$

Consequently, from (8) and using (11):

$$p_t = \overline{m} - y^* + \frac{\delta}{1+\delta}\varepsilon_t \tag{13}$$

The solutions for y_t and p_t consist of an expected part (y^* and $\overline{m} - y^*$, respectively) and an unexpected part (functions of ε_t). Rational expectations has incorporated anything known at $t-1$ with implications for p and y at time t into the expected part, so that the unexpected part is purely unpredictable.

This model, though simple, has an interesting implication, first pointed out by Sargent and Wallace (1975). The solution for y_t is invariant to the parameters of the money supply rule. Output would in this model be at its normal level in the absence of surprises, which here are restricted to monetary surprises. If the government attempts to stabilise output by changing the money supply rule to, say,

$$m_t = \overline{m} - \beta(y_{t-1} - y^*) + \varepsilon_t \tag{14}$$

then still the solution for output is (12), because this money supply rule is incorporated into people's expectations at $t-1$ and cannot cause any surprises. The only effect is on expected (and so also actual) prices:

$$E_{t-1}p_t = \overline{m} - \beta(y_{t-1} - y^*) - y^* = \overline{m} - y^* - \frac{\beta}{1+\delta}\varepsilon_{t-1} \tag{15}$$

$$p_t = \overline{m} - y^* - \frac{\beta}{1+\delta}\varepsilon_{t-1} + \frac{\delta}{1+\delta}\varepsilon_t \tag{16}$$

Note that this will raise the variance of prices around their long-run value $\overline{m} - y^*$ by $(\frac{\beta}{1+\delta})^2\sigma^2$. This is illustrated in Figure 2.2, where we start this

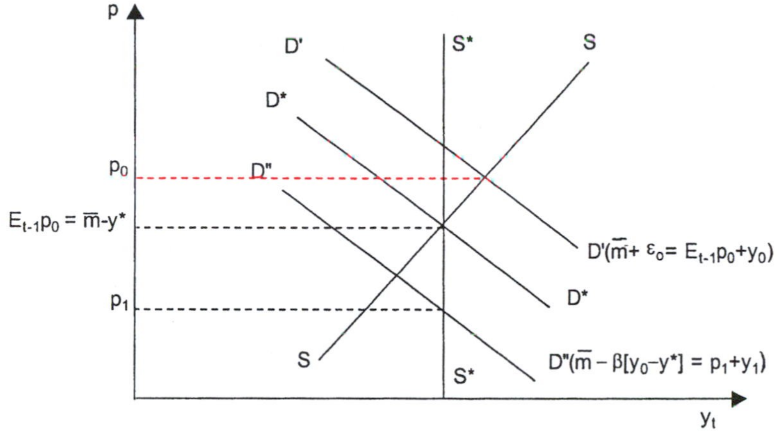

Figure 2.2: A simple model with an interventionist monetary rule

model out from steady state at period $t-1$, where $E_{t-1}p_0 = \overline{m} - y^*$, $E_{t-1}y_0 = y^*$; let there be a shock in period 0, ε_0.

The solution for $(p_0,\ y_0)$ is the same as before. But now the government responds in period 1 with a money supply contraction, reducing m to $\overline{m} - \frac{\beta}{1+\delta}\varepsilon_0$; this shifts the aggregate demand curve to $D''D''$. But because producers know in period 0 that this reaction will occur, they work out the intersection of their expected supply S^*S^*, and the expected demand, $D''D''$, correctly anticipating that $p_1 = \overline{m} - \frac{\beta}{1+\delta}\varepsilon_0 - y^*$. Where these curves intersect is accordingly expected output and prices.

This of course contradicts the well-known results for models with backward-looking expectations whereby stabilization policy by government can reduce fluctuations in output, provided the government chooses the appropriate monetary target. For example, suppose we had assumed in accordance with the popular practice of the 1960s that expectations of the price level were formed adaptively. The adaptive expectations hypothesis is that:

$$x_t^e - x_{t-1}^e = \mu(x_{t-1} - x_{t-1}^e) \qquad 0 < \mu < 1 \tag{17}$$

or that expectations of x_t change by some positive fraction, μ, of last period's error. This can be written equivalently as:

$$\begin{aligned} x_t^e &= \mu x_{t-1} + (1-\mu)x_{t-1}^e = \mu x_{t-1} + (1-\mu)[\mu x_{t-2} + (1-\mu)x_{t-2}^e] \\ &= \mu \sum_{i=0}^{\infty} (1-\mu)^i x_{t-1-i} \end{aligned} \tag{18}$$

by continuous substitution for $x^e_{t-2}, x^e_{t-3} \cdots$

Substituting p^e_t for $E_{t-1}p_t$ in our simple model of (7) to (9) turns it into an orthodox dynamic model to be solved by standard methods. Equation (8) becomes:

$$p_t = \mu \sum_{i=0}^{\infty} (1-\mu)^i p_{t-1-i} + \delta(y_t - y^*) \qquad (2.8^a)$$

We can see that expected prices depend not on the planned money supply but on past events (past prices), which were known to the government last period. Consequently the government can plan a money supply for this period confident that it will not be 'frustrated' by a response from expectations. They can set a target m^*, such that $y_t = y^*$. This will be a target which accommodates prices at their expected level, delivering $p_t = p^e_t$; for $(8)^a$ assures us that when $p_t = p^e_t$, $y_t = y^*$. By (7), when $p_t = p^e_t$ and $y_t = y^*$, then:

$$m^* = p^e_t + y^* = \mu \sum_{i=0}^{\infty} (1-\mu)^i p_{t-1-i} + y^* \qquad (19)$$

We now find that the solution for output depends on the deviations of money supply from this optimal target:

$$y_t = y^* + \frac{1}{1+\delta}(m_t - m^*) \qquad (20)$$

These deviations may be due either to unpredictable errors, ε, as in the rational expectations (RE) case, or to a policy failure to plan m_t at m^*; in other words:

$$m_t - m^* = \varepsilon_t + m^T - m^* \qquad (21)$$

where m^T is the actual policy target. But in this adaptive model both affect output, whereas in the RE version only ε, the error term, does. In other words, the monetary policy chosen affects output not, as in the RE case, merely the monetary surprise.

In subsequent chapters we shall be examining this RE model and a number of considerably more complex RE models whose properties will differ from this one substantially. Nevertheless it is a common feature of all these models that there is an important difference between the effects of an anticipated and of an unanticipated change in any exogenous variable; by contrast, in models where expectations are formed adaptively (or as any fixed function of past data) it makes no difference. This is probably the most fundamental result of rational expectations. It is the nature of the difference of these effects that forms the detailed study of RE models.

The method of solution set out above (the 'basic' method) will suffice for all RE models in which there are expectations (at any date in the past) of current events only. To repeat, this method involves three steps:

1. Solve the model, treating expectations as exogenous.
2. Take the expected value of this solution at the date of the expectations, and solve for the expectations.
3. Substitute the expectations solutions into the solution in 1, and obtain the complete solution.

RE MODELS WITH EXPECTATIONS OF FUTURE VARIABLES (REFV MODELS)

It will very often, in fact almost invariably, be the case — in the nature of economic decisions which, as we have seen, involve a view of the future — that expectations of future events, whether formed currently or in the past, will enter the model. For these REFV models, our basic method must be supplemented and it can be replaced by more convenient alternatives.

For example, add to our previous simple model the assumption made by Cagan (1956) in his influential study of hyperinflation, that the demand for money responds negatively to expected inflation (we can think of this as approximating the effect of interest rates on money demand in less virulent inflations). Let the model now be:

$$m_t = p_t + y_t - \alpha(E_{t-1}p_{t+1} - E_{t-1}p_t) \; (\alpha > 0) \tag{22}$$

$$p_t = E_{t-1}p_t + \delta(y_t - y^*) \tag{8}$$

$$m_t = \overline{m} + \varepsilon_t \tag{9}$$

We keep (8) and (9) as before. In (22) expectations of inflation in the current period are regarded as formed on the basis of last period's (quarter's) information; as in (8) we are appealing to an information lag.

Let us use our basic method and see how it has to be adapted for this model. Step 1 (solving given expectations as exogenous) gives us:

$$\overline{m} + \varepsilon_t = p_t + \frac{1}{\delta}(p_t - E_{t-1}p_t) + y^* - \alpha(E_{t-1}p_{t+1} - E_{t-1}p_t) \tag{23}$$

This is the same intersection (p_t, y_t) as in Figure 2.1, except for the extra term $-\alpha(E_{t-1}p_{t+1} - E_{t-1}p_t)$ which shifts $D'D'$ relative to what is shown there.

To find $E_{t-1}p_t$ and $E_{t-1}p_{t+1}$ we now take expectations of the model at $t-1$ (step 2) to yield:

$$\overline{m} - y^* = (1+\alpha)E_{t-1}p_t - \alpha E_{t-1}p_{t+1} \tag{24}$$

Equation (24) can solve for $E_{t-1}\, p_t$ in terms of $\overline{m}$, y^*, and $E_{t-1}p_{t+1}$. But this is not a solution because $E_{t-1}p_{t+1}$ is not solved out; we appear to have shifted the problem into the future.

To solve for $E_{t-1}p_{t+1}$ we may lead the model by one period (for example, write (22) as $m_{t+1} = p_{t+1} + y_{t+1} - \alpha(E_t p_{t+2} - E_t p_{t+1})$) and take expectations of it at $t-1$ as before. This yields analogously:

$$\overline{m} - y^* = (1+\alpha)E_{t-1}p_{t+1} - \alpha E_{t-1}p_{t+2} \tag{25}$$

We have now solved for $E_{t-1}p_{t+1}$ in terms of m, y^*, and $E_{t-1}p_{t+2}$ again shifting the problem into the future. This naturally leads us to solving for expected values using the method of forward iteration proposed by Thomas Sargent. We write (25) as:

$$E_{t-1}p_{t+1} = \frac{1}{1+\alpha}(\overline{m} - y^*) + \frac{\alpha}{1+\alpha}E_{t-1}p_{t+2} \tag{26}$$

Substitute successively (forwards) for $E_{t-1}p_{t+2}$, $E_{t-1}p_{t+3}$ and so on in (26) to obtain:

$$E_{t-1}p_t = \frac{1}{1+\alpha}\sum_{i=0}^{N-1}\left(\frac{\alpha}{1+\alpha}\right)^i(\overline{m} - y^*) + \left(\frac{\alpha}{1+\alpha}\right)^N E_{t-1}p_{t+N} \tag{27}$$

Let $N \rightarrow \infty$ and assume (as seems natural) that $E_{t-1}p_{t+i}$ is stable, so that $E_{t-1}p_{t+N} \rightarrow$ its equilibrium as $N \rightarrow \infty$. Since $\left(\frac{\alpha}{1+\alpha}\right)^N \rightarrow 0$ also as $N \rightarrow \infty$ the final, remainder, term in (27) disappears and (27) becomes:

$$E_{t-1}p_t = \frac{1}{1+\alpha}\sum_{i=0}^{\infty}(\frac{\alpha}{1+\alpha})^i(\overline{m} - y^*) = \overline{m} - y^* \tag{28}$$

We can reach the same result by using the forward operator, B^{-1} (B is the backward operator that instructs us to lag the variable but not the expectations date, unlike L which instructs us to lag both).

Write (24) as:

$$(1+\alpha)\left(1 - \frac{\alpha}{1+\alpha}B^{-1}\right)E_{t-1}p_t = \overline{m} - y^* \tag{29}$$

It follows that:

$$E_{t-1}p_t = \frac{1}{1+\alpha}\frac{\overline{m}-y^*}{1-\frac{\alpha}{1+\alpha}B^{-1}} = \frac{1}{1+\alpha}\sum_{i=0}^{\infty}\left(\frac{\alpha}{1+\alpha}B^{-1}\right)^i(\overline{m}-y^*)$$
$$= \overline{m}-y^* \quad (30)$$

In this particular case, the exogenous variables are constant. However, Sargent's method can be generalised; for example suppose that the money supplies were exogenously given to us (it might be that each period the central bank's policies are reassessed in the light of a variety of current information including bank announcements and the result is most simply written down as a new set of projections each time.) The model is the same, (22) and (8), except for the omission of (9).

(23) now becomes:

$$m_t = p_t + \frac{1}{\delta}(p_t - E_{t-1}p_t) + y^* - \alpha(E_{t-1}p_{t+1} - E_{t-1}p_t) \quad (31)$$

Subtracting from this its expected value at $t-1$ yields:

$$p_t - E_{t-1}p_t = \frac{\delta}{1+\delta}(m_t - E_{t-1}m_t) \quad (32)$$

which tells us that the solution for prices depends on the revision to the money supply planned at t plus expected prices.

To find expected prices take expectations of (31):

$$E_{t-1}m_t - y^* = (1+\alpha)(E_{t-1}p_t) - \alpha(E_{t-1}p_{t+1}) \quad (33)$$

from which we obtain using the forward operator:

$$E_{t-1}p_t = [\frac{1}{1+\alpha}\sum_{i=0}^{\infty}(\frac{\alpha}{1+\alpha})^i E_{t-1}m_{t+i}] - y^* \quad (34)$$

In other words the whole path of future monetary policy foreseen at $t-1$ determines expected prices for t.

We have now seen how in a rational expectations model the expected future affects expectations of the present. Plainly the direction of causation is from the (expected) future to the (expected) present. We note that (24) is a difference equation which had to be 'solved forwards' by iteration into the future; the present depends on the future via a stable root, $\frac{\alpha}{1+\alpha}$. However, it is possible — though on reflection odd — to look at the relationship differently, as one where the expected present affects the expected future. Looking at it this way draws attention to the possibility that a rational expectations model may have self-generating explosive paths or 'bubbles'.

Suppose we go back to (24) and (25). We could have carried on in this way indefinitely and it is easy to see that we would have obtained a series of equations which could be written as a sort of difference equation:

$$\overline{m} - y^* = (1+\alpha)E_{t-1}p_{t+i} - \alpha E_{t-1}p_{t+i+1} \ (i \geqslant 0) \quad (35)$$

This is actually a difference equation in a variable p^e_{t+1}, defined to be p_{t+i} as expected from $t-1$:

$$p^e_{t+i+1} - \frac{1-\alpha}{\alpha} p^e_{t+i} = -\frac{1}{\alpha}(\overline{m} - y^*) \ (i \geqslant 0) \tag{36}$$

The solution of this first-order non-homogenous difference equation is familiarly:

$$p^e_{t+i} = \overline{m} - y^* + [p^e_t - (\overline{m} - y^*)](\frac{1+\alpha}{\alpha})^i \ (i \geqslant 0) \tag{37}$$

where $\overline{m} - y^*$ is the equilibrium of p_t (the 'particular' solution), $\frac{1+\alpha}{\alpha}$ is the unstable root (note that it is the inverse of the stable forward root when we solved the model forwards) and $p^e_t - (\overline{m} - y^*)$ is the constant (determined by the initial value p^e_t) in the 'general' solution. Here we are solving the model 'backwards' from the future to the present in the sense that the (expected) future is depending on the (expected) present; the same root that was stable when the model was solved forwards is now unstable when the model is solved backwards.

This can be understood from Figure 2.3. Here we have drawn the long-run Phillips curve, S^*S^*, and the aggregate demand curve, D^*D^*, on the assumption that prices are not expected to change ($E_{t-1}\Delta p_{t+1} = 0$). On this assumption the expected price level is $\overline{m} - y^*$ as before (see Figure 2.1). But we can rewrite the expected solution of equations (22) and (9) as $E_{t-1}\Delta p_{t+1} = \frac{1}{\alpha}(E_{t-1}p_t + y^* - \overline{m})$ which shows that if expected aggregate demand ($E_{t-1}p_t + y^*$) exceeds the expected money supply, $\overline{m}$, then it must be because prices are expected to rise; and vice versa. So to the right of D^*D^*, prices are expected to rise, and to its left they are expected to fall, as shown by the arrows on Figure 2.3. Since output is always expected to be y^* on S^*S^*, the possible solution for $E_{t-1}p_t$ and subsequent $E_{t-1}p_{t+1}$ are shown by the arrows on S^*S^*. One such solution is shown by the intersection of the $D'D'$ dashed curve showing the expected aggregate demand curve, when prices are expected to rise.

CHOOSING A UNIQUE DEMAND PATH

Equation (37) and Figure 2.3 give an infinite number of solution paths for p^e_{t+i} $(i \geqslant 0)$. For we are free to choose any value of p^e_t we like; the model does not restrict our choice. Another way of looking at (37) is to say that we can choose any future value for any p^e_{t+i} we wish and work back from that to a solution for p^e_t. We could already have guessed that this would be so from (24) for, to obtain the expectation of a current value, we were compelled to take a view about $E_{t-1}p_{t+1}$. Any view of

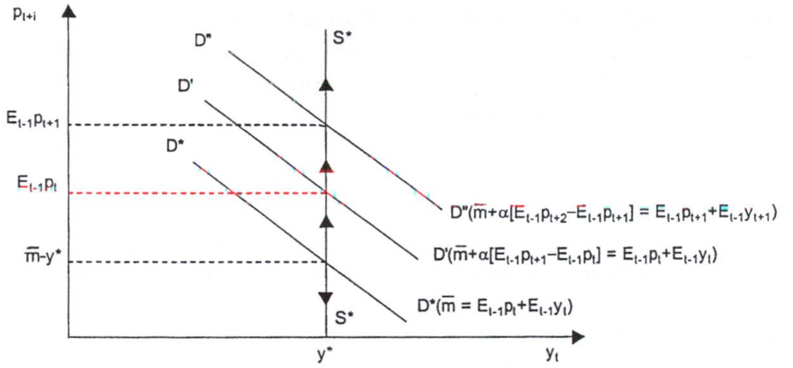

Figure 2.3: The solution expected at $t-1$ of a simple REFV model, illustrated for an unstable path

this future will then compel a present which is consistent with it; any set of expectations is therefore self-justifying.

REFV models (that is, the vast majority) would be little better than curiosa if they did not carry with them additional restrictions sufficient to define a unique solution; for they would merely assert in effect that 'anything can happen provided it is expected, but what is expected is arbitrary'. Worse still, as (37) illustrates, these paths for events can be unstable; in fact, our model here implied that all paths for prices except that for which $p_t^e = \overline{m} - y^*$, explode monotonically as shown in Figure 2.4. Thus our particular REFV model would assert that only by accident would an equilibrium price level be established, otherwise prices would be propelled into either ever-deepening hyperdeflation or ever-accelerating hyperinflation, even though money supply is held rigid! (Output in this model is always expected to be equilibrium.) While such an assertion may appeal to some it has not impressed those who have espoused RE models; they have looked instead for additional restrictions.

We have already hinted at the source of an additional restriction in our model by noting the instability of all but one path. It is clear that the unstable paths are in some sense absurd. The question is: what would prevent them? It has to be the case that behaviour would alter in such a way as to prevent them.

Consider, for example, the path of ever-accelerating hyperinflation anticipated fully now (on the basis of last period's information). People deciding how much money to hold for transactions would expect now that in so many years they will need truckfuls of money to buy the daily groceries; they would therefore find an alternative means of carrying out transactions to avoid the investment in trucks they will otherwise anticipate. They would use beans or cows or sophisticated forms of barter to replace the old money. Ultimately the old money would not be used at all; prices would be defined in the new money, say beans.

But money has an issuer; it may be a bank or a government. The issuer derives profits from people's use of its money issue, and it will pay them to avoid its replacement. This it can only do by stopping any such hyperinflation 'bubbles' occurring. It turns out that a commitment on the issuer's part to put an end to any such inflation at some point, by decreasing the money supply at a sufficient rate to offset any decline in real money balances held, will do the trick. For if people expect that inflation will stop at some period $t+N$ (at which the bank will 'step in'), then this implies an arresting of the very ongoing process that sustains the earlier path. Real money balances desired in $t+N$ will now be higher than anticipated in that path, so inflation must be lower in $t+N$. But if this is so, then real money balances in $t+N-1$ will be similarly higher, so also inflation will be lower then; and so on. The whole path will be invalidated.

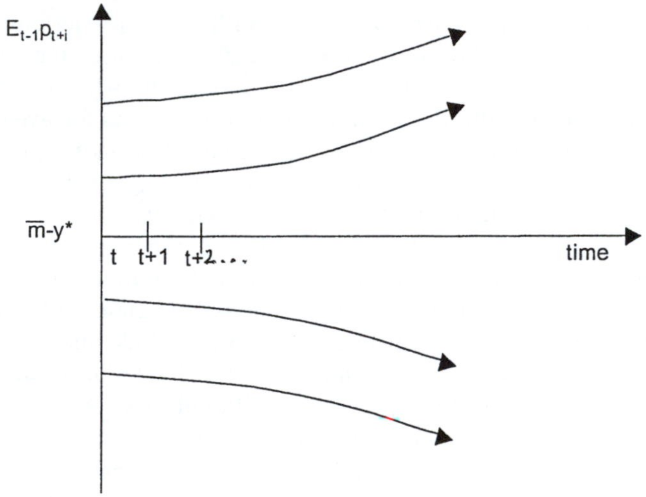

Figure 2.4: The solution paths for the price level expected at $t-1$, as in equation (37)

In fact we can show this formally by imposing on the difference equation (37) the condition that :

$$p^e_{t+i+1} - p^e_{t+i} = 0 \ (i \geqslant N) \tag{38}$$

and letting (37) run from $N \leqslant i \geqslant 0$, since $t+N$ is the period when the bank's new regime takes over. Using (37) for $i = N$, we have:

$$\overline{m} - y^* = p^e_{t+N} + \alpha(p^e_{t+N} - p^e_{t+N+1}) = \text{by (38) } p^e_{t+N} \tag{39}$$

By (37) this implies:

$$\overline{m} - y^* = \overline{m} - y^* + [p^e_t - (\overline{m} - y^*)]\left(\frac{1-\alpha}{\alpha}\right)^N \tag{40}$$

or:

$$p^e_t = (\overline{m} - y^*) \tag{41}$$

It can be seen that (41) when applied to (37) selects the unique stable path for p^e_{t+i} so that:

$$p^e_{t+1} = \overline{m} - y^* \ (i \geqslant 0) \tag{42}$$

An analogous argument can be constructed for the path of ever-deepening hyperdeflation. In this case people will 'demand' infinite amounts of money because its return is infinite in the long term; this implies that the money will be hoarded and disappear from circulation. The bank or government will wish to prevent this (because otherwise some other money will come into existence) by issuing money until the profit rate on the issue has returned to a normal level, that is the rate of deflation is zero. The knowledge that the issuer will go on issuing money until this occurs acts to impose the same condition (38) on the model.

We have constructed verbal arguments to justify the imposition of a 'terminal condition' such as (38) in our model. These arguments appeal to forces not explicitly in the model, but which would be brought into play by certain types of behaviour apparently allowed for by the model. These forces will differ from model to model; for example we may appeal to legal controls or supervisory agencies to ensure 'orderly markets', or to competitive forces[1], or to precepts upon government itself. But an RE model with expectations of the future (REFV model) is incomplete

---

[1] For example, in the competitive equilibrium model of the labour market of Lucas and Sargent, as set out in, for example, Sargent (1979a, chapter 16) the transversality conditions of households and firms supply the necessary terminal conditions. These conditions are necessary for optimality; in other words, explosive paths for labour supply and demand are not followed by households or firms because they are suboptimal.

without some forces of this kind to supply an additional restriction, such as the terminal condition here.

Another way of describing our 'terminal' condition would be as a 'side' or 'transversality' condition: all these express the same idea, that there is an additional restriction on the model, here coming from government or central bank behaviour designed to rule out what is from their (or society's) viewpoint an undesirable outcome, in this instance for the monetary environment. We will come across other such transversality conditions later in this book (for example, on private or government borrowing designed to rule out unsustainable and thus undesirable borrowing paths).

Our terminal condition (38) has the effect in the model here of selecting the unique stable path. For REFV models with such a unique stable path like the one here (that is, with the 'saddlepath' property, so called because any deviation from this path is unstable), the imposition of terminal stationarity on the expectations ensures the selection of this path. For such models, it is therefore only necessary to specify as a side condition on the model that the solutions be stable or stationary; this condition is referred to variously in the literature as the 'stability' or 'stationarity' or 'convergence' condition, or 'ruling out speculative bubbles' or 'boundedness'. We appealed to it when we used the forward iteration or operator method above; to obtain that solution we had to assume that the expected price sequence was stable.

We have now completed step (2) in our solution procedure, albeit in a more complex manner than before; call it step (2′). We proceed to step (3) and substitute for $E_{t-1}p_t$, $E_{t-1}p_{t+1}$ into (23). It turns out in this model that the solution is the same as for our earlier model, as the reader can easily verify.

We may now review our basic method for solving REFV models:

1. Solve the model, treating expectations as exogenous.

2. Take the expected value of this solution at the date of the expectations. If the model generates a unique stable path for the expectational variables, impose the stability condition, and derive this solution for the expectations. Do so either by the forward iteration or the backward difference equation method.

3. Substitute the expectations solutions into the solution in 1 and obtain the complete solution.

BUBBLES

The significance of the terminal condition that enforces stability can be seen by considering 'bubbles' or 'will o' the wisp' variables. Suppose we had no such terminal condition. Then it can be seen that it can be rational to expect at $t-1$ any price level for t provided one also expects an ever-exploding price level for the future, the 'bubble'.

It is possible to add arbitrary variables to the solution of REFV models provided they obey certain processes dictated by the coefficients in the model's future expectations (see, for example, Canzoneri, 1983; and Gourieroux et al., 1982).

For example, take the model we have been looking at, of (22), (8) and (9). Suppose people believe at $t-1$, for no good reason, that prices would be affected by $(\frac{1+\alpha}{\alpha})^i E_{t-1} z_{t+i}$ where:

$$E_{t-1} z_{t+i} = z_{t-1} \tag{43}$$

(that is, z_t is a martingale). Their belief, though 'irrational', would formally be validated by the model, since

$$E_{t-1} p_{t+i} = (\overline{m} - y^*) + (\frac{1+\alpha}{\alpha})^i E_{t-1} z_{t+i} \tag{44}$$

is a solution to the model, as can be verified by substituting (44) and (43) into (24). Any 'will o' the wisp' variable, z_{t-1}, could therefore produce an irrational solution to an REFV model by this self-validating process.

This is simply an implication of the indeterminacy of p_t^e we noted earlier in commenting on equation (37); so we can write $p_t^e - (\overline{m} - y^*) = \mu_{t-1}$ where μ_{t-1} is anything. However, the solution to the bubble problem is one and the same as that of the indeterminacy and instability problem: we have to impose an additional restriction on the model to ensure determinacy and stability. Since the exploding bubble must at some point violate the terminal condition, the whole path collapses back to the unique stable solution.

This terminal condition approach to ruling out bubbles is similar in effect to McCallum's suggestion (1983) that a 'minimum set of state variables' (MSV) be imposed on the solution; that is, one eliminates as many state variables as possible from the solution while still maintaining consistency with the rational expectations constraint. In effect the minimum set excludes any such extraneous variables that enter as bubbles. We would argue that the justification of imposing MSV lies in the optimizing transversality conditions on the agents in the model. However, of course in practice the procedures deliver the same solution.

OTHER METHODS OF SOLUTION FOR REFV MODELS

Not surprisingly there are several other methods for finding the unique stable solution to an REFV model which has one. We shall explain two in detail because they have been widely used: the Muth method of undetermined coefficients and the Lucas method of undetermined coefficients.

The Muth Method of Undetermined Coefficients

The Muth method starts from the proposition that the general solution of our model can be written (via the Wold decomposition — see the time-series annex at the end of the book):

$$p_t = \overline{p} + \sum_{i=0}^{\infty} \pi_i \varepsilon_{t-i} \tag{45}$$

$$y_t = \overline{y} + \sum_{i=0}^{\infty} \phi_i \varepsilon_{t-i} \tag{46}$$

where $\overline{p}$, $\overline{y}$ are the equilibrium values of p_t, y_t. Note that this way of writing the solution assumes that there are no expected future exogenous variables or else that they can be entirely substituted out in terms of current and past events. This implies that the Muth and Lucas methods are not entirely general (in particular it means that the forward root is solved backwards and so appears in its inverse, unstable, form), but they are useful for the wide class of models where this assumption is valid.

Let us focus on the solution for p_t, since that for y_t follows easily enough. $\overline{y} = y^*$ and $\overline{p} = \overline{m} - y^*$ by setting $E_{t-1}p_t = E_{t-1}p_{t+1} = p_t = \overline{p}$ and $y_t = \overline{y}$ in the model.

Having found the equilibrium in terms of the constants, we now drop these from the model and define (p_t, y_t) in deviations from equilibrium. The model can now be written in terms of p_t as:

$$\varepsilon_t = (1 + \frac{1}{\delta})p_t + (\alpha - \frac{1}{\delta})E_{t-1}p_t - \alpha E_{t-1}p_{t+1} \tag{47}$$

Using (45):

$$p_t = \sum_{i=0}^{\infty} \pi_t \varepsilon_{t-i} \tag{48}$$

$$E_{t-1}p_t = \sum_{i=1}^{\infty} \pi_i \varepsilon_{t-i} \tag{49}$$

$$p_{t+1} = \sum_{i=0}^{\infty} \pi_i \varepsilon_{t-i-1} = \sum_{i=1}^{\infty} \pi_{i+1} \varepsilon_{t-i} \tag{50}$$

$$E_{t-1} p_{t+1} = \sum_{i=1}^{\infty} \pi_{i+1} \varepsilon_{t-i} \tag{51}$$

Equations (49) and (51) follow from (48) and (50) respectively because $E_{t-1}\varepsilon_t = E_{t-1}\varepsilon_{t+1} = 0$.

Substituting (48)–(51) into (47):

$$\varepsilon_t - \left(1 + \frac{1}{\delta}\right) \sum_{i=0}^{\infty} \pi_i \varepsilon_{t-i} - \left(\alpha - \frac{1}{\delta}\right) \sum_{i=1}^{\infty} \pi_i \varepsilon_{t-i} + \alpha \sum_{i=1}^{\infty} \pi_{i+1} \varepsilon_{t-i} = 0 \tag{52}$$

Each ε_{t-i} can be any number so that (52) can hold if and only if the set of the coefficients on ϵ_t, on ϵ_{t-1}, on ϵ_{t-2} ...., each individually sums to zero. These sets must satisfy:

$$(\text{on } \varepsilon_t) 1 - \left(1 - \frac{1}{\delta}\right) \pi_0 = 0 \tag{53}$$

$$(\text{on } \varepsilon_{t-i}, i \geqslant 1) - (1 + \alpha)\pi_i + \alpha \pi_{i+1} = 0 \tag{54}$$

Equation (54) is a homogeneous, difference equation in π_i with the same root as (27) above, and an analogous solution:

$$\pi_i = \pi_1 \left(\frac{1 + \alpha}{\alpha}\right)^{i-1} \quad (i \geqslant 1) \tag{55}$$

Note that the forward root here is being 'driven backwards' artificially. In (55) again we see that there are an infinity of solutions chosen here by selecting π_1 arbitrarily and that only one is stable, namely that where $\pi_1 = 0$, which of course stops the forward root operating backwards in an unstable manner.

Invoking the stability condition we set $\pi_1 = 0$, so that $\pi_i = 0$ $(i \geqslant 1)$. From (53) we obtain $\pi_0 = \frac{\delta}{1+\delta}$. Our solution in p_t is therefore:

$$p_t = \overline{m} - y^* + \left(\frac{\delta}{1 + \delta}\right) \epsilon_t \tag{56}$$

as before.

The Muth method becomes unwieldy for larger models where there are several errors like ε_t for each of which a sequence of coefficients must be determined, but it is often convenient for small illustrative models, and we shall use it frequently for this purpose.

Lucas Method of Undetermined Coefficients

A variant of the Muth method of undetermined coefficients has occasionally been used (for example, Barro, 1976; Lucas, 1972a) whereby the solution for the endogenous variables, instead of being written in terms of the constants and the errors, is written in terms of the 'state' variables, that is, current and past values of the exogenous variables (including the error terms of the model equations) and past values of the endogenous variables. (It therefore is like the Muth method in assuming that expected future exogenous variables can be reduced to current and past events; it, too, therefore drives the forward root backwards.) The need to include all the state variables can make this method unnecessarily complicated, as the example of this model shows.

Write the solution for p_t (on which we focus) as

$$p_t = \pi_1 \varepsilon_t + \pi_2 p_{t-1} + \pi_3 y_{t-1} + \pi_4 \varepsilon_{t-1} + \pi_5 \overline{m} + \pi_6 y^* \tag{57}$$

We have:

$$\overline{m} + \varepsilon_t = p_t + \frac{1}{\delta}(p_t - E_{t-1}p_t) + y^* - \alpha(E_{t-1}p_{t+1} - E_{t-1}p_t) \tag{58}$$

Use (57) to generate $E_{t-1}p_t$, $E_{t-1}p_{t+1}$ and substitute for these and p_t in (58), obtaining:

$$\begin{aligned}\overline{m} + \varepsilon_t = \pi_t \varepsilon_t + \pi_2 p_{t-1} + \pi_3 y_{t-1} + \pi_4 \varepsilon_{t-1} + \pi_5 \overline{m} + \pi_6 y^* + \frac{1}{\delta}(\pi_1 \varepsilon_t) \\ + y^* - \alpha[(\pi_2 - 1)(\pi_2 p_{t-1} + \pi_3 y_{t-1} + \pi_4 \epsilon_{t-1} + \pi_5 \overline{m} + \pi_6 y^*) \\ + \pi_3 y^* + \pi_5 \overline{m} + \pi_6 y^*]\end{aligned} \tag{59}$$

We used $E_{t-1}y_t = y^*$ in this, from the Phillips curve. Now by the same argument as with the Muth method, the terms in each of the state variables must equate. So we have:

$$(\text{terms in } \varepsilon_t)\text{: } 1 = \pi_1 + \frac{1}{\delta}\pi_1$$

yielding:

$$\pi_1 = \frac{1}{1 + \frac{1}{\delta}} = \frac{\delta}{1 + \delta} \tag{60}$$

$$(\text{terms in } p_{t-1})\ 0 = \pi_2 - \alpha(\pi_2 - 1)\pi_2 = \pi_2(1 + \alpha) - \alpha\pi_2 \tag{61}$$

from which there are two solutions for $\pi_2 = 0, \frac{1+\alpha}{\alpha}$. Of these, $\frac{1+\alpha}{\alpha}$ (the forward root again being artificially driven backwards) violates the stability condition and is ruled out, leaving $\pi_2 = 0$.

$$\text{(terms in } y_{t-1}\text{)}\ 0 = \pi_3 - \alpha(\pi_2 - 1)\pi_3, \text{ implying } \pi_3 = 0 \tag{53}$$

$$\text{(terms in } \varepsilon_{t-1}\text{)}\ 0 = \pi_4 - \alpha(\pi_2 - 1)\pi_4, \text{ implying } \pi_4 = 0 \tag{54}$$

Given these solutions, the terms in $\overline{m}$ and y^* yield $\pi_5 = 1$, $\pi_6 = -1$. Hence we have obtained, if by a somewhat round-about route, the solution for p_t; that for y_t follows simply using the Phillips curve.

Clearly the method of solution is a matter purely of convenience. We have discussed several methods, all of which have been extensively used according to the problem and tastes of the problem solver. All have their advantages and disadvantages and are worth the reader's while to understand.

THE TECHNIQUES IN APPLICATION: A MORE COMPLICATED EXAMPLE

We now use a slightly more elaborate REFV model (with a unique stable solution) to illustrate further the application of these solution methods. The model here is 'fully dynamic', that is to say it returns to its steady state gradually after a shock rather than immediately as our previous models did. As such it is a prototype for many macro models used in practical analysis.

We retain our Cagan-style money demand equation but date the expectations at t for convenience in the money market[2]. We also retain our simple money supply equation (9); but we allow for adjustment costs in the response of output to unexpected price changes (our Phillips curve). So now we have a new model:

$$m_t = p_t + y_t - \alpha(E_t p_{t+1} - p_t)\ (\alpha > 0) \tag{62}$$

$$y_t - y^* = \frac{1}{\delta}(p_t - E_{t-1}p_t) + \mu(y_{t-1} - y^*) = \frac{1}{\delta}\frac{(p_t - E_{t-1}p_t)}{1 - \mu L} \tag{63}$$

$$m_t = \overline{m} + \varepsilon_t \tag{64}$$

where we have used the backward lag operator, L, in rewriting (63) to facilitate our subsequent operations.

[2]This dating of expectations implies that agents in the money and bonds markets have access to all current information whereas those in the goods and labour markets only have access to last period's — not a set-up with much theoretical appeal. Exactly what information which agents have is discussed carefully below (especially in the following chapters, 3 and 4). Here we make this assumption merely to illustrate our techniques with less complication.

Basic Method

Let us apply our adjusted method, focusing on the solution for p_t. Step 1 gives, substituting for (63) and (64) into (62):

$$\overline{m} + \varepsilon_t = (1+\alpha)p_t + y^* + \frac{1}{\delta}\frac{(p_t - E_{t-1}p_t)}{1-\mu L} - \alpha E_t p_{t+1} \tag{65}$$

Rearranging and multiplying through by $(1-\mu L)$ yields:

$$(\overline{m} - y^*)(1-\mu) + \varepsilon_t - \mu\varepsilon_{t-1} = -\alpha E_t p_{t+1} + \left(1+\alpha+\frac{1}{\delta}\right)p_t + \left(\alpha\mu - \frac{1}{\delta}\right)E_{t-1}p_t - (\mu+\alpha\mu)p_{t-1} \tag{66}$$

Notice that the lag of $E_t p_{t+1}$ is $E_{t-1}p_t$ and not, for example, p_t or $E_{t-1}p_t$.

We now move to step (2′), where we must find $E_t p_{t+1}$ and $E_{t-1}p_{t+1}$. Accordingly, first we take expectations at $t=1$ to obtain:

$$(\overline{m} - y^*)(1-\mu) - \mu\varepsilon_{t-1} = -\alpha E_{t-1}p_{t+1} + (1+\alpha+\alpha\mu)E_{t-1}p_t - (\mu+\alpha\mu)p_{t-1} \tag{67}$$

and:

$$(\overline{m} - y^*)(1-\mu) = -\alpha E_{t-1}p_{t+i+1} + (1+\alpha+\alpha\mu)E_{t-1}p_{t+i} - (\mu+\alpha\mu)E_{t-1}p_{t+i-1}\ (i \geqslant 1) \tag{68}$$

The solution of (68) is:

$$E_{t-1}p_{t+i} = (\overline{m} - y^*) + A_1\left(\frac{1+\alpha}{\alpha}\right)^i + A_2\mu^i\ (i \geq 0) \tag{69}$$

where A and B are determined by the initial values $E_{t-1}p_{t+1}$, $E_{t-1}p_t$. However, we have only one equation (67), to determine both $E_{t-1}p_{t+1}$ and $E_{t-1}p_t$, so that there is an infinity of paths, all but one unstable (this situation of a unique stable path from which movement in any direction is unstable is known as the 'saddlepath' property). Impose the stability condition, then set $A_1 = 0$ with the result that $A_2 = E_{t-1}p_t - (\overline{m} - y^*)$ so defining:

$$E_{t-1}p_{t+1} = \overline{m} - y^* + [E_{t-1}p_t - (\overline{m} - y^*)]\mu \tag{70}$$

We can now use (67) to solve for $E_{t-1}p_t$ as:

$$E_{t-1}p_t = (\overline{m} - y^*)(1-\mu) - \frac{\mu}{1+\alpha}\varepsilon_{t-1} + \mu p_{t-1} \tag{71}$$

We can infer immediately from (71) that:

$$E_t p_{t+1} = (\overline{m} - y^*)(1-\mu) - \frac{\mu}{1+\alpha}\varepsilon_t + \mu p_t \tag{72}$$

This can be verified by leading (67) one period, taking expectations at t, and repeating the operations in (68) to (71) but advanced one period.

We have now completed step 2′ and proceed to step 3, substituting $E_{t-1}p_t$ and $E_t p_{t+1}$ from (71) and (72) into (66), to obtain after collecting terms:

$$p_t = (\overline{m}-y^*)(1-\mu) - \frac{\mu}{1+\alpha}\varepsilon_{t-1} + \mu p_{t-1} + \frac{1+\alpha-\alpha\mu}{(1+\alpha)(1+\alpha-\alpha\mu+\frac{1}{\delta})}\varepsilon_t \tag{73}$$

This model and its solution are illustrated in Figure 2.5. The initial shock to demand, ε_t, shifts the aggregate demand curve out to DD along the SS, short-run Phillips, curve. The position of DD takes account of $E_t p_{t+1}$, the expected value of next period's price level. This expectation solution is found by locating the unique stable path (the analogue of the algebra in equations (69) to (71)). The D^*D^* curve shows the combinations of (p, y) for which prices are not expected to change: the equation of the LM curve (62) is written as $E_t \Delta p_{t+i+1} = \frac{-1}{\alpha}(\overline{m} - E_t p_{t+i} - E_t y_{t+i}$ $(i \geqslant 1)$. The S^*S^* curve shows the combinations of (p, y) for which output is not expected to change: the Phillips curve, (63), is written as $E_t \Delta y_{t+i} = (\mu - 1)(E_t y_{t+i} - y^*)$ $(i \geqslant 1)$.

The arrows show the implied motion of (p, y) where they take values off these curves; the line with arrows pointing along it towards the steady-state equilibrium at the intersection of D^*D^* and S^*S^*, is the saddlepath, the unique stable solution. $E_t p_{t+1}$ jumps from p_t on to this line at the point where it intersects $S'S'$, the expected vertical Phillips curve given by the gradual adjustment of y_t back to y^*; going through this point accordingly in an aggregate demand curve, $D'D'$, whose equation is $\overline{m} - E_t y_{t+1} + \alpha E_t p_{t+2} = (1+\alpha)E_t p_{t+1}$. $D'D'$ looks forward to $E_t p_{t+2}$ which can be found in a similar way as the point on the saddlepath intersected by $E_t y_{t+2}$. Accordingly (p, y) are expected to converge at the rate μ on $(\overline{m} - y^*,\ y^*)$ along this saddlepath, after their initial shock to $(p_t,\ y_t)$.

The basic method using the Sargent forward operator approach

We proceed as above up to (68). Sargent now rewrites (68) as:

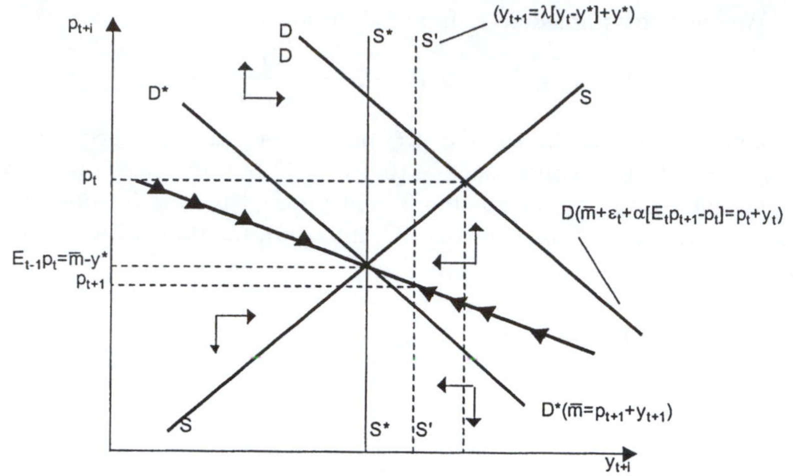

Figure 2.5: The solution of a fully dynamic model when a shock, ε_t, disturbs equilibrium

$$\begin{aligned}
\frac{-1}{\alpha}(\overline{m}-y^*)(1-\mu) &= \left[B^{-1} - \left(\frac{1+\alpha}{\alpha}+\mu\right) + \left(\frac{1+\alpha}{\alpha}\right)\mu B\right] E_{t-1}p_{t+i} \\
&= \left(B^{-1} - \frac{1+\alpha}{\alpha}\right)(1-\mu B)E_{t-1}p_{t+i} \\
&= -\frac{1+\alpha}{\alpha}\left[1 - \left(\frac{\alpha}{1+\alpha}\right)B^{-1}\right](1-\mu B)E_{t-1}p_{t+i} \quad (i \geqslant 1) \qquad (74)
\end{aligned}$$

Now we can write (74) as:

$$\left(\frac{1}{1+\alpha}\right)\frac{(\overline{m}-y^*)(1-\mu)}{\left(1-\frac{\alpha}{1+\alpha}B^{-1}\right)} = (1-\mu B)E_{t-1}p_{t+i} \quad (i \geqslant 1) \qquad (75)$$

If we impose stability, this yields setting $i = 1$:

$$E_{t-1}p_{t+1} = \mu E_{t-1}p_t + (\overline{m}-y^*)(1-\mu) \qquad (76)$$

which yields the rest of our solution as before.

The Sargent method thus represents a convenient extension of operator techniques to REFV models. ‘Backward roots’ (entering because of lagged adjustment) are projected backwards, that is, kept in the form $1/(1-\mu B)$, ‘forward roots’ (entering via expected future variables) are projected forwards, that is, transformed to $1/\left(1-\frac{\alpha}{1+\alpha}B^{-1}\right)$; this procedure, under the stability condition, gives us the same result as before, but in a very compact manner.

Sargent's method is particularly useful for dealing with delayed shocks which are nevertheless anticipated from a date before they occur; so far we have considered only contemporaneous, unanticipated shocks. But, for example, it may become known now that the government plans to raise the money supply sharply in two years' time for some reason to do with anticipated public finance difficulties.

To allow for such a possibility let us in (64) allow ε_t to be a shock which may be related to previous events, whereas before it was assumed to be unrelated. Now moving through the previous steps of our solution, we find that (66) is the same. Taking expectations at $t-1$, however, yields:

$$(\overline{m}-y^*)(1-\mu)+E_{t-1}\varepsilon_t-\mu\varepsilon_{t-1}=-\alpha E_{t-1}p_{t+1} \\ +(1+\alpha+\alpha\mu)E_{t-1}p_t-(\mu+\alpha\mu)p_{t-1} \quad (77)$$

and so:

$$(\overline{m}-y^*)(1-\mu)+E_{t-1}\varepsilon_{t+i}-\mu E_{t-1}\varepsilon_{t+i-1}=-\alpha E_{t-1}p_{t+i+1}+ \\ (1+\alpha+\alpha\mu)E_{t-1}p_{t+}i-(\mu+\alpha\mu)E_{t-1}p_{t+i-1} \quad (i\geq 1) \quad (78)$$

Sargent's (74) now becomes:

$$-\frac{1}{\alpha}(\overline{m}-y^*)(1-\mu)-\frac{1}{\alpha}(1-\mu B)E_{t-1}\varepsilon_{t+i}= \\ \left(1-\frac{1+\alpha}{\alpha}B\right)(1-\mu B)B^{-1}E_{t-1}p_{t+i} \quad (i\geqslant 1) \quad (79)$$

And (75):

$$(\overline{m}-y^*)(1-\mu)+\frac{1}{1+\alpha}\frac{1-\mu B}{1-(\frac{1+\alpha}{\alpha}B)^{-1}}E_{t-1}\varepsilon_{t+i} \\ =(1-\mu B)E_{t-1}p_{t+i} \quad (i\geq 1) \quad (80)$$

The left-hand side of this can be written:

$$(\overline{m}-y^*)(1-\mu)+\frac{1}{1+\alpha}\sum_{j=0}^{\infty}(\alpha/1+\alpha)'(E_{t-1}\varepsilon_{t+i+j}-\mu E_{t-1}\varepsilon_{t+i-1+j})$$

which implies for the case of $i=1$ the solution for:

$$E_{t-1}p_{t+1}=\mu E_{t-1}p_t+(\overline{m}-y^*)(1-\mu)+1/(1+\alpha) \\ \sum_{j=0}^{\infty}[\alpha/(1+\alpha)]^j\,(E_{t-1}\varepsilon_{t+j+1}-\mu E_{t-1}\varepsilon_{t+j}) \quad (81)$$

We can also use (77) to solve for $E_{t-1}p_t$ as:

$$E_{t-1}p_t = (\overline{m} - y^*)(1-\mu) + \frac{1}{1+\alpha}E_{t-1}\varepsilon_t - \frac{\mu}{1+\alpha}\varepsilon_{t-1} + \mu p_{t-1} + \frac{1}{1+\alpha}\sum_{j=0}^{\infty}\left(\frac{\alpha}{1+\alpha}\right)^{j+1}(E_{t-1}\varepsilon_{t+j+1} - \mu E_{t-1}\varepsilon_{t+j}) \quad (82)$$

Now we see that the future shocks foreseen at $t-1$ for $t+j$ enter the expected solution for p_t with a coefficient of

$$\left.\frac{1}{1+\alpha}\right]\left[\left(\frac{\alpha}{1+\alpha}\right)^j - \mu\left(\frac{\alpha}{1+\alpha}\right)^{j+1}\right] = \left(\frac{\alpha}{1+\alpha}\right)^j\left(1-\mu\frac{\alpha}{1+\alpha}\right)\left(\frac{1}{1+\alpha}\right)$$

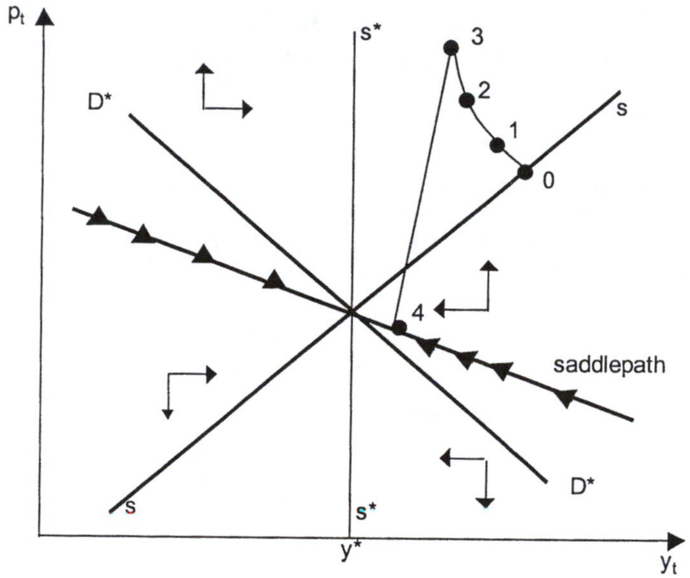

Shock ε_t occurs at $t=3$, anticipated at $t=0$. Numbers show the solution at each date, $t=0$, 1, ...

Figure 2.6: The effect of an unanticipated shock

Hence the forward root is 'thrown forwards', acting as a weight on the foreseen shock which diminishes the further ahead the shock occurs.

This is illustrated in Figure 2.6 for a positive demand shock anticipated at time t for three periods ahead. At t (= 0 on the figure) the expected future shock to demand raises prices unexpectedly, increases supply (a movement along SS), and stimulates demand (a shift in DD) because the rise in future prices relative to present prices reduces the demand for money, so increasing money expenditure. Demand continues to rise in $t = 1$ and $t = 2$ because future prices exceed current prices by a greater amount in $t = 1$ than $t = 0$ and in $t = 2$ than in $t = 1$; this is dictated by the dynamics (shown by the phase arrows) in that part of Figure 2.6. At $t = 3$, the shock occurs and increases demand further. Prices in $t = 4$ are expected to drop to exactly where they would have been (along the saddlepath) had the original shock to demand been an unanticipated one at $t = 0$ sufficient to stimulate output by the same amount as the anticipated shock did; so in $t = 3$, there are conflicting forces on demand, the positive effect of the $t = 3$ shock more than offsetting the effect from the expected future decline in prices. It is a useful exercise to assign numbers to the parameters and plot the resulting path as in figure 2.6.

Muth method

The Muth method, though not particularly intuitive, is probably the easiest to apply for this model. The general solution for p will be as before

$$p_t = \overline{p} + \sum_{i=0}^{\infty} \pi_i \varepsilon_{t-i} \tag{83}$$

and it remains that:

$$\overline{p} = \overline{m} - y^* \tag{84}$$

Box 2.1

The algebra for the illustration works out as follows if for convenience we set $E_{t-1}p_t = p_{t-1} = y_{t-1} = \varepsilon_{t-1} = \varepsilon_t = \overline{m} = y^* = 0$:

$$p_t = [\frac{\alpha}{1+\alpha+\frac{1}{\delta}}]E_t p_{t+1} \text{ from (65)}$$

$$E_t p_{t+1} = (\frac{1}{1+\alpha})(\frac{\alpha}{1+\alpha})^2(1-\mu\frac{\alpha}{1+\alpha})\varepsilon_{t+3} + \mu p_t \text{ from (82)}$$

led by one period and taking expectations at time t so that:

$$p_t = qx_t \text{ and } E_t p_{t+1} = (1+\mu q)x_t$$

where

$$\begin{aligned} x_t &= (\frac{1}{1+\alpha})(\frac{\alpha}{1+\alpha})^2(1-\mu\frac{\alpha}{1+\alpha})\varepsilon_{t+3}, \\ q &= \frac{\alpha}{1+\alpha-\alpha\mu+\frac{1}{\delta}} \end{aligned}$$

Again from (82)

$$\begin{aligned} E_t p_{t+2} &= \mu E_t p_{t+1} + \frac{1+\alpha}{\alpha}x_t = [\mu + \mu^2 q + \frac{1+\alpha}{\alpha}]x_t \\ E_t p_{t+3} &= \mu E_t p_{t+2} + \frac{1+\alpha}{\alpha}x_t = \\ & [\mu^2 + \mu^3 q + \mu(\frac{1+\alpha}{\alpha}) + (\frac{1+\alpha}{\alpha})^2]x_t \\ E_t p_{t+4} &= \mu E_t p_{t+3} - \mu\left(\frac{1}{1+\alpha}\right)\varepsilon_{t+3} \\ &= \mu\left\{ \begin{array}{c} \mu^2 + \mu^3 q + \mu\left(\frac{1+\alpha}{\alpha}\right) + \left(\frac{1+\alpha}{\alpha}\right)^2 - \\ \left(\frac{1+\alpha}{\alpha}\right)^2\left(\frac{1+\alpha}{1+\alpha-\alpha\mu}\right) \end{array} \right\} x_t \\ E_t p_{t+5} &= \mu E t p_{t+4} \end{aligned}$$

Both $E_t p_{t+4}$ and $E_t p_{t+5}$ are negative.

We now substitute in (66) dropping constants to obtain the identities in the ε_{t-i} from:

$$\varepsilon_t - \mu\varepsilon_{t-1} = -\alpha\sum_{i=0}^{\infty}\pi_{i+1}\varepsilon_{t-1} + \left(1+\alpha+\frac{1}{\delta}\right)\sum_{i=0}^{\infty}\pi_i\varepsilon_{t-i} + \left(\alpha\mu - \frac{1}{\delta}\right)\sum_{i=1}^{\infty}\pi_t\varepsilon_{t-i} - (\mu+\alpha\mu)\sum_{i=1}^{\infty}\pi_{t-1}\varepsilon_{t-1} \quad (85)$$

The identities emerge as

$$(\varepsilon_t):\ \ 1 = -\alpha\pi_1 + \left(1+\alpha+\frac{1}{\delta}\right)\pi_0 \quad (86)$$

$$(\varepsilon_{t-1}):\ \ -\mu = -\alpha\pi_2 + (1+\alpha+\alpha\mu)\pi_1 - (\mu+\alpha\mu)\pi_0 \quad (87)$$

$$(\varepsilon_{t-i}, i \geqslant 2):\ \ 0 = -\alpha\pi_{i+1} + (1+\alpha+\alpha\mu)\pi_i - (\alpha+\alpha\mu)\pi_{i-1} \quad (88)$$

Applying the stability condition to the solution of (88):

$$\pi_i = A_1\left(\frac{1+\alpha}{\alpha}\right)^{i-1} + A_2\mu^{i-1} \ \ (i \geqslant 2) \quad (89)$$

sets $A = 0$, so that:

$$\pi_i = \pi_1 \mu^{i-1} \quad (i \geqslant 2) \tag{90}$$

Substituting this into (86) and (87) gives:

$$\pi_0 = \frac{1 + \alpha - \alpha\mu}{(1+\alpha)(1 + \alpha + \frac{1}{\delta} - \alpha\mu)} \tag{91}$$

$$\pi_1 = \frac{-\mu}{\delta(1+\alpha)(1 + \alpha + \frac{1}{\delta} - \alpha\mu)} \tag{92}$$

We can easily verify that this is the solution arrived at previously.

A MORE GENERAL WAY OF LOOKING AT AN REFV MODEL

We have been considering models with exogenous ('forcing') processes — here the money supply — that consist of a constant and a current shock. For most of the time we have assumed that the shock could not be predicted; here the unstable root was ruled out by our terminal condition. Then we looked at the case where one period's shock was known some periods in advance; here we showed that the unstable root determines how this shock works back to affect the present — in effect the root is 'thrown forward' and becomes stable when working backwards from the future. It is time to generalise the solution method we have been using to any sort of exogenous process.

To illustrate such a general method we take a variant of our earlier models:

$$m_t = p_t + y_t - \alpha(E_{t-1}p_{t-1} - E_{t-1}p_t) \tag{93}$$

$$y_t = y^* + \delta(p_t - E_{t-1}p_t) + \mu(y_{t-1} - y^*) \tag{94}$$

which will be recognised as a Cagan-style money demand function with inflation expectations dated at $t-1$ and a New Classical supply curve with persistence. Now let m_t be an exogenous process of a completely general sort: each period there is a new realization of m_t and a new set of $E_t m_{t+i} (i \geqslant 1)$. We will make no restrictions on how this set $(m_t,\ E_{t+i})$ changes at each t.

Consider the expectation at $t-1$ of this model:

$$E_{t-1}m_t = (1+\alpha)\left.\ 1 - \frac{\alpha}{1+\alpha}B^{-1}\right] E_{t-1}p_t + E_{t-1}y_t \tag{95}$$

$$E_{t-1}y_t = y^* + \mu\delta\frac{(p_{t-1} - E_{t-1}p_{t-1})}{(1-\mu L)} \tag{96}$$

Let $p_t - E_{t-1}p_t = \eta_t$; we can easily solve for η_t as

$$\frac{1}{1+\delta}(m_t - E_{t-1}m_t) = \eta_t \tag{97}$$

by taking deviations from expected values across the model; this is a function of the purely unpredictable element (the innovation) in m_t.

Returning to our model above we can write the solution for $E_{t-1}p_t$ as:

$$\begin{aligned} E_{t-1}p_t = {} & \frac{E_{t-1}m_t}{(1+\alpha)(1-\frac{\alpha}{1+\alpha}B^{-1})} - y^* - \\ & \frac{\mu\delta\eta_{t-1}}{(1+\alpha)\left(1-\frac{\alpha}{1+\alpha}B^{-1}\right)(1-\mu L)} \\ = {} & \frac{1}{1+\alpha}\sum_{i=0}^{\infty}\left(\frac{\alpha}{1+\alpha}\right)^i (E_{t-1}m_{t+i} - E_{t-1}y_{t+i}) \end{aligned} \tag{98}$$

where

$$E_{t-1}y_{t+i} = y^* + \mu\delta\sum_{j=i}^{\infty}\mu^j\eta_{t-1-j+i} = y^* + \mu^{i+1}(y_{t-1} - y^*);$$

note that the expectations of future innovations are by definition zero.

Thus our solution automatically throws the term in α forwards (because it relates the present to expected future events) and the term in μ backwards (because it related the present and the expected future to past events). We can see that the general solution has a forward and a backward component, for each of which one of the roots of the model is appropriate.

The model requires, for stability, that both $\mid \frac{\alpha}{1+\alpha} \mid \prec 1$ and $\mid \mu \mid \prec 1$; both of these would be imposed as a matter of specification normally. Looking back over our previous discussion of uniqueness and will o' the wisp variables, we can also see that in these conditions the terminal condition will both ensure uniqueness and rule out bubbles.

Forward and backward roots: an examination

We can see that in the model we have been using — with slight differences in dating of the expectations — we have obtained an equation of the form:

$$\ldots = \left[-\alpha B^{-1} + (1+\alpha+\alpha\mu) - (1+\alpha)\mu B\right] E_{t-1}p_{t+i} \tag{99}$$

If this is solved backwards we write it as:

$$... = -\alpha \;\; 1 - \left(\frac{1+\alpha}{\alpha} + \mu\right))B - \left(\frac{1+\alpha}{\alpha}\right))\mu B^2\Big] B^{-1} E_{t-1} p_{t+i} \quad (100)$$

The roots are then plainly $\frac{1+\alpha}{\alpha}$ and μ. These we recognise as the forward root, $\frac{\alpha}{1+\alpha}$, solved backwards and so inverted, and the backward root, μ.

If the difference equation is solved forwards we write it as:

$$... = -\mu(1+\alpha) \;\; 1 - \left(\frac{\alpha}{1+\alpha} + \frac{1}{\mu}\right) B^{-1} - \left(\frac{\alpha}{1+\alpha}\right) \frac{1}{\mu} B^{-2}\Big] B E_{t-1} p_{t+i} \quad (101)$$

The roots are then $\frac{1}{\mu}$ and $\frac{\alpha}{1+\alpha}$ which we recognise as the forward root solved forwards and the backward root, μ, solved forwards and so inverted.

Plainly to obtain the appropriate solution as permitted by the terminal condition, we solve the forward root forwards and the backward root backwards as we have seen, obtaining:

$$... = (1+\alpha)\left(1 - \frac{\alpha}{1+\alpha} B^{-1}\right)(1-\mu B) E_{t-1} p_{t+i} \quad (102)$$

Equivalently we can obtain this appropriate solution by factorising

$$\begin{aligned} -\alpha B^{-1} + (1+\alpha+\alpha\mu) - (1+\alpha)\mu B = k_0(1-k_1B^{-1})(1-k_2B) = \\ -k_0k_1B^{-1} + k_0(1+k_1k_2) - k_0k_2B \quad (103) \end{aligned}$$

where the undetermined coefficients are given by

$$k_0k_1 = \alpha; \; k_0(1+k_1k_2) = 1+\alpha+\alpha\mu; \; k_0k_2 = \mu(1+\alpha) \quad (104)$$

Solving (96) for k_1 yields:

$$k_1^2 - \left(\frac{\alpha}{1+\alpha} + \frac{1}{\mu}\right) k_1 - \left(\frac{\alpha}{1+\alpha}\right) \frac{1}{\mu} = 0 \quad (105)$$

(the characteristic equation of the model solved forward) whence $k_1 = \frac{\alpha}{1+\alpha}, \; \frac{1}{\mu}$.

Alternatively solve (104) for k_2 to obtain:

$$k_2^2 - (\frac{1+\alpha}{\alpha} + \mu)k_2 - (\frac{1+\alpha}{\alpha})\mu = 0 \quad (106)$$

(the characteristic equation solved backwards) yielding $k_2 = \frac{1+\alpha}{\alpha}, \; \mu$.

To find the stable solution we select the stable values of each root, forward (k_1), and backward (k_2).

STABILITY PROBLEMS IN RATIONAL EXPECTATIONS MODELS

When we considered adaptive expectations models we were concerned about whether they were stable or not. Clearly these were backward-looking models and this question amounted to whether the roots, all of them backward, were stable; if they were not, then we would naturally assume the specification was wrong, since we look for models that are stable, reflecting what we take to be a stable reality (if it were not, it should have exploded — yet it hasn't). With rational expectations models stability, as we have seen, involves in the two-root case both the forward and backward roots being stable when driven respectively forwards and backwards. If either is unstable, there is instability (either expected future events produce unstable current effects or past events produce unstable expected future effects). Let us consider them in turn: first, the case where the forward root is unstable — commonly known as the uniqueness problem.

The Uniqueness Problem: the unstable forward root

When the forward root is unstable, it is easiest to see what is happening in the simple model of equations (22), (8) and (9) at the beginning of the section on REFV models. Let us suppose that for some reason α in our model is negative and < -0.5. Suppose, for example, that there is a rigid relationship of money to average transactions in a period; and that precautionary transactions demand is positively related to the rate of inflation, because of the irregularity of price changes and the correlation between the size of these changes when they occur and the inflation rate (for example, I go to the doctor and find he had just put up his price by 30 per cent). This is implausible but not impossible.

Here we have, taking expectations at $t-1$, looking at the solution forwards:

$$\frac{\overline{m}-y^*}{1+\alpha}=\left(1-\frac{\alpha}{1+\alpha}B^{-1}\right)E_{t-1}p_t \tag{107}$$

Plainly, the forward sum$(\overline{m}-y^*)/\left(1-\frac{\alpha}{1+\alpha}B^{-1}\right)$ does not converge. Equally if we look at the equation backwards we have:

$$-\frac{\overline{m}-y^*}{\alpha}=\left(1-\frac{1+\alpha}{\alpha}B\right)E_{t-1}p_{t+1} \tag{108}$$

from which it follows that:

$$E_{t-1}p_{t+i}=\overline{m}-y^*+A\left(\frac{1+\alpha}{\alpha}\right)^i \quad (i\geqslant 1) \tag{109}$$

where $A = E_{t-1}p_t - (\overline{m} - y^*)$

This has a multiplicity of stable paths since $\left|\frac{1+\alpha}{\alpha}\right| < 1$: there is no unique stable path, hence the 'non-uniqueness' label of this case. Previously we used the stability condition to choose the unique stable path. However, now all the paths in (109) are stable, as shown in Figures 2.7 and 2.8, because we have rigged it so that $\left|\frac{1+\alpha}{\alpha}\right| < 1$. The stability condition is incapable of selecting a unique solution, therefore. This problem was first pointed out by Taylor (1977); and so far as we know there is nothing to rule out the possibility that REFV macroeconomic models will have an infinity of stable paths.

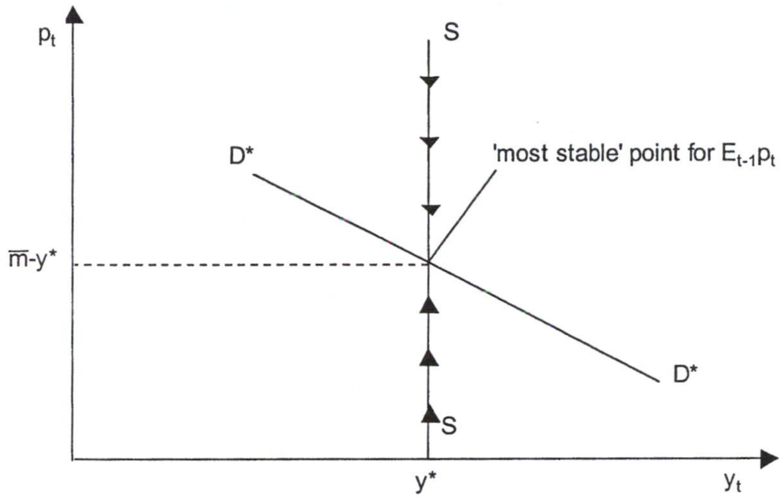

Figure 2.7: The uniquness problem in (p_t, y_t) space

There is no generally agreed procedure among those using REFV models for this problem, other than to avoid using the ones with this property. One solution has, however, has been suggested by Minford et al. (1979) — to impose a terminal condition as we do in a normal model. Needless to say any 'solution' must somehow do violence to the model as specified since it is literally unstable. However, the economy may be, for some peculiar but genuine reason (as exemplified above), like this at least for a while: then could the terminal condition remove undesirable price level instability, as it did in the same model in its normal set-up? It turns out that it does indeed impose a unique stable solution. Thus we set:

$$E_{t-1}p_{t+N} = E_{t-1}p_{t+N+1} \tag{110}$$

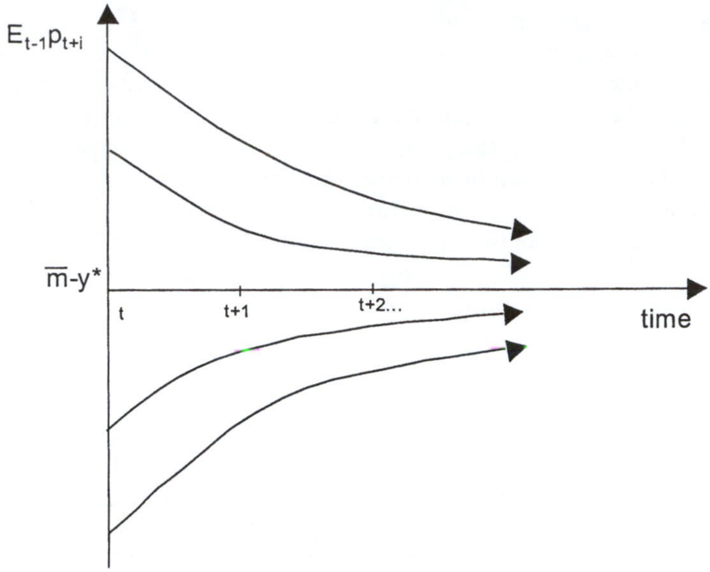

Figure 2.8: The uniqueness problem in (p_t, t) space

Using the forward solution we find that this implies

$$\frac{\overline{m} - y^*}{1+\alpha} = E_{t-1}p_{t+N} - \frac{\alpha}{1+\alpha}E_{t-1}p_{t+N+1} \tag{111}$$

whence $E_{t-1}p_{t+N} = \overline{m} - y^*$.

Via backwards recursion we obtain:

$$E_{t-1}p_{t+N-1} - \frac{1+\alpha}{\alpha}E_{t-1}p_{t+N} = \frac{\overline{m} - y^*}{1+\alpha} \tag{112}$$

whence $E_{t-1}p_{t+i} = \overline{m} - y^*$ $(i \geqslant 0)$.

Using the backwards solution, our terminal solution implies :

$$A\left(\frac{1+\alpha}{\alpha}\right)^{N+1} + \overline{m} - y^* = A\left(\frac{1+\alpha}{\alpha}\right)^{N} + \overline{m} - y^* \tag{113}$$

which is strictly valid only when $A = 0$. Thus also:

$$E_{t-1}p_{t+i} = \bar{m} - y^*(i \geqslant 0)$$

Note that just as in the case of our normal model, a bubble can be added to this solution, namely $(\frac{1+\alpha}{\alpha})^i E_{t-1}z_{t+i}$, but in this case it is an 'imploding bubble'. The terminal condition rules this out here, as it did the exploding bubble of our normal case. The justification for such a condition might seem strained in this case. Yet upon consideration it is equally justifiable. Non-uniqueness (forward instability and imploding bubbles) must cause quite as serious problems as backwards instability and exploding bubbles. For the endogenous variables may in each period jump by unpredictably large (strictly unbounded) amounts; even though they will subsequently be expected to return to equilibrium, in all subsequent periods there will be shocks with infinite variance. Such uncertainty would be likely to provoke changes in behaviour sufficient to create an incentive for the money issuer to make a commitment such as is set out in the terminal condition. This commitment would then limit the uncertainty as we have seen, to that associated with the 'most stable' path — a result much in the spirit of a suggestion by Taylor (1977) that the least variance path will be selected by 'collective rationality'[3].

Let us now apply this same approach to the more complicated model we used above:

$$m_t = p_t + y_t - \alpha(E_{t-1}p_{t+1} - E_{t-1}p_t) \tag{114}$$

$$y_t = y^* + \delta(p_t - E_{t-1}p_t) + \mu(y_{t-1} - y^*) \tag{115}$$

$$m_t = \bar{m} + \varepsilon_t \tag{116}$$

This yields a reduction in terms of prices and expected prices of:

$$\begin{aligned}(\overline{m} - y*)(1-\mu) + \varepsilon_t - \mu\varepsilon_{t-1} = p_t - \mu p_{t-1} - \alpha E_{t-1}p_{t+1} + \alpha\mu E_{t-2}p_t \\ + \delta(p_t - E_{t-1}p_t) + \alpha E_{t-1}p_t - \alpha\mu E_{t-2}p_{t-1}\end{aligned} \tag{117}$$

Let us assume, as we shall see we must, that $\left|\frac{1+\alpha}{\alpha}\right| \succ |\mu|$. First solve the model forwards and impose the terminal condition to obtain:

$$E_{t-1}p_{t+N} = \overline{m} - y^* - \mu^{N+1}(y_{t-1} - y^*) \tag{118}$$

The backwards recursion proceeds:

$$E_{t-1}p_{t+N-1} = \frac{\alpha}{1+\alpha}E_{t-1}p_{t+N} + \frac{1}{1+\alpha}[\overline{m} - y^* - \mu^N(y_{t-1} - y^*)] \tag{119}$$

[3]There have been other suggestions, like Taylor's, as to how society would select such a path. Peel (1981) argues that the monetary authorities will select a feedback rule generating uniqueness; however, it is not clear that they do select such rules in practice. McCallum (1983) argues that the solution chosen, when framed according to the Lucas undetermined coefficients method, will contain only the minimum set of state variables (his MSV procedure). This, we would argue, would be a result of the sort of government commitment we refer to. In practical terms MSV and terminal conditions deliver the same solution.

ultimately reaching:

$$E_{t-1}p_t = \overline{m} - y^* - \left\{ \left(\frac{\alpha\mu}{1+\alpha}\right)^N + \frac{1}{1+\alpha}\left[\begin{array}{c} \left(\frac{\alpha\mu}{1+\alpha}\right)^{N-1} + \left(\frac{\alpha\mu}{1+\alpha}\right)^{N-2} + \ldots \\ + \frac{\alpha\mu}{1+\alpha} + 1 \end{array} \right] \right\} \mu(y_{t-1} - y^*) \quad (120)$$

which, letting N be large (where for convergence $\left|\frac{1+\alpha}{\alpha}\right| \succ |\mu|$)

$$\simeq \overline{m} - y^* - \frac{1}{1+\alpha(1-\mu)}\mu(y_{t-1} - y^*) \quad (121)$$

The same result is obtained using the backward solution; take expectations of (117) at $t-2$ to obtain:

$$\frac{-(1-\mu)}{\alpha}(\overline{m} - y^*) = E_{t-2}p_{t+1} - (\frac{1+\alpha}{\alpha} + \mu)E_{t-2}p_t + \mu(\frac{1+\alpha}{\alpha})E_{t-2}p_{t-1} \quad (122)$$

whose solution is:

$$E_{t-2}p_{t+i} = \overline{m} - y^* + A_1(\frac{1+\alpha}{\alpha})^{i+1} + A_2\mu^{i+1} \quad (i \geqslant 1) \quad (123)$$

with initial values $E_{t-2}p_t$ and $E_{t-2}p_{t-1}$.

The terminal condition forces the constant on the root with the highest modulus (that is, $\frac{1+\alpha}{\alpha}$) to be zero, whence:

$$E_{t-2}p_{t+i} = \overline{m} - y^* + [E_{t-2}p_{t-1} - (\overline{m} - y^*)]\mu^{i+1} \quad (i \geqslant 0) \quad (124)$$

whence also:

$$E_{t-1}p_{t+i+1} = \overline{m} - y^* + [E_{t-1}p_t - (\overline{m} - y^*)]\mu^{i+1} \quad (i \geqslant 0) \quad (125)$$

Substitute for $E_{t-1}p_{t+1}$ from (125) into (114), take expectations at $t-1$ of (114)–(116), and reduce to obtain:

$$(\overline{m} - y^*) = E_{t-1}p_t + \mu(y_{t-1} - y^*) - \alpha[(1-\mu)(\overline{m} - y^*) + \mu E_{t-1}p_t] \quad (126)$$

whence:

$$E_{t-1}p_t = \overline{m} - y^* - \frac{1}{1+\alpha(1-\mu)}\mu(y_{t-1} - y^*) \quad (127)$$

as with the forward solution.

There is no solution if $\left|\frac{1+\alpha}{\alpha}\right| \prec |\mu|$. (123) now sets $A_2 = 0$ which gives:

$$E_{t-1}p_{t+1} = (1 - \frac{1+\alpha}{\alpha})(\overline{m} - y^*) + \frac{1+\alpha}{\alpha}E_{t-1}p_t$$

Repeating the operations which gave (127), we now find that:

$$E_{t-1}p_t = \frac{\mu}{\alpha}(y_{t-1} - y^*)$$

implying:

$$E_{t-1}p_{t+1} = \frac{\mu}{\alpha}(E_{t-1}y_t - y^*) = \frac{\mu^2}{\alpha}(y_{t-1} - y^*)$$

When this is substituted again into (114)–(116) we obtain:

$$E_{t-1}p_t = \frac{\overline{m} - y^*}{1+\alpha} + \frac{\mu(1-\mu)}{1+\alpha}(y_{t-1} - y^*) \qquad (128)$$

There is therefore no solution for $E_{t-1}p_t$ by contradiction. (If $\left|\frac{1+\alpha}{\alpha}\right| = |\mu|$, the terminal condition cannot impose a unique solution and (120) does not converge; so again there is no solution.)

What we have seen is that provided $\frac{\alpha}{1+\alpha}$ is not too unstable (ie. provided that $\left|\frac{\alpha}{1+\alpha}\right| \prec \left|\frac{1}{\mu}\right|$), the terminal condition will force a stable solution and rule out implosive bubbles.

The case of an unstable backward root

We can illustrate this case with the model we have just used. Here $|\mu| \succ 1$ in which case output is expected to explode — clearly an inadmissible model in general since the backward sums $\delta\varepsilon_t / [(1+\delta)(1-\mu L)]$ do not converge.

In this case, too, however, there is a reason for seeking some sort of a solution. Such a model cannot be ruled out for an episode (for example moving between two stable models in a general non-linear model — as discussed in the supply-side chapter *a propos* of virtuous and vicious circles and more generally in the Time-Series Annex). We therefore need to face up to the problems for inflation and monetary policy in such an episode. We have justified our terminal condition as a restriction placed on behaviour by the monetary authorities to prevent undesirable price outcomes. So here we ask if a terminal condition will produce acceptable price behaviour.

We can in fact simply use our workings in the previous section, while noting here that $\alpha/(1+\alpha) \prec 1$. Again we require for a solution that

$(1+\alpha)/\alpha \succ |\mu|$: that is, that here the backward root not be too unstable. Thus if $\alpha/(1+\alpha) \succ 1$ (our last case of an unstable forward root) then $(1+\alpha)/\alpha \prec 1 \prec |\mu|$ and so there can be no solution with a terminal condition.

However with $(1+\alpha)/\alpha \succ |\mu|$ we obtain the same solution as above, namely:

$$E_{t-1}p_{t+i+} = \overline{m} - y^* - \mu^{i+1}\frac{1}{1+\alpha(1-\mu)}(y_{t-1} - y^*) \quad (i \geqslant 0) \qquad (129)$$

This shows clearly that a terminal condition will solve for a price path, that it will be unique, but that it will be unstable matching the instability in output — we might label this as 'controlled price instability'.

What we have shown about models with stability problems is that, by introducing a terminal condition justified by monetary policy reactions, we will in many cases — where the instability is not too severe — find unique solutions: if the instability is too severe, there will be no solution at all under a terminal condition. In our particular model with two roots, 'not too severe' means $(1+\alpha)/\alpha \succ |\mu|$. This implies that if both forward and backward roots are unstable there is no solution, since $(1+\alpha)/\alpha \prec 1 \prec |\mu|$. More general models with more roots have to be examined case by case if they have instability of either sort, using the analytical techniques we have described in this chapter.

CONCLUSIONS

This has been a chapter designed to equip the reader with the techniques to solve rational expectations models in a manner useful to applied work[4]. We have shown how to use four main methods of solution: a basic method, both with the Sargent forward operator and with the model solved backwards, and the Muth and Lucas undetermined coefficients methods. We have also discussed the criterion for choosing a unique solution in these models, free of extraneous or 'will o' the wisp' variables. The criterion we propose, namely that terminal conditions are imposed on the model (some external 'transversality condition'), is widely accepted in practice The effect of this condition is to ensure a stable path free of extraneous variables or bubbles. Practical methods

[4]There are a number of descriptions of solution methods available in the literature (see, e.g., Shiller 1978; and the useful Aoki and Canzoneri, 1979). For more complex applications than those considered in this chapter, the reader will invariably use numerical methods on the computer.

of solution used vary (see for example Wallis et al., 1985). However all of them are approximations to the analytic bubble-free solution we have been setting out above.

APPENDIX 2A: WHEN ADAPTIVE EXPECTATIONS ARE RATIONAL

Suppose that a series is generated by the ARIMA(0, 1, 1) process (see time-series annex at the end of the book):

$$y_t = y_{t-1} + u_t - j u_{t-1} \tag{1}$$

where u_t is a Gaussian white noise process and j a positive constant.

The rational expectation $E_{t-1}y_t$ of (1) is given by:

$$E_{t-1}y_t = y_{t-1} - j u_{t-1} \tag{2}$$

From (1):

$$y_t - y_{t-1} = (1 - jL)u_t \tag{3}$$

where L is the lag operator.

Substituting for u_{t-1} from (3) into (2) we obtain:

$$E_{t-1}y_t = y_{t-1} - j\left(\frac{y_{t-1} - y_{t-2}}{1 - jL}\right)$$

so that:

$$E_{t-1}y_t - jE_{t-2}y_{t-1} = y_{t-1} - jy_{t-2} - j(y_{t-1} - y_{t-2}) \tag{4}$$

Subtracting $E_{t-2}y_{t-1}$ from both sides of (4) and rearranging we obtain

$$E_{t-1}y_t - E_{t-2}y_{t-1} = \quad \{y_{t-1} - E_{t-2}y_{t-1}\} \tag{5}$$

where $\quad = 1 - j$

Notice also from (5) that:

$$E_{t-1}y_t = \frac{y_{t-1}}{(1 - (1 - \quad)L)} = \frac{(1-\lambda)y_{t-1}}{(1 - \lambda L)}$$
$$= (1-\lambda)(1 + \lambda L + \lambda^2 L^2 + \lambda^3 L^3 + \ldots +)y_{t-1} \tag{6}$$

where $\lambda = 1 - \quad$ so that $\lambda = j$.

Equation (5) will be recognised as an adaptive expectations process. In other words if a variable is described by an ARIMA(0, 1, 1) process then adaptive expectations can be rational expectations if the coefficient of adaptation is equal to $1 - j$.

More generally we should note that a variety of mechanistic forms of expectation formation can be rational in a particular model structure. For instance regressive expectations are rational in the Dornbusch overshooting model considered in Chapter 14. The point is, of course, that these mechanistic expectations mechanisms will, in general, cease to be rational if policy regimes change.

Two interesting examples where adaptive expectations are rational are in models proposed by Sargent and Wallace (1973) and Muth (1961).

The Sargent–Wallace model of a hyperinflation

The demand for real balances has the form:

$$\log\left(\frac{M_t}{P_t}\right) = \alpha\pi_t^e + \gamma Y + \varphi + u_t \quad \alpha < 0, \quad \gamma > 0. \tag{6}$$

where M is the demand for nominal balances (assumed equal to supply), P is the price level, π_t^e is the public's expectation of future inflation, so $\pi_t^e = E_t \log P_{t+1} - \log P_t$, is assumed known. Y is real income assumed constant and u_t is a stochastic error term with an average value of zero. α, γ and φ are parameters.

Taking the first difference of (6) we obtain

$$\mu_t = \pi_t + \alpha(\pi_t^e - \pi_{t-1}^e) \tag{7}$$

where $\mu_t = \log\left(\frac{M_t}{M_{t-1}}\right)$ is the rate of change of the money supply and $\pi_t = \log\left(\frac{P_t}{P_{t-1}}\right)$ is the rate of inflation. It is assumed that $u_t - u_{t-1} = \eta_t$ where η_t is a white noise error.

Adaptive expectations (here current expectations of future inflation) can be written here as:

$$\pi_t^e = \frac{(1-\lambda)\pi_t}{1-\lambda L} \tag{8}$$

Substituting (8) into (7) we obtain the solution for π_t as:

$$\{[1+\alpha(1-\lambda)] - [\lambda + \alpha(1-\lambda)]L\}\pi_t = (1-\lambda L)\mu_t - (1-\lambda L)(1-L)u_t \tag{9}$$

so that the current inflation rate is determined by distributed lags of changes in the money supply and of the disturbance in the demand function.

To provide a rationalization of how adaptive expectations could have the rationality property, suppose the rate of monetary expansion is governed by the process:

$$\mu_t = \frac{(1-\lambda)\pi_t}{1-\lambda L} + \varepsilon_t \tag{10}$$

where ε_t is a white noise disturbance.

Substitute from (10) into (9) for μ_t to obtain

$$\{[\lambda + \alpha(1-\lambda)] - [\lambda + \alpha(1-\lambda)]L\}\pi_t = (1-\lambda L)\left[\varepsilon_t - (u_t - u_{t-1})\right] \tag{11}$$

Equation (11) can be rewritten as

$$[\lambda + \alpha(1-\lambda)]\,(1-L)\,\pi_t = (1-\lambda L)\,[\varepsilon_t - (u_t - u_{t-1})] \tag{12}$$

Now $\frac{1-L}{1-\lambda L} \equiv 1 - \frac{(1-\lambda)L}{1-\lambda L}$ so that (12) can be rewritten as:

$$\pi_t = \frac{(1-\lambda)\pi_{t-1}}{1-\lambda L} + [\lambda + \alpha(1-\lambda)]^{-1}\,[\varepsilon_t - (u_t - u_{t-1})] \tag{13}$$

Recalling that $u_t - u_{t-1} = \eta_t$ the rational expectation of (13) is given by:

$$E_{t-1}\pi_t = \frac{(1-\lambda)\pi_{t-1}}{1-\lambda L} \text{ implying that } E_t\pi_{t+1} = \pi_t^e = \frac{(1-\lambda)\pi_t}{1-\lambda L} \tag{14}$$

In other words if the money supply process is (10) the adaptive expectations will be rational. The question is why should the money supply process follow (10) in a hyperinflation. It is typically assumed that in a hyperinflation period the authorities print money to finance their nominal expenditure, assuming the level of real government expenditure, G, is constant. This assumption is captured in continuous time (where $\dot{x} = \frac{\partial x}{\partial t}$) by:

$$\frac{\dot{M}(t)}{P(t)} = G$$

or

$$\frac{\dot{M}}{M} = \frac{PG}{M} \tag{15}$$

In continuous time the demand for real balances is given by:

$$\frac{M}{P} = f\,[\pi^e(t)] \tag{16}$$

so that substituting (16) into (15) gives

$$\frac{\dot{M}}{M} = \frac{G}{f(\pi^e)} \tag{17}$$

Assuming a unique solution to (17) a linear discrete-time approximation to (17) is given by

$$\mu_t = E_t\pi_{t+1} + \varepsilon_t \tag{18}$$

where ε_t is assumed to be a white noise error term.

Assuming rational expectations (10) is equivalent with (18) (since $E_t\pi_{t+1} = \frac{(1-\lambda)\pi_t}{1-\lambda L}$).

Consequently Sargent and Wallace have demonstated how adaptive expectations can be rational in a hyperinflationary period.

We also note from (7) and (18) that

$$E_t\pi_{t+1} + \epsilon_t = \pi_t + \alpha(\pi_t^e - \pi_{t-1}^e) + \phi_t \tag{19}$$

or

$$\pi_t^e = \pi_t + \alpha(\pi_t^e - \pi_{t-1}^e) + \phi_t - \varepsilon_t \tag{20}$$

If expectations are adaptive:

$$\pi_t^e = \frac{(1-\lambda)\pi_t}{1-\lambda L} \tag{8}$$

Substituting (8) into (20) for π_t^e, π_{t-1}^e we obtain

$$\frac{(1-\lambda)\pi_t}{1-\lambda L} = \pi_t + \alpha(1-L)\frac{(1-\lambda)\pi_t}{1-\lambda L} + \phi_t - \varepsilon_t \tag{21}$$

Simplifying (21) we obtain

$$\pi_t - \pi_{t-1} = -\left[(\lambda + \alpha(1-\lambda)^{-1}(1-\lambda L)(v_t)\right] \tag{22}$$

where v_t is the composite white noise error, $v_t = \phi_t - \varepsilon_t$

The process (22) is an ARIMA(0, 1, 1) as required for adaptive expectations of inflation to be rational.

Agricultural prices

The adaptive expectations assumption was widely employed in modelling of agricultural markets (see Nerlove, 1958) since models embodying this assumption were readily able to generate stable cyclical fluctuations. It is useful to illustrate how an agricultural model embodying rational expectations can also readily exhibit such fluctuations in price or how price series for storable commodities can approximately follow a random walk.

We employ the model of Muth (1961). We write the model as follows (all means are put to zero for simplicity):

$$q_t^d = -\beta p_t \tag{23}$$

$$q_t^s = \gamma E_{t-1}p_t + u_t \tag{24}$$

$$I_t = \alpha(E_t p_{t+1} - p_t) \tag{25}$$

$$q_t^d + \rho I_t = q_t^s + \rho I_{t-1} \tag{26}$$

where q_t^d, q_t^s are quantity demanded and supplied, respectively, p_t is price, I_t is a speculative inventory and u_t is an error process; α, β, γ and ρ are constants. In this model it is assumed that storage of a commodity is possible, and that storage, transactions costs and interest rates are negligible. Consequently, a speculative inventory exists which depends on the anticipated capital gain from holding the stock. The parameter α, which measures the response of inventory demands to expected price changes, is a function of the degree of risk aversion and the conditional variance of prices in Muth's exposition (also see Turnovsky, 1983).

Because storage can occur, equilibrium does not require that current production (supply) equals current consumption demand. Equation (26) represents the market equilibrium condition. A parameter ρ (= 1 or 0) is introduced for analytical convenience: if storage occurs it is equal to unity; otherwise if we set $\rho = 0$ and $\alpha = 0$, we have the standard, no storage, market clearing model.

Substitution of equations (23), (24) and (25) into (26) yields the reduced form:

$$-\beta p_t + \rho\alpha(E_t p_{t+1} - p_t) = \gamma E_{t-1} p_t + \rho\alpha(E_{t-1} p_t - p_{t-1}) + u_t \qquad (27)$$

Assume initially that u_t is white noise. Solve this model under rational expectations using the Lucas method of undetermined coefficients.

If we let

$$p_t = a p_{t-1} + b u_t \qquad (28)$$

for $\rho = 1$ we obtain by substitution

$$b = \frac{1}{a\alpha - (\alpha + \beta)} \text{ and } a = 1 + 0.5 \ \frac{(\beta + \gamma)}{\alpha}\Big] - 0.5 \left\{ 2 + \frac{(\beta + \gamma)}{\alpha}\Big]^2 - 4 \right\}^{0.5} \qquad (29)$$

with $0 < a < 1$.

The solution for prices (28) is of interest. Price exhibits serially correlated fluctuations around its mean value when u_t, a variable which represents exogenous influences, is random. The reason for this is that inventories smooth out the effects of disturbances (shocks) to demand or supply. Consider, for instance, an abnormally good harvest due to favourable weather. In a market without storage, the additional supply will impact on market price in the current period. However with an inventory demand, speculators will buy some of the harvest, since the price in the future will, *ceteris paribus*, be greater than today, as weather returns to its normal expected value. This procedure will generally dampen price fluctuations. In addition the shock in the current period will have an impact in future periods which in this context is another way of saying that price movements will exhibit serial correlation.

Equation (28) also leads to another insight, as pointed out by Muth. As the importance of inventory speculative demands dominate a market relative to flow demands or supplies (as is likely over short periods of time) and consequently α becomes large relative to β or γ then (29) implies that a will become close to one. Consequently, price will approximate a random walk. This is an empirical feature often noted in price series for storable commodities in high frequency data. We also note that in this model the rational expectation of price is a fixed multiple of last period's price, though the coefficient is a function of the parameters of the model. In general, rational price expectations will be a function of lagged prices, though not in a mechanistic fixed fashion as occurs in an adaptive expectations model. Muth, however, did use a special case of the above model to illustrate how an adaptive expectations scheme could be rational. If we let $\rho = 0$ and $\alpha = 0$ we obtain the reduced form of the market clearing model given by

$$-\beta p_t = \gamma E_{t-1} p_t + u_t \tag{30}$$

Suppose that the error process is serially correlated so that

$$u_t = u_{t-1} + v_t \tag{31}$$

where v_t is white noise.

Consequently the rational expectation of (30) is given by

$$-(\beta + \gamma) E_{t-1} p_t = u_{t-1} \tag{32}$$

If we lag (30) one period and substitute for u_{t-1} in (32) we obtain

$$-(\beta + \gamma) E_{t-1} p_t = -\beta p_{t-1} - \gamma E_{t-2} p_{t-1} \tag{33}$$

Adding $(\beta + \gamma) E_{t-2} p_{t-1}$ to the left- and right-hand side of (33) we obtain after simplification the adaptive expectations scheme

$$E_{t-1} p_t - E_{t-2} p_{t-1} = \frac{\beta}{\beta + \gamma} (p_{t-1} - E_{t-2} p_{t-1}) \tag{34}$$

Notice from (30) and (32) that

$$-\beta p_t = -\frac{\gamma u_{t-1}}{\beta + \gamma} + u_t = \left(1 - \frac{\gamma L}{\beta + \gamma}\right) u_t \tag{35}$$

Differencing (35) and substituing for u_t from (31) we obtain

$$p_t - p_{t-1} = -\beta^{-1} \left(1 - \frac{\gamma L}{\beta + \gamma}\right) v_t \tag{36}$$

so that as required prices follow an ARIMA(0, 1, 1) process.

Finally it is interesting to consider the properties of a simple adaptive scheme when it is not rational. Consider the Wold decomposition for a variable

$$p_t = \overline{p}_t + \sum_{i=0}^{\infty} \pi_i u_t \tag{37}$$

where $\overline{p}_t$ is the mean component which could include a deterministic trend.

For ease of exposition consider the simplest adaptive expectation, namely

$$p_t^e = p_{t-1} = \overline{p}_{t-1} + \sum_{i=0}^{\infty} \pi_i u_{t-i} \tag{38}$$

The forecast error is given by

$$p_t - E_{t-1}p_t = \overline{p}_t + \sum_{i=0}^{\infty} \pi_i u_t - (\overline{p}_{t-1} + \sum_{i=0}^{\infty} \pi_i u_{t-i}) \tag{39}$$

In the case where $\overline{p}$ is a constant so $\overline{p}_t = \overline{p}_{t-1}$, we observe that the adaptive forecast is unbiased, since the average value of the forecast error is zero. However the forecast is inefficient in general since the right-hand side of (39) being a function of past information implies that the forecast error is correlated with information known at the time expectations were formed. If $\overline{p}_t$ contains a deterministic trend so that $\overline{p}_t = a + bt$, then $\overline{p}_t - \overline{p}_{t-1} = b$ so that from (39) the adaptive forecast will exhibit systematic bias and inefficiency.

3

Partial Information and Signal Extraction

To this point, we have assumed that people had access to all relevant information on events up to a certain date in forming their expectations: for example $E_t x_t$ or $E(x_t \mid \Phi_t)$ implied they know the whole contents of Φ_t, the information set relating to period t and before. If they did not have access to Φ_t, then they might have access to Φ_{t-1}, the previous period's information set. However, there is an intermediate possibility, which we have up to now ignored but which has important implications for the behaviour of people with rational expectations. This possibility is that they know a part of Φ_t only, as well as all of Φ_{t-1}. For example, each individual might know the prices of certain goods which he or she trades (but not the general price level). This is 'micro' information. As for macro or aggregate information, in many economies capital market information, such as exchange rates or interest rates, is available essentially instantaneously.

When endowed with such partial knowledge, agents face a statistical inference problem. Observation of the current values of macroeconomic variables, given knowledge of the variance of disturbances in the economy, allows them to form an optimal expectation of the currently unobserved random variables using Kalman filter methods (Kalman, 1960). In particular, if a variable z is observed which is the sum of two random variables (u, e) i.e.:

$$z_t = u_t + e_t \tag{1}$$

then the current expectations of u and e are respectively given by

$$E_t(u_t) = \frac{\sigma_u^2}{\sigma_u^2 + \sigma_e^2} z_t \tag{2}$$

$$E_t(e_t) = \frac{\sigma_e^2}{\sigma_u^2 + \sigma_e^2} z_t \tag{3}$$

where σ_u^2, σ_e^2 are the known variances of the disturbances (Graybill, 1961, has a fuller discussion). The coefficient on z_t in (2) or (3) can be thought of as that of a simple ordinary least squares regression of u_t on z_t (carried out over an infinite sample).

The purpose of this chapter is to consider two examples of how partial information alters the solution of rational expectations models; these will both illustrate the method of solution and explain the workings of two models important in their own right. The first example is the Phillips curve in Lucas' (1972b) 'islands story', where people know individual prices but not the general price level — a case of partial micro information. The second example is a general macro model where people have some capital market information — a case of partial macro information.

THE NEW CLASSICAL PHILLIPS CURVE

In the original formulation of the Phillips curve (Phillips, 1958; Lipsey, 1960), as we saw in chapter 1, short-run rigidity of wages and prices and so market disequilibrium was assumed. The curve related the change in wages to a measure of excess demand at wages that were not clearing the market. This relationship was later 'augmented' by Phelps (1970) and Friedman (1968) with the addition of expected inflation: the idea was that people were bidding up wages at a rate expected to reduce excess demand but since excess demand would only fall if wages rose in real terms, nominal wages must be bid up by an amount equal to the expected necessary rise in real wages plus the expected rise in general prices. To the resulting wage equation was usually added a price equation relating prices to costs, from which a Phillips curve in price inflation could be obtained.

The New Classical reinterpretation consists of five elements:

1. The labour market is assumed to clear: there is no wage rigidity.

2. People and firms observe prices in their own markets continuously but observe prices in other markets after a time lag. This implies that firms continuously observe the prices of their inputs and outputs, workers only their wages and some local prices (e.g. of groceries for which they continuously shop). Workers must form an expectation of the general price level.

3. Workers have rational expectations and in particular use signal extraction to infer the current general price level from the local prices they observe.

4. Workers' supply of labour has a substantial elasticity to current real wages; this is usually supported by the idea of intertemporal substitution of labour supply (although it could also occur when labour has a reservation wage for other reasons, such as unemployment benefits or 'shadow economy' earnings).

5. Firms continuously maximize profits; they relate prices to (marginal) cost, capital usually being taken as fixed, and they hire labour to the point at which its marginal value product equals its wage.

These ideas were developed by Lucas in a series of papers (Lucas and Rapping, 1969, Lucas, 1972a, b, 1973). They can be seen as a response to the difficulties of integrating rational expectations into the original Phillips curve formulation: it is hard to see why rational workers and firms should permit rigidity of wages and prices. Later, as we shall see in chapter 4, Keynesian theorists attempted to overcome this difficulty by the assumption of nominal contracts of long maturity; that assumption is not easy to reconcile with the idea of voluntary contracting by agents free to exploit all opportunities for trade, and Lucas' theory has the advantage of full consistency with that paradigm (one can also think of it as a model in which there are fully contingent wage contracts).

Let us begin with workers' intertemporal substitution. If one writes down a worker-consumer's general utility function, including terms in both consumption and leisure now and in all future periods, the first-order conditions for a maximum will among other things set the marginal rate of transformation between present and future labour supply equal to the gross real rate of interest — for an application see Sargent (1979a, chapter 16).

This is illustrated in Figure 3.1, where for simplicity the worker is assumed to have a fixed present value of consumption, $\overline{c}$, which can be achieved in a two-period life by working either this period or next: his indifference curves between leisure (work) are tangent to the trade off between minimum current and future hours required to achieve $\overline{c}$. $\overline{c}$ divided by next period's expected real wages, w^e_{t+1}, and multiplied by $1+r$ (the gross real interest rate) gives the number of hours needed to provide $\overline{c}$ by working entirely in $t+1$ and borrowing against that income to consume in t. The tangency condition is:

$$\frac{U'_{t+1}.w^e_t}{U'_t.w^e_{t+1}} = \frac{1}{1+r}$$

where U' is the marginal utility of leisure.

Hence for a normally behaved utility function, higher current real wages will have an income effect if 'permanent' real wages rise as well, diminishing work effort, and a substitution effect (relative to future real wages), raising it. Lucas' argument is that these movements in current real wages generally leave permanent real wages unchanged and so the substitution effect is dominant, and large enough to account for the empirically observed Phillips curve correlation between prices and output.

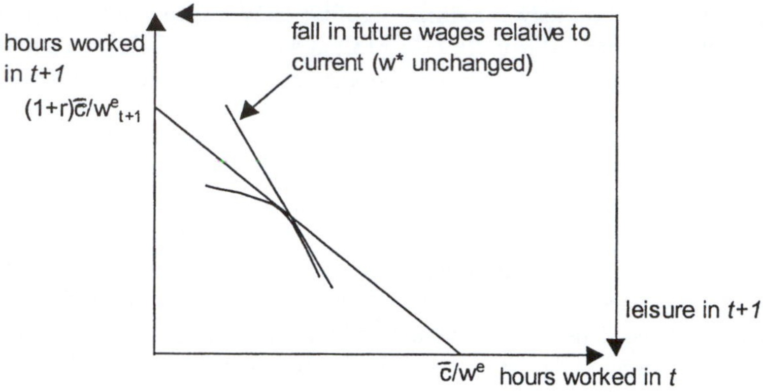

Figure 3.1: Intertemporal substitution by workers

Firms' profit maximization leads, as discussed in chapter 1, to a downward-sloping demand for labour from the first-order condition that the marginal product of labour, f', equals the real wage, or $f' = W/P$, which in the simplest case where labour is the only variable factor also expresses the price = marginal cost condition, $P = \frac{W}{f'}$; if f is a normally behaved production function, f'will fall as labour input increases.

The complete Phillips curve derivation is illustrated in figure 3.2, a four quadrant diagram due to Parkin and Bade (1988), first introduced in chapter 1 as Fig.1.1. Quadrant (a) shows the labour (L) market: the supply by workers is conditional on expected (log) prices, p^e(as well as permanent real wages, w^*, and r, both of which we hold constant here), the demand by firms depends on their own actual prices, which they continuously observe. Quadrant (b) shows the short run production function relating output ($Y = \exp y$) to labour, capital being fixed. Quadrant (c) transfers the implied output to quadrant (d), which summarizes the resulting PP relationship between (*log*) prices, p, and output. This is illustrated for an increase of p from $p_0 = p^e$ to p_1, with workers continuing to expect prices of $p^e = p_0$. This raises labour demand to $D'D'$ but leaves the supply curve where it is. Employment expands and more output is produced: the rise in prices has raised wages and so 'fooled' workers into thinking they are being paid higher real wages, so supplying more labour to firms who are actually enjoying lower real wage costs.

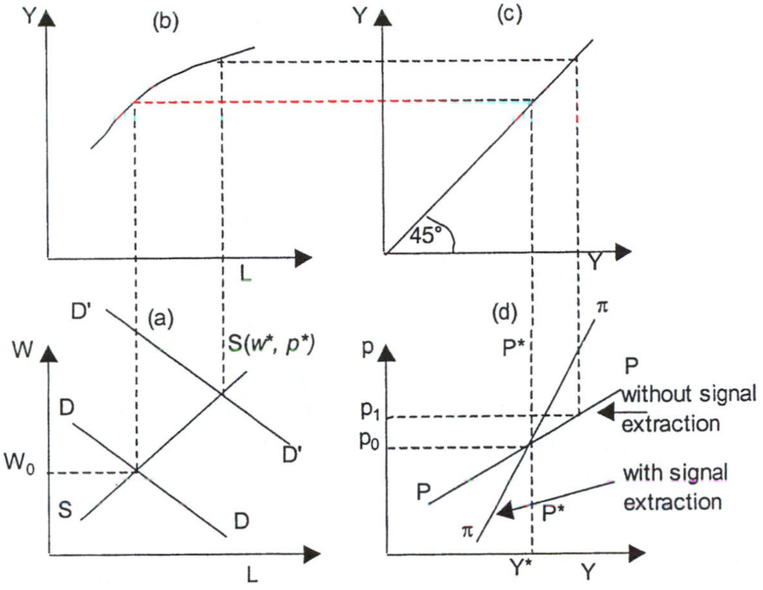

Figure 3.2: The New Classical Phillips curve

Suppose p_1 is maintained in the next period and p^e rises to this new level, then SS too shifts upwards. It will do so by exactly the same (vertical) distance as DD, namely a rise in W that is of the same proportion as the rise in p; this leaves both actual and expected real wages the same as at our starting point, and hence labour supply and demand will be the same as then. The resulting relationship between p and y, the 'long-run' Phillips curve obtained when $p = p^e$, is shown as P^*P^* and is vertical: consistently with neo-classical theory in which people and prices care about real quantities and relative prices, having no 'money illusion', rises in prices when fully anticipated or perceived have no real impact. In this simple model with no lags or adjustment in production or labour supply the economy is at its natural rate when $p = p^e$.

Let us write the resulting Phillips curve relationship between y and p (the log of respectively output and prices) as:

$$y_t - y^* = \frac{1}{\delta}(p_t - p_t^e) \tag{4}$$

This immediately brings out the formal equivalence between the traditional Phillips curve we used in chapter 2, in which prices are the dependent variable, and the New Classical formulation here in which output is. Although the derivations are clearly different, the result is formally the same.

Now let us graft on to this process the one assumption we have so far left out, signal extraction. Workers can use their current information on local prices they observe in their regular shopping to improve their expectation of the general price level. Denote the ith (of N) group of workers' (log) local price as p_{it} and assume that it is governed by

$$p_{it} = v_{it} + p_t \tag{5}$$

where v_{it} is a random error with variance of σ_v^2.

The problem faced by the ith group of workers is to forecast $p_t - E(p_t \mid \Phi_{t-1})$ from $p_{it} - E(p_{it} \mid \Phi_{t-1})$ where $\Phi_{\ t-1}$ is all last period's data assumed available to all i groups by the current period. To do this, they compute the least squares regression of $p_t - E_t(p_t \mid \Phi_{t-1})$ on $p_{it} - E(p_{it} \mid \Phi_{t-1})$ and predict from it.

We know that

$$p_t = \sum_{i=1}^{\infty} x_i \epsilon_{t-1} + p^* \tag{6}$$

$$E(p_t \mid \Phi_{t-1}) = \sum_{i=0}^{\infty} \pi_i \epsilon_{t-1} + p^* \tag{7}$$

and

$$E(p_{it} \mid \Phi_{t-1}) = E[(p_t + v_{it}) \mid \Phi_{t-1}] = E(p_t \mid \Phi_{t-1}) \tag{8}$$

since all i groups have the same $t-1$ information and cannot predict v_{it} from it. So our regression will be:

$$\pi_0 \epsilon_t = \phi_0 + \phi(\pi_0 \epsilon_t + v_{it}) \tag{9}$$

Assuming our workers had a large sample, so that we can ignore sampling error for simplicity, they will obtain (all i groups since σ_v^2 is the same for all v_{it}) $\phi_0 = 0$ because ϵ_t and v_{it} have zero means, and

$$\phi = \frac{E(\pi_0 \epsilon_t, v_{it})}{E(\pi_0 \epsilon_t, v_{it})^2} = \frac{\pi_0^2 \sigma^2}{\pi_0^2 \sigma_\epsilon^2 + \sigma_v^2}$$

Armed with this regression, the ith group's current expectation of p_t, $p_{t,i}^e = E(p_t \mid \theta_{it}, \Phi_{t-1})$ where θ_{it} is this period's data available in the current period to the ith worker, now can be written as:

$$p_{t,i}^e = E(p_t \mid \Phi_{t-1}) + \phi(p_{it} - E[p_t \mid \Phi_{t-1}]) \tag{10}$$

Averaging expectations over all i groups gives us:

$$p_t^e = \frac{\sum_i p_{t,i}^e}{N} = (1-\phi)E(p_t \mid \Phi_{t-1}) + \phi p_t \qquad (11)$$

In passing, notice that p_t^e implies an average expectation of ϵ_t. Since all i groups know that $p_t = \pi_0 \epsilon_t + E(p_t \mid \Phi_{t-1})$, their expectation of ϵ_t will be given by:

$$\begin{aligned} E(\epsilon_t \mid \theta_{it}, \Phi_{t-1}) &= \frac{E(p_t \mid \theta_{it}, \Phi_{t-1}) - E(p_t \mid \Phi_{t-1})}{\pi_0} \\ &= \frac{p_{t,i}^e - E(p_t \mid \Phi_{t-1})}{\pi_0} = \frac{\phi(p_{it} - E(p_t \mid \Phi_{t-1})}{\pi_0} \end{aligned} \qquad (12)$$

Averaging (12) over all i gives:

$$\epsilon_t^e = \frac{\phi \pi_0 \epsilon_t}{\pi_0} = \phi \epsilon_t \qquad (13)$$

We may now integrate p_t^e into our New Classical Phillips curve:

$$y_t - y^* = \frac{1}{\delta}(p_t - p_t^e) = \frac{(1-\phi)}{\delta}[p_t - E(p_t \mid \Phi_{t-1})] \qquad (14)$$

The dashed curve in figure 3.2 shows the resulting full New Classical Phillips curve: signal extraction steepens its slope, since now as actual prices rise workers react by altering p_t^e.

Let us work out the values of ϕ and π_0 for a simple model:

$$\overline{m} + \epsilon_t = p_t + y_t \qquad (15)$$

$$y_t - y* = \frac{(1-\phi)}{\delta}[p_t - E(p_t \mid \Phi_{t-1})] \qquad (16)$$

Using the Muth solution we obtain: $\pi_i = 0$ $(i \geq 1)$ and $\pi_0 = \delta/(\delta + 1 - \phi)$. The slope of the Phillips curve is $\frac{1-\phi}{\delta}$ and must lie between 0 and $\frac{1}{\delta}$, since $0 < \phi < 1$.

With ϕ as given above, we can see that the solution for π_0 and ϕ is in general a cubic, with the extreme values of $\pi_0 = 1$, $\phi = 1$ (vertical Phillips curve) and $\pi_0 = \frac{\delta}{1+\delta}$, $\phi = 0$ (the PP curve in Figure 3.2).

The main implication of signal extraction is therefore that the Phillips curve's slope depends on the behaviour of monetary policy. This determines $\pi_0 \epsilon_t$ in our simple models to this point; but even in more complex models where many influences impact on the 'surprise' term $(p_t - E(p_t \mid \Phi_{t-1}))$, including all demand and supply shocks, money supply shocks will still play a major role (a more complex model of this sort in which the problem is to disentangle permanent from temporary money supply shocks is set out by Brunner et al. (1980). If the money supply is volatile, then workers will assume that the current movements in prices they observe are largely monetary in origin: ϕ will be close to 1 as $\pi_0^2\sigma_\epsilon^2$ is large relative to σ_v^2 . The Phillips curve will be close to vertical. By contrast, countries with monetary stability will have flatter Phillips curves, with workers interpreting local price movements as predominantly relative price movements. Lucas (1973) turned up convincing evidence of this in a large cross-country sample of Phillips curves; and much subsequent evidence has confirmed it. One particularly obvious way in which the Phillips curve steepens is through the spread of indexation in countries with poor monetary control: indexation for a group of workers typically replaces p_t^e by a weighted average of $p_t^e$and p_t (or p_{t-k} where k is made as small as possible given information-gathering costs). Ironically, though, in countries with extreme monetary volatility indexation is handicapped both by the necessary lag in information and by poor or even fraudulent government information about the general price level.

THE SUPPLY SIDE: INTEGRATING MACRO WITH MICRO

Most of this book is concerned with the behaviour of the economy in response to monetary shocks, in the sense of shocks which disturb the absolute price level. These set up reactions through the Phillips or supply curve on output and so on other variables, for example in the way we have just examined. Yet there is a wide variety and scale of real shocks, which, regardless of their effects on the price level, cause important effects on the economy. One of the key changes in our thinking produced by the rational expectations hypothesis has been a renewed emphasis on the 'supply side'; that is, the mechanisms through which the economy responds to real shocks.

One branch of rational expectations research, real business cycle theory, dismisses monetary shocks altogether as a source of variation in output, explaining it entirely in terms of real shocks (e.g. Kydland and Prescott, 1982; Long and Plosser, 1983); these economists argue that people have sufficiently up-to-date information on the price level to avoid being fooled as in the New Classical supply curve and that any contracts they sign are fully indexed to the price level, again avoiding any real effects of unexpected price changes as in the New Keynesian supply curve. The price level on this view will vary if the money supply increases (e.g. through expansion in bank credit and deposits) but this will have no real effects. Only if there is some shock to payments technology which disturbs real plans (for example, by credit controls creating a 'credit crunch') will monetary shocks have a real effect: but this is not a normal money supply shock in our terms.

The real business cycle school may or may not be going too far in denying any effect of monetary shocks: testing its assertions is difficult because it can in principle account for the same correlations we observe, such as that between prices and output in the Phillips curve, by appealing to reverse causation — real shocks move output, which induces monetary expansion, which raises prices. Nevertheless, what is undoubtedly important is the focus on real shocks and the supply side as of primary interest to macroeconomists. We have just set out a basic model of the supply side, to explain the full New Classical model. This model can be developed to explain unemployment in terms of people's voluntary choices confronted with the opportunities they face (not necessarily attractive ones of course); a further factor which may frustrate their choices however is the power of unions. Analysis of unemployment along these lines for the UK is to be found in Minford et al. (1983) and Layard and Nickell (1985), for Germany in Davis and Minford (1986) and for a variety of other countries in Bean et al. (1986). In chapter 9 we discuss these supply-side issues further; and in chapter 11 we set out a full real business cycle model.

Rational expectations has re-united macro- and microeconomics into a single subject. Keynes (1936) divided off, indeed created, the subject of macroeconomics with its own aggregate laws, not derivable from micro behaviour and subject to regular aggregate 'market failure'. Since his intervention we have learned much about aggregate behaviour, which had never previously been much studied by the classical economists. Essentially, rational expectations has enabled us to account for macro behaviour in terms of micro laws.

CAPITAL MARKETS AND PARTIAL MACRO INFORMATION

We now consider our second example of signal extraction. Here we assume that there is no useful local information (σ_v^2 is large relative to σ_ϵ^2) but that there is current macro information from capital markets. Clearly a relevant model of most economies will contain both sorts of information but it helps our exposition to focus on each separately.

Our illustrative example supposes that people know the interest rate currently. They wish to derive from this estimates of other current macroeconomic variables — the price level and output, and so on. They do this just as in the local information case by prediction from a regression of these variables on the interest rate, any variable x_t being expressed as $x_t - E(x_t \mid \Phi_{t-1})$. Again, as in the local case, the regression parameters enter the model through their effect on the expected variables: there is an additional feedback in the model from current events to expectations, altering the impact effect of shocks to the economy.

This is a much more complicated signal extraction problem than the earlier one we considered in the Lucas supply curve where the general price level had to be extracted from the local price. There the only information people have is the local price and the equation relating this to the general price (5). Here they have information on a 'global' (economy-wide) variable, interest rates, and all the equations of the global (macro) model. Hence any view they form of the shocks driving the global interest rate must be consistent with what the model would produce; it must also be the case that the actual shocks (which will in general differ from what they expect) must via the model produce this same interest rate. This is a highly complicated consistency condition.

To get an intuitive understanding of what is happening, it is useful to consider diagrammatically how the economy behaves when this sort of signal extraction is going on; and to compare it with the usual situation we have discussed up to now where no global signal extraction is going on.

It is of some interest to compare the reaction of this 'economy', based on the model of equations (17)–(20) below, when R_t is known with that when R_t is not known. Table 3.1 shows the reactions of output to the three shocks as derived below from that model. When R_t is not known, all shocks have 'normal' positive effects on output. However, the sizes of the coefficients are quite different when R_t is known. This is hardly surprising since now output responds both to expected shocks and to the difference of shocks from their expected levels. Now even the sign of effect can be different for the various shocks. We can understand this as follows.

	u_t	v_t	e_t
y_t (R_t not known)	W	$a(\frac{c}{\alpha})W$	aW
y_t (R_t known)	$\phi_u + \frac{\phi_v}{1+a}$	$\phi_e - a\phi_u$	$a\phi_u + \frac{a\phi_v}{1+a}$
where $W = \frac{1}{1+a(1+\frac{c}{\alpha})}$			

Source: Model equations (17)–(20)

Table 3.1: Output Reactions to Shocks

Suppose the noise in e_t dominates; then $\phi_e \to 1$, $(\phi_u, \phi_v) \to 0$ and u_t has no effect because $E_t u_t \to 0$, $E_t v_t \to 0$. Suppose noise in v_t dominates; then $(\phi_e, \phi_u) \to 0$ and v_t has no effect. But suppose noise in u_t dominates; then $E_t v_t \to 0$, $\phi_u \to 1$, so that $\frac{\partial(v_t + E_t u_t)}{\partial v_t} = -a$. Hence a demand shock has a negative effect on output if supply shocks predominate, because agents misinterpret the effect of the positive demand shock on interest rates as that of a negative supply shock; expected prices consequently rise more than actual prices and supply of output is reduced.

Similar 'peculiarities' can occur in the reactions of p_t and R_t; Table 3.2 documents them. It is worth stressing therefore that the economy's behaviour in response to shocks can be 'paradoxical' if the shocks are 'misinterpreted'. Such effects are well known at the level of everyday comment (cf. the behaviour of the UK economy in 1980, when the interest rates were interpreted as responding to 'overshooting' of its target by the money supply; subsequently it turned out that the money supply, truly measured, had contracted substantially). It is of interest that they can be rationalized within a stylized framework.

One such case is illustrated in figures 3.3 and 3.4. In figure 3.3, it is assumed that a negative monetary shock, e_t, occurs but that R_t is not currently known; so normal results are obtained. The LM curve shifts leftwards in the upper (R_t, y_t) half, shifting left the aggregate demand curve in the lower (p_t, y_t) half. Prices and output fall and the interest rate rises; expectations of course are undisturbed.

	u_t	v_t	e_t
$p_t(R_t$ not known$)$	$-(1+\frac{c}{\alpha})W$	$\frac{c}{\alpha}W$	W
$p_t(R_t$ known$)$	$-S$	$(1+a)S-1$	$1-aS$
$R_t(R_t$ not known$)$	$-\frac{a}{\alpha}W$	$(1+\frac{ac}{\alpha})W/\alpha$	$-\frac{a}{\alpha}W$
$R_t(R_t$ known$)$	A	B	D

$$S = \frac{\alpha+c}{\alpha(1+c)}\phi_u + \frac{c+\alpha(1+c)}{\alpha(1+c)(1+\alpha)}\phi_v + \frac{c(1-\mu)}{\alpha(1+c(1-\mu))}\phi_e$$

Source: Model equations (17)–(20)

Table 3.2: Price and Interest Rate Reaction to Shocks

In figure 3.4 the same shock occurs when R_t is currently observed (so that $E_t p_t$ now reacts); we illustrate the paradoxical case just discussed where people expect only variations in the supply shock, u_t, to be of any significance, so they misinterpret the shock as a negative supply shock. The left side of figure 3.4 shows actual outcomes, the right side shows expected ones: across the two sides expected outcomes are of course the same. The expected outcome is a rise in the interest rate and in prices, together with a fall in output because of a negative u_t. The rise in $E_t p_t$

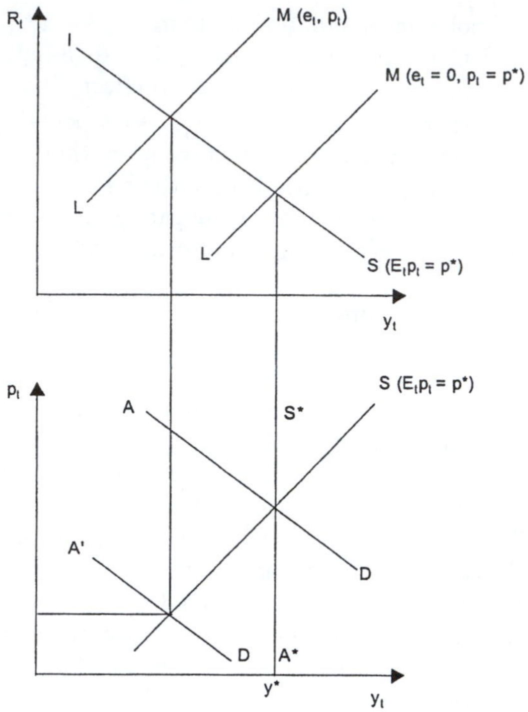

Figure 3.3: The case where R_t is not currently observed and a negative e_t shock occurs

shifts both the expected IS and LM curves, IS^e and LM^e, along the $ISLM^e$ curve which plots their intersection as Ep_t changes. In (E_tp_t, E_ty_t) space, the AS curve shifts leftwards from the fall in E_tu_t, along A^eD^e, the expected aggregate demand curve.

The actual outcome can be broken down into two parts: the shifts in the curves because E_tp_t rises, and the shifts because e_t falls. The rise in E_tp_t shifts the AS curve up and the AD curve leftwards in (p, y) space, the latter being produced by the IS curve shifting leftwards in (R, y) space. The fall in e_t shifts the LM leftwards in (R, y) space and so the AD leftwards in (p, y) space. These various shifts are shown on the graphs by labelling each curve according to the value of e_t, p_t and Ep_t.

In effect, the expected supply shock drives expected prices up (because of fears of shortage) so that even though prices may fall by much the same as in the normal case, the contraction in output is much greater. In this example, the misinterpretation of the monetary shock has se-

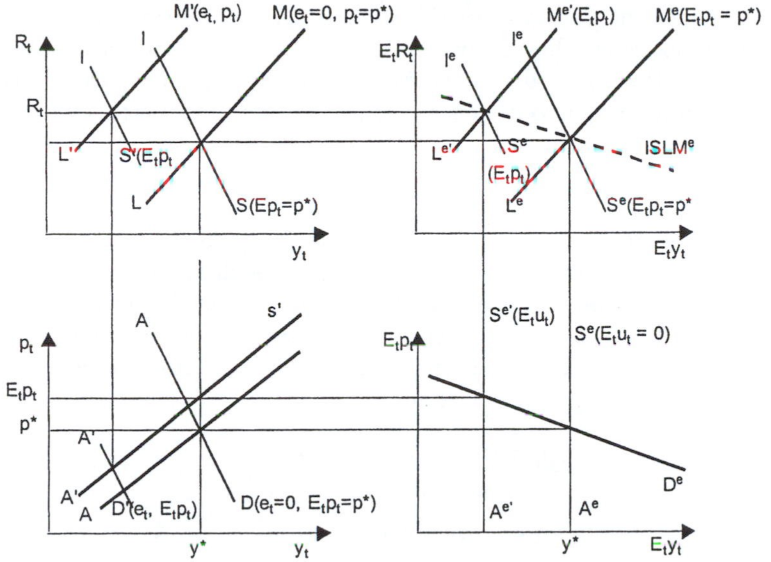

A negative ε_t shock occurs, but σ^2_v, σ^2_e are small so that a u_t shock is expected ($\phi_u \to 1$).
The ε_t shock is interpreted as a u_t shock ($E_t p_{t+1} = p^*$, i.e. $\mu = 0$)

Figure 3.4: The case where R_t is currently observed

riously worsened recession (somewhat reminiscent of the 1980 British recession).

We have seen how the economy behaves. But how in detail does one extract a signal about the shocks in this economy? First, we need to know the variance of the different shocks (we assume for simplicity that they are unrelated; if not, we also need their covariances): this tells us the unconditional probability distribution of each shock. Second, we need to know the effect each shock would have — via the model — on interest rates: with this extra knowledge we can extract the probability distribution of each shock conditional on the observed value of the interest rate, and so the conditional expected value of the shock.

Plainly, as we have seen in the diagrammatic example, the expected values of the various shocks influence the behaviour of the economy: in our example the shock expected was overwhelmingly the supply shock and this caused the economy's agents to expect a high price level when hit by a demand shock. Hence the effect of the shocks on the economy depend on the signal extraction people make; and so the effects and the signal extraction formula are set simultaneously by the structure of the model and the variances of the shocks. We now show one method for solving out what they are within the sort of model we have been using hitherto: this method has the benefit of showing transparently the interdependence between signal extraction, the model structure and the shock variances. In practical applications, however, we would recommend the use of a computer algorithm (developed in Matthews et al., 1994a, b).

To give our example enough complexity to be of interest we move to a fairly general macro model. We express all variables in deviations from equilibrium; so all constants such as $\overline{m}$ and y^* are dropped. For short, $E_t x_t$ is used to represent the current expectation conditional on last period's full data and this period's partial data (consisting of R_t, the interest rate). The model is:

$$y_t = a(p_t - E_t p_t) + u_t \tag{17}$$

$$m_t = p_t + y_t - cR_t \tag{18}$$

$$m_t = \mu m_{t-1} + e_t \tag{19}$$

$$y_t = -\alpha R_t + \alpha E_t p_{t+1} - E_t p_t + v_t \tag{20}$$

u_t, v_t and e_t are independent random shocks with known variances σ_u^2, σ_v^2 and σ_e^2; (17) is aggregate output supply; (18) is money demand; (19) is money supply; (20) is demand for aggregate output.

To solve this model, we first obtain a basic equation in the errors as deviations from their expected values. Taking expectations of (17) and subtracting the result from (17) yields:

$$y_t - Ey_t = a(p_t - E_t p_t) + u_t - E_t u_t \tag{21}$$

Equating (18) with (19) and following the same procedure as with (17) yields:

$$e_t - E_t e_t = p_t - E_t p_t + y_t - E_t y_t - c(R_t - E_t R_t) \tag{22}$$

Equation (20) analogously gives:

$$y_t - Ey_t = -(R_t - ER_t) + v_t - E_t v_t = v_t - E_t v_t \tag{23}$$

since $R_t = E_t R_t$, R_t being known. Simple manipulation then yields our basic equation in the errors:

$$(1 + a)(v_t - E_t v_t) = a(e_t - E_t e_t) + u_t - E_t u_t \tag{24}$$

This formal restriction across the expected and actual values of the errors results from the fact that people know R_t. Therefore the actual solution of R_t (based on the actual and expected errors) must coincide with the expected solution (based only on the expected errors). The parameters α and c drop out because when deviations from expectations are taken these multiply variables that must be zero (since $R_t = E_t R_t$, $E_t(E_t P_t) = E_t P_t$, $E_t(E_t P_{t+1}) = E_t P_{t+1}$).

This linear model has a general linear solution for R_t in terms of the current shocks and lagged information:

$$R_t = Au_t + Bv_t + De_t + Zm_{t-1} \tag{25}$$

A, B, D and Z are the coefficients to be solved for. Consequently, using the Graybill (1961) formula, the best estimates of u_t, v_t, e_t, given $R_t - Zm_{t-1}$ are:

$$E_t u_t = \frac{1}{A}\phi_u(Au_t + Bv_t + De_t) \tag{26}$$

$$E_t v_t = \frac{1}{B}\phi_v(Au_t + Bv_t + De_t) \tag{27}$$

$$E_t e_t = \frac{1}{D}\phi_e(Au_t + Bv_t + De_t) \tag{28}$$

where

$$\phi_u = \frac{A^2\sigma_u^2}{X}; \phi_v = \frac{B^2\sigma_v^2}{X}; \phi_e = \frac{D^2\sigma_e^2}{X}$$

and

$$X = A^2\sigma_u^2 + B^2\sigma_v^2 + D^2\sigma_e^2$$

Substituting (26), (27) and (28) into (24) we obtain:

$$(1+a)v_t - ae_t - u_t = \{(1+a)\frac{\phi v}{B} - \frac{a\phi e}{D} - \frac{\phi u}{A}\}(Au_t + Bv_t + De_t) \tag{29}$$

Since v_t, e_t and u_t may each be any real number, (3.29) is only satisfied, in the usual manner of undetermined coefficients, if the coefficients on each alone add up to zero, that is if for example

$$1 = \phi_v - \frac{aB}{(1+a)D}\phi_e - \frac{B}{(1+a)A}\phi_u \quad (\text{on } v_t) \tag{30}$$

Further, since we know that $\phi_v + \phi_e + \phi_u = 1$ it follows at once similarly that

$$\frac{D}{A} = a; \frac{D}{B} = -\frac{a}{1+a}; \frac{A}{B} = -\frac{1}{1+a} \tag{31}$$

Consequently

$$\phi_u = \frac{\sigma_u^2}{X'}; \phi_v = \frac{(1+a)^2\sigma_v^2}{X'}; \phi_e = \frac{a^2\sigma_e^2}{X'} \tag{32}$$

where

$$X' = \sigma_u^2 + (1+a)^2\sigma_v^2 + a^2\sigma_e^2$$

The full solution of this model can now be found. From (17), (18) and (19) we have:

$$p_t + a(p_t - E_t p_t) + u_t - cR_t = e_t + \mu m_{t-1} \tag{33}$$

from which we obtain, taking expectations and using $R_t = E_t R_t$:

$$R_t = \frac{1}{c}(E_t p_t + E_t u_t - E_t e_t - \mu m_{t-1}) \tag{34}$$

Equating (17) and (20), taking expectations and substituting for R_t from (34) we get:

$$E_t u_t - E_t v_t = -\frac{\alpha}{c}(E_t p_t + E_t u_t - E_t e_t - \mu m_{t-1}) - \alpha E_t p_t + \alpha E_t p_{t+1}$$

and rearranging:

$$E_t p_{t+1} - \left(\frac{1+c}{c}\right) E_t p_t = \frac{\alpha + c}{\alpha c} E_t u_t - \frac{1}{\alpha} E_t v_t - \frac{1}{c} E_t e_t - \mu / c m_{t-1} \tag{35}$$

Following Sargent's procedure (see chapter 2), we write the left hand side of (35) as

$$-\frac{1+c}{c} \ 1 - \frac{c}{1+c} B^{-1} \Big] E_t p_t$$

where B is the backward operator instructing one to lag variables but not the expectations date (e.g. $BE_t P_t = E_t P_{t-1}$). Equation (35) can now be written as:

$$\begin{aligned} E_t p_t = &-\left(\frac{c}{1+c}\right)\left(\frac{1}{1-\frac{c}{1+c}B^{-1}}\right) \\ &\left(\frac{\alpha+c}{\alpha c} E u_t - \frac{1}{\alpha} E v_t - \frac{1}{c} E \epsilon_t - \frac{\mu}{c} m_{t-1}\right) = \\ &-\frac{\alpha + c}{\alpha(1+c)} E_t u_t + \frac{c}{\alpha(1+c)} E_t v_t + \frac{1}{1+c} E_t e_t \\ &+ \frac{\mu}{1+c} \sum_{i-0}^{\infty} \left\{\frac{c}{1+c}\right\}^i E_t m_{t-1+i} \end{aligned} \tag{36}$$

Since $E_t m_{t-1+i} = m_{t-1}, \mu m_{t-1} + E_t e_t, \mu^2 m_{t-1} + \mu E_t e_t, \ldots$ for $i = 0, 1, 2, \ldots$ (36) becomes:

$$E_t p_t = \frac{-(\alpha + c)}{\alpha(1+c)} E_t u_t + \frac{c}{\alpha(1+c)} E_t v_t + \frac{1}{1+c(1-\mu)} E_t e_t + \frac{\mu}{1+c(1-\mu)} m_{t-1} \quad (37)$$

whence:

$$E_t p_{t+1} = \frac{\mu^2 m_{t-1} + \mu E_t e_t}{1+c(1-\mu)} \quad (38)$$

To find R_t substitute from (37) into (34) to obtain

$$R_t = \frac{-(1-\alpha)}{\alpha(1+c)} E_t u_t + \frac{1}{\alpha(1+c)} E_t v_t - \frac{1-\mu}{1+c(1-\mu)} E_t e_t - \frac{\mu(1-\mu)}{1+c(1-\mu)} m_{t-1} \quad (39)$$

We can write

$$E_t u_t = \phi_u Q_t; E_t v_t = -\frac{\phi_v}{1+a} Q_t; E_t e_t = \frac{\phi_e}{a} Q_t \quad (40)$$

where

$$Q_t = u_t - (1+a) v_t + a e_t$$

Hence

$$A = -\frac{1-\alpha}{\alpha(1+c)} \phi_u - \frac{1}{\alpha(1+c)(1+a)} \phi_v - \frac{1-\mu}{a[1+c(1-\mu)]} \phi_e$$

$$B = -(1+a)A;$$

$$D = aA \quad (41)$$

What we see therefore in these solutions is a striking complexity in the contemporaneous response of the economy to shocks. That complexity is due to the fact that the shocks go through an 'interpretation filter' — signal extraction — which modifies their 'direct' effect, that is their effect in a world where people have no global information. Thus for as long as people do not have full information, the course of the economy is contemporaneously influenced by what they think are the shocks driving it. This influence persists after they have discovered what the shocks were, because of the lagged effects in the model: however of course this persistence also applies to the direct effects of the shocks. We can therefore describe global signal extraction as a further contemporaneous transmission mechanism of shocks, over and above their direct transmission mechanism.

CONCLUSIONS

We have seen that signal extraction has potentially important effects on economic behaviour. How people interpret shocks conditions their behaviour whether in the slope of the Phillips curve or more generally. In this chapter we have illustrated these effects and shown how models can be solved allowing for the signal extraction feedback. In subsequent chapters we shall be applying the techniques of chapters 2 and 3 to the analysis of a variety of policy issues.

Part II

Evaluating Government Policy

4

Stabilization Policy — Can we?

In this chapter we will outline the implications for stabilization policy if people form their expectations rationally. Stabilization policies are typically defined as policies aimed at reducing (usually the variance of) output or employment deviations from their full-employment ('natural' or 'equilibrium') levels. This is the definition we will use primarily, though we will occasionally widen it to policies designed to stabilise a wider menu of macro variables (such as inflation).

We will consider government use both of the budget (tax rates and spending- 'fiscal policy') and of the money supply ('monetary policy'). We will treat a monetary policy of interest rate setting as equivalent to some money supply policy (rather like in trade theory import quotas are treated as equivalent to tariffs which vary with market conditions).

As this point is important (given that central banks usually do use rules for setting interest rates) and not immediately obvious, let us consider two examples of this. In the first case, suppose the interest rate behaviour of the government or central bank (henceforth 'the government') is

$$R_t = \alpha(y_{t-1} - y^*) + \beta(m_t - m^*) + \eta_t \tag{1a}$$

Then we can rewrite it as a money supply rule:

$$m_t = m^* + \frac{1}{\beta}R_t - \frac{\alpha}{\beta}(y_{t-1} - y^*) - \frac{1}{\beta}\eta_t \tag{1b}$$

In the second case, assume that the interest rate behaviour does not directly include the money supply. Here we have to introduce other relationships in the model to determine the implied money supply behaviour. So let

$$R_t = \alpha(y_{t-1} - y^*) + \eta_t \tag{1c}$$

and suppose the demand for money is simply $m_t = -\beta R_t$

Then the implied money supply rule is

$$m_t = -\alpha\beta(y_{t-1} - y^*) - \beta\eta_t \tag{1d}$$

In other words we can rewrite any interest rate behaviour as an implied behaviour of the money supply, and regard the government as obeying that 'money supply rule'.

The vexed question now arises of what government policies are 'rules', which 'discretionary', and which 'fixed rules'. However from the viewpoint of rational expectations we can distinguish between that part of government behaviour which is a surprise (cannot be predicted from known past events) and that part which is a predictable response to past events; furthermore within the surprise element we will distinguish between that part which responds predictably to contemporaneous events and that part which is contributed by the government's own unpredictability. The description of the predictable part of the behaviour is the 'rule' governing its behaviour; the rest is the 'surprise' element in policy. Within the rule element, the government could respond to past events actively or it could refuse to respond at all; the former is often called a 'feedback' response, the latter a 'fixed target' rule. Perhaps the best-known example of this last is Milton Friedman's proposal that the government should adopt a policy of a fixed growth rate of the money supply (Friedman, 1968).

It is possible for feedback rules to be simple or complex, depending on exactly how governments set about stabilization. In the 1970s for example it was quite usual for governments to make detailed forecasts every so often of what would happen with different settings of policy instruments; and then to adjust the settings to obtain the most desirable forecast — 'optimal control policy'. This is sometimes referred to as 'discretion' or 'fine-tuning'.

The relationship between past events and policy reaction resulting from this process would be complex; but it could in principle be written down. More recently governments have lost faith in such forecasting procedures (for reasons we discuss in chapter 6) and have used simpler rules of policy reaction — to one or at most a few lagged variables. It is rules like these we shall focus on as typical of feedback response or 'flexible rules'. (Notice in passing that flexibility cannot, as some might think casually, consist in a government changing its mind every period on how it will react to past events; if it did, it would have entirely unpredictable behaviour — policy would be a pure surprise.)

We will also examine the government response to contemporaneous events. It is usual to suppose that governments can observe these no better than any private person (we will also consider the case where it has superior information below). However, there are ways policy can respond to events without the government directly observing them: we describe these as 'automatic' responses. For example taxes (and benefits) respond to incomes through the tax/benefit system, without the government doing anything (i.e. changing tax or benefit rates). Similarly, the money supply (or interest rates) may respond automatically and simultaneously to income under the particular rule in force, without a contemporaneous decision by the government. These policy responses may well be important stabilizers (or indeed destabilizers).

MODELS WITH THE SARGENT–WALLACE SUPPLY CURVE

An early result, due to Sargent and Wallace (1975), is that stabilization policy has no impact on either real output or unemployment in classical equilibrium models if they embody a supply function relating deviations of output to surprise movements in the price level, and further that both private and public agents (a) have identical information sets and (b) are able to act on these information sets. We discussed this result briefly in chapter 2 in the context of a simple monetary model, which we now extend somewhat.

Consider the following simple model:

$$y_t = -\alpha(R_t - E_{t-1}p_{t+1} + E_{t-1}p_t) + \mu_f(y_{t-1} - y^*) \tag{2}$$

$$y_t = y^* + \beta(p_t - E_{t-1}p_t) \tag{3}$$

$$m_t = p_t + y_t - cR_t + v_t \tag{4}$$

$$m_t = \overline{m} + \mu_m(y_{t-1} - y^*) + u_t \tag{5}$$

α, β, μ_f, μ_m, and c are constants (μ_f, μ_m would typically be negative in Keynesian policy rules), u_t and v_t are random errors, R_t is the nominal interest rate.

Equation (2) is the aggregate demand schedule. It includes a fiscal feedback response $\mu_f(y_{t-1} - y^*)$ representing government counter-cyclical variations in spending or tax rates.

Equation (3) is the Sargent and Wallace Phillips (or supply) curve. This is derived as in chapter 3. The only difference is that it assumes that people can obtain no useful information about the general price level from their current local prices; so there is no signal extraction in this case — hence the dating of expectations at $t-1$. The same assumption is used throughout the model. It turns out, as we shall see later, to be an important restriction.

Another way of looking at (3) is as an 'old' Keynesian expectations-augmented Phillips curve in which inflation equals expected inflation plus an effect of excess demand proxied by $y - y^*$: we can rewrite it as $\pi_t - E_{t-1}\pi_t[= p_t - p_{t-1} - (E_{t-1}p_t - p_{t-1})] = \frac{1}{\beta}(y_t - y^*)$. Sargent and Wallace stressed that their result could be viewed as an implication of orthodox Keynesian models, if rational expectations were substituted for adaptive expectations.

Equation (5) is a money supply rule with a feedback response

$$\mu_m(y_{t-1} - y^*)$$

On substituting (2) for R_t into (4) and equating (5) to the result, we obtain:

$$\overline{m} + \mu(y_{t-1} - y*) + w_t = p_t + (1 + \frac{c}{\alpha})y_t - c(E_{t-1}p_{t+1} - E_{t-1}p_t) \quad (6)$$

where $w_t = u_t - v_t$ and $\mu = [\mu_f(\frac{c}{\alpha}) + \mu_m]$. Substitution of (3) into (6) for y_t and y_{t-1} yields :

$$\begin{aligned} \overline{m} + \beta\mu(p_{t-1} - E_{t-2}p_{t-1}) + w_t = p_t + (1 + \frac{c}{\alpha})\beta(p_t - E_{t-1}p_t) \\ - c(E_{t-1}p_{t+1} - E_{t-1}p_t) + (1 + \frac{c}{\alpha})y^* \quad (7) \end{aligned}$$

To solve (7) for prices, we use the Muth solution method discussed in chapter 2, writing:

$$p_t = \overline{p} + \sum_{i=0}^{\infty} \pi_i w_{t-i} \quad (8)$$

We find that the identities yield:

$$\overline{p} = \overline{m} - (1 + \frac{c}{\alpha})y^* \quad (9)$$

$$(\text{terms in } w_t) \quad 1 = \pi_0[1 + \beta(1 + \frac{c}{\alpha})] \quad (10)$$

The identities in the other errors are irrelevant for our purposes here. Since

$$p_t - E_{t-1}p_t = \pi_0 w_t \quad (11)$$

substitution in (3) yields

$$y_t = y^* + \beta\pi_0 w_t \quad (12)$$

From (10) we see that π_0 does not depend on either μ_m or μ_f and consequently we see from (12) that systematic monetary policy does not influence the variance of output in this model. Unanticipated monetary change is of course equal to $m_t - E_{t-1}m_t$.

Since $E_{t-1}m_t = \overline{m} + \mu m(y_{t-1} - y^*)$,

$$m_t - E_{t-1}m_t = u_t \tag{13}$$

which is a component of w_t. Consequently, unanticipated monetary policy does influence output in the Sargent-Wallace model but not anticipated monetary policy.

This result stems from the nature of the supply curve. Output is set by supply considerations (relative prices, technology, producers' preferences, etc.) and is only influenced by macroeconomic events if these cause surprise movements in absolute prices which in turn are partially (mis-) interpreted as relative price movements. Government by definition cannot plan surprises (if it tried to, the 'surprise' would be — under our assumptions here — part of available information at $t-1$ and so would be fully anticipated, and no surprise at all); its feedback responses are planned variations in net spending or money supply.

A basic extension of the result occurs if there are adjustment costs in supply; allowance for these in a standard way (e.g. a quadratic cost function) adds a term $+j(y_{t-1} - y^*)$to (3) $(0 < j > 1)$. A shock to output now persists, and in principle the business cycle in output can be accounted for by the interaction of a variety of shocks with such a 'persistence mechanism' (various forms of it have been suggested by Lucas, 1975; Sargent, 1976; Fischer, 1980b; Barro, 1980).

Even though a macroeconomic shock now affects output for the indefinite future, it is still impossible for fiscal or monetary feedback rules to affect its variance because they can neither affect the impact of the shock itself, being a surprise, nor alter the adjustment parameter which determines the lagged effects, this parameter being fixed by technology, etc. We leave the demonstration of this — by substituting for y_t and y_{t-1} in (7) from the new supply curve in (3) — as an exercise for the reader.

DIFFERENT INFORMATION SETS

It is crucial for this neutrality proposition that, even in a model embodying a Sargent-Wallace supply curve, both private and public agents have the same information set.

If, for example, the government has an information superiority, then it can use this to modify the 'surprise' faced by the private sector. For suppose private agents have access only to last period's data in the current period, but the government knows the true price level (assume it collects price statistics over the period and waits before releasing them). Then it may in principle let its net spending or the money supply react to this information; its reactions will modify the price surprises to suppliers. Formally, add $-a_f(p_t - E_{t-1}p_t)$ into (2) and $-a_m(p_t - E_{t-1}p_t)$ into (5) where a_f, a_m (both positive) are fiscal and monetary responses respectively. To simplify matters set $\mu_f = \mu_m = 0$. Equation (7) now becomes

$$\overline{m} - (a_m + \frac{ca_f}{\alpha})(p_t - E_{t-1}p_t) + w_t = p_t + (1 + \frac{c}{\alpha})(p_t - E_{t-1}p_t) - c(E_{t-1}p_{t+1} - E_{t-1}p_t) + (1 + \frac{c}{\alpha})y^* \quad (14)$$

so that from the terms in w_t we have:

$$\pi_0 = \frac{1}{1 + (1 + \frac{c}{\alpha})\beta + a_m + \frac{ca_f}{\alpha}} \quad (15)$$

from which it is apparent that the higher a_m, a_f the smaller the price surprise and hence the output variance.

One may ask, however, why a government in possession of macro information should not release it rapidly as an alternative to implementing such (presumably costly) rules. If it did so, private agents would be able to make better informed judgements about current macroeconomic events, increasing the economy's stability. In the example here, if price data are released rapidly, then p_t will be effectively known in period t and the economy will be in continuous equilibrium — perfect stability!

A further information asymmetry, which may violate neutrality and has had some attention (Turnovsky, 1980; Weiss, 1980), is that where one group of private agents has superior information to that possessed by suppliers and by the government. To illustrate this possibility, modify the aggregate demand schedule (2) in the above model to

$$y_t = -\alpha(R_t - E_t p_{t+1} + p_t) \quad (16)$$

The interpretation of this aggregate demand schedule (16) is that investors have instantaneous access to current information on all relevant macro data while other agents, such as the government or suppliers of goods receive this information with a one-period lag.

In defence of this idea, it is argued that agents in regular contact with asset markets receive global information (such as interest rates and asset prices) almost instantaneously, by contrast with those in the labour market.

Substitution of (16) into our model in place of (2) yields the following reduced form:

$$\overline{m} + \mu\beta(p_{t-1} - E_{t-2}p_{t-1}) + w_t = (1+c)p_t + (1+\frac{c}{\alpha})(p_t - E_{t-1}p_t)$$
$$- cE_t p_{t+1} + (1+\frac{c}{\alpha})y^* \quad (17)$$

where $\mu = (\mu_m + \mu_f c/\alpha)$ as before. Using the Muth solution the identities are given by:

$$\overline{p} = \overline{m} - (1+\frac{c}{\alpha})y^* \quad (18)$$

(terms in w_t)

$$1 = \pi_0(1 + c + \beta(1+\frac{c}{\alpha}) - c\pi_1 \quad (19)$$

(terms in w_{t-1})

$$\mu\beta\pi_0 = \pi_1(1+c) - c\pi_2 \quad (20)$$

(terms in $w_{t-i},\ i \geq 2$)

$$0 = \pi_i(1+c) - c\pi_{i+1} \quad (21)$$

Equation (21) defines an unstable process. Consequently applying the stability condition, we set $\pi_i = 0$ $(i \geq 2)$. Therefore we can simultaneously solve (18) and (19) to obtain π_0 and π_1. The important point is that π_0, the coefficient on the current innovation, will depend on μ; consequently the variance of output depends on the feedback rules.

The basis of this result is that the agents in the goods market with superior information demand goods this period in reaction to expected future prices because these affect the real interest rate they expect to pay. Even though expected future output is invariant to the feedback rule, expected future prices are not in these models — clearly not, since the *demand* for output is affected by feedback and this in turn has to be equated with given output supply by prices and interest rates. So current demand for goods is affected by the feedback parameters via their effect on expected future prices, and the response of goods demand, and so of prices and so of output, to shocks is correspondingly modified. The government can thus exploit these agents' information without itself having access to it. This second asymmetry result is, however, subject to questioning of a similar type to the first: namely, the basis for the restriction of such macroeconomic information to one set of agents. The case for macroeconomic information on individual markets being so restricted seems more secure, although this is communicable through asset prices.

But macroeconomic information, once available, is a public good which, first, it is usual for the government to insist be made available at low cost; second, even if it is not so provided, it would pay the possessors to divulge it for a fee to other agents, since this maximizes the overall possibilities for its exploitation; third, asset prices themselves will communicate this information indirectly to other agents. The model just used furthermore makes the strong assumption that people operating in asset markets know *all* current macro data (this is implicit in taking expectations based on current period data), which is clearly implausible.

In short, the overall set-up here is generally implausible in both the asymmetry and the comprehensiveness of the group's information set.

PARTIAL INFORMATION

The result above can be refined to deal with the two objections under certain conditions. Suppose we let everyone in the economy have access to some partial current information, as discussed in chapter 3. When that information is micro, it turns out that flexible rules will affect the variance of output. The reason is the same as in the Turnovsky-Weiss case: people react to current shocks because they have incomplete information but the flexible policy rule affects expected future prices, which in turn condition those reactions. Of course, if people could disentangle from their current information exactly what the current money supply shock was, then they could protect their real wages, relative prices and real supplies and demands against mere monetary noise, and a flexible money supply rule would be ineffective; but they cannot, and so it is effective. As for a flexible fiscal rule, that too is effective provided people cannot disentangle the shocks well enough to predict the current price level exactly: in other words, they have less than full current information, which is guaranteed by assumption.

To illustrate policy effectiveness in the presence of micro partial information, take the model of chapter 3, equations (15) and (16), in which people know their local prices only (models of this sort with policy effectiveness were first set out in Marini (1985, 1986) and Minford, 1986). Let us modify the model equation (15) by the addition of a flexible money supply response to output, $-\mu(y_{t-1} - y*)$and a Cagan-style demand response to expected inflation. The model now becomes:

$$\overline{m} + \epsilon_t - \mu(y_{t-1}y*) = p_t + y_t - \alpha(E_t p_{t+1} - E_t p_t) \tag{22}$$

$$y_t - y* = \frac{1-\phi}{\delta}(p_t - E[p_t \mid \Phi_{t-1}]) \tag{23}$$

where as before $\phi = \frac{\pi_0^2\sigma_\epsilon^2}{\pi_0^2\sigma_\epsilon^2+\sigma_v^2}$. Using the Muth solution method and our previous results that $E_t\epsilon_t = \phi\epsilon_t$, we can substitute for y_t from (23) into (22) to obtain:

$$\overline{m} + \varepsilon_t - \mu\frac{(1-\phi)}{\delta}\pi_0\epsilon_{t-1}$$
$$= \sum_{t=0}^{\infty} \pi_i\epsilon_{t-1} + y* + \frac{(1-\phi)}{\delta}\pi_0\epsilon_t - \alpha(\pi_1\phi\epsilon_t - \pi_0\phi\epsilon_t)$$
$$+ \sum_{i=1}^{\infty}(\pi_{i+1} - \pi_i)\epsilon_{t-i} \quad (24)$$

$$\text{(terms in } \epsilon_t) \qquad 1 = \pi_0\frac{1}{\delta}(1-\phi)\pi_0 - \alpha(\pi_1\phi - \pi_0\phi) \quad (25)$$

$$\text{(terms in } \epsilon_{t-1}) \qquad -\frac{\mu}{\delta}(1-\phi)\pi_0 = \pi_1 - \alpha(\pi_2 - \pi_1) \quad (26)$$

$$\text{(terms in } \epsilon_{t-i},\ i \geq 2) \qquad 0 = (1+\alpha)\pi_{i-i} - \alpha\pi_{i+1} \quad (27)$$

Imposing the terminal condition $\pi_N = 0$ $(N > 2)$ yields $\pi_i = 0$ $(i \geq 2)$; $\pi_1 = -\mu(1-\phi)\pi_0/\delta$; and

$$\pi_0 = \frac{1}{1 + \frac{1-\phi}{\delta} + \alpha\phi + \frac{\alpha\mu\phi(1-\phi)}{\delta(1+\alpha)}} \quad (28)$$

It is clear from (28) that the parameter μ of the flexible rule affects π_0 and so output's response to the monetary shock, which is $\frac{(1-\phi)\pi_0}{\delta}$. It turns out, when ϕ is substituted out in terms of π_0, that (28) is a quintic in π_0. Computer solutions for a wide variety of possible parameter values indicate that π_0 has only one real root, which is reduced as μ rises: this yields the commonsense result that the more policy 'leans against' the recent business cycle, the more it stabilizes output. Suppose a monetary expansion, ϵ_t, raises output through a surprise rise in prices, this causes an expected money supply contraction through the flexible rule, implying expected future price deflation, which in turn raises the current demand for money, lowers that for goods and so partially counteracts the upward pressure on current prices exerted by the current monetary expansion.

The process is illustrated in figure 4.1. $A'D'$ shows the aggregate demand curve shift from ϵ_t alone. But next period's AD curve, A_1D_1, shifts leftwards generating an expected price fall to E_tp_{t+1}. This also shifts current aggregate demand to A_0D_0. The path of prices and output

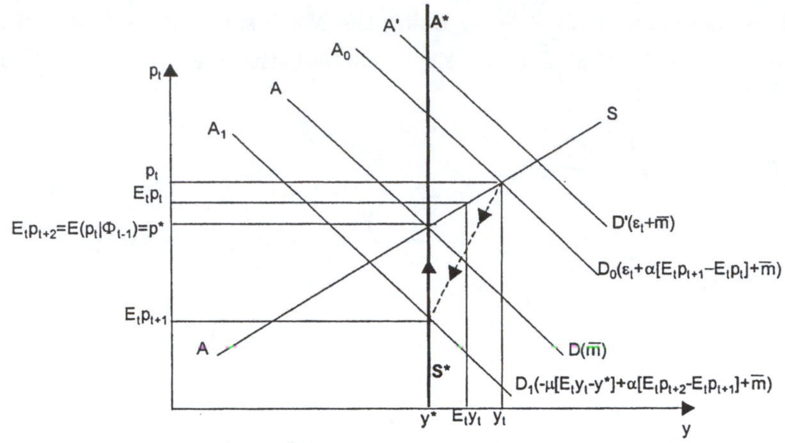

Figure 4.1: A monetary shock, ε_t, with a monetary feedback rule and local price information

is marked by the arrows. The point of the illustration is to show that y_t rises to less than it would reach without the rule.

When people have only partial macro information as in our second model in chapter 3, equations (17)–(20), this same effect does not in fact occur. Consider the effect of μ the flexible response of money to past events, in that model. While the solution for prices and interest rates reflects the response parameter, μ, that for output does not. The reason is that the current information on interest rates allows people to work out exactly what the effect of the feedback response is on expected future prices; since it can be worked out exactly, it is impounded into $E_t p_t$ and cannot affect output, which depends on producers being surprised by prices. In effect, in figure 3.4 whatever change in $E_t p_t$ is produced by feedback (affecting $E_t p_{t+1}$), it shifts both the AS and AD curves vertically by the same amount, leaving y_t and $E_t y_t$ the same.

However, when people have both micro information on local prices and macro information on interest rates, effectiveness is restored (see, for example, Barro, 1980; King, 1982). Let us take as a representative model this same model, equations (17)-(20) of chapter 3, and add local price information, so that $p_{it} = p_t + v_{it}$: this is essentially the model of Barro (1980). There are now two pieces of information, p_{it} and R_t. For simplicity, let $v_t = 0$ so that there are only two macro errors, e_t and u_t.

Plainly both p_{it} and R_t will be used to estimate e_t and u_t. In this case we would have

$$E_t u_t = \alpha_u p_{it} + \beta_u R_t \tag{29}$$

$$E_t e_t = \alpha_e p_{it} + \beta_e R_t \tag{30}$$

where the αs and βs would be derived from the regressions of u_t and e_t on p_{it} and R_t; $R_t = Au_t + De_t + Zm_{t-1}$ and $p_{it} = q_0 u_t + \pi_0 e_t + v_{it} + \pi_m m_{t-1}$.

It turns out from the regression formulae that:

$$\alpha_u = \frac{DK}{\Delta} \tag{31}$$

$$\alpha_e = -\frac{AK}{\Delta} \tag{32}$$

$$\beta_e = \frac{q_0 K + D\sigma_v^2 \sigma_e^2}{\Delta} \tag{33}$$

$$\beta_u = \frac{-\pi_0 K + A\sigma_v^2 \sigma_u^2}{\Delta} \tag{34}$$

where $\Delta = (q_0 D - A\pi_0)^2 \sigma_u^2 \sigma_e^2 + \sigma_v^2 (A^2 \sigma_u^2 + D^2 \sigma_e^2)$ and $K = (q_0 D - A\pi_0)\sigma_u^2 \sigma_e^2$.

It follows that

$$A\alpha_u + D\alpha_e = 0 \tag{35}$$

and

$$D\beta_e + A\beta_u = 1 \tag{36}$$

Equation (24) holds as before so that here

$$ae_t + u_t = aE_t e_t + E_t u_t \tag{37}$$

Substituting from $E_t e_t$ and $E_t u_t$ gives:

$$ae_t + u_t = [(a\alpha_e + a_u)q_0 + (q\beta_e + \beta_u)A]\, u_t + [(a\alpha_e + \alpha_u)\pi_0 + (\alpha\beta_e + \beta_u)D]e_t \tag{38}$$

yielding two identities in u_t, e_t as

$$1 = q_0 a\alpha_e + \alpha_u q_0 + a\beta_e + A\beta_u \tag{39}$$

$$1 = \alpha_e \pi_0 + \frac{a_u \pi_0}{a} + D\beta_e + \beta_u \frac{D}{a} \tag{40}$$

Letting, from (35), $\alpha_u = -\frac{D}{A\alpha_e}$ and, from (36), $\beta_u = \frac{1}{A} - \frac{D\beta_e}{A}$, and substituting these into (39) and (40) implies that $\frac{D}{A} = a$.

Consequently the regression coefficients simplify to

$$\alpha_u = \frac{aK}{\Delta}; \alpha_e = -\frac{K}{\Delta}; \beta_e = \frac{q_0 K + a\sigma_v^2\sigma_e^2}{A\Delta}; \beta_u = \frac{-\pi_0 K + \sigma_v^2\sigma_u^2}{A\Delta}$$

where $K = (aq_0 - \pi_0)\sigma_u^2\sigma_e^2$ and $\Delta = (aq_0 - \pi_0)^2\sigma_u^2\sigma_e^2 + \sigma_v^2(\sigma_u^2 + a^2\sigma_e^2)$.

The solution is then worked out for R_t as before in chapter 3 yielding

$$A = -\frac{(1-\alpha)(1-aW)(1+c[1-\mu]) + \alpha(1+c)(1-\mu)W}{X};$$

$$D = \frac{-(1-\alpha)a(1+c[1-\mu])V + \alpha(1+c)(1-\mu)(1-V)}{X}$$

where $W = \frac{a\sigma_v^2\sigma_e^2}{\Delta}; V = \frac{\sigma_v^2\sigma_u^2}{\Delta}$ and $X = \alpha(1+c)(1+c[1-\mu])$.

Finally, using the expression for $p_t = \pi_0 e_t + q_0 u_t + m_{t-1}$, π_0, q_0 and π_m are found by the undetermined coefficients method.

We then find that

$$y_t = (1 - aW)u_t + aVe_t \tag{41}$$

It turns out therefore that μ indeed enters the determination of $y_t = E_t u_t$ because it affects the weight of R_t and p_{it} in forming expectations of u_t and so also π_0, q_0, A, D.

AUTOMATIC STABILIZERS: AN ASIDE

Before going on to consider alternative assumptions about the supply curve we digress briefly to discuss the potential goal of 'automatic' stabilizers. By an automatic stabilizer we mean a mechanism in which a variable (for instance, tax liabilities) responds to current income levels, and therefore provides an automatic and immediate adjustment to current disturbances.

This is to be distinguished from policy actions in response to global information, such as we have been considering hitherto; 'automatic' implies that the response is effected at the microeconomic level, without recourse to macroeconomic information or to higher political authority. Tax liabilities, when tax rates are set, are of this sort: only the taxpayer, his income and the tax man are involved. In the monetary area, certain open market procedures — such as pegging central bank liabilities by Treasury bill sales — also fall into this category. The work of Poole (1970) on monetary policy in a closed economy and of Parkin (1978) on monetary and exchange rate intervention in an open economy can be regarded as dealing with these types of stabilizer.

McCallum and Whittaker (1979) considered the properties of automatic tax stabilizers and showed that they do influence the variance of output. Their point can most easily be demonstrated by writing the aggregate demand schedule as:

$$y_t = \alpha'(R_t - E_{t-1}p_{t+1} + p_t) - \sigma_t y_t \tag{42}$$

where t is the direct tax elasticity and σ is the elasticity of spending to temporary variations in tax liabilities. The tax elasticity,

$$t = \frac{\partial \ln(\text{tax receipts})}{\partial \ln(\text{output})} = \frac{(\frac{\partial \text{tax}}{\partial \text{output}})}{(\frac{\text{tax}}{\text{output}})}$$

is the marginal tax rate divided by the average tax rate.

If we define

$$\alpha = \frac{\alpha'}{1 + \sigma t} \tag{43}$$

then the solution of the model (42), (3), (4) and (5) is the same as (9) and (10), but where α is defined as here in (43). Consequently the solution for output is not independent of the automatic stabilizer, given this orthodox aggregate demand function;[5] a higher tax elasticity reduces the variance of output. However, although a high tax elasticity contributes to a reduction in output fluctuations, it does so at the cost of distortions to the operations of markets at the micro level: the highest tax elasticity of all is obtained when the marginal rate is 100 per cent!

The role of automatic stabilizers of this sort is quite distinct from that of feedback policy, although sometimes they are confused in popular discussion. It is, as we have seen, preserved within the Sargent and Wallace model considered above. However, there is one interesting set of conditions under which a particular monetary stabilizer is ineffective. This is where people have access to the same partial macro (or micro) information responded to by the monetary authorities.

Consider an 'automatic response' to the current interest rate, as discussed by Poole (1970), in the context of the macro model with partial macro information in chapter 3, equations (17)-(20). Suppose we rewrite the money supply function (19) as

$$m_t = \mu m_{t-1} + \eta R_t + e_t \tag{3.19'}$$

Assume first that the monetary authorities can respond at a micro level (e.g. in the treasury bill market) to a market interest rate, with the effect aggregated over the whole security market of ηR_t; assume also that no one observes the aggregate interest rate, R_t. Then the effect is to augment c, whenever it occurs in the solution, to $c' = c+\eta$ (flattening the LM curve). This will, as Poole suggested, dampen the effect of money and supply shocks, u_t and e_t, and augment that of demand shocks, v_t, as can be verified from the first line of table 3.1.

Now suppose R_t to be known to all as partial macro information; then the same policy (now no longer a response to micro data, but one to macroeconomic information) has no effect on output at all, as can be seen from the second line of table 3.1 where c does not enter.

We therefore have the result that interest rate stabilization is rendered ineffective (on output) in a Sargent -Wallace framework when the interest rate is universally observed. The reason is that any such response in impounded into $E_t p_t$ (because people can work out the money change due to ηR_t) and cannot affect the surprise element $p_t - E_t p_t$.

This would not be true of any variable to which the monetary authorities could respond at a micro level and which was not universally observed, as in the case above with R_t when unobserved. In this case people could not work out the money change to this response, and it could affect the surprise element, $p_t - E_t P_t$. However, plausible candidates for such a variable are hard to think of.

Nevertheless, the interesting possibility is introduced by macro information that the authorities can reduce the variance of output by raising the variance of the money supply shock, e_t, i.e. by deliberately making larger rather than smaller mistakes. Previously this was impossible; higher $vare$ necessarily implied higher $vary$ since e_t entered y_t additively. But now $vare$ affects the coefficients of the y expression via ϕ_u, ϕ_v, ϕ_e.

Consider the asymptotic variance of y, σ_y^2. Substituting for ϕ_u, ϕ_v, ϕ_ϵ from (32) in the y expression (table 3.1, line 3) we obtain:

$$\sigma_y^2 = \sigma_v^2 + [\frac{a^2\sigma_e^2 - a\sigma_u^2}{X'}]^2 + [\frac{\sigma_u^2 + (1+a)\sigma_v^2}{X'}]^2[\sigma_u^2 + a^2\sigma_e^2] \qquad (44)$$

Now we find that as $\sigma_e^2 \to \infty$ and $\phi_e \to 1$, $\sigma_y^2 \to \sigma_v^2$ (the variance of the demand shock). In this case, the variance of output is dominated by the variance of demand shocks because suppliers become totally unresponsive to prices, believing them to reflect solely 'noise' in the money supply. It is clear that this may reduce the variance of output compared to the no-monetary-noise model; thus as $\sigma_e^2 \to 0$,

$$\sigma_y^2 \to \frac{a^2\sigma_v^2(\sigma_u^2)^2 + [\sigma_u^2 + (1+a)\sigma_v^2]^2\sigma_u^2}{[\sigma_u^2 + (1+a)^2\sigma_v^2]^2} \qquad (45)$$

which, depending on σ_u^2 and a, can exceed σ_v^2.

Yet it can be shown that σ_y^2 is an inappropriate indicator of welfare and that the optimal policy is, commonsensically, to minimize σ_e^2 (that is, for the central bank cashiers to make as few and as small mistakes as possible).

Abstracting from the usual problems (public goods, externalities, incomplete markets, etc.) the Pareto-optimal situation under uncertainty is one of Walrasian equilibrium when all the shocks are known to all agents (this is discussed at greater length in chapter 5). In the context of our model output would in this situation be simply $y_t = u_t$, because $E_t p_t = p_t$and u_t, the supply shock, would shift our vertical supply curve fully along the quantity axis.

The optimal outcome under uncertainty, under normal assumptions for social welfare, is one which minimizes the variance of output from this outcome, as well as ensuring that this is the expected outcome: that is, such that $E_t y_t = E_t u_t$ and $\sigma^2_{yu} = E(y-u)^2$ is a minimum. All rational expectations outcomes, whatever the information set, guarantee that $E_t y_t = E_t u_t$. The problem therefore reduces to choosing σ^2_e to minimise σ^2_{yu}. However $\sigma^2_{yu} = a^2 E(p_t - E_t p_t)^2$, so that the optimal policy is equivalently to minimise the variance of unanticipated price changes σ^2_{pe}.

Using our earlier expression for y_t (table 3.1, line 3), we find that

$$(p_t - E_t p_t) = \frac{y_t - u_t}{a} = \frac{\begin{array}{c} -[\phi_e + a(1-\phi_u)]u_t + ((1+a)\phi_u + \phi_v)ae_t \\ +[(1+a)\phi_\epsilon - a(1+a)\phi_v)]v_t \end{array}}{a(1+a)} \tag{46}$$

Hence

$$\sigma^2_{pe} = \frac{\begin{array}{c} [\phi^2_e + a^2(1-\phi_u)^2 + 2a\phi_\epsilon(1-\phi_u)]\sigma^2_u + [(1+a)^2\phi^2_u + \phi^2_v \\ +2(1+a)\phi_u\phi_v]a^2\sigma^2_\epsilon + [(1+a)^2\phi^2_e + a^2(1+a)^2\phi^2_u \\ -2a(1+a)^2\phi_e\phi_u]\sigma^2_v \end{array}}{[a(1+a)]^2} \tag{47}$$

As $\sigma^2_e \to 0$, we find that

$$\sigma^2_{pe} \to \frac{\sigma^2_v \sigma^2_u}{\sigma^2_u + (1+a)^2\sigma^2_v} \tag{48}$$

and that as $\sigma^2_e \to \infty$

$$\sigma^2_{pe} \to \frac{\sigma^2_v + \sigma^2_u}{a^2} \tag{49}$$

The ratio of (36) to (35), K, is given by

$$K = \frac{(\sigma^2_v + \sigma^2_u)[\sigma^2_u + (1+a)^2\sigma^2_v]}{a^2\sigma^2_v\sigma^2_u} > 1 \tag{50}$$

so that the low extreme dominates the high extreme.

We can also show that minimizing σ_e^2 minimizes σ_{pe}^2; for $\frac{\delta\sigma_{pe}^2}{\delta\sigma_e^2} > 0$ throughout the range of σ_ϵ^2.

Differentiating (47) yields:

$$\frac{\delta\sigma_{pe}^2}{\delta\sigma_\epsilon^2} = \frac{\begin{array}{c}\phi_u^2\phi_e[1+a^2+2a(\phi_e+\phi_v)]+4a^2\phi_u^2\phi_v+\phi_v^2\phi_e \\ +4a\phi_e\phi_u\phi_v+(\phi_u+\phi_v)[(1+a)\phi_u+\phi_v]^2\end{array}}{(1+a)^2} > 0 \quad (51)$$

Hence welfare is unambiguously maximised by minimising the variance of the money supply, as we would instinctively expect to be the case.

MODELS WITH LONG-TERM NON-CONTINGENT CONTRACTS: THE NEW KEYNESIAN PHILLIPS CURVE

One of the assumptions required for anticipated monetary policy to have no effect on output in the Sargent-Wallace model is that agents are able to act on their information sets. If we have a situation where, for instance, private agents cannot respond to new information by changing their consumption, wage-price decisions, etc., as quickly as the public sector can change any (at least one) of its controls, then scope once again emerges for systematic stabilization policy to have real effects. This insight was developed principally by Fischer (1977a, b) and Phelps and Taylor (1977) in the context of multi-period non-contingent wage or price contracts.

Suppose we have a situation where all wage contracts run for two periods and the contract drawn in period t specifies nominal wages for periods $t+1$ and $t+2$. At each period of time, half the labour force is covered by a pre-existing contract. As long as the contracts are not contingent on new information that accrues during the contract period, this creates the possibility of stabilization policy. Firms respond to changes in their environment (say, unpredictable changes in demand which were unanticipated at the time of the pre-existing contract) by altering output and employment at the pre-contracted wage; only contracts which are up for renewal can reflect prevailing information. If the monetary authorities can respond to new information that has accrued between the time the two-period contract is drawn up and the last period of the operation of the contract, then systematic stabilization policy is possible. In other words, while there are no information differences between public and private agents, the speed of response to the new information is different.

The essentials of this argument involve replacing the Sargent-Wallace supply equation (3) with one based on overlapping contracts. Suppose, following Fischer (1977 a, b), that wages are set for two periods so as to maintain expected real wages constant at a 'normal' level. Denote (the log of nominal) wages set in period $t-1$ for period t as ${}_{t-i}W_t$. Then

$$ {}_{t-i}W_t = E_{t-i}p_t \tag{52} $$

(where the log of normal real wages is set to zero) and current nominal wages are

$$ W_t = 0.5({}_{t-2}W_t + {}_{t-1}W_t) = 0.5(E_{t-2}p_t + E_{t-1}p_t) \tag{53} $$

Now let output supply be a declining function of the real wage (from firms maximizing profits subject to a production function with labour input and some fixed overheads):

$$ y_t = -q(W_t - p_t) + y^* \tag{54} $$

We derive from these the new supply equation:

$$ y_t = 0.5q[(p_t - E_{t-2}p_t) + (p_t - E_{t-1}p_t)] + y^* \tag{55} $$

This equation, the New Keynesian (NK) Phillips curve, and its derivation are illustrated in figure 4.2 (for $Y = \exp y$), which also contrasts it with the New Classical (NC) Phillips curve, in a diagram also taken from Parkin and Bade (1988). In figure 4.2, as p rises from its expected level p_0 to p_1, $MPL+p$ (the wage offer for labour where MPL is the log of labour's marginal product) shifts: under NC nominal wages are bid up along SS, under NK wages are fixed at the contract level W_0. Hence the NK Phillips curve, S_{NK}, is flatter than the NC Philips curve, S_{NC}.

Let us use (55) in place of (43), together with the rest of the model (2), (3) and (5); then it can conveniently be written in terms of the Muth solution as:

$$ y_t = q(\pi_0 w_t + 0.5\pi_1 w_{t-1}) + y^* \tag{56} $$

The model solution equation can now be written:

$$ \begin{aligned} \overline{m} + q\mu(\pi_0 w_{t-1} + 0.5\pi_1 w_{t-2}) + w_t &= p_t + q(1+\frac{c}{\alpha})(\pi_0 w_t + 0.5\pi_1 w_{t-1}) \\ &- c(E_{t-1}p_{t+1} - E_{t-1}p_t) + (1+\frac{c}{\alpha})y^* \end{aligned} \tag{57} $$

The identities in the w_{t-i} are now:

(terms in w_t) $$ 1 = \pi_0[1 + q(1+\frac{c}{\alpha})] \tag{58} $$

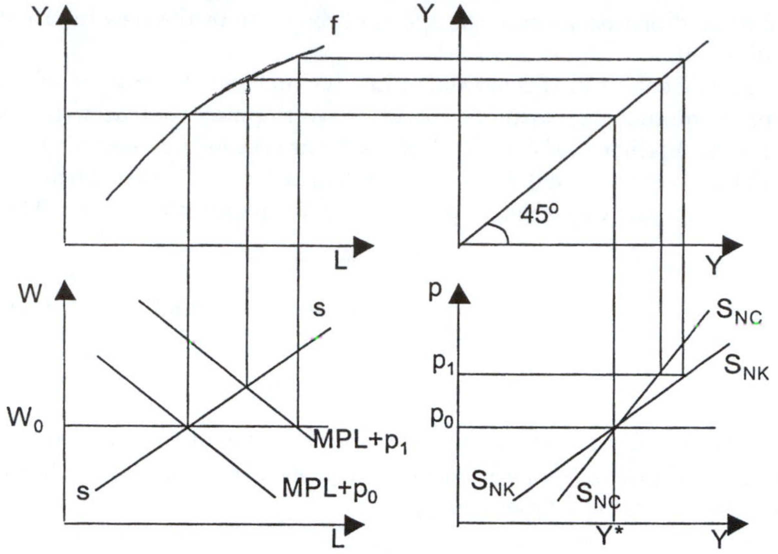

Figure 4.2: The New Keynesian Phillips curve (contrasted with the New Classical)

$$\text{(terms in } w_{t-1}) \qquad \mu q \pi_0 = \pi_1 + 0.5q(1+\frac{c}{\alpha})\pi_1 - c(\pi_2 - \pi_1) \quad (59)$$

$$\text{(terms in } w_{t-2}) \qquad 0.5q\mu\pi_1 = \pi_2 - c(\pi_3 - \pi_2) \quad (60)$$

$$\text{(terms in } w_{t-i},\ i \geq 3) \qquad 0 = (1+c)\pi_i - c\pi_{i+1} \quad (61)$$

Equation (61) gives $\pi_i = 0$ $(i \geq 3)$ applying the stability condition, whence we can solve the other three equations for π_2, π_1, π_0. μ enters the solution for π_1 and π_2 and, since π_1 enters the output supply equation, μ therefore influences the variance of output. In fact in this particular example, it will raise the variance; minimum variance occurs where $\mu=$ 0, since this sets $\pi_1=\pi_2=\pi_0$.

The model is illustrated in figure 4.3. With feedback, $\mu \neq 0$, we obtain the path shown. Suppose there is a temporary aggregate demand shock in $t = 0$, shifting AD to A_0D_0. The supply curve, S^*S^*, whose position is fixed by $E_{t-2}p_t = E_{t-1}p_t = p*$, does not move; we reach point 0. Next period, aggregate demand is shifted by negative feedback on y_0 to A_1D_1. Half the workers have now renegotiated wages in $t = 0$ with $E_0p_1 = p_1$ (their expectations of p_1 in period 0), So the supply curve shifts to S_1S_1. Next period aggregate demand shifts to A_2D_2 as feedback now raises it in response to y_1. All workers have renegotiated wages, fully expecting $p_2 = E_0p_2$ (there is no further surprise in prices relative to wage negotiations); so $y_2 = y^*$. In period 3, finally, feedback stops so both aggregate demand and supply return to normal, that is A^*D^* and S^*S^*.

Of course, the diagram shows clearly that had the aggregate demand curve not reacted with feedback, then in period 1 it would have returned to A^*D^* and workers would not have needed to renegotiate wages, staying on S^*S^*. Thus the path would have been direct from point 0 to point 3, clearly more stable than the path with feedback.

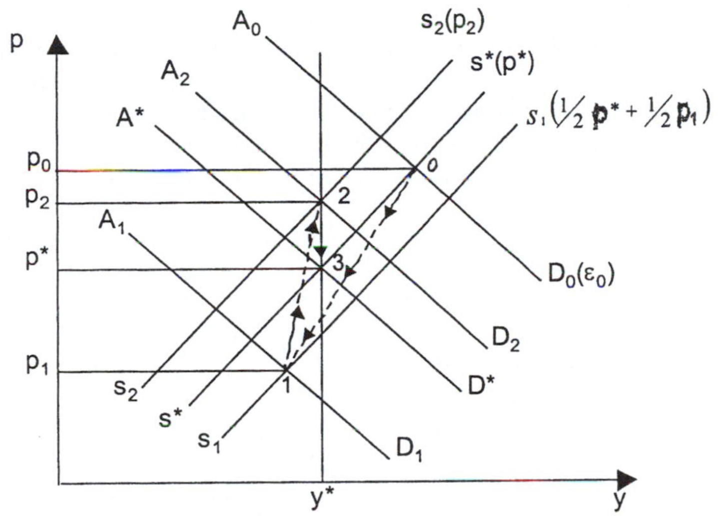

The path with feedback is shown by numbers; the path without feedback is 0, 3, 3...

Figure 4.3: The effectiveness of feedback response in the New Keynesian model

This example illustrates the obvious point that the case for stabilization policy does not rest with showing effectiveness; it is also necessary to show optimality. Nevertheless, it is easy to construct examples where $\mu \neq 0$ minimizes output variance; the reader should investigate one such as an exercise, namely when an adjustment term $+j(y_{t-1} - y*)$ is added to (55). The reader should find that, while π_o is unaltered, the expression for π_1 becomes:

$$\pi_1 = \frac{q\mu\pi_0 + j(\pi_0 - 1)}{1 + c(1 - j)} + 0.5q(1 + \frac{c}{\alpha} - \frac{c\mu}{1+c})] \qquad (62)$$

Since $j(\pi_0 - 1) < 0$, the optimal value of μ found by minimising the variance of $y - y^*$, sets $E_0(y_{t+1} - y*) = 0$ after a shock in $t = 0$, implying that $\pi_0 j + \pi_1 = 0$. It turns out that the optimal value of $\mu = \frac{-j(1+c)}{0.5q}$ is negative, representing the normal 'leaning into the wind' response.

Models with overlapping contracting have been developed by Taylor (1979a, b, 1980) in a series of papers in order to show that important features of the business cycle can be captured by integrating this type of supply curve into standard macroeconomic analysis, and to analyse optimal policy design in such an economy.

Three points of weakness remain in this approach. First, the theoretical basis of non-contingent contracts, in which the nominal wage or price is fixed and quantity is set by demand, has not been established to universal satisfaction. One approach is to assume that in incomplete markets nominal wage contracts offer insurance against real shocks. Another approach is to assume 'menu costs', that is transactions costs in fixing, negotiating and changing prices which are reduced by periodic contracts: this approach (assumed by earlier authors such as Barro (1972), Mussa (1981) and Canzoneri (1980)) has been explored theoretically by, for example, Rotemberg (1983) and Parkin (1986). What is harder to establish is how large these menu costs are and why, given that non-contingent contracts risk losses in the face of shocks, the contracts do not build in contingency clauses (which may be less expensive to write in than the potential losses they avoid). The humdrum answer may be that people are approximately risk neutral for small risks and so reduce menu costs by writing non-contingent contracts that expose them totally to these risks: they only bother with contingency clauses (or other insurance) for the large risks. This tallies with other insurance practices, such as excess clauses and no claims bonuses, which effectively exclude the small risks.

If this is so, then the appearance of non-contingent contracts may be deceptive, the second weakness in this approach. They may be truly non-contingent for only rather trivial shocks. Indeed, closer inspection reveals that actual contracts are exceedingly complex once implicit elements are taken into account. For example, they will typically include bonus, discount and lay-off elements for quantity variation, and indexation (whether formal or informal via shop-floor renegotiation) is frequently found.

The third and related weakness is that, if the authorities were systematically to exploit these contracts in a way not envisaged at the time the contracts were set, then this would presumably lead to differences in the way contracts were written (contract length and indexation clauses are clearly endogenous). In the limit, if the government systematically exploited them in a way that altered agents' outcomes excessively from what they wished, then long-run contracts would be written in such a way that they were equivalent to a succession of single-period contracts so that the scope for stabilization policy would disappear.

For all these reasons (we revert to these issues in chapter 6) there remains considerable doubt as to whether non-contingent contracts can be regarded as a firm basis for modelling and policy formulation. Nevertheless, in practice they are widely used in macroeconomic modelling, since they both appear to be widely used and do pick up usefully the short-term nominal rigidity observed in wages: clearly this implies that we must treat analysis based on such models with caution — but then what is new about that?

One final point: the 'New Keynesian' and 'New Classical' supply curves are often presented as a contrast between 'disequilibrium' and 'market clearing' approaches. This can be misleading. The fact that people may sign non-contingent contracts does not imply either that they are in disequilibrium or that markets do not clear when shocks occur later on during the contract period. Obviously they were aware this could happen (hence no 'disequilibrium') and planned not to vary their price in response to changed demand (hence their supply is elastic, 'clearing' the market). We are dealing with a different (non-auction) market structure entered into voluntarily by rational agents: this implies different properties in response to shocks, that is all. It is quite different from the Keynesian or old Phillips curve assumptions set out in chapter 1.

NEW CLASSICAL MODELS WITH INTERTEMPORAL SUBSTITUTION

The last group of models we wish to examine for feedback effectiveness is New Classical models with intertemporal substitution fully operative. The earlier New Classical models of this chapter suppressed one mechanism, the role of real interest rates in varying labour supply; empirically, this mechanism itself is of doubtful significance but in the open economy movements in real interest rates are associated with movements in the real exchange rate, and these are found to have powerful effects on labour supply, as is discussed in chapter 8. We can think of this closed economy mechanism as a proxy for that powerful open economy mechanism. It has some interesting theoretical implications for policy effectiveness.

As explained in chapter 3, the New Classical supply function is derived from workers or consumers maximizing expected utility subject to a life-time budget constraint (a nicely tractable set-up, which has been explored by Sargent (e.g. 1979a, chapter 16), is the quadratic utility function with quadratic adjustment costs). From such a framework one can obtain a formal supply of labour equation of the form:

$$n_t = f(w_t^e, w_{t+1}^e - w_t - r_t, n_{t-1}) \tag{63}$$

where w is the real wage, n is labour supply (both in logarithms) and r is the real interest rate, which we now treat as a variable. The e superscript denotes expected at time t. The information set assumed in this is last period's macroeconomic information and each worker also observes at the micro level his or her current nominal wages; but we assume that no micro information is usable for signal extraction about macro data. So $w_t^e = W_t - E_{t-1}p_t = w_t + p_t - E_{t-1}p_t$ where W_t is nominal wages (in logs). The first term in (4.63) represents the long-term effect of rising wages on supply, while the second represents intertemporal substitution with a single-period 'future' for simplicity; the third represents costs of adjustment. w_{t+1}^e is standing in for the whole future path of real wages and it will be helpful for our purpose here to treat it as a constant, 'the future normal real wage'.

Let us write the equation in (log) linear form as:

$$n_t = \sigma_0 + \sigma_1(w_t + p_t - E_{t-1}p_t) + \sigma_2 r_t + j n_{t-1} (0 < j < 1) \tag{64}$$

Now juxtapose this with a demand for labour function (65) derived from a simple Cobb-Douglas production function, $y_t = \delta k_t + (1-\delta)n_t$, with a fixed overhead element k_t

$$n_t = y_t - w_t \tag{65}$$

from (65) and the production function we have

$$n_t = k_t - \frac{1}{\delta} w_t \tag{66}$$

or

$$w_t = -\delta n_t + \delta k_t \tag{67}$$

Substituting for w_t from this into (64) gives

$$n_t = \frac{1}{1+a} \frac{a k_t + \sigma_0 + \sigma_2 r_t + \sigma_1(p_t - E_{t-1}p_t)}{1 - qL} \tag{68}$$

where $q = \frac{j}{1+a}$; $a = \delta\sigma_1$.

Using (66) gives us:

$$y_t = (1 - qL)\delta k_t + \frac{1-\delta}{1+a}[ak_t + \sigma_0 + \sigma_2 r_t + \sigma_1(p_t - E_{t-1}p_t)] + qy_{t-1} \tag{69}$$

The steady state values of r_t and y_t (r^*, y^*) will depend on the whole model while k_t we assume to be held constant here; for simplicity we will normalize them all at zero in what follows.

Now write the full model as:

$$y_t = -\alpha r_t + \mu_f(y_{t-1}) \tag{70}$$

$$y_t = dr_t + \beta(p_t - E_{t-1}p_t) + qy_{t-1} \tag{71}$$

$$m_t = p_t + y_t - cR_t + v_t \tag{72}$$

$$m_t = \overline{m} + \mu_m y_{t-1} + u_t \tag{73}$$

$$R_t = r_t + E_{t-1}p_{t+1} - E_{t-1}p_t \tag{74}$$

Equation (70) is the IS curve with the fiscal feedback parameter μ_f. (71) is the supply curve with d, β, q taken from (69) (e.g. $d = \frac{1-\delta}{1+a}\sigma_2$). (72) is money demand, (73) is money supply with feedback parameter, μ_m. (74) is the Fisher identity.

We can immediately establish by (70) and (71) that fiscal feedback is effective, but monetary feedback is not. We obtain

$$r_t = -\frac{\beta(1-\mu_f L)}{(a+d)(1-\frac{q\alpha+\mu_f d}{a+d}L)}(p_t - E_{t-1}p_t) \tag{75}$$

This expression for r_t then can be substituted into (70) to obtain y_t: clearly the reaction of y_t to unanticipated prices depends importantly on μ_f but not on μ_m. As for $p_t - E_{t-1}p_t$, this is quickly found as:

$$p_t - E_{t-1}p_t = \frac{a+d}{a+d+\beta(\alpha+c)}(u_t - v_t) \tag{76}$$

The intuition behind this result is that fiscal policy is causing *intertemporal substitution* of supply, in order to offset the 'cyclical' effects of shocks. Incidentally, this effect of fiscal feedback is quite independent of whether government bonds are net wealth (discussed in chapter 7). For example, even if private consumption depends only on permanent income and not on transitory income, the government expenditure pattern over time could be altered without affecting the present value of the tax stream, so altering the pattern of total demand over time. Of course, if private consumption depends also on transitory income, then alteration of the temporal pattern of taxes, holding the present value of the tax stream constant, would also have this effect. Such alteration of the patterns of aggregate demand over time then sets off the movement in real interest rates which creates intertemporal substitution in supply.

These points are illustrated in figure 4.4, where it is assumed that $q \approx 0.5$ and $\mu_f \approx -1$; the diagram is in $(r,\ y)$ space instead of the more usual $(p,\ y)$ space, to focus on real interest rate movements. Initially, we assume some money supply shock drives prices up, unexpectedly shifting the SS New Classical Supply curve rightwards; real interest rates drop to point 0 along the original IS curve. Now, if there were no fiscal feedback, $\mu_f = 0$, the SS curve would shift back to S^*S^* at the rate of 50 per cent of $(y_{t-1} - y^*)$ per period. The path would be traced by the arrows along the I^*S^* curve. With fiscal feedback, the IS shifts leftwards to I_1S_1 reaching point 1, where output is at y^*; hence in period 2 we return to to I^*S^* (plainly faster in this example than that with no feedback). The path of output is seen to be fully determined by this diagram; monetary feedback policy enters neither curve, so is ineffective. Only the shock to the money supply enters through $p_t - E_{t-1}p_t$.

The ineffectiveness of monetary feedback policy is negated by the introduction of wealth effects into the IS curve (or the supply curve). Assume that consumers hold long maturity bonds with fixed coupons denominated in money terms: these must be government bonds in this closed economy, since any private sector bonds would net out in a consolidated private sector balance sheet. If we treat these government bonds as net wealth (chapter 7), then variations in the price level brought about by monetary policy, future government expenditure constant, will alter the real value of these and so net wealth and spending.

The point can be seen by adding the term $f(\bar{b} - p_t)$ into (70)[1]. We set $\mu_f = 0$ since fiscal policy will remain effective as before; and to simplify the algebra here we set $q = 0 = \bar{b}$. Using (70) and (71) we now obtain:

$$r_t = -f'p_t - \beta'(p_t - E_{t-1}p_t)(77) \qquad (77)$$

where $f' = \frac{f'}{\alpha+d}$, $\beta' = \frac{\beta}{\alpha+d}$. Equating (72) and (73) and substituting into the result (77) for r_t and (71) for y_t we obtain the following equation

[1] $\bar{b}$, the example here, would be the log of a perpetuity bond issue at £100 face value which promises to pay £100xR_t (R_t being the perpetuity rate of interest) for all future periods; its present value will always be £100. The point made here goes through for all types of nominal bonds; only if bonds are indexed will it not do so, for the obvious reason that the path of prices becomes irrelevant to the value of net wealth.

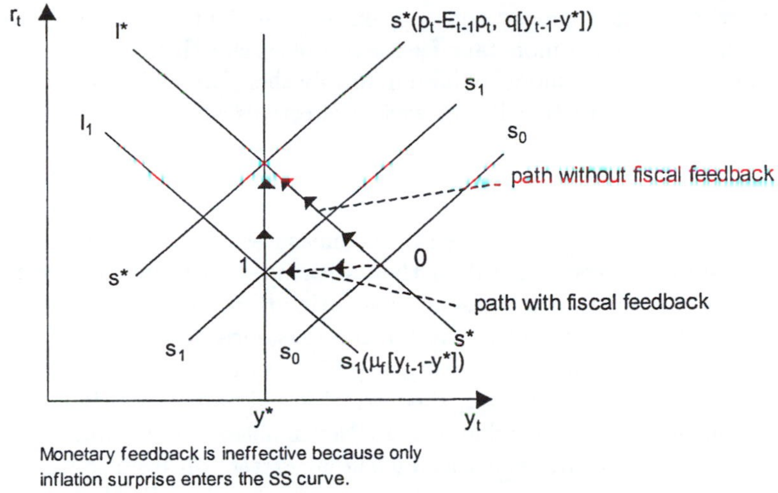

Figure 4.4: The effectiveness of fiscal policy with intertemporal substitution of supply

in p_t:

$$(1 - f'd + f'c)p_t + f'\mu_m d p_{t-1} - cE_{t-1}p_{t+1} + cE_{t-1}p_t +$$
$$(\beta - \beta'd + \beta'c)(p_t - E_{t-1}p_t) - \mu_m(\beta - \beta'd)(p_{t-1} - E_{t-1}p_{t-1})$$
$$= \overline{m} + u_t - v_t \quad (78)$$

If $p_t = \sum_{i=0}^{\infty} \pi_i w_{t-i} + \overline{p}$ where $w_t = u_t - v_t$ then the identities in the w_{t-i} are:

$$(w_t) \qquad [(1 - f'd + f'c) + (\beta - \beta'd + \beta'c)]\pi_0 = 1 \quad (79)$$

$$(w_{t-1}) \quad (1 - f'd + f'c)\pi_1 + f'\mu_m\pi_0 - c\pi_2 + c\pi_1 - \mu m(\beta - \beta'd)\pi_0 = 0 \quad (80)$$

$$(w_{t-i},\ i \geq 2) \qquad \pi_{i+1} - (\frac{1 - f'd}{c} + 1 + f')\pi_i - \frac{f'\mu_m d}{c}\pi_{i-1} = 0 \quad (81)$$

Suppose (81) has a unique stable root δ: then $\pi_2 = \delta\pi_1$ where δ depends on μ_m. π_1 also depends on μ_m from (80). Now output is given by (71) using (77), as:

$$y_t = -df'p_t + \alpha\beta'(p_t - E_{t-1}p_t) \quad (82)$$

from which it is apparent that μ_m enters the solution for output too. Wealth effects make monetary feedback policy effective.

The full classical model of labour supply therefore yields two interesting propositions. First, without wealth effects fiscal feedback is effective but monetary feedback is not (this is noted by Sargent, 1979a, chapter 16). Secondly, with wealth effects both are effective. Again, this by no means establishes that feedback rules are beneficial. Sargent (1979a), for example, shows that if welfare is measured by the sum of identical consumers' expected utility, then with no wealth effects zero fiscal feedback is optimal in the case of quadratic utility and production functions. That issue we defer. As for the existence of wealth effects, on which the effectiveness of monetary policy turns, that too is an issue requiring separate discussion; theoretically and empirically it is at this point an open question (chapter 7). Nevertheless, as a minimum it is of some interest that, even without signal extraction from local prices, new classical models in general give scope for fiscal feedback and across a potentially broad class also give scope for monetary feedback. This is contrary to the impression given (no doubt unintentionally) by much of the early literature, although subsequently corrected by Lucas and Sargent (1978).

CONCLUSIONS

We have shown in the context of equilibrium linear models that there is one main set of assumptions under which neither monetary nor fiscal feedback policies have an impact on the variance of output: these are a New Classical (or old Keynesian with rational expectations) Phillips curve of the sort assumed by Sargent and Wallace, without signal extraction from local prices, without intertemporal substitution in supply induced by real interest rates, and without information asymmetries. It would be turgid and counter-productive to list here again all the conditions under which effectiveness of either fiscal or monetary feedback policy is or is not preserved.

The general proposition in this chapter is that rational expectations as such do not rule out counter-cyclical policy, but rather they alter its impact[2], leaving it as an empirical matter whether they do or do not re-

[2]This viewpoint is in principle reinforced by work (e.g. Dickinson et al., 1982) which has taken up a suggestion of Shiller (1978) and shown that if a non-linear version of the Sargent-Wallace supply function replaced their original linear version then even retaining all other assumptions, stabilization policy is feasible. Clearly non-linearity will be a typical feature of models of national economies; neverthe-

duce the variance of relevant macroeconomic variables, and as a further issue whether they do or do not improve welfare. We also considered automatic stabilizers briefly and showed that their distinct role was not nullified by rational expectations, except in the specific New Classical case where people have current access to the same information that triggers the stabilizing mechanism; in this case output will be invariant because people will incorporate the response into their price expectations. Once it is appreciated that stabilization policy is in general not ruled out by rational expectations models, whether New Classical or not, the issue of whether the economy is subject to 'disequilibrium' (a misnomer for non-contingent contracts) ceases to be of special significance: it is just one of a number of questions that have to be confronted in the detailed specification of a rational expectations model. It is the rationality of expectations itself that carries the really powerful implications for the nature of the impact of stabilization policy.

---

less, it seems doubtful that this source of stabilization leverage is of much practical importance.

5

Stabilization Policy — Should we?

In Chapters 3 and 4 we discussed the potential effectiveness (for output) of stabilization policy by which we mean feedback policy rather than 'automatic stabilizers' which will generally be effective for reasons we explained. We have shown that in general such policy can be effective. The question then arises of whether any such policy is optimal and, if so, how it should be designed. In practice we will focus on monetary policy, since fiscal policy is generally regarded as too slow in implementation and too uncertain in effect to be useful (besides the concern that varying spending programmes and tax rates may cause micro distortions). In this chapter we will discuss the issue of optimality: should we stabilize the economy? In the next we will discuss practical issues of design.

We will discuss two issues that bear on optimality: the welfare criterion and the question of credibility (or 'time inconsistency'). The first concerns whether it is not better to leave the economy alone, letting it react in accordance with the decisions of private agents; has the government reason to believe it can improve on these? The second issue concerns the problems raised by the government's natural desire to manipulate the economy in order to please its electorate; this may lead to the abandonment of inflation pledges in order to stimulate economic activity. Thus governments may find it hard to pursue a consistent anti-inflation policy and this will undermine its credibility.

THE WELFARE CRITERION

The yardstick of welfare that is most widely used by economists is the Pareto criterion. Pareto optimality is the condition in which no one can be made better off without someone else being made worse off; it can be illustrated for a two-person world by an Edgeworth box diagram (figure 5.1), in which the 'contract curve' joins the points of tangency of the two sets of indifference curves, these points being all Pareto-optimal. If it is then assumed that distributional considerations are absent, either because they do not matter or because the government achieves the socially desired distribution at all times, there can be a unique Pareto optimum for the specified distribution, illustrated by the circled dot in figure 5.1.

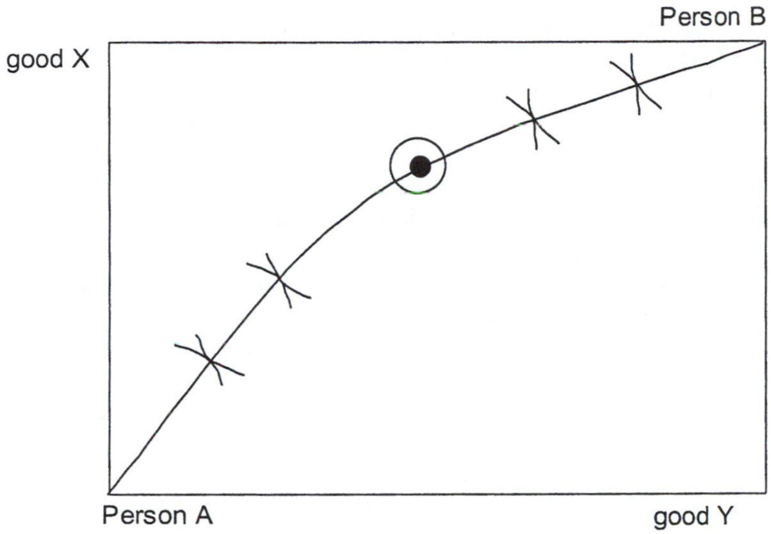

Figure 5.1: An Edgeworth box diagram

The proof that, for a given distribution function there exists a unique Pareto optimum has been established for an economy with well-behaved preferenes and technology in a Walrasian equilibrium when markets are competitive and complete and there are no distortions (discrepancies between private social costs due, for example, to externalities); the proof is due to Arrow, Debreu and Hahn (see Arrow and Hahn, 1971). In an economy of this type, the steady-state level of output at the Pareto optimum would be the y^* in our models.

Of course, in actual economies, with incomplete and some monopolistic markets and with distortions, y^*, the equilibrium level of output, will not be at a Pareto optimum. However, it is usual in macroeconomics to assume that these problems are the province of 'micro' policies, and that there should be no attempt by macroeconomic policy to push y systematically away from y^*; indeed we have already seen that any such attempt in an adaptive expectations model would cause ever-accelerating or ever-decelerating prices and in a rational expectations model would be completely frustrated. Instead y^* is taken, from the viewpoint of macroeconomic policy, to be the optimum output level in a steady state (it is, strictly, the 'second-best' optimum — but the best that can be achieved with macroeconomic policy instruments).

Supposing this to be so, the question arises of what is the optimum short-run output level. In Keynesian disequilibrium models with adaptive (or other backward-looking) expectations, if output is less (or more) than y^*, this is involuntary and suboptimal, the result of 'market failure'; hence the variation of output around y^* is a natural criterion for minimization.[1] Since output tends to y^* in the long run but y^* will typically be growing over time, we can measure this variation as the variance of output around its moving trend $\text{var}(y - y*)$. This is what we focused on in the discussion of effectiveness in chapter 4.

Sometimes in these models other measures have also been included in the minimand to represent the costs due to loss of consumer surplus not included in GDP — for example, the variance of inflation or interest rates as proxies for consumer and financial uncertainty. However, it is usually assumed in the context of stabilization policy that the variations in these costs across alternative policies are relatively small; this would also be our assumption.

In equilibrium models with adaptive expectations (such as the one implicit in Milton Friedman's, Friedman, 1968), output deviations from y^* arise because of expectations errors which could have been avoided by efficient use of available information. Again $\text{var}(y - y*)$ is a natural minimand because agents would wish they had made output decisions on the basis of good forecasts.

In equilibrium models with rational expectations, however, y only departs from y^* because of unavoidable expectations errors. Such models include the New Keynesian ones of chapter 4, because the nominal wage contracts in these models are voluntarily negotiated, in the full knowledge that when shocks occur the response to them will be constrained by the contract. (This leaves open the possibility that monetary policy can improve the private sector's feasible outcomes from its contract structure — we assume not here but return to the issue in chapter 6.)

Output is always at its 'desired' level in these models in the sense that, given available information, agents are maximizing their welfare subject to their private constraints, including the effects of shocks and associated expectations errors. Then, provided the level of distortion in

---

[1] If output, however, changes for supply reasons (e.g. crop failure), this would naturally be added into y^* and the variation computed around this adjusted figure.

the economy does not vary with $(y-y^*)$, government cannot improve and may reduce welfare by reducing $var(y - y^*)$ for the simple reason that it was already being maximized; an example of this is given by Sargent (1979, chapter 16) in a classical labour supply model where fiscal policy is effective because of intertemporal substitution, as discussed in chapter 4, and the same point has been stressed by Beenstock (1980).[2]

The proviso that the level of distortion does not vary with $(y-y^*)$will be violated in practice when unemployment benefits do not vary with wages; for when depressive shocks reduce output and employment, the gap between the private and social costs of unemployment will increase.

A simple way of evaluating the social gain to stabilization policy is shown in figure 5.2. Assume that the undistorted supply of labour would be at L^+; it is entirely inelastic. Assume also that if employed it could be put to work at the normal wage of w^*, this representing its social product because there is some long-term project (e.g. building a road) whose return is the same in slump as in boom. Then assume that policy can either stabilise employment (output) in face of shocks entirely at L^* or allow employment to vary to L_1 on the upside and L_2 on the downside. The extra employment has social utility, since it gets people closer to the optimum, L^+. We can measure the social loss as $w^*(L^+ - L)$.

We now notice from figure 5.2 that an upward shock has less absolute effect on employment than a downward shock because the supply curve gets progressively flatter as wages fall, getting closer and closer to the benefit level. This implies that as the economy fluctuates the average level of employment falls. It follows that the social loss is on average greater too. So plainly fluctuations lower welfare.

Policy makers would of course like to keep the economy at L^+, minimising fluctuations around this point. However, stabilization policies which attempt to boost L over L^* (y above y^*) systematically will be frustrated in the attempt and will create other problems for the economy (inflation in the case of monetary policy and high taxation in the case of fiscal policy). Hence $var\ (y - y^*)$ is the minimand subject to the constraint that stabilization policies are not on average biased away from y^*.

To sum up, in rational expectations models, there are prima facie reasons to believe that in general stabilization policy, even if effective, will not improve welfare, the main exception being where distortions are correlated with the cycle; the importance of this exception will vary with the nature of the benefit system.

---

[2]This situation is not one of full Pareto-optimality, as markets are incomplete and distortions assumed to exist; however, it is a situation of restricted Pareto-optimality (second-best), under the provisos given.

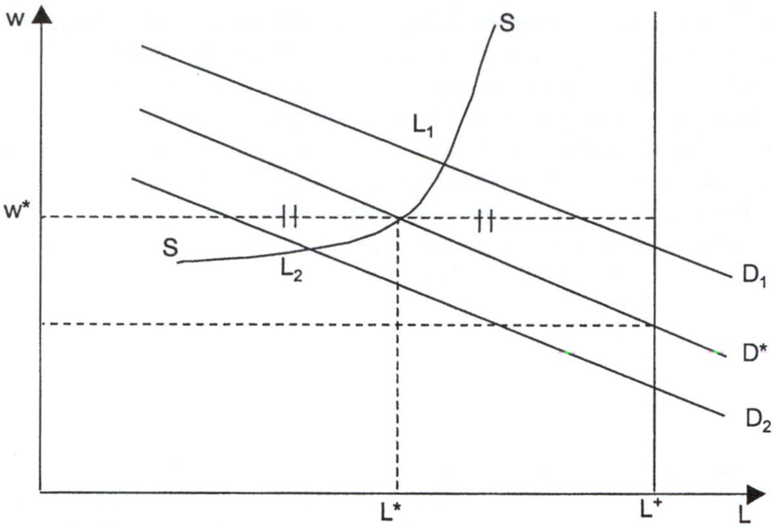

Figure 5.2: Benefit distortions and stabilization

This fundamental argument for stabilization policy is in principle also an argument for a change in the benefit system. Of course, if for some reason the benefit system cannot in practice be changed, then stabilization policy is justified on the 'second best' grounds we have described. But this does not imply that one should uncritically accept the system and the costs it incurs, even with stabilization policies to mitigate them.

OPTIMAL ECONOMIC POLICIES AND TIME INCONSISTENCY

A crucial feature of an economy with rational expectations is that current outcomes and the movement of the system's state depend in part upon anticipated future policy decisions.

The same feature will obviously not occur when expectations are formed in a backward-looking manner, since in these circumstances current outcomes and the movement of the system's state depend only upon current and past policy decisions and upon the current state: they need to allow for the full effects on private behaviour of people's expectations about the outcomes of the rules (we discuss this issue, often known as

Lucas' Critique, in chapter 6). However, having computed the rules appropriately, policy-makers face a further difficulty — or opportunity — if they are not bound in some way to stick to the rule they so compute but people expect them to stick to it nevertheless. For after one period of operating this rule, people have made certain commitments, expecting the rule to prevail; the policy maker now faces a new situation, in that he can exploit these commitments in making policy afresh. Such policy behaviour is known as 'time-inconsistency'.

Of course, matters will not rest there, since the people, thus tricked and exploited, will be less willing to believe that the fresh policy rule will prevail without yet further twists. There is also the question of whether people would have been willing to believe the original policy rule in the first place if the policy-makers could wriggle out of it. Finally, we may ask why policy-makers should wish to trick people in this way 'for the social good' — on the face of it, it is peculiar that social good can be achieved by trickery. However, we defer these developments of the argument until after an explanation of the mechanism behind time-inconsistency.

Kydland and Prescott (1977) showed how, in a dynamic economic system in which agents possess rational expectations, the optimal policy at time $t = 0$, which sets future paths for the control variables (taxes, subsidies, monetary growth), implies values of the control variables at some later time $t+i$, that will not be optimal when policy is re-examined at $t+i$, even though the preferences of agents are unchanged. This they called the time inconsistency of optimal plans.

Two examples (given by Kydland and Prescott, 1977; Fischer, 1980b) relate to examinations and patent policy. Optimal policy at the beginning of a course is to plan to have a mid-session exam. However, on the morning of the exam when all student preparation is complete, the optimal policy is to cancel the exam, saving the students the trouble of writing and the lecturer the trouble of grading. Optimal policy may analogously be to withdraw patent protection after resources have been allocated to successful inventive activity on the basis of continued patent protection.

The argument's formal structure can be seen in a simple two-period problem presented by Kydland and Prescott. Let $\pi = (\pi_1, \ \pi_2)$ be a sequence of policies for periods 1 and 2 and $x = (x_1, \ x_2)$ be the corresponding sequence for economic agents' decisions. The social objective function is given by

$$S(x_1, x_2, \pi_1, \pi_2) \tag{10}$$

Consider first the situation with backward-looking expectations, where no time inconsistency arises. For simplicity we will assume an absence of stochastic error terms, which does not affect the argument. In this case the model is:

$$x_1 = x_1(\pi_1) \tag{11}$$

$$x_2 = x_2(x_1, \pi_2) \tag{12}$$

The policy maker maximizes (1) subject to this model, meeting the first order conditions of a maximum (we assume the S function is well-behaved so that second-order conditions are met):

$$0 = \frac{\partial S}{\partial \pi_1} = \left(\frac{\partial S}{\partial x_1} + \frac{\partial S}{\partial x_2} . \frac{\partial x_2}{\partial x_1} \right) \frac{\partial x_1}{\partial \pi_1} + \frac{\partial S}{\partial \pi_1} \tag{13}$$

$0 = \frac{\partial S}{\partial \pi_2} = \frac{\partial S}{\partial x_2} . \frac{\partial x_2}{\partial \pi_2} + \frac{\partial S}{\partial \pi_2}$

The solution of (2) to (5) defines the optimal values of π_1 and π_2 (and the implied x_1 and x_2) which the policy maker chooses at the beginning of period 1. At the end of period 1, x_1 and π_1 have occurred, exactly as the model predicted and the policy maker intended, respectively. So at this point, were he to recompute his optimal second period policy π_2, he would simply solve (3) and (5) for π_2 and x_2. Since x_1 and π_1 are as implied by the complete four-equation solution earlier, the truncated solution for π_2 and x_2 conditional on them will also be the same as before (any reader doubtful of this should check this result with any set of four simultaneous equations). So the policy maker will automatically continue with his planned policy under the case of backward-looking expectations.

Now consider how rational expectations affect the situation, under the (artificial) assumption that people believe the policy-maker's announced plans. The model now changes because the outcome in period 1 is affected by expectations of period 2 policy

$$x_1 = x_1(\pi_1, \pi_2) \tag{14}$$

$$x_2 = x_2(x_1, \pi_2) \tag{15}$$

The policy maker's maximization at the start of period 1 is now given by

$$0 = \frac{\partial S}{\partial \pi_1} = \left(\frac{\partial S}{\partial x_1} + \frac{\partial S}{\partial x_2} . \frac{\partial x_2}{\partial x_1} \right) \frac{\partial x_1}{\partial \pi_1} + \frac{\partial S}{\partial \pi_1} \tag{16}$$

$$0 = \frac{\partial S}{\partial \pi_2} = \frac{\partial S}{\partial x_2} . \frac{\partial x_2}{\partial \pi_2} + \frac{\partial S}{\partial \pi_2} + \{ \frac{\partial S}{\partial x_1} + \frac{\partial S}{\partial x_2} . \frac{\partial x_2}{\partial x_1} \} \frac{\partial x_1}{\partial \pi_2} \tag{17}$$

Equation (8) is the same as (4) under adaptive expectations, but (9) adds to (5) the last term, which reflects the public's rational anticipation of π_2 and its effect on period 1 events, x_1. The policy maker obviously wants that effect to be optimal.

At the end of period 1, when x_1 and π_1 have become history, the policy maker can re-optimize his setting of π_2 and, if he does so, his appropriate first-order condition is:

$$0 = \frac{\partial S}{\partial \pi_2} = \frac{\partial S}{\partial x_2}.\frac{\partial x_2}{\partial \pi_2} + \frac{\partial S}{\partial \pi_2} \tag{18}$$

which reverts to (5). In other words, having influenced expectations in period 1, he now can neglect any effect of π_2 on the x_1 outcome (just as was the case throughout with adaptive expectations). He solves for π_2, x_2 from (7) and (10), given π_1, x_1 (and previously planned π_2, x_2) from (6) to (9).

Obviously the solution for π_2, x_2 will be different from the previous plan (it would be the same if and only if (10) were identical to (9)). Hence his optimal plan is necessarily time inconsistent.

In macroeconomic policy time inconsistency arises because of the desire among policy makers to exploit the Phillips curve short-run trade-off between output and inflation. If they merely carry forward the money supply plans everyone expects, output will be at the natural rate, y^* (as will unemployment). However, they would ideally prefer higher output (as stressed by Hillier and Malcolmson, 1984) because of the presence of distortions (such as unemployment benefits discussed earlier) which mean that private decisions generate too low an output and employment. So it is optimal to raise money supply growth (and inflation) above its expected level to stimulate output.

Take the following example, using a heavily simplified macro model; the example originally comes from Barro and Gordon (1983). Let the government set money supply growth, g_t, and assume that inflation is equal to this (one can think of this as the government using the money supply to target inflation directly). Output is determined by the Phillips curve:

$$y_t = y^* + \theta(g_t - g_t^e) \tag{19}$$

g_t^e is people's rational expectation of money supply growth formed before the t-period opens.

The government's (and also the social) utility function is:

$$U_t = -(y_t - ky^*)^2 - s(g_t - g^*)^2 \quad (k > 1) \tag{20}$$

$ky^*(> y^*)$ and g^* are the government's ideals for output and inflation, respectively.

Suppose the government announces its planned money growth in $t-1$; it is believed and therefore equals g_t^e. But then it is able to change its mind at the beginning of t, after g_t^e has been set, so that a different g_t can be delivered. The set-up is quite artificial, as we pointed out earlier and will shortly discuss.

Before the period the government maximizes U_t with respect to g_t, subject to the Phillips curve and $g_t = g_t^e$. In this case $y_t = y^*$ and the maximum is:

$$0 = \frac{\partial U_t}{\partial g_t} = -2s(g_t - g^*) \tag{21}$$

whence $g_t = g^*$.

However, once period t has begun, the government can re-optimize, maximizing U_t with respect to g_t again subject the Phillips curve, but now given $g_t^e = g^*$. Substituting for y_t from (12) in (11) gives:

$$U_t = -[(1-k)y^* + \theta(g_t - g^*)]^2 - s(g_t - g^*)^2 \tag{22}$$

Maximizing this we get:

$$0 = \frac{\partial U_t}{\partial g_t} = -2[(1-k)y^* + \theta(g_t - g^*)]\theta - 2s(g_t - g^*) \tag{23}$$

so that

$$g_t = g^* + \frac{\theta(k-1)y^*}{s + \theta^2} \tag{24}$$

Actual money supply growth is more stimulatory than expected as the government exploits the Phillips curve. Figure 5.3 illustrates this.

The concentric ellipses in figure 5.3 are the government's (society's) indifference curves, with B denoting its 'bliss point'. $P_L P_L$, $P_s P_s$ are respectively the long-run Phillips curve and the short-run, conditional on $g_t^e = g^*$ (we will return to $P_s' P_s'$ and point c). Point a is the optimal plan before period t opens. Point b is the optimal action after it opens.

As our heavy earlier hints have indicated, there is an artificiality in the assumptions which permit the government to fool rational private decision makers in this way. Even though it is for the general good, private individuals will try to avoid being fooled in this way, because as individuals that is their best decision. That is precisely what a distortion involves: the outcome of best private plans does not coincide with the social optimum.

Another way of stating this is to say that individuals will, in forming rational expectations, take account of the government's incentive not to carry through its announced plan. If people know the model, then they know the government's utility function and that it will maximize it.

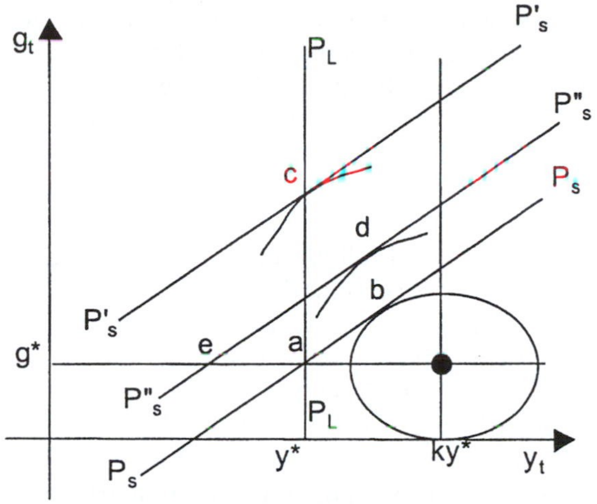

Figure 5.3: Time-inconsistent exploitation of the Phillips curve

They will be in a position to work out what the government will actually do as opposed to what it says it will do.

In our example, this has radical results. People form their expectations, g_t^e, by working back from what the government will do in period t given those expectations. The government will maximize U_t subject to the Phillips curve and g_t^e whatever it is. Substituting (11) into (12) gives:

$$U_t = -[(1-k)y^* + \theta(g_t - g_t^e)]^2 - s[g_t - g^*]^2 \tag{25}$$

and setting $\frac{\partial U_t}{\partial g_t} = 0$ solves for:

$$g_t = \frac{sg * + \theta^2 g_t^e + \theta(k-1)y^*}{s + \theta^2} \tag{26}$$

This is the rule people know the government will actually follow, regardless of its pious intentions. Therefore to form a rational expectation in period $t-1$ people take expectations of (18): in so doing they ensure that $g_t^e = E_{t-1}g_t$. Therefore they solve:

$$E_{t-1}g_t = \frac{sg * + \theta^2 E_{t-1}g_t + \theta(k-1)y^*}{s + \theta^2} \tag{27}$$

from which it emerges that:

$$g_t^e = E_{t-1}g_t = g^* + \frac{\theta(k-1)y^*}{s} \tag{28}$$

When the government comes to execute its optimal rule (18), whatever it may have announced in advance, it will find that it will generate money supply growth exactly as people expected, $g_t = g_t^e$ as in (20). This can be established by substituting (20) for g_t^e into (18) and solving for g_t.

In figure 5.3, this is point c, where $y_t = y^*$ on the long run Phillips curve. Yet the government has reached a tangency point of an indifference curve to the short run Phillips curve, $P_s'P_s'$, through that point.

What we see here is a combination of two factors. First, rational expectations is ensuring that in the absence of shocks people are not surprised so that their private output plans are not frustrated: $y_t = y^*$ on the long-run Phillips curve and $g_t = E_{t-1}g_t$. This is a restoration of Sargent and Wallace's principle of policy ineffectiveness in the context of a standard Phillips curve.

Secondly, the government is pursuing a particularly destabilizing rule for inflation. Instead of responding to past output, itself a rule that destabilizes money growth and inflation in the presence of shocks (but not here where shocks have been assumed away), it is responding to expectations of inflation in the attempt to stimulate output above its natural (inevitable) level. In other words, whatever money supply growth people may expect it to inject in an attempt to stimulate the economy, it goes one better in its attempt to reach tangency with the short-run Phillips curve. The process is only arrested by the escalating costs of inflation. It can be seen from figure 5.3, where the vertical distance between points b and c is given by $(k-1)\frac{\theta^2}{s(s+\theta^2)}$, that as the cost of inflation, s, tends to zero, point c tends to infinity.

Consequently, on top of any moderate destabilization of inflation that may occur if it also attempts to respond to past output, the government may produce a very large destabilization of inflation through this type of response. The solution forced by the conflict between the government's determination to reach tangency with the short-run Phillips curve and the people's rational expectations is the point c where both are finally satisfied.

In this case the 'time-inconsistency' of the government's optimal plans has been marginalized by people's rational expectations, because any 'plans' the government may form before period t opens are irrelevant. The only 'plan' of any interest is the computed outcome of the government's true rule. If we refer to this as the government's true plan, then we can say that it is time consistent, because it will be followed through in period t.

Clearly, this time-consistent result of the interaction between the government's rule and people's rational expectations delivers poor social utility. If somehow the government could achieve point a (the result of its original time-inconsistent optimal plan, had it been carried forward), that would be better, since it would achieve lower inflation together with $y_t = y^*$ as in c. Point b is better still but no longer available because of rational expectations.

In terms of the general two-period problem set out in the model of equations (1), (6) and (7), the equivalent of point a is the solution of equations (8) and (9) together with the model where the government determines its optimal plan assuming its own credibility. The equivalent of point b is the solution of (10) and (7) given x_1 and π_1 as determined by this original optimal plan and the full model — here it 'backslides'. The equivalent of point c is given by the joint solution of (10) and (18) with the model, where its future backsliding is fully taken into account in its decision for first-period policy and in the behaviour of private agents.

We have now exposed the artificiality of our original assumption that people automatically believe the plans the government announced at the start of the first period. In fact they will only believe them if the government commits itself in advance to carry them out, on pain of a penalty at least as great as any gain from backsliding. This penalty has to be administered by some agency outside the government's control: otherwise the government could abrogate the penalty. This incidentally creates a difficulty for a sovereign democratic government: if it is sovereign, may it not refuse to submit to any penalty, even one it agreed to? Clearly if it does not surrender its sovereignty over this matter then it cannot enjoy a point such as a in figure 5.3. Without an effective and sufficient penalty, the only possible point is c: not only b but also a is ruled out. (Point c, the 'time-consistent' policy case in this literature, would in the literature of contracts be called the 'self-enforcing' or 'incentive-compatible' case. In effect if no contract can be enforced against the interests of one party, then the only possible contract is one that this party will carry out anyway — Hart, 1983. The parallel here in policy is that no enforceable contract specifying a penalty can be drawn up with the policy maker.)

Since a is preferable to c, it is in the interest of policy-makers to find a mechanism for effective commitment. Various mechanisms have been suggested. The most widely canvassed is a constitutionally independent central bank such as the Bundesbank (set up after the Second World War) in Germany and the Federal Reserve Board in the USA; we shall explore this carefully below. Another is to join a currency board system of fixed exchange rates (as in the sterling area) whereby one's money supply is controlled by the dominant currency of the system: the European Monetary System evolved into the euro-area partly for this reason. In the case where the government itself controls its own money supply within a floating exchange rate system, the British government since the Second World War being one example, it may seek to create political embarrassment from backsliding.

The Thatcher government's Medium Term Financial Strategy — MTFS — was of this type. It set targets for the money supply and public sector deficit for a rolling four-year period: these targets and the associated commitments to reduce inflation were emphasized by the government as a litmus test of its fitness to govern. The implication was that the public should not re-elect it if it failed: clearly a dangerous commitment to fail on from a political viewpoint.

These mechanisms all have the key deficiency that governments are sovereign and cannot be bound by past commitments; therefore they will naturally re-optimise and whatever hurdles are put in their way they will contrive to leap over them — thus the time-inconsistency problem reappears (McCallum, 1995). Democratic governments for example have the power to change constitutions or to leave currency boards. They can plainly run public sector deficits, which ultimately may drive them to print money to avoid the rising cost of debt finance: central bank obstruction in these circumstances will be over-ruled, with the ultimate threat of removing the bank's independence. The Thatcher MTFS confronted the issue of deficits, and by making the public its judge also avoided the constitutional issue. The question still remained over how far it could get away with backsliding: for example, could it not have tried to persuade the public at an election that somewhat higher inflation then planned was for their good because it allowed lower unemployment (point b in figure 5.3)?

This deficiency implies that there is with each of these mechanisms some probability of effectiveness, some of backsliding; let us leave on one side for now where these probabilities might come from and how they might be assessed. The resulting solution will reflect these probabilities. Let us pursue this in the context of our inflation-unemployment trade-off example.

Suppose the government commits incompletely to a plan of $g_t = g^*$ so that there is a probability, π, of its pursing a backsliding policy g_t^b (that is, maximizing U_t given whatever expectations, g_t^e, have been formed on the basis of its 'commitment'). The consequential expectations, g_t^e, will be:

$$g_t^e = \pi g_t^b + (1-\pi)g^* \tag{29}$$

To calculate g_t^b, we substitute for g_t^e in U_t obtaining

$$U_t = -[(1-k)y^* + \theta(g_t - \pi g_t^b - (1-\pi)g^*)]^2 - s(g_t - g^*)^2 \tag{30}$$

so that its backsliding strategy is given by setting $0 = \frac{\partial U_t}{\partial g_t}$ which yields:

$$g_t^b = g^* + \frac{\theta(k-1)y^*}{s + \theta^2(1-\pi)} \tag{31}$$

(Our procedure, it will be recalled, is to maximize with respect to g_t, given g_t^b, then to set $g_t^b = g_t$ in the resulting first-order condition, and solve for g_t^b.)

It follows that:

$$g_t^e = g^* + \frac{\pi\theta(k-1)y^*}{s + \theta^2(1-\pi)} \tag{32}$$

The resulting situation is illustrated in Figure 5.3 by the Phillips curve $P_s'' P_s''$ and is worked out in Box 5.1. The outcome will either be d if the government backslides or e if it does not. Point d is clearly better than c (it may or may not be worse than a, depending on the size of s, the government's dislike of inflation and the extent of credibility in the uncertain case); backsliding when you have uncertain commitment is better than when you have none, but you might have been better off with totally certain commitment.

Box 5.1

THE VIRTUE OF (EVEN SOME) CREDIBILITY

When credibility is total, then

$$g_t = g_t^e = g^*$$

and

$$U_t = -[(1-k)y^*]^2 = U_a$$

i.e. utility in case a in Fig.5.3.

When there is no credibility (case c), we obtain

$$U_c = U_a(1 + \frac{\theta^2}{s})$$

After laborious substitutions we obtain for the backsliding case d under imperfect credibility

$$U_d = U_a(\frac{s(s+\theta^2)}{(s+\theta^2[1-\pi])^2})$$

and in case e (follow-through with g^*),

$$U_e = U_a(\frac{s+\theta^2}{s+\theta^2[1-\pi]})^2$$

Comparing U_e with U_c and U_d with U_a, we obtain in both cases an ambiguous ranking:

$$\frac{U_e}{U_c} = \frac{U_d}{U_a} = \frac{s(s+\theta^2)}{(s+\theta^2[1-\pi])^2}$$

Subtracting the denominator from the numerator yields:

$$\theta^2[s(2\pi-1) - \theta^4(1-\pi)^2]$$

so that $U_e \succ U_c$ and $U_d \succ U_a$ if for example π is high or if $\pi \succ 0.5$ and s is high or θ is low (it requires that $\pi \succ 0.5$).
The probability-weighted average of U_d and U_e is

$$U_w = \pi U_d + (1-\pi)U_e = U_a(\frac{s+\theta^2}{s+\theta^2[1-\pi]})$$

which is worse than U_a and better than U_e.

Point *e*, following through on uncertain commitment, though clearly worse than *a* and *d*, may or may not be greater than *c*. However the expected (probability-weighted) utility of points *d* and *e* is better than *c* and worse than *a*. It follows that some commitment, however uncertain, is better than no commitment at all, because it gets the government on to a lower Phillips curve, so a better trade-off: expectations of money supply growth, g_t^e, are reduced.

Uncertainty about whether the government will backslide for some reason is unavoidable given its sovereignty. The essential source of the uncertainty is whether the penalty triggered by backsliding (over-riding the central bank, being politically embarrassed by higher inflation, etc.) will be bigger than the gain from it (lower unemployment, higher output at the expense of somewhat higher inflation).

As we have seen, it pays the government to make a tough commitment to g^*. But no government can bind its successor, or even itself at a future date. If its preferences change (a new government or new ministers), or if circumstances change (an unexpected fall in y^*, for example), the penalty may not be sufficient.

Modelling this uncertainty is clearly difficult. Various attempts have been made. One, initiated by Backus and Driffill (1985 a,b), has focused on uncertainty about government preferences. The government may turn out to be 'wet' or 'dry' (respectively caring about both inflation and unemployment, and caring only about inflation): the probability, π, of backsliding (the effect of 'wetness') is constantly re-assessed in the light of policy actions.

The difficulty with this approach is to motivate, first, these differences in preferences and, second, the private sector's lack of knowledge about them. If we probe more deeply into the basis of politics — we do more on these lines in Chapter 8 below — we can see that parties wish to win votes, by appealing to popular preferences (those of the median voter), and they may also have 'ideology' (that is beliefs about what should be done allied to the belief that they can make this attractive to voters). Possibly we could define a wet government as one that wished to appeal to the median voter; a dry one as one that ideologically favoured zero inflation regardless of short-term popularity. Yet this raises the question: if voters truly reward reflationary time-inconsistency at the polls, would it be rational for a government to be dry, so guaranteeing loss of office?

Box 5.2

UNKNOWN PREFERENCES AND REPUTATION — A SIMPLE EXAMPLE

A government gets elected for a two-period term (a 'period' lasts two years). There are two sorts of politician: 'wet' with utility function (seen from the start of any term of government they might have)

$$U_w = -\frac{1}{2}\pi_t^2 + a(y_t - \overline{y}) + \delta[-\frac{1}{2}\pi_{t+1}^2 + a(y_{t+1} - \overline{y})]$$

and 'dry' with utility function

$$U_d = -\frac{1}{2}\pi_t^2 - \frac{1}{2}\delta\pi_{t+1}^2$$

where in both cases $\delta \succ 1$ (because the second period is closest to the next election). The economy consists of a Phillips Curve

$$y_t = b(\pi_t - \pi_t^e)$$

and π_t^e is formed rationally with information at $t-1$ (the log of the natural rate, y^*, has been normalised at 0). The private sector is assumed to know nothing at all about the politicians' preferences, so that the initial probability of the government being wet, $prob_w = 0.5$; it then looks for clues from government behaviour.

The dry-politician government would maximize its utility ($\frac{\partial U_d}{\partial \pi_t} = \frac{\partial U_d}{\partial \pi_{t+1}} = 0$) by setting $\pi_t = \pi_{t+1} = 0$. The wet-politician government faces a choice. If it chooses $\pi_t \succ 0$ in t, then the private sector will know in forming period $t+1$ expectations that the government is wet ($prob_w = 1$); if it chooses $\pi_t = 0$, the private sector will still be in the dark and $prob_w = 0.5$ still. in period $t+1$ it no longer matters whether the private sector knows because the period after the election $(t+2)$ does not count: politicians only care about winning the election. Hence maximizing U_w with respect to π_{t+1} yields simply

$$0 = \frac{\partial U_w}{\partial \pi_{t+1}} = -\pi_{t+1} + abor\pi_{t+1} = ab$$

Maximizing U_w with respect to π_t involves choosing the highest of two utilities, cases A and B:

(A) if $\pi_t = 0$: $U_w^A = -ab\pi_t^e - a\overline{y} + \delta[-\frac{1}{2}(ab)^2 + ab(ab - \pi_{t+1}^{e,A}) - a\overline{y}]$

(B) if $\pi_t \succ 0$, then the wet government will choose the π_t that maximizes u_w, that is $0 = \frac{\partial U_w}{\partial \pi_t} = -\pi_t + ab$ so $\pi_t = ab$ (remembering that π_{t+1}^e will be invariant to π_t if $\pi_t \succ 0$.) Its utility will then be:

$$U_w^B = -\frac{1}{2}(ab)^2 + ab(ab - \pi_t^e) - a\overline{y} + \delta[-\frac{1}{2}(ab)^2 + ab(ab - \pi_{t+1}^{e,B}) - a\overline{y}]$$

Subtracting U_w^A from U_w^B gives us:

$$U_w^B - U_w^A = -\frac{1}{2}(ab)^2 + (ab)^2 - \delta ab(\pi_{t+1}^{e,b} - \pi_{t+1}^{e,a})$$

which clearly depends on private expectations formed in t for $t+1$. In case A, people will still not know the government is wet and so $\pi_{t+1}^{e,A} = 0.5ab$; in case B people will know and so $\pi_{t+1}^{e,B} = ab$. So

$$U_w^B - U_w^A = \frac{1}{2}(ab)^2 - \delta ab(\frac{1}{2}ab) = \frac{1}{2}(ab)^2(1-\delta) \prec 0$$

Hence it pays a wet government to pretend it is dry in period t: $\pi_t = 0$, so 'building reputation' – before exploiting its reputation in the run-up to the election with a pre-election reflation. We can now incidentally work out π_t^e. Since people know that a wet government would choose this strategy, of zero inflation in the first period, therefore $\pi_t^e = 0$; both governments would therefore choose zero inflation, leaving people no way of distinguishing when forming expectations for the second period.

This is known as a situation of 'pooling equilibrium' in period t because both types of politician choose the same, 'pooled', outcome. However, the set-up assumes that the dry government is indifferent to being indistinguishable from a wet government in the first period. This is true above because the dry government's utility is unaffected by y_{t+1} and so by π^e_{t+1}.

Yet this is improbable since in winning the next election the dry government would be helped by lower unemployment and so by a lower π^e_{t+1}. We can allow for this by letting its preferences now be:

$$U_d = -\frac{1}{2}\pi_t^2 + \delta[-\frac{1}{2}\pi_{t+1}^2 + \alpha(y_{t+1} - \overline{y})]$$

where $\alpha \prec a$

In this, much more complicated, case the dry government also has a choice: it can choose $\pi_t = 0$ as before, knowing a wet government would match it or it can choose a π_t that is so *negative* in the first period that a wet government would find it too expensive to pretend and match it. If the dry government were to choose the latter strategy, we would have a 'separating equilibrium' where the wet governmentr does not pretend and hence cannot 'build reputation'; instead the private sector knows at once what sort of government it faces.

Consider the possibilities for the dry government:

(i) It chooses $\pi_t = 0$. By so doing it permits a wet government to pretend, as we know from the above steps it would.

(ii) The dry government chooses $\pi_t \prec 0$, such that the wet government would find it not worth pretending. To find out how negative π_t would have to be we check out the critical π_t just above which the wet government gives up pretending, call this π_t^*. π_t^* is such that $U_w^A = U_w^B$

So if $\pi_{wt} = \pi_t^*$, then $\pi_{t+1}^{e,A} = \frac{1}{2}ab$ and

$$U_w^A = -\frac{1}{2}(\pi_t^*)^2 + ab(\pi_t^* - \pi_t^e) - a\overline{y} + \delta[-\frac{1}{2}(ab)^2 + ab(ab - \frac{1}{2}ab) - a\overline{y}]$$

If $\pi_{wt} = ab$, then $\pi_{t+1}^{e,B} = ab$ and

$$U_w^B = -\frac{1}{2}(ab)^2 + ab(ab - \pi_t^e) - a\overline{y} + \delta[-\frac{1}{2}(ab)^2 - a\overline{y}]$$

Setting $U_w^A = U_w^B$ and cancelling terms gives us:

$$\pi_t^{*2} - 2ab\pi_t^* - (\delta - 1)(ab)^2 = 0$$

the unique negative solution of which is: $\pi_t^* = ab(1 - \sqrt{\delta})$
We now ask whether it would pay the dry government to choose this, so forcing the wet government to stop pretending, or instead choose $\pi_t = 0$, so allowing it to pretend (for the dry to choose anything in between would be the worst of both worlds since it would suffer from negative inflation as well as permitting pretence). We compare U_d^A $(\pi_t = 0)$ with U_d^* $(\pi_t = \pi_t^*)$, so that $\pi_{t+1}^{e,0} = \frac{1}{2}ab$ and $\pi_{t+1}^{e,*} = 0$. We obtain:

$$U_d^* - U_d^A = \frac{1}{2}(ab)^2[\frac{\delta\alpha}{a} - (1 - \sqrt{\delta})^2]$$

Considering this problem we can see at once that we require $\delta \succ 1$ and $\alpha \succ 0$ for a separating equilibrium to be possible. $\delta = 1$ implies $\pi_t^* = 0$; $\alpha = 0$ implies that $U_d^* \succ U_d^A$. Fig. 5.4 below shows the conditions (for $\delta \succ 1$) under which we get a separating equilibrium: where $\frac{\alpha}{a} \succ \frac{(1-\sqrt{\delta})^2}{\delta}$. For example, assuming $\delta = 2$ (the pre-election performance is twice as important for the election as the post-election one), then α needs to be only 9% of a; so the dry government needs to care about pre-election unemployment only a very little relative to a wet one.

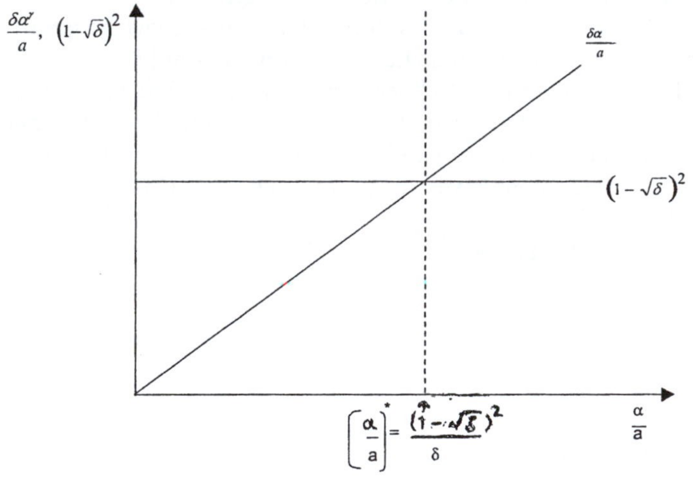

Figure 5.4: The Backus–Driffill model

As for revelation of preferences, Vickers(1986) showed that in many circumstances it would pay the dry government to signal its nature by some extreme act of dryness that a wet government would find too costly to imitate. In this case there would be a 'separating equilibrium' in which wage bargainers would know exactly what sort of government they faced. This question is explored in the example in Box 5.2.

Another approach, initiated by Barro and Gordon (1983), assumes that preferences are known and constant and that the penalty for backsliding is a 'loss of reputation', whereby the private sector (wage bargainers) disbelieve the government's announced plans for a certain period of time and assume the government will backslide during this period. The penalty is arbitrary in the Barro and Gordon model but we could reduce the arbitrariness by assuming for example that private disbelief continues until there is a change of membership in the government (e.g. an election cycle).

During the period of lost reputation, the government is considered to suffer the point c. This penalty is in general less than the gain to backsliding on g^* as an announced plan. People work out the announced plan ($g_t^p > g^*$) such that the penalty is just sufficient to offset any gain from backsliding. This is of course the plan that the goverment will also choose. It produces a point on the vertical Phillips curve between a and c. This is worked out in Box 5.3.

Box 5.3

REPUTATION THROUGH PRIVATE SECTOR WITHDRAWAL OF BELIEF

The government has an infinite-horizon utility function at t:

$$U_t = \sum_{i=0}^{\infty} \delta^i \{-\frac{1}{2}\pi_{t+i}^2 + a(y_{t+i} - \overline{y})\} \qquad \delta \prec 1$$

and faces a Phillips Curve

$$y_t = b(\pi_t - \pi_t^e)$$

π_t^e is formed rationally at $t-1$ for t according to the following agreed private sector one-period punishment strategy:
(1) if $\pi_{t-1} \succ \pi_{t-1}^e, \pi_t^e = ab$ (the government's discretionary chocie)
(2) if $\pi_{t-1} = \pi_{t-1}^e, \pi_t^e = \pi^a$, acredible government target announced in $t-1$ for t, t for $t+1$ etc (provisionally assumed constant).

Under (1) the government 'forfeits credibility', under (2) it 'achieves credibility'.
We start this game off by assuming that $\pi_{-1} = \pi^e_{-1}$.
Knowing the private strategy the government chooses a plan at -1 for $t \geq 0$. It has two basic strategies to compare:
(a) It can announce and deliver π^a throughout – a permanent follow-through strategy.
(b) It can cheat in even periods and suffer punishment in odd periods (cheating in odd ones must be worse than this because the gains are delayed). When it cheats it will choose $\pi = ab$ because this maximizes its (cheating) utility as we have seen.
Under (a) its utility is:

$$U_t^a = \frac{1}{1-\delta}[-\frac{1}{2}(\pi_a)^2 - a\overline{y}]$$

Under (b) it is:

$$U_t^b = \sum_{i(even)}^{\infty} \delta^i\{-\frac{1}{2}(ab)^2 + ab(ab - \pi_a) - a\overline{y}\} + \sum_{i(odd)}^{\infty} \delta^i\{-\frac{1}{2}(ab)^2 - a\overline{y}\}$$

Remembering that

$$\sum_{i(even)}^{\infty} \delta^i = 1 + \delta^2 + \delta^4 + ... = \sum_{i}^{\infty} \delta^{2i} = \frac{1}{1-\delta^2}$$

and analogously

$$\sum_{i(odd)}^{\infty} \delta^i = \frac{\delta}{1-\delta^2}$$

we obtain

$$U_t^b = \frac{1}{1-\delta^2}[\frac{1}{2}(ab)^2(1-\delta) - (1+\delta)a\overline{y} - ab\pi^a]$$

whence $\left(\text{remembering } \frac{1}{1-\delta^2} = \frac{1}{(1-\delta)(1+\delta)}\right)$

$$U_t^a - U_t^b = -\frac{1}{2(1-\delta)}\{(\pi^a)^2 - \frac{2ab}{1+\delta}\pi^a + \frac{(1-\delta)}{(1+\delta)}(ab)^2\}$$

The situation is illustrated by Figure 5.5 which shows U^a and U^b as functions of π^a, the credible target. $U^a = U^b$ at two points: $\pi^a = \frac{ab(1-\delta)}{1+\delta}$; ab (these are found as the solutions to the quadratic in

π^a that comes from setting $U^a = U^b$). Any point to the left of the first is not credible because it would pay the government to cheat. Any point between the first and second provides less utility than the first and so will not be chosen by the government. Therefore the first point, $\frac{ab(1-\delta)}{1+\delta}$, is the only feasible one: at it the government will never cheat, because the loss of utility from losing credibility next period just offsets the gain from cheating. Plainly π^a is a constant as assumed (as can be checked by seeing that this holds in every period).

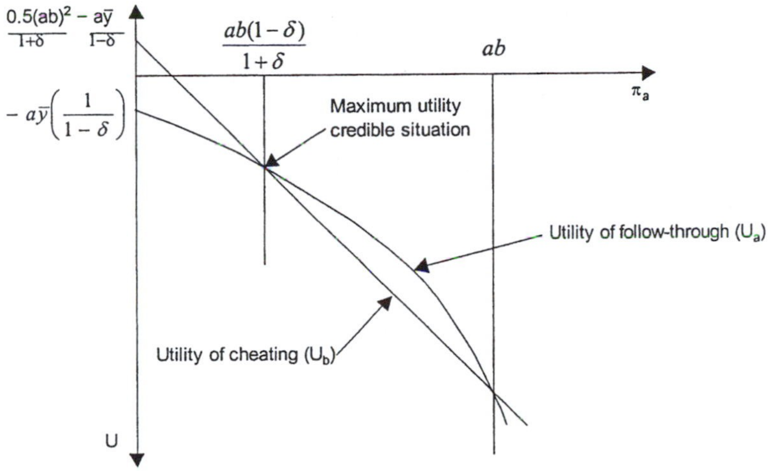

Figure 5.5: The Barro-Gordon model of credibility

This idea on its own simply works out what would happen if the penalty for backsliding on a plan were less than the penalty needed to prevent backsliding on g^*. The result is a steady $g_t^e = g_t > g^*$. The government would in fact be better off if it could somehow persuade people to disbelieve it for longer!

Uncertainty of a sort can be introduced by introducing shocks to the economy's natural rate or to the government's preferences which cause the government to choose a new g_t^e equilibrium, after initially reneging. As we have seen it will always pay the government to choose a permanent non-punishment equilibrium as soon as it can. If $g_t > g_t^e$, the government loses credibility: future g_t defaults to point c until credibility is restored. It then reverts to $g_t = g_t^e > g^*$ until the next shock producing $g_t > g_t^e$.

The difficulty with this approach is how to define and motivate a co-ordinated, non-arbitrary strategy on the part of private agents for 'triggering' belief or disbelief — their 'punishment strategy'. These agents, it must be remembered, are not voters here, but wage bargainers. Why should they collectively come together to agree a punishment strategy instead of getting on with their own private business? One can think of reasons if workers are represented by a single union or a well-integrated set of unions; and this case has been explored by Herrendorf and Neumann (1998). But in general the case is unconvincing.

We have therefore reviewed two approaches to uncertainty — one emphasizes the uncertainty of government preferences, the other that of the changing environment. Both are attempts to model the evolution of credibility, viewed as the possible selection by the government of either low inflation or reflationary policy. However both have arbitrary elements in them which make them unconvincing in general as an account of why governments choose to inflate or not.

More recently economists have returned to the original Kydland-Prescott model and attempted to embed it in a rational political process. There have been two main strands of thought.

The first is an institutional model of politics. In this approach it is assumed that institutions matter and do in practice constrain governments, including democratic ones. So it is accepted here that governments will be prone to time-inconsistency, implicitly because this will appeal to voters whose preferences are such as in the Barro-Gordon set-up. But there are difficulties for governments in overturning institutional barriers — they are for example seen as 'high-handed' or 'arbitrary' and therefore governments like to be seen as acting within the conventions; even if they could overthrow them, they will not do so lightly because it requires costly legislative time and ministerial energy.

These authors (the earliest of whom is Rogoff, 1985) suggest that the electorate may well accept some institutional reform, if it can be shown to have good long-term effects. Then the reform once made it will be respected by future governments. They suggest therefore establishing the institution of an independent central bank, with a remit (or 'institutionalized preferences' which could be summarised in the degree of 'inflation toughness' of the Governor) to give more attention to inflation than would be given by politicians reflecting popular preferences.

The earlier work gave no real role to stabilization since there were no shocks shifting the Phillips curve itself; only demand shocks introduced by monetary policy and inflation and causing output to move up and down the Curve. In this revival of the idea of Bank independence Phillips curve shocks (which could come from supply or from demand via other elements entering the curve, such as the exchange rate or real interest rates driving inter-temporal substitution) were introduced so that the government has another reason for varying inflation besides the desire to raise output above the natural rate: to stabilize the economy in the face of shocks.

The resulting set-up is illustrated in figure 5.6 (the same as figure 5.5 above, except that the Phillips curve is now stochastic). The voter, as represented by the government, has 'normal' preferences with a dislike of both inflation and unemployment. Unrestrained, these would produce the poor time-consistent outcome c on our original figure — high average inflation; however it would also stabilize shocks as shown at points f and g. Reflecting on their institutions however voters realize that this systematic result of the political process is not as good as could be achieved if institutional restraint was exercised through an independent central bank that was free to react to shocks and yet limited in its tolerance of inflation. (One might ask here why not look at other constitutional restraints? The answer would be that a purely constitutional law would lack the necessary flexibility Since we are setting the institution up for the long term we are concerned about its effect on expected (average) future social (i.e. the voters') utility. We vary a until this is maximized; it turns out (see Box 5.4) that this occurs somewhere between 0 (total intolerance of inflation) and popular preferences. Inflation would be zero at the first but stabilization would also be nil; at the second the inflation bias would be at its worst but stabilization would be at its most effective. A compromise is necessary.

Box: 5.4

THE INSTITUTIONAL APPROACH TO THE INDEPENDENT CENTRAL BANK

Suppose society has the utility function:

$$U_s = -\frac{1}{2}[\pi_t^2 + \alpha(y_t - \overline{y})^2]$$

and faces a Phillips Curve

$$y_t = c(\pi_t - \pi_t^e) + u_t$$

where u_t consists of shocks on the Phillips curve from supply and also demand (via real interest rates or exchange rates which enter the inflation/labour supply process) with variance σ^2. The institutional reformer wishes to choose a central bank set of 'preferences' (shorthand for the remit given in the central bank legislation) in order to mazimize society's expected utility (i.e. the average over the future – long – period during which the legislation will hold), that is

$$EU_s = -\frac{1}{2}[E\pi_t^2 + \alpha E(y_t - \overline{y})^2]$$

To motivate the set-up consider two extreme instructions to the central bank which we summarise as giving the central bank a set of preferences of the form:
(i) not to care at all about unemployment ($a = 0$)
(ii)to behave as if it had the same preferences as society ($a = \alpha$)
Using the central bank's first order conditions,
under (i) $\pi_t = 0 = \pi_t^e$ and so $EU_s = -\frac{1}{2}\alpha[\overline{y}^2 + \sigma^2]$
under (ii) $\pi_t = \frac{\alpha c^2 \pi_t^e + \alpha c\overline{y} - \alpha c u_t}{1+\alpha c^2}$. It follows that $\pi_t^e = ac\overline{y}$ so that $\pi_t = \alpha c\overline{y} - \frac{\alpha c}{1+\alpha c^2}u_t$ and $y_t = \frac{1}{1+\alpha c^2}u_t$ so $EU_s = -\frac{1}{2}\{\overline{y}^2(\alpha + \alpha^2 c^2) + (\frac{\alpha}{1+\alpha c^2})\sigma^2\}$
Compared with case (i), case (ii) offers a clear reduction in the effects of shocks due to the Bank's active stabilisation response, but a rise in the effect of $\overline{y}$ (the 'distortionary gap' between desired full employment output and its natural rate), due to the Bank's frustrated attempt to stimulate output beyond its natural rate; this latter being the effect on expected utility of the inflation bias.
We can now generalise the problem and find a compromise Bank preference for lower unemployment, letting $0 \prec a \prec \alpha$
This will produce analogously from the Bank's first order condition

$$\begin{aligned} \pi_t &= ac\overline{y} - \frac{ac}{1+ac^2}u_t \\ y_t &= \frac{1}{1+ac^2}u_t \end{aligned} \tag{33}$$

and society will enjoy

$$EU_s = -\frac{1}{2}\left\{[\alpha + a^2c^2]\overline{y}^2 + \frac{\alpha + a^2c^2}{(1+ac^2)^2}\sigma^2\right\}$$

From this we can construct figure 5.7 where we show how EU_s varies with a. As $a \to \alpha$, the effect of the shocks falls as stabilisation rises but the inflation bias rises too. The two together reach a maximum at $\widehat{a}$. From $0 = \frac{\partial EU_s}{\partial a}$ we find the equation for $\widehat{a}$ is:

$$\frac{\widehat{a} - \alpha}{\widehat{a}(1+\widehat{a}c^2)^3} = \frac{\overline{y}^2}{\sigma^2}$$

which reveals that $\widehat{a}$ rises as σ^2 rises relative to $\overline{y}^2$. The reason is that the bigger the shocks are relative to the distortionary gap, the more the gain to stabilizing relative to the cost in higher inflation bias.

All this assumes the central bank's remit must be to maximize something of the same form as society's utility. But of course institutional design need not be restricted to this. Walsh (1995) pointed out that one could add a linear term to u_B; selected so that when this was maximized, inflation bias could be eliminated but optimal stabilization could be achieved. Let $U_B = -\frac{1}{2}(\pi_t^2 + \alpha[y_t - \overline{y}]^2) - \lambda\pi_t$ and set $\lambda = \alpha c\overline{y}$. The first order conditions now yield:

$$\begin{aligned} \pi_t &= -\frac{\alpha c}{1+\alpha c^2}u_t \\ y_t &= \frac{1}{1+\alpha c^2}u_t \\ EU_s &= -\frac{1}{2}[\alpha\overline{y}^2 + \frac{\alpha}{1+\alpha c^2}\sigma^2] \end{aligned}$$

which represents the first best result for society (shown as F on the diagram).

Some other ways of getting the same result are to adjust U_B by inserting an inflation target, π^*, that is artificially low or by setting a side-condition that inflation not be varied from its proper target except in response to shocks. These results can be extended to the more realistic case where output is persistent; in this case the optimal contract contains state-contingent restrictions — see the Appendix to chapter 11 on dynamic programming.

Recently it has been realized that institutional preferences[3] can be

[3] A number of authors have also considered objective functions that are non-quadratic in inflation and output deviations. For instance Orphanides and Wilcox (1996) consider the opportunistic approach of the central banker. Proponents of this approach hold that when inflation is moderate but still above the long-run objective, the Central Banker should not take deliberate anti-inflation action, but rather should wait for external circumstances – such as favorable supply shocks and unforeseen recessions – to deliver the desired reduction in inflation. While waiting for such circumstances to arise, the Central Banker should aggressively resist incipient increases in inflation. The policy maker who is endowed with these preferences gives higher weight to stabilizing output when inflation is low, but higher weight to inflation when inflation is above target. Such an approach is motivated by the views expressed by leading Central Bankers. For instance in testimony before the Senate committee that

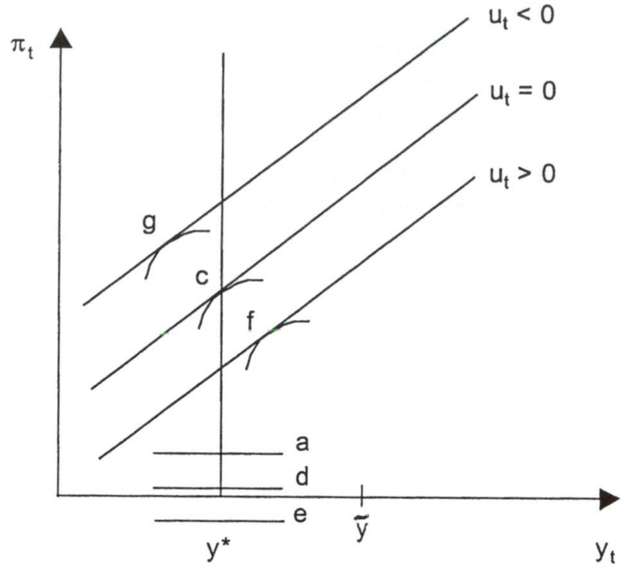

Figure 5.6: A tough central bank (a, d, e) and one with the same preferences as society (g, c, f)

rewritten so that the central bank delivers both zero inflation and maximum stability. In principle this is easily done (Walsh, 1995) by adding a

---

was meeting to consider his nomination to the Federal Reserve Board, former Vice Chairman Blinder summarized his views on this issue as follows:

'If monetary policy is used to cut our losses on the inflation front when luck runs against us, and pocket the gains when good fortune runs our way, we can continue to chip way at the already-low inflation rate.' [Blinder, 1994, p.4].

Nobay and Peel (1998) consider the case where Central Bankers have an asymmetric objective function. This is motivated in part by the European Central Bank's announced objectives according to which inflation should not be above 2 per cent, but is allowed to be below that level.

Specification of such asymmetric preferences leads to terms in the variance of inflation or output impacting on expected inflation. In particular there is a deflationary bias in the ECB example. Essentially the Central Bank has to shoot for a lower expected rate of inflation to allow for the conditional variance of shocks.

Other authors (see e.g. Beetsma and Jensen, 1997; Briault, Haldane and King, 1996) have explored the implications of assuming that the Central Banker's preferences, though quadratic, are uncertain. In particular the weight on say inflation has a stochastic component. Such specifications have implications for expected inflation and the efficacy of inflation targets as opposed to inflation taxes (Walsh, 1995) from a welfare perspective.

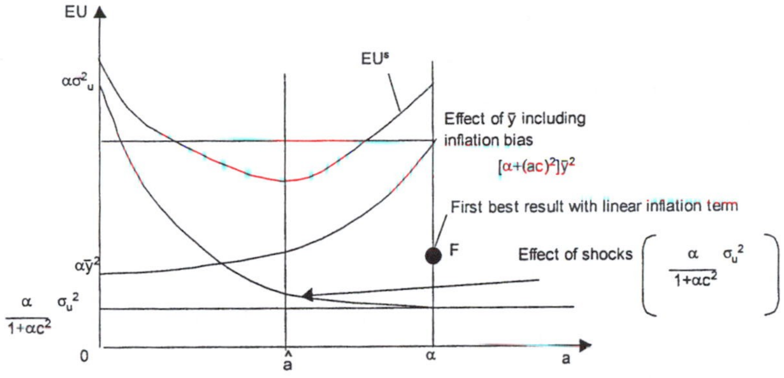

Figure 5.7: Choosing the optimal central bank preference parameter (a)

linear inflation target into the bank's preferences (it can be thought of as forcing an extra linear penalty on inflation); this can then be chosen to force the inflation bias to zero while the a parameter is left at the social preference value so guaranteeing that stabilization is maximized. There are other ways that this can be expressed such as telling the bank to stabilize the economy optimally subject to average inflation (i.e. inflation in the absence of shocks) being equal to target.

This is the institutionalist view. However it is challenged by those who argue that it only artificially 'solves' the time-inconsistency problem (McCallum, 1995). It relies on institutional restraint to prevent governments doing what suits them. Yet suppose that a government is restrained on one occasion by the cost of overriding the constitution; will it not find a way of doing it somehow at less cost in the future? Popular opinion will be forever straining at the leash demanding that its politicians deliver lower unemployment by a 'little bit of inflation'. When politicians are rewarded by popularity will they not in the end do whatever is necessary to gain it?

The institutionalists reply that popular opinion is also in favour of the reform when 'in institutional mode'. Yet this is inconsistent; popular opinion cannot be one thing in one mode and another thing when voting in elections. Either it wants restraint or it does not; it cannot do both at the same time.

One is driven to reject institutionalism as superficial, and failing to address the problem at its roots. The Institution is like the *deus ex machina* with which the Greek dramatists often ended their plays, just as a convenient device to end them but without inherent justification.

Greek audiences accepted it because they understood what it stood for: viz a way of giving the audience the moral of the story (delivered by the god). We have to probe deeper to see if a similar basis can be found for the institutional story.

To find one, we go to political economy and ask whether it could provide a solution. This second strand of thought is a fairly recent reaction to the institutionalist approach (Minford, 1995; Romer and Romer, 1997). Institutionalism has produced some empirical evidence in its favour (for example Cukierman, 1992), showing a correlation between the degree of Bank independence and the rate of inflation. This can be criticized on two levels. First, the definitions of independence are themselves influenced (implicitly if not explicitly) by success in keeping inflation down; the degree of 'toughness' (independence) of a central bank is necessarily evidenced by inflation itself. The example can be given here of the Bundesbank which always scores the most highly on measures of independence; however in strict terms it has no real independence as it could be nationalised by a simple majority of the lower house of parliament (the Bundestag). Its power comes, as board members will frequently say, from its support in public opinion. Second, correlation cannot prove causation here; it may be that as public opinion becomes disenchanted with inflationary policies, it decides to 'institutionalize' this by setting up an independent central bank.

The revisionist view is precisely this: that the electorate begins to understand the time-inconsistency problem as a potential source of inflation, much as an alcoholic understands that his short-term giving-in to the craving for the bottle is the cause of his disease. Wishing to ensure that inflation is kept low on average in spite of the desirability of low unemployment and of stabilizing the economy, it redesigns its own voting reflexes to reward politicians appropriately. It will henceforth penalize 'reflation' whose aim is to stimulate the economy beyond its natural rate; but it will reward stabilizing monetary policy, defined as that which, while reacting to shocks in a stabilising manner, does not on average drive output beyond the natural rate. The electorate does this because it recognises that its 'preferences' (as expressed in these rewards and penalties) are the root cause of political behaviour.

This view requires that the electorate is coordinated in some way so that its punishment strategy can be formulated and exercised. But this is not difficult to understand. We speak of the anti-inflationary 'climate of opinion' in Germany, or in the USA and Britain since the 1970s; what we mean is the popular reflexes that, no doubt heavily influenced by 'informed opinion', underlie voting behaviour.

Furthermore this view leads us to the practical case for an independent central bank: that it is an efficient low-cost way of organising the execution of monetary policy in line with such a public opinion of the problem — just as having independent courts is for the law, or privately-run (privatised) companies is for business. We can say that it does 'institutionalize' the solution effectively. In other words it tells us how we can make sense of the institutionalist case which in itself solves nothing. The solution of the time-inconsistency problem is at the basic level of public understanding, just as that of alcoholism is at the level of personal understanding. Without understanding no solution is possible. With it any set-up for monetary policy would in principle work (just as an alcoholic has many means in principle for stopping drinking to destruction); but a central bank is a convenient method in many ways (just as joining a group like Alcoholics Anonymous is for alcoholism). Empirically it makes sense of the wide variety of institutions under which countries have had both low and high inflation (Romer and Romer, 1997); an independent central bank is neither necessary nor sufficient for low inflation. It merely happens to be convenient for it in a democracy.

CONCLUSIONS

We began this chapter by asking whether there was any case in principle for the government to intervene in the business cycle via variations in interest rates or money supply growth. After all private agents have access to the same information as the government and their decisions would be expected, in the absence of micro distortions, to reflect social as well as private costs and benefits. However we identified the crucial distortions in the labour market (notably the presence of unemployment benefit) that made unemployment non-reflective of social costs; since the business cycle will under these conditions give more unemployment on the downside than less unemployment on the upside, greater cycle variability will produce a higher average distortion. Hence successful stabilization policy would reduce damaging unemployment on average.

We then set out the problem of time inconsistency as a cause of excessive inflation; the point being that governments, having started out with a sensible aim for low inflation, will have an incentive to stimulate the economy further than this in order to bring unemployment down closer to full employment. People, knowing this incentive, then react by raising their inflation expectations to the point where governments just have no further incentive to inflate; this of course means that inflation is higher than the target while at the same time the economy does no better on unemployment — 'stagflation'. Various models of inflation 'credibility' have been built on the idea that private agents may react to past behaviour in forming views of whether a government will in the future succumb to the temptation to 'reflate'; these models are attempts to see whether the natural operation of private markets and reputation can reduce this governmental tendency. However these models are unsatisfactory in a variety of ways and economists have turned to other ways of resolving the problem. Many economists and policy-makers called for the power over monetary policy to be either withdrawn totally from government (for example by a constitutional clause or by fixing the exchange rate to an external monetary anchor) or delegated to an independent central bank with a strictly limited mandate for stabilization and an overriding obligation to control inflation. This of course means that the power of monetary policy to stabilize is largely jettisoned. Some institutionalists have tried to deal with this problem by arguing that politics will generate institutions, most naturally an independent central bank, to restrain politicians' reflation instincts (as encouraged by popular opinion) while still allowing the flexibility to deal with shocks. The Bank's charter can be tuned to deliver the first-best combination of low inflation and output stability. However this is only a solution of the time-inconsistency problem in a superficial sense because it can only work if public opinion tolerates it and does not clamour for an override when reflation is attractive. We argued that the true solution of the problem lies in public opinion itself: understanding how it must reward and penalise political behaviour over monetary policy. Given such understanding, a convenient but in no way essential way to organise monetary policy is then via an independent central bank accountable to public opinion for generating low inflation and output stability.

6

Practical issues of effective stabilization

In the last chapter we asked whether there was a case for monetary policy to stabilize the economy: we concluded that there was. In this chapter we ask what in practice must be done to carry out this stabilization function successfully. We begin with the issue that has haunted policy makers since rational expectations became widely accepted: Lucas' critique of policy choice (Lucas, 1976) which makes the point that the models being used for the formulation of policy rules may well not remain constant as these rules are reset because the behaviour modelled depends on expectations which themselves depend on the rules. Dealing with this critique turns out to be an elusive business. Many economists have however persuaded themselves that models with overlapping wage (and sometimes price) contracts have sufficient constancy under changing rules to be reasonably reliable as a guide to policy formulation. A large literature has grown up using such models to test different sorts of rules. We look at these tests and other ways of evaluating policy in practice.

THE LUCAS CRITIQUE OF POLICY EVALUATION

It was Lucas (1976) who first pointed out that if expectations are formed rationally, then unless the estimated equations used by model builders to evaluate the consequences of alternative government policies are genuinely structural or behavioural, the implications of such simulations or evaluations may be seriously flawed. The essential insight of Lucas is that, when expectations are formed rationally, agents react to the behaviour of government. Consequently, unless the equations estimated by the model builder are structural, the coefficients in equations which are estimated over one policy regime will implicitly depend on the parameters of the government policy rule in operation. Consequently, the evaluation of alternative policies can be quite misleading.

Let us take as an example the following simple model, with overlapping contracts (so that stabilization policy is effective), a quantity theory demand for money function and a money supply rule that responds to past output. All the variables are measured in deviations from their normal values.

$$y_t = \beta(p_t - 0.5[E_{t-1}p_t + E_{t-2}p_t]) \tag{1}$$

$$m_t = p_t + y_t \tag{2}$$

$$m_t = \mu y_{t-1} + \varepsilon_t \tag{3}$$

The solution is

$$y_t = \frac{\beta}{1+\beta}\varepsilon_t + \frac{0.5\mu\beta^2}{(1+\beta)(1+0.5\beta)}\varepsilon_{t-1} \tag{4}$$

from which it is immediately apparent that the optimal monetary response is nil ($\mu = 0$).

What we have just done is to set out the model in its 'structural' form (that is, in terms of its underlying relationships). But suppose we had written the model in a 'reduced' or solved form, with each variable in terms only of its ultimate determinants after all the model's relationships have worked themselves out in the current period. Equation (4) is such a form, but since the error term, ε_t, is not directly observable (it is an implication of equation (3), we could write (4) in terms of observable ultimate determinants m_t and y_{t-1} (using $\varepsilon_t = m_t - y_{t-1}$ from (3)) as:

$$y_t = \sigma_1 m_t + \sigma_2 m_{t-1} + \sigma_3 y_{t-1} + \sigma_4 y_{t-2} \tag{5}$$

where $\sigma_1 = \frac{\beta}{1+\beta}$; $\sigma_2 = \frac{0.5\mu\beta}{(1+\beta)(1+0.5\beta)}$; $\sigma_3 = -\mu\sigma_1$; $\sigma_4 = -\mu\sigma_2$.

Having recovered this relationship from the data, we could compute the optimal monetary policy for time t, given what has already occurred in $t-1$ (the planning period). It is obvious that we must set m_t so as to make $y_t = 0$ (we have one instrument, m_t, and one target, y_t, so the problem here is simple) or:

$$m_t = -\frac{1}{\sigma_1}(\sigma_2 m_{t-1} + \sigma_3 y_{t-1} + \sigma_4 y_{t-2}) \tag{6}$$

According to our relationship (5), this feedback rule for money supply ought to deliver zero fluctuation in output. However, in fact it may deliver worse fluctuations even than the feedback rule (3) the central bank was previously following! Actual money supply will be given by (6) plus ε_t, which is the unpredictable error in executing monetary intentions. The resulting rule can be written as:

$$m_t = \mu y_{t-1} + \frac{\varepsilon_t}{1 + \frac{0.5\mu\beta}{1+0.5\beta}L} \tag{7}$$

(using our knowledge of the σ_i in terms of the model's structural parameters). When this is substituted into the model, we find the new solution for y_t as

$$y_t = \frac{\beta}{1+\beta}\varepsilon_t + \frac{0.5\mu\beta^2}{(1+\beta)(1+0.5\mu\beta)^2}\varepsilon_{t-1} \tag{8}$$

Here output is far from perfectly stabilized with respect to past events — though it will in this instance be slightly more stable.

Where we went wrong was that we used the reduced form to calculate the optimal rule. But that reduced form itself depends on the monetary rule because the rule influences (rational) expectations and so economic behaviour (this problem would not arise in adaptive expectations models, where the effect of money on output does not depend on the rule itself). So the reduced form will not remain constant (as assumed) as we change the rule towards the 'optimum'. Hence we must compute a false optimum.

The policy maker using these methods of optimal control is doomed to go on recomputing his 'optimal' rule as his 'model' constantly changes: it will not necessarily converge to a constant rule and model, however, nor is there any guarantee that it will get any better over time. It could get worse, or alternatively better and worse. In general, we cannot say.

The problem we have just described is not too difficult to solve. Once the policy maker recognizes that the model underlying (5) is a rational expectations model consisting of (1) to (3), he will use the appropriate method and set $\mu = 0$! Estimating the structural parameters of the model is a technical problem not in principle more difficult than estimating the reduced form parameters (we discuss the problem briefly in chapter 16).

DEEP STRUCTURE

We have assumed that (1) and (2) are truly 'structural', that is, that they are invariant to the policy maker's rule. However, this may well not be so. People's behaviour is itself the result of optimizing subject to constraints of budgets and technology; policy rules will typically change their budget constraints because expected future prices and incomes will depend in general on the economy's behaviour which in turn depends on the rules. Equations (1) and (2) express people's resulting behaviour in demand and supply functions; these may therefore alter as policy rules alter. Rational expectations implies that the vast majority of the economic relationships econometricians typically estimate are not strictly structural.

A simple example of this arose with the model of equations (22) and (23) in chapter 4, where we assumed signal extraction from local prices. We saw that output depended on the stabilization parameter, μ:

$$y_t - y^* = \frac{\frac{(1-\phi)}{\delta}}{1 + \frac{(1-\phi)}{\delta} + \alpha\phi + \frac{\alpha\mu\phi(1-\phi)}{\delta(1+\alpha)}} \varepsilon_t \tag{9}$$

It might seem from this that for maximum stability μ should be pushed as high as technically feasible (implying dramatic monetary contraction in booms, expansion in recessions). However, this conclusion treats ϕ as a structural parameter. It is not, since we know that $\phi = \frac{\pi_o^2\sigma_\varepsilon^2}{\sigma_v^2+\pi_o^2\sigma_\varepsilon^2}$, the slope of the Phillips curve, depends on the extent to which the variance of local prices reflects local shocks and overall monetary instability. To compute the appropriate value of we must allow for this as discussed in chapter 4.

Lucas' critique therefore raises deep difficulties for econometricians attempting to recover from the data relationships which are usable for policy making.

One reaction to this problem has been to assert that only the parameters of preferences and technology ('deep structure') will be regime-invariant and that macroeconomists should therefore estimate these. Some early examples are Hansen and Sargent (1980) and Sargent (1978, 1981). A research methodology along these lines is now in full swing. This work models agents at the microeconomic level as intertemporal optimizers subject to the constraints of budget and technology, and attempts to retrieve the parameters of the (aggregated) utility and production functions. In chapters 11-13 we set out some key features of these 'representative agent' models. The problem is to find a way of embedding sufficient detail into the constraints facing agents to allow these models to confront the data successfully.

The models use estimates of utility and production function parameters derived from microeconomic studies (usually of large cross-sectional data sets). Processes for shocks (error terms) to technology and preferences are then estimated from the time series when restricted by the results of these studies. The success of a model in predicting the facts of the business cycle is evaluated by comparing the second and higher moments of the predicted and actual series: techniques of statistical inference from this comparison are not yet widely in use, though available, whether because of the high costs of using them or because the model practitioners do not feel that such stringent testing is appropriate, given the models' relative infancy. Whether such models yet have sufficient dynamic structure to be useful for evaluating stabilization policy is still a matter of debate. However, they do have the clear strength that, being in principle invulnerable to the Lucas critique, they should give a useful guide to the longer-run effects of policies once people have understood the new environment.

Models of this general equilibrium type are widely used in evaluating such policy issues as the effects of world tariff reduction rounds or the introduction of funded private pensions. But for this purpose the interest is in the long-run steady state results and often we have reasonable confidence in at least the rough magnitude of the long-run parameters to be used. The problem with using these general equilibrium models for evaluating stabilization policy is that the parameters of importance are the dynamic ones that govern lags of response — that is, those of expectations and adjustment principally; these have generally been retrieved from time-series estimation as in cross-section there is usually not enough time variation to estimate response to change. However, in recent years 'panel' data-sets (where there is variation across agents and also over time) have offered the promise of resolving this problem.

A second school of thought, of which a major proponent is Sims (1980), asserts that there is no practical possibility of policy evaluation and the best we can achieve is the estimation of time-series models whose parameters will shift in an unpredictable way with regime change. He has proposed the estimation of simultaneous time-series models (i.e. where each variable depends on its past and also on the past of the other variables in the model). These 'Vector Autoregression' (VAR) models have proved extremely popular as ways of summarising an economy's behaviour. The difficulty with them is of interpretation: plainly they are not structural and so inferring what the structural relations may be that underlie these solved-out time-series relationships requires the assumption of 'identifying restrictions', in other words the modeller must assume some structural model. The method however means that the links between the structural model and the VAR parameters are complex; in practice the structural parameters cannot be retrieved solely from the VAR estimation. Again, this strand of thought has prompted a huge research programme to refine the method.

A final reaction has been to model expectations explicitly, but to continue to treat as structural the parameters of such macroeconomic model equations as the consumption and investment functions; this approach has been adopted for example in the Liverpool model (chapter 16) and other examples are Blanchard and Wyplosz (1981), Taylor (1979a) and Holly and Zarrop (1983). It is recognized by these authors that the parameters of these equations will change as regimes change, but it is argued that the major impact of regime change will be felt in the expectations variables, while that on the parameters themselves, except for quite violent regime change, may be of second order importance. Nevertheless, these models have increasingly attempted to introduce 'micro-founded' equations, thereby getting closer to deep structure. This approach has tended to dominate hitherto, practical policy evaluation mainly being done using models of this type, with on the face of it reasonable success in the past decade in controlling both inflation and output fluctuations; we discuss the results in the next section.

We end this section, therefore, in a cautious vein: policy evaluation is certainly difficult, but various researches are in hand which may offer scope for better evaluation in the future.

EVALUATING POLICY IN NEW KEYNESIAN MODELS WITH OVERLAPPING WAGE/PRICE CONTRACTS

In practice many modellers in the 1990s work with overlapping contract models of the New Keynesian type which we discussed in chapter 4. As we have seen these models exhibit a high degree of nominal rigidity which enables monetary policy to be effective in stabilizing the economy.

A simple framework for looking at this work is the New Keynesian model of chapter 4, discussed earlier in this chapter (equation 55), together with the assumption that the government or central bank controls aggregate demand through monetary policy. In that set-up, let us ignore the time-inconsistency issue, as we argued was appropriate at the end of chapter 5; we will assume that there is some mechanism, such as that of popular disapproval, restraining the government from trying to exploit the Phillips Curve by systematically stimulating the economy beyond its natural rate. So the government's actions are restricted to varying policy in response to shocks to the economy, as summarised in the Phillips curve shock (remembering this can reflect the whole menu of supply and demand shocks through intertemporal substitution or exchange rate effects on the supply of labour and output). Since this set-up is known, people will also know the rule, and hence will form their inflation expectations knowing it will hold; therefore inflation expectations over the long term are equal to the inflation target, while in the short term they depend on the speed with which inflation converges on the target, as determined by the parameters of the model including policy. Our New Keynesian supply curve is:

$$y_t = \sigma(p_t - 0.5[E_{t-1}p_t + E_{t-2}p_t]) + \gamma y_{t-1} + u_t \tag{10}$$

where y_t is the log deviation from the natural rate (i.e. $y^* = 0$).

In practice of course models used for policy evaluation are more complicated than this. But this simple model is sufficient to illustrate the nature of the choices available. What emerges is a trade-off between the variability of inflation and the variability of output; not of course between the average levels of output and inflation between which there is no (long-run) trade-off — the average level of output is its natural rate and the average level of inflation is its target value, varying which will of course make no difference to output. But inflation changes can accommodate shocks to some degree and so dampen down their effect on output; this reduces output variation at the cost of raising inflation variation.

We saw in chapter 5 that if there is a social welfare function which includes the squared variations in inflation and output around their target and natural rate respectively then expected social welfare will depend on the variances of inflation and output. The optimal feedback response of inflation to the shock (which we assume is held to for as long as the model prevails) will then as we saw depend on the degree of dislike of output variation and on the slope of the Phillips Curve. The flatter the slope (the higher c) the less the response required; the greater the dislike of output variation (α) the higher the response.

One can interpret this social welfare function — which is certainly widely used by central banks in practice — as reflecting on the one hand the individual agent's dislike of inflation uncertainty (in creating consumption uncertainty which needs then to be insured at some cost) and on the other hand the social cost of unemployment variation, as discussed above in chapter 5. Various efforts have been made to produce such micro-based justifications (e.g. Rotemberg and Woodford (1998), Woodford (1998), and Minford, Nowell and Webb (1999)). If one uses this interpretation it follows that reducing the extent of the unemployment benefit subsidy to unemployment would reduce the extent of the distortion from unemployment variation and so reduce the size of α and the need for activist monetary accommodation. However, few societies appear to have reached this situation; and the consensus among policymakers is that monetary policy ought to stabilize output fairly actively. Witness for example the behaviour in 1997-8 of the Federal Reserve Board in response to the Asian Crisis or that of the Bank of England's

Monetary Policy Committee to the threat of recession in autumn 1998; in both cases quite sharp cuts in interest rates were made in order to avert recession.

In recent policy therefore, as dominated by this New Keynesian framework, active feedback monetary response has been prevalent. To implement this response central banks have favoured using interest rate rather than money supply rules. Demand for broad money functions have proved unstable in the world of deregulated banking that has generally prevailed in the 1980s and 1990s; while narrow money demand functions, though immune to deregulation, have proved vulnerable to technological change (credit cards and cash machines), to movement in the black economy, and to increasing use of home notes in foreign economies (e.g. 'dollarization' in Israel and Russia). As the interpretation of money supply movements became more uncertain central banks have relied increasingly on direct evaluation of economic conditions and a response via interest rates (this implies some equivalent money supply response — but evaluating it is of course uncertain when demand functions are unstable).

In chapter 5 (and the appendix to chapter 11, on dynamic programming) we derive the optimal response of inflation to the Phillips curve shock on the assumption that this can be exactly delivered by interest rate movements; the optimal response to other shocks is nil on this assumption. In practice however the shocks cannot be observed and interest rate policy cannot deliver an exact inflation outcome; and so a choice must be made between rules (of reasonable simplicity) that respond to observable variables, usually inflation and output themselves. This choice can be made by embedding these rules in a model of the economy and checking the resulting variances of output and inflation (either analytically or by stochastic simulation).To see what sort of interest rate response would be optimal on this basis, assume that aggregate demand depends on real interest rates (an IS curve expressed in nominal terms; using interest rates bypasses the LM curve):

$$p_t + y_t = -\beta r_t \tag{11}$$

where p_t is in log deviations from the (moving) price level target and r_t is in deviations from the natural real rate of interest.

We use prices in place of inflation and a moving price level target in place of an inflation target as this simplifies our exposition. (To re-express policy in terms of inflation targeting would introduce more complicated dynamics.)

We now write the interest rate rule as:

$$r_t = \mu_p p_{t-1} + \mu_y y_{t-1} \tag{12}$$

(To turn this rule into one for nominal interest rates one simply adds in the expected inflation rate.) We can set the solution up using the Muth method, with $p_t = \sum_{i=0}^{\infty} q_i u_{t-i}$, by substituting from (10) and (12) into (11) for y_t and r_t, to obtain

$$(1+\beta\mu_y L)([1+\sigma q_0]u_t + 0.5\sigma q_1 u_{t-1}) + (1-\gamma L)(1+\beta\mu_p L)\sum_{i=0}^{\infty} q_i u_{t-i} = 0 \quad (13)$$

Collecting terms then gives us:

$$(u_t) \qquad q_0 = \frac{1}{1+\sigma} \quad (14)$$

$$(u_{t-1}) \qquad q_1 = \frac{\beta(\mu_p - \mu_y - \gamma)}{(1+\sigma)(1+0.5\sigma)} \quad (15)$$

$$(u_{t-2}) \qquad q_2 = -q_1(0.5\beta\mu_y\sigma + \beta\mu_p - \gamma) + (\gamma\beta\mu_p)q_0 \quad (16)$$

$$(u_{t-i},\ i \geqslant 3) \qquad q_i = -(\beta\mu_p - \gamma)q_{i-1} + (\gamma\beta\mu_p)q_{i-2} \quad (17)$$

Now turn to the variance of output. Because

$$y_t = \frac{(1+\sigma q_0)u_t + 0.5q_1 u_{t-1}}{1-\gamma L} = (1+\sigma q_0)u_t + \sum_{i=1}^{\infty}(1+\sigma q_0 + \frac{0.5q_1}{\gamma})\gamma^i u_{t-i} \quad (18)$$

the variance of output is

$$vary_t = \{(1+\sigma q_0)^2 + (1+\sigma q_0 + \frac{0.5q_1}{\gamma})^2 \frac{\gamma^2}{1-\gamma^2}\}\sigma_u^2 \quad (19)$$

By contrast the variance of prices is:

$$varp_t = \sum_{i=0}^{\infty} q_i^2 \sigma_u^2 \quad (20)$$

Policy cannot affect q; but it does affect all other q_i. The optimal set of these for minimising $varp_t$ are $q_i = 0 (i \geqslant 1)$. The optimal set for minimising $vary_t$ is $(1+\sigma q_0 + \frac{0.5q_1}{\gamma}) = 0$, that is $q_1 = \frac{-\gamma}{0.5(1+\sigma)}$, implying that

$$\mu_y = \mu_p - \gamma + \frac{\gamma(1+0.5\sigma)}{0.5\beta} \quad (21)$$

whereas for $q_1 = 0$ we must have

$$\mu_y = \mu_p - \gamma \tag{22}$$

Hence there is a trade-off between $vary_t$ and $varp_t$, involving the choice of q_1. This is a general feature of these models (Taylor, 1999; Clarida, Gali and Gertler, 1999) in respect of the Phillips Curve shock, u_t. Plainly, in such models r_t should aim to offset any 'pure' demand shocks (i.e. any shock to equation 11) entirely, since they must add to the variances of either prices or output or both; however, in practice matters are not so simple since as we have seen demand shocks will also enter u_t (via supply or cost effects induced by interest rates or exchange rates). So the trade-off between the two variances is pervasive across most relevant shocks and should therefore show up in stochastic simulations of models for a complete set of shocks. One can see that a society that cared a lot about output fluctuation would set a $\mu_y$close to (21) and then find a μ_p that minimised q_i^2 $(i \geqslant 2)$ subject to this. Clearly the closeness of μ_y to (21) would depend on how much society cared about output variability.

Rather than find the optimal μs for this particular, illustrative and highly simplified model, we report on findings from full models about the results of stochastic simulations with interest rate rules of the form of (12). Rules of this type have been called Taylor rules after John Taylor who first propagated them having completed a spell on the US Council of Economic Advisers, where he felt the need to come up with a 'monetarist' rule that did not rely on targeting the money supply given its instability — the original suggestion for such rules was by Henderson and McKibbin (1993). Econometric work has found that rules of this type fit central bank behaviour quite well; this does not necessarily mean that they actually adopted these rules but rather that whatever rule they did adopt produces interest rate behaviour of this sort (Minford et al. (2001), show that a wide variety of monetary rules can produce an appearance of a Taylor rule). Given that economic behaviour varies with the policy regime, we should be rather cautious in translating results for Taylor Rules into equivalent results say for money supply rules. But we will assume in what follows that having a coefficient on output in a Taylor rule is qualitatively at least similar to having a feedback coefficient on output in a money supply rule.

In a recent article Taylor (1999) compared various parameterizations of such rules within a variety of econometric models of different economies (containing many complexities omitted here but obeying the basic logic of our simple model) and concluded that a quite simple rule, $i_t = 1.5\pi_t + 0.5y_t + i_0$, did best out of those investigated. His results show that if the lagged interest rate is included with a coefficient of unity (so

Standard deviations* of	Inflation	Output	Interest Rate
Output Coefficient = 0.5	2.13	1.94	2.82
Output Coefficient = 1.0	2.16	1.63	3.03

*average across nine models; % p.a. for inflation and interest rate; % for output.

Table 6.1: Average behaviour of rules of nine models

that it is the change of the interest rate that reacts to output and inflation) then in models without rational expectations the results are often unstable; this is because the interest rate keeps on rising in response to a stubborn inflation shock and since expectations of the future effect on inflation fall only slowly, interest rates overreact. It is possible to reduce the variance of output by increasing the coefficient on output to 1.0 say. But the cost is a slightly higher variance of inflation and a much higher variance of interest rates. The average behaviour with these two rules across all the nine models examined is shown in Table 6.1

There is therefore some evidence of a trade-off in estimated models between output and inflation variability; also between output and interest rate (instrument) variability, the latter naturally rising as rules are more 'activist' with regard to stabilising the business cycle (i.e. with a higher output coefficient). Different central banks adopt varying positions along these trade-offs, with the more 'conservative' ones adopting lower output coefficients; during 2000 Mr. Wim Duisenberg, the chairman of the new European Central Bank (ECB), for example, stated that the ECB would not be 'activist'. However, it is too early to say whether its policies will adhere closely to this position in practice.

During the 1990s central bank practice, following this sort of behaviour — whatever its degree of activism —, appears also to have been successful, both in curbing inflation and in preventing large swings in economic activity, at least in the Anglo-Saxon world and in Europe. Japan has had an unhappy decade of persistent recession after the 'bubble-bursting' monetary squeeze at its start and the Asian Crisis of 1997 caused a massive recession in Asia; but these developments were limited in their impact on the rest of the OECD and much of the credit for that seems to be due to effective monetary policy.

CALVO CONTRACTS

A popular device for modelling long-term nominal contracts is due to Calvo (1983). Price-setters (or wage-setters, analysed analogously) operate under imperfect competition where if prices were flexible they would be continuously set as a mark-up on marginal cost. They are assumed to face a menu cost of changing their price: this takes the form of a lump sum cost which acts as a threshold. If some unexpected shock to costs exceeds this threshold, they will change their price and set it to the newly expected marginal cost. It is assumed that there is a constant probability, $1-\xi$, of such a shock for each (identical) price-setter. The expected losses at $t=0$ of the hth price-setter can be written:

$$\sum_{t=0}^{\infty} E_0 \beta^t [p_t^h - (1+m)c_t^h]^2 \tag{23}$$

where m is the mark-up and c is the marginal cost.

The first-order condition with respect to the decision to set his price at $\widetilde{p}_0^h$ then implies:

$$\widetilde{p}_0^h = (1+m)(1-\beta\xi)\sum_{t=0}^{\infty}(\beta\xi)^t E_0 c_t^h \tag{24}$$

In other words the reset price is equal to a weighted average of all future expected marginal costs plus the mark-up. This expression is justified as follows. Consider the losses associated with the decision to set $\widetilde{p}_0^h$. For $t=0$, $\widetilde{p}_0^h$ can be freely set and so the loss is $[\widetilde{p}_0^h-(1+m)c_0^h]^2$. At $t=1$ there is a ξ chance of being unable to change his prices from $\widetilde{p}_0^h$ and a $1-\xi$ chance of being able to reset it, in which case any loss is not to do with today's decision; hence the expected loss at $t=1$, due to today's decision, is $\beta\xi[\widetilde{p}_0^h-(1+m)E_0c_1^h]^2$. Similarly at $t=2$, there is a ξ^2 chance of being unable to change it from $\widetilde{p}_0^h$ in either $t=1$ or $t=2$; there is a $(1-\xi)^2$ of being able to change it in both periods, a $\xi(1-\xi)$ chance of changing it in $t=1$ but not in $t=2$, and similarly of not changing it in $t=1$ but doing so in $t=2$. In all these last theree cases nothing decided for $t=0$ affects the losses which are due to decisions taken in later periods. So the expected loss at $t=2$ due to the decision at $t=0$ is $\beta^2\xi^2[\widetilde{p}_0^h-(1+m)E_0c_2^h]^2$. Analogously at $t=i$ it is $\beta^i\xi^i[\widetilde{p}_0^h-(1+m)E_0c_i^h]^2$. Equation (23) will only contain these terms in $\widetilde{p}_0^h$ in other words. So differentiating it with respect to $\widetilde{p}_0^h$ yields the first-order condition above. In general at time t the hth's agent's decision is therefore:

$$\widetilde{p}_t^h = (1+m)(1-\beta\xi)\sum_{i=0}^{\infty}(\beta\xi)^i E_t c_{t+i}^h \tag{25}$$

Across the population $1-\xi$ will on average reset their prices in exactly the same way, and ξ will retain last period's price, hence $\widetilde{p}_t^h=\widetilde{p}_t$, $E_t c_{t+i}^h = E_t c_{t+i}$ and

$$p_t - p_{t-1} = (1-\xi)(\widetilde{p}_t - p_{t-1}) \tag{26}$$

Now let $(1-m)E_t c_{t+i} = \delta E_t(y_{t+i} - y^*_{t+i})$, that is marginal costs are a rising function of output (and approximately linear in the region of y^*_t, the natural rate of output). Then we can rewrite (26) as:

$$\pi_t = p_t - p_{t-1} = \frac{(1-\xi)(1-\beta\xi)\delta(y_t - y^*_t)}{1-\beta\xi B^{-1}} - (1-\xi)p_{t-1} \tag{27}$$

where B^{-1} is the forward operator, leading the variable but not the date of expectation. Hence, multiplying through by the expression in the forward operator and collecting terms, we obtain

$$\pi_t = \frac{\beta\xi}{1-\beta\xi(1-\beta\xi)}E_t\pi_{t+1} + \frac{\delta(1-\xi)(1-\beta\xi)}{1-\beta\xi(1-\beta\xi)}(y_t - y^*_t) - \frac{(1-\xi)(1-\beta\xi)}{1-\beta\xi(1-\beta\xi)}p_{t-1} \tag{28}$$

This is the Calvo forward-looking Phillips Curve in which effectively the whole path of future output (marginal costs) affects current price rises.

In what we did above we implicitly assumed that price-setters were resetting their prices when expected general inflation was zero; the idea is that the shocks they face are relative, micro, shocks. If they expect rises in the general price level, then it is usual to argue that, being general, all would be expected to raise their own prices in line. It would be like a general relabelling or indexing of prices that would not incur the menu cost, which arises from getting out of line with others. Thus all authors (e.g. Erceg, Henderson and Levin, 2000; Christiano, Eichenbaum and Evans, 2002) add on an 'updating term' to allow for general expected (or 'core') inflation. Thus π_t is to be read as $\pi_t - \overline{\pi}_t$ where $\overline{\pi}_t$ is this expected general inflation rate. Strictly therefore we should write:

$$\pi_t = \overline{\pi}_t + \frac{\beta\xi}{1-\beta\xi(1-\beta\xi)}E_t(\pi_{t+1} - \overline{\pi}_{t+1}) + \frac{\delta(1-\xi)(1-\beta\xi)}{1-\beta\xi(1-\beta\xi)}(y_t - y^*_t) - \frac{(1-\beta\xi)(1-\xi)}{1-\beta\xi(1-\beta\xi)}(p_{t-1} - \overline{p}_{t-1}) \tag{29}$$

where the last term is usually neglected of small order. $\frac{\beta\xi}{1-\beta\xi(1-\beta\xi)}$ can be greater or less than one (so that the forward sums converge provided that $(y_t - y^*_t)$ converges at a rate γ such that $\gamma\frac{\beta\xi}{1-\beta\xi(1-\beta\xi)} \prec 1$).

$\overline{\pi}_t$ can be thought of as the rate of general indexation; for that reason some authors (e.g. Christiano et al., 2002) write it as π_{t-1} to allow for a lag in indexation; this introduces lagged inflation as well as expected future inflation into the Phillips Curve. It must be confessed however that there is some confusion on this point; clearly, for example, if $\overline{\pi}_t = E_t\pi_t = \pi_t$ and $E_t\overline{\pi}_{t+1} = E_t\pi_{t+1}$, the relationship dissolves. If we introduced an information lag, so that $\overline{\pi}_t = E_{t-1}\pi_t$, then it becomes the standard surprise inflation Phillips Curve of Lucas, Sargent and Wallace discussed *passim* in earlier chapters.

Equation (28) is typically used in New Keynesian models with an IS curve and an interest-rate-setting rule, so that the causation runs from the interest rate to output and so to inflation; notice that the rule must drive output back to y^* faster than $\frac{\beta\xi}{1-\beta\xi}$ to avoid inflation divergence. Rotemberg and Woodford (1999) have argued in favour of 'super-inertial' interest rate rules of the form:

$$r_t = \frac{1}{\lambda}r_{t-1} + a(y_t - y_t^*) + b(\pi_t - \pi^*) \tag{30}$$

where $\lambda \prec 1$. The reason is that only very small reactions of interest rates are required to stabilise output and inflation because these reactions are not only very long-lasting but also diverge so that output and inflation are driven rapidly back to their targets by the prospect of such interest rate paths. However, as we saw above, with backward-looking influences on behaviour, such super-inertia creates possible instability.

Calvo-style Phillips Curves have a form that is analytically tractable but their interpretation in the context of ongoing inflation is problematic. When underlying inflation is zero, one can under certain assumptions write the representative agent's welfare as a linear combination of the variance of inflation (which creates relative price distortions disturbing consumption) and the variance of the output gap (which disturbs employment and so leisure) — e.g. Gali and Monacelli (2002). This then justifies the standard approach to optimal monetary policy which involves trading off the variance of inflation and the output gap, in the manner used in earlier sections.

DOES THE LUCAS CRITIQUE AFFECT NEW KEYNESIAN (TAYLOR) RULES?

However, even if this monetary policy devised using New Keynesian methods has apparently been successful, we must ask whether this success is stable or could be undermined by some parameter shift of the sort implied by the Lucas Critique. For the models assume that the parameters (of Phillips and IS curves) remain constant even though the monetary regime is being altered towards an optimum.

We saw in the first section of this chapter that the Phillips curve slope in particular depended on the variability of inflation. The more activist the monetary policy, the higher this variability; and hence the the steeper the Phillips Curve (the lower σ). This in turn implied that activism should be more moderate than implied with a fixed slope of the Phillips Curve. (In other words excess activism would actually, by steepening the Phillips Curve, make the combined variability of inflation and output worse.) The calculations reported by John Taylor do not take account of this extra loop of effect on the economy's behaviour; and we may reasonably expect, given this argument, that the rules understate the response to inflation (i.e. interest rates should keep inflation closer to target instead and not be so influenced by output fluctuation).

This line of thinking might also lead us to consider other aspects of monetary policy that could affect the slope of the Phillips Curve. In a recent paper Minford, Nowell and Webb (1999) pointed out that the persistence of shocks to the price level within the period of overlapping contracts has the effect of raising the variance of real wages within the contract period — because the more persistent the shock the more are contracted nominal wages disturbed from their intended average level over the contract period. This persistence could be expected to produce a high level of indexation which would greatly steepen the Phillips Curve; there is strong evidence of widespread indexation or equivalent practices since the 1970s with no real sign of any reduction during the low-inflation 1990s. In terms of quarterly monetary policy it implies that central banks should pay a great deal of attention to keeping prices on average in the contract period close to the trajectory expected — effectively targeting the price level not the inflation rate. A rule that targets inflation (or indeed the growth rate of the money supply) implies that the price level will be non-stationary (i.e. has an infinite variance in the long run). Such total long-run uncertainty must undoubtedly carry economic costs.

What these, and no doubt other related issues of parameter variation, indicate is that the optimization of monetary policy is a still more complicated matter than these New Keynesian methods imply. The classical economists set great store by the certainty of the price level in both the short and long run, in order to underpin the efficiency of the market price signalling process; they put no emphasis on activist monetary policy, believing that a constancy of prices (and they thought by implication the money supply) would generate sufficiently stabilizing output behaviour by the private sector. Since Keynes monetary policy has increasingly been pressed into service to stabilize output. What we have yet to work out is how great a conflict there is between these two aspirations for monetary policy.

CONCLUSIONS

In this chapter we accepted that monetary policy could effectively stabilize output fluctuations and also that there was at least in principle a case for so using it, at least to some degree; we thus turned to a consideration of what that degree might be in practice and how to calculate the appropriate rule of behaviour, whether for interest rates or for the money supply. We began by setting out the key practical problem of such calculations: Lucas' critique of macro models whose parameters would shift in response to changing monetary rules. Clearly to calculate the appropriate response we must know the parameters of the model that will occur under every relevant monetary rule; this means in effect that we must know the parameters of the underlying structural model of the economy (i.e. the one with the parameters that will not shift in response to a changing environment). From that model — even if we do not use it directly — we can work out what will happen to the parameters of any other model that we do use directly. Just relying on estimated reduced form models would be insufficient because we would know they must change with changing monetary rules as the expectations implicit in them changed. Unfortunately the problem of parameter shift runs deep: IS/LM/Phillips Curve models with rational expectations solved explicitly are still vulnerable because their supply and demand parameters are those of optimising behaviour and with different rules the optimal behaviour changes. We discussed three main approaches to the problem. First, to build new models whose parameters were those of tastes and technology (presumably immune to policy change); this is empirically difficult because these parameters can only be observed indirectly. Second, to abandon any pretence of structural models by estimating time-series models whose parameters are easily recoverable; and to design policy rules that are robust to any possible variations in these parameters. The problem here is that we have little way of knowing how big these parameter variations might be in the absence of a structural model to predict them. Third, to assume that IS/LM/Phillips Curve models' parameters (with overlapping New Keynesian contracts) are in practice reasonably immune to relevant variations in monetary rules. Much practical work has been done with such models to find optimal interest rate (Taylor) rules; and this work has been very influential on central bank practice with apparently successful results in the 1990s. The question with which we concluded was whether these rules were in spite of these hopes vulnerable to Lucas' critique (given the extent of indexation and equivalent practices that could steepen the Phillips Curve); at this stage we offer a guarded 'yes' to this question (the evidence also suggests that indexation or equivalent practices are extremely widespread) and suggest that future work may give a stronger role to price level stability.

7

Fiscal Policy and the government budget constraint

Up to now we have discussed fiscal policy as an element of demand management, separate from monetary policy and useable both as an automatic stabiliser and for feedback policy. However, the main focus of our discussion of stabilization policy has been on monetary policy, which in practice has been almost exclusively the instrument governments have used for this purpose. In this chapter we consider the role of and contraints on fiscal policy in more detail. We start with accounting, the implications of the government budget constraint; then go on to various models of how fiscal policy affects the economy; finally we turn to policy implications.

GOVERNMENT SOLVENCY AND THE GOVERNMENT BUDGET CONSTRAINT

The first question we must ask about government tax, any resources it raises by printing money with consequent inflation (its 'seigniorage'), its spending and its borrowing is: what are the limits on a government's actions? These limits are implied by its budget constraint, which relates these elements. It can conveniently be thought of as the borrowing required to finance the budget deficit, the gap between spending, inclusive of debt interest, and tax plus seigniorage. Sometimes it is useful to refer to the 'primary' deficit which is spending *excluding* debt interest, less tax. To keep the exposition as simple as possible we will assume that all debt is one-period indexed bonds, the number of which we denote by b_t: such a bond is a promise to pay (next period, $t+1$) £1 plus the rate of inflation and a real rate of interest, r_t; hence its face value today is always £1. Later we will discuss complexities introduced by nominal bonds.

Let us define the budget constraint then as:

$$b_{t+1} - b_t = g_{t+1} - \tau_{t+1} + r_t b_t - \frac{H_{t+1} - H_t}{P_{t+1}} = d_{t+1} + r_t b_t \qquad (1)$$

where d_t is the primary deficit (in real terms); g_t, τ_t are respectively real government spending excluding debt interest and real taxation; and H_t is the monetary base (government's own monetary liabilities) and so the real value of its increase is the seigniorage. This equation plainly tells us how debt will accumulate as the government runs primary deficits . We can project it into the future and track out the implications of such policies for debt.

However, matters do not end there since plainly debt must eventually be paid off. 'Eventually' here could in practice mean at a future date which is constantly postponed — in other words, the government does not actually pay it off by any particular date because it continually persuades its creditors to take more debt ('rolling it over'). Thus we can let the date of repayment be infinitely far in the future; nevertheless we assume that that day is some time in the future. We can put this another way: if a government is seen to be in a position where it will never pay its debts and so will have to default, then it will be violating the terms of its debt and so of its budget constraint: it will be insolvent. We will assume that the government does not behave in this way. (We will deal later with what happens if it does and a default is expected.)

On this assumption the government's outstanding debt defines the limits on its future deficits. It can only issue debt that is 'backed' by future primary surpluses exactly sufficient to pay it off with its interest. If its debt is so backed, then it is said to be solvent. Solvency is guaranteed if the government budget constraint is met at all times.

This can be seen by repeated forward substitution for b_{t+i} in (1); we will assume a constant real interest rate, r. So

$$b_t = \frac{s_{t+1} + b_{t+1}}{1+r} \qquad (2)$$

where s_t is the primary surplus. Continuing to substitute for b_{t+i} we obtain:

$$b_t = \sum_{i=1}^{N} \frac{s_{t+i}}{(1+r)^i} + \frac{b_{t+N}}{(1+r)^N} \qquad (3)$$

If we now let N go to infinity and impose the condition that the debt will eventually be paid off (which we interpret as above: that the government may roll over its debts but is expected not to default, that is to be in a position to pay them off some time), then the last term goes to zero and we obtain:

$$b_t = \sum_{i=1}^{\infty} \frac{s_{t+i}}{(1+r)^i} \tag{4}$$

which is the solvency condition.

In fact, we note from (3) that the condition for the remainder term to go to zero is weaker than that debt should be totally paid off at some (indefinite) date: it is merely that real debt should grow less rapidly than the real rate of interest. This shows a peculiarity of infinite time: that the government not only need never pay off its debts but may even raise its debt, provided the growth rate does not exceed the rate of interest. Buiter (1999) has called this the great 'puzzle' of fiscal arithmetic. Plainly if the economy has a finite life then when it ends debts must be paid off: everyone will wish to use up their wealth in consumption (or transfer it to another economy) before the end. The same applies if the economy has a finite life whose end is constantly postponed.

In fact there is some difficulty in assuming the economy comes to an end; for behaviour being forward-looking, those of our theories that have people acting in the interests partly of their descendants would fail were the economy to stop — the meaning attached by people to life's purposes would be drained away, as would the incentive to maintain any of society's institutions or infrastructure. Our assumption is that people act as if they only care about themselves, in which case they would simply consume all they have before the economy's and their end; implying that the government must also pay off its debt, since people will call it in and consume it. However, law and order (which rely on social institutions being respected) might also break down. The end of the economy is effectively the end of its inhabitants' world; imagining how people would behave if the world were to end is hard, if not meaningless (an amusing attempt is in Douglas Adams, 1978, 'The restaurant at the end of the universe' where the whole point is that people cannot really imagine the end).

This seems to force us to consider time which is truly infinite — that is, where the economy never stops. In this situation how can we interpret the constraint that the government must simply have its debt grow at less than the rate of interest? Clearly it may be asked to pay it off (unlike money, where it knows it will never be asked to redeem its fiat currency). Anyone redeeming state debt will force the government to sell the debt to someone else: solvency then requires that when resold it has a present value equal to its face value (at least equal — implicitly we assume that if its present value was greater, then taxes would be cut or spending raised, in effect redistributing the excess back to the citizens.) On reflection, this is no more troublesome as a way of avluing government paper than the way we value say private equity (the present value of future dividends).

Government debt in other words is sold at a price that reflects its 'value' that is, its discounted stream of primary surpluses, its cash flow available for paying interest and repayment on the debt. The transversality condition on b_{t+N} forces exactly this condition on that future debt.

It may be useful to illustrate this point with an example. Consider three cases.

First, let debt be increasing faster than the rate of interest. By definition:

$$\Delta b_t = rb_{t-1} - s_t \tag{5}$$

Because $\frac{\Delta b_t}{b_{t-1}} > r$, s_t must be negative. This is the case of Ponzi finance, where debt is run up to pay off interest and pay for extra net spending.

Suppose this situation prevails from time $t+N+1$, where the remainder term of (7.3) cuts in, and let s be constant and negative. Then the present value of b_{t+N} at time $t+N$ can be written by discounting future surpluses as:

$$\text{p.v.of } b_{t+N} = s[\frac{1}{1+r} + ... + \frac{1}{(1+r)^{N+1}} + ...] = \frac{s}{r} \tag{6}$$

Plainly, s being negative the debt will be valueless.

More generally, let debt be growing at the constant rate $g(> r)$, so that $\frac{\Delta b_t}{b_{t-1}} = r - \frac{s_t}{b_{t-1}} = g$ and thus $\frac{s_t}{b_{t-1}} = -(g-r)$ is constant, implying that primary surpluses are both negative and also growing at the same rate as debt, g.

Then the present value of b_{t+N} becomes:

$$\begin{aligned}\text{p.v.of } b_{t+N} &= \frac{s_{t+N+1}}{b_{t+N}}\frac{b_{t+N}}{1+r} + \frac{s_{t+N+2}}{b_{t+N+1}}\frac{b_{t+N+1}}{(1+r)^2} + ... \\ &= b_{t+N}[-(g-r)][\frac{1}{1+r} + \\ &\quad \frac{1+g}{(1+r)^2} + \frac{(1+g)^2}{(1+r)^3} + ...] \\ &= -\frac{(g-r)}{1+g} b_{t+N} \sum_{i=1}^{\infty} \frac{(1+g)^i}{(1+r)^i} = -\infty \end{aligned} \tag{7}$$

The present value of the government's future cash flow in (6) is negative and in (7) is infinitely negative; in both cases its debt at $t+N$,

b_{t+N}, is valueless. In other words it will be impossible to issue debt at $t+N+1$, b_{t+N+1}, to pay off b_{t+N}; it follows that b_{t+N} itself could not have been issued, given this was known. And so on, back down the chain to the present time, t. In period t the government will be unable to issue any more debt, b_{t+1}, and will therefore default on its current debt, b_t.

Secondly, consider the case where $g = r$. Then (7) equals 0. There are neither primary deficits or surpluses from $t + N$.

The accumulated debt, b_{t+N}, has no value, as there is no future cash flow to service it; hence there is also insufficient cash flow from t onwards to pay off the current debt, b_t. The government is not therefore solvent; it will again be unable to issue new debt and will default on b_t.

Thirdly and finally, consider the case where $g < r$. Then (7) becomes finite and equal to b_{t+N}, in other words its face value. Hence the present value at t of future surpluses from $t + N + 1$ onwards in this case is equal to that of the debt which will have been accumulated up to that point by previous deficits, b_{t+N}. The government's outstanding debt is therefore 'backed': the government could pay off its debt at any time (by just surrendering its cash flow to creditors). The essential point is that with $g < r$, there is a primary surplus from $t + N + 1$ which starts equal to $(r - g)b_{t+N}$ and grows at the same rate, g, as debt (hence in effect remaining equal to this growing value).

The government's solvency or transversality condition can therefore be seen to be the commonsense condition that at all times the debt must be backed by primary surpluses with a present value equal to the debt's face value.

If this were not to be satisfied then the market would react by marking the debt's price below face value. Call this price D_t. At all points of time this price will move to make the market value of government debt equal to its present value. Hence we can write the price equation as:

$$D_t = \frac{\sum_{i=1}^{\infty} \frac{s_{t+i}}{(1+r)^i}}{b_t} \tag{8}$$

What this means is that a government can issue debt which is not fully backed by its future policies but only at a price that reflects this. We have been dealing with these policies as if they are fully known in advance. In this case when future policies change from those that are solvent to those that offer inadequate present value, there will be an immediate and sudden fall in the price of outstanding debt below its face value. In other words, if the government announces policies which mean it cannot pay its debts, it is as if it is 'writing down' the obligations (coupons etc.) on those debts; which of course implies that their present value, D_t (their price in the market-place) is correspondingly lowered.

In practice, when future surpluses are uncertain, we can think of r as the pure risk-free real interest rate and D_t as the risk discount factor (in present value) on expected future surpluses when valued at the risk-free rate (their 'face value' as we have put it). Thus equivalently we could value these expected future surpluses at the risk-free rate *plus* the risk-free premium implied by D_t, that is, at the market rate of interest on government bonds. This would be the bonds' market value. This is the usual situation in the bond market where a government is following an official policy of servicing its debt fully (no default). When a government defaults, that is announces it will no longer pay its interest and repayment obligations on old bonds in full, then D_t is marked in the market as an explicit discount (e.g. 20 pence in the pound) on the old bonds when valued at the rate of interest applicable to any fresh debt the government might raise.

THE 'FISCAL THEORY OF THE PRICE LEVEL'

In the past few years a surprising literature has grown up claiming that the (general consumer) price level, P_t, can be determined by fiscal policy — for example, Sims (1994) and Woodford (1995) and see Buiter (1999) for a critique on which this section draws. The claim can be seen quite simply by considering equation (4) above, the solvency condition. In that equation assume that instead of issuing indexed bonds the government has outstanding nominal bonds, so that $b_t = \frac{B_t}{P_t}$; let B_t be the market value of these bonds in money terms, computed by the normal discounting method given current interest rates (thus for example if bonds were perpetuities paying £1 each period their present value would be the number of these bonds divided by R_t the long-term rate of interest). Now suppose the government makes plans for future primary surpluses (on the RHS of the equation) whose present value is lower than the real value of the debt — this policy these authors call 'non-Ricardian' (if the government plans an RHS equal to debt's real value, a 'Ricardian' policy, then none of the following is relevant; the price level is then not claimed to be affected by fiscal policy — this use of 'Ricardian' has nothing to do with our later discussion of 'Ricardian Equivalence') . The Fiscal Theory states that prices will adjust to reduce the real value of the debt to equality with this RHS in order to produce solvency at the new real value; in effect this adjustment is a devaluation of the debt in response to fiscal policies that do not give it sufficient 'backing'.

One oddity of this theory is that it implies the price level will be overdetermined under the usual assumption that the government sets the level of the money supply as well as its rate of growth (seigniorage). To avoid this the theory assumes that the government sets the interest rate and not the level of the money supply; it does set seigniorage however (hence we can think of the interest rate path being set by a rule that targets the growth of the money supply or inflation and possibly real variables also). In a flexible-price economy this leaves the price level indeterminate because the choice of interest rate only sets real money balances demanded and cannot fix the split of these between nominal money supply and prices. Thus the Fiscal Theory claims that in such a situation the fiscal plans will set prices via (4) as above.

We can immediately note that this argument does not work in a model where prices are sticky (as in overlapping wage contracts) and there is some Phillips Curve mechanism translating excess demand into current inflation; for in this case an interest rate rule will fix the price level because it will fix excess demand, so inflation and so given past prices the current price level. So in this case, too, as in the flexible-price case where money supply is set, there would be overdetermination of the price level.

Overdetermination of a variable is fatal to a theory because it implies an internal inconsistency. Thus we can say at once that for many possible economies the Fiscal Theory of the price level will produce an incoherent theory overall. Furthermore, we can see from our discussion in the above section that the Fiscal Theory leaves out the way in which insolvency is dealt with by bond markets, viz. an adjustment of the bond price itself (D_t), not of the (goods) price level over which bond markets have no control.

Can we accept the Fiscal Theory as a possible mechanism for determining the price level where it is left indeterminate by an inadequately-specified interest rate rule? Not really, because the bond market, facing an equation (4) that was not satisfied, would have two degrees of freedom — either adjusting D_t or P_t. Hence either the price level or the bond price would be indeterminate. The model under these policies would thus be inadequate to explain a world in which both are seen to be determinate. Implictly Fiscal Theorists impose $D_t = 1$ to resolve this problem: but this is not merely arbitrary, it is at variance with the facts of debt downgrade (that is, a rise in the risk-premium added to the risk-free rate).

The Fiscal Theory therefore does not solve the problem of price level indeterminacy due to an inadequately-specified interest rate rule; such a world cannot therefore apply since we observe determinate prices. Under other assumptions it produces overdetermination of the price level — and thus must also be rejected. Buiter has called this theory a 'fallacy' — a correct assessment in our view if we interpret it in the bald way we have set it out above.

There is however a constructive way to think of the theory: as defining a particular combination of fiscal and monetary policies. By such a combination we mean a set of government plans that, given existing debts and projected real interest rates,

(a) set primary surpluses through spending and tax plans

(b) set the money supply (either directly or indirectly via plans for interest rates and prices).

We can distinguish four types of plan:

1. 'Classical' monetary policy leadership: the money supply is set implying a price level sequence (or alternatively an interest rate rule targeting inflation or the money growth rate from a given initial price level: this implies a determinate money supply sequence). Fiscal policy sets surpluses required to validate the real debts given this price sequence.

2. 'Sargent-Wallace fiscal leadership' (discussed further below under 'selfish overlapping generations'): here the *current* money supply is set to fix current prices but fiscal policy implies deficits which require a further inflation (and implied price level) sequence to validate the debt, so defining the future money supply sequence (or equivalent interest rate rule alternative as in type 1 policy).
Both policy types 1 and 2 are 'Ricardian' in terms of the fiscal theory.

3. 'Non-Ricardian' fiscal leadership: fiscal policy implies deficits and an inflation path is set via *future* money supply growth (or implicit future interest rate policy); to validate the debt a *current* price level rise is required, implying a current money supply jump (or equivalent current interest rate policy). Hence type 3 is to be understood as fiscal leadership like type 2, only whereas 2 fixes current prices via monetary policy, 3 fixes future inflation via monetary policy; thus in 2 future monetary policy must reflect fiscal requirements whereas in 3 current monetary policy must do so via a jump in the levels of both money and prices.
In none of the above cases does the government plan a default which leaves:

4. 'Planned default': here fiscal policy implies deficits while monetary policy fixes a price path that cannot validate the debt. The consequence is that the debt is automatically devalued by a fall in its

own price, D_t. This is the case of deliberate outright default without resort to 'indirect default' via price-devaluation (3) or inflation tax (2).

(1)–(4) is thus a classification of possible fiscal-monetary strategies. The 'fiscal theory' can then be thought of as drawing attention to 3. The essential point is that behind monetary policy lies a fiscal constraint: the government in the end has to plan how this will be met and the monetary (and hence price) consequences, present and future, are one part of this.

MODELS OF FISCAL EFFECT

The Ricardian equivalence model

In considering how fiscal policy might affect the economy, we begin with the model of 'Ricardian equivalence', named after Ricardo, who suggested the model without really believing it. If we assume that households have an infinite life, that all taxes are lump-sum (so creating no distortions), and that markets are complete (no unrealised opportunities for insurance or lending exist), then household consumption will depend, through intertemporal optimization, on the real rate of interest and permanent income. It follows that government spending plans will require a certain permanent level of taxation-plus-seigniorage in line with our previous discussion. Let us hold seigniorage constant as it is to do with monetary policy. If the government varies the pattern of taxation between periods, it will make no difference to this required permanent level. Cutting taxes in the present by TC_t for example will simply imply more taxes later, by an amount equal in present value to the tax cuts: for the extra debt issued will be rolled up with interest until future extra taxes are raised to pay it off, say in $t + N$. When they are, the accumulated extra debt will be equal to $TC_t(1 + r)^{t+N}$ and its present value will therefore be this discounted by the same interest rate, thus simply TC_t. This implies that households will treat the extra bonds they hold as not providing them with any extra wealth; thus government bonds are said to have no 'wealth effect'.

This is not to be confused with the idea that government spending changes have no effect: they will in principle. A higher permanent level of spending, the increase spread equally across periods, will raise permanent taxation and so lower permanent income by an equal amount. However, even Though they must reduce their permanent consumption by this amount, households may not reduce their spending in the current period by it; for example if interest rates are currently very high so that current consumption is low, they may reduce consumption proportionately in all periods given the pattern of interest rates, which in turn implies only a small absolute cut in the current period. Hence there would be a 'balanced budget multiplier' effect here, putting interest rates up still further.

If government spending is increased temporarily, with permanent spending held constant, then households will not change their consumption at given interest rates, so implying a rise in aggregate demand which will put upward pressure on interest rates. So the pattern of government spending over time will affect demand and the economy and the permanent level of government spending may also do so. The Ricardian Equivalence point applies to the pattern of taxation.

Its implications are that fiscal policy, interpreted as bond-financed tax changes, has no effect on the economy. Since there are also no distortions to be affected as taxes are speeded up or deferred through borrowing changes, it is a matter of supreme indifference in this model whether the government runs deficits or not in financing its spending plans. The only element in fiscal policy that matters is the level of those plans and their pattern over time. However it is usual to define fiscal policy to exclude this (considering it as allocative or strategic policy) and to refer to the extent of deficits: on this definition fiscal policy is irrelevant to aggregate demand.

Plainly too there is no relation in this model between deficits and monetary policy; a higher deficit requires no extra money supply growth to reduce the strain of financing it by bonds as there is no strain because private agents spend the same and so provide extra savings exactly equal to the required extra borrowing. Nor does a higher deficit increase interest rates, tightening monetary conditions (as in the IS-LM models we have used up to now). Monetary policy can be chosen entirely independently of fiscal policy (the only relation would be with the *permanent* level of taxes, which being lump-sum impose no distortions whereas seigniorage creates distortionary costs through money demand).The Ricardian assumptions can of course be relaxed, to dilute this harsh implication of a zero wealth effect. First, if taxes are not lump-sum, then a change in their intertemporal pattern will cause distortions, which will have real effects. We will discuss below (model (c)) how this alters the situation.

Secondly, we may appeal to various failures in the 'complete markets' assumption. These are not likely to have a large effect quantitatively; but one example is given in Box 7.1.

Box: 7.1

AN EXAMPLE OF MARKET INCOMPLETENESS: INCOMPLETE INSURANCE.

Suppose each individual faces considerable uncertainty about how much tax he and his heirs will pay; he does not know future income, future family size, the possibility of emigration, etc. Let us ignore emigration, in which case the change in tax prospects will have no impact on him; this no doubt affects only a minority. Let us assume that the tax system, as is typically the case in Western economies, is progressive; also assume that people are identical and risk averse. Suppose everyone receives the same transfer and holds it in the form of bonds. Then the individual will perceive his and his heirs' potential net income after tax as follows: at the one extreme they will be poor, receive the bond interest, but pay little tax, from there progressing with higher income towards the other extreme where they will be rich, receive the bond interest, and pay a lot of tax. If taxes are raised they will pay little more if poor, but significantly more if rich. This effect of a high covariance between tax and income is illustrated in figure 7.1 (for a simplified distribution with only 'poor' and 'rich' states of equal probability).
We are interested in the change in the 'certainty equivalent' of each man's future net income after tax, by this we mean the sure income that would yield him the same utility as the income possibilities he actually faces. Before the bond transfer and consequent future tax liability, let him have an expected net income of Ey, the average of his 'poor' and 'rich' states; the expected utility of this is EU_0 and the certainty equivalent is y_0. After the bond transfer, everyone's expected net income remains the same because the tax payments averaged across the two states must equal the bond interest receipts for the government's budget to balance in the future. But now each person will be better off than before when poor (he received the bond interest but his extra tax burden is less than this), and worse off than before when rich (his extra tax burden exceeds the bond interest); the arrowed line on figure 7.1 joins these two states, and, because of the insurance he receives in effect, his expected utility rises to EU_1 and his certainty equivalent income to y_1 so that the bond transfer

increases private wealth. Barro (1974) has further pointed out that, if the tax rate is raised when taxes go up to pay for the bond interest, then this increases the progressiveness of the tax system and this insurance effect is enhanced, as illustrated by the dashed line with higher expected utility EU_2 and certainty equivalent income y_2. Clearly this insurance effect of bond issue would be eliminated if the private insurance market already provided full insurance. However, this is unlikely because of incentive incompatibility (see e.g. Hart, 1983); full insurance gives the insured person an incentive to lie about his poverty or fraudulently to avoid trying to be rich.

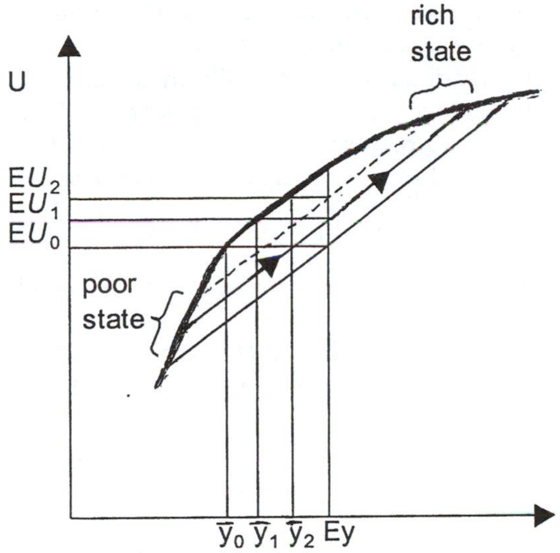

Figure 7.1: Certainty equivalent and expected net income after tax

Thirdly, we may drop the assumption of infinite life; this in practice is the most important relaxation. Plainly current households' members do not live for ever. But Barro (1974) has shown in a model of overlapping generations that, if each person leaves a bequest, then everyone acts as if he is infinitely lived. The reason is that the transfer he receives diminishes the utility of his heirs while raising his current resources. Yet he has already decided, having left them a bequest, that his optimal course is to give them their previous utility at the expense of his current resources; therefore he will raise his bequest in order to offset the government's action, in effect saving the whole of the transfer for his heirs. The transfer, by not changing his opportunity set, leaves his net wealth and behaviour unchanged.

If he has not planned a bequest, then the level of utility he desires for his heirs cannot be established; the transfer may or may not push their utility below his desired level. Hence we cannot establish how much, if at all, he will offset the transfer by saving.

It is of interest that the lack of bequests might not matter, because a 'bequest' could be negative (parents could receive transfers from their children) as well as positive, a continuous variable; hence the government transfer would always be offset. What matters is that one generation cares about the other, so that the government's redistribution from one to the other is offset (accidental bequests, e.g. because death comes unexpectedly early, are beside the point).

Barro's argument can be shown formally by simply setting out each generation's lifetime budget constraint. Suppose first of all that there is no government borrowing or taxation; then generation 1 has a life-time budget constraint viewed at $t+1$ (when this generation is old) of

$$y^1_{t+1} + y^1_t(1+r) = c^1_{t+1} + c^1_t(1+r) + q^1_{t+1} \tag{9}$$

where q^1_{t+1} is its bequest to generation 2, made at the end of $t+1$ period; $y =$ income, $c =$consumption, both in real terms, and r is the real rate of interest (assumed constant over time in this base-case situation). Superscripts denote the generation. Generation 2's lifetime budget constraint viewed from period $t+1$ is:

$$\frac{y^2_{t+2}}{1+r} + y^2_{t+1} + q^1_{t+1} = \frac{c^2_{t+2}}{1+r} + c^2_{t+1} + \frac{q^2_{t+2}}{1+r} \tag{10}$$

Now let the government transfer the amount b_t in t to generation 1, then young, and announce the plan to tax generation 2 by $T^2_{t+1} = b_t(1+r)$ when it is young, in $t+1$, meanwhile offering b_t bonds at t to the loan market. Then the two generations' constraints become:
(gen. 1)

$$y^1_{t+1} + y^1_t(1+r) + b_t(1+r) = c^1_{t+1} + c^1_t(1+r) + q^1_{t+1} \tag{11}$$

(gen. 2)

$$\frac{y^2_{t+2}}{1+r} + y^2_{t+1} + q^1_{t+1} - b_t(1+r) = \frac{c^2_{t+2}}{1+r} + c^2_{t+1} + \frac{q^2_{t+2}}{1+r} \tag{12}$$

If generation 1 had already optimally planned a bequest designed to give generation 2 a certain lifetime consumption possibility while leaving itself with a certain other one, then the government's action, if not offset somehow, will raise its own consumption while reducing that of generation 2, which is by implication suboptimal. However, if generation 1 raises its bequest exactly by the amount of the transfer grossed up by interest received from putting it into savings, then both generations will be exactly as well off as it originally planned; hence the transfer is saved by generation 1, which thereby buys the bonds the government offers.

The Model of Selfish Overlapping generations: Unpleasant Monetarist Arithmetic

Whether generations are linked with each other in Barro's sense is an empirical matter. It may vary across and within societies. It seems reasonable to explore a model which is at the other end of the spectrum from the Ricardian and assumes each generation cares only about itself. Such a model is for example used by Sargent and Wallace (1981) in a paper designed to investigate the upper limit of deficits when money supply growth is being held down by 'monetarist' policies.

In their overlapping-generations (OLG) model, debt is held by the young, to be redeemed from them when old (the old will only wish to consume, in the absence of heirs). In such a model the government clearly cannot borrow more from the young than their current income. We will consider below (Chapter 12) the detailed workings of such a model. But plainly the pattern of taxation can have large effects in it; for example a tax cut financed by borrowing throughout the lives of the current generation, so that taxes are raised on the next generation, or perhaps indefinitely deferred, must raise the consumption of the current generation as it will raise its permanent income.

Let us turn to the connection of fiscal with monetary policy. As we will see in Chapter 12, borrowing in an OLG model is limited by the capacity of the younger generation to lend; the old will not lend since they wish to consume all their wealth before they die. The young will lend as much as they can be induced to through higher interest rates; let us assume that the government is deterred from raising interest rates above some normal level, r, by the higher debt servicing costs this will imply. Then at this interest rate there will be some maximum amount the young are willing to lend: call this the government's debt ceiling.

Now consider how the ceiling on debt would affect a simple macro model. Suppose that GDP, N (also standing for the population by an appropriate choice of indices), grows at the rate n per year and that the real rate of interest, r, is constant and greater than n. Let H^* = rate of growth of money, $'$ = per capita value, π = rate of inflation, P = price level, b_t = the value of one-year indexed bonds. Write the demand for high-powered money, H, in the quantity theory manner as:

$$H_t = hP_tN_t \tag{13}$$

so that $H_t^* = \pi_t + n$. Suppose now that at time $t = 1$ new intentions are announced and carried out, for future fiscal and monetary policy; the announcement (fully believed) changes the present real value of bonds to b_1 as prices and interest rates react. There are then two phases of policy: 'transition' from $t = 2, ..., T-1$, and 'terminal' from $t = T, ...,$. During the transition phase policies may be different from their terminal phase when they must be in steady state. The government budget constraint is from $t = 2$ onwards:

$$b_t - b_{t-1} = d_t + rb_{t-1} - \frac{H_t - H_{t-1}}{P_t} \tag{14}$$

Expressing (14) in per capita terms, dividing all though by N_t, gives:

$$\frac{b_t}{N_t} = \frac{d_t}{N_t} - \frac{H_{t-1}}{P_tN_t}\frac{H_t - H_{t-1}}{H_{t-1}} + \frac{(1+r)b_{t-1}}{(1+n)N_{t-1}} \tag{15}$$

Using $P_tN_t = (1 + H_t^*)P_{t-1}N_{t-1}$, this becomes

$$b'_t = d'_t - \frac{hH_t^*}{1 + H_t^*} + (1 + r - n)b'_{t-1} \tag{16}$$

Since $r > n$ this is an explosive difference equation if interest-exclusive deficits and monetary targets are pursued independently. Suppose that during transition a constant H^* and d are chosen: these policies are monetarist so that H^* is 'low' but fiscal policy is 'expansionary', so that $d' > \frac{hH^*}{1+H^*}$. The set limit on this per capita stock of debt b', discussed above, is now bound to be reached at some point. At the date when this occurs, $b'_t = b'$, then policies have to change so as to ensure:

$$0 = b'_{t+1} - b'_t = d' - \frac{hH^*}{1 + H^*} + (r - n)b'_t \tag{17}$$

that is, that real bonds do not change any more. However, the policies could have been chosen so as to change before this, so that $b'_t < b'$ at this point. In general, the terminal date T, for the switch to a sustainable policy with unchanging per capita debt can be chosen freely from $t = 2$ onwards, so that H_T and d_T, the terminal or steady state policies are governed by:

$$0 = b'_T - b'_{T-1} = d'_T - \frac{hH_T^*}{1 + H_T^*} + (r - n)b'_{T-1}(b'_T \quad b') \tag{18}$$

The point is that there is a trade-off between the transitional policies (including the length of time they are pursued) and the terminal policies because the transitional policies affect the terminal stock of debt:

$$b'_{T-1} = (1+r-n)^{T-2} b'_1 + \sum_{i=2}^{T-1} (1+r-n)^{i-2} \left(d' - \frac{hH^*}{1+H^*} \right) \tag{19}$$

The trade-off implies each of the following:

1. If the government wishes to maintain a constant interest-exclusive deficit $d' = d'_T$, then the smaller is current (transitional) money supply growth, the larger will future money supply growth H_T^* have to be. Given fiscal 'profligacy', there is therefore a trade-off between current and future inflation.

2. If the government wishes to maintain constant money supply growth H^*, then the higher are the transitional deficits the larger are the future surpluses that will be required. Given monetary discipline, there is therefore a trade-off between current and future fiscal discipline.

The message is, in short, that tough monetary policies require tough fiscal policies (called by Sargent and Wallace 'unpleasant monetarist arithmetic').

The role of long-dated nominal bonds

We have so far neglected the term in b'_1, the value of real bonds after the policies are announced; implicitly we have suggested that b'_1 was quite small. This then allows scope for policy makers to choose between trade-offs 1 and 2 above. If, however, b'_1 is large, and close to b', then there is little scope for choice; the policy makers are forced to go rapidly to steady state fiscal-monetary policies, hard as these must be.

If the government bonds are nominal and short-dated, then the revaluation due to policies of lower inflation will be small unless the change is drastic; hence for example on a one-year nominal bond b_0, the change in value will be $-b_0(H^* - H_0^{*e})$ where H_0^{*e} is the money supply growth expected before the policy change. If the bonds are indexed as we assumed above, then the revaluation will be nil (given the fixed real interest rate assumption).

If the bonds are long-dated, the revaluation effect can be very large. For example, take a bond paying a fixed money amount, M_K, on maturity at $t = K$. The present value of this at $t = 1$ expected at $t = 0$ was $b_0 = \frac{M^K}{(1+R_0)^{K-1}}$ where $R_0 = H_0^{*e} + r - n$ was the nominal interest rate at $t=0$; the actual present value at $t=1$ is then $\frac{M^K}{(1+R_1)^{K-1}}$ where $R_1 = H_K^* + r - n$ and $H_K^* = \frac{T-1}{K-1}H^* + \frac{K-T}{K-1}H_T^*$ (that is, a weighted average of the transitional and the terminal H^*). Hence the unanticipated capital revaluation on such a bond is $-b_0(K-1)(H_K^* - H_0^{*e})$. For a credible anti-inflation policy where $H_K^* = H_T^* = n$, this revaluation will be a $K-1$ multiple of the terminal fall in inflation, and create the necessity for harsh fiscal discipline with much greater rapidity.

Definitions of the 'deficit'

Several definitions of the government 'deficit' are in use: inclusive or exclusive of debt interest and, if inclusive, inclusive of either nominal or real debt interest. We can re-express the restrictions placed on fiscal policy in terms of these different definitions.

Consider a version of the government budget constraint expressed in nominal terms in the steady state:

$$\Delta H_t + \Delta B_t = (g-\tau)P_t N_t + R_t B_t \tag{20}$$

B is the nominal market value of bonds (in steady state interest rates will not be changing), R is the market nominal interest rate, τ the tax rate and g the share of government spending in GNP (both assumed constant); H, P, π and N are respectively money supply, prices, inflation and GNP as before.

From our previous analysis, we constrain the ratio of debt to GDP to a constant in steady state so that:

$$\frac{\Delta B_t}{B_t} = \pi + n(\text{the growth of nominal GNP}) \tag{21}$$

Equation (20) can be written as:

$$\frac{\Delta H_t}{H_t}\frac{H_t}{P_t N_t} + \frac{\Delta B_t}{B_t}\frac{B_t}{P_t N_t} = g - t + \frac{B_t}{P_t N_t}R_t \tag{22}$$

So that using (21):

$$\frac{\Delta H_t}{H_t} = \overline{v}[g - \tau + \overline{b}(r-n)] \tag{23}$$

where $\overline{v}$ is the equilibrium velocity of money and $\overline{b}$ the equilibrium ratio of debt to GNP.

Equation (23) says that the steady state growth rate of money depends upon the ratio to GNP of the steady state deficit inclusive of real debt interest (sometimes called the 'inflation-adjusted real deficit'), minus an allowance for growth, $\bar{b}n$. We can also note that since in equilibrium $\frac{\Delta H_t}{H_t} = \pi + n$,

$$(\pi + n)(H_t + B_t) = R_t B_t + (g - \tau) P_t N_t \tag{24}$$

or

$$\frac{\Delta H_t}{H_t} = \pi + n = \frac{R_t B_t + (g - \tau) P_t N_t}{H_t + B_t} = \frac{PSBR_t}{P_t N_t} \frac{P_t N_t}{H_t + B_t} \tag{25}$$

which says that money growth equals the public sector borrowing requirement (PSBR) to GNP ratio times the 'velocity' of government net financial liabilities ('outside money', discussed in the next section).

Equations (23) and (25) are of course exactly equivalent, although one uses the inflation-adjusted deficit while the other uses the unadjusted deficit. However, when (23) is used to assess what fiscal policy must be used to validate a certain counter-inflationary monetary policy (e.g one to reduce $\Delta H_t/H_t$ to n from some high level), great care must be taken to include in $\bar{b}$ the effects of falling inflation and interest rates on the value of outstanding bonds; this adjustment can be very large as we saw above when a large proportion of these bonds are non-indexed and of long maturity, so that large cuts in the government deficit excluding interest may be necessary. When (25) is used, the implications are more transparent since nominal debt interest will not change except for short maturity stocks, which are rolled over before inflation comes down. These remarks are relevant to the debate on the Thatcher government's Medium Term Financial Strategy, which did not always carefully observe this point (for example, Buiter and Miller (1981) incorrectly argued that the fiscal policies were 'unnecessarily' restrictive using a crude adjustment for current inflation on debt at current market value).

Given the overall policy requirement of fiscal-monetary consistency, the application in any situation will be largely a question of what is politically feasible. This is particularly true of the short-run time path immediately on announcement. It may well be wise, for example, to cut public spending rapidly as money supply growth is cut, even though this implies a 'real' budget surplus (that is, inclusive of real debt interest) in the first few years because during this period debt interest on long-dated stock is still offset by high inflation. This real surplus will disappear as soon as inflation comes down, because the debt interest on long-dated stock will fall away only very slowly. Then, with the spending cuts done, the budget deficit will be at steady state levels and some of the debt revaluation (on the long-dated stock) will have been worked off by the previous real surpluses; this is an illustration of the previous section's discussion.

A Neo-Keynesian model with wealth effects

We can embed the logic of the OLG model above with its wealth effects of government bonds within a conventional IS-LM model of the type we used in earlier chapters; the advantage of doing so is that while the conclusions of the OLG analysis follow also in this conventional model, it can additionally be used for analysis of short-term stabilization policy. To illustrate these points we represent the government budget constraint in a different but convenient way. Private sector net financial wealth consists, in a closed economy (which we continue to assume), of government bonds and high powered money (the 'monetary base', consisting of the notes and coins issue plus commercial banks' deposits with the central Bank), that is, government net financial liabilities. These are known as 'outside money' (following an earlier literature — e.g. Patinkin, 1965; Metzler, 1951; Gurley and Shaw, 1960). Bank deposits are 'inside money' in that banks are a private sector institution; their deposits are therefore both assets and liabilities of the private sector, cancelling out in net terms.

Let f be the stock of government net financial liabilities (hence government debt) in real terms (that is, deflated by the consumer price index). f will rise for two reasons: first, a government deficit will create new liabilities, and second, the existing stock of liabilities will be subject to capital gains, as the price of bonds rises or the consumer price index falls. We write:

$$\Delta\theta_t = \frac{\Delta f_t}{f_{t-1}} = \frac{d_t}{\overline{b}} - (q\Delta R_t + \Delta p_t) \tag{26}$$

where d is the (total, inclusive of debt interest) government deficit as a fraction of GDP, $\overline{b}$ is the ratio of government debt to GDP, $q =$ is the proportionate response of long-term bond prices to the long-term interest rate (R); and $\theta = log f$. The unit coefficient on p_t (the log of the price level) reflects our assumption that all government liabilities are denominated in money terms. We will view (26) with $\overline{b}$, q held constant at some average value as an appropriate approximation.

To (26) we add a relationship determining the supply of high-powered money (in logs), which we shall write as m (which we can also treat as total money, reflecting the convenient and conventional assumption that there is a fixed 'money multiplier' between the two). We write:

$$\Delta m_t = \frac{\Phi}{\overline{b}}(d_t - \overline{d}) + \Delta\overline{m} + \epsilon_t \tag{27}$$

where $\overline{d}$ is the equilibrium (steady state) government deficit as a fraction of GDP, ϵ is an error term, and $\Delta\overline{m}$ is the equilibrium rate of growth of money. Equation (27) states that out of equilibrium money supply will have an independent random component (to which we could add other independent temporary determinants of money if we wished) as well as a component responding to the temporary component of the deficit. Given (26), (27) implicitly also determines the supply of nominal bonds as the difference between nominal financial assets and the monetary base.

Equation (27) focuses on two aspects of monetary policy with which we shall proceed to deal. First, how far does the equilibrium growth rate of money reflect the government deficit? Secondly how far should the money supply growth rate be varied (over the 'cycle') as budgetary financing needs change? In other words, what are the links between fiscal and monetary policy, first in, and second out, of steady state? This distinction is an important one in rational expectations models, as we shall see.

We begin with behaviour out of steady state.

Stability and Bond-Financed Deficits Out of Steady State

One issue that was given great prominence from the early 1970s until the general acceptance of rational expectations was the possibility of instability in models with wealth effects, if budget deficits are bond-financed. This can be illustrated in a simple fixed-price *IS-LM* model without rational expectations (a log-linear adaptation of Blinder and Solow's 1973 model). We use non-stochastic continuous time and abstract from the steady-state relationship between money and deficits by setting $\overline{d} = \Delta\overline{m} = 0$:

$$y_t = k\theta_t - \alpha r_t + \phi d_t \tag{28}$$

$$m_t = \overline{p} + \delta y_t - \beta r_t + \mu\theta_t \tag{29}$$

$$\dot{\theta}_t = \frac{d_t}{\overline{b}} - q\,\dot{r}_t \tag{30}$$

$$d_t = \overline{g} - \tau y_t \tag{31}$$

$$\dot{m}_t = \frac{\Phi}{\overline{b}} d_t \tag{32}$$

$\overline{g}$, government expenditure as a fraction of GDP, includes debt interest: this formulation assumes that other expenditure is reduced as debt interest rises. If it were not, the instability under bond finance discussed below would be severely worsened. τy_t measures marginal tax receipts as a fraction of GDP and hence τ is the income elasticity of taxation minus one: initial average tax receipts are netted out of $\overline{g}$. $\dot{}$ denotes the time derivatives. Because prices are fixed at $\overline{p}$, r_t is both the nominal and real interest rate. Equations (28) and (29) are the *IS* and *LM* curves with wealth effects; (30)–(32) are the budget constraint and money supply relationship for this model.

The model solves for y_t and r_t given θ_t. Using (32) and (30) gives $\dot{m}_t = \Phi\ (\theta_t + q\ \dot{r}_t)$ so that $m_t = \Phi(\theta_t + qr_t) + K_m$, where K_m is an arbitrary constant. Substituting for m_t from this into (29) and for d_t from (31) into (28) yields the equations for y_t and r_t. Substituting the solution of them for y_t and r_t into (30) yields the equation of motion for θ_t as:

$$\dot{\theta}_t = \frac{-\frac{\tau}{b}(k\beta - \alpha\mu + \Phi kq + \Phi\alpha)}{(1+\phi\tau)(\beta + q\mu) + \delta(\alpha + qk)}\theta_t \tag{33}$$

For stability we require $(k\beta - \alpha\mu + \Phi kq + \Phi\alpha) > 0$. Clearly if money supply is held constant regardless of the deficit, i.e $\Phi = 0$ (bond financed deficits), then we must have $k\beta > \alpha\mu$, which raises the possibility of instability if there are relatively strong wealth effects in the LM curve. $\Phi > 0$ reduces the possibility; Blinder and Solow and others have accordingly advocated money-financed deficits as a means of avoiding possible instability.

This instability is illustrated in Figure 7.2. In addition to the IS and LM curves we have drawn in a 'WW' curve, which is the equation of the budget constraint, (30), showing the level of output where $\dot{\theta}_t = 0$, that is. there are no changes in wealth. For $\dot{\theta}_t = 0$, we must have both $d_t = 0$ and $\dot{r}_t = 0$; $\dot{r}_t = 0$ automatically when $\dot{\theta}_t = 0$ because as we have seen, r_t and y_t (the intersection of the IS and LM curves) depend on θ_t and cease to move when θ_t stops moving. This level is $\overline{y} = \frac{\overline{g}}{\tau}$since from (31) $d_t = 0$ at this point. To the right of the WW curve, $\dot{\theta}_t$ is falling (and rising to the left). The IS curve shifts leftward as θ_t falls but the LM curve shifts rightwards. Instability under bond-financing ($\Phi = 0$) occurs when the intersection moves rightwards (and down) that is, $k\beta < \alpha\mu$, as the effect of θ_t on y_t (from equations (28) and (29)) is

$$\frac{k\beta - \alpha\mu}{\beta + \alpha\delta}$$

This can be seen diagramatically by noting that the rightward shift of the LM is $\mu\theta$, the leftward shift of the IS is $k\theta$; but the flatter the IS curve (the higher α) the more the LM curve shift dominates the output movement, and vice versa the flatter the LM curve (the higher β).

We pointed out that there is additional instability if one assumes government expenditure is fixed and does not fall to offset debt interest. The interested reader can work this case out, using in place of (31):

$$d_t = \overline{g} - \tau y_t + \overline{r}\overline{b}\theta_t + \overline{b}r_t \tag{30$'$}$$

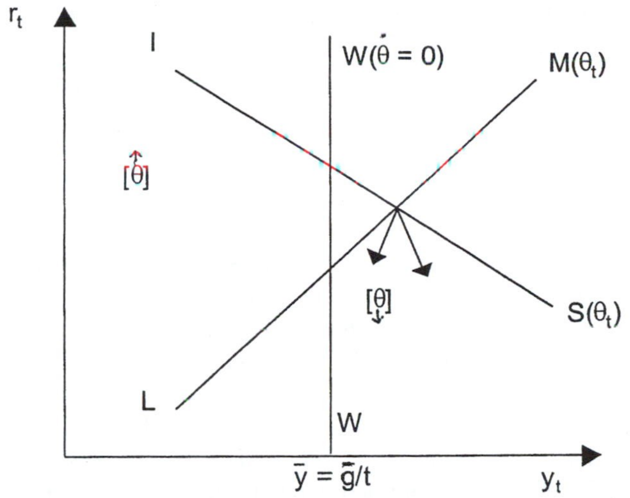

Figure 7.2: Instability with bond-financed deficits

where the last two terms approximate debt interest around some average interest rate, $\bar{r}$, and an average financial asset to GDP ratio, $\bar{b}$. The reader will find that the equivalent of (33) contains a number of extra positive terms in the numerator, increasing the chances of instability.

Under rational expectations, however, this Blinder-Solow argument carries less force. To convert their model into a rational expectations form, it is sufficient to recognize that the valuation of financial assets is forward-looking, that is, it depends on expectations of future interest rates; for convenience, now use discrete time. Returning, for example to the model given by (28) to (32), replace (30) and (32) by:

$$\triangle\theta_t = \frac{1}{\bar{b}}d_t - q(E_t r_{t+1} - E_{t-1} r_t) \tag{29'}$$

$$\triangle m_t = \frac{\Phi}{\bar{b}}d_t \tag{31'}$$

If the model is now solved by the methods of chapter 2, we obtain (if we drive the forward root backwards) a second-order characteristic equation in which one of the roots (the inverted forward root) should be absolutely greater than unity for a unique stable (saddlepath) solution (i.e. having both forward and backward roots stable). The roots involve all the coefficients and there is no general condition to ensure the saddlepath property.

If $\Phi = 0$, the characteristic equation $x_t + ax_{t-1} + bx_{t-2} = 0$ with roots σ_1, σ_2 has:

$$a = -(\sigma_1 + \sigma_2) = -1 + \frac{D + \frac{\tau}{b}(k\beta - \alpha\mu)}{q[\delta k + (1 + \phi\tau)\mu]}$$

$$b = \sigma_1\sigma_2 = -\frac{D}{q[\delta k + (1 + \phi\tau)\mu]} \qquad (34)$$

where $D = (1 + \phi\tau)\beta + \delta\alpha$.

Since $b < 0$, the roots cannot be complex, and at least one of the roots must be negative (alternating motion) and the other positive (monotonic motion) which is consistent with a saddlepath. For example, take the following parameter values, which approximate those of the Liverpool model of the UK:

$\beta = 2,\ \phi = k = \delta = 1,\ \tau = 0.3,\ \alpha = 0.5,\ q = 3,\ \mu = 0,\ \frac{1}{b} = 2$

These give $b = -1.03$, $a = 0.43$. Hence the roots are σ_1, σ_2 = 0.82, −1.25: the monotonic saddlepath (figure 7.3a). Had we found by contrast $\mu = 5$ so that $k\beta < \alpha\mu$, we would have had σ_1, σ_2 = 1.015, −0.135; again a saddlepath, but this time with alternating motion (figure 7.3b).

Interestingly, in the particular example here, the $k\alpha < \alpha\mu(\mu = 5)$ is actually more stable in that, although it is alternating, the absolute value of the stable root is much lower than in the case of $\mu = 0$. Computer examination of a wide range of values for the parameters suggests that problems with saddlepath stability arise whether $k\beta >$ or $< \alpha\mu$.

If $k\beta > \alpha\mu$, there is saddlepath stability when q or μ are low (otherwise the roots have a tendency to be both less than unity in absolute value: a 'non-uniqueness' problem). If $k\beta < \alpha\mu$, there is saddlepath stability when q is high (or in some cases when μ is high, even though q is low); otherwise the roots tend to be both greater than unity. The two typical cases of saddlepath stability are shown in figure 7.3

We conclude this section negatively: there is no compelling reason within rational expectations models to believe that the cyclical or short-run component of monetary policy ought to be influenced by fiscal policy. The decision, for example, whether to pursue a constant money supply growth rate through the cycle even though the budget deficit will be moving cyclically, can be taken on other grounds, notably those appropriate to stabilization policy. We now turn to the steady state component of the money supply rule, where the situation is quite different.

Long-term monetary targets

We now take the previous model, but abstract from short-run behaviour while reinstating the possibility of steady state inflation. We have in

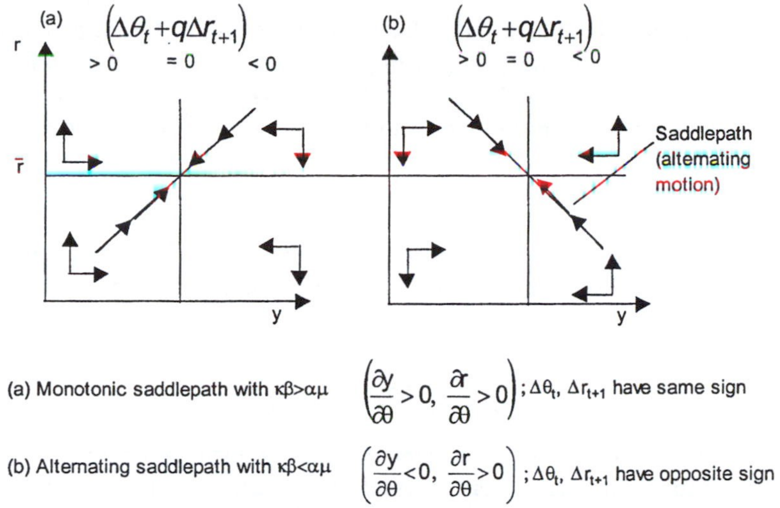

Figure 7.3: Two possible types of motion under rational expectations

equilibrium (* values are equilibrium ones):

$$y^* = k\theta^* - \alpha r^* + \phi\bar{d} \tag{35}$$

$$m^* = p^* + \delta y^* - \beta R^* + \mu\theta^* \tag{36}$$

$$\Delta\theta^* = \frac{1}{\bar{b}}\bar{d} - q\Delta R^* - \Delta p^* \tag{37}$$

$$\bar{d} = \bar{g} - \tau y^* \tag{38}$$

$$R^* = r^* + \Delta p^* \tag{39}$$

$$\Delta m^* = \Delta\overline{m} \tag{40}$$

We assume y^* is exogenously given as the natural rate in an (omitted) Phillips Curve.

The question we wish to ask is: can $\Delta\,\overline{m}$ be chosen independently of $\bar{d}$? For simplicity assume a steady state growth rate of zero ($\Delta y^* = 0$), although this does not affect the argument. Assume also that $\bar{d}$ and $\Delta\overline{m}$ are chosen to be constants.

The first thing to notice is that, if in steady state both real interest rates and inflation are constant, then at once we have $\Delta R^* = 0$ from (39), $\Delta\theta^* = \frac{\alpha}{k}\,\Delta\, r^* = 0$ from (35); then from (36) and (40) we have $\Delta\overline{m} = \Delta m^* = \Delta p^*$, while from (37) we have $\frac{1}{\bar{b}}\bar{d} = \Delta p^*$. It then follows that $\frac{1}{\bar{b}}\bar{d} = \Delta\overline{m}$; monetary and fiscal policy have to be 'consistent', that is the rate of money supply growth has to be equal to the deficit as a fraction of financial assets, $\frac{1}{b}\overline{d}$. This in turn is equal to the rate at which nominal financial assets are growing $(\triangle\theta^* + \triangle p^*)$; hence if money is growing at this rate, so also are bonds. Consistent monetary and fiscal policy hence implies that money and nominal bonds must be growing at the same rate.

What happens if they do not? Suppose for example we place a terminal condition on inflation reflecting a government inflation target achieved via money supply growth. So inflation will be constant in steady state. We may then derive by a similar procedure to the one already used:

$$\triangle r^* = \frac{k}{k(\beta + q) + \alpha(1-\mu)}\left(\frac{1}{b}\overline{d} - \triangle\overline{m}\right) \tag{41}$$

In other words, if the government (given its terminal condition on inflation) fails to pursue consistent fiscal and monetary policy, real interest rates will take the strain and eventually either (rising r^*) government expenditure would have to contract to zero (taxes rise to absorb the whole of GNP) or (falling r^*) real interest rates would become negative — neither of which is possible. Of course a sensible government will wish to stop any such tendency well before any such stage is threatened.

This argument has been conducted on the assumption that $\overline{d}$ is set, with changing interest payments on debt being offset by changes in government spending or taxes; if one assumes instead that government spending and tax rates are unaltered, then the steady state inflation rate under consistent policy, $\frac{1}{b}\overline{d} = \triangle\overline{m}$, depends on the level of government spending and taxes chosen; the algebra of this is more complex (see Minford et al., 1980), and the inflation resulting from any initial rise in the deficit is much greater than in the analysis above, because the eventual deficit is compounded by the rise in interest payments, but the essential message remains that there must be consistency between fiscal and monetary policy in steady state.

To conclude, wealth effects imply a constraint across the steady state components of fiscal and monetary policy, though not the short-run components. Hence in (27) $\triangle\,\overline{m} = \frac{1}{b}\overline{d}$, whereas we are free to write any short-run response function or error process besides. What we have done in this section is to show within a conventional *IS-LM* model with wealth effects essentially the same result as derived in the overlapping generations framework of Sargent and Wallace — that there are close connections between fiscal and monetary policy choices in the long run, but that in the short run there is considerable flexibility in their relationship.

A model with distortionary taxation: the optimal pattern of borrowing

We have seen that if a government wishes to achieve a certain money supply growth rate (to reach a desired inflation rate), then it is limited in the steady state (or 'average') deficit it can pursue at the same time. Nevertheless, provided it is willing to make up temporary deficits in excess of this with future deficits that fall short of it (even running into surpluses), then as we have seen it can still achieve its monetary objectives. The question we now ask is: what is a desirable pattern of such temporary deficits and surpluses?

In chapter 4 we looked at this issue from the point of view of stabilization policy ('demand management'). We concluded first, that tax rates acted as an effective automatic stabilizer and that this was desirable, if the tax rates were an unavoidable microeconomic distortion and if unemployment was distorted upwards in cyclical troughs by the benefit system; secondly that activist, 'feedback', fiscal policy was also effective and could also be beneficial on similar grounds. But we now consider the issue abstracting from the business cycle and stabilization policy. We use the criterion of optimal public finance alone: that is, we consider the distortionary costs of taxation. In order to do this, we shall drop the assumption that taxes are lump sum, and assume instead that each period there is an average (= marginal) tax rate, T_t. Such distortionary taxation implies that even in an economy with infinitely-lived households (or where each generation cares about the others) the pattern of deficits and borrowing affects consumer surplus and so private wealth, by creating variation in the extent of the tax distortions over time and hence in their present discounted value. It turns out that there is an optimum pattern which minimizes this present discounted loss of surplus.

Suppose that output, N, is (apart from temporary effects of tax rate variation) continuously at $\overline{N}$, so that stabilization is not of interest, and for simplicity suppose further that $\overline{N}$ is constant, real government spending is constant at $\overline{G}$, and money supply growth is constant at μ. As in the Sargent-Wallace example, let the demand for money be given by the quantity theory as:

$$H_t = hP_t\overline{N} \tag{42}$$

and the budget constraint be given by:

$$b_t - b_{t-1} = G - T_t(1-\epsilon)\overline{N} + rb_{t-1} - \frac{H_t - H_{t-1}}{P_t} \tag{43}$$

where b_t are indexed one-period bonds with a constant real interest rate, r, as at the start of this chapter and note that $T_t(1-\epsilon)\overline{N}$ deducts tax revenue lost as output responds to the tax rate with an elasticity ϵ (assumed constant). We can rewrite the budget constraint, following (4) as:

$$b_{t-1} = \frac{1}{1+r}\left[\sum_{i=0}^{\infty}\left(\frac{1}{1+r}\right)^{i}\left(T_{t+i}(1-\epsilon)\overline{N} - \overline{G} + \frac{h\overline{N}\mu}{1+\mu}\right)\right]$$
$$= \frac{\frac{h\overline{N}\mu}{1+\mu} - \overline{G}}{r} + \sum_{i=0}^{\infty}\left(\frac{1}{1+r}\right)^{i+1} T_{t+i}(1-\epsilon)\overline{N} \quad (44)$$

This says that the outstanding value of bonds must be equal to the present value of taxation less the present value of government spending (net of inflation tax revenue). This is the constraint on the pattern and total of taxation — due to the solvency constraint.

Now examine the distortion costs of taxation. By the usual consumer surplus triangle analysis, we can write the present value of these costs at the end of $t-1$, C_{t-1}, as:

$$C_{t-1} = \sum_{i=0}^{\infty} \frac{1}{2} T_{t+i}^{2} \varepsilon \overline{N}\left(\frac{1}{1+r}\right)^{i+1} \quad (45)$$

The optimal tax rates are discovered by minimizing C_{t-1} subject to the tax constraint. Form the Lagrangean:

$$L = C_{t-1} + m[K - \sum_{i=0}^{\infty}\left(\frac{1}{1+r}\right)^{i+1} T_{t+i}(1-\epsilon)\overline{N}] \quad (46)$$

where $K = b_{t-1} + \frac{\overline{G} - \frac{h\overline{N}\mu}{1+\mu}}{r}$. The first-order condition is:

$$0 = \frac{\partial L}{\partial T_{t+i}} = T_{t+i}\epsilon - m(1-\epsilon) \quad (47)$$

Since ε and m are fixed constants, this yields

$$T_{t+i} = T = \frac{m(1-\epsilon)}{\varepsilon} \quad (48)$$

This result, due to Lucas and Stokey (1983), extends Ramsey's (1927) rule that commodity tax rates should be inversely proportional to their demand elasticities. In other words, the optimal tax rate, T, is a constant if the output elasticity is constant over time. We can work out what it must be by solving for $T_{t+i} = T$ in the taxation constraint as:

$$T(1-\epsilon) = \frac{rb_{t-1}}{\overline{N}} + \frac{\overline{G}}{\overline{N}} - \frac{h\mu}{1+\mu} \quad (49)$$

The constant tax yield is that which will pay the interest on the outstanding stock of debt plus the government spending bill net of the inflation tax. Hence the stock of debt is held constant by optimal taxation. (If GDP was growing and government spending constant as a fraction of it, then the constant tax rate formula would imply that debt would also be constant as a fraction of GDP. The reader may like to rework the optimal tax rate problem with GDP growing at the rate n, using the budget constraint formulation of equation (16). He should find that the steps are identical, except that $r - n$ is substituted for r and bonds and government spending are expressed as fractions of GDP; the optimal tax rate remains constant.)

To put optimal tax rates another way, remember that optimality requires the intertemporal rate of transformation between revenues to equal that between welfare costs; that is,

$$\left(\frac{\delta C_{t-1}}{\delta T_{t+1}}\right) / \left(\frac{\delta R_{t-1}}{\delta T_{i+1}}\right) = \left(\frac{\delta C_{t-1}}{dT_{t+i+1}}\right) / \left(\frac{\delta R_{t-1}}{\delta T_{t+i+1}}\right) \tag{50}$$

where $R_{t-1} = \sum_{t=0}^{\infty} (\frac{1}{1+r})^{i+1} T_{t+i}(1-\epsilon)\overline{N}$ is the present value of revenues. In words this states that the (discounted) marginal cost per unit of (discounted) revenue gained from raising the tax rate in period $t+i$ must equal that from raising the tax rate in period $t+i+1$. The former (LHS) is $\frac{T_{t+i}\varepsilon}{m(1-\epsilon)}$, the latter (RHS) is $\frac{T_{t+i+1}\varepsilon}{m(1-\epsilon)}$ — in each the numerator is the contemporaneous welfare cost, the denominator the contemporaneous tax yield, of a penny rise in the tax rate. Notice that since both the welfare cost and the tax yield are discounted, the discount factor drops out.

Figure 7.4 illustrates this. It is assumed that workers have a constant marginal product MPL. The supply curve, SS, shows the output they produce as their marginal real wage, w, rises, increasing their hours input into the overall production function. The tax rate, T, depresses their marginal take home pay by Tw. The triangles of consumer surplus are minimized in total area when they are equal: as one increases from this point, the other decreases by less because their area depends on the square of the tax rate. The height of the triangle is measured by T_{t+i}, which is also a measure of the loss per unit of extra revenue raised.

CONCLUSIONS

We have considered the role of fiscal policy in three basic models: with Ricardian equivalence (where there are complete markets, infinitely-lived

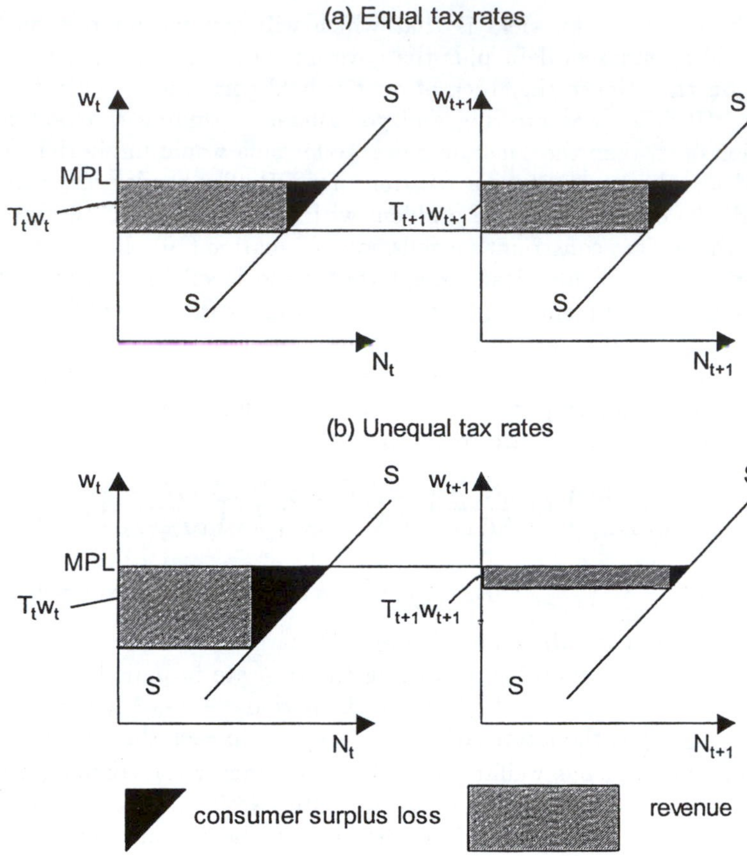

Figure 7.4: The optimality of a constant tax rate

households and non-distorting, i.e. lump-sum, taxes), and then in two main cases without it, the first with overlapping generations with finite life that do not care about each other, and the second where they do (and so behave like infinitely-lived households) but there are distorting taxes.

In the first Ricardian equivalence model the pattern of taxes and borrowing does not matter. The only constraint on the government is its solvency; if it violates this condition with its tax, spending and monetary policies then the markets will mark its debt down in value until the condition is met (in other words the debt value factors in expected default). Monetary policy sets the rate of inflation and should if properly conducted also fix the price level. Fiscal policy then must set taxes and spending so that solvency is ensured.

In the second model with unconnected overlapping generations we saw that there are important links between fiscal and monetary policy due to the fact that patterns of public borrowing affect the current generation's wealth. These links do not involve short-run behaviour, that is, over the economic cycle; independent fiscal and monetary responses to the cycle do not in general cause instability (or non-uniqueness) under rational expectations. By contrast, with adaptive expectations and wealth effects, coordination may be necessary even in the short run to avoid instability. It is in steady state that fiscal and monetary policy must be 'consistent', that is, the growth rate of real government bonds must be reduced to the rate of growth of GDP (assuming this is the rate at which the demand for bonds will grow in steady state at constant real interest rates).

In the final model, with distortionary taxation and infinitely-lived agents, the pattern of borrowing and taxation affects consumer surplus (and so private wealth) and we find that the optimum tax rate that minimises this loss of surplus is planned to be constant over time from the present state, given past and current shocks ('tax-smoothing'). As new shocks arrive, the tax rate adjusts to maintain the same future constancy, with borrowing taking up the resulting difference between taxes and spending.

So, summarising, we can say that given the choice of monetary targets to set prices fiscal policy is significantly constrained, to achieve solvency, to ensure long-run consistency between debt and money holdings, and to achieve optimality in tax patterns. We have moved a long way from the models of the 1970s where fiscal policy could be freely set, the only result being 'crowding out' via interest rate movements.

8

The political economy of democracy

One of the major developments in the public choice literature in the past two decades has been the construction and empirical testing of models that consider the interaction of the preferences of government and electors and the behaviour of the economy.

Important early examples of this work are the papers by Nordhaus (1975), MacRae (1977) and Frey and Schneider (1978a, b). A key assumption of this work is that expectations are formed in an error learning or adaptive manner. The purpose of this chapter is to consider the implications that the rational expectations hypothesis has for the behaviour or role of the authorities; we assume that both the authorities and the voters have rational expectations. This raises the interesting issues of whether there is scope for differences in economic policy between different political parties and of how voters will react to differences in policy and economic performance.

We begin by outlining the early work in the public choice literature, which is based on adaptive expectations. We then consider the rational expectations alternative.

THE NORDHAUS MODEL

Perhaps the most interesting model of the adaptive expectations vintage is Nordhaus (1975). The Nordhaus model is based on the Downs (1957) hypothesis that governments have an over-riding goal of winning the next election. Hence they obey the 'median voter theorem' (namely, that their policies will be designed with maximum appeal to the floating voter who will decide the election) and are consequently concerned to maximize their popularity over the period of office. This has the implication that both parties will offer identical policies, since they will be driven by competition for the median voter to offer a policy which will win him or her over: identical policy will give each party an equal chance of winning, which is the equilibrium.

Their popularity is assumed to depend on a number of key economic variables, notably the rate of inflation and unemployment. It is further assumed that voters, in evaluating the history of inflation and unemployment, give highest weight when voting to the current rates of both then current. The government is assumed to maximize its popularity subject to the constraint that the rate of inflation, the rate of unemployment and the expected rate of inflation are linked via an expectations-augmented Phillips curve. Finally it is assumed that price expectations are formed adaptively. The Nordhaus model thus has the following mathematical structure (in continuous time).

Maximize

$$P = \int_0^T G(u,p)(1+r)^t \tag{1}$$

subject to the constraints:

$$p = g(u) + p^e \tag{2}$$

$$Dp^e = \phi(p - p^e) \tag{3}$$

where p is the rate of inflation (p^e the expected rate), u is the rate of unemployment, r is the discount rate (*positive* to reflect voter myopia), G and g are functions, ϕ is a positive constant, and D is the differential (rate of change) operator such that, e.g. $Dx = dx/dt$. Equation (1) is the government's objective function.

Popularity, P, is maximized between the time of arrival in office (0) and the time of the next election (T). Equation (2) is the augmented Phillips curve and equation (3) the adaptive expectations mechanism.

Clearly the optimal paths of unemployment and inflation will depend on the precise choice of functions $G(.)$ and $g(.)$. Nordhaus specifies an objective function:

$$G(.) = -\alpha p - \frac{\beta}{2}u^2 \tag{4}$$

and a linear augmented Phillips curve:

$$g(u) = a - bu \tag{5}$$

where α, β, a, b are positive constants.

The mathematics required to solve this problem is outside the scope of this book (see e.g. Cass and Shell, 1976). It turns out that the path of the unemployment rate between elections implied by its solution has the form shown in figure 8.1.

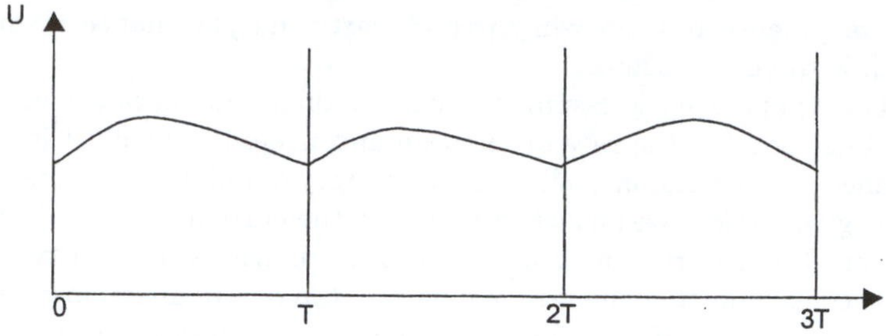

Figure 8.1: The Political Business Cycle

The essential implication then of this work is that governments deliberately cause a business cycle so that, at the date of election, they are in the most favourable position with respect to voters' preferences; hence on arriving in office, they raise unemployment to initiate a reduction in inflation, then after two years or so they stimulate the economy to reduce unemployment in time for the election date, leaving their successor to cope with the rise in inflation that is the lagged result of this policy.

While the optimal pattern of inflation or unemployment does depend on the precise choice of functional forms, the essential insight of Nordhaus, that governments may have a vested interest in creating business cycles, will survive these and other changes (such as the length of the electoral period T; see Chappell and Peel, 1979). The assumption that government popularity depends on variables such as the rate of inflation or unemployment has received some empirical support. In particular Frey and Schneider (1978a, b) have reported empirical work for a variety of different countries, such as the United Kingdom, the USA and West Germany, in which a measure of government popularity, typically based on opinion polls, is found to be significantly related to such economic variables.

Subsequent work (e.g. Borooah and Van der Ploeg, 1982; Chrystal and Alt, 1981; Pissarides, 1980; Minford and Peel 1982a; Harte et al., 1983, Gartner,1994), showed that the work of Frey and Schneider is not statistically robust with respect to changes in the sample period or the economic variables chosen. This is perhaps not too surprising. Economists, when analysing agents' choice between alternatives, are concerned to stress the appropriate relative prices. This point has typically been neglected in the empirical work on government popularity. The alternative hypothesis is best outlined by Tullock (1976), who writes: 'Voters and customers are essentially the same people. Mr. Smith buys and votes; he is the same man in the supermarket and in the voting booth. There is no strong reason to believe his behaviour is radically different in the two environments. We assume that in both he will choose the product or candidate he thinks is the best bargain for him.'

When we also recognize that voters are expressing preferences for different policies over the life-time of a government, it is clear that the relevant choice should reflect expectations of future policy differences between parties. From this perspective the conventional work is implicitly assuming that expectations of the future paths of economic variables under the party in power are formed adaptively and that the paths of economic variables under the alternative parties are considered by electors as fixed.

RATIONAL EXPECTATIONS AND REPUTATION

It is possible to motivate a political business cycle by reference to the new literature on reputation and partial information, discussed in earlier chapters. Suppose that before the run-up to the election, the government has acquired a good reputation for monetary prudence and that there is partial information about current events, with people observing current economic activity but not observing current policy variables, such as the money supply and government spending. Votes are cast according to people's assessment of the equilibrium levels of output and inflation as rationally expected, but they have a signal extraction problem.

In this vein, let election popularity (the voting balance) be given by:

$$P_t = -(Ey_t - k\overline{y}_{t-1})^2 - f(Eg_t - \pi^*)^2 \tag{6}$$

where $\overline{y}$ is equilibrium output ($k > 1$ reflects the people's desire for a better supply side), and g is the equilibrium level of inflation and also of policy levers (money supply growth and the fiscal deficit behind it).

Let

$$\overline{y}_t = \overline{y}_{t-1} + \epsilon_t \tag{7}$$

ϵ_t is random, partly the result of past policies whose fruits cannot be accurately forecast. Actual output (observed) is given by a Phillips curve where g_t^e is the people's expectations of government policy based on its reputation:

$$y_t = \overline{y}_t + \theta(g_t - g_t^e) \tag{8}$$

But

$$g_t = g_t^e + m_t \tag{9}$$

where m_t is the unforeseen policy change unobserved by the public but known by government.

The public's signal extraction gives

$$E\overline{y}_t = \overline{y}_{t-1} + \phi(y_t - \overline{y}_{t-1}) = \overline{y}_{t-1} + \phi[\epsilon_t + \theta(g_t - g_t^e)] \quad (10)$$

$$Eg_t = g_t^e + Em_t = g_t^e + \frac{(1-\phi)(y_t - \overline{y}_{t-1})}{\theta} = g_t^e + \frac{(1-\phi)}{\theta}(\epsilon_t + \theta(g_t - g_t^e)) \quad (11)$$

The government now maximizes P_t (subject to g_t^e, ϵ_t, $\overline{y}_{t-1}$ given) with respect to g_t in the election run-up by setting $0 = \frac{\partial P_t}{\partial g_t}$ and this first-order condition yields

$$g_t = \frac{\{\phi(k-1)\theta\overline{y}_{t-1} - (1-\phi)f(g_t^e - \pi^*) - [\phi^2\theta + \frac{f(1-\phi)^2}{\theta}]\epsilon_t\}}{\phi^2\theta^2 + f(1-\phi)^2} + g_t^e \quad (12)$$

g responds positively to target output ($k\overline{y}_{t-1}$), and positively to a bad supply shock (negative ϵ_t), although it is restrained by 'bad reputation', high g_t^e. So there is a tendency for monetary policy to expand pre-election, especially if the supply side is bad.

The government would in this model aim to build up its reputation after an election; then in the run-up it would 'use up' some of this reputation. Clearly there are strict limits to the policy boost that can be delivered in this way; these fall far short of the crude swings in policy optimal under the Nordhaus model. Nevertheless, there is still a basis here for a political business cycle under rational expectations. Models of a similar structure are to be found in Cukierman and Meltzer (1986 a, b), Alesina and Sachs (1988) and Alesina et al. (1997) for example.

The intuition behind this and other such models can be appreciated if one asks: would any government like to go into an election during a recession? Clearly no one can be sure of what is truly the reason for the economy's bad performance; and some blame is bound to rub off on the government. Yet the very transparency of this motivation could undermine even this limited political business cycle model. Suppose that everyone knows the government will maximize P_t in the run up to an election. Then reputation-building is useless and the policy unravels.

First, take the model as at present set up. People would form their expectation g_t^e not by observing past actions but by taking expectations of (12) and setting $E_{t-1}g_t = g_t^e$. The result is

$$g_t^e = \pi^* + \frac{\phi(k-1)\theta}{(1-\phi)f}\overline{y}_{t-1} \quad (13)$$

When the government comes to maximize (6) knowing ϵ_t but initially supposing the public does not know it, it would choose in general:

$$g_t = g_t^e + q\epsilon_t \tag{14}$$

But the public will know that this is the government's current policy because it knows the government's preferences. Therefore it will know that

$$y_t = \overline{y}_{t-1} + (1 + \theta q)\epsilon_t \tag{15}$$

where q is the government's known response to ϵ_t. So the public will in fact be able to infer the value of ϵ_t and so $Eg_t = g_t$, $E\overline{y}_t = \overline{y}_t$.

(The only case where this will not be so is if $q = -\frac{1}{\theta}$; in this case the public will be unable to judge the size of the shock at all because the government is deliberately stopping output from reacting to the supply-side shock at all. However, should the government choose this then the public will know that, although there will in general have been some shock to the supply side they are unable to know what it is; their best guess in this case is any value at all, a completely flat distribution. We should assume therefore that the popularity function is undefined at this point and by implication worse than one that is defined.)

This being so, the whole problem changes. Now there is no signal extraction problem; instead,

$$P_t = -(\overline{y}_t - k\overline{y}_{t-1})^2 - f(g_t - \pi^*)^2 \tag{16}$$

The government's maximizing strategy is simple: $g_t = \pi^*$. There is no political business cycle again: straightforward honesty is the best policy.

Clearly this argument implies an extraordinarily perceptive voting public and clear knowledge of the government's motivation. Both must be in doubt. Given the paradox of voting (see next section), let alone the costs of investing in good information extraction as a voter, there are reasons to doubt such rationality. Government motives may be obscure, given the ideological factor; or they may deliberately be obscured as in the Backus and Driffill (1985 a, b) model.

Nevertheless, this case of unravelling at least serves to show that full rational expectations with known government objectives does remove the political business cycle. It provides a useful benchmark, and cautions that the political business cycle, at least if practised too vigorously, is likely to self-destruct.

We now turn to the central issues of what might determine voting and party policies if voters have this full (benchmark) rationality.

A RATIONAL EXPECTATIONS MODEL OF VOTERS AND PARTIES

We proposed a model (Minford and Peel, 1982a) in which the expectations of voters and the authorities are both assumed to be rational. We argue that the marginal costs of information gathering can be regarded as sufficiently low for the representative voter to develop an informed opinion of the future path of economic variables. One simple mechanism (and there are probably some others) by which this can occur is via public forecasts. Forecasts of inflation and output from forecasting groups (for instance, in the UK the Treasury, the National Institute of Economic and Social Research, and the Liverpool Research Group, besides a plethora of City of London institutions) will represent informed opinion and are given widespread publicity by newspapers and television, which the voters obtain at negligible marginal cost. While these public forecasts will differ to some extent, they will tend to be correlated and voters' expectations, as conditioned by them, will more closely approximate rational expectations than some mechanistic adaptive alternative.

Although the typical voter may face low costs of gathering information and opinions this does not explain why he votes. The direct marginal benefits of voting, in the sense that an individual vote will influence the electoral outcome, appear a priori to be less than the marginal costs of voting. Indeed, the 'paradox of voting' is that, because the effect of one vote on the election outcome is negligible, the voter obtains no expected marginal gain from voting. However, the most attractive rationale for rational voting is the 'civic' recognition by voters that democracy cannot function unless many people vote (see Mueller, 1979, for a fuller discussion of these issues). In game-theoretic terms, democratic behaviour is a game with rules, one set of which governs voting; such games evolve from social discovery processes (for a discussion of such evolutionary processes see Sugden, 1986). Voters are expected to vote according to their own preferences; since most have only the vaguest idea of the 'nation's good' and little ability to evaluate it, they are expected to evaluate the effect of party policies on their own individual or household interests, where they should have a keen and accurate perception. Then the electoral process aggregates these votes into a popular preference for one party's policies. A number of authors (e.g. Meltzer and Richard, 1981, 1983) have emphasized that such 'voting with one's pocket' opens up the possibility of 'rent-seeking' by voter coalitions with a vested interest: politicians then have to weigh up their ability to attract (organized) votes from vested interests against their chance of appealing to the (disorganized) votes of the ordinary voters. We return below to the effects this choice may have on party platforms.

Controversy, into which we cannot enter here, surrounds what sort of process delivers the better results. Anglo-Saxon systems of first-past-the-post deliver strong mandates, which notably Popper (1988, 1945/66) has defended as providing a strong capacity of electorates to get rid of governments. Continental systems of proportional representation deliver governments which can only survive by consensus between coalition partners. The Anglo-Saxon systems have produced large-scale swings of policy, with 'experiments' on a grand scale. The continental systems have produced a slowly changing compromise set of policies, which never became as socialist as, say, the UK when socialism was fashionable in the 1960s but neither moved so rapidly towards deregulation and free markets as the socialist tide receded in the 1980s.

Given our assumptions about the information set of agents, we follow a number of different authors in supposing that political parties in part pursue economic policies which are broadly in accordance with the objective economic interests and subjective preferences of their 'class', defined as their core political constituency. For instance, Johnson (1968) writes: 'From one important view, indeed, the avoidance of inflation and the maintenance of full employment can most usefully be regarded as conflicting class interests of the bourgeois and proletariat, respectively, the conflict being resolvable only by the test of relative political power in the society.'

Robinson (1937) also writes: 'In so far as stable prices are regarded as desirable for their own sake, as contributing to social justice, it must be recognised that justice to the rentier can be achieved only by means of the injustice to the rest of the community of maintaining a lower level of effective demand than might otherwise be achieved. We are here presented with a conflict of interests...and actual policies are largely governed by the rival influences of the interests involved.'

While clearly we do not accept the assumption made in both these comments that output is demand-determined, they do usefully highlight the importance of rival organised interest groups in the political process.

VOTERS

We assume that there are three relevant sets of voters: Labour (Democrats), Conservatives (Republicans) and floating voters. The supporters of each party come from different parts of the electorate (for example, 'labourers' and 'capitalists', see Hibbs, 1978). The stylized assumption is that Labour voters primarily hold human capital and the Conservatives primarily financial capital, while floating voters have large amounts of both.

The current utility function of the voters is written in quadratic form as:

$$C_t = c_1 p_t + c_2 p_t^2 + c_0 \qquad \text{(Conservative)} \qquad (17)$$

$$V_t = v_1 p_t + v_2 p_t^2 + v_3 y_t + v_4 y_t^2 + v_0 \qquad \text{(Floating)} \qquad (18)$$

$$L_t = l_1 y_t + l_2 y_t^2 \qquad \text{(Labour)} \qquad (19)$$

where c_1, c_2, v_1, v_2, v_4, l_2 are negative and c_0, v_0, v_3, l_1 positive constants; y is disposable labour income.

The floating voter who determines the election outcome is assumed to express his voting intentions (up to and including the time he votes in the election) according to which party is expected to give him greater utility from the time of the next election onwards. Formally he takes the expectation $E_t V_T$ (which is taken as a proxy for his expected utility for all time beyond the election) conditional on each party's policies in turn, $E_t V_T^L$, $E_t V_T^C$ (Labour and Conservative respectively); he casts his vote for Labour if $E_t V_T^L > E_t V_T^C$ and vice versa. In aggregate it is assumed that voters are distributed around the typical floating voter, yielding a cumulative voters' balance function of the form:

$$B_t = b(E_t V_T^G - E_t V_T^O) + h_t \qquad (20)$$

where G denotes 'government' and O 'opposition'; h_t is an error process for non-economic omitted variables. Taking expectations of (19) for the government yields:

$$E_t V_T^G = v_1 E_t p_T + v_2 E_t p_T^2 + v_3 E_t y_T + v_4 E_t y_T^2 \qquad (21)$$

these being the expected outcomes (that is, under the current government).

Doing the same (a 'counterfactual' expectation) for the opposition and subtracting from (21) gives:

$$E_t V_T^G - E_t V_T^O = \beta_1(E_t p_T - \overline{p}) + \beta_2(var_T p - \overline{varp}) + \beta_3(E_t y_T - \overline{y}) + \beta_4(var_T y - \overline{vary}) \qquad (22)$$

where $varp$, $vary$ are the variances of p and y around their expected values and $\overline{p}$, $\overline{y}$, $\overline{varp}$, $\overline{vary}$ reflect the relevant expectation and variances of the opposition.

Unlike previous voting functions, this formulation is explicitly forward-looking in inflation and income and it includes variances of the relevant economic variables. In their related empirical work Minford and Peel (1982a) use the perhaps unsatisfactory proxy of time trends for the opposition party's policies and there is clearly scope for the use of more subtle alternatives. Using Gallup data for the United Kingdom over the period 1959-75, they produce evidence that (22) performs in a more satisfactory manner than the conventional Frey-Schneider alternative. However, in later empirical work on the UK, West Germany and Sweden, Harte (1986) finds that these voting functions are as unstable as their non-rational predecessors. Similar instability is found, with alternative functions under rational expectations, by Borooah and Van der Ploeg (1982). This instability is not difficult to explain in terms of Lucas's (1976) critique. These voting functions are, in spite of their forward-looking, terms 'reduced-form' expressions in which the effects of voter preferences, the model and the exogenous processes linking policy (in each party), as well as the economic environment, are jointly solved out. Even if preferences are unchanged, then other elements will change and shift the voting functions. The instability does not necessarily invalidate the theory but it should make us modest in our expectations of estimating it.

A side implication of this approach is that voter preferences will gradually change with their economic interests. For example, '*embourgeoisement*', carrying with it the wider accumulation of non-human capital (including home and share ownership), will increase the size of the 'capitalist' class relative to the 'labour' class. Strong evidence of this change has been produced for the UK (Crewe, 1988). There is also evidence in opinion poll data from 1987, at a time when Labour policies were still designed to appeal to traditional labour voters, that share ownership was significantly correlated with voting Tory; with privatization having greatly extended share ownership (from 8 to 25 per cent of the population), this could have been an important electoral factor.

EMPIRICAL EVIDENCE ON POPULARITY

The empirical evidence on the relationship between political popularity, as measured in opinion polls, and economic variables is, as we have seen, clearly suggestive that the relationships are unstable. Besides the Lucas critique, this instability could also be due to omission of key variables: for instance social issues such as health or education are omitted from the regressions, and could often be important. In addition variables that measure the opposition's policies are difficult to operationalise and as a consequence rarely formally considered in the econometric analyses, but again must be relevant to the voting decision. For these types of reasons it is perhaps not surprising that the estimated functions display such marked instability. Recent work by Box-Steffensmeier and Smith (1996), Byers, Davidson and Peel (1997, 2000) points to a different statistical reason for the instability. Employing popularity data for a large number of different countries and political parties, they obtained the striking result that popularity could be parsimoniously modelled as a fractionally integrated process, ARFIMA process (Granger and Joyeaux, 1980) — see the Time-Series Annex at the end of the book for statistical background to this and the following discussion.

The ARFIMA (p, d, q) process is given by:

$$x_t = (1 - L)u_t \tag{23}$$

where u_t is a stationary ARMA (p, q) process, and d is non-integer.

ARFIMA processes have the property that the autocorrelation function exhibits hyperbolic decay rather than the eventually exponential decay of the stationary ARMA, or I(0), process, and enables ARFIMA processes to model dependence between observations at long range. But at the same time and in contrast with the I(1) or unit root case, these processes exhibit eventual mean reversion. In fact Byers, Davidson and Peel (1997, 2000) found a remarkable similarity between the estimated d for different countries; they were all around 0.7 and the error term was, in most cases, white noise. An estimate of d that lies between 0.5 and unity carries the implication that the series is non-stationary but ultimately mean-reverting. The finding of such a process has important implications for trying to 'explain' popularity by conventional regression analyses using economic variables. It has been shown (Tsay and Chung, 1996; Marmol, 1998) that the 'spurious regression' phenomenon best known in connection with unit root processes extends to fractional processes. Variables such as inflation and interest rates have also been shown to be fractional, if not unit root processes, see for example Baillie, Chung and Tieslau (1996). Therefore, simple regression t values may be misleading.

Byers, Davidson and Peel (1997) explained the fractional result in the following manner. They hypothesised for simplicity that voters fall into two stylized categories: the committed and the uncommitted. The committed individuals are those with strong party allegiances. They are motivated by conviction or group solidarity, and their voting intentions are generally insensitive to news. They will support their party of choice through good times and bad. The uncommitted individuals, in contrast, who are usually called 'floating voters', tend to award their votes on the basis of performance. Newspaper headlines can sway their voting intentions considerably, although, by the same token, the effect of news is typically transitory and will tend to average out in the long run. The current voting intentions of the floating voters are on the whole a poorer predictor of future voting intentions than those of the committed voters. These features of the voting population are captured in the model by assuming that the logarithm of the odds in favour of an individual expressing an intention to vote for a particular party evolves as a first-order AR process, with a parameter that takes a value close to 1 for committed voters, and substantially below 1 for the floating voters. Consider a population of voters, each characterized by a particular value of the AR coefficient on the interval [0, 1]. If the distribution of these coefficients is as they hypothesize, a result due to Granger (1980) implies that the average of a large sample of individual voting intentions (after a logistic transformation) should behave similarly to a fractionally integrated process. This means that it should exhibit long memory, unlike a stationary ARMA process, in spite of being eventually mean-reverting.

The Byers, Davidson and Peel explanation of the fractional property of popularity data is not based on a formal theoretical model with explicit utility underpinnings. It is suggestive that a model that can capture the fractional property of popularity data may need to acknowledge differing degrees of 'habit' amongst heterogeneous voters. In their interpretation it is news about economic variables that drives popularity changes, not their actual values. They report empirical evidence consistent with this interpretation. Their empirical findings may be consistent with alternative underpinnings but at the least are a challange to the 'traditional' models explaining popularity. The fractional property of voting responses implies they are stable and predictable in the long run but respond to news in the short run.

One extraordinary regularity survives in all models (certainly for the UK): the mid-term swing of polled opinion away from the governing party, and back again as the election approaches. This quasi-seasonal effect is routinely incorporated into voting functions, but no explanation for it exists. The usual rationalization is in terms of a 'costless protest': the electorate use polls (and by-elections) to signal their preferences for modifications of government policy. This does not amount to a desire to change the government, so that as the election approaches, true preferences re-emerge.

EXPLAINING PARTY POLICY

We would like to explain differing party policy within a rational expectations framework. According to Downs' median voter theorem noted above, party policies should be the same: however, a party is formed by activists with strong views on policy and it is faced with a choice of a likely win by giving these views up or a less likely win while keeping the chance of implementing them now or later when the public may have been persuaded. We can think of this as maximizing expected utility over the future where the utility from implementing policies rises as they get closer to the party's principles but the short-term chances of winning (and therefore of implementing them) rise as the platform gets closer to the centre. Hence each party will choose some compromise electoral manifesto but measurably to the 'left' or 'right' of the median voter.

We can tie these ideas in with another strand of the public choice literature: this considers the power of vested interests, distinguished by their high motivation and efficient organization. Olson (1965, 1982) argues that they are more effective than ordinary voters, including median or floating ones, whose interests are less intensely affected by general tax or expenditure changes; hence ordinary voters devote less attention (costly information gathering and assessment) to the issues and vested interests prevail over policy. Such vested interests will attempt to influence all parties but because of their 'class interest' will have most influence with one party typically. Such influence tends to reinforce the tendency for party policies to differ.

We assume that the authorities are faced with an economy in which there is no long-run trade-off between inflation and output, but where, in the short run, fiscal and monetary policy can stabilize the economy by appropriate choice of feedback rules; these are assumed to be effective on the grounds of, for example, contracts, as discussed in chapter 4. The absence of a long-run trade-off does not, however, avoid a choice of the long-run budget deficit and, of course, the implied monetary growth rate. It might seem that all parties would have as their long-run target zero inflation, and hence choose targets for the budget deficit and money supply growth to go with this. This is clearly not the case, however, once we recognize that a budget deficit with inflation implies a different incidence of the existing tax burden from one with zero inflation, since an unanticipated shift to high inflation on the accession of a new government will lower the capital value of nominal government debt. This will expropriate debt holders to the advantage of the general taxpayer, who now pays less tax.

We assume for formal purposes, very simply, that each party maximizes the expected value at the next election date of a weighted average of the utility of its own supporters and that of the floating voter. The expectation is formed at time $t = 0$, the time of strategy choice, and it is supposed that this choice occurs only once in each period between elections and then cannot effectively be changed. We suppose that a party has had its 'honeymoon' period, has had to react to the pressures of office and after about half a year of its term has settled down and then chooses its strategy. The other party has by this time settled in opposition and also chooses its strategy. Once chosen the parties cannot with credibility change them.

Formally then, for example, the Conservative party maximizes:

$$\mu E_0 C_T + (1 - \mu) E_0 V_T \tag{24}$$

where μ is the weight given to its own supporters. The function will be expected to be maximized at time T, the time of the election. In principle it ought to be expected utility from this date onwards, with a suitable discount factor, but, for empirical purposes this is considered needlessly complicated, given that we have ruled out expected future changes in policy programmes.

Equation (24) is maximized subject to the voters' preferences and their model of the economy. The formal mathematics of this is somewhat complicated (see Minford and Peel, 1982a). However, the implication of the analysis is important. This is that different political parties, who represent different class interests, will pursue different policies. In particular party policies will differ significantly, not only in budget and money supply targets but also in feedback coefficients according to the interaction between voter preferences and the model structure. Labour reaction functions will, relative to Conservative reaction functions, embody a higher steady state budget deficit and be more responsive to real rather than nominal shocks.

Quite clearly the precise form of reaction function will be dependent on the true model of the economy and the nature of voter preferences. However, the point of our study remains valid, namely that in an economy with rational expectations on the part of both government and voters, there is scope for systematic policy differences between different political parties.

Empirical results on UK reaction functions for the period 1959-75 support the model in that significant differences between the political parties were discovered. Harte et al. (1983) also confirmed the fruitfulness of the approach, and found significant statistical differences in reaction functions between the parties in the UK, Sweden and West Germany. Differences in reaction functions with respect to political variables have also been found in a number of other countries (e.g. Alesina, Roubini and Cohen, 1997).

These results conflict with the median voter theorem, which predicts the same policies for each party. This theorem is therefore rejected by the data for first-past-the-post democracies, for which it was constructed. For proportional representation systems, the theorem would apply to the parliamentary party holding the balance of power; for these democracies, there is stronger evidence of party policy convergence, with the differences in Sweden and Germany appearing less marked than in the UK and USA.

Although there are party differences in policy, nevertheless the median voter (or party) theorem embodies an important principle: of policy convergence towards the centre. This principle has inspired a number of studies investigating how far the interests of this median or 'swing' group of voters (or their party) influence particular, as opposed to general economic, policies. Are particular taxes designed to shift the tax burden away from these voters? Are government expenditures fixed to benefit them? Models which answer 'yes' include that of Meltzer and Richard (1981, 1983), who also find evidence for these forces.

RELATED ISSUES AND CURRENT RESEARCH

Political economy, the topic of this chapter, is a burgeoning area of research, for two reasons. First, the government is an agent with objectives, whose actions are of obvious importance: modelling them should be superior to treating policy as exogenous or a fixed feedback rule. Secondly, analytical and computational tools have improved to the point where it is feasible to compute the equilibria in games between governments and the public or other governments.

Much of this research has already been discussed. But two topics deserve emphasis.

In chapter 5, we discussed the issue of time-inconsistency and the incentives both to cheat on promises if believed and, once people realize this incentive, to find a mechanism which ensures promises are carried out. Models of reputation under imperfect information are attempts to explain variations in credibility between total public gullibility on the one hand and total cynicism on the other; such models can produce a political business cycle, as we have seen.

They may also produce strategies to bind successor governments into policies which benefit the current government. A high inherited level of public debt, for example, may restrain a future socialist government (when it comes to re-optimize) from increasing public expenditure; a conservative government might then push tax cuts further than otherwise in order to reduce tax rates and public spending in the long term, should it lose power. Models supporting such strategies are to be found in Alesina and Tabellini (1989, 1990) and Persson and Svensson (1987).

The question of how policy promises can be enforced, by voting behaviour or by other parties or by constitutional structures, is also important, since good policies typically involve making promises which are then kept. Rogoff and Sibert (1988) consider voters punishing the government, although this involves the difficulty of why individual voters should bother, given their lack of power to influence anything individually (as in the voting paradox above). Alesina (1987) considers strategies where the other party deters promise-breaking in an inter-party pact ('bipartisan policy'): this may not apply well to controversial policy areas, such as public spending and inflation. Tabellini (1987) considers the role of independent, overlapping governors in an independent central bank. A good survey of all these issues is to be found in Alesina (1989).

The second topic concerns the source of inflation itself. Much existing literature assumes inflation is motivated by governments needing inflation revenue or seigniorage to finance exogenous public spending, with the extent of the inflation tax being determined by an optimizing choice across tax patterns, to minimize the welfare and collection costs of taxation. Yet this approach is at variance with the considerations of political interest suggested in this chapter. Instead, inflation may serve the interests of the dominant voter and the party that represents him — as explored in Minford and Peel (1982a) and Minford (1988). On this view, inflation and its associated high interest rates, high inflation variance and expansionary public spending-cum-deficit programmes, is not an accident or the result of Keynesianism, but a deliberate strategy. The elimination of these policies will occur, not through better understanding nor through constitutional devices (which can always be over-ridden by a democratic majority) but through the formation of a new dominant voter coalition with different interests. This effect on macroeconomic policies parallels the effects explored by Meltzer and Richard (1981, 1983) and Olson (1965, 1982) on distributional and micro policies.

CONCLUSIONS

Recent work in the public choice literature has considered the interaction of the preferences of the government and electors and the behaviour of the economy. This early work assumed that expectations are formed adaptively and generated one key conclusion, namely that the authorities may deliberately create a business cycle. When expectations are formed rationally, the authorities may still be able to generate a political business cycle, provided there is imperfect information and uncertainty about their objectives; however, the scope is more limited and can disappear altogether as information improves.

Another key result of the public choice literature is the median voter theorem, according to which party policies should be essentially the same, because they are designed to capture the floating voter. However, there is more empirical support for an alternative theory in which parties attempt to maximize the expected future utility, not only of floating voters but also of their own class-based supporters and associated vested interests. This will give rise to systematic differences in the parties' reaction functions.

We also considered the way in which government popularity and voting behaviour has been modelled. We suggested that the conventional approach based on past economic indicators was deficient in ignoring expectations of future economic variables and the behaviour of the opposition. However, because of the importance of non-economic factors, it is unlikely that functions based solely on economic variables will generate statistically robust results; the evidence to date confirms this lack of robustness.

Finally, we considered research on how voter coalitions and vested interests may influence the strategies of political parties towards a whole range of variables — inflation, public spending, public debt and subsidies, to name but a few. Modern analytical and computational tools offer us the chance of a better understanding of the causes of government strategy.

APPENDIX 8A: DIFFERENCES IN ECONOMIC POLICIES OF POLITICAL PARTIES AND CENTRAL BANK INDEPENDENCE

We analysed above the implications of a model in which it was assumed that different political parties, who represent different class interests, will pursue different policies. This assumption may also have implications both for the operation of an independent central bank (see chapter 5) and the interpretation of the empirical evidence on the impact of independent central banks on economic outcomes as pointed out by e.g. Waller (1989) and Alesina and Gatti (1995).

Essentially if economic policies differ between parties then rational expectations of future economic variables will reflect electoral uncertainty. For example inflation expectations for a period in which there is an election will be given by

$$Ep = jEp^l + (1 - j)Ep^c \tag{1}$$

where j is the (assumed exogenous) probability of election of party l and Ep^c and Ep^l are expected inflation under the two parties.

To illustrate formally some implications we employ the model of Alesina and Gatti (1995) as set out in Alesina, Roubini and Cohen (1997).

They assume that the utility functions of the two parties have a standard quadratic form and are given by:

$$U^l = -0.5p^2 - 0.5b^l(y - y^*)^2 \tag{2}$$

and

$$U^c = -0.5p^2 - 0.5b^c(y - y^*)^2 \tag{3}$$

where $y^*$is the target level of output, assumed equal for the two parties to make the algebra simpler. Similar considerations apply to the target rate of inflation, assumed to be zero for each party b^c is assumed to be smaller than b^l so that the Conservative party gives relatively less weight to output stabilization and more to inflation than the Labour party.

The supply function is given the simple form

$$y = p - Ep + u \tag{4}$$

where u is a random shock. The natural rate of output is set to zero. Thus y is the output gap.

Assume that expectations are formed over a period that includes an election.

Employing the same methodology and timing of events as outlined above we obtain the first-order conditions for maximising U^l, and U^c given the supply function and Ep as

$$-p^l - b^l(p^l - Ep + u - y^*) = 0 \tag{5}$$

and

$$-p^c - b^c(p^c - Ep + u - y^*) = 0 \tag{6}$$

Substitution for Ep from (1) gives two simultaneous equations that can be solved for $p^c$and p^lrespectively as

$$p^l = \frac{b^l(1+b^r)y^*}{1+b^l(1-j)+jb^c} - \frac{b^l u}{1+b^l} \tag{7}$$

and

$$p^c = \frac{b^c(1+b^l)y^*}{1+b^l(1-j)+jb^c} - \frac{b^c u}{1+b^c} \tag{8}$$

When party l is in power output is given by

$$y = p^l - Ep + u \tag{9}$$

so that output under party l, substituting for p^l and Ep from (7) and (1) respectively is given by

$$y^l = \frac{(1-j)(b^l - b^c)y^*}{1+b^l(1-j)+jb^c} + \frac{u}{1+b^l} \tag{10}$$

The same procedure gives the output for party c as

$$y^c = \frac{-j(b^l - b^c)y^*}{1+b^l(1-j)+jb^c} + \frac{u}{1+b^c} \tag{11}$$

The variance of output, σ_y^2, is given by

$$\sigma_y^2 = jE(y^l - Ey)^2 + (1-j)E(y^c - Ey)^2 \tag{12}$$

since $Ey = 0$ substitution yields the solution for σ_y^2 as

$$\sigma_y^2 = \frac{j(1-j)(b^l - b^c)^2(y^*)^2}{(1+b^l(1-j)+jb^c)^2} + \frac{j}{(1+b^l)^2} + \left.\frac{(1-j)}{(1+b^c)^2}\right] \sigma_u^2 \tag{13}$$

where σ_u^2 is the variance of u.

The variance of inflation, σ_p^2, is given by

$$\sigma_p^2 = jE(p^l - Ep)^2 + (1-j)E(p^c - Ep)^2 \tag{14}$$

Substitution from (1), (7) and (8) gives

$$\sigma_p^2 = \frac{j(1-j)(b^l - b^c)^2(y^*)^2}{(1+b^l(1-j)+jb^c)^2} + [\frac{j(b^l)^2}{(1+b^l)^2} + \frac{(1-j)(b^c)^2}{(1+b^c)^2}]\sigma_u^2 \qquad (15)$$

Finally expected inflation is given by

$$Ep = \frac{b^c(1+b^l) + j(b^l - b^c)}{1+b^l(1-j)+jb^c} \qquad (16)$$

Equation (13) is the essential insight of Alesina and Gatti. The variance of output is decomposed into two parts. The first is the result of electoral uncertainty. Naturally it disappears when $j = 0$ or 1; the variance is also increasing in $b^l - b^c$, so that the greater the difference in policies between the two parties the greater the variance of output. It is also interesting that the variance of output is not independent of the target level of output as is the case when there is no political uncertainty. The second term reflects the impact of the variance of the economic shock.

It is also interesting to note from (10) and (11) that the average value of the output gap is no longer zero under the different regimes. The conservative regime will experience a negative output gap on average whilst the labour regime will experience a positive one.The result of Alesina and Gatti is important for interpretation of empirical work. We showed above how appointment of a conservative central banker would result in a higher variance of output than the first best. However in comparison to the outcome under political uncertainty the variance of output could be lower, depending upon the various parameters. This point is important both as a potential argument for the introduction of an independent central bank and when interpreting the empirical evidence on the economic effects of central banks.

Alesina and Gatti (1995) also consider the interesting issue of whether both parties could be better off appointing an independent central banker with a given b rather than the non-cooperative outcomes defined by equations (13), (15) and (16). They suggest that this can be the case.

9

Unemployment, productivity and growth

The modern macroeconomic model implies that the economy is converging on its natural rate at some speed determined by for example overlapping contracts or adjustment costs. Therefore the natural rates of output and unemployment become of central interest.

Much of the literature of the 'supply side' dwells on productivity and growth, but this neglects the important issue of unemployment which has been a particular problem in Europe. This has importance beyond the narrow issue of the number of people unemployed because of its social significance: politicians attach great importance to 'curing unemployment' because of its obvious unpopularity with voters. Unfortunately they tend to alight on measures that address the symptoms, not the disease; notably 'work-sharing', reducing participation (by for example early retirement or 'family policies' designed to keep women at home), reducing working hours, or indeed reducing productivity growth and the penetration of new technology. The reason they pick such policies is that the original disease, as we shall argue below, is due to their erecting 'social' support mechanisms that raise labour costs; it follows that cures based on 'labour market deregulation' (i.e. eliminating or bypassing such support) have no appeal to them. Instead they put their faith in measures that they think may mitigate the side-effects, in unemployment, of their (desirable) social policies.

This tendency of high unemployment to be accompanied by such policies is illustrated in Table 9.1. This shows at the end of the 1990s how low participation and low working hours tended to accompany the high unemployment in Germany, France and Italy. In Italy for example were the participation rate to be at the US level with no other changes unemployment would be around 30%. Table 9.2 following shows some evidence that these countries have also experienced a relative slowdown

	Unemployment (%) *	Participation+ Total (%)	(55–64	Working Hours**
US	4.6	66.4	57.2	1943
Japan	4.4	62.6	66.2	2014
UK	4.6	63.9	51.5	1826
Germany	10.6	55.0	42.6	1557
France	11.5	55.6	36.1	1612
Italy	12.3	47.2	28.3	1790

Sources
* (Economist) mid 1998 **1992, Manufacturing
(US Bur. Lab. Stats, Washington DC)
+ Total: 1990 (US Bur. Lab. Stats, Washington DC);
55-64 Yr Olds: 1995 (OECD)

Table 9.1: Labour Market Performance

in productivity growth in the 1980s and 1990s from the earlier postwar period; this suggests that their productivity growth too may have been held back by such policies.

UNEMPLOYMENT

Our focus in this section is on the natural rate, not on the cyclical behaviour of unemployment. The latter has to be explained in the context of the business cycle models of earlier chapters. The natural rate is the equilibrium to which these cycles tend. Milton Friedman (1968) remarked in his AEA lecture in 1968 that it was the equilibrium 'ground out by the Walrasian system' of real demands and supplies. However, it never really occurred to macroeconomists to model it until much later; Friedman, Phelps (1970) and others using the natural rate concept effectively treated it as a natural constant. It was not until the early 1980s in the UK where unemployment rose above 10% with no apparent tendency to fall that models began to be formulated of a changing natural rate. The first effort was by Minford (1983); he took the classical labour supply set-up of earlier chapters and added the idea of a permanent unemployment benefit, payable without any check on work availability (a peculiarly European concept). The result was to tilt the labour supply curve so that the real wage offer never fell below the benefit. This had the effect of creating the 'real wage rigidity' identified for example by Bruno and Sachs (1985) in their account of the 1973–4 oil crisis (figure 9.1). Note too that with such benefits one can account also for the cyclical behaviour of real wages and unemployment; real wages are procyclical, rising in the upswing and lifting people out of benefit, falling in the downswing so that people go on to benefit.

Hence unemployment tends to breed policies that inhibit participation and productivity growth. Our discussion therefore begins with unemployment. It goes on to the optimal size of government. It ends with growth itself.

	1960–1973	%		1979–1994	%
1	Japan	5.5	1	Ireland	2.6
2	Portugal	5.4	2	Finland	2.5
3	Ireland	4.6	3	Spain	1.7
4	Italy	4.4	4	Portugal	1.6
5	Finland	4.0	5	UK	1.5
6	Belgium	3.8	6	Denmark	1.3
7	France	3.7	7	France	1.3
8	Netherlands	3.4	8	Belgium	1.2
9	Spain	3.2	9	Japan	1.1
10	Austria	3.1	10	Netherlands	1.1
11	Germany	2.6	11	Sweden	1.0
12	UK	2.6	12	Austria	0.9
13	Greece	2.5	13	Italy	0.9
14	USA	2.5	14	Australia	0.8
15	Denmark	2.3	15	USA	0.5
16	Australia	2.2	16	Germany	0.4
17	Switzerland	2.1	17	Canada	-0.1
18	Norway	2.0	18	Norway	-0.1
19	Sweden	2.0	19	Switzerland	-0.2
20	Canada	1.9	20	Greece	-0.3

Source: OECD (1996) as cited in Crafts (1997)

Table 9.2: Total Factor Productivity (TFP) Growth in the Business Sector (% per annum)

In the figure one can see how the normal marginal product of labour schedule can interact with this distorted labour supply schedule to generate equilibrium unemployment. Should the benefit rise relative to productivity, unemployment will result. That is, people will voluntarily refuse to take available wage offers because benefits are preferable. They are 'unemployed' in the sense that they are not working but are 'available for work': thus in response to the usual survey questions they would be counted as wanting work (if at the 'right wage' but this is not generally included in the assessment) and some governments also would count them as unemployed because they are in receipt of unemployment benefit. In any case the unemployment is recognizable as what causes social dissatisfaction.

The labour market model can be generalised to include the effects of union power, taxes of all sorts, and employer and employee national insurance contributions (which in Europe are largely taxes in nature). When placed within the general equilibrium of an open economy one obtains natural rates of output, real wages and the real exchange rate as well as employment and unemployment (see chapter 10). Later versions have proliferated; in the UK Layard and Nickell (1985) estimated a similar model, and Bean et al (1986) attempted to extend it to other European countries which began to experience rising unemployment UK-style during the late 1980s and 1990s. It turns out that in each country there are substantial idiosyncracies in the social support mechanisms, complicating effective modelling of the natural unemployment rate. Nevertheless a large amount of empirical work, both cross-section (Burda, 1988, was the first to exploit the variation across European countries and show the importance of long-duration benefits) and time-series evidence (Layard, Nickell and Jackman, 1991, survey much of it) seemed to confirm that these mechanisms, particularly the length of time benefits were available and their ease of eligibility, were responsible for persistently high unemployment in Europe. By the end of the 1990s a general consensus had appeared, embodied in the OECD secretariat, that 'labour market flexibility' was the key to reducing equilibrium unemployment.

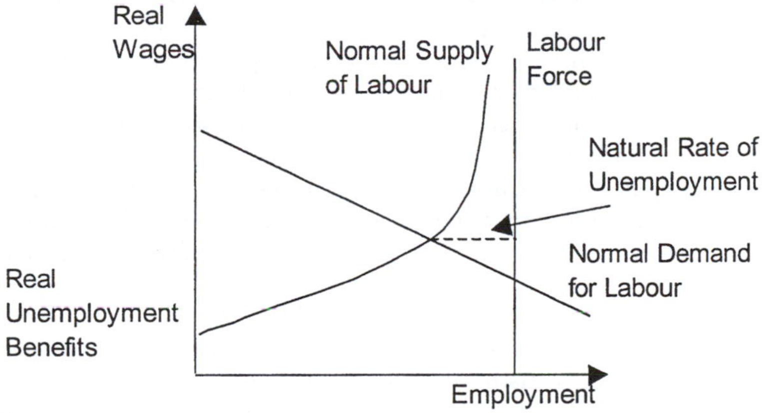

Figure 9.1: The natural rate of unemployment

Much of the traditional literature on unemployment emphasises search behaviour (e.g. Lancaster, 1979; Nickell, 1979). In the absence of a permanent unemployment benefit such behaviour would make sense; we could model a steady flow of job separations, with people searching for some average time determined in the usual search-optimising manner. This would give rise to an unemployment equilibrium of the rate of flow times the length of search; e.g. if 20% of the workforce separate each year and spend three months searching, this would yield an unemployment rate of 5% (0.2×0.25=0.05). We can think of this as a 'frictional' rate of unemployment; plainly in a well-functioning economy the natural rate should be such a frictional rate. The very high and long-lasting levels of unemployment seen in Europe during the late 1980s and early 1990s are not well explained in these terms, however; these high natural rates are better explained in terms of the model above, in which the long-term unemployed cannot be said in any meaningful way to be 'searching'.

Thus a first set of policies to generate high activity should be those of labour market flexibility.

THE OPTIMAL ROLE OF GOVERNMENT

It is plain that government provides some useful services. These services (such as law and order and infrastructure) could be provided privately but it is more efficient in practice to provide them publicly; that is, for 'public goods' there is a direct saving of resources from eliminating the duplication, the transactions costs and the under-use from private provision. However, there is also a cost in public provision: that distorting taxes must be raised to pay for the service. Though lump-sum taxes without a distorting effect are possible, they are so unpopular that in practice governments do not raise them to any serious extent (when the UK government brought in the 'poll tax' in the late 1980s to replace the 'rate', a tax on property values, it contributed to the fall of Margaret Thatcher; subsequently the tax was withdrawn in favour of a banded property tax).

We can model these two sides of public spending in terms of the labour market and the production function: public spending raises productivity but causes a distortion in labour supply — figure 9.2. A helpful way of summarising the twin effects as government spending (G) rises as a fraction of GDP stems from the Laffer Curve (figure 9.3) which shows tax revenue as a function of the tax rate (tax revenue = public spending). At low levels of spending, the tax rate is low and the marginal distortion cost of taxation (which rises with the square of the tax rate according to the standard consumer surplus formula) is correspondingly low, while the marginal benefit of government spending is high. With efficiency raised by the spending and low tax-distorting inefficiency, the revenue yield relative to the tax rate is high. As spending and the tax rate rises, this relative yield falls, as the marginal benefit of the spending falls and the marginal distorting cost rises. The optimal tax rate and size of government is given by T_0; as spending rises above this point, we move towards the revenue-maximising tax rate $T_{\max}$ where any further rise in the tax rate yields no extra revenue and so permits no extra spending. Thus whatever its motives no government can rationally operate to the right of this point.

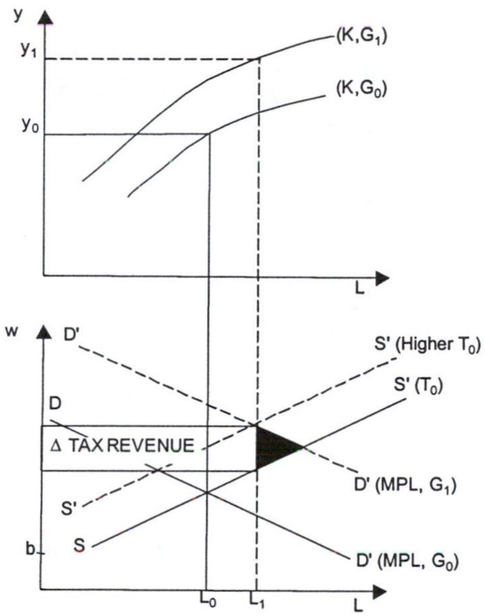

Figure 9.2: Public spending distorts the labour supply

This, useful as it is conceptually, tells us nothing in practice about where the optimal tax rate is. If we neglect very poor countries in Africa and elsewhere with poor infrastructure, there seem to be three main groups: Asian emerging-market countries with low tax rates (around 20%), good basic infrastructure but limited provision of welfare services and social insurance like unemployment benefit and public health care; an Anglo-Saxon group with medium tax rates (35-40%) and fairly extensive welfare services/social insurance; and a European group with

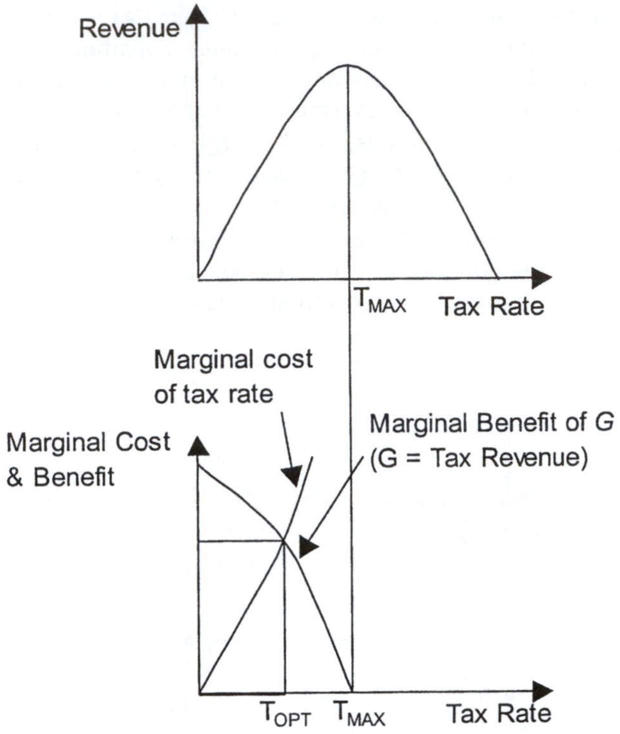

Figure 9.3: The Laffer curve

high tax rates (around 50%) and very extensive social insurance. The essential problem with the latter group is, as we saw in the last section, that generous social insurance distorts labour supply. Furthermore, the high marginal tax rates implied have substantial effects on work incentives for taxpayers on top rates at least; evidence from the US (Lindsey, 1987a, b; Feldstein, 1995) and the UK (Minford and Ashton, 1991) suggest that high earners' hours respond strongly to rising marginal rates so that higher-band tax revenues are likely to fall, putting them on the wrong side of the Laffer Curve (this is without including the effects of tax avoidance and evasion, and of migration or 'brain drain'). It is true that a degree of social insurance may make workers more willing to be flexible in job choice and location (for example the combination of no unemployment benefit and strong unions, as in Italy, may make it extremely difficult to close plants.) Nevertheless in a rich society most people would be willing to pay for higher than basic levels of health insurance, pensions and education; if the state provides these basic levels but no more, there is a basis for cutting tax rates to somewhere between the Anglo-Saxon and the Asian rates. Such a move has proved to be popular in the UK with pensions for example. If acceptable politically, it enables the economy to have a less distorting tax system with the reduction in government provision offset by higher private provision.

Government spending as % of GDP	
Anglo Saxon / Oriental	
USA	36.7*
Japan	36.7*
UK	43.5**
Continental European	
Germany	51.0**
France	54.3*
Italy	53.2**
* 1995 ** 1996	

Table 9.3: Public Expenditure Shares in GDP

GROWTH

Exogenous growth

Let us start by discussing a world with exogenous growth, the original standard framework of growth theory in which the size of the labour force and the progress of technology are both given by forces beyond the control of households or their governments (which respond to their wishes in some sense, let us assume).

Consider first the whole world economy. Represent its production possibilities in the simplest way as Cobb-Douglas:

$$y_t = A_t L_t^{\alpha} K_t^{1-\alpha} \tag{1}$$

For simplicity we will set depreciation to zero. Now, recalling that in equilibrium desired savings equal desired investment, we can follow Harrod and Domar to obtain the basic equation of growth equilibrium:

$$S = s(r)Y = I = k(r)\Delta Y = k(r)gY \tag{2}$$

where k is the capital-output ratio, $\frac{K_t}{Y_t}$; or

$$\frac{s(r)}{k(r)} = g \tag{3}$$

We can show that growth, g, is exogenously given by technological progress and the growth of the labour force; hence (3) will solve for the real interest rate, r:

$$r_t = (1-\alpha)\frac{K_t}{Y_t}; \text{that is, } k(r) = \frac{r_t}{1-\alpha} \tag{4}$$

$$w_t = \alpha\frac{L_t}{Y_t} \tag{5}$$

are the first-order conditions. Substituting for endogenous capital in the production function gives us:

$$Y_t = A_t^{\frac{1}{\alpha}} L_t \left(\frac{1-\alpha}{r_t}\right)^{1-\frac{1}{\alpha}} \tag{6}$$

Assuming that there is a steady state with a constant real interest rate and growth rate, then taking log first differences of (6) yields the growth rate as:

$$g = \frac{1}{\alpha}g_A + g_L \tag{7}$$

where $g_A(g_L) =$ growth of A (L).

From (4) this is the growth rate also of capital. With the real interest rate given by (3), (6) yields the level of output, (4) the level of capital, and (5) the real wage consistent with full employment of the labour force, L.

If we now consider an open economy facing a world capital market with given world real interest rate, then everything is the same except that now with r_t exogenous (3) is replaced by:

$$\frac{s(r)}{k(r) + \frac{NFI}{Y_t}} = g \tag{8}$$

which serves to determine NFI, net foreign investment (alias the current account surplus).

We have assumed implicitly that each country has its own technology. But we could add a mechanism of 'technological catch-up' whereby technological knowledge flows from high- to low-technology countries (via a variety of possible channels — e.g. licencing, corporate take-over, or multi-national company investment in low-wage countries using their own technology to exploit low wage costs). This catch-up would produce faster growth of A until it had caught up with best practice internationally. This 'convergence' is the focus of empirical work by Barro and Sala-i-Martin (for example, 1998) — note the caveats of Quah (1993).

Endogenous growth

One can investigate more complicated functional forms and also do empirical work on the 'sources of growth' (e.g. Denison, 1974) but essentially this was the long and the short of 'growth theory' under these exogeneity assumptions. It is against this background that one can consider 'endogenous growth'. The assumption in this case is that the growth rate is a matter of choice (whether by individual households or their governments). In some sense this seems quite right. There are huge differences in growth rates, both between countries at the same time and within the same country at different periods of history (Parente and Prescott, 1999, provide a clear overview of the 'stylised facts' of growth). These differences seem to be the result of choices within these countries.

Of course two questions arise. What proximate mechanism produces growth? And how do people formulate their choices (that in turn feed into the mechanism) in the light of it? These two questions are closely intertwined.

On the first question of mechanisms there is now a huge literature theorising on possible ones. One can perhaps single out three as front runners — though it must be stressed that empirical testing has lagged way behind the theory (not least because of the great difficulties of identification in this area where so many different mechanisms are at work, all of them related in both causal directions with growth) so that we are still largely in our armchairs on this issue.

The first is increasing returns to scale over sections of the production function — P. Romer (1986). Suppose one accepts that in nature at some comprehensive level of description there are constant returns essentially on logical grounds: if you double every single ingredient that is producing something then in principle you should double output since all you are doing is replication — putting the same thing side by side with itself must give you double. Nevertheless in practice not everything is included in the production function, there are always uncosted factors ('commons', resources that are uncharged for because they are not scarce in the given situation) and also as size changes so does the nature of the operation. For example in 'virgin territories' land is free; then the increasing penetration of people can reap increasing returns as thresholds of exploitability are passed. A similar thing appears to happen with all new technologies (Mansfield, 1968); they follow an S-shaped curve of productivity. In the early stages productivity grows slowly because the technique is poorly implementable with little learning and few users; as more users join and learning increases, productivity rises rapidly; finally as all its uses are exploited productivity growth tails off.

These ideas underpin specifications of the production function with increasing returns — most easily represented by making the technology parameter, A_t, depend on size of output. Assuming that the stock of labour is exogenous, then the increasing returns can be exploited by increasing the capital stock.

A second main route is to model A_t as accumulated knowledge, with knowledge production an industry in its own right (the R&D sector).

The third, closely related, route is to include human capital (skills of the workforce as opposed to pure technological knowledge) in the production function (Lucas, 1988). One can then treat it as investment requiring, like physical capital, savings to create it (though in this case not recorded financial savings but rather the substitution of 'creative' for non-creative leisure), in which case the model's behaviour is essentially like that of the Solow model; but because it downgrades the contribution of 'pure labour' in favour of human capital it implies that saving has a bigger effect on growth and so can account more easily for growth differences between countries (D. Romer, 1996, section 3.11). Or we can attribute human capital to learning-by-doing, so that it increases with the level of output say (more precisely with the accumulation of output experience). As with increasing returns one can think of this as a way by which size raises the technology parameter, A_t.

Having discussed mechanisms, we turn to the second, crucial question of how choices are formulated: if people could predict exactly how their and other people's investments would interact and could coordinate these choices, then one could envisage a country's (a social planner's) strategy to exploit ('internalise') these increasing returns. If on the other hand choices are uncoordinated and each regards the investments of others as given and unpredictable, then the increasing returns are 'external' to individual choice; people will preserve the same first-order condition as above but increasing returns will come from them happening to invest together for reasons of say perceived improvement in technology. It is more normal (and clearly more realistic) to make this latter assumption that people act singly so that these effects, through either mechanism, are external. We make this assumption initially in order to illustrate the workings of the typical endogenous growth model.

In what follows we shall formally use the open economy assumption and treat the real interest rate as exogenously set in world markets. (One can also think of the interest rate as reacting in a closed economy, the world say, to clear the market for savings and investment; in this case r_t will have a varying steady state value, provided there is a steady state, as growth varies.) This departs from the frequently-met assumption of a fixed savings rate; but it is both more realistic and simpler to handle and in any case the essential properties of the models are unaffected.

We give two examples, using the model as already set up but adding an explicit equation for A_t. Our second will illustrate the knowledge-production model. The first illustrates the increasing returns and the learning-by-doing human capital models: we represent both mechanisms by the simple device of making technology a function of size

$$A_t(Y_t) = \exp^{\pi t} Y_{t-1}^{\gamma} \tag{9}$$

where π and γ are positive constants. The lag is there to bring out some simple dynamics. If we now substitute into the production function both this and the optimal capital stock from (4) we obtain:

$$Y_t = (\exp \frac{\pi}{\alpha} t) Y_{t-1}^{\gamma/\alpha} L_t \left(\frac{r_t}{1-\alpha}\right)^{\frac{1-\alpha}{\alpha}} \tag{10}$$

implying that:

$$g_t = \frac{\pi}{\alpha} + \frac{\gamma}{\alpha} g_{t-1} + g_L \tag{11}$$

If $\gamma \geq \alpha$, then this will be an explosive difference equation and growth explodes correspondingly; no steady state exists until presumably at some point γ drops to below α. If and when $\gamma \prec \alpha$, then the model converges on steady state growth which is:

$$g = \frac{\alpha}{\alpha - \gamma} \left(\frac{1}{\alpha}\pi + g_L\right) \tag{12}$$

and the corresponding output is:

$$y_t = \left(\exp \frac{\pi}{\alpha - \gamma} t\right) L_t^{\frac{\alpha}{\alpha-\gamma}} [\frac{1-\alpha}{r_t}]^{\frac{1-\alpha}{\alpha-\gamma}} \tag{13}$$

What we see here is two exciting results. First, that growth can 'take off' in an explosive burst, feeding on itself. Second, that even when it is not (or no longer) explosive, growth will settle down to a 'multiplier' on the exogenous sources of growth. From a policy viewpoint any government action that could promote such exogenous sources of growth would be prima facie desirable, since the private consumption cost would presumably be exceeded by the 'multiplied' effect of the action (and certainly would be far exceeded if explosive growth is triggered). For example suppose government-financed training increased human capital, inserting a multiplicative term h_t into (9). Then the level of output would rise by $h_t^{\frac{1}{\alpha-\gamma}}$; so provided the tax cost is less than this it would be desirable, abstracting from distributional issues. Similar arguments could be applied to public infrastructure spending that contributed directly to the profitability of investment (so raising A_t). Examples could be extended easily to many aspects of public spending — e.g. on health, policing, social care. Via their contributions to human capital or the productivity of private capital they could generate large multiplied benefits. This discussion follows familiar long-standing discussions of public spending whenever an 'externality' is identified. The difficulties with the line of argument are also familiarly those of identifying the benefits with any degree of certainty. Here we have only the haziest idea even of the functional forms that might embody these externalities let alone the size of the parameters; empirical work has barely begun to generate plausible estimates.

The second example we consider is that of knowledge accumulation via an R&D industry; it has essentially the same sort of implications. We follow D. Romer's (1996) simplification of models due to P. Romer (1990), Grossman and Helpman (1991), and Aghion and Howitt (1992). Now let A_t be produced by some fixed fraction, a_L, of the labour force (we ignore capital for simplicity) according to

$$\frac{\partial A_t}{\partial t} = a_L L_t A_t^{\theta} \tag{14}$$

Substituting capital demand into our production function gives us:

$$Y_t = A_t^{1/\alpha}(1 - \alpha_L) L_t \left(\frac{r_t}{1-\alpha}\right)^{1/\alpha} \tag{15}$$

(where Y_t is the output available for consumption and investment, excluding R&D) from which:

$$g = \frac{1}{\alpha} g_A + g_L \tag{16}$$

as in the Solow case. The difference is now that g_A is endogenous.

(14) is a first-order differential equation in A_t which is explosive if $\theta \geq 1$. Hence in this example as in the first we may have explosive bursts of growth until θ falls below 1. Once $\theta \prec 1$, we have:

$$g_{A,t} = \frac{\frac{\partial A_t}{\partial t}}{A_t} = a_L L_t A_t^{\theta - 1} \tag{17}$$

so that

$$\frac{\partial \ln g_{A,t}}{\partial t} = g_L + (\theta - 1) g_{A,t} \tag{18}$$

In the steady state where $\frac{\partial \ln g_{A,t}}{\partial t} = 0$, this implies

$$g_A = \frac{g_L}{1-\theta} \tag{19}$$

so that steady state growth of output is as before a multliplier of exogenous growth factors:

$$g = \left[1 + \frac{1}{\alpha(1-\theta)} \right] g_L \tag{20}$$

The policy implications are analogous with respect to intervention in R&D. If somehow resources can be diverted to this industry, by a rise in a_L for example, then the immediate loss in output is soon more than made up for by the rise in A_t, possibly an explosive one for a time. Nevertheless, such seductive implications must be qualified by our empirical ignorance of the parameters as well as of the mechanisms generating effective R&D.

These two examples must suffice to illustrate the proliferation of models with features of this type. The general implication of these models is that with uncoordinated private agents there are potentially massive externalities in activities generating 'growth agents' such as knowledge, human capital, and agglomeration and other sources of increasing returns.

Suppose instead that private choices are coordinated in some way. This could happen in different ways. Government coordination is one; as it involves detailed knowledge of the potential gains from new technological applications and investments, this is not a main candidate except for rather basic elements of a joint strategy such as infrastructure. Plainly however in any coordination the government is likely to have some role to play, if only in agreeing to get out of the way (e.g. in monopoly regulation). Probably the main way in which coordination might occur is intra-industry joint ventures; there are many examples of such collaboration between competitors (such as in the airline industry to develop internet booking systems or in the telecommunications industry to develop the new generation of mobile phones and handheld computers). One should also not discount popular coordination, now more achievable via the internet.

Assuming such coordination, one can think of a representative household (like a social planner) optimising its intertemporal utility by choosing a particular growth strategy given all these sources of self-reinforcing growth. This clearly produces a highly complex private optimising problem in which all the opportunities and constraints are internalised; of course if the economy could offer explosive growth, this will imply a massive free lunch and a coordinated jump to a hugely richer world where convergence once more has returned and normal maximization can be resumed. The role for government in this set-up is different from the externality case just considered. Here government has no business spending any resources since there are no ('external') opportunities not already exploited by the private sector/government coordination. In these circumstances government regulations, taxes and other interventions would inhibit the private sector from exploiting available opportunities. In crude terms, where there are large incentives to exploit potential new technologies, the private sector will take larger risks and invest more resources than where taxes are high and regulations are stringent. Interestingly, Parente and Prescott concluded that some such x-factor of the degree of non-intervention promised the best hope of explaining the stylised facts of growth.

This emphasises the importance of social institutions and policy frameworks, within which in general households take decentralised decisions in their own private interests and yet may have an effective way of internalising some externalities. The idea that somehow societies automatically internalise all externalities flies in the face of the obvious evidence of huge differences in the success of different societies in achieving growth. There is plenty of evidence that institutions evolve over time instead of being the direct object of social choice (Sugden, 1986). They are the result either of unprompted social interaction or of some political process. In the last section of this chapter we discuss what light 'political economy' can shed on success and failure in producing institutions that are good for the supply side of the economy.

THE POLITICAL ECONOMY OF THE SUPPLY SIDE

There is a massive literature on the creation and evolution of the institutions that favour or inhibit capitalist growth. North (1981) charted the way in which protestant dissent in the low countries and the UK produced the first industrial revolutions; Lal (1998) has gone further back to show how competition in Europe between nation states under the edicts of Papal Christendom gave capitalism its secure basis. In two important books, the late Mancur Olson (1965 and 1982) set out the mechanism by which vested interest groups could prevent the general good (in the second he argued that as nations become older they acquire more powerful vested interests as networks and clubs have longer to form and become entrenched); essentially they can exercise discipline over their members who have strong interests at stake, whereas the general public have too little incentive individually to understand how their own interests are prejudiced by the action of these groups. Hence for politicians to mobilise opinion in favour of reform is costly and uncertain; whereas these groups can offer them rewards, both personal and political, for pushing forward their own agendas — an activity known as 'rent-seeking', in which existing rents are diverted instead of being augmented by productive action. This basic idea has led to a substantial applied research agenda (e.g. St. Paul, 1996, on the difficulties of modifying costly firing regulations in Europe, and Tullock et al., 2000, for a survey of US work).

However, there are examples of supply-side reforms being undertaken in spite of vested interest opposition. Three such are the wide-ranging reforms of the Thatcher conservatives over the 1980s and 1990s in the UK, and in the US the Carter deregulation of the 1970s and the Reagan tax reforms of the 1980s. On these occasions it proved possible for politicians to build a sufficient coalition in public opinion to support reform.

So there is a tension between the strengths of vested interests and the power of public opinion in asserting its general interests. A political economy of institutions should attempt to model this tension. In chapter 8 we already reviewed the political economy of macroeconomic policy; central to this were models of voting behaviour. It is natural to extend these to supply-side issues — which we can define as microeconomic issues with macroeconomic consequences.

Many detailed approaches are possible. Here we illustrate them by taking one possible model, that of the floating voter lying between 'capitalists' and 'workers' as in the model of Minford and Peel (1983) reviewed in chapter 8. The workers, it will be remembered, obtained their income stream from human capital, whose value was badly affected by unemployment but largely hedged against inflation; the capitalists obtained theirs from financial and physical capital which was largely unaffected by unemployment but vulnerable to inflation. We can see similar dichotomies of interests between these two groups in respect of supply-side issues; unemployment benefits will appeal to workers but be disliked by capitalists who will pay much of the bill in return for no reward, redistributive taxation will be the same, as will be such things as minimum wages, workers' rights and firing restrictions. Let us assume that the effects of an improvement in the general good of the economy is too small in normal circumstances to affect the voting behaviour of each group relative to its sectional (rent-seeking) interest; thus each group normally votes its selfish pocket. We can imagine a status quo in which the vested interests of each group of voters are represented respectively by unions and employers' associations; the floating voter is some weighted combination of the two groups, which therefore votes a weighted average pocket. The question then is how shocks to the economy may alter the political equilibrium represented by this floating voter.

As hints towards the outcome, we may reflect on how — as noted at the start of this chapter — downward shifts in general economic prosperity have triggered increased intervention (more benefits, taxation and regulation). The Great Depression in the US famously unleashed both the Roosevelt New Deal interventions and massive protection. During the 1980s in continental Europe the rise of unemployment brought increased regulation of the labour market — for example reduced working hours — that reduced participation as well. At the same time we may also note that crises and very poor economic performance can trigger reform because voters suspend their normal voting patterns, so obviously atrocious has the general state of the economy become that it pays them more to restore its health than to gain a rent-seeking interest.

This sort of voting behaviour might suggest a model for change in the political equilibrium according to some indicator of general economic performance, say unemployment. We could assume that at very low rates of unemployment (good performance) the floating voters are predominantly capitalist, with little concern for unemployment (because prosperity has enhanced holdings of non-human capital and reduced the risk to human capital); at high but not catastrophic rates they are predominantly workers, with high concern (the risk to human capital has risen and holdings of non-human capital have been devalued); and that at catastrophic rates they switch from normal voting patterns to become concerned with maximising the general good. Suppose we focus on a representative supply-side issue, like the level and duration (overall 'generosity') of real unemployment benefits, B_t. This points to a model of change in B_t being a quadratic in the rate of unemployment, U_t, or say:

$$\Delta \ln B_t = \alpha(U_{t-1} - c) - \beta(U_{t-1})^2 \tag{21}$$

so that initially a rise in unemployment above some critical rate, c, would trigger demands for higher benefits; but as unemployment rose, the general good element would become more of a restraining factor, until ultimately voters demanded reform and benefits were cut. One could postulate similar mechanisms affecting other supply-side policies; for example the tax rate would tend to rise as benefit bills rose with intermediate unemployment, but be cut once the crisis had hit, while demands for regulations would tend to mirror demands for benefits.

If we combine this with a standard model of (long-term) unemployment, as set out earlier in this chapter:

$$\ln U_t = \sigma \ln B_t + U_0 \tag{22}$$

we obtain the interesting non-linear relationship:

$$\frac{\Delta U_t}{U_{t-1}} = \Delta \ln U_t = \sigma\alpha(U_{t-1} - c) - \sigma\beta(U_{t-1})^2 \tag{23}$$

or

$$U_t = (1 - \sigma c)U_{t-1} + \sigma\alpha(U_{t-1})^2 - \sigma\beta(U_{t-1})^3 \tag{24}$$

This is just an example of the sort of model one might use to simulate the tendency of the political equilibrium to add supply-side damage on top of a bad shock, perhaps from demand; producing a 'vicious circle'; but also of the phenomenon of drastic reform prompted by disaster that causes vested interests to set their narrow aims aside. Depending on how rapidly the economy improves after such reform, a virtuous circle can result as unemployment drops sufficiently for demands for restored benefits to disappear. What we are suggesting here is that good macroeconomic management has a crucial role in supporting good supply-side policy; just as earlier we saw that poor supply-side policy may create pressures for inflationary macroeconomic policies. There are intimate linkages through political economy between the two sorts of policies; and these links have the capacity to create both vicious and virtuous circles of economic performance.

CONCLUSIONS

In this chapter we have extended our discussions of macroeconomics outside the area of monetary and fiscal policy and the 'demand side', in which the natural rates of output and unemployment are taken as given by exogenous supply factors; and we have focused on the determinants of these factors themselves. We began by setting out a theory relating persistent unemployment (dominated by a large number of long-term unemployed) to the interaction of generous long-duration unemployment benefits with taxes and other labour market distortions, like union powers. We then looked at the determinants of growth and productivity, in the 'new theory' of endogenous growth that has been built on the Solow model. Finally, we reviewed some evidence that, paralleling the links from poor supply-side performance to inflationary policies discussed in chapters 5 and 8, there appear to be links from severe business cycle shocks to poor supply-side policies, the most notable example being the Great Depression. We suggested that political economy models could account for these links too, embodying the tension between voting along vested interest lines and voting, perhaps under conditions of crisis, along lines dictated by general welfare. These models should be able to account for the phenomenon of vicious and virtuous circles in economies' behaviour generated by these linkages.

Part III

Extending and Deepening the Models — the Open Economy and Micro-foundations

10

The Macroeconomics of an Open Economy

All economies are of course open to trade and capital transactions with others; only the world economy is not. So in principle, the models we have dealt with to this point are all to be considered as models of the world economy. Even the United States, once blithely treated as 'closed' by the majority of macroeconomists, has been recognized in the past two decades at least to be importantly affected by international influences.

These influences are transmitted through the balance of payments which records the transactions of a country's residents with residents elsewhere. The current account records all transactions with non-residents which alter the net assets of residents, that is, transactions that require payment. Exports of goods and services and receipts of factor income from abroad (interest, profits and dividends, and remitted rents or wages) increase residents' net worth: if residents do not receive direct payment by cash or cheque, then they receive IOUs in some form. Imports decrease residents' net worth. Exports net of imports, the current account balance, therefore measures the change in residents' net worth as a result of transactions with 'foreigners', non-residents. This implies that movements in the current account have net wealth effects wherever in the domestic economy wealth matters — notably spending, possibly the demand for money and the supply of labour.

The capital account of the balance of payments records the capital counterpart of all current transactions (that is, payment in some form by a drawdown of assets against foreigners) and also all transactions with non-residents which do not alter net assets of residents but rather reshuffle them: for example, borrowing from or lending to them (a swap of a loan liability for cash), equity issues (a swap of the ownership of physical assets for cash), direct purchase of physical assets or 'direct investment' (a swap of physical assets for cash) or combinations of these

	Assets		Liabilities
1	Physical capital	4	Government bonds (inc. Treasury bills)
2	Value of cumulated current deficits	5	Currency in hands of banks and public
3	Reserves		

Table 10.1: Consolidated bank / government balance sheet

(like equity purchase financed by borrowing). It follows that the net change in the capital account (the rise in net assets) is exactly equal to the current account balance. By convention a rise in assets is recorded with a minus sign so that the capital and current account balances thus sum to zero.

Within the capital account, transactions with the central bank are singled out. The central bank's net foreign asssets, the 'foreign exchange reserves', can finance purchases and sales of the domestic currency, usually for reasons of exchange rate policy. Apart from net interest earned or capital gains, which are typically small enough to neglect, the reserves will only rise or fall because of these sales or purchases, that is, foreign exchange intervention.

The reserves have monetary significance. If we think of the central bank as the monetary arm of the government, issuing money and holding reserves for it, then we can write the consolidated bank/government balance sheet as in Table 10.1

Items 1 and 2 are the result of the government's past decisions to invest (1) and to consume more than its revenue (2). These are financed by borrowing (item 4) or currency issue (5). Changes in item 3, the acquisition of foreign assets (net), must be similarly financed by new borrowing or currency issue, given the inherited items 1 and 2. In change terms we can write:

$$\triangle M = \triangle R + DEF - \triangle B \tag{1}$$

where M = currency issue, R = reserves, DEF = the government's investment and consumption less revenue ('total' deficit, or 'borrowing requirement'), B = bonds outstanding. DEF and B can be computed either inclusive or exclusive of capital gains or losses. The essential point of (1) is that if there is foreign exchange intervention, $\triangle R$, to sell the domestic currency, this will increase the money supply, $\triangle M$, unless there is an offsetting open market operation, in this case the sale of bonds, $\triangle B$, for currency.

We can immediately link this to the exchange rate regime. Under fixed exchange rates, the central bank stands ready to maintain the exchange rate with whatever intervention is needed. At this exchange rate, the economy will throw up a current account, $CURBOP$, and a balance, $CAPBOP$, on all capital transactions not involving the central bank (or 'capital balance' for short). By definition the current account balance, being the net acquisition of foreign assets, must of course be equal to the balance of net foreign assets transactions recorded in the capital account, including transactions in the foreign exchange reserves. By the balance of payments convention noted above (an application of double-entry book-keeping), assets acquired are recorded with a negative sign in the capital account, liabilities with a positive sign. This implies that all non-reserve transactions which would increase the reserves, by requiring payments from foreigners, are positive, and vice versa.

Hence

$$CURBOP + CAPBOP = \triangle R \tag{2}$$

It follows that the supply of money is affected through (1) by whatever reserves movements are thrown up at the fixed exchange rate.

A floating exchange rate is defined by the absence of foreign exchange intervention: $\triangle R = 0$. Hence the rate has to move to whatever level will continuously force the current and capital accounts together to zero.

A useful way to approach the open economy aspects then is to set up models of the current and capital account respectively.

THE CURRENT ACCOUNT: TWO MODELS

There are two main models of trade flows in the short or medium run. The first assumes that products are non-homogeneous and produced under imperfect competition: the products of British firms differ from those of German firms, say, even in the same market. The second assumes that products are homogeneous and produced under perfect competition: prices for British and German output of the same product are equalized across all world markets (that is, in any given market they will be equal, though transport costs will cause prices of both to differ between markets).

Let us take each model in turn, in each case treating home costs and prices as given: we will revert to this 'supply' aspect shortly. All prices will be expressed in home currency so that the exchange rate is implicit in the foreign prices.

Imperfect Competition

The imperfect competition model is illustrated in figure 10.1. XX shows the demand for exports by non-residents (shifted by world trade, WT), MM that for imports by residents (shifted by domestic demand, D). The ϕM curve shows the real value of imports as $P_H/P_F(=1/\phi)$ varies.

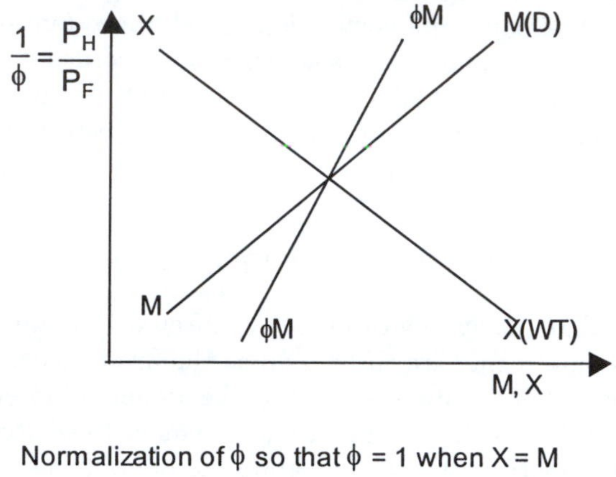

Figure 10.1: The imperfect competition model of the current account

This is the familiar model of import and export demand, encountered in the majority of macro models. The resulting current account equation is:

$$CURBOP = P_H X(WT, P_H/P_F) - P_F M(D, P_H/P_F) \tag{3}$$

In real terms

$$\frac{CURBOP}{P_H} = X - \phi M \tag{4}$$

where $\phi = P_F/P_H$ is the inverse of the terms of trade. It is usually found in empirical work (e.g. by Stern et al., 1976) that the current account improves after a few years when the terms of trade worsen (as could occur with a devaluation that is not fully offset by a rise in home prices), although in the short run because of lags in the response of trade volumes the current account may worsen (the 'J-curve'). The condition for improvement (the Marshall-Lerner condition) can be written in terms of elasticities as:

$$\varepsilon_x + \varepsilon_m - 1 > 0 \tag{5}$$

This applies exactly when trade is initially in balance ($X = \phi M$) and is derived straightforwardly from:

$$0 < [\delta(\frac{CURBOP}{P_H})/\delta\phi] \cdot \phi/X = \frac{\delta X}{\delta\phi} \cdot \frac{\phi}{X} - \phi \cdot \frac{\delta M}{\delta\phi} \cdot \frac{\phi}{\phi M}$$

$$- M \cdot \frac{\phi}{\phi M} = \varepsilon_x + \varepsilon_m - 1 \quad (6)$$

remembering that $\varepsilon_m = - \frac{\delta M}{\delta\phi} \cdot \frac{\phi}{M}$ is positive by the elasticity convention.

Perfect Competition

The perfect competition model is illustrated in figure 10.2. We take non-traded goods ('home') prices, P_{NT}, as given in this case; traded prices, P_T, are of course set by world market conditions. A devaluation, not offset fully by a rise in home prices, will raise P_T relative to P_{NT}. Domestic demand, D, depending overall on output, y, and wealth, θ, is split between traded and non-traded goods by relative prices, P_{NT}/P_T. The supply of non-traded goods, at given P_{NT}, rises or falls to meet demand for them (in practice market-clearing will require that P_{NT} move to equilibrate the two). The supply of traded goods will depend on traded prices relative to home prices (and costs): we will assume throughout that capital stocks are fixed (although this can easily be varied to obtain long run solutions; see the appendix).

The current account equation we obtain is:

$$CURBOP = P_T(Q_T[P_{NT}/P_T] - D_T[D, P_{NT}/P_T]) \quad (7)$$

where we have aggregated over exported and imported products; in fact $P_T Q_T = P_{XT}Q_{XT} + P_{MT}Q_{MT}$ (similarly $P_T D_T$), so if there is an improvement in the terms of trade, P_{XT}/P_{MT}, the current account would improve, with no consequence for trade volumes provided P_{NT}/P_T remained constant — unlike the imperfect competition model. A fall in P_{NT}/P_T (due say to a devaluation not fully offset by a rise in P_{NT}) will unambiguously improve the current account in both the short and the long run — unlike the effects of the analogue, a terms of trade change in the imperfect competition model.

HOME PRICES: THE SUPPLY SIDE

We held home prices constant to study the partial equilibrium determination of the current account, largely from the demand side. We now discuss how home prices in the two models are determined, and also the general demand-supply equilibrium of the model.

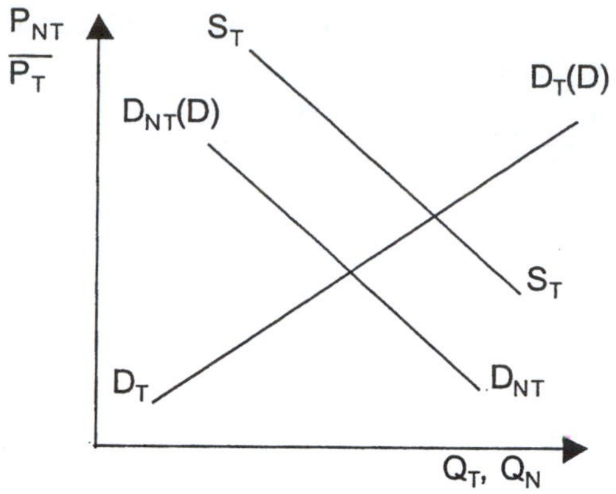

Figure 10.2: The perfect competition model of the current account

Imperfect competition

Figure 10.3 illustrates this in the imperfect competition model (it is a diagram adapted from the earlier Parkin and Bade diagram of figure 3.2). In the bottom left hand quadrant, the labour supply curve slopes upward as the real consumer wage, W deflated by the consumer price index, π, rises. $\pi = P_H^{\alpha} P_F^{1-\alpha}$., that is, it is a weighted average of home goods prices and imported prices. The demand for labour however reacts to the real producer wage,

$$\frac{W}{P_H} = \frac{W}{\pi} \cdot \frac{\pi}{P_H} = \frac{W}{\pi} \cdot (\frac{P_F}{P_H})^{1-\alpha}$$

so as $(P_H/P_F) = e$ rises, $\frac{W}{P_H}$ the real producer wage falls relative to the real consumer wage and the demand for labour rises, shifting DD rightwards. The higher employment is translated, by the production function and the 45° line in the top two quadrants, into an open economy supply curve, OS in the bottom right-hand quadrant. Finally, we use figure 10.1 to derive a curve showing combinations of e and D that give current account equilibrium: that is, where the XX and ϕM curves cross each other as D is varied. The resulting curve is the XM in the bottom right quadrant of Figure 10.3: note that since along it, $D = y$ (implied by current account equilibrium), we can draw it in e, y space.

When these relationships are put together, we can see in figure 10.3. that e_0, y_0, L_0, $(W/\pi)_0$ are the general equilibrium, conditional on the capital stock (we can also let this vary: for this long-run case, see the appendix).

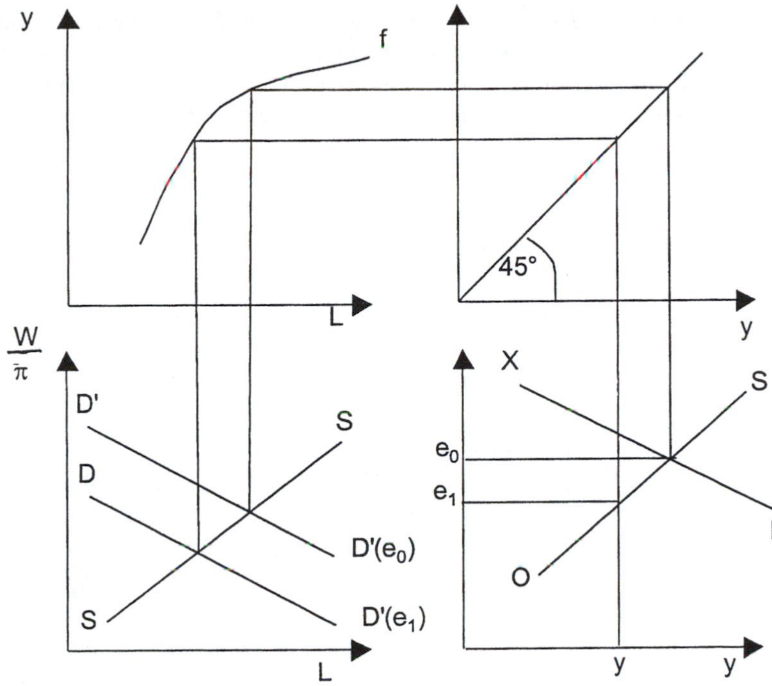

Figure 10.3: Supply and Demand in the Open Economy under imperfect competition (capital stock fixed)

Perfect Competition

Figures 10.4 and 10.5 explain how the perfect competition open economy supply curve is derived. Figure 10.4 shows the demand for labour by traded and non-traded goods industries: the non-traded demand is assumed to be more elastic that the traded, because factor proportions are more malleable, given the capital stock, than in manufacturing (hotel porters versus machine operatives). Since

$$\pi = P_{NT}^{1-\alpha} P_T$$

it follows that

$$W/\pi = (W/P_{NT})(P_{NT}/P_T)^{\alpha}$$

and also that

$$W/\pi = (W/P_T)(P_{NT}/P_T)^{-(1-\alpha)}$$

This implies that if P_{NT}/P_T (which now becomes the real exchange rate, e) rises, then at a given W/π, producer real wages rise for the traded goods sector, to w'_T, but fall for the non-traded sector, to w'_{NT}. Overall, under our assumption, the demand for labour would then rise, just as in figure 10.3.

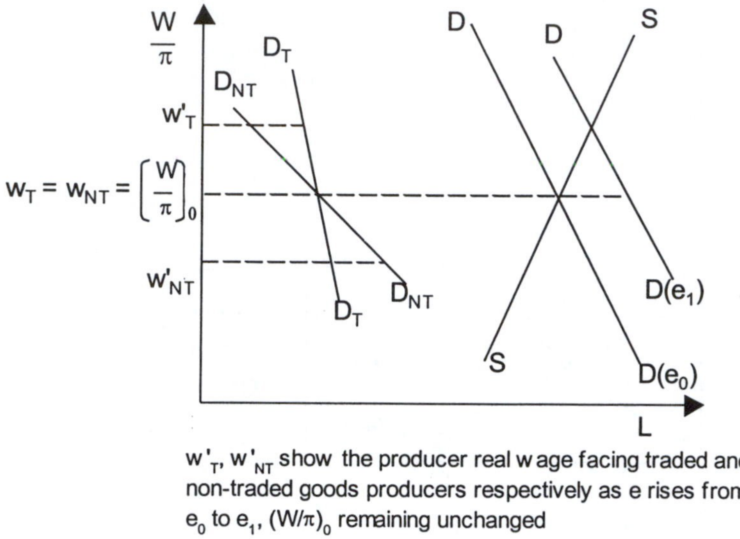

Figure 10.4: The labour market under perfect competition (capital stock fixed)

Figure 10.5 then takes up the rest of the story, as in figure 10.3. In the top left-hand quadrant is shown the production function for the whole economy (f) as well as those for traded and non-traded goods: clearly one can trace out production in each of these two sectors as well, from their demands for labour in figure 10.4.

The XM curve in figure 10.5 is derived from figure 10.2 by varying D and tracing out the P_{NT}/P_T values for which there is an intersection between demand and supply for traded goods (current account equilibrium). As with the derivation of the XM in figure 10.3, $D = y$ at these values so that we can draw the relationship as between P_{NT}/P_T and y. General equilibrium is at the intersection of the XM and OS curves, at e_0, y_0, L_0, $(W/\pi)_0$.

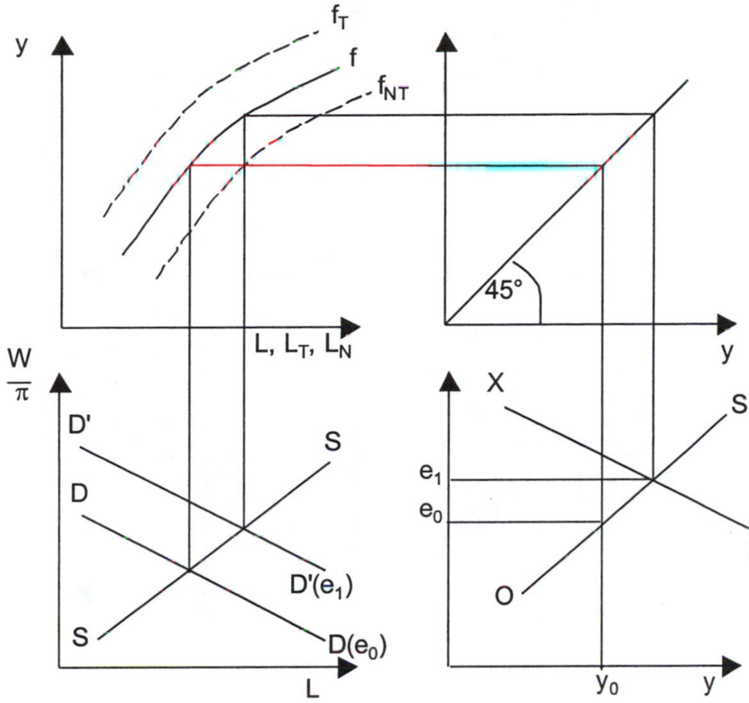

Figure 10.5: Supply and Demand under perfect competition (capital stock fixed)

The open economy supply curve (OS) and the effect of prices

The OS curve we have just derived can be thought of as the equivalent of y^* in the closed economy Phillips curve: that is, it is the state of the economy when there are no price surprises (including prices different from those built into wage contracts for the New Keynesian case).

The analysis when there are price surprises is the same as in the closed economy case, only here the OS curve shifts in e, y space — a presentational difference only. Figure 10.6 illustrates the resulting open economy 'Phillips curve' effect.

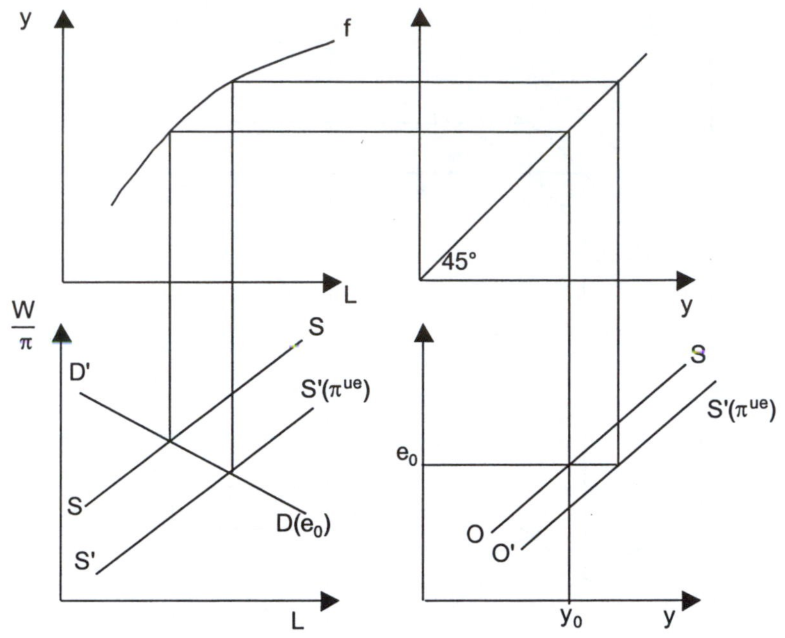

Figure 10.6: A price surprise shifts the OS curve: the open economy Phillips curve effect

THE CAPITAL ACCOUNT AND THE REST OF THE OPEN ECONOMY MODEL

We shall see in Chapter 14 (where we deal with efficient markets) that, as a result of portfolio diversification, the equilibrium price or return on an internationally traded asset is (possibly totally) insensitive to variations in its supply. In the case of interest rates, this gives rise to the uncovered interest parity condition:

$$R_t = R_{F,t} - (E_t S_{t+1} - S_t) \tag{8}$$

This safe return on one-period bonds (in domestic currency terms) is the benchmark for all other domestic asset returns: if the yield is sensitive to the supply of domestic assets, one can add to (8) an extra term in the stock of net foreign assets, and possibly also total assets, inclusive too of the physical capital stock. However, empirically such terms are rarely significant and we ignore them here.

It is useful to rewrite (8) in real terms:

$$
\begin{aligned}
r_t = R_t - E_t\pi_{t+1} + \pi_t = R_{F,t} - E_t\pi F_{,t+1} + \pi_{F,t} \\
- (E_tS_{t+1} + E_t\pi_{t+1} - E_t\pi_{F,t+1}) + (S_t + \pi_t - \pi_{F,t}) \\
= r_{f,t} - E_te_{t+1} + e_t \quad (9)
\end{aligned}
$$

where r is the real interest rate and e the real exchange rate defined in this section as the (log) ratio of the consumer price deflators. (9) is the 'BB curve' of the Mundell-Fleming model (Mundell, 1960; Fleming, 1962) along which the foreign exchange market is always clearing.

Whether we have the perfect competition model or the imperfect competition model, this definition of the real exchange rate will do equally well. In the perfect competition model, $\pi - \pi_F = (1-\alpha)P_{NT} + \alpha P_T - \pi_F$ (all prices are now expressed in logs). If $\pi_F = P_T$, then $\pi - \pi_F = (1-\alpha)(P_{NT} - P_T)$. In general $\pi_F = \delta P_T + (1-\delta)P_{F,NT}$ and $\pi - \pi_F = (1-\alpha)(P_{NT} - P_T) + (1-\delta)(P_T - P_{F,NT})$. Clearly in all cases $\pi - \pi_F$ picks up the movement of domestic non-traded prices relative to foreign traded prices converted into domestic currency. In some circumstances there will also be an error reflecting an equivalent movement abroad.

In the imperfect competition model,

$$
\begin{aligned}
\pi - \pi_F &= \alpha P_H + (1-\alpha)P_F - \delta P_F - (1-\delta)P_H = \\
&\quad (\alpha + \delta - 1)(P_H - P_F)
\end{aligned}
$$

where $\alpha > 0.5 < \delta$. Here $\pi - \pi_F$ is a transform of the terms of trade, the real exchange rate in this model.

In either case we will incorporate coefficients $(1-\alpha)$ and $(\alpha+\delta-1)$ into the coefficients of e_t in the IS, XM and OS curves in the rest of the model, to which we now turn. We can modify the IS curve as:

$$y_t = -\alpha r_t - \delta e_t + k\theta_t + \overline{d} \quad (10)$$

where θ = net nominal wealth, including now net foreign assets, and e enters because of the effect on demand of the current account. The LM curve becomes:

$$m_t = \pi_t + ny_t - \beta R_t \quad (11)$$

Now let us ignore government bonds as net wealth; we can then write the current account as

$$\triangle\theta_t = -qe_t - \mu y_t \quad (12)$$

Add the definition

$$e_t = \pi_t + S_t - \pi_{F,t} \quad (13)$$

the open economy supply curve:

$$y_t = \sigma e_t + p(\pi_t - E_{t-1}\pi_t) \tag{14}$$

and the definition of real interest rates:

$$r_t = R_t - (E_t\pi_{t+1} - \pi_t) \tag{15}$$

Equations (9) to (15) make up a seven equation model determining y, e, r, θ, π, R and either m (S fixed: fixed rates) or S (m fixed: floating rates). The solution can be found by the methods in chapter 2: it turns out that the characteristic equation is second order. We will assume that the solution is well-behaved, with both forward and backward roots stable.

Here, rather than find the solution algebraically, we use a graphical method. We can note (from the solution) that $E_te_{t+1} = je_t + \varepsilon_t$ where ε_t is a combination of the current shocks to the model and j is the stable backward root. Now use (9), the BB curve, to eliminate r_t in favour of e_t throughout the model. When we do this substitution in the IS curve we are obtaining Parkin and Bade's (1988) $ISBB$ curve, the IS curve when the foreign exchange market is cleared. Notice that this $ISBB$ curve shifts with θ_{t-1}, the previous stock of net foreign assets (we eliminate θ_t in terms of e_t, y_t and θ_{t-1} in (12).

The XM and OS curves have been derived earlier. This leaves the determination of prices in the right-hand quadrant. Under fixed exchange rates ($S = \overline{S}$) we can use (13) to obtain prices along the 45° line, FX. Under floating, prices are determined by (11) using (9) as follows:

$$\pi_t = m_t - ny_t + \beta(r_{F,t} + E_t\pi_{t+1} - \pi_t + (1-j)e_t - \varepsilon_t) \tag{16}$$

So the slope of the FL curve is (given by the solution $E_t\pi_{t+1} = j\pi_t + \eta_t$ η_t being a combination of shocks, like ε_t in the analogous solution of $E_te_{t+1} = je_t + \varepsilon_t$)

$$\frac{\delta e_t}{\delta \pi_t} = \frac{1+\beta(1-j)}{\beta(1-j)} > 1$$

Finally we can illustrate how the model works, with a temporary fiscal shock, shifting the $ISBB$ curve temporarily to the right. This is shown under floating in Figure 10.7 by the dashed lines. The $ISBB$ shifts out the $ISBB_1$. This raises output, shifting the FL curve to F_1L_1, lowering prices and so shifting the OS curve left to O_1S_1. This creates a current account deficit (equilibrium in period 1 is to the right of the XM curve); note that the XM curve partitions the e, y space between falling θ (to its right) and rising θ (to its left). Thus θ falls so that next period, the $ISBB$ shifts leftwards to $ISBB_2$. Also in period 2 the OS

curve returns to OS_1 (π^{ue} now being zero), while the FL curve shifts to the right with falling output. From period 2, the $ISBB$-OS intersection lies to the left of the XM; so θ continues to rise (at the rate $1-j$, along the stable path) until eventually it reaches the XM curve.

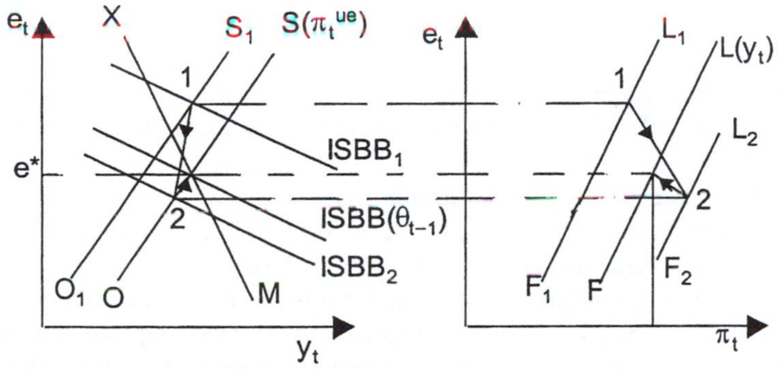

Figure 10.7: The full open economy and a fiscal shock under floating rates

The same fiscal shock is shown for fixed rates in figure 10.8. It can be seen that apart from the effect on prices, which may fall under floating but must rise under fixed, the effects are quite similar. The real exchange rate, real interest rates and output rise; and these rises are later reversed.

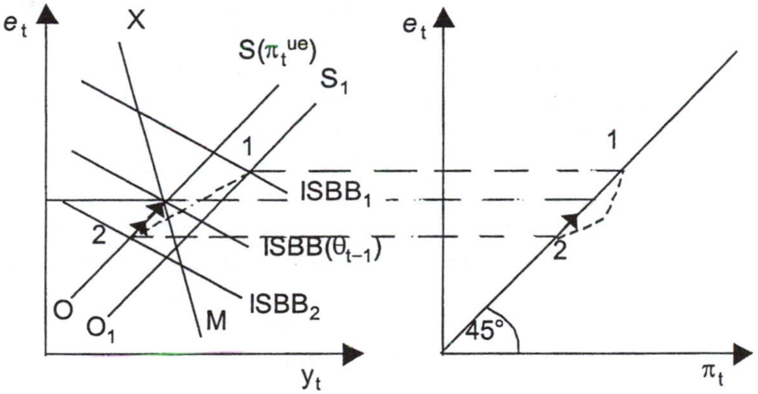

Figure 10.8: A fiscal shock under fixed rates

Needless to say, this model represents just the barest bones of a fully specified open economy model. But it should clarify the key elements, before the encrustation of complications from adjustment lags, contracts and the rest.

CONCLUSIONS

The open economy model is of key importance in applied macroeconomics, since all economies (except the world) are open! This chapter has extended the earlier analysis to capture the main essentials of openness.

The current account determines movements in net foreign assets, a key element of national wealth; these impact on spending. The current account depends on demand and relative prices; either relative home/foreign prices (under imperfect competition) or relative traded/non-traded prices (perfect competition). These relative prices are in turn determined by supply conditions interacting with demand: the open economy supply curve is derived analogously to the Phillips curve in the closed economy, but wages react additionally to the changing relative foreign prices.

The capital account (excluding the central bank's operations) has monetary importance: together with the current account it determines the demand for and supply of money. If the central bank does not intervene in the foreign exchange market, then demand must equal supply: the exchange rate moves to ensure this — floating rates. Consumer prices are then determined by the domestically set money supply, interacting with the demand for money. If the central bank intervenes, to hold the exchange rate — fixed rates — the reserves will adjust to equal the gap between demand and supply: but changes in the reserves will change the money supply through the central bank's balance sheet. With market efficiency, the reserves will adjust so rapidly as capital flows to take immediate advantage of any uncovered interest differential, that the central bank loses all, even short term, control of the money supply. When all these factors are put together, the open economy model shows how the economy can be stimulated termporarily, with the real exchange rate and real interest rate moving in sympathy with output and the price level, but that losses of net foreign assets cause it to reverse this stimulus in order to restore the economy's original wealth.

It can be seen that under floating exchange rates an open economy has essentially the same structure as the closed-economy models we analysed earlier: the floating exchange rate adjusts to insulate domestic monetary policy from foreign monetary policy. The main differences are that the effects of interest rates are reinforced by the real exchange rate which rises with the real interest rate, and that there are additional spillovers from foreign shocks. However, the decision to fix the exchange rate causes a radical alteration in the behaviour of the economy by subordinating its monetary conditions to foreign monetary policy: its nominal interest rates are fixed abroad.

APPENDIX 10A LONG-RUN EQUILIBRIUM IN THE OPEN ECONOMY

In the long run, the capital stock is variable. It is natural to assume constant returns to scale, since there is a tendency for industries to be driven to operate at their lowest cost level by the processes of international competition: if there were decreasing returns to scale, industries would contract and if increasing, they would expand until constant returns were achieved. As for external returns to scale, there is pressure to internalize these externalities and similarly to drive industry operations to the minimum cost point: even if the externalities are at the national level, forces operate to internalize them through national policy.

Imperfect Competition

Assuming constant returns to scale and mobile international capital, figure 10.3 is redrawn for the long-run figure 10.9. Now in the labour market there is a unique feasible real consumer wage that can be paid given the terms of trade and the international cost of capital ($\overline{r}$). Because $P_H = W^{\beta}(\overline{r}P_F)^{1-\beta}$ and $\pi = P_H^{\alpha}P_F^{1-\alpha}$, therefore:

$$\frac{W}{\pi} = \frac{W}{P_H^{\alpha}P_F^{1-\alpha}} = \frac{P_H^{1/\beta}(\overline{r}P_F)^{-(1-\beta)/\beta}}{P_H^{\alpha}P_F^{1-\alpha}} = (P_H/P_F)^{(\frac{1}{\beta}-\alpha)}\overline{r}^{(1-\frac{1}{\beta})}$$

(note that $\frac{1}{\beta} > 1 > \alpha$; capital goods are assumed to be imported but this does not affect the essential argument).

As e rises from e_0 to e_1, so the feasible real consumer wage rises; labour supply increases. Also $\frac{W}{P_H} = [\frac{P_H}{\overline{r}P_F}]^{(\frac{1}{\beta}-1)}$ also rises, so that labour input per unit of output is reduced and the production function shifts upwards. The open economy supply curve is accordingly flatter in the long run than in the short.

Perfect competition

Figures 10.10 and 10.11 show the long run equilibrium of the perfect competition model. As in the short run we have $\pi = P_{NT}^{1-\alpha}P_T^{\alpha}$. But in the long run under constant returns we also have

$$P_T = W^{\delta}(\overline{r}P_T)^{1-\delta} \tag{1}$$

$$P_{NT} = W^{\beta}(\overline{r}P_T)^{1-\beta} \tag{2}$$

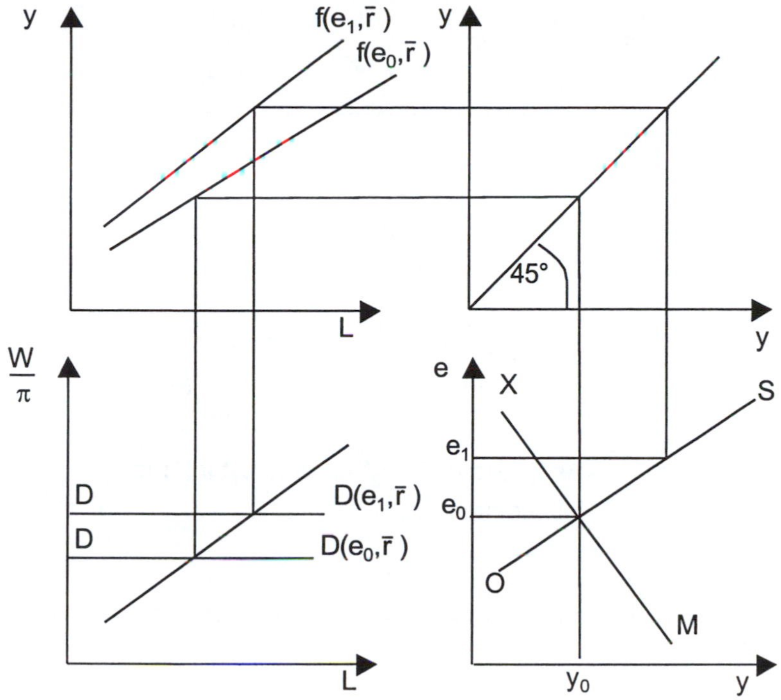

Figure 10.9: The open economy under imperfect competition in the long run

Together these two imply that $e = \frac{P_{NT}}{P_T} = \bar{r}^{1-(\beta/\delta)}$. Using the definition of π, they also imply that

$$W/\pi = \bar{r}^{-\frac{1-\beta+\alpha[\beta-\delta]}{\delta}} \tag{3}$$

So assuming that π is set by domestic monetary conditions, these three equations determine W, P_T, P_{NT} as functions of π and $\bar{r}$; in other words, $\bar{r}$ determines real consumer wages (W/π), the real exchange rate, $e = P_{NT}/P_T$, and real product wages, (W/P_T, W/P_{NT}). Figure 10.A.2 shows how from e^* (given by $\bar{r}$), any slight rise in e would lead to an infinite expansion of the traded goods industry, and vice versa; assume for these purposes that labour is in infinitely elastic supply at some W and that P_{NT} is given by (2) so that non-traded industry expands to whatever is required by demand. As demand is varied, traded goods are made available by this process (P_T rising or falling) to keep the current account in balance. This yields the flat XM curve in Figure 10.11.

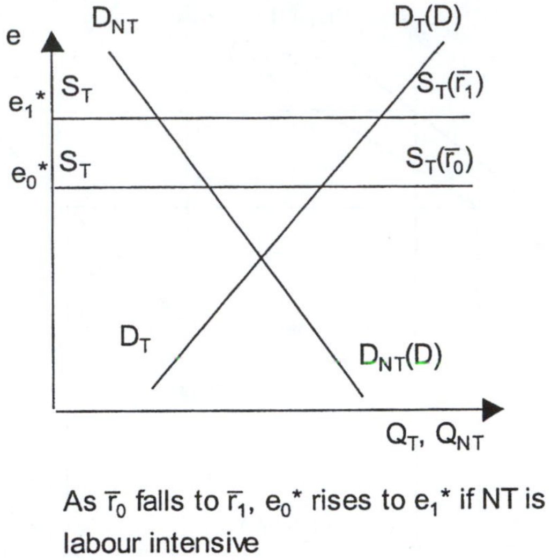

Figure 10.10: The perfect competition model of the current account in the long run

Turning now to constraints on labour supply, we see in Figure 10.A.3 how at each e^* (corresponding to a certain $\bar{r}$) there is a unique real consumer wage, $(W/\pi)^*$; any rise of $(W/\pi)^*$ above this reduces the output of both industries, and also their demand for labour, to zero, since it exceeds labour's long run unique marginal product. At this $(W/\pi)^*$ there is a particular labour supply which defines the level of employment and output. If we assume that the non-traded sector is labour-intensive (β is larger than δ), then as $\bar{r}$ rises, both e and W/π fall. This is the assumption made in Figures 10.10 and 10.11, giving an upward-sloping long-run OS curve (otherwise it would slope downwards). What we are seeing here is the standard Heckscher-Ohlin-Samuelson model result that a rise in the cost of capital raises the relative price of the capital-intensive industry and lowers the real wage.

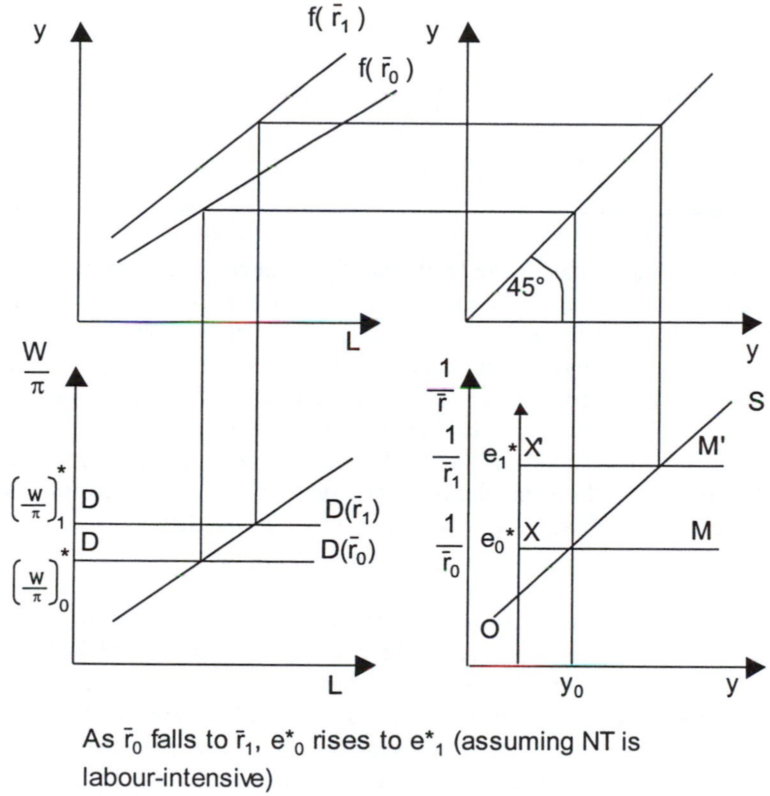

Figure 10.11: Supply and demand under perfect competition in the long run

11

Representative agent models in cashless economies

Macroeconomic models have traditionally been constructed from aggregate demand and supply relationships. These relationships are in turn justified by 'micro-foundations': that is to say, it is shown that people or firms (agents) maximizing their utility or expected utility would on average behave according to these relationships. To obtain aggregate from individual behaviour, assumptions have been made about the distribution of preferences and technological idiosyncracies: often, appeal can be made to the central limit theorem, which says that the mean of N independent random variables has a normal distribution, with a standard deviation equal to that of the component variables divided by $\sqrt{N}$.

Nevertheless, the parameters of these relationships are only loosely tied to the parameters of the preferences and technology of individual agents. We saw this earlier when discussing Lucas' critique (Lucas, 1976) of econometric models: certain of the model's parameters will shift under changes of policy regime or other exogenous variable processes. Yet we would like to have models which can be used to evaluate the effects of just such changes. This argues the need for models whose parameters are solely those of preferences and technology, so-called 'deep structure'.

In response to this need, a variety of models have been produced which make dramatically simple assumptions about preferences and technology, in order to make a complete treatment practicable. Often technology is reduced to stochastic per capita endowments of a single consumption good and consumers are treated as identical representative agents.

These models are obviously no use for traditional forecasting and policy analysis where we try to predict and control particular sequences of events. But this is not the use for which they are intended. Rather it is to model an economy in the sense of mimicking and so understanding its (average) time-series properties when shocked; from a policy viewpoint, this should guide us towards policies which improve those properties. This is a long term perspective. With it tends to go the view that economists and policy makers should only be concerned with these average properties over the long term and not with short term sequences of events.

There are horses for courses. In practice, whether they ought to be or not, economists are called upon to help in both the short- and the long-term aspects of problems. Provided they are honest about the shortcomings of the tools they use in both contexts, we can see no objection to them earning their living doing both. For this reason, we have presented the more traditional models already and now proceed to give an account of these deep structure models. Inevitably, it is too short to be more than an introduction (see Sargent, 1987, for a fuller treatment).

THE BASIC STRUCTURE OF A REPRESENTATIVE AGENT MODEL

In these models the representative household maximizes expected utility subject to its budget constraint; the government spends, levies taxes and prints money subject to its budget constraint; and markets clear, imposing general equilibrium. From this structure it is possible to derive relationships between the stochastic shocks and macroeconomic outcomes, such as consumption, interest rates and prices.

Consumer Maximization

Take first the household's decision. In a non-stochastic world it would typically be assumed to maximize a time-additive utility function:

$$U = \sum_{t=0}^{\infty} \beta^t u(c_t) \tag{1}$$

c_t is consumption, and u is a well-behaved utility function with positive and diminishing marginal utility of consumption. Let its budget constraint be:

$$A_{t+1} = R_t(A_t + y_t - c_t) \tag{2}$$

where A_t is wealth at the beginning of period t, R_t is the interest rate (gross, inclusive of capital repayment), and y_t is income. A_0 and y_t are given.

Using the Lagrangean method, we can write the maximand as:

$$L = u(c_0) + \beta u(c_1) + \beta^2 u(c_2) + ... + \mu_0[A_1 - R_0(A_0 + y_0 - c_0)]$$
$$+ \mu_1[A_2 - R_1(A_1 + y_1 - c_1)] + \mu_2[A_3 - R_2(A_2 + y_2 - c_1)] + ... \quad (3)$$

yielding the first-order conditions with respect to the consumer's choice variables $c_0, c_1, ...; A_1, A_2, ...$ as :

$$0 = \frac{\delta L}{\delta c_0} = u'(c_0) + \mu_0 R_0; \; 0 = \frac{\delta L}{\delta A_1} = \mu_0 - \mu_1 R_1$$

$$0 = \frac{\delta L}{\delta c_1} = \beta u'(c_1) + \mu_1 R_1; \; 0 = \frac{\delta L}{\delta A_2} = \mu_1 - \mu_2 R_2 \quad (4)$$

where $u' = \frac{\delta u}{\delta c}$.

Equation (4) yields a string of relationships between the marginal utility of consumption in one period and the next:

$$u'(c_t) = \beta R_t u'(c_{t+1}) \quad (5)$$

The household equates its marginal rate of transformation

$$u'(c_t)/\beta u'(c_{t+1})$$

with the gross rate of interest, a result illustrated in figure 11.1.

As figure 11.1 and equation (5) suggest, one can split up the consumer's problem into a sequence of two-period decisions. Given $(A_t + y_t)$, he decides c_{t+1} relative to c_t: that is, he can either decide c_{t+1} if he has already decided on c_t or c_t if he must consume c_{t+1}. This splitting up of the decision problem is known as dynamic programming. In dynamic programming, each period's consumption is first solved given the last period's consumption, wealth and income: finally the initial consumption level is set so that all assets are ultimately consumed.

For many purposes we shall only need to consider the first stage of the decision process. Occasionally, dynamic programming solutions are presented backwards from the future (that is, consumption in one period is solved given consumption in the next period): this method is convenient if there is some fixed terminal point from which one can work back (at which for example the consumer dies, leaving a fixed or no bequest). But it is obviously only a presentational matter whether one period's consumption is seen as depending on last period's or next period's.

The consumer decides what to do one period at a time, and in principle he can recompute his decision for the next period when it comes: he decides c_0 this period (with a plan for $c_1, c_2, \ldots$), next period he decides

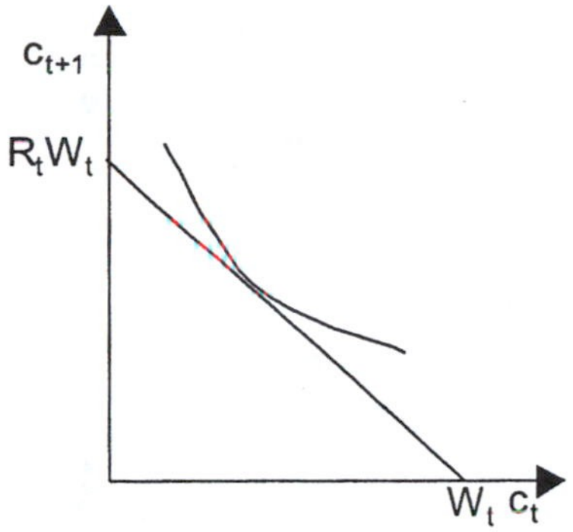

Figure 11.1: Intertemporal consumer choice

c_1 (given c_0, then in the past, and with a plan for c_2, $c_3, \dots$). Of course in this problem with no stochastic shocks he will always stick to his original plan (this is not to be confused with the time inconsistency of policy makers who can influence other people's decisions and then recompute: our consumer only affects himself). He might as well decide at the start on his consumption plan and just carry it out without further thought.

We now turn to a stochastic environment, where in each period a particular shock is realized. The consumer will have decided on consumption in the previous period based on his expectation across all possible shocks. He will also have a plan for his consumption in future periods; this will be a contingency plan, in which his consumption will depend on which shocks occur. Since he does not actually have to decide irrevocably on future consumption until the period involved, this contingency approach is the optimal one: he maintains his flexibility until the last possible moment. Then as the shocks are realized, he picks the relevant branch of his contingency plan. Figure 11.2 illustrates.

We can think of this equivalently as the consumer either recomputing his best expected plan each period or as computing at the start a total contingency plan and carrying it out as the shocks are realized: the point is that the consumer is making use of his potential flexibility in the face of shocks by deferring decisions on actual consumption until he has to take them.

The consumer is assumed to maximize expected utility in this envi-

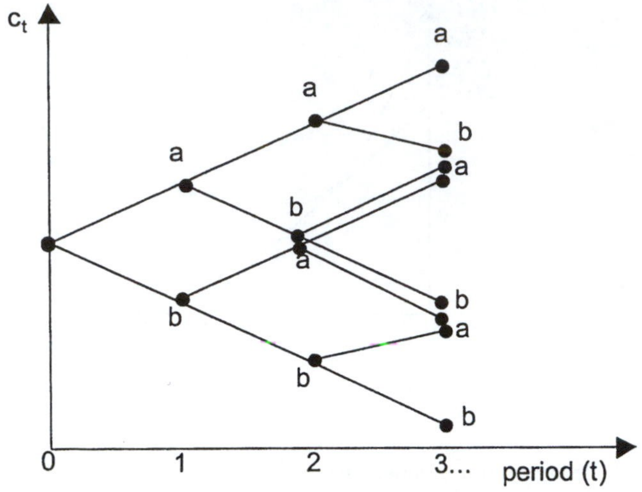

Figure 11.2: Contingency plan for consumption, with the shock each period taking two values (a, b)

ronment, or

$$U_0 = E_0 \sum_{t=0}^{\infty} \beta^t u(c_t)$$

subject to $A_{t+1} = R_t(A_t + y_t - c_t)$, where $R_t = R(1 + \varepsilon_t)$ for example but y_t is a known series. We can now use the principle of dynamic programming and take each period's decision separately.

We can write U_0, substituting c_1 out from the constraints, as:

$$U_0 = u(c_0) + E_0 \beta u(R_0[A_0 - c_0] + y_1 - A_2/R_1) + E_0 \beta^2 u(c_2) + ... \quad (6)$$

Maximizing this with respect to c_0 (A_0 given) gives:

$$0 = \frac{\delta U_0}{\delta c_0} = u'(c_0) + E_0 \beta u'(c_1)(-R_0)$$

or

$$u'(c_0) = E_0 \beta R_0 u'(c_1) \quad (7)$$

Analogously at $t = 1$, the consumer maximises U_1 (A_1 given) to obtain:

$$u'(c_1) = E_1 \beta R_1 u'(c_2) \quad (8)$$

and in general:

$$u'(c_{t)} = E_t \beta R_t u'(c_{t+1}) \tag{9}$$

which is the expected analogue of (5). By the law of iterated expectations it follows that:

$$E_0 u'(c_t) = \beta E_0 R_t u'(c_{t+1}) \tag{10}$$

We can reach this general result more compactly by using expected Lagrangeans, taking the expectations operator through the Lagrangean multipliers.

Let the consumer be faced with a given realization A_t; then he can choose c_t, c_{t+1}, A_{t+1} to maximise (at t) U_t subject to the constraint, or the expected Lagrangean,

$$\begin{aligned} L = U_t + E_t\{\mu_t(A_{t+1} - R_t[A_t + y_t - c_t]) + \\ \mu_{t+1}(A_{t+2} - R_{t+1}[A_{t+1} + y_{t+1} - c_{t+1}]) + ...\} \end{aligned} \tag{11}$$

$$0 = \frac{\delta L}{\delta c_t} = \beta_t u'(c_t) + E_t \mu_t R_t \tag{12}$$

$$0 = \frac{\delta L}{\delta A_{t+1}} = E_t \mu_t - E_t \mu_{t+1} R_{t+1} \tag{13}$$

$$0 = \frac{\delta L}{\delta c_{t+1}} = E_t \beta_{t+1} u'(c_{t+1}) + E_t \mu_{t+1} R_{t+1} \tag{14}$$

Equation (9) follows by substitution.

GENERAL EQUILIBRIUM

Equation (9) can be turned into a pricing formula for an asset. Suppose the asset yields an uncertain dividend, d_{t+1}, and has a current price, p_t, so that

$$R_t = \frac{p_{t+1} + d_{t+1}}{p_t} \tag{15}$$

Then

$$u'(c_t) = E_t \beta (\frac{p_{t+1} + d_{t+1}}{p_t}) u'(c_{t+1})$$

or

$$p_t = \frac{\beta}{u'(c_t)} E_t u'(c_{t+1})(p_{t+1} + d_{t+1}) \tag{16}$$

Since all consumers are identical, the only way this asset will be held (by anyone and everyone) is for (15) to hold.

One way to create a simple economy with an asset market is to follow Lucas' tree model (Lucas, 1978). Let the only asset be an identical tree, one initially at t belonging to each consumer, who has no other source of income. Let each tree produce non-storable fruit, an all-purpose consumption good, in the quantity d_t. Let the number of trees belonging to each consumer be S_t; the supply of trees per consumer is $\overline{S} = 1$.

Fruit can be exchanged for trees at the price p_t (units of fruit per tree). But Walras' Law implies that if the fruit market is in excess demand, the tree market is in excess supply. Therefore market clearing across the whole economy (trees and fruit) implies that

$$c_t = d_t \tag{17}$$

Equations (15) and (16) therefore constitute our model of the economy, yielding the compact form:

$$p_t = \beta \frac{1}{u'(d_t)} E_t u'(d_{t+1})(p_{t+1} + d_{t+1}) \tag{18}$$

Substituting successively for $E_t p_{t+1}$, $E_t p_{t+2}$, ... and using the law of iterated expectations ($E_t E_{t+i} = E_t$), yields:

$$\begin{aligned} p_t = E_t &\left. \frac{\beta u'(d_{t+1})}{u'(d_t)} d_{t+1} + \beta^2 \frac{u'(d_{t+1})u'(d_{t+2})}{u'(d_t)u'(d_{t+1})} d_{t+2} + \ldots \right] \\ &= E_t \sum_{j=1}^{\infty} \beta^j \frac{u'(d_{t+j}))}{u'(d_t)} d_{t+j} \end{aligned} \tag{19}$$

Depending on the form of the utility function, one can solve for p_t as a function of the current and expected d. One convenient case is where $u(c_t) = lnc_t$ so that $u'(c_t) = \frac{1}{c_t}$, in which case

$$p_t = E_t \sum_{j=1}^{\infty} \beta^j d_t = \frac{\beta}{1-\beta} d_t \tag{20}$$

In this case the asset price varies with whatever stochastic process drives the harvest of fruit.

THE GOVERNMENT BUDGET CONSTRAINT

In this general equilibrium framework with no money, let us introduce a government issuing debt, bonds, each of which pays next period one unit of the fruit, regardless; b_{t+1} is the number of such bonds outstanding at t (b_t the number issued in $t-1$). Its budget constraint will be

$$g_t - T_t + b_t = b_{t+1}/R_{1t} \tag{21}$$

where g_t = government spending per capita, T_t = taxes per capita (an equal poll tax), R_t = the one-period-ahead rate of return on debt .

For this debt to be held, it must be as with trees that

$$u'(c_t) = \beta E_t R_t u'(c_{t+1}) \tag{22}$$

Since R_t is certain, this implies

$$R_t^{-1} = \beta \frac{E_t u'(c_{t+1})}{u'(c_t)} \tag{23}$$

Now market clearing of the fruit market implies:

$$c_t + g_t = d_t \tag{24}$$

The consumer's budget constraint is

$$d_t S_t - c_t - T_t + b_t + p_t S_t = \frac{b_{t+1}^d}{R_{1t}} + p_t S_{t+1}^d \tag{25}$$

where S_t is his existing holding of trees and S_{t+1}^d is his desired holding of trees for next period.

Using the two budget constraints, (20) and (24), and fruit market clearing, (23), Walras' Law reappears for debt and trees together:

$$\frac{b_{t+1}}{R_t} + p_t S_t = \frac{b_{t+1}^d}{R_t} + p_t S_{t+1}^d \tag{26}$$

Since debt and trees are perfect substitutes at the R_t given by (22) and p_t given by (18), any excess supply of debt (excess demand for trees) is eliminated by an infinitesimal movement in either p_t or R_t.

The Ricardian equivalence result immediately follows in this model, that taxes are irrelevant, to consumption from (23), and to interest rates and asset prices:

$$R_t^{-1} = \beta \frac{E_t u'(d_{t+1} - g_{t+1})}{u'(d_t - g_t)} \tag{27}$$

$$p_t = \sum_{j=1}^{\infty} \beta^j \frac{E_t u'(d_{t+j} - g_{t+j}) d_{t+j}}{u'(d_t - g_t)} \tag{28}$$

Only the path of GDP and government spending matters. This is because households are infinitely-lived so that the pattern of (lump-sum) taxes does not affect their life-time consumption possibilities or permanent income.

THE PRICING OF CONTINGENT CLAIMS

We saw earlier (equation 15) that the price of an asset paying a stochastic dividend, d_t, was:

$$p_t = \beta E_t \frac{u'(c_{t+1})(p_{t+1} + d_{t+1})}{u'(c_t)} \tag{29}$$

The price and the dividend is in units of the consumption good, 'fruit' or whatever. Now consider a claim which pays out one unit of the consumption good in $t+1$ when the state of the economy, some vector x_{t+1}, has a value between x_0 and x_1. By extension of (28) its value will be:

$$q_t[x_0 \quad x_{t+1} \quad x_1] = \frac{\beta}{u'(c_t)} \int_{x_0}^{x_1} u'(c_{t+1}[x_{t+1}]) f(x_{t+1}, x_t) dx_{t+1} \tag{30}$$

$f(x_{t+1}, x_t)$ is the probability density function over x_{t+1} (given that x_t has occurred); integrating the area under this function gives the probability of x_{t+1} lying in the range x_0 to x_1. Equation (29) says that the price of a contingent claim is the marginal utility of one unit next period, relative to this period's marginal utility if x_{t+1} lies in the range, times the probability of its lying in that range.

Equation (29) allows any contingent claim to be priced. One simply specifies the range of contingency, evaluates the marginal utility of consumption in that contingency, multiplies by the pay-off in units of the consumption good, and weights each part of the range by its probability. Equation (29) can also be derived directly from the consumer's maximum problem subject to a budget constraint containing the contingent claim: this is left as an exercise for the interested reader.

Contingent claims which nest other contingent claims within them (for example, a claim on two-period ahead consumption given x_{t+2} and x_t) must be consistent with the claims nested within them; otherwise arbitrage opportunities occur. Hence, for example, a claim on consumption two periods ahead must have the same price today as the current price of a one-period ahead claim on consumption two periods ahead times the current price of a claim on consumption one-period ahead. This is exactly analogous to the arbitraging of interest rates of n-period ahead maturity with the n one-period interest rates for the intervening periods.

GOVERNMENT BONDS AS NET WEALTH: MODELS WITH INTERTEMPORAL AND GEOGRAPHIC CONSTRAINTS

We saw above that, subject to the solvency condition, a government could borrow as much or as little as it liked with no effect on the economy, assuming its taxes were lump sum (distortionary taxes are another matter as we showed in chapter 7, where we discussed the Lucas-Stokey optimal tax-smoothing proposition) — this is Ricardian equivalence. Yet a number of authors have been impressed with the role that a government-issued liability could perform by intermediating between people who may not be willing to lend directly to each other for some reason: they will still be willing to lend to a government which in turn may transfer, or lend, to others. Of course, such government bonds will generally affect economic outcomes and be net wealth.

Two main sets of reasons have been advanced why people would be unwilling to lend to some other people: one is death (the young will not lend to the old because the old have no incentive to pay it back after death), the other is geographic isolation (members of one tribe will not lend to members of another if they cannot see them again to reclaim the debt).

OVERLAPPING GENERATIONS MODELS

Samuelson's overlapping generations model, used (see chapter 7) by Barro (1974) with a bequest motive in order to re-establish Ricardian equivalence, has been used extensively by Neil Wallace and his colleagues under the assumption of inter-generational indifference (no bequests) to establish a role for government liabilities.

Suppose all generations are made up of N identical agents, whose income stream in perishable consumption units is $y - \varepsilon$ and ε in their youth and old age respectively: $0 < \varepsilon < y/2$ so that they obtain more income when young than old. Consumption when young and old is respectively $c_t^h(t)$ and $c_t^h(t+1)$ for the hth agent of generation t. Assume there is no investment opportunity other than a loan market, but that the government has no borrowing, tax or spending programme initially. Then we can easily show that there will be no lending by agents when young, l_t^h, at all: the old will not lend (because they will not be alive to be paid back) or borrow (because they cannot pay back when dead).

Assume the consumer maximizes a logarithmic utility function

$$U_t^h(c_t^h(t), c_t^h(t+1)) = \ln c_t^h(t) + \ln c_t^h(t+1) \tag{31}$$

subject to

$$\begin{aligned} y - \varepsilon - c_t^h(t) &= l_t^h \\ \varepsilon + [1 + r(t)]l_t^h &= c_t^h(t+1) \end{aligned} \tag{32}$$

where $r(t)$ is the net rate of interest, to be determined by the clearing of the loan market (this by Walras' Law also clears the goods market). His Lagrangean is therefore:

$$\begin{aligned} J = \ln c_t^h(t) + \ln c_t^h(t+1) + \mu_t^h(t)[y - \varepsilon - c_t^h(t) - l_t^h] \\ + \mu_t^h(t+1)\{\varepsilon + [(1 + r(t)]l_t^h - c_t^h(t+1)\} \end{aligned} \tag{33}$$

The first-order conditions yield:

$$c_t^h(t) = \frac{c_t^h(t+1)}{1 + r(t)} \tag{34}$$

The consumer's life-time constraint is:

$$c_t^h(t) + \frac{c_t^h(t+1)}{1 + r(t)} = y - \varepsilon + \frac{\varepsilon}{1 + r(t)} \tag{35}$$

so that

$$c_t^h(t) = \frac{y - \varepsilon}{2} + \frac{\varepsilon}{2(1 + r(t))} \tag{36}$$

and

$$l_t^h = \frac{y - \varepsilon}{2} - \frac{\varepsilon/2}{1 + r(t)} \tag{37}$$

Market-clearing requires that $\sum_h l_t^h = 0$ and hence $l_t^h = 0$ since all agents are identical. Consequently

$$1 + r(t) = \frac{\varepsilon}{y - \varepsilon} < 1 \tag{38}$$

Negative interest rates are required to induce people to consume all of their youthful income, since no one is available to make a loan to.

Now let the government borrow (a one-period loan) to spend in the first period only, the sum $G(1) = N[\frac{y}{2} - \varepsilon]$; it pays off its debt from taxes (τ) on the young in period T. Its budget constraint is:

$$G(t) + L^g(t) = \sum \tau_{t-1}^h(t) + \sum \tau_t^h(t) + [1 + r(t-1)]L^g(t-1) \quad (39)$$

where $L^g(t)$ is the loan it takes out in t and it starts with $L^g(0) = 0$. In this case, this implies

$$\begin{aligned} G(1) &= -L^g(1) = N\left[\frac{y}{2} - \varepsilon\right]; \\ L^g(t) &= [1 + r(t-1)]L^g(t-1) \ \{T > t \geq 2\} \end{aligned}$$

and

$$\sum_h \tau_T^h(T) = -[1 + r(T-1)]L^g(T-1), \text{ setting } L^g(T) = 0 \quad (40)$$

The loan market equilibrium in period 1 is now:

$$0 = L^g(1) + \sum_h l_1^h = -N\left[\frac{y}{2} - \varepsilon\right] + N \left[\frac{y - \varepsilon}{2} - \frac{\varepsilon/2}{1 + r(1)}\right] \quad (41)$$

which is only satisfied if $r(1) = 0$. This government intervention has therefore raised interest rates by siphoning off the young's expenditure into loans. Subsequently, the government debt remains constant: $L^g(2) = L^g(1)$, which implies that $r(2) = 0$; and so on until T, when $L^g(T) = 0$ but the tax bill reduces the income of the young, and $0 = \sum_h l_t^h$ gives $1 + r(T) = \frac{\varepsilon}{y/2}$. Thereafter of course the equilibrium gives $r(t) = \frac{\varepsilon}{y - \varepsilon}$ $(t > T)$ as in (37).

The implications for consumption patterns of this intervention are beneficial to every generation except the Tth and beyond. Generations less than T now consume:

$$c_t^h(t) = \frac{y}{2} = c_t^h(t+1) \quad (42)$$

whereas previously they consumed $y - \varepsilon$ and ε respectively in t and $t+1$. Figure 11.3 illustrates the improvement in their welfare. The 45° line yy shows each generation's consumption possibilities when young and old, provided there is some mechanism (like the government loan sequence above) to ensure that when it transfers resources to the old, the same will be done by the next generation to it. Clearly the optimal point is along the 45° line from the origin.

The Tth generation is worse off, as its consumption pattern becomes $\frac{y}{2}$ in youth (because of the tax bill) and in old age. The following generations are of course unaffected.

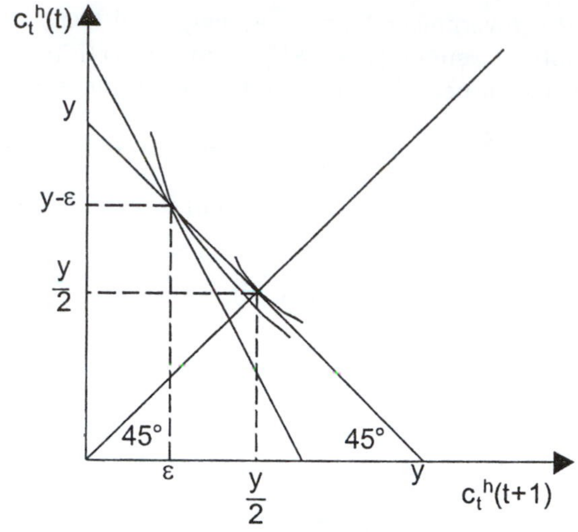

Figure 11.3: The welfare effect of consumption smoothing on the OLG model

This would therefore appear not to be a Pareto-improving policy across all generations. However, in an economy with an infinite life, it can be made so by deferring repayment of the government debt indefinitely: the Tth generation then never arrives. In this case the government bond issue is a source of net wealth to the country, even if the initial output diverted to government spending, $G(1)$, is thrown away!

The gain, to repeat, lies in the ability of government bonds to effect loans from the young generation to the old. The young invest in government debt, the old pay it off; but they do not have to deal with each other directly. Notice that this government loan sequence effects exactly the same as a pay-as-you-go pension scheme, taxing the young by $y - \varepsilon - \frac{y}{2}$ and giving this as a pension to the old; so here a loan market in government debt is all that is needed to enable people to make their own pension provision efficiently.

GEOGRAPHY: THE BEWLEY–TOWNSEND MODEL

A similar point about the usefulness of government debt can be made about two communities, each with uneven income patterns over time, but which are separated in space rather than by time as the above generations are. Let community A people have an income stream in perishable consumption units of $y - \varepsilon$ and ε (a variable harvest say) while community B people have the stream ε and $y - \varepsilon$, in even and odd periods respectively. All A and B people share identical preferences. But the A people will not lend to the B people, or vice versa, because the two groups rarely meet (they may trade but one group having traded, their next trading session is with another group); Bewley (1980) and Townsend (1980) suggest a 'turnpike' with A and B people passing each other in opposite directions, meeting once but never again. The A and B people both live for $T + 1$ periods (where we can allow $T \to \infty$); assume there are N each. It is obvious that A people will consume in even and odd periods $y - \varepsilon$ and ε respectively, B people ε and $y - \varepsilon$; their consumption pattern will be as uneven as their income pattern. As with our overlapping generations model, a government which borrows can smooth their consumption.

Write its budget constraint per capita as:

$$g_t + l_t^g = \tau_1 + (1 + r(t-1))l_{t-1}^g \quad (T \geq t \geq 0, \text{ given } l_{-1}^g = 0) \tag{43}$$

The government levies the same tax, τ_t on everyone; g_t and l_t^g are per capita spending and one-period loans.

Each hth consumer maximizes

$$\sum_{t=0}^{T} \beta' u(c_t^h)$$

subject to

$$c_t^h + l_t^h \quad y_t^h + (1 + r(t-1))l_{t-1}^h \quad (T \geq t \geq 0$$

given $l_{-1}^h = 0$).

The market equilibrium in loans is:

$$\frac{1}{2}l_t^A + \frac{1}{2}l_t^B + l_t^g = 0 \tag{44}$$

Let us for maximum simplicity assume the government merely acts as a lender and borrower, and does not use its tax or spending powers. Then $l_t^g = 0$ (net) for all t and it follows from market equilibrium that

$$c_t^A + c_t^B = y \tag{45}$$

The consumer's optimum in the usual way yields:

$$\frac{u'(c_t^h)}{u'(c_{t+1}^h)} = \beta(1 + r(t)) \tag{46}$$

Hence since from (44) $c_t^B = y - c_t^A$

$$\frac{u'(c_t^A)}{u'(c_{t+1}^A)} = \frac{u'(y - c_t^A)}{u'(y - c_{t+1}^A)} = \beta(1 + r(t)) \tag{47}$$

It follows that $c_t^A = c_{t+1}^A$ and $1 + r(t) = \frac{1}{\beta}$: full consumption smoothing with the rate of interest equal to the rate of time preference. Imposing the terminal condition that all loans must be paid off (so that the present values of consumption and income are equal), and letting $T \to \infty$, yields

$$\frac{c^A}{1 - \beta} = \frac{y - \varepsilon(1 - \beta)}{1 - \beta^2} \tag{48}$$

This is the result of equating the present values of A's constant infinite consumption stream and of A's alternating infinite income stream, starting $y - \varepsilon$. Hence

$$c^A = \frac{y - \varepsilon(1 - \beta)}{1 + \beta}$$

and

$$c^B = \frac{\beta y + \varepsilon(1 - \beta)}{1 + \beta} \tag{49}$$

This outcome is illustrated in figure 11.4, a box diagram with A's preferences running from the bottom left-hand corner and B's from the top right. Because of positive time preference, their indifference curves have a slope of $-\beta$ along the 45° line between these two corners (compare Figure 11.1 where the slope is -1); A and B agents being identical, their contract curve lies along this 45° line. The autarchic point is at a; the optimum at b is where the budget line going through a with the slope $-(1 + r)^{-1} = -\beta$ cuts the contract curve.

The point about the role of public debt here is that it enables *trade* ('geographic smoothing'). With each community made up of infinitely-lived households, then government borrowing (and its tax pattern over time) will make no difference to the pattern of consumption and asset prices — that is, there is Ricardian equivalence. Government debt here creates net wealth only to the extent that it facilitates trade: it is acting like the capital account of the balance of payments. However, if the capital account is already operating, this effect of government debt disappears.

THE REAL BUSINESS CYCLE MODEL

In chapter 3 we referred to the research agenda of 'real business cycles' (RBC), in which the shocks driving the business cycle are identified as

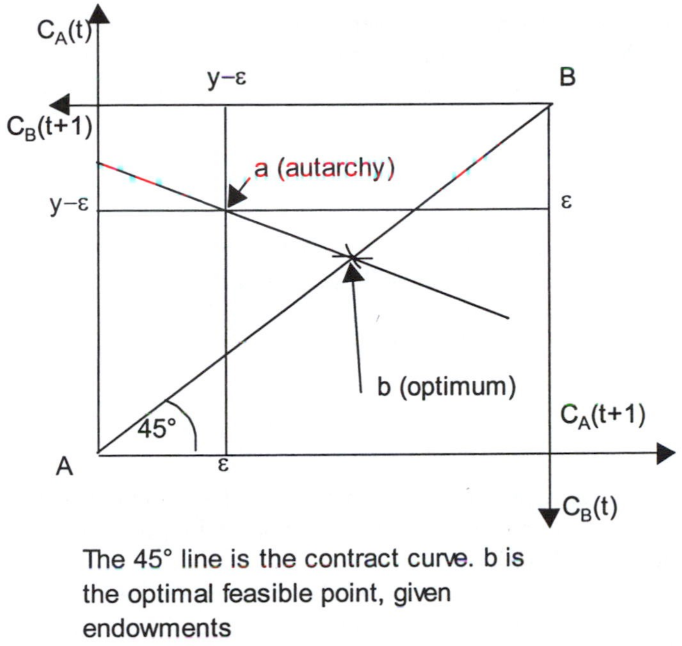

Figure 11.4: The Bewley–Townsend model

coming from productivity and tastes rather than from monetary policy; the reason being that rational agents with access to good up-to-date information will not either sign nominal contracts or suffer information lags about prices sufficient to generate a forward-sloping AS curve — in effect the RBC AS curve is vertical. Even though nowadays we would generally 'augment' such a model with nominal rigidities that would give monetary shocks a role, this uncompromising agenda has produced a large volume of work and insights into the economy's behaviour following Kydland and Prescott (1982), the prime instigators: a large selection is provided by Hartley et al. (1998).

In early post-war macroeconomic thought productivity growth was treated as a smooth and predictable 'deterministic trend', that is a (normally loglinear) time trend; so were changes in tastes that for example through changing labour supply affected output growth. Thus the economy could be thought of as a time trend of 'potential output' with business cycle movements around it:

$$y_t^* = \gamma t + y_0^* \tag{50}$$

The movements around it were seen as due to demand shocks. The RBC model denies this; shocks to potential output are random walks with drift (with possibly additional serial correlation which we ignore for simplicity)

$$\Delta y_t^* = \gamma + \eta_t \tag{51}$$

Here γ is the deterministic trend (the drift), but the key point is that potential output is also constantly being shocked upwards or downwards by permanent changes in tastes (leisure preference) and productivity (for example upwards by innovation, downwards by a new technology that outdates existing capital). If we integrate (50), we obtain:

$$y_t^* = \gamma t + y_0^* + \sum_{i=t-1}^{0} \eta_{t-i} \tag{52}$$

which shows that potential output reflects the cumulant of past shocks to technology and tastes (dominated probably by productivity shocks to the production function).

When one thinks about the matter, it is clear that this rather than (49) must be correct, since technological change is by definition unpredictable and yet once it has occurred its effect is permanent and (unless and until some new change) irreversible. The seminal piece of empirical work that showed (50) fitted the facts better than (49) was Nelson and Plosser (1982).

Given that the progress of potential output is random, this source of shocks can also disturb the economy in the short run, with the assistance of propagation mechanisms. First, investment in the new technology will be spurred by its arrival; the additional capital will take time to build, generating a delayed stimulus to demand. Second, consumer-workers will adjust their consumption and work-plans in response to the new income prospect and real interest movements. The business cycle results from the interplay of these reactions within a market-clearing environment (that is, one where agents are free to make all mutually-beneficial trades).

Plainly there is nothing to stop us adding nominal rigidities to this model; but RBC theorists reject these additions as theoretically ill-founded since people will not wish to subject themselves to additional (money) shocks when they can set prices in relative terms, either by reacting promptly to any changes in money prices or by indexation. RBC modellers claim their models can capture the properties of the business cycle without these additions. A large empirical literature has grown up around these claims, using techniques that are generally different from classical regression: in particular RBC modellers reject forecasting as a valid test of a model. A model should be a mock-up of the economy, to provide insight into how the economy works; thus its 'cyclical properties' should be like those of the economy. This does not imply one can forecast the economy well from a given initial situation, because one cannot forecast the shocks that will occur. RBC modellers favour comparing the unconditional moments of the model's simulations with those of the economy: especially the second moments, the variances and co-variances of key variables like output, employment, interest rates, wages and prices.

We now write down a simple RBC specification. So far our representative agent models have taken the capital stock (e.g. 'trees') as given: income has come as 'endowments' or 'fruit'. Nor have we included labour supply. Essentially we have explored models designed to shed light on particular issues — such as asset pricing and the wealth effects of government borrowing; these models have had both infinitely-lived people, equivalent (as in Barro, 1974) to overlapping generations of mortals who care about their predecessors or their successors or both, and overlapping generations who did not care either way. RBC models draw on both; but the main group assume the former.

So we begin with with a representative household maximizing expected utility from consumption, c_t, and leisure, $1 - L_t$, at time 0:

$$E_0 \sum_{t=0}^{\infty} \beta^t \frac{\{c_t^{\gamma}(a_t[1 - L_t])^{1-\gamma}\}^{1-\rho}}{1 - \rho} \tag{53}$$

where this utility function, usually chosen, is of the Constant Relative Risk Aversion (CRRA) type, with a Cobb-Douglas relation between consumption and leisure (γ is the share of market activity in the total of consumption plus leisure value and a_t is a (leisure) preference shock). All units in the model are per head of population.

The representative firm, owned by the representative household, has a Cobb-Douglas production function with a time-to-build lag between the decision to invest in a capital project and its appearance as capital. The household chooses to consume or to invest in either real bonds or the firm's capital projects. Hence its budget constraint is

$$c_t + I_t + b_t = A_t K_t^{\alpha} L_t^{1-\alpha} - T_t + b_{t-1}(1 + r_{t-1}) \tag{54}$$

where

$$I_t = \sum_{i=1}^{4} k_i s_{t-i+4} \tag{55}$$

$$K_t = (1 - \delta)K_{t-1} + s_{t-4} \tag{56}$$

We have assumed that projects take four periods to complete. Here s_{t-4} for example is the project started at $t-4$, which is then completed in four parts, $k_1 - k_4$, each of these being a proportion. Thus s_{t-4} is completed by t, when it appears in the capital stock, K_t; besides this addition there is depreciation δ. I_t, investment, is the sum of the spending on projects in train: $k_4 s_t$, $k_3 s_{t-1}$, $k_2 s_{t-2}$, $k_1 s_{t-3}$. It is assumed that a project once started is then taken through to completion: naturally enough because of the large sunk cost of a completed section.

Finally, we have a government which spends on necessary public goods and raises taxes:

$$b_t = G_t - T_t + b_{t-1}(1 + r_{t-1}) \tag{57}$$

Market-clearing in goods is:

$$c_t + I_t + G_t = A_t K_t^{\alpha} L_t^{1-\alpha} \tag{58}$$

This model is highly nonlinear and cannot be solved analytically, except via a (perhaps unacceptably inaccurate) linear approximation. To illustrate the ideas of such a model we use a simpler set-up in which capital is continuously variable with a one-period lag of installation. This changes the consumer's budget constraint to:

$$c_t + K_t - (1-\delta)K_{t-1} + b_t = A_t K_{t-1}^{\alpha} L_t^{1-\alpha} - T_t + b_{t-1}(1 + r_{t-1}) \tag{59}$$

We will also simplify by assuming that households' decision to supply labour is predetermined (perhaps by some decision made a long time before on patterns of education and work); hence L_t itself becomes the preference shock and we drop a_t. The Lagrangean the household maximizes at time 0 now becomes:

$$\Lambda = E_0 \sum_{t=0}^{\infty} \beta^t \frac{\{c_t^{\gamma}(1-L_t)^{1-\gamma}\}^{1-\rho}}{1-\rho} + \lambda_t\{c_t + K_t - (1-\delta)K_{t-1} + b_t - A_t K_{t-1}^{\alpha} L_t^{1-\alpha} + T_t - b_{t-1}(1 + r_{t-1})\} \tag{60}$$

The first-order conditions are:

$$0 = E_0\{\beta^t[c_t^{\gamma}(1-L_t)^{1-\gamma}]^{-\rho}\gamma c_t^{\gamma-1} + \lambda_t\} \tag{61}$$

$$0 = E_0\{\lambda_t - \lambda_{t+1}(1 + r_t)\} \tag{62}$$

$$0 = E_0\{\lambda_t - (1-\delta)\lambda_{t+1} - \lambda_{t+1}A_{t+1}L_{t+1}^{1-\alpha}\alpha K_t^{-(1-\alpha)}\} \tag{63}$$

These imply the decision for $t = 0$ variables is:

$$c_0 = E_0 c_1 \beta(1 + r_0)^{\frac{-1}{1-\gamma}} \left\{\frac{c_1^{\gamma}(1-L_1)^{1-\gamma}}{c_0^{\gamma}(1-L_0)^{1-\gamma}}\right\}^{\frac{\rho}{1-\gamma}} \tag{64}$$

$$K_0 = \frac{E_0(\alpha\lambda_1 A_1)^{\frac{1}{1-\alpha}} L_1}{\{E_0\lambda_1(r_0+\delta)\}^{\frac{1}{1-\alpha}}} \tag{65}$$

where

$$\lambda_1 = \frac{\gamma\beta(1-L_1)^{-\rho(1-\gamma)}}{c_1^{1-\gamma(1-\rho)}}$$

Taking logs of this we obtain:

$$\ln K_0 = \ln E_0(\alpha\lambda_1 A_1)^{\frac{1}{1-\alpha}} L_1 - \frac{1}{1-\alpha}\ln(r_0+\delta) - \frac{1}{1-\alpha}\ln E_0\lambda_1 \tag{66}$$

Let us now assume that $\Delta \ln A_t = \eta_t$ and $\Delta \ln L_t = \epsilon_t$ where both these errors are normal and iid. We can now make use of the fact that when $\ln Z_t$ is normally distributed with an innovation x_t then approximately

$$\ln E_{t-1} Z_t = E_{t-1} \ln Z_t + 0.5 var(x_t) \tag{67}$$

Hence

$$\ln K_0 = \frac{1}{1-\alpha}\ln A_0 + \ln L_0 - \frac{1}{1-\alpha}\ln(r_0+\delta) + \overline{K}_0 \tag{68}$$

where

$$\overline{K}_0 = \frac{1}{1-\alpha} + 0.5\text{var}\{(\alpha\lambda_1 A_1)^{\frac{1}{1-\alpha}} L_1\} - \frac{0.5}{1-\alpha}\text{var}(\lambda_1)$$

is a constant which depends on the variances of the two errors and their covariances with λ.

We can generalise these conditions by letting $0 = t$ (in other words, the period 0 we have been planning from can be any period, t; the plan will then treat 0 as t, 1 as $t+1$ and so on). Hence we can generalise (67) as:

$$\ln K_t = \frac{1}{1-\alpha}\ln A_t + \ln L_t - \frac{1}{1-\alpha}\ln(r_t+\delta) + \overline{K}_0 \tag{69}$$

It follows from the production function that:

$$\ln Y_t = \ln A_t + (1-\alpha)\ln L_t + \frac{\alpha}{1-\alpha}\ln A_{t-1} + \alpha \ln L_{t-1} - \frac{\alpha}{1-\alpha}\ln(r_{t-1}+\delta) + \alpha\overline{K}_0 \tag{70}$$

To solve for interest rates we use the first-order condition for consumption (63) (letting $0 = t$, $1 = t+1$) with (68) for the capital stock and (69) for output, the exogenous process for government spending and substitute them all into the market-clearing equation (57). This is a nonlinear expression in which the expected path of interest rates as seen from period t must ensure that markets clear given public spending plans while consumption is intertemporally smoothed via investment and bond holding. This path (most accurately found via a computer algorithm) will be approximately a saddlepath like our solutions in chapter 2 with forward-looking expectations; plainly there is scope here as there for long drawn-out dynamics from the interaction of adjustment and rational expectations. It is possible to make some rough linear approximations but we do not pursue that here — enough has been done to show that one can obtain solutions for output and the other key macro variables exhibiting both variability and persistence that in principle at least could mimic a real economy — as explored in the empirical literature.

CONCLUSIONS

In this chapter we have examined the behaviour of representative agent models in a cashless society. We have seen that where loan and other contingent claim markets are complete, these claims are priced so that the expected future discounted marginal utility of consumption equals its current marginal utility. Since all agents are identical, consumption must equal (perishable) output in every period. If a government enters the market, then Ricardian equivalence holds: only government spending affects consumption and asset yields. Government debt is irrelevant to real outcomes.

Government debt becomes relevant if some constraint on market completeness prevents optimal loan trades being made between agents. Two such constraints were considered: overlapping generations without a bequest motive where the young will not lend to the old; and communities which are spatially separated so that loans cannot be reliably recovered. In both cases a government which borrows to finance a deficit can achieve intermediation between surplus and deficit agents. In the first case, Ricardian equivalence is eliminated; in the second case Ricardian equivalence still holds for the pattern of government borrowing over time but government willingness to borrow and lend enables trade to occur, in effect proxying the capital account of the balance of payments (chapter 13); of course if capital transactions are already possible, this role for government debt evaporates.

We ended the chapter by setting up a Real Business Cycle model whose aim is to mimic the economy's cyclical properties without appealing to anything other than maximizing behaviour by entirely rational and well-informed agents — it is assumed that they either are well-informed about general price movements or can easily index their own wages and prices to general prices. In this model government policy only matters for the business cycle to the extent that government spending fluctuates: there is Ricardian equivalence so that tax rates are irrelevant and monetary policy is entirely ineffective. The literature exploring this model empirically has not surprisingly generated considerable controversy which continues on many fronts.

APPENDIX 11A THE TECHNIQUE OF DYNAMIC PROGRAMMING

Suppose we write a maximization problem at time $t = 0$ as follows:
Maximize at $t = 0$

$$M = \sum_{0}^{T} \beta^t r(x_t, u_t) + \beta^{T+1} R(x_{T+1}) \tag{1}$$

where (x_0 is given)

$$x_{t+1} = g(x_t, u_t) \tag{2}$$

The r function is the value or return produced in period t; R is the terminal r function, the value in the last period, which the agent is assumed to be unable to affect with his instrument from $T + 1$ onwards. x_t is the state (e.g. of the economy) variable; it may be a vector of variables but we will treat it for simplicity as a single variable. u_t is the variable to be used as the instrument of maximization. The g function is the model of the economy relating the state at $t + 1$ to the previous state and the instrument. There is no uncertainty.

The dynamic programming method is to maximize M in two-period segments, taking the results from other periods as being already maximized. It thus breaks down the problem into T problems. For convenience, start with segment T:
Maximize

$$\beta^T [r(x_T, u_T) + \beta R(x_{T+1})] \tag{3}$$

This takes x_T as given (in effect by separate maximization of previous segments) and, since there is no u_{T+1} by assumption, it must be maximized by choice of u_T. This gives rise to the following first-order condition:

$$0 = \frac{\partial r(x_T, u_T)}{\partial u_T} + \beta \frac{\partial R_{T+1}}{\partial x_{T+1}} \frac{\partial g(x_T, u_T)}{\partial u_T} \tag{4}$$

Since r, g and x_{T+1} are all functions of x_T and u_T, this gives us a maximizing solution for u_T in terms of x_T:

$$\widehat{u_T} = h_T(x_T) \tag{5}$$

Denote the maximizing value of x_{T+1} correspondingly $\widehat{x}_{T+1}$. Then our T segment becomes:

$$[r(x_T, \widehat{u}_T) + \beta R(\widehat{x}_{T+1})] = V_T(x_T) \tag{6}$$

$V_T(x_T)$ is the 'value function' as seen at time T; by this is meant the function which, given x_T, extracts the most value from *subsequent* uses of the instrument (i.e. here u_T).

We must now repeat the operation for the $T-1$ segment:

$$[r(x_{T-1}, u_{T-1}) + \beta V_T(x_T)] \tag{7}$$

where $V_T(x_T)$ is the present value at T of the last, T, segment since this part is what needs to be maximised at $T-1$, having had its maximizing u_T chosen (and so has been reduced, after solving for u_T in terms of x_T, to an expression solely in x_T). Thus we maximise at $T-1$ an expression that already allows for the effect of future maximization at T. Again we obtain the first-order condition:

$$0 = \frac{\partial r(x_{T-1}, u_{T-1})}{\partial u_{T-1}} + \beta \frac{\partial V_T}{\partial x_T} \frac{\partial g(x_{T-1}, u_{T-1})}{\partial u_{T-1}} \tag{8}$$

This again solves for:

$$\widehat{u}_{T-1} = h_{T-1}(x_{T-1}) \tag{9}$$

Again we can rewrite the $T-1$ segment as:

$$[r(x_{T-1}, \widehat{u}_{T-1}) + \beta V_T(\widehat{x}_T)] = V_{T-1}(x_{T-1}) \tag{10}$$

$V_{T-1}(x_{T-1})$ analogously is the value function seen at $T-1$; plainly it includes the value function at T within it, discounted by β. We may continue backwards along the time segments obtaining:

$$[r(x_{T-2}, \widehat{u}_{T-2}) + \beta V_{T-1}(\widehat{x}_{T-1})] = V_{T-2}(x_{T-2})$$
$$[r(x_{T-3}, \widehat{u}_{T-3}) + \beta V_{T-2}(\widehat{x}_{T-2})] = V_{T-3}(x_{T-3}) \tag{71}$$
$$\vdots$$
$$[r(x_0, \widehat{u}_0) + \beta V_1(\widehat{x}_1)] = V_0(x_0) \tag{11}$$

$V_0(x_0)$ is the maximised value of M, that is, when the whole path of x_1, x_2, , x_{T+1} has been maximized by the path of u_0, u_1, .., u_T.

This segment-by-segment technique is highly convenient for thinking about uncertainty. It is usual to assume that at each period the agent can change his current and future instrument settings. If we think of him maximizing the expected value of (1), then he will at T choose a $\hat{u}_T$ that maximizes the expected value of (4), and (6) will be the discounted value function, as expected at T; this will be his contingency plan for T. $V_0(x_0)$ will then be the expected value function at $t = 0$; and within it will be nested expectations at $t = 1$, $t = 2$, ..., $t = T$. We can then use the law of iterated expectations to convert the expression into an expected value at $t = 0$.

Reverting to the case of no uncertainty, we can see that it implies in (9) an optimising rule relating the instrument to the state. Plainly if we can find this rule, then we can substitute it into M in (1) and so find the value function, the maximum value our agent can obtain. Such a rule, which in general will not be time-invariant, would be:

$$\widehat{u}_T = h_T(x_T) \tag{12}$$

In the case of uncertainty, this rule is to be found from the expected first-order condition and it becomes a rule for a contingency plan relating the planned instrument to whatever the state then turns out to be: thus $\hat{u}_T$ becomes the contingent plan value of u_T. If we take expectations of (12), it will give the expected instrument as a function of the expected state.

In practice, with models of any complexity there are no available analytical techniques for finding the contingent-plan rule or the value function: the problem has to be solved numerically via the computer. In this respect, the situation is worse than for the linear rational expectations models we mainly considered in chapters 1-7; for these the analytic techniques exist and can be written down, even if in practice they too are usually found by the computer. For dynamic programming problems the form of the contingent rule has to be guessed in the first place; to minimize complexity, set-ups are often converted into linear models with quadratic maximands, for which the form of the rule is known. However, most of the representative agent models being used in modern research are highly non-linear; so such a conversion carries a cost in brutal approximation.

To gain an understanding of solution paths the computer will generate, it is helpful to work through a simple set-up.

Let a household maximize

$$\sum_{t=0}^{T} \beta^t \ln c_t \tag{13}$$

subject to

$$A_{t+1} = R_t(A_t - c_t) \tag{14}$$

$A_{T+1} = 0; A_0,\ R_t(t = 0,\ 1, \dots ,\ T)$ are given. R_t is the gross real rate of interest.

Here the household has a finite life and will leave no bequest. We keep its problem to the simple one of deciding how to spend an initial stock of wealth, A_0, through its lifetime. In terms of our previous notation, we define the state as A_t and the instrument, u_t, as the amount of wealth unconsumed in period t, or 'savings' for short: $u_t = A_t - c_t$. Thus $A_{t+1} = R_t u_t$.

Starting with the last period, T, plainly there will be no savings: $0 = A_{T+1} = R_T(u_T)$ so that

$$c_T = A_T \tag{15}$$

(a corner solution where all remaining assets are consumed).

The value function at T is therefore:

$$V_T(A_T) = \ln c_T = \ln A_T = \ln R_{T-1} u_{T-1} \tag{16}$$

We now maximize the $T-1$ segment:

$$\ln(A_{T-1} - u_{T-1}) + \beta \ln R_{T-1} u_{T-1} \tag{17}$$

with respect to u_{T-1}.

The first-order condition is (in the standard way equating the marginal utility of consumption today with β times the marginal utility of consumption the next period times the real interest rate):

$$0 = \frac{-1}{A_{T-1} - u_{T-1}} + \frac{\beta}{u_{T-1}} = \frac{\beta A_{T-1} - (1+\beta) u_{T-1}}{u_{T-1}(A_{T-1} - u_{T-1})} \tag{18}$$

so that

$$u_{T-1} = \frac{\beta}{1+\beta} A_{T-1} \tag{19}$$

that is,

$$c_{T-1} = \frac{1}{1+\beta} A_{T-1} \tag{20}$$

The $T-1$ value function is now:

$$\begin{aligned} V_{T-1}(A_{T-1)} &= \ln\left(\frac{1}{1+\beta} A_{T-1}\right) + \beta \ln\left(R_{T-1} \frac{\beta}{1+\beta} A_{T-1}\right) \\ &= \beta \ln \beta - (1+\beta)\ln(1+\beta) + \beta \ln R_{T-1} \\ &\qquad + (1+\beta)\ln A_{T-1} \end{aligned} \tag{21}$$

Now maximize the $T-2$ segment with respect to u_{T-2} :

$$\ln(A_{T-2} - u_{T-2}) + \beta[\beta \ln \beta - (1+\beta)\ln(1+\beta) + \beta \ln R_{T-1}$$

$$+ (1+\beta)\ln(R_{T-2}u_{T-2})]$$

The first-order condition yields analogously:

$$u_{T-2} = \frac{\beta(1+\beta)}{1+\beta(1+\beta)}A_{T-2} \text{ or } c_{T-2} = \frac{1}{1+\beta(1+\beta)}A_{T-2} \tag{22}$$

Proceeding now to maximize the $T-3$ segment with respect to u_{T-3} yields:

$$u_{T-3} = \frac{\beta[1+\beta(1+\beta)]}{1+\beta[1+\beta(1+\beta)]}A_{T-3} \text{ or } c_{T-3} = \frac{1}{1+\beta[1+\beta(1+\beta)]}A_{T-3} \tag{23}$$

Hence we discover that the ratio of savings to wealth starts very close to unity, declines slowly at first, and then plunges sharply in the final years of life. Notice that even in this simple set-up the reaction rule is not constant, the reason being that the end-of-life constraint forces wealth to be completely used up; in order to smooth consumption the share of wealth consumed must rise over the lifetime (figure 11.5).

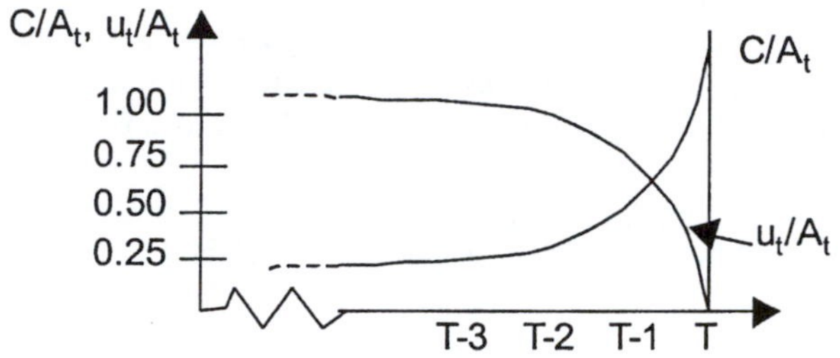

Figure 11.5: Consumption of wealth over lifetime

To find a constant rule requires a problem that does not change over time; an infinite lifetime in this case. If we now change the above problem to an infinite horizon one of maximising at $t = 0$:

$$\sum_{t=0}^{\infty} \beta^t \ln c_t \tag{24}$$

subject to

$$\lim_{t \longrightarrow \infty} A_T = 0; A_{t+1} = R_0(A_t - c_t) = R_0 u_t$$

This assumes that the implied one-period interest rate at $t = 0$, R_0, also applied at all future dates (that is, there is a flat term structure).

We can now guess at a constant reaction function and the corresponding value function. Let us try for V_T the same logarithmic form as the consumption function (since consumption will be related to wealth and therefore welfare at T related to the log of wealth):

$$V_T(A_T) = k \ln A_T + k_0 \tag{25}$$

and

$$u_T = aA_T \tag{26}$$

where k, k_0 and a are unknown and to be found out through the method of undetermined coefficients. To check our guess we derive the first-order condition and then implied value function; if correct, we can solve for the unknown coefficients when we compare these functions with our guessed ones. Using our guess, we maximise with respect to u_T the T-period segment:

$$V_T(A_T) = \ln c_T + \beta V_{T+1}(A_{T+1}) \tag{27}$$

where $V_{T+1}(A_{T+1})$ must be given by (25).

We find the first-order condition of (27) as:

$$u_T = \frac{\beta k}{1 + \beta k} A_T \tag{28}$$

We now substitute this into (27) and compare the result with (25):

$$\begin{aligned} V_T(A_T) &= \ln\left(\frac{1}{1+\beta k}A_T\right) + \beta k \ln(R_0 u_T) + \beta k_0 \\ &= \ln\left(\frac{1}{1+\beta k}A_T\right) + \beta k \ln\left(R_0 \frac{\beta k}{1+\beta k}A_T\right) + \beta k_0 \\ &= \beta k \ln \beta k - (1+\beta k)\ln(1+\beta k) + \beta k \ln R_0 + (1+\beta k)\ln(A_T) + \beta k_0 \end{aligned} \tag{29}$$

When set equal to the guessed solution, (25), this yields our undetermined coefficients as:

$$k = \frac{1}{1-\beta}$$

and

$$k_0 = \frac{\beta k \ln \beta k - (1+\beta k)\ln(1+\beta k) + \beta k \ln R_0}{1-\beta} = \frac{\beta \ln \beta + (1-\beta)\ln(1-\beta) + \beta \ln R_0}{(1-\beta)^2}$$

and

$$a = \frac{\beta k}{1 + \beta k} = \beta$$

Hence we have successfully found a constant rule and value function:

$$V_T(A_T) = \frac{1}{1-\beta}\ln A_T + \frac{\beta\ln\beta + (1-\beta)\ln(1-\beta) + \beta\ln R_0}{(1-\beta)^2} \tag{30}$$

$$u_T = \beta A_T \tag{31}$$

$$c_T = (1-\beta)A_T \tag{32}$$

APPENDIX 11B USING DYNAMIC PROGRAMMING TO CHOOSE THE OPTIMAL MONETARY POLICY UNDER OUTPUT PERSISTENCE

In chapter 5 we considered the issue of choosing optimal monetary policy and of time inconsistency. Because the Phillips Curve had no output persistence, the problem could be solved using static optimization. However, suppose that the Phillips Curve exhibits persistence as follows:

$$y_t = \rho y_{t-1} + \alpha(\pi_t - \pi_t^e) + \epsilon_t \tag{1}$$

where π_t^e is the rational expectation of inflation for t formed with $t-1$ information; it is also under commitment the inflation rate chosen and announced by the monetary authority.

Commitment

The set-up is that the central bank has scope to react to shocks- implicitly because the wage contract underlying this Phillips Curve is longer than the publication/reaction time to the shock. Using the usual loss function the value function under commitment is:

$$V(y_{t-1}) = Max(wrt\pi_t, \pi_t^e)E_{t-1}\{-0.5(\pi_t - \pi^*)^2 - 0.5\lambda(y_t - y^*)^2 + \beta V(y_t)\} \tag{2}$$

The value function form that works for the quadratic loss is also quadratic:

$$V(y) = \gamma_0 + \gamma_1 + 0.5\gamma_2 y^2 \tag{3}$$

Under commitment there is an additional constraint that the policy instrument choice at $t-1$ is also to be rationally expected because it will be followed through:

$$E_{t-1}\pi_t = \pi_t^e \tag{4a}$$

and also

$$\pi_t = E_{t-1}\pi_t + b\epsilon_t \tag{4b}$$

which uses the property of rational expectations and b is an undetermined coefficient (here it will be the chosen maximising response of monetary policy to the supply shock).

Hence maximise

$L_t (= \{-0.5(\pi_t - \pi^*)^2 - 0.5\lambda(y_t - y^*)^2 + \beta V(y_t)\} + \mu(\pi_t - b\epsilon_t - \pi_t^e)$ where we have used the combined constraint of (4a) and (4b)), to obtain the two first order conditions, the usual one in π_t and then the second $0 = \frac{\partial E_{t-1} L_t}{\partial \pi_t^e}$ respectively:

$$\pi_t = \pi^* - \alpha(\lambda - \beta\gamma_2)[\rho y_{t-1} + \alpha(\pi_t - \pi_t^e) + \epsilon_t] + \alpha\lambda y^* + \beta\gamma_1\alpha + \mu \quad (5)$$

and

$$\mu = \alpha(\lambda - \beta\gamma_2)\rho y_{t-1} - \alpha\lambda y^* - \beta\gamma_1\alpha \quad (6)$$

Substituting for the Lagrange multiplier, μ, from (6) into (5) and taking expectations at $t-1$ yields (via the commitment constraint):

$$E_{t-1}\pi_t = \pi^* = \pi_t^e \quad (7)$$

Hence (5) now yields the optimal inflation rule under commitment:

$$\pi_t = \pi^* - \frac{\alpha^2(\lambda - \beta\gamma_2)}{1 + \alpha^2(\lambda - \beta\gamma_2)}\epsilon_t \quad (8)$$

To find the value function, one could equate (3) for lagged output with the RHS of (2) once the optimal values of π_t and y_t are substituted in the RHS. But as we are only interested in γ_2 in this case we can take the first derivative of each side of (2) with respect to y_{t-1} and equate these expressions (the first derivative of two sides of an equality are equal via the 'envelope theorem'). Differentiating the LHS of (2) yields $\gamma_1 + \gamma_2 y_{t-1}$. The RHS of (2), remembering that once optimised we take expectations of it, is differentiated as:

$$\rho^2(\lambda - \beta\gamma_2)y_{t-1} + \rho\lambda y^* + \rho\beta\gamma_1$$

from which it follows, equating the LHS derivative with the RHS derivative, that:

$$\gamma_1 = \frac{\rho\lambda y^*}{1 + \rho\beta}$$

and

$$\gamma_2 = \frac{-\rho^2\lambda}{1 - \beta\rho^2}$$

Hence:

$$\pi_t = \pi^* - \frac{\alpha\lambda}{1 + \alpha^2\lambda - \beta\rho^2}\epsilon_t$$

Notice that the supply shock response in now larger because of the need to stabilise future output which will now be affected by the persistence term.

Discretion

Now the problem is

$$Max(wrt\ \pi_t)\{-0.5(\pi_t - \pi^*)^2 - 0.5\lambda(y_t - y^*)^2 + \beta V(y_t)\} \quad (9)$$

where now π_t^e is simply the rational expectation of t-inflation formed at $t-1$.

Using the same value function, the first-order condition yields:

$$\pi_t = \frac{1}{1+\alpha^2(\lambda - \beta\gamma_2)}\{\pi^* + \alpha^2(\lambda - \beta\gamma_2)\pi_t^e - \alpha(\lambda - \beta\gamma_2) [\rho y_{t-1} + \epsilon_t] + \alpha\lambda y^* + \beta\alpha\gamma_1\} \quad (10)$$

Taking expectations yields:

$$E_{t-1}\pi_t = \pi^* - \alpha(\lambda - \beta\gamma_2)[\rho y_{t-1}] + \alpha\lambda y^* + \beta\alpha\gamma_1 \quad (11)$$

Hence

$$\pi_t = \pi^* - \alpha(\lambda - \beta\gamma_2)[\rho y_{t-1}] + \alpha\lambda y^* + \beta\alpha\gamma_1 - \frac{\alpha(\lambda - \beta\gamma_2)}{1+\alpha^2(\lambda - \beta\gamma_2)}\epsilon_t = a - b\epsilon_t - cy_{t-1} \quad (12)$$

where a, b and c are implicitly defined.

Now set $\frac{\partial V(y_{t-1})}{\partial y_{t-1}} = \gamma_1 + \gamma_2 y_{t-1}$ (the derivative of the supposed value function wrt y_{t-1})

$$V(y_{t-1}) = E_{t-1}\{-0.5(a - \pi^* - b\epsilon_t - cy_{t-1})^2 - 0.5\lambda(y_t - y^*)^2 + \beta[\gamma_0 + \gamma_1 y_t + 0.5\gamma_2 y_t^2]\} \quad (13)$$

where $y_t = \rho y_{t-1} + [1 - \alpha b]\epsilon_t$

Hence

$$\frac{\partial V(y_{t-1})}{\partial y_{t-1}} = c(a - \pi^*) + \rho\lambda y^* + \rho\beta\gamma_1 - \{c^2 + \rho^2[\lambda - \beta\gamma_2]\}y_{t-1} \quad (14)$$

Equating coefficients between this and the supposed value function derivative yields:

$$\gamma_1 = c(a - \pi^*) + \rho\lambda y^* + \rho\beta\gamma_1$$

and

$$\gamma_2 = -\{c^2 + \rho^2[\lambda - \beta\gamma_2]\}$$

For values where the model is well-behaved the lowest negative root of this quadratic is relevant (see Svensson, 1997) and we obtain the optimizing value of $\widehat{c}$ (and $\widehat{\gamma_2}$). This can then be substituted into the expression for γ_1 to yield:

$$\gamma_1 = \frac{\lambda y^*(\rho + \alpha\widehat{c})}{1 - \beta(\rho + \alpha\widehat{c})}$$

The basic point is that there is an inflation bias $= \frac{\lambda y^*}{1-\beta(\rho+\alpha\widehat{c})} + \widehat{c}y_{t-1}$. Also the response to the current supply shock is excessive because the future inflation bias also depends on today's output; so it needs to be stabilised more strongly. To eliminate these twin problems the monetary authority must be prevented from following a (lagged) feedback rule, since just as in the Sargent and Wallace ineffectiveness result such a feedback component is fully anticipated by wage/price setters and impounded into $E_{t-1}\pi_t$. However, provided the feedback rule is off 'current' output, there is no bias and the optimal stabilization can be achieved; implictly the justification for a feedback off current output is that there are long-term contracts so that the authorities can react to events before the wage/price setters. Hence this set-up can be considered as a simplified overlapping-contract Phillips Curve, where in effect the wage/price setters all contract simultaneously at the start of the period.

Svensson (1997) considers ways this can also be achieved through Walsh contracts, Rogoff 'twisting of preferences', altering the inflation target and the output target. It is obvious that the Walsh contract must be state-contingent to eliminate the lagged output element in the inflation bias. The same is true of the output target; it must now be equal to the 'short-run natural rate', ρy_{t-1}.

However, altering the inflation target to be state-contingent, while it removes the inflation bias, does not restore the optimal response to the supply shock. Because it introduces a remainder term (the square of output appears now additionally because it enters the inflation target) into the utility function, it leads to an over-strong response to the shock, over-stabilising output. In this case the 'intriguing' result occurs that if the authority is made more 'weight-conservative' together with a state-contingent inflation target, the conservativeness can offset this over-reaction, so that the optimal result is restored.

The basic point remains that in practice the central bank must be induced to react only to current shocks and not to lagged information already incorporated into people's contract decisions. This does in practice then require a decision on the relevant length of the 'current' period; new information arriving within this period should be reacted to, previous not. On the logic of long-term contracts overturning the Sargent-Wallace result (Minford and Peel, 2001), this should be the longest period for which nominal contracts are written.

12

Money in representative agent models

What is money? This seems an odd question to ask. Clearly it is the physical item — dollar bill, beads, gold coins — used to pay for goods in order to avoid the 'double coincidence of wants' required in barter exchange. The classic theory of its emergence without social 'invention' is due to Menger (1892) who develops an evolutionary model. In this a good with appropriate characteristics (transportability, wide use etc.) is requested in exchange for goods by sellers secure in the knowledge that someone else will want it in exchange for the goods they may wish to buy — see White (1999). In fulfilling this function money will not pay interest because of the inconvenience involved; money holdings would have to be dated on their face to pay interest, like bearer bonds. But given the frequency with which money changes hands, for each bearer to get interest due of a few pennies would involve obviously bigger transactions costs. (Mrs. Grocer has to give you interest on your pound note when you pay for your bread, after allowing for when you acquired it — an unhappy lady.)

Other theories of how it emerged are of interest but appear in the end not to dominate Menger's insight. We discuss Wallace's (1980) overlapping-generation, OLG, model below; in it money has a store-of-value role in the absence of bonds. As a store of value money has the serious problem that it does not pay explicit interest. Even in primitive societies without paper bonds there are ways of storing value that yield expected return — cattle, inventories, crop credit arrangements etc.. There is an analogous problem with money as a store of value in the Bewley–Townsend turnpike model.

The search-theoretic models of Kiyotaki and Wright (1989, 1991, 1993) are of great interest and essentially a contribution to Mengerian theory. They derive the optimal search strategy of a representative agent within an environment where there are a variety of goods which may function as money, fiat currency being one but with no intrinsic value, the others (commodity moneys) having intrinsic value. They look for Nash equilibria with different moneys. Of course the problem with these equilibria is how one rather than another is selected. Menger's evolutionary model implicitly assumes in addition some sort of adaptiveness; people 'gravitate' towards the initially most promising commodity money and later as the attractions of fiat money become evident (or the interests of a monopoly currency provider, more likely, become dominant) they 'jump' to a fiat currency equilibrium. In their 1993 paper Kiyotaki and Wright show formally that fiat currency adoption is on a knife-edge; if most people decide to adopt it everyone will, but if few think of doing so, noone will. Selgin (1997) shows that a spontaneous move to fiat currency is unlikely if there is adaptive learning; rather, people are likely to adopt commodity money first as the closest alternative to barter and then stay with it. These models can be thought of as the beginnings of a formalization of Menger's ideas.

Suppose we accept the evolutionary theory of money's emergence. Then by the same evolutionary principles we would expect money's functions in time to be performed by new means. Means of payment emerge that use money as a unit of account but for most of the time avoid using money as a means of payment — clearing systems, bank accounts, deposit accounts with nonbank intermediaries, e–money vouchers and so on. The original physical money is the 'base' of this system of 'credit payment' (so-called because you pay with an interest-bearing balance) besides defining the unit (see White (1999) again for a compact history of intermediation along these lines).

As this evolution proceeds we should observe that competition between intermediaries drives the rewards to these functions of money down to the cost of provision for each. So effecting payment via a clearing system will command a competitive fee, while holding a deposit will command the rate of interest: there is 'unbundling' whereby we can consider deposits as held for their returns as stores of value and payment as a separate service done for a fee. Cash alone, being provided by a monopoly supplier (the government typically), will not be subject to competition by assumption within its 'domain'; however, even here evolution may be producing competition as it becomes easier (via the internet for example) to use alternative units of account with general acceptability.

Hence to introduce 'money' into representative agent models we must ask what our purpose is: to model a particular earlier stage of monetary evolution or to attempt to model 'modern times' (or indeed the possible future)? In what follows we introduce several examples of money in the economy, starting with models which we view as historical in intention and going on to models of the here-and-now. Finally we discuss where some tendencies in monetary policy and in potential competition between monetary authorities might lead in macroeconomic behaviour.

We begin with models which treat money as a store of value (it may also be a means of payment but so is any other asset or any good). Representative agent models face a fundamental difficulty in this case: money, defined as a non-interest bearing asset, has no role to play unless one is created for it by an artificial constraint. Consider the models of chapter 11. In models like Lucas', with infinitely-lived agents, there is nothing to stop trades in fruit (different sorts presumably) being paid for by an interest-bearing claim on fruit-in-general. In the Bewley-Townsend model, with parallel communities, government bonds can be used in payment. In the OLG models, again government bonds can be used. So money is inferior to interest-bearing claims and will have no value.

Accordingly, these models have a problem. To resolve it, the Bewley-Townsend model assumes away government bonds, leaving money as the only asset (possibly a government liability). We are presumably to assume that this is a very primitive economy in which there is no legal or other infrastructure to support lending and borrowing.

OLG models attempt an optimizing-agent explanation in the presence of a full menu of assets. They accept that money must offer a yield equal to that of bonds, or it cannot be held (will become valueless, with the 'price level' in terms of it becoming infinite). Then equilibria must involve a rate of inflation (or equivalent money creation and distribution to existing holders) equal to the rate of interest.

It is not obvious what application these models have. The OLG assumption (with no bequests) breaks up inter-generational links and opens up a role for government as an inter-generational intermediary, as we saw in chapter 11 with government bonds. It is frankly difficult to see why a government would print money in such a world when bonds can be issued. (A competitive banking system paying interest on money would be a different matter.) However, a number of these models have grafted on to the OLG constraint additional constraints: that only money (no bond) exists, and that there are regulatory requirements to use it (e.g. to pay taxes). (Incidentally, this regulatory theory of money, presumably motivated by the government's desire for revenue, is the nearest any of these models gets to an optimizing theory of why money exists.) These constraints place such OLG models alongside the Bewley-Townsend one as examinations of economies at a rather early stage of monetary evolution.

INTRODUCING MONEY INTO BEWLEY–TOWNSEND AND OLG MODELS

In chapter 11 we showed that both the Bewley-Townsend and OLG models gave government bonds a role in intermediating between groups which would not lend to each other. However, government bonds are a relatively sophisticated instrument, coming late in economic evolution. Money came first, as a government-backed medium of exchange and store of value. It is interesting to ask how these economies would behave if there were only money to perform this intermediary function.

If money is the only available store of value, then to achieve the optimal consumption-smoothing (that is, intermediation) that bonds achieved (in chapter 11) we require prices to be falling at the rate of time preference.

Consider now the Bewley-Townsend model. Consumers with T-period lives maximize

$$J = \sum_{t=0}^{T} \beta^t u(c_t) - \mu_t^h (p_t c_t + m_t^h - p_t y_t - m_{t-1}^h) \quad (1)$$

with $m_{-1}^A = 0$, $m_{-1}^B = m$ given; A agents receive $y^A = \varepsilon$ (odd periods), $y - \varepsilon$ (even); B agents receive $y^B = y - \varepsilon$ (odd), ε (even). The first-order conditions are:

$$0 = \frac{\delta J}{\delta c_t} = \beta^t u'(c_t) - h_t p_t \quad (2)$$

$$\frac{\delta J}{\delta m_t^h} = -\mu_t^h + \mu_{t+1}^h = 0 \text{ for } m_t^h > 0$$

$$0 \text{ for } m_t^h = 0 \quad (3)$$

$$0 = \frac{\delta J}{\delta m_t^h} = -\mu_t^h = 0 \text{ for } m_T^h > 0$$

$$0 \text{ for } m_T^h = 0 \quad (4)$$

The last, terminal, condition implies that for money to be held in T (as it must be for market clearing, i.e. $N_A m_T^A + N_B m_T^B = M$), then $-\beta^T u'(c_T)/p_T = 0$. But with $\beta^T u'(c_T) > 0$ (since $c_T < \infty$, there can be no saturation of wants), p_T must be infinite: money will all be spent in the last period until it is worthless. Working back to $T-1$, since $\mu_T^h = 0$, so will $\mu^h_{T-1} = 0$, and money will become worthless throughout. So to have a monetary economy we have to let $T \to \infty$. Agents live forever (a parable for the household which treats the interests of its descendants as its own, subject to the constant rate of time preference, β).

In this case, the terminal condition becomes for $m^h_T > 0$,

$$lim_{T\to\infty}(-\mu^h_T) = 0$$

If prices are falling at the rate $1-\beta$, we know that all agents will smooth their consumption optimally (as in chapter 11); consumption will be constant. Whichever agents are holding money at time t have

$$\frac{u'(c_t)}{p_t} = \frac{\beta u'(c_{t+1})}{p_{t+1}} \tag{5}$$

But A and B agents hold money in alternate periods (as we saw with bonds in chapter 11). Hence (5) holds in alternate periods for A and B agents: so it always holds for one set of agents. Therefore since c_t and u' are constant, $\frac{p_{t+1}}{p_t} = \beta$. Unfortunately, this violates the terminal condition, since $\mu^h_t = \frac{\beta^t u\prime}{p_0 \beta^t}$ and therefore $lim_{T\to\infty}(-\mu^h_T) = \frac{-u\prime(c_t)}{p_0} \neq 0$ (unless $p_0 = \infty$).

What this means is that as time goes on the present value of money holdings (discounted by the rate of time preference) does not diminish: so people find they have surplus money and spend it. This raises p_T and the path before it, and p does not fall by $(1-\beta)$ each period. This solution is therefore not an equilibrium. It follows that the Pareto-optimal solution in this model is impossible if only money, not bonds, exists.

Only equilibria where prices fall more slowly than $(1-\beta)$ are possible. One such equilibrium is a constant price one: this is obviously interesting as one of the features encouraging the evolution of money would be its stability in purchasing power. Figure 12.1 illustrates how price stability (offering a zero rate of return) achieves less than perfect consumption smoothing.

Let p be constant at $\overline{p} = 1$. Then A agents for example who get ε in odd periods will consume c^{**} in odd periods, c^* in even ($c^{**} \prec c^*$), so that

$$\frac{u'(c**)}{u'(c*)} = 1/\beta \tag{6}$$

B agents consume c^{**} in even periods, c^* in odd (with (6) holding as for A agents). $c^{**} + c^* = y$ for both sets of agents, so that $c^* = y - c^{**}$. Since there are the same numbers ($N = N_A = N_B$) of each, this also satisfies market clearing.

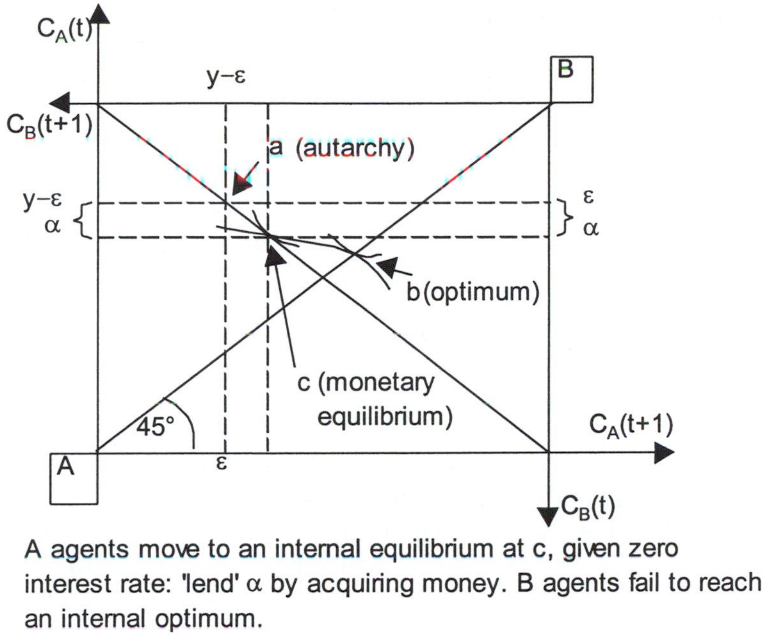

Figure 12.1: Monetary equilibrium with a static price level in the Bewley–Townsend model

B agents will hold enough money at the end of odd periods to buy c^{**}in the even periods, but will run this money balances down totally in the even period. The reason is that in the even period $u'(c^{**}) > \beta u'(c^*)$, so that they would rather spend then than wait and will exhaust their money holdings in the attempt: in terms of the first order conditions, they are at a corner solution with $m_t^h = 0$ (t even). A agents follow the same pattern in the alternate period. The result is that the money supply is passed from A to B each period.

It is possible to get to Pareto-optimal equilibrium if some way can be found to pay interest on money while still satisfying the terminal condition. For example, if prices fall at $1 - \beta$ per period and the money supply is reduced at this rate also by lump sum taxes, then this condition will be satisfied. But it is of course a highly artificial scenario, hardly suited to the idea that this is a primitive economy.

MONEY IN THE OLG MODEL

In the OLG example of chapter 11, we found that, if the government borrowed to finance a transfer to the initial old generation, and chose this transfer well, it could perfectly smooth each generation's consumption pattern across its youth and old age. By failing ever to pay off the loan it maintains this perfect smoothing for ever. The real interest rate is zero; because the economy is not growing, this is in this example the Pareto-optimal outcome. In this model if the economy were growing at the rate n, the Pareto-optimum would be where $r = n$.

This is illustrated in figure 12.2, which shows the zero-saving equilibrium (consumption is $y - \varepsilon$ in youth and ε in old age) with $r = r_o$ and the feasible reallocation along the line $-(1+n)$, achieved when $r = n$. This reallocation is feasible because the next generation is $(1+n)$ times the current; so if δ consumption is transferred by each of the young to the old each period, then each of the old, being less in number, will enjoy $\delta(1+n)$. By giving up consumption to the old today then the young guarantee an old age in which they will enjoy $\delta(1+n)$. (To achieve this equilibrium, the government must increase its debt and spending each period at the rate n).

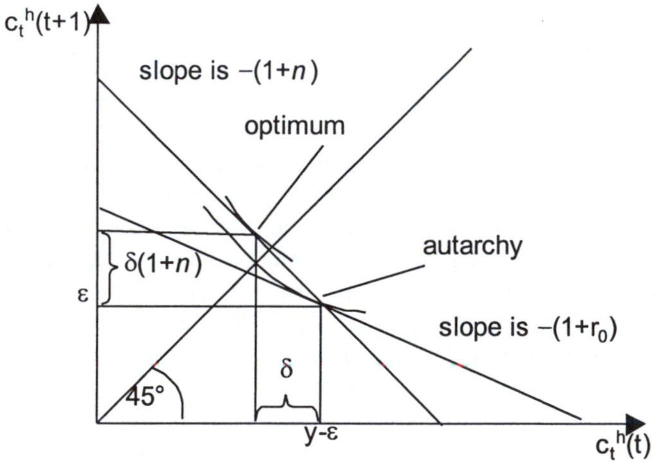

Figure 12.2: Feasible reallocation of consumption from zero savings (autarchy) to optimal intergenerational lending in government bonds — the overlapping generations model with growth, π.

In the example of chapter 11, where $n = 0$, and bonds paid zero interest, we could easily think of money performing exactly the same function as bonds. Let the government issue currency, $H(t)$, instead of bonds and let the price level be $p(t)$. Then we can treat $\frac{H(t)}{p(t)} = -L^g(t)$ as equivalent to the previous bonds, and the equilibrium would be the same. If currency issue were to be kept constant at H_0, $p(t)$ would then be constant at p_0: $\frac{p(t+1)}{p(t)} = 1$, implying a zero interest rate on money, the Pareto-optimal equilibrium as before.

So in this case, money could perform the same consumption-smoothing function as bonds, justifying its role in early societies with no growth and an unsophisticated financial market. It would also be possible for any government to swap bonds for money with no effect on anything (prices, consumption, interest rates) in the economy: there is no need for the new mix of bonds and money $H'(t) + L^{g\prime}(t)$ to change $p(t)$ since $\frac{H'(t)}{p(t)} + L^{g\prime}(t) = \frac{H(t)}{p(t)} + L^g(t)$ and, given that government liabiliies are the same overall, nothing else changes either. This is the 'real bills' doctrine, that open market operations altering the supply of money have no effect.

Matters become more complicated in growing economies, where the optimal $r = n > 0$. Here it will often be the case that a monetary equilibrium cannot be optimal. Essentially, this is because in a monetary equilibrium prices would have to be falling at the rate n. Yet the government must run a deficit in order to permit intermediation between generations. To finance this it must issue more and more currency, which will be inconsistent with falling prices.

However, there will usually exist suboptimal monetary equilibria. A large literature exists exploring the properties of such equilibria: for an introduction to it see Sargent (1987).

The main difficulty with using OLG models for the study of monetary economies is their emphasis on money as a store of value: this and the arbitrage between money and other financial assets produces somewhat strange results. For primitive static economies without alternatives to money, however, OLG monetary models offer interesting insights.

THE CASH-IN-ADVANCE MODEL

To resolve the problem of money's value in a model of a modern economy, it is simply assumed that money is needed for transactions. Money here is the physical unit of cash; all other assets and liabilities are bonds, physical assets, or claims to them (e.g. equities). It is assumed that to make transactions cash is required. In one such model, Lucas', there is a 'cash-in-advance' constraint (following Clower, 1965), whereby it is assumed that spending can only be carried out with money, which must therefore be accumulated in advance (Lucas, 1980).

Similar to this, and used in other models of the same general type, is the assumption that money 'has utility' and is an argument of the consumer's utility function. Effectively, this is being justified by the Clower constraint, and is merely an alternative way of expressing it, implying a degree of substitutability of money in transactions, whereas the cash-in-advance model assumes none.

If money has no use, it becomes valueless. This is obvious enough. Consider some cowrie shells which are stated by some village chieftain to be currency: if no one needs them in order to exchange goods (and they are useless for any other purpose), then there are two possibilities. One is that they have a value in exchange: but if so, they will be spent in order to obtain that value from the goods for which they can be exchanged. Since everyone will get rid of them in this way, they fall in value until they are worthless — the other possibility.

This is worth briefly demonstrating. Suppose the chieftain (government) issues currency of M per capita and will spend $\frac{M}{p_0} = g_0$ where p_t= the price level, g_0 = government spending in period 0: the government spends no more, $g_t = 0$ $(t \geq 1)$. If there exist other assets with a gross return R_t, then for currency to be held it must have an equal return so that

$$\frac{p_t}{p_{t+1}} = R_t = \frac{q_{t+1} + d_{t+1}}{q_t} \tag{7}$$

where q_t is the price of the assets (trees) and d_t their dividend (fruit). Now consider the consumer's budget constraint when the market equilibrium holds:

$$q_t\overline{s} + \frac{M}{p_t} + d_t = c_t + q_t\overline{s} + \frac{m_{t+1}}{p_t} \ (t \geq 1) \tag{8}$$

where $\overline{s}$ = the number of trees per capita and m_{t+1}= the number of currency units held for period $t+1$.

Since $c_t = d_t$ by goods market equilibrium, it follows that $\frac{M}{p_t} = \frac{m_{t+1}}{p_t}$; that is, $\frac{M}{p_t}$ is never spent, but it grows at the rate $(R_t - 1)$ each period, so that its present discounted value is $\frac{M}{p_t}$ of course.

It follows that if there is market equilibrium the consumer can only spend d_t in every period; and yet if $\frac{M}{p_t} > 0$, he will fail to spend all his wealth over his infinite lifetime; that is, he will spend all except $\frac{M}{p_t}$ (in present value). This is sub-optimal. The consumer will therefore attempt to spend more than d_t, which will drive the price level to infinity. Since $1/p_1 = 0$, money will not be held in period 0, so that $1/p_0 = 0$, and the government will be unable to spend anything ($g_0 = 0$).

In order to give money value, it must be given a source of usefulness. As we have seen, one way to point to this is through the Clower constraint, revived by Lucas (1980).

In Lucas' model each household has to acquire money *before* going to buy goods for consumption. Then while one member is shopping for consumption, the other householder is selling the household product for money, which is taken into the next period. Then that part of it not needed for shopping is exchanged for income-yielding assets; and the whole sequence is repeated, starting again with shopping/selling later in that period.

Begin at the start of a period, where the houshold has money, $\frac{M_t}{p_t}$, and assets: one tree, $s_{t-1} = 1$ whose price is $r_t(x_t)$, and government nominal debt $\frac{l_t^h(x_t)}{p_t}$, where x_t is the state of the economy (the vector of current endogenous and exogenous variables). All quantities are measured per capita: everyone now goes into a securities-trading session where assets are acquired and taxes are paid. The market-clearing conditions for this are:

$$m_t^p + m_t^g = M_{t+1} \tag{9}$$

$$s_t = 1 \tag{10}$$

$$l_{t+1}^h(x_{t+1}) = l_{t+1}(x_{t+1}) \tag{11}$$

where M_{t+1} and $l_{t+1}(x_{t+1})$ are respectively the money supply and government claims issued by the government and m_t^p, $l_{t+1}^p(x_{t+1})$ the private sector's demand for these; m_t^g is the government's demand for money.

Having acquired money, government and private agents go into a goods trading session in which household products are sold for money to government and household consumers:

$$p_t d_t = m_t^p + m_t^g \tag{12}$$

is the household income carried into the next period in the form of a money holding. d_t is the harvest per tree.

$$p_t g_t = m_t^g \tag{13}$$

$$p_t c_t = m_t^p \tag{14}$$

are the government's and household's consumption respectively. (We will assume that the nominal rate of interest is positive so dominating the zero return on money — so that consumers never hold more money than they plan to spend. Hence (14) is an equality.)

Equations (12)-(14) imply that the goods market clears:

$$p_t c_t + p_t g_t = p_t d_t \tag{15}$$

and money-market clearing (9) then implies the Quantity Theory:

$$M_{t+1} = p_t d_t \tag{16}$$

Now consider the household's consumption decision in this framework.

It maximizes $E_{t=0} \sum_{t=0}^{\infty} \beta' u(c_t)$ subject to

$$\begin{aligned} \theta_t(x_t) &\geq \frac{m_t^p}{p_t} + \tau_t + r_t(x_t)s_t + \frac{1}{p_t}\int l_{t+1}^p(x_{t+1})n(x_{t+1}, x_t)dx_{t+1} \\ m_t^p &= p_t c_t \end{aligned}$$

$$\theta_{t+1}(x_{t+1}) = \frac{p_t d_t s_t}{p_{t+1}} + r_{t+1}(x_{t+1})s_t + \frac{l_{t+1}^p(x_{t+1})}{p_{t+1}} + \frac{m_t^p - p_t c_t}{p_{t+1}} \tag{17}$$

Equation (17) states that the household's beginning period real wealth, $\theta_t(x_t)$, must be spent on money, taxes (τ_t), and government claims (at current price $n(x_{t+1}, x_t)$ for contingency x_{t+1}); that consumption can only be carried out by money; and that next period's beginning wealth will be produced by this period's income (in the form of money $=p_t d_t s_t$) deflated by next period's prices, next period's value of the trees and government claims acquired this period, and the value of any money acquired by the household before the goods trading session but not used for consumption then. However our assumption that the nominal return on bonds is positive implies that there will be no such surplus money balance, because money is only useful for buying consumption goods, and the cash-in-advance constraint is binding: $m_t^p = p_t c_t$.

The consumer's Lagrangean is then:

$$\begin{aligned} L &= E_{t=0} \sum_{t=0}^{\infty} \beta^t u(c_t) - \mu_t\{(c_t + T_t + r_t(x_t)s_t & (18) \\ & + \frac{1}{p_t}\int l^p t_{+1}(x_{t+1})n(x_{t+1}, x_t)dx_{t+1} - \frac{d_{t-1}f_{t-1}s_{t-1}}{p_t} & (19) \\ & - r(x_t)s_{t-1} - \frac{l_t^p(x_t)}{p_t}\} & (20) \end{aligned}$$

The first order conditions yield:

$$n(x_{t+1}, x_t) = \frac{\beta u'(d_{t+1} - g_{t+1})M_{t+1}d_{t+1}}{u'(d_t - g_t)M_{t+2}d_t} f(x_{t+1}, x_1) \tag{21}$$

$$r_t(x_t) = \int \left\{ \frac{\beta u'(d_{t+1} - g_{t+1})}{u'(d_t - g_t)} \right\} . \tag{22}$$

$$\left\{ r_{t+1}(x_{t+1}) + \frac{M_{t+1} d_{t+1}}{M_{t+2}} \right\} f(x_{t+1}, x_t) dx_{t+1} \tag{23}$$

Equation (19) is the price of a nominal bond which pays out when x_{t+1} occurs and it is set just as it was earlier, as the expected domestic marginal utility of consumption in that event relative to its current marginal utility; except that in this case it is the marginal utility of consumption of a nominal rather than a real unit that is assessed, so that it is deflated by the price level when x_{t+1} occurs. (Of course $c_t = d_t - g_t$ by the market-clearing condition.)

Equation (20) is the price of a real asset (the tree). Again the pricing method is the same as before but now the asset's dividend is in monetary form ($p_t d_t$) as it can only be exchanged for money. So apart from the expected future real price, $\int r_{t+1}(x_{t+1}) f(x_{t+1}, x_t) dx_{t+1}$, its value depends on the expected value of the dividend received this period but spent next, $\int \frac{d_t p_t}{p_{t+1}} f(x_{t+1}, x_t) dx_{t+1}$.

What effects does government policy have on this economy?

The government's budget constraint is:

$$g_t = \tau_t + \frac{1}{p_t} \int l_{t+1}(x_{t+1}) n(x_{t+1}, x_t) dx_{t+1} - \frac{l_t(x_t)}{p_t} + \frac{M_{t+1} - M_t}{p_t} \tag{24}$$

Government policy consists of choosing sequences for g_t, τ_t and M_t, conditional on x_t, and consistently with (21). Now because in this economy the output must be shared between government and private consumption, it is impossible for consumption to be affected by the pattern of taxation or money supply, given the government consumption sequence. However, the money supply sequence (and so also the taxation sequence if it is altered as a result) does affect the real value of real assets (trees). Hence there are real effects of monetary policy and taxation, because the returns from real assets can only be enjoyed by being exchanged for money and then spent. It follows that if there was investment in this economy, but the returns from investment could only be enjoyed by exchange for money, then private consumption would be affected by taxation and monetary policy: the mix between private investment and consumption would be changed. Only if there were an investment vehicle (such as an indexed bond) offering consumption possibilities quite independent of the price level would this cease to be the case. But such a vehicle may be ruled out in this cash-in-advance world (even on an indexed bond the indexed dividend has to be paid at a particular time to be exchanged later for goods in monetary exchange).

UNPLEASANT MONETARIST ARITHMETIC REVISITED

Let us return to the question addressed in chapter 7: whether tighter money today will reduce inflation permanently in the absence of changes in government spending and tax sequences. We can rewrite the government budget constraint:

$$K = \frac{M_1 - M_0}{p_0} + \sum_{j=1} \int q(x_{t+j}, x_t) \frac{(M_{t+j+1} - M_{t+j})}{p_{t+j}} dx_{t+j} \tag{25}$$

where K is the present value of the $(g_t - \tau_t)$ sequence and $q(x_{t+j},\ x_t) = \frac{\beta' u'(c_{T+j})}{u'(c_t)} f(x_{t+j},\ x_t)$ is the present (t-period) real discounted value of a unit of consumption if x_{t+j} occurs (that is, it is a contingent real discount rate).

Using the quantity theory, we can rewrite this:

$$K = d_0 - \frac{M_0}{p_0} + \sum_{j=1} \int q(x_{t+j}, x_t)(d_{t+j} - p_{t+j-1} d_{t+j-1}/p_{t+j}) dx_{t+j} \tag{26}$$

If M_1 is lowered, p_0 falls (M_0 is given), so $\frac{M_0}{p_0}$ rises and there is a lower current inflation tax which must be offset by a higher future inflation tax (p_{t+j}/p_{t+j-1}): but because $q(x_{t+j},\ x_t)$ is of the order $\beta^{\,j}$ (c_{t+j} being random and stationary), future inflation has to be higher by the order β^{-j}.

POSSIBLE MODERN EVOLUTIONS OF MONEY AND MONETARY POLICY: THE REEMERGENCE OF COMMODITY MONEY?

In chapter 6 we considered the evidence on optimal monetary (interest rate) feedback policy. We saw that rules in which monetary conditions reacted to deviations of inflation and output from their respective targets (of 'low' inflation and the natural rate) gave good results in conditions where people signed overlapping wage (or price) contracts of some given structure. However, the question arises whether these rules remain optimal when this structure is endogenous; we suggested there that this was not so but rather one found that rules offering price stability (that is, where any excess over the inflation target — which need not be zero — is clawed back in subsequent periods) produced a gain in macro stability because people lengthened the period for which nominal contracts would be signed. A formal rule of this sort would be one with a price-level target in which there was, for example, full clawback of a quarterly inflation error in the following quarter. This is examined in Minford et al. (2001) where the details can be found. The rule is analogous to a commodity standard in which if prices rise, implying that the relative price of the commodity, say gold, has fallen, then less gold is produced, driving the price up again and the general price level down again. With fiat money being targeted on the general price level in terms of money, the supply of money would react more rapidly than gold production under the gold standard; for example, suppose that productivity rose, raising the supply of goods and so driving down the price level, then the money supply would rise in the following period to accommodate this productivity increase, pushing prices back up again.

If households are using their wage contract structure to help minimize the variance of their consumption pattern, then they should react to this greater certainty in prices by reducing the indexation element (or equivalently lengthening their contract period). This will mean (see figure 12.3) that the aggregate supply curve will be flatter (more nominal rigidity) and the aggregate demand curve will be steeper (less reaction of money demand to rising prices because less effect on wages; and so less monetary tightening caused by rising prices, so less fall in output and employment). This in turn implies that real shocks have less effect on both output and prices. So provided pure monetary shocks are kept low this is a recipe for general macro stability.

CONCLUSIONS

Money is a commodity used as a unit of account and a means of payment. Its evolutionary origin most likely lies in the emergence of a commodity with the right characteristics to avoid the double coincidence of wants implied by barter. Its evolution proceeded towards the modern competitive banking system in which money remains the unit of account, issued by a monopoly government, but its payments function has largely been taken over by clearing systems based on credit, in which people can earn interest on their assets as well. Its evolution continues today, with the monopoly role of government in deciding the unit of account possibly coming under competitive threat from other governments and even perhaps the private sector. The models we focus on in this chapter are intended to understand how money interacts with the economy at different stages of monetary evolution. The Bewley-Townsend model

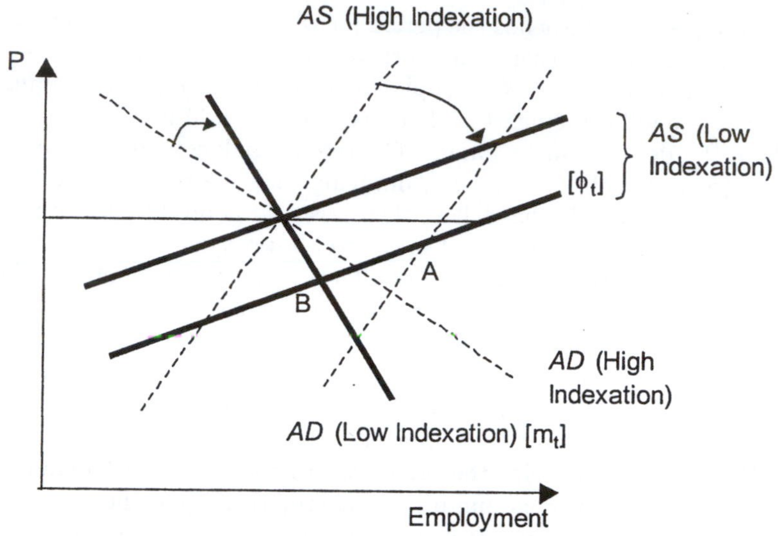

Figure 12.3: The effect of reduced indexation on slopes of AS and AD curves [ϕ_t = productivity shock; m_t = monetary shock]

explains how money permits two parallel (primitive) communities which are too remote from each other to lend directly to each other, to lend indirectly via money holding in the absence of interest-bearing instruments issued by a government or some trusted international intermediary. The OLG model shows how money can be a store of value which permits one generation to lend to the next indirectly again in the absence of bonds: however in a growing economy there are difficulties in achieving a monetary equilibrium which is Pareto optimal. The last model we looked at, Lucas' model of cash-in-advance, simply assumes money is needed for transactions; given that, it models how an economy with its full panoply of other financial instruments would behave. Because returns on other assets have to be turned into money before they can be enjoyed, changes in monetary policy can alter the expected rate of return on these and so have real effects. Finally, we considered how money and monetary policy might develop; currently we observe overlapping wage (and price) contracts which make it optimal to pursue rules of monetary reaction to deviations from inflation and output targets. However, if contracts are endogenous, as surely they are over some time period, then it may well be desirable to pursue price-level stability; this lengthens contracts and creates greater automatic stability in the economy.

13

Open economy representative agent models

In chapter 10 we explained open economy macroeconomics within a standard macro model of the aggregate demand/supply sort. This model is widely used by macroeconomists for policy and forecasting. Nevertheless it has no explicit micro-foundations and economists have wished to analyse open economy issues in the same way as in the models of the last two chapters. In this chapter we extend some of those models to the open economy. There is a huge degree of complexity possible in such models as a wide array of features special to the open economy can be incorporated (for a full account see Obstfeld and Rogoff, 1996). We limit ourselves rather strictly here and aim to get the reader familiar with some essential elements. In particular we will invariably assume a small open economy facing world markets (one can then easily think of that world economy being effectively a closed economy as in the last two chapters, uninfluenced by its small neighbour).

THE OPEN ECONOMY IN THE CASHLESS OLG MODEL

A natural way to begin thinking about the open economy is in terms of overlapping generations trying to save for their old age. Whereas in chapter 11 this was only possible if the government stepped in with its borrowing, with the open economy it is possible without a government, through the balance of payments. Let there be one sort of perishable good traded throughout the world. We adopt the OLG model of chapter 11 but now allow lending overseas by the young generation, l_t^h, which is then repaid to it when old — as before the old must consume all the resources they have.

The household maximizes the logarithmic utility function

$$U_t^h(c_t^h(t), c_t^h(t+1)) = \ln c_t^h(t) + \ln c_t^h(t+1) \quad (1)$$

subject to $y - \varepsilon - c_t^h(t) = l_t^h$ and $\varepsilon + [1 + r(t)]l_t^h = c_t^h(t+1)$, where $r(t)$ is the world net rate of interest, exogenous to this economy. Its Lagrangean is therefore:

$$J = \ln c_t^h(t) + \ln c_t^h(t+1) + \mu_t^h(t)[y - \varepsilon - c_t^h(t) - l_t^h] \\ + \mu_t^h(t+1)\{\varepsilon + [(1 + r(t)]l_t^h - c_t^h(t+1)\} \quad (2)$$

The first-order conditions yield:

$$c_t^h(t) = \frac{c_t^h(t+1)}{1 + r(t)} \quad (3)$$

The consumer's life-time constraint is:

$$c_t^h(t) + \frac{c_t^h(t+1)}{1 + r(t)} = (y - \varepsilon) + \frac{\varepsilon}{1 + r(t)} \quad (4)$$

so that

$$c_t^h(t) = \frac{y - \varepsilon}{2} + \frac{\varepsilon}{2(1 + r(t))} \quad (5)$$

and

$$l_t^h = \frac{y - \varepsilon}{2} - \frac{\varepsilon/2}{1 + r(t)} \quad (6)$$

We now consider market clearing in the open economy when there is no money, only credit notes denominated in terms of the single good. Our small economy residents can make a loan to foreigners, allowing them to consume home endowments in return for repayment with interest next period; any repaid loans' proceeds will be used on consumption of foreigners' endowments. It is plain that any net loans made will be equal to net home endowments not consumed at home, that is, net exports: we assume in the standard small-economy way that the net loan and net export supplies by our residents make no difference to the world price of loans (the interest rate) or of the single good. So market clearing for our small economy is automatic at world prices via the balance of payments which gives:

$$l_t^h - l_{t-1}^h(1 + r(t-1)) = y - c_t^h(t) - c_{t-1}^h(t) \quad (7)$$

One can imagine these external transactions taking place on the beach where foreigners come to trade; all sales by young residents are settled by credit notes and all credit notes held by old residents are repaid with interest by supplies of goods.

We can now consider the behaviour of our small country's balance of payments on the assumption that the world interest rate is constant at r. With each generation's endowments in youth and old age constant, each young generation will consume and lend the same as the next: hence $l_t^h = l_{t-1}^h = l^h$. Also $c_t^h(t) = c^h$ and $c_t^h(t+1) = c^h(1+r)$ are constant.Since the population of each generation is assumed in (7) to be constant at N, it follows from (7) that the current account of the balance of payments,

$$y - c^h - c^h(1+r) + rl^h = l_t^h - l_{t-1}^h = 0 \tag{8}$$

is in continuous balance.

However this would plainly alter if there was growth, say in population N at the rate n, still assuming constant r. In this case each generation has a constant per capita consumption when young and old, and so also constant borrowing when young — the same as in equation (8). But each generation is $(1+n)$ times the previous one in size.Then the balance of payments equation would become:

$$(1+n)l^h - l^h(1+r) = (1+n)(y - \epsilon - c^h) + \epsilon - c^h(1+r) \tag{9}$$

What this shows is that this country will have a persistent current account balance of payments surplus of, using (6):

$$nl^h = \frac{n}{2}\left\{y - \epsilon\left(1 + \frac{1}{1+r}\right)\right\} \tag{10}$$

This is because the young are always more in number than the old so that their aggregate savings exceed the aggregate dissaving of the old (being only equal when their numbers are equal). It follows by the same argument that if population were declining then the country would be in persistent deficit.

What we see is that the focus of this model is on the dynamics of population and the endowment. The balance of payments is an automatic financing mechanism about which there is no particular concern; its surpluses and deficits will reflect these underlying dynamic factors.

Suppose we return to the constant population/endowment model and examine whether the government could create problems for the balance of payments. The government's budget constraint is:

$$G(t) + L^g(t) = \sum \tau_{t-1}^h(t) + \sum \tau_t^h(t) + [1 + r(t-1)]L^g(t-1) \tag{11}$$

where $\sum \tau_{t-1}^h(t)$ and $\sum \tau_t^h(t)$ are the t-period lump-sum taxes raised respectively on the $t-1$ and t generations.

The household's budget constraint now must deduct the taxes payable from its income in each period:

$$c_t^h(t) = \frac{y - \varepsilon - \tau_t^h(t)}{2} + \frac{\varepsilon - \tau_t^h(t+1)}{2(1 + r(t))} \tag{12}$$

and

$$l_t^h = \frac{y - \varepsilon - \tau_t^h(t)}{2} - \frac{\varepsilon - \tau_t^h(t+1)}{2(1 + r(t))} \tag{13}$$

Now the balance of payments becomes:

$$L^g(t) + l_t^h - l_{t-1}^h - L^g(t-1) = y - c_t^h(t) - G(t) - c_{t-1}^h(t) + r(t-1)(l_{t-1}^h + L^g(t-1)) \tag{14}$$

with the capital account on the left-hand side of the equal sign and the current account on the right. From this we can see that if the taxes collected on the young and on the old each remain constant, like endowments, population and interest rates, then households will lend a constant amount ($l_{t-1}^h = l_t^h$), and the capital and current accounts will be in balance if the government balances its budget ($L_t^g = L^g(t-1)$). The difference then from the closed economy OLG model is that now the government has no beneficial role in borrowing because the private sector can smooth its consumption without its assistance. Nevertheless of course if the government borrows and so creates a current account deficit, it means it must repay it by reduced spending or extra taxes later; there is no 'balance of payments problem' unless there is a possibility that it will not. But this in turn would be spotted by foreign lenders offering the loans so that what one sees here is a process of smoothing of household and government spending undertaken by foreign lenders in an entirely voluntary, self-enforcing process. It is not difficult to embed temporary or permanent shocks into this model to see the smoothing effect via balance of payments deficits and surpluses.

AN OPEN CASH-IN-ADVANCE MODEL WITH DYNASTIC HOUSEHOLD

The OLG model focuses on longer-term savings decisions and so highlights the role of the balance of payments in smoothing the effects of long-lived shocks to population and GDP. For short-term analysis of the business cycle however it is not much help. For this we naturally turn to one of the models of chapter 12, Lucas' cash-in-advance model, where the household is assumed to be infinitely-lived (that is, to be 'dynastic' in that it cares about the welfare of its descendants). We retain the basic set-up that households, government and foreigners decide in the first half of each period on all financial transactions, including the acquisition of money to buy goods in the home economy and now foreign money to buy foreign goods. We now add a second, foreign, 'country' — the rest of the world. The home and foreign goods are not, as in our OLG model, the same; they compete for the custom of households in the two countries.

Each country has a stock of trees, one per capita. We will allow these trees to be owned by foreigners (capital movements), in fractions, so that in effect 'equity' can be held in someone else's tree — one purchases a fraction of it. This is of no consequence in a closed economy where everyone is identical and so ends up with the same tree; however in the open economy people can buy parts of trees in other countries and as each country has different conditions this may well happen.

The representative household in the home country maximizes in period 0 for example a logarithmic utility function in consumption of home and foreign goods and of leisure:

$$U_0 = E_0 \sum_{t=0}^{\infty} \beta^t (\ln c_t + \ln c'_t + \alpha \ln l_t) \tag{15}$$

subject to

$$p_t c_t + \frac{p^*_t c'_t}{e_t} + p_t r_t s_t + \frac{p^*_t r^*_t}{e_t} s'_t = p_{t-1} y_{t-1} + p_t r_t s_{t-1} + \left\{ \frac{p^*_t r^*_t}{e_t} + p^*_{t-1}(1 - l^*_{t-1})^{\pi} d^*_{t-1} \right\} s'_{t-1} + T_t \tag{16}$$

$$y_t = (1 - l_t)^{\pi} d_t s_t \tag{17}$$

$$m_t \geq p_t c_t \tag{18}$$

$$m'_t \geq p^*_t c'_t \tag{19}$$

where an asterisk denotes 'foreign' and a prime denotes the demand by a home resident for something foreign; c is consumption (hence c' is home consumption of the foreign good); l is leisure; m is demand for home money (m' of foreign money); s is the demand for trees and r is their real price; p is prices; e the exchange rate (foreign currency per unit of home currency); y is output; d is the fruit crop of the tree when the household is working at full stretch ($l = 0$); T is the money transfer from the government.

We use the same sequencing as in chapter 12; the household has to use the proceeds of income in the last period (plus its government transfer and asset disposals) to acquire goods this period; income depends on work, with elasticity π. The consumer makes plans to hold money and assets during the financial sub-period. We assume the leisure plan is then carried out during the production-and-shopping subperiod that follows: shocks to the fruit yield are revealed in this subperiod so that consumption plans may be frustrated by price changes.

Assuming as usual that money's zero nominal return is dominated by the expected nominal return on trees, so that the cash-in-advance constraint is binding, the first-order conditions are:

$$\frac{c_t'}{c_t} = \frac{p_t e_t}{p_t^*} \tag{20}$$

$$E_t \frac{[p_t(1-l_t)^\pi d_t + p_{t+1} r_{t+1}]}{r_t p_t} = E_t \frac{c_{t+1} p_{t+1}}{\beta c_t p_t} \tag{21}$$

$$\frac{\alpha}{l_t} = E_t \frac{\beta \pi p_t d_t (1-l_t)^{\pi-1} s_t}{p_{t+1} c_{t+1}} \tag{22}$$

$$E_t \left\{ \frac{p_{t+1}^* r_{t+1}^* + p_t^*(1-l_t^*)^\pi d_t^*}{p_t^* r_t^*} \right\} \frac{e_t}{e_{t+1}} = E_t \left\{ \frac{p_{t+1} r_{t+1} + p_t(1-l_t)^\pi d_t}{p_t r_t} \right\} \tag{23}$$

the first is the home/foreign goods consumption trade-off; the second that of present versus future consumption; the third that between leisure and future consumption; the last is that between home and foreign trees (uncovered interest parity in nominal terms).

The foreign household has exactly analogous utility and first-order conditions.

The government's budget constraint is:

$$M_t - M_{t-1} = T_t \tag{24}$$

Market clearing gives us:

$$s_t = 1 = s_t^* \tag{25}$$

$$M_t = m_t + m_t^{*\prime} = p_t(c_t + c_t^{*\prime}) = p_t d_t \tag{26}$$

$$M_t^* = m_t^* + m_t' = p_t^*(c_t^* + c_t') = p_t^* d_t^* \tag{27}$$

$$m_t^{*\prime} + p_t r_t \Delta s_t^{*\prime} - p_{t-1}(1-l_{t-1})^{\pi} d_{t-1} s_{t-1}^{*\prime} = \frac{m_t'}{e_t} + \frac{r_t^*}{e_t}\Delta s_t' - \frac{p_{t-1}^*(1-l_{t-1}^*)^{\pi} d_{t-1}^* s_{t-1}'}{e_t} \quad (28)$$

This last is the balance of payments constraint, that foreigners' demand for home money (home exports) and extra home trees minus their earnings from their previous stock of home trees be equal in terms of the same currency to home households' demand for foreign money (home imports) and extra foreign trees minus their earnings from their previous stock of foreign trees. It shows that there is scope for one economy to smooth its consumption for example in the face of a poor crop by selling shares of its trees to foreigners; buying them back later in a good year. This model is in fact rather similar to that of chapter 10, even though the latter had no micro-foundations. It is more complex to solve both because of its non-linearity and because it is a two-country case; to solve it analytically would require either linearising or loglinearising it. (A simpler version without capital flows is solved analytically with some loglinear approximation in Minford, 1995). However our main purpose here is to show its structure.

A SMALL-COUNTRY VERSION

Now let us simplify this to make it possible to derive a tractable analytic solution. First, let us treat leisure as a constant; then let both fruit yield and the money supply be random variables around a constant mean,

$$d_t = \overline{d}(1+\varepsilon_t) \quad (29)$$

and

$$M_t = \overline{M}(1+\eta_t) \quad (30)$$

Then rewrite contemporaneous utility as

$$u_t = \ln v_t \text{ where } v_t = \{c_t^{-\rho} + \alpha c_t'^{-\rho}\}^{\frac{-1}{\rho}} \quad (31)$$

$$\text{so that } U_0 = E_0 \sum_{t=0}^{\infty} \beta^t \ln v_t \quad (32)$$

Third, turn this into a small-country model, by assuming that the Rest of the World (the other country) consumes a fixed proportion of the home country's produce, x^*, and does not hold its trees; its prices of goods, p^*, and of trees, r^*, and its tree yield, d^*, are exogenous (and constant).

This implies the new first-order conditions are:

$$\frac{c'_t}{c_t} = (\alpha RXR_t)^{\sigma} \tag{33}$$

$$E_t\frac{(\frac{p_t}{p_{t+1}}d_t + r_{t+1})}{r_t} = \beta^{-1}E_t(\frac{c_{t+1}}{c_t})^{\rho+1}\frac{v_{t+1}}{v_t} \tag{34}$$

$$E_t\frac{[\frac{p_t}{p_{t+1}}d_t + r_{t+1}]}{r_t} = E_t\left(\frac{r^* + d^*}{r^*}\frac{RXR_t}{RXR_{t+1}}\right) \tag{35}$$

where $\sigma = \frac{1}{1+\rho}$ and $RXR_t = \frac{p_t e_t}{p_t^*}$ is the real exchange rate. (34) is uncovered interest parity in real terms, obtained from (23) which is in nominal terms in the manner of chapter 10, equation (9).

The home country's residents now only obtain foreign goods over and above their exports and the return on their foreign trees, by selling some foreign trees, so the balance of payments equation becomes:

$$\frac{m'_t}{e_t} + \frac{r^*p^*(s'_t - s'_{t-1}) - d^*p^*s'_{t-1}}{e_t} = m_t^{*\prime} = p_t x^* d_t \tag{36}$$

and so

$$c'_t + r^*\Delta s'_t - d^*s'_{t-1} = RXR_t x^* d_t \tag{37}$$

Market-clearing implies

$$M_t = m_t = p_t(c_t + x^*d_t) = p_t d_t \tag{38}$$

so that

$$c_t = d_t(1 - x^*) \tag{39}$$

and

$$p_t = \frac{M_t}{d_t} \tag{40}$$

as before.

The import function is from (32) and (38):

$$c'_t = (\alpha RXR_t)^{\sigma}c_t = (\alpha RXR_t)^{\sigma}d_t(1 - x^*) \tag{41}$$

It follows that

$$v_t = c_t[1 + (\alpha RXR_t)^{-\sigma\rho}]^{-\frac{1}{\rho}} \tag{42}$$

Equating the right hand sides of (33) and (34), and using (31) and (41), we obtain:

$$\frac{E_t(\frac{1+(\alpha RXR_{t+1})^{-\sigma\rho}}{1+(\alpha RXR_t)^{-\sigma\rho}})^{-\frac{1}{\rho}}(\frac{d_{t+1}}{d_t})^{\rho+1}}{E_t(\frac{RXR_t}{RXR_{t+1}})} = \beta\left(\frac{r^* + d^*}{r^*}\right) \tag{43}$$

Leading this one period forwards but taking expectations at t still, we would find:

$$\frac{E_t(\frac{1+(\alpha RXR_{t+2})^{-\sigma\rho}}{1+(\alpha RXR_{t+1})^{-\sigma\rho}})^{-\frac{1}{\rho}}}{E_t(\frac{RXR_{t+1}}{RXR_{t+2}})} = \beta\left(\frac{r^* + d^*}{r^*}\right) + c_0 \tag{44}$$

where c_0 is (minus) the constant of a Taylor series second order approximation of the left-hand side (in d_{t+1} and d_{t+2}) around $\overline{d}$. From (43) it is plain that RXR must be constant from $t+1$ onwards if we assume for simplicity that $\beta(\frac{r^*+d^*}{r^*}) = 1$, that is, domestic time preference is equal to the world rate of interest) and that c_0 is small enough to neglect. The left-hand side of (43) is unity with a constant RXR; but if RXR were expected to rise (fall) then the left hand side would be greater (less) than unity. To find out this constant value, we can solve backwards from the terminal value (at T, $T \to \infty$) when the transversality condition that $\Delta s_T^{*\prime} = 0$ and $d_T = \overline{d}$ is met; then we can solve from the balance of payments condition (36) that:

$$c'_T = RXR_T x^* \overline{d} + d^* s'_{T-1} \tag{45}$$

Using the import function (40) yields us

$$(\alpha RXR_T)^\sigma (1 - x^*)\overline{d} = RXR_T x^* \overline{d} + d^* s'_{T-1} \tag{46}$$

Linearising the left hand side around the presumed equilibrium $\overline{RXR}$ we obtain:

$$\sigma(1 - x^*)\overline{d}(\alpha\overline{RXR})^{\sigma-1} RXR_T + f_0 = RXR_T x^* \overline{d} + d^* s'_{T-1} \tag{47}$$

where f_0 is a constant; so that

$$RXR_T = \frac{d^* s'_{T-1} - f_0}{\overline{d}\{\sigma(1 - x^*)(\alpha\overline{RXR})^{\sigma-1} - x^*\}} \tag{48}$$

In this we assume that σ is large enough for the denominator to be positive; this is required for stability, as otherwise a rising real exchange rate (relative home to foreign prices) would cause the current account to improve. Since from period $t+1$ the real exchange rate is constant it follows that

$$RXR_{t+i} = \frac{d^* s'_{T-1} - f_0}{\overline{d}\{\sigma(1 - x^*)(\alpha\overline{RXR})^{\sigma-1} - x^*\}} \text{ for } i = 1, 2, ..., T \tag{49}$$

Going back to (42), rewrite it as

$$\frac{E_t(1+(\alpha RXR_{t+1})^{-\sigma\rho})^{-\frac{1}{\rho}}}{E_t(\frac{1}{RXR_{t+1}})} = \beta\left(\frac{r^*+d^*}{r^*}\right)d_t^{\rho+1}RXR_t\{1+(\alpha RXR_t)^{-\sigma\rho}\}^{-\frac{1}{\rho}}+c_1$$

where c_1 analogously to c_0 results from the Taylor Series approximation (for the terms in d_{t+1}) around $\overline{d}$. We can see in this equation that with the left-hand side now fixed, a positive shock to GDP lowers the real exchange rate for one period and also by (34) the real return on home trees. Net exports rise (the rise in output raises exports and imports by similar amounts assuming that x^* and α are of similar size; the fall in RXR then assures that imports will fall back from this level), so that foreign trees are acquired. The following period the real exchange rate rises back to a permanent level higher than the pre-shock rate, since foreign stocks of trees are permanently higher.

This example under our assumptions gives the typical boom/bust cycle; because the extra output cannot all be sold abroad more has to be sold domestically which forces people to spend more generally this period (this is effected by the falling real exchange rate driving down the implicit home real interest rate, made up of the world real rate minus the expected appreciation of the real exchange rate).

The role of money in this model is restricted to determining, apart from the current price level, the current real price of trees. Money does not affect the real exchange rate, which is a limitation on this model. We could give it a bigger role by reintroducing a leisure reaction as in the previous model; or we could introduce nominal wage/price rigidity via overlapping wage contracts for example as discussed extensively in earlier chapters for the closed economy. Obstfeld and Rogoff (1996) set out a representative agent model with menu costs of price setting in their last chapter; the characteristics of this model are quite like those of the Dornbusch-style models of chapter 10 above but the complexity required to obtain them is a huge order higher. Increasingly economists are finding that the 'deep structure' models required to model the world in a useful way are far too complex to handle in practice; this then impels them to write down a set of linear approximations, typically of the IS/LM/Phillips-curve form, which are derived from the deep structure model. But of course this was exactly what the original proponents of these models believed they were doing originally — that is, deriving from some theoretical structure some useable macro approximations. We seem to have come full circle! It is good to know one can derive these IS/LM models from micro-foundations but having done so the practical policy maker will want mainly to use models like those of chapter 10 or versions with more elaborate nominal rigidities.

CONCLUSIONS

We have set out here a variety of deep structure open economy models to give an idea of how they are built and what the balance of payments is doing in a deep structure way — viz helping an open economy to smooth consumption and to engage in arbitrage across world markets. Such models are useful exercises for understanding the underlying processes involved in open economy macroeconomics. However in practice except for policy or simulation exercises involving large-scale regime changes it is usual for economists to use the models of the type of chapter 10, which have their origins in the Mundell-Fleming model of the 1960s but have since been 'stretched' to incorporate the modern developments of rational expectations, supply functions, and nominal rigidities in wage-price setting.

Part IV

Confronting Models with Facts

14

Testing the Rational Expectations Hypothesis

In the remainder of this book, we consider the ways in which the RE hypothesis has been tested empirically. We begin in this chapter with the efficient market hypothesis, which is a joint hypothesis made up of rational expectations and a hypothesis about how expected returns are determined. In chapter 15, we discuss the evidence assembled by Robert Barro and others to test whether output is determined by the New Classical model or not. In chapter 16, we review direct tests of rational expectations using survey data on actual expectations; we then turn to the estimation of complete rational expectations models. Some such models are 'deep structure' (where the parameters are those of tastes and technology, presumably invariant to changes in the processes driving the exogenous variables including policy) but most are 'shallow structure', the parameters being those of aggregate supply and demand curves.

The purpose of this chapter is to consider the relationship between the concepts of financial market efficiency and rational expectations. A particular feature of financial markets is that trading can occur, in principle, almost continuously, and the market price is free to move to eradicate any imbalance between demand and supply. Furthermore since the assets traded (stocks, bonds, commodities) can be resold or traded in future periods it follows that financial markets are, more obviously than others, speculative in the technical sense that expectations of future asset prices affect current asset prices.

We begin this chapter by defining the concept of an efficient capital market and setting out models for the determination of normal or equilibrium asset returns and also the implications of rational expectations for the determination of asset prices. A brief review of the empirical evidence for efficiency in asset markets together with the problems faced in interpretation of the empirical evidence is also presented.

EFFICIENCY, PERFECTION AND ASSET PRICING IN CAPITAL MARKETS.

A capital or asset market is defined to be efficient when prices (e.g. stock prices, bond prices or exchange rates) fully and instantaneously reflect all available relevant information. Fama (1970) has defined three types of market efficiency, according to the extent of the information reflected in the market:

1. Weak-form efficient: A market is weak-form efficient if it is not possible for a trader to make abnormal returns by developing a trading rule based on the past history of prices or returns.

2. Semi-strong-form efficient: A market where a trader cannot make abnormal returns using a trading rule based on publicly available information. Examples of publicly available information are past money supply data, company financial accounts, or tipsters in periodicals.

3. Strong-form efficient: Where a trader cannot make abnormal returns using a trading rule based on any information source, whether public or private.

These three forms of efficiency represent a crude partitioning of all possible information systems into three broad categories, the precise boundaries of which are not easily defined. However, they are useful, as we shall see, for classifying empirical research on market efficiency. As their names suggest, strong-form efficiency implies semi-strong efficiency which in turn implies weak-form efficiency, while of course the reverse implications do not hold.

It is useful to distinguish between the concept of an efficient capital market and that of a perfect capital market. A perfect capital market could be defined as one in which the following conditions hold (see Copeland and Weston, 1988):

1. Markets are informationally efficient, that is information is costless and it is received simultaneously by individuals.

2. Markets are frictionless, that is there are no transactions costs or taxes, assets are perfectly divisible and marketable and there are no constraining regulations.

3. There is perfect competition in product and securities markets, that is agents are price-takers.

4. All individuals are rational expected-utility maximizers.

If conditions 1 to 4 were met (and assuming no significant distortions elsewhere in the economy), the capital market would be allocationally efficient, in that prices would be set to equate the marginal rates of return for all producers and savers, and of course consequently savings are optimally allocated. The notion of capital market efficiency is therefore much less restrictive. An element of imperfect competition in product markets would imply capital market imperfection; nevertheless, the stock market could determine a security price which fully reflected the present value of the stream of expected future monopoly profits. Consequently the stock market could still be efficient in the presence of imperfection.

Asset prices, in order to give the correct signals to traders, must fully and instantaneously reflect all available information. However, as pointed out by Grossman and Stiglitz (1976, 1980), it cannot be the case that market prices do fully and instantaneously reflect all available information. If this were so, agents would have no incentive for collecting and processing information, since it would already be reflected in the price, which each individual is assumed to be able to observe costlessly. It is the possibility of obtaining abnormal profits in the course of arbitraging which provides the incentive to collect and process new information. In the Grossman and Stiglitz model, individuals choose to become informed or remain uninformed, and in equilibrium each individual is indifferent between remaining uninformed on the one hand, and collecting information (or buying the expertise of brokers), so becoming informed, on the other. This is because after deducting information costs each action offers the same expected utility.[1]

---

[1] Hellwig (1982) challenges the Grossman and Stiglitz proposition that the informativeness of market prices in equilibrium is bounded away from full informational efficiency. Hellwig points out that this proposition rests on the assumption that agents learn from current prices at which transactions have actually been completed. This is a model in which investors learn from past equilibrium prices but not from the auctioneer's current price offer. Hellwig is able to show that if the time span between successive market transactions is short, the market can approximate full informational efficiency arbitrarily closely and yet the return to being informed remains bounded away from zero. This results from the fact that informed agents can utilize this information before uninformed agents have an opportunity to infer it from current market prices.

Hellwig also pursues the implications that arise if one relaxes the assumption that agents cannot assure themselves of being informed in a given period, but rather agents choose the frequency on average at which they obtain information. It appears that

Nevertheless, a reasonable interpretation of empirical tests of the efficient model hypothesis is, given that the data are collected at discrete intervals, that the process of arbitrage has occurred within the period. Consequently the implications of different available information can then be analysed without modelling the process of arbitrage itself (Begg, 1982) and this is the usual assumption in empirical work.

RATIONAL EXPECTATIONS AND MARKET EFFICIENCY

The semi-strong-form efficient markets model, i.e. that based on publicly available information, is an application of the concept of rational expectations, although this was not stressed in the early literature on efficiency, which goes back much further than the rational expectations literature. If expectations are non-rational, then publicly available information will not be reflected in asset prices and systematic abnormal profit opportunities will be available. This can be seen simply enough by noting that market agents have to know the model governing prices (or act as if they know it) in order to eliminate abnormal expected returns; if the model governing expected prices is different from that governing actual prices, there will be systematic abnormal returns available in the market.

Strong-form efficiency also implies that agents have rational expectations, since they must know how to use all sorts of private information as well as public; where strong-form efficiency differs from semi-strong is about the effects of private information on the market (fully discounted in strong-form, not at all in semi-strong).

Not quite the same is true of weak-form efficiency. In this case, since they make efficient use only of the past history of prices, they must know the time series model governing prices; strictly speaking this does not imply knowledge of the underlying structural model, since there will be generally insufficient identifying restrictions. Nevertheless, in practice, with limited samples and structural change, recovery of the time-series parameters by market agents from the data can effectively be ruled out. It is therefore natural, if not necessary, to assume in this case too that agents have rational expectations and so know the underlying model, from which they are then able to derive the time-series parameters.

While, therefore, market efficiency can be regarded as implying ratio-

---

relaxing such assumptions leaves his main result above unimpaired — see also the survey by Jordan and Radner (1982).

nal expectations, rational expectations does not imply market efficiency. Market efficiency is a joint hypothesis about expectations and market behaviour (specifically, the model of equilibrium expected returns). The main hypothesis about behaviour is the capital asset pricing model (see below); and in empirical tests more detailed assumptions must also be made about how equilibrium returns will move. Further hypotheses concern the behaviour of the agents with access to different sets of 'available' information. Under weak-form efficiency, active market participants are assumed to make effective use only of the past history of prices in their market; one theoretical basis for this has been in the costs of obtaining and processing wider information (Feige and Pierce, 1976). Under semi-strong-form efficiency, the assumption made is the usual one in rational expectations macro models that active agents use all publicly available information, presumed to be useable at zero or low cost. Finally, in the strong-form case it is assumed that those agents with access to private information deploy or indirectly influence funds to eliminate expected returns from this source of information; there are, however, problems with this, since private information cannot be sold at a fair price (once divulged it is valueless, but before divulgence it is impossible for the buyer to assess) and those with access have, by definition, in general only limited funds.

Because all definitions of market efficiency invoke the concept of abnormal returns, we are required for empirical work to have a theory of the equilibrium expected rate of return for assets. Tests of market efficiency are conducted after allowance for the equilibrium rate of return. If the riskiness of an asset does not change over time (or conversely if its risk changes randomly over time) then, for example, weak-form efficiency implies that there should not be an extrapolative pattern in the time series of returns. If there were a recurring pattern of any type, traders who recognized the pattern would use it to make abnormal profits. The very effort to use such patterns would, under the efficiency hypothesis, lead to their elimination.

THE CAPM MODEL OF EQUILIBRIUM EXPECTED RETURNS

The equilibrium expected return on assets is a central topic in modern portfolio theory and the interested reader is directed to, for example, Copeland and Weston (1988) for a full discussion (Allen, 1985, provides a helpful introduction). The following brief account of one such and widely used theory, the capital asset pricing model (CAPM), must suffice here.

Only if traders are risk-neutral[2] will they be indifferent to the variability of the returns (i.e. the risk) on their portfolio. Risk-averse individuals will be concerned about aggregate portfolio risk and will require a risk premium on each asset (or class of assets). By combining assets in the portfolio it is possible to diversify away some of the risk (the 'unsystematic' risk) associated with an asset. However, to the extent that the returns on an asset move with the market, there will be a component of risk (systematic risk) that cannot be diversified away. Assuming optimal portfolio diversification, the risk premium reflects the asset's systematic risk and hence its contribution to the overall variability of returns on the portfolio. This premium will be included in the equilibrium expected rate of return on this asset, in addition to the general rate of return on the portfolio.

The algebra of the CAPM theory is straightforward. All investors are assumed, as in standard portfolio analysis, to maximize their expected utility subject to their portfolio wealth constraint: this yields for each investor an optimally diversified holding of each asset in terms of the expected returns on all assets. It is convenient to aggregate this equation across investors and refer to the result as the asset demand of a 'typical' investor (but this does not imply that all investors are the same; it is merely an expression indicating averaging). The CAPM's contribution is then to note that at any time there will be a certain stock of each asset outstanding in the market which must be held in equilibrium. To be held, its expected return (and so its price) must satisfy the asset demand equation of the typical investor: in other words, this equation is turned round and solved for the necessary expected return in terms of the outstanding asset quantity. As the quantity of each asset rises, however risky it may be, it contributes only a little to the total risk on the whole market portfolio because it forms only a small part of this diversified whole; hence the rise in necessary expected return (fall in price) is negligible and we can talk of 'the' required expected return on an asset, independently of its quantity outstanding. Clearly this must not be pushed too far: some assets (e.g. dollar liabilities in currency

---

[2] Consider an individual faced with a possible gamble; he may choose either to receive 100 for sure, or to toss a coin and receive 50 if heads occur and 150 if tails occur. The expected outcome of this latter choice is $100 = 0.5(50) + 0.5(150)$. The question is: will the individual prefer the actuarial value of the gamble (this it its expected outcome) with certainty or will he prefer the gamble itself? If he prefers the gamble he is a risk lover; if he is indifferent he is risk neutral; and if he prefers the sure outcome he is risk averse. It is also possible to compute the maximum amount of wealth an individual would be willing to give up in order to avoid the gamble. This is the notion of a risk premium (see Pratt, 1964; Arrow, 1971; Markowitz, 1959).

portfolios) are outstanding in very large quantities and their risk cannot be fully diversified away.

Assume three assets, one of which yields a safe return . The typical investor maximizes the expected utility of end-of-period wealth, $E_t U(W_{t+1})$, with respect to w_1 and w_2 subject to the budget constraint

$$W_{t+1} = w_1 R_{1t} + w_2 R_{2t} + (1 - w_1 - w_2) R_t \tag{1}$$

where w_i is the share in the investor's portfolio of asset i, R_{it} is the actual return during the period, $W_{t+1}$is his end-period wealth expressed as an index (beginning period wealth = 1), U is his utility function ($U' > 0$, $U'' < 0$), and E_t is his expectation formed at the beginning of the period when he takes his investment decision.

Take a Taylor series expansion of $U(W_{t+1})$ around $E_t(W_{t+1})$:

$$U(W_{t+1}) = U(E_t W_{t+1}) + U'.(W_{t+1} - E_t W_{t+1}) + 0.5U''.E_t(W_{t+1} - E_t W_{t+1})^2 + ... \tag{2}$$

Ignoring terms of higher order than two, (see e.g. Kraus and Litzenberger (1976), Hwang and Satchell (1997) or Harvey and Siddique (2000) for some implications of higher moments) or alternatively assuming that the agent's utility function only depends on the first two moments, the expectation of this is:

$$E_t U(W_{t+1}) = U(E_t W_{t+1}) + U'.(E_t W_{t+1} - E_t W_{t+1}) + 0.5U''.E_t(W_{t+1} - E_t W_{t+1})" \tag{3}$$

which is equal to

$$U(w_1 E_t R_{1t} + w_2 E_t R_{2t} + \{1 - w_1 - w_2\} R_t) + 0.5U''(w_1^2 \sigma_1^2 + w_2^2 \sigma_2^2 + 2 w_1 w_2 \sigma_{12}) \tag{4}$$

where $\sigma_{ij} = E_t([R_{it} - E_t R_{it}][R_{jt} - E_t R_{jt}])$, the covariance between the returns of assets i and j, and σ_i^2 = the variance of i's return.

The first order conditions with respect to w_1 and w_2 respectively are:

$$U'[E_t R_{1t} - R_t] = U''[w_1 \sigma_1^2 + \sigma_{12} w_2] \tag{5}$$

and

$$U'[E_t R_{2t} - R_t] = U''[w_2 \sigma_2^2 + \sigma_{12} w_1] \tag{6}$$

$$\frac{-U''}{U'} = p \tag{7}$$

p is defined as a measure of absolute risk aversion.

We can express (5) and (6) in the CAPM form with required expected asset returns as the dependent variable (the standard portfolio analysis has the asset shares as the dependent variables): w_1 and w_2 are given by the outstanding stocks of assets 1, 2 and the safe asset in the overall market.

Rearranging (5) the expected return on asset 1 for example is :

$$E_t R_{1t} = R_t + p(w_1 \sigma_1^2 + w_2 \sigma_{12}) = R_t + pw(x_1[\sigma_1^2 - \sigma_{12}] + \sigma_{12}) \quad (8)$$

and on asset 2

$$E_t R_{2t} = R_t + p(w_2 \sigma_2^2 + w_1 \sigma_{12}) = R_t + pw(x_2[\sigma_2^2 - \sigma_{12}] + \sigma_{12}) \quad (9)$$

where x_1 is the share of asset 1 in the risky part of the market portfolio, $x_1 = \frac{w_1}{w}$, $x_2 = \frac{w_2}{w}$, and w is the share of the risky part in the total market ($w = w_1 + w_2$). Suppose we regard asset 1 as being a single asset and asset 2 as being a portfolio of all assets in the risky market, that is essentially 'the' risky market portfolio. Then (8) reveals that the expected return on a single asset consists of the safe return plus a risk premium reflecting risk aversion (p), the overall share of risky assets in the whole market (w) and the covariance between asset 1 and the risky market (σ_{12}), 'systematic risk': there is also a small component in the risk premium for the extent to which risk on asset 1 exceeds this covariance ('diversifiable risk'), but this has a negligible effect because it is multiplied by x_1, the small share of asset 1 in the risky market. So provided asset 1 is small in relation to the market, its risk can be virtually totally diversified away and barely affects the expected return.

Suppose we now let asset 2 embrace the whole risky market. Then $x_2 = 1$ and we have from (9):

$$E_t R_{mt} = R_t + pw\sigma_m^2 \quad (10)$$

where m is the whole risky portfolio so that in this case $\sigma_2^2 = \sigma_m^2$. From this it follows that:

$$pw = \frac{(E_t R_{mt} - R_t)}{\sigma_m^2} \quad (11)$$

This means we can rewrite asset 1's required return, substituting (10) into (8), as

$$E_t R_{1t} = R_t + \frac{\{x_1[\sigma_1^2 - \sigma_{1m}] + \sigma_{1m}\}}{\sigma_m^2}(E_t R_{mt} - R_t) \quad (12)$$

or more generally for any asset

$$E_t R_{it} = R_t + \beta_i (E_t R_{mt} - R_t) \quad (13)$$

where we assume the weight x_i is small enough to be ignored and so

$$\beta_i = \frac{\sigma_{im}}{\sigma_m^2} \tag{14}$$

$E_t R_{mt} - R_t$ is the excess return required on a unit of the average portfolio: it is therefore 'the cost of average risk'. Individual assets command higher or lower excess returns according to their 'beta', β_i, which measures their systematic risk, the covariance of the ith asset with the market portfolio, divided by the variance of the market portfolio — as illustrated in figure 14.1.

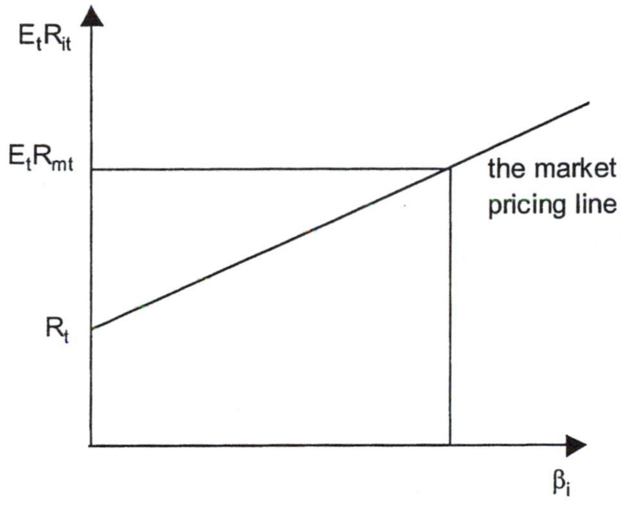

Figure 14.1: The Pricing of a Security

OTHER MODELS OF EQUILIBRIUM EXPECTED RETURNS

A related idea to the CAPM assumes that aggregate market risk is dominated by several sources of risk: principal component analysis can be used to separate these out. Thus there is not one but several market 'risks' or variables which are uncorrelated (for example, one variable might be a measure of the world business cycle, another might be the North-South terms of trade): the expected return associated with taking each risk is priced exactly as above — now think of 'asset 1' and 'asset 2' as being respectively 'exposure' to 'risk 1' and 'risk 2': that is, you buy £1 worth of assets combined in such a way that their return is correlated perfectly with variable 1, and similarly for variable 2. These fundamental risks being priced, each asset is then priced, by arbitrage, according to its amount of each risk. This is the arbitrage pricing theory (APT), due to Ross (1976).

CONSUMPTION CAPM

In chapters 11 and 12 we set out Lucas' theory of asset pricing. The first-order condition for the optimal consumption and portfolio decision is given by equation (9) in chapter 11 as

$$u'(c_t) = E_t\beta(1 + R_{it})u'(c_{t+1}) \tag{15}$$

where we have generalised the model to allow for the real gross return, $1 + R_{it}$, on the ith asset'[3]

Recalling that the covariance of X and Y denoted by $covXY$ is by definition $covXY \equiv E(X - EX).(Y - EY) \equiv EXY - EX.EY$ (we also note in passing that $cov(1 + X,\ Y) = covXY$), we can write the unconditional form of (15) as

$$E(1 + R_{it}) = \frac{(1 - cov(1 + R_{it}.K_{t+1}))}{EK_{t+1}} \tag{16}$$

---

[3] If we write the budget constraint as

$c_t + p_t s_{t+1} + q_t b_{t+1} = (p_t + d_t)s_t + b_t$

where b_t represents holdings of the riskless asset, s_t represents holdings of the risky asset, p_t is the price of the risky asset, q_t is the normalised price of the riskless asset. The optimization yields

$$u'(c_t) - \lambda_t = 0 \tag{1}$$
$$-\lambda_t q_t + \beta E_t \lambda_{t+1} = 0 \tag{2}$$
$$-\lambda_t p_t + \beta E_t(p_{t+1} + d_{t+1})\lambda_{t+1} = 0 \tag{3}$$

where λ_t is the Lagrange multiplier.
These conditions, 1-3, yield

$$\begin{aligned} 1 &= \beta E_t \frac{u'(c_{t+1})}{q_t u'(c_t)} \\ 1 &= \beta E_t \quad \frac{(p_{t+1} + d_{t+1})u'(c_{t+1})}{p_t u'(c_t)}\Bigg] \end{aligned}$$

noting that $q_t^{-1} = (1 + R)$ where R is the risk-free real rate. p, s can be generalized to any asset as in the text.

where $K_{t+1} = \frac{\beta u'(c_{t+1})}{u'(c_t)}$ is called the stochastic discount factor or pricing kernel.

For a risk free real interest rate R_t^f the covariance term is zero so that

$$E(1 + R_t^f) = \frac{1}{EK_{t+1}} \tag{17}$$

For the portfolio of assets we have that

$$E(1 + R_{mt}) = \frac{(1 - cov(R_{mt}, K_{t+1}))}{EK_t} \tag{18}$$

We can employ (16), (17) and (18) to obtain

$$E(R_{it}) - R_t^f = -(1 + R_t^f)cov(R_{it}, K_{t+1}) \tag{19}$$

and

$$E(R_{it}) - R_t^f = \frac{[covR_{it}, K_{t+1}](ER_{mt} - R_t^f)}{cov(R_{mt}, K_{t+1})} \tag{20}$$

Equation (20) illustrates that an asset's expected real return in excess of the risk free rate is higher the more negative the covariance between the asset and the ratio of marginal utilities. This is because when consumption is smaller, marginal utility is higher. An asset with a more negative covariance thus implies that the return is lower when consumption is low. This is the precisely the state however when wealth is more valued; consequently the agent requires a higher risk premium to hold the asset. This model of the relationship between expected returns is known as the consumption CAPM. Equation (20) shows the relationship to the ordinary CAPM where covariances with the pricing kernel replace those with the market portfolio.

To make the model empirically operational we have to specify the error structure of the model and the form of the utility function.

Consider the implications of the model if

$$u(c_t) = \frac{c_t^{1-\delta} - 1}{1 - \delta} \tag{21}$$

where δ is a constant and is called the coefficient of relative risk aversion.[4] This function has the convenient property that it nests the linear case, $\delta = 0$, and the logarithmic form, $\delta = 1$. (The latter case is found by employing L'Hopital's rule when $\delta = 1$.)

For this function

$$\frac{u'(c_{t+1})}{u'(c_t)} = (\frac{c_{t+1}}{c_t})^{-\delta} \tag{22}$$

In addition we assume that consumption and asset returns are jointly conditionally lognormally distributed. This allows us to make use of the fact that for a conditionally lognormally distributed variable, Y,

$$\ln E_t(Y) = E_t[\ln Y] + 0.5var_t[\ln Y] \tag{23}$$

Taking logarithms of (15) and employing (23) we obtain

$$\begin{aligned} E_t \ln(1+R_{it}) = &-\ln\beta + \delta E_t(\ln c_{t+1} - \ln c_t) \\ &- 0.5\{\text{var}\ln(1+R_{it}) + \delta^2 \text{var}(\ln \frac{c_{t+1}}{c_t})) \\ &- 2\delta \text{cov}(\ln(1+R_{it})\ln(\frac{c_{t+1}}{c_t}))\} \end{aligned} \tag{24}$$

(Note let $Y_t = \frac{(1+R_{it})u'(c_{t+1})}{u'(c_t)}$ so from (15), $\ln(1) = \ln\beta + \ln(E_t Y_t)$. Then use (22) and (23) to obtain

$$\begin{aligned} 0 \quad = \quad & \ln\beta + E_t(\ln(1+R_{it}) - \delta\ln(\frac{c_{t+1}}{c_t})) + 0.5\{\text{var}(1+R_{it}) + \\ & \delta^2\text{var}(\frac{c_{t+1}}{c_t}) - 2\delta\text{cov}(\ln(1+R_{it})\ln(\frac{c_{t+1}}{c_t}))\} \end{aligned}$$

Rearranging this expression gives (25))

If the real rate of interest on an asset, R_t^f, is risk free (24) simplifies to

$$\ln(1+R_t^f) = -\ln\beta + \delta E_t(\ln c_{t+1} - \ln c_t) - 0.5(\delta^2\text{var}(\ln\frac{c_{t+1}}{c_t}) \tag{25}$$

When there is a nominal asset yielding a certain nominal rate, N_t, we can employ the definition of the real rate of interest for this asset, say, $1 + R_{Nt}$, as

$$1 + R_{Nt} \equiv \frac{(1+N_t)P_t}{P_{t+1}} \tag{26}$$

where P is the price level.

Substitution of (26) in (15) and employing the same method as above gives us the required nominal return on the safe nominal asset, assuming conditional normality, as:

$$\begin{aligned} \ln(1+N_t) = &-\ln\beta + E_t(\ln P_{t+1} - \ln P_t) + \delta E_t(\ln c_{t+1} - \ln c_t) \\ &- 0.5(\delta^2\text{var}(\ln\frac{c_{t+1}}{c_t}) + \text{var}(\pi) + 2\delta cov(\ln\frac{c_{t+1}}{c_t}, \pi)) \end{aligned} \tag{27}$$

where $\pi = \ln(P_{t+1}) - \ln(P_t)$

We observe from (25) that the riskless real rate has a linear relationship with the expected change in real consumption. If the riskless real rate is assumed constant we can rearrange (25) with expected changes in consumption as the left hand side variable. This is the relationship estimated by Hall (1978): under rational expectations changes in consumption should be orthogonal to information dated prior to the information set conditioning expectations.

From (27) we observe that the safe nominal asset responds with a unit coefficient to expected inflation and is also determined by terms which reflect inflation risk premia.

Subtracting (25) from (24) we obtain

$$E_t \ln(1+R_{it}) - \ln(1+R_t^f) + 0.5var(1+R_{it}) = \delta cov\left(\ln(1+R_{it}), \ln(\frac{c_{t+1}}{c_t})\right) \quad (28)$$

or that

$$\ln E_t \frac{(1+R_{it})}{(1+R_t^f)} = \delta cov\left(\ln(1+R_{it}), \ln(\frac{c_{t+1}}{c_t})\right) \quad (29)$$

The implication of this model is that risk premia are determined by the covariation between the asset and changes in consumption times the coefficient of relative risk aversion.

Because the covariance term is relatively small in actual data, empirical tests of this model have not been able to explain the excess return on stocks over bonds, on average some 6% in the US over 100 years and large in other countries as well (see Campbell, 1996), without assuming a possibly implausibly large coefficient of relative risk aversion (well in excess of 10). This has become known as the equity premium puzzle after the pioneering contribution of Mehra and Prescott (1985). Recent contributions have suggested a variety of mechanisms that might resolve the puzzle. These include more general specifications of the utility function (e.g. Epstein and Zin, 1989, 1991), the introduction of habit formation (e.g. Constantinides, 1990; Campbell and Cochrane, 1999, 2000), survivor bias (e.g. Brown, Goetzmann and Ross, 1995), peso problems (see below; Rietz, 1988), heterogeneous agents (e.g. Constantinides and Duffie, 1996). Many of these ideas are superbly set out in Campbell, Lo and MacKinlay (1997).

DETERMINATION OF ASSET PRICE BEHAVIOUR UNDER RATIONAL EXPECTATIONS

We next consider the implications of the assumption of rational expectations for the behaviour of asset prices. Consider the return to holding an asset over the period t to $t+1$, say a share. We have

$$R_{t+1} = \frac{P_{t+1} + D_{t+1}}{P_t} - 1 \tag{30}$$

where D_{t+1} is any dividend or payment in the period and P_t, P_{t+1} is the price of the asset at time t and $t+1$.

We assume initially for simplicity that investors are risk neutral so that via arbitrage expected returns are equal to those on a riskless asset with a real rate of interest, $\overline{R}$, assumed constant, so that $E_t R_{t+1} = \overline{R}$.

Since P_t is part of the current information set, the expectation of (30) when rearranged is given by

$$P_t = \frac{1}{(1+\overline{R})} E_t P_{t+1} + \frac{1}{(1+\overline{R})} E_t D_{t+1} \tag{31}$$

Assuming rational expectations and solving this model forwards N periods we obtain

$$P_t = E_t \sum_{i=1}^{N} \frac{D_{t+i}}{(1+\overline{R})^i} + \frac{E_t P_{t+N}}{(1+\overline{R})^N} \tag{32}$$

In the absence of speculative bubbles (see below) we assume that the last term goes to zero as we let N go to infinity. In this case the current asset price is equal to the expected value of the stream of dividends into the indefinite future. This term is the fundamental of the process which we can call F_t.

Under these assumptions we have that:

$$P_t = E_t \left[\sum_{i=1}^{\infty} \frac{D_{t+i}}{(1+\overline{R})^i} \right] \tag{33}$$

We can write (33) in the equivalent form

$$P_t = E_t \left[\sum_{i=1}^{\infty} \frac{D_{t+i}}{(1+\overline{R})^i} \right] + \frac{D_t}{1+\overline{R}} - \frac{D_t}{1+\overline{R}} + \frac{E_t D_{t+1}}{(1+\overline{R})^2} - \frac{E_t D_{t+1}}{(1+\overline{R})^2} + \frac{E_t D_{t+2}}{(1+\overline{R})^3} - \frac{E_t D_{t+2}}{(1+\overline{R})^3} + \dots \tag{34}$$

Rearranging (34) we have that

$$P_t = E_t\left[\sum_{i=1}^{\infty}\frac{\Delta D_{t+i}}{(1+\overline{R})^i}\right] + \frac{D_t}{1+\overline{R}} + \frac{E_tD_{t+1}}{(1+\overline{R})^2} + \frac{E_tD_{t+2}}{(1+\overline{R})^3} + \dots \tag{35}$$

so that using (33) we can rewrite (35) as

$$P_t = E_t\left[\sum_{i=1}^{\infty}\frac{\Delta D_{t+i}}{(1+\overline{R})^i}\right] + \frac{D_t}{1+\overline{R}} + \frac{P_t}{1+\overline{R}} \tag{36}$$

Multiplying through by $1+\overline{R}$ and rearranging we obtain the alternative form

$$P_t = \frac{D_t}{\overline{R}} + \frac{1}{\overline{R}}E_t\left[\sum_{i=1}^{\infty}\frac{\Delta D_{t+i}}{(1+\overline{R})^{i-1}}\right] \tag{37}$$

Equation (37) shows that the current price of the stock is equal to the dividend divided by $\overline{R}$ plus a term in the discounted stream of expected future changes in dividends. In this form the model is amenable to empirical testing in the form of cointegration analysis (see Time-Series Annex). If dividends are a non-stationary process but changes in dividends are stationary then the stock price is cointegrated with dividends with coefficient $\frac{1}{\overline{R}}$.

An insightful special case of the above model arises when dividends are expected to grow at a constant rate g.

For this case

$$E_tD_{t+i} = (1+g)E_tD_{t+i-1} = (1+g)^iD_t \tag{38}$$

Substituting (38) in (33) we obtain

$$P_t = \frac{(1+g)D_t}{(1+\overline{R})} + \frac{(1+g)^2D_t}{(1+\overline{R})^2} + \frac{(1+g)^3D_t}{(1+\overline{R})^3} + \frac{(1+g)^4D_t}{(1+\overline{R})^4} + \dots \tag{39}$$

We can rewrite (39) as

$$P_t = \frac{(1+g)D_t}{(1+\overline{R})}\quad 1 + \frac{(1+g)}{(1+\overline{R})} + \frac{(1+g)^2}{(1+\overline{R})^2} + \frac{(1+g)^3}{(1+\overline{R})^3} + \dots\Big] \tag{40}$$

Recalling that $\frac{1}{1-x} = 1 + x + x^2 + x^3 + \dots$.. for $|\, x \,| < 1$ and assuming that $g < \overline{R}$ (as it must be since the stock price is not infinite) we can rewrite (40) as

$$P_t = \frac{(1+g)D_t}{(1+\overline{R})}\left\{\frac{1}{1-\frac{(1+g)}{(1+\overline{R})}}\right\} = \frac{(1+g)D_t}{\overline{R}-g} \tag{41}$$

This form is the Gordon growth model. It demonstrates the important point that if $\bar{R}$ is close to g then small permanent changes in $\overline{R}$ can have a major impact on the stock price.

The assumption made in the derivation of the asset price (33) is that expected stock returns are equal to a constant risk-free real rate of interest (in the context of CAPM say a constant real rate plus a constant risk premium). Relaxing this assumption in the above framework results in the loss of analytic tractability since expectations would be of a non-linear form. It is interesting to note an approximation for the case of a variable return that preserves tractability which was initially employed by Campbell and Shiller (1988 a, b).

Taking logarithms of (30) we have that

$$\ln(1+R_{t+1}) = \ln(P_{t+1}+D_{t+1}) - \ln(P_t) = \ln(P_{t+1}) - \ln(P_t) + \ln\left(1+\frac{D_{t+1}}{P_{t+1}}\right) \quad (42)$$

Noting that $\frac{D_{t+1}}{P_{t+1}} = \exp[\ln D_{t+1} - \ln P_{t+1}]$ we can rewrite (42) as

$$r_{t+1} = p_{t+1} - p_t + \ln(1+\exp(d_{t+1}-p_{t+1})) \quad (43)$$

where lower case letters now represent logarithms so that $r_t = \ln(1+R_t)$

Letting $z_t = d_{t+1} - p_{t+1}$ and taking a first-order Taylor expansion of the last term in (43) around the mean value of $\overline{z}$ we obtain

$$r_{t+1} = p_{t+1} - p_t + \ln(1+\exp(\overline{z})) + \frac{\exp(\overline{z})}{1+\exp(\overline{z})}[d_{t+1} - p_{t+1} - \overline{z}] \quad (44)$$

Rearranging (44) we obtain

$$r_{t+1} = \frac{p_{t+1}}{1+\exp(\overline{z})} + \frac{\exp(\overline{z})d_{t+1}}{1+\exp(\overline{z})} - p_t + \ln(1+\exp(\overline{z})) - \frac{\overline{z}\exp(\overline{z})}{1+\exp(\overline{z})} \quad (45)$$

Letting $\lambda = \frac{1}{1+\exp(\overline{z})}$ and noting that $\frac{1-\lambda}{\lambda} = \exp(\overline{z})$ and $1-\lambda = \frac{\exp(\overline{z})}{(1+\exp(\overline{z}))}$ we can rewrite (45) as

$$r_{t+1} = \lambda p_{t+1} + (1-\lambda)d_{t+1} - p_t - \ln(\lambda) - (1-\lambda)\ln\left(\frac{1-\lambda}{\lambda}\right) \quad (46)$$

or

$$r_{t+1} = \lambda p_{t+1} + (1-\lambda)d_{t+1} - p_t + \delta \quad (47)$$

where $\delta = -\ln(\lambda) - (1-\lambda)\ln\left(\frac{1-\lambda}{\lambda}\right)$

For a constant dividend-price ratio

$$\lambda = \frac{1}{1 + \frac{D}{P}} \tag{48}$$

The average value of the dividend price ratio observed in economies shows that the value of λ will be close to unity, around 0.96 in the US for example, so that in (47) the weight on the log price is close to one and that on log dividends closer to zero. Clearly the approximation will be more accurate the smaller the variation in the log dividend price ratio. Analysis by Campbell and Shiller (1988a) is suggestive that the approximation does not produce gross violations of reality, particularly at the monthly level of analysis. Essentially the approximation provides analytical tractability at the cost of some error in the statement of average returns. From an empirical perspective dividends appear to be more parsimoniously explained as a loglinear rather than a linear time-series process and this is an advantage of the approximation method.

We can take expectations of (47) and solve forward to obtain

$$p_t = \frac{\delta}{1-\lambda} + E_t\left[\sum_{i=0}^{\infty} \lambda^i \left[(1-\lambda)\, d_{t+i+1} - r_{t+i+1}\right]\right] \tag{49}$$

where we assume once again in the absence of speculative bubbles that the term $E_t \lambda^{\infty} p_{t+\infty}$ is zero.

We observe from (49) that the current log stock price is higher the higher expected future dividends and the lower expected future returns (i.e. the stock discount factors).

We can transpose (49) following the type of procedure outlined above (34) to obtain the equivalent form

$$p_t = \frac{\delta}{1-\lambda} + d_t + E_t\left[\sum_{i=0}^{\infty} \lambda^i \left(\Delta d_{t+i+1} - r_{t+i+1}\right)\right] \tag{50}$$

(Hint: in (49) add inside square brackets the term $d_t - d_t + \lambda d_{t+1} - \lambda d_{t+1} + \lambda^2 d_{t+2} - \lambda^2 d_{t+2} + - + \lambda^n d_{t+n} - \lambda^n d_{t+n}$, rearrange in terms of Δd_{t+1+i}. The terms in $d_t + \lambda d_{t+1} + \lambda^2 d_{t+2} + ... + \lambda^n d_{t+n}$then can be substituted out.)

Equation (47) is useful for illustrating another point.Taking expectations at time t of (47) and subtracting the resultant from (47) we obtain

$$r_{t+1} - E_t r_{t+1} = \lambda(p_{t+1} - E_t p_{t+1}) + (1-\lambda)[d_{t+1} - E_t d_{t+1}] \tag{51}$$

If we lead (50) one period, take expectations of it at time t and subtract the resultant from it, we obtain an expression for $p_{t+1} - E_t p_{t+1}$ which we substitute in (51) to obtain

$$r_{t+1} - E_t r_{t+1} =$$

$$\lambda \left\{ \begin{array}{c} d_{t+1} - E_t d_{t+1} + E_{t+1} \left. \sum_{i=0}^{\infty} \lambda^i \left(\Delta d_{t+2+i} - r_{t+2+i} \right) \right] \\ -E_t \left. \sum_{i=0}^{\infty} \lambda^i \left(\Delta d_{t+2+i} - r_{t+2+i} \right) \right] \end{array} \right\}$$

$$+ (1-\lambda)(d_{t+1} - E_t d_{t+1}) \quad (52)$$

Recognising that $d_{t+1} - E_t d_{t+1} = E_{t+1} d_{t+1} - E_{t+1} d_t - (E_t d_{t+1} - E_t d_t)$ under the information assumptions of the model, i.e. d_t is observable at time t, d_{t+1} at $t+1$, so $E_{t+1} d_{t+1} = d_{t+1}$, $E_t d_t = d_t$, we can rewrite (52) in the form presented by Campbell (1991) namely

$$\begin{aligned} r_{t+1} - E_t r_{t+1} &= E_{t+1} \sum_{i=0}^{\infty} \lambda^i \Delta d_{t+1+i} - E_t \sum_{i=0}^{\infty} \lambda^i \Delta d_{t+1+i} \\ &\quad - [E_{t+1} \sum_{i=1}^{\infty} \lambda^i r_{t+1+i} - E_t \sum_{i=1}^{\infty} \lambda^i r_{t+1+i}] \\ &= (E_{t+1} - E_t) \sum_{i=0}^{\infty} \lambda^i (\Delta d_{t+1+i} - \lambda r_{t+2+i}) \quad (53) \end{aligned}$$

Equation (53) is informative. We observe that unexpected stock returns are a function of revisions of expected future changes in dividends and revisions of stock discount factors. Further, *ceteris paribus* an upward revision in expectations of future returns leads to a fall in the price today since for a given dividend stream this can only be generated from a lower price today. The equation also demonstrates how revisions of expectations into the indefinite future impact on the current innovation in returns. Under rational expectations these revisions are news. However this creates a problem in empirical work which endeavours to estimate the impact of empirical measures of news on unanticipated asset returns. Clearly the impact of current news can have an ambiguous impact on unanticipated returns depending on the implications it has for future revisions to expectations. For example the news that the current money stock is higher than anticipated could be interpreted as a signal for future tightening of money stock or a move to a more relaxed regime. Similarly output figures higher than anticipated could signal the end of a slump or the beginning of an inflationary episode. This implies that without knowledge of current and future policy regimes empirical estimates of the impact of current news will be 'non-structural' so that the estimated coefficients may be difficult to interpret.

We can illustrate two other important implications for the potential behaviour of asset prices and returns using a modified example borrowed from Campbell, Lo and Mackinlay (1997).

Assume that the log of dividends is generated by the process

$$d_{t+1} = \rho d_t + u_{t+1} \tag{54}$$

where u_{t+1} is a random variable and$\mid \rho \mid < 1$. So we assume that dividends are a stationary process in this example.

Further assume that the stock discount factor is generated by

$$E_t r_{t+1} = \overline{r} + y_t \tag{55}$$

where $\overline{r}$ is a constant and y_t is generated by the process

$$y_t = \alpha y_{t-1} + v_t \tag{56}$$

where $\mid \alpha \mid < 1$ and v_t is a random variable.

y_t is an observable variable and might represent changing risk. Given these assumptions we can substitute in (50) to obtain the solution for the price of the asset. The log price of the asset (50) is given by

$$p_t = \frac{\delta}{1-\lambda} + E_t \left\{ \sum_{i=0}^{\infty} \lambda^i \left[(1-\lambda)\, d_{t+1+i} - r_{t+1+i} \right] \right\} \tag{57}$$

The first term in the braces, substituting for future dividends, is given by

$$\begin{aligned}(1-\lambda)[E_t d_{t+1} + \lambda E_t d_{t+2} + \lambda^2 E_t d_{t+3} + \ldots] = \\ (1-\lambda)[\rho d_t + \lambda \rho^2 d_t + \lambda^2 \rho^3 d_t + \ldots]\end{aligned} \tag{58}$$

and the second term by

$$\begin{aligned}-\{E_t r_{t+1} + \lambda E_t r_{t+2} + \lambda^2 E_t r_{t+3} + \ldots\} = \\ -\{\overline{r} + y_t + \lambda(\overline{r} + \alpha y_t) + \lambda^2(\overline{r} + \alpha^2 y_t) + \ldots\}\end{aligned} \tag{59}$$

so that substituting in (57) we obtain

$$p_t = \frac{\delta}{1-\lambda} + d_t \frac{(1-\lambda)\rho}{1-\lambda\rho} - \frac{\overline{r}}{1-\lambda} - \frac{y_t}{1-\lambda\alpha} \tag{60}$$

(recalling again that $\frac{1}{1-x} = 1 + x + x^2 + x^3 + \ldots$ for $\mid x \mid < 1$)

We can substitute (60) into (47) to obtain the solution for the one period stock return as

$$\begin{aligned} r_{t+1} = \lambda \left(\frac{\delta}{1-\lambda} + d_{t+1} \frac{(1-\lambda)\rho}{1-\lambda\rho} - \frac{\overline{r}}{1-\lambda} - \frac{y_{t+1}}{1-\lambda\alpha} \right) + (1-\lambda) d_{t+1} \\ - \left(\frac{\delta}{1-\lambda} + d_t \frac{(1-\lambda)\rho}{1-\lambda\rho} - \frac{\overline{r}}{1-\lambda} - \frac{y_t}{1-\lambda\alpha} \right) + \delta \end{aligned} \tag{61}$$

Using (54) and (56) and simplifying this gives

$$r_{t+1} = \overline{r} + u_{t+1} + y_t - \frac{\lambda v_{t+1}}{(1-\lambda\alpha)} \tag{62}$$

The solution for log prices illustrates that when the variability of y_t is small, so that the variability of expected returns is small, this does not imply that the variability of prices need be small. This is because the denominator of the term in y_t can be small. More formally, assuming the covariance between y_t and d_t is zero, we have from (60) that the variance of prices is given by

$$\sigma_p^2 = \frac{\sigma_y^2}{(1-\lambda\alpha)^2} + \frac{(1-\lambda)^2\rho^2}{(1-\lambda\rho)^2}\sigma_d^2 \text{ where } \sigma_y^2 = \frac{\sigma_v^2}{1-\alpha^2} \tag{63}$$

where $\sigma_d^2 = \frac{\sigma_u^2}{1-\rho^2}$is the variance of dividends.

Clearly σ_y^2 can be small but σ_p^2 large.

We can also solve for the reduced form ARMA time-series representation (see Time-Series Annex) of log returns and log prices in our example.

Using the lag operator, and substituting for y_t we obtain for returns

$$r_{t+1} = \overline{r} + u_{t+1} + \frac{v_t}{(1-\alpha L)} - \frac{\lambda v_{t+1}}{(1-\lambda\alpha)} \tag{64}$$

Multiplying out the lag operator we obtain

$$r_{t+1} = \alpha r_t + \overline{r}(1-\alpha) + u_{t+1} - \alpha u_t + \frac{v_t}{(1-\lambda\alpha)} - \frac{\lambda v_{t+1}}{(1-\lambda\alpha)} \tag{65}$$

The summation of the two error terms on the right hand side of (65) can be rewritten as a moving average error process of order one so that observed returns follow an ARMA (1, 1) process. Depending upon the covariance between news in dividends and news in returns the process can exhibit positive or negative autocorrelation.

Employing a similar process for changes in asset prices we obtain the ARMA representation for the level of the log asset price as (where L is the lag operator)

$$\begin{aligned} &p_t(1-\rho L)(1-\alpha L) \\ &= \frac{(\delta-\overline{r})(1-\alpha)(1-\rho)}{(1-\lambda)} + \frac{(1-\lambda)\rho u_t(1-\alpha L)}{1-\lambda\rho} u_t - \frac{v_t(1-\rho L)}{(1-\lambda\alpha)} \end{aligned} \tag{66}$$

so that the level of the log of the asset price is described by an ARMA(2, 1) in this example.

Although both returns and asset prices are forecastable in this example there can be no presumption that the market is inefficient. The crucial element in the definition is that *abnormal* returns should not be forecastable in an efficient market. We will observe another example of this next where the exchange rate has a predictable path in the Dornbusch overshooting model even though the market is efficient by construction.

OPEN ECONOMY MODELS WITH EFFICIENT FINANCIAL MARKETS

In Chapter 10 we set out the general behaviour of macro models of the open economy with efficient markets and New Classical price behaviour, under fixed and floating exchange rates. Here we focus in more detail on the behaviour of nominal exchange rates under floating, under varying assumptions about price behaviour. This will illustrate the role of financial efficiency per se in open macro models.

Our model is based on that outlined by Dornbusch (1976) in his seminal paper. For simplicity it is assumed that there is perfect capital mobility between countries (i.e. transactions costs are negligible and international assets are perfect substitutes). Consider initially a risk-neutral agent who is faced with the choice between holding a domestic or foreign bond for the duration of one period (say 90 days). The nominal rates of interest in the foreign country and in the domestic country are given by R_t and R_t^F respectively. Since the bonds are perfect substitutes, asset market equilibrium requires that the expected rates of return on the two bonds be equal. This expected rate of return has two components. The first component is the interest rate on the bond, which we can assume to be known at t; the second component is the expected capital gain or loss from exchange rate changes during the 90-day period.

It follows that the speculative condition for equilibrium, known as uncovered interest arbitrage is:

$$R_t = R_t^F + (E_t S_{t+1} - S_t) \tag{67}$$

where R_t, R_t^F are the domestic and foreign nominal interest rate, S_t is the logarithm of the current exchange rate (here domestic units per foreign unit) and $E_t S_{t+1}$is the expectation of the rate in period one (90 days in our example). A rise in S_t in our notation here represents a depreciation of the home currency. Equation (67) therefore implies that the interest rate differential in favour of domestic bonds must be equal to the expected depreciation of the exchange rate.

For example, if the domestic currency pays 12 per cent interest (per 90 days) and the foreign currency pays 4 per cent interest, a domestic investor buying foreign currency at the beginning of the period and converting back at the end of the period will, assuming the domestic currency depreciates by 8 per cent, expect to finish up with sufficient domestic currency to make him indifferent between holding domestic or foreign bonds.

There is also a forward market for foreign exchange in many exchange rates (i.e. traders can at time t contract to trade foreign currency at time $t+1$). In the forward market, large transactors are required to put up only very small amounts of money as 'margin requirements', so there is no need to discount. Consequently, using a similar argument to the one above, arbitrage implies the covered interest arbitrage condition that

$$R_t = R_t^F + (F_t - S_t) \tag{68}$$

where F_t is the logarithm of the forward exchange rate at time t for period $t+1$. We note that the covered condition is riskless and holds via arbitrage regardless of the manner in which expectations are formed. Uncovered arbitrage is a speculative condition, hence the explicit assumption of risk-neutral investors. Equating the covered and uncovered condition we obtain that $F_t = E_t S_{t+1}$ so that the forward rate is a direct measure of the market's expectation of the future exchange rate. The properties of the forward rate as a predictor of future spot rates has been a focus of much empirical research as we will discuss below.

In the Dornbusch model it is assumed that prices in goods or labour markets are in the short term 'sticky' with respect to changes in market conditions. This could, for instance, be because of the existence of multi-period wage or price contracts as in the New Keynesian model. It follows from this assumption that purchasing power parity does not hold in the short run. Purchasing power parity (PPP) or the 'law of one price', states that in the absence of transport costs and other transactions costs international arbitrage in goods should eliminate differentials between the prices of goods in different countries. We discussed in chapter 10 on the open economy how this would not hold in the short run but should hold in the long run, whether traded goods are homogeneous across countries or differentiated and imperfectly competitive (PPP in the long run but not the short is confirmed by numerous empirical tests, e.g. Taylor et al., 2001).

Under PPP we would have:

$$S_t = p_t - p_t^F \tag{69}$$

where p, p^F are the logarithms of the domestic and foreign price level.

With perfect capital mobility and PPP, from (67) and (69), the equalization of expected real rates of interest immediately follows:

$$R_t - (E_t p_{t+1} - p_t) = R_t^F - (E_t p_{t+1}^F - p_t^F) \tag{70}$$

Absence of PPP in the short run means that we may examine the behaviour of the real exchange rate, x, defined as:

$$x_t = S_t - p_t + p_t^F \tag{71}$$

For simplicity we assume that output (in logs), real interest rates, foreign interest rates and the foreign price level (in logs) are fixed and normalised to zero; but this does not affect the features of the model on which we focus here. The model is given by

$$R_t = E_t S_{t+1} - S_t \tag{72}$$

$$m_t^s = m_t + \overline{m} = p_t - \delta R_t \tag{73}$$

$$p_t - p_{t-1} = k(S_t - p_{t-1}) + u_t \tag{74}$$

where m_t is a random monetary shock around $\overline{m}$, the constant average money supply, and u_t is a supply shock. Equation (73) is a conventional demand for money function equated to money supply. Equation (74) is an *ad hoc* price adjustment mechanism which captures the hypothesis that the price level responds sluggishly to changes in the exchange rate, via aggregate demand and its effects on the volume of net trade. The specification has the convenient property that when $k = 1$, PPP holds instantaneously apart from the current supply shock.

When PPP holds instantaneously the model can be rearranged to give

$$S_t = \frac{\delta E_t S_{t+1}}{(1+\delta)} + \frac{m_t^s - u_t}{(1+\delta)} \tag{75}$$

Equation (75) will be recognised to have the same form as (31) above. We solve this model under the assumption that agents have full current information. The reduced form for the model is given by

$$k\overline{m} + m_t - (1-k)m_{t-1} = kS_t + u_t - \delta(E_t S_{t+1} - S_t) + \delta(1-k)(E_{t-1}S_t - S_{t-1}) \tag{76}$$

Following the procedures outlined in chapter 2, the solution for the exchange rate in the full-information case is given by[4]

$$S_t = (1-z)\overline{m} + zS_{t-1} + a_o m_t + a_1 m_{t-1} + a_2 u_t \tag{77}$$

where z is the stable root of the equation:

$$\delta z^2 - z(\delta(1-k) + k + \delta) + \delta(1-k) = 0 \tag{78}$$

and $a_0 = \frac{1}{k+\delta(1-z)+\delta(1-k)}$, $a_1 = -(1-k)a_0$, $a_2 = \frac{-1}{k+\delta(1-z)}$

We notice from (77) that, in the long run, when $S_t = S_{t-1}$, the elasticity of the exchange rate with respect to an increase in the permanent level of money supply is unity. In other words, in the long run the exchange rate depreciates by the change in $\overline{m}$. Given that $\overline{m}$ is a constant (72) implies that R is zero in the long run, and hence (73) that prices have the same response to $\overline{m}$ as the exchange rate. Equation (74) implies that in the long run PPP must hold. Leading (77) one period and taking expectations we obtain:

$$E_t S_{t+1} - S_t = (1-z)(\overline{m} - S_t) + a_1 m_t \tag{79}$$

Equation (77) defines an expectations mechanism known as regressive expectations. It informs us that when the equilibrium exchange rate is above the current exchange rate, then expectations are revised upwards and vice versa. The fact that regressive expectations can by choice of the regressive parameter $(1-z)$ be rational is one implication of this Dornbusch model. However, we should note that this property can hold in rational expectations models only where there is one stable root; it does not hold generally.[5]

We can substitute (77) into (71) and (73) to obtain

$$S_t = \frac{\overline{m}[1+\delta(1-z)] + m_t - u_t - (1-k)p_{t-1}}{k+\delta(1-z)} \tag{80}$$

[4] For the real interest rate differential to be constant, as investigated by Mishkin (1981), an infinitely large intertemporal substitution response is required for either α or β. The evidence does not support such responses; it is therefore not surprising that Mishkin concludes from his reduced-form work that the differential varies over time. Similar arguments apply to variation of the real interest rate within a closed economy, as investigated by Fama (1975) for the USA; this evidence has now been found (by Nelson and Schwert, 1977) to support non-constancy, which again is not surprising. We may also note that the size of variation in both the differential and the closed (e.g. world) economy level of real interest rates cannot be suggested a priori; nor can the length of time to convergence (determined by z in this model as influenced by all the parameters).

[5] Relative risk aversion (RRA) is defined as $RRA = \frac{-c_t u''(c_t)}{u'(c_t)} = \delta$ for the specification of the utility function.

Equation (80) illustrates another key insight of Dornbusch.

The impact of a change in the permanent level of money supply ($\overline{m}$) in the short run, ceteris paribus, is greater than unity except when $k = 1$ and consequently greater than the long-run impact. This phenomenon is known as 'overshooting'. The rationale for this effect is that because, in the short run, prices are at a point in time sticky or adjusting slowly, the only way the money market can remain in equilibrium as the permanent level of the money supply is increased is for the interest rate to fall. However, a falling interest rate has to be associated with an expected appreciation of the currency. Consequently the current exchange rate has to depreciate further than its long-run value in order to give rise to anticipations of an appreciation as it moves to its ultimate long-run value.

This mechanism is illustrated diagrammatically in figure 14.2. Suppose that at time $t = 0$ the pound/dollar rate is \$1 = £1. At time $t = N$ the authorities increase the level of the money supply by 100 per cent. In the long run this causes the pound to depreciate against the dollar to \$1 =£2.0. However, in the short run the pound depreciates further, to say \$1 = £2.50 and then follows the arrowed path back to long-run equilibrium. We notice that along the arrowed path the pound is appreciating, but has always depreciated relative to $t = 0$. The possibility that efficient assets markets, in conjunction with sticky wages or prices, could give rise to volatile behaviour of asset prices was a principal insight of Dornbusch and has been influential (see e.g. Buiter and Miller, 1981).

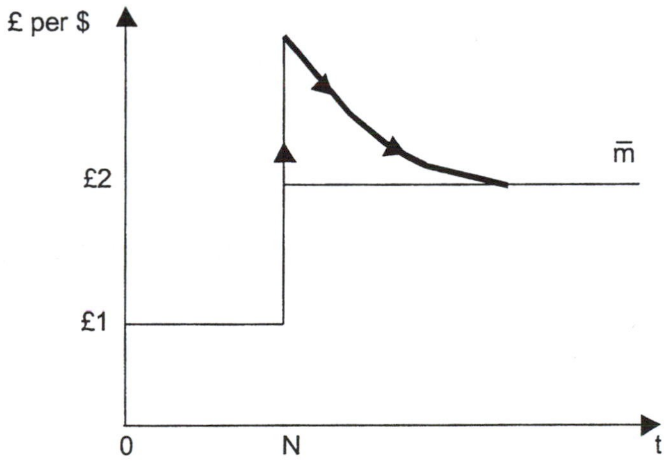

Figure 14.2: Exchange Rate Overshooting

We should also note from the solution for the exchange rate that, while a positive monetary shock causes a depreciation of the currency, its impact can be greater or less than unity, but since $\overline{m}$ has not changed, there will always be an 'overshoot' of the long-run equilibrium. The Dornbusch result applies to permanent (unanticipated) changes in the money stock ($\overline{m}$).

Another important feature of the model is that the exchange rate has a predictable path (77). However uncovered arbitrage was assumed in the model consequently the asset market is efficient since expected abnormal returns (in this example deviations from uncovered interest arbitrage) are not predictable. This is another example where predictability of an asset price does not violate market efficiency. In particular the exchange rate does not follow a random walk, though this is sometimes assumed in empirical work.

A number of authors have attempted to test the Dornbusch model (see e.g. Driskill, 1981; Frankel, 1979; Haache and Townsend, 1981; Demery, 1984), by examining the properties of reduced-form exchange rate equations derived from structural models of the Dornbusch type. The empirical results the authors report are unfavourable to the model. However there are a number of problems with these tests, the main one being that they all assume the regressive form for expectations, which is in general incorrect (Minford and Peel, 1983). For example, Haache and Townsend (1981) and Frankel (1979, 1982) specify models in which lagged adjustment or wealth effects are introduced into the demand for money function or lagged adjustment is introduced into the interest arbitrage condition; in these specifications, expectations will not be regressive. Box 14.1 shows that overshooting also can, but does not necessarily, occur in equilibrium models.

Box 14.1

EXCHANGE RATE OVERSHOOTING IN EQUILIBRIUM MODELS

We now examine whether exchange rate overshooting, which occurs in the Dornbusch model as a result of disequilibrium in goods or labour markets, must always be regarded in a real economy as occurring as a consequence of such features. We will demonstrate that this is not the case. Overshooting can indeed occur in equilibrium open economy models. In order to explain this, we adopt the model of the previous section.

In keeping with the equilibrium framework, we assume that all agents form expectations on the basis of the same set of macro information. This we date at $t-1$, and for simplicity ignore current global information (but this does not alter our point).

Hence the exchange market equilibrium condition becomes:

$$E_{t-1}S_{t+1} - S_t = R_t \tag{1}$$

and the real interest rate differential, r, is defined as:

$$r_t = R_t - E_{t-1}p_{t+1} + p_t \tag{2}$$

(We have for simplicity set the foreign real interest rate to zero.)

Demand for money is:

$$m_t = p_t + y_t - \lambda R_t \tag{3}$$

Money supply is:

$$\Delta m_t = \epsilon_t + \Delta \overline{m}_t + \Delta v_t \tag{4}$$

where

$$\Delta \overline{m}_t = u_t \tag{5}$$

This money supply function now allows not only for (unanticipated) temporary changes in the level of money (v) and once-for-all changes in the level (ϵ) but also for once-for-all changes in the steady state rate of increase (u). It will thus permit us to examine the different reactions to these shocks. (note $m_t = \sum_{i=0}^{\infty} \epsilon_{t-i} + \overline{m}_t + v_t$ where $\overline{m}_t = \sum_{i=0}^{\infty} u_{t-i}$)

From the definition of real interest rates and the real exchange rate, $x_t = S_t - p_t$, and from (1) we have:

$$(R_t - E_{t-1}p_{t+1} + p_t) = E_{t-1}S_{t+1} - E_{t-1}p_{t+1} - (S_t - p_t) = E_{t-1}x_{t+1} - x_t \tag{6}$$

i.e. the real interest differential must equal the expected real depreciation.

Now complete the model with an IS and Phillips curve:

$$y_t = -\alpha r_t + \delta x_t \tag{7}$$

$$y_t = \beta r_t + \gamma(p_t - E_{t-1}p_t) + \sigma y_{t-1} \tag{8}$$

Equation (8) has the full classical form discussed in chapter 3. Note that neither α nor β is infinite, so that r will vary. The model has been set up so that $y = r = x = 0$ in equilibrium. Notice that it belongs to the same Mundell-Fleming family as that of chapter 10. Define the superscript '^{ue}' as 'unanticipated at t-1'; hence for example $p_t^{ue} = p_t - E_{t-1}p_t$. Equations (6)–(8) can be solved as a recursive block in terms of p_t^{ue} to give:

$$x_t = \mu x_{t-1} + \pi_0 p_t^{ue} + (\pi_1 - \mu\pi_0)p_{t-1}^{ue} \tag{9}$$

where $\pi_0 = \frac{\gamma}{\alpha+\beta+\delta}$, $\pi_1 = \sigma\pi_0\frac{\alpha+\delta}{(\alpha+\beta)(1-\mu)+\delta}$ and μ is the (assumed unique) stable root of the characteristic equation

$$\mu^2 - (1 + \frac{\alpha\sigma + \delta}{\alpha + \beta})\mu + \frac{\sigma(\alpha + \delta)}{\alpha + \beta} = 0 \tag{10}$$

r and y have similar solutions: a first-order moving average in p^{ue} and first-order autoregressive coefficient μ. From (3) using these, we obtain:

$$p_t^{ue} = qm_t^{ue} \tag{11}$$

$$x_t^{ue} = \pi_0 qm_t^{ue} \tag{12}$$

where $q = \frac{1}{[1+\lambda+\lambda\pi_0+(\alpha+\delta)\pi_0]}$ is greater than 0 and less than 1. The nominal exchange rate depreciation is:

$$S_t^{ue} = x_t^{ue} + p_t^{ue} = q(1 + \pi_0)m_t^{ue} \tag{13}$$

where $m_t^{ue} = \epsilon_t + u_t + v_t$
We can usefully rewrite

$$q(1 + \pi_0) = \frac{\alpha + \beta + \delta + \gamma}{(\alpha + \beta + \delta)(1 + \lambda) + \gamma(\lambda + \alpha + \delta)} \tag{14}$$

which makes it clear that the value is positive and greater or less than unity depending on all the impact parameters (however if $\lambda + \alpha + \delta$ is greater than 1 then it must be less). Notice that overshooting properties occur in the broad sense that both the nominal and the real exchange rate depreciate in a 'volatile' manner in response to positive money shocks.
For the case where the money supply is growing over time we define overshooting as a reaction of the nominal exchange rate by a greater

proportion than the change in the (current) equilibrium nominal exchange rate, i.e. that which would prevail were the present money supply difference to be maintained in perpetuity, apart from elements expected to be reversed (v_t).

On this basis, we can determine from (13) that:

1. The exchange rate may respond more than proportionately to a once-for-all change in m (ϵ_t), and so the equilibrium exchange rate. This is the overshooting considered by Dornbusch (1976), which deals with surprise shifts in the permanent level of m.

2. It also may respond more than proportionately to a rise in m which is due to a permanent rise in its growth rate (u), However, since there is no way that speculators can distinguish between ϵ and u shocks when they occur, the reactions to both are the same.

3. It also responds to a temporary change in m (v), which on our definition does not change the equilibrium exchange rate. This is also a form of overshooting, though not that dealt with by Dornbusch.

All these types of overshooting in response to monetary shocks are qualitatively the same as those in the 'sticky price' models of Dornbusch and Frankel, yet they emerge from an equilibrium model. By altering our assumptions about the availability of current global information, these results could be easily 'enriched' to give a variety of potential overshooting responses; substantial overshooting is exhibited in empirical application by an equilibrium model of the UK economy (Minford, 1980, the Liverpool model). To sum up, volatility of the nominal exchange rate (overshooting), as well as of the real exchange rate and real interest differentials, is not prima facie evidence of 'price stickiness', 'disequilibrium' or 'inefficiency' in goods or labour markets.

Distinguishing Equilibrium from Disequilibrium Models of the Exchange Rate?

For good measure we can show that, on the basis of a reduced form exchange rate equation on its own, it is not possible to determine whether it comes from an equilibrium or disequilibrium model. For this purpose, we set up two models identical in all respects except in their 'supply' behaviour.

The first model is the one just dealt with; it consists of the demand for money function (3), money supply function (4), efficient market condition (1), and IS curve (7) and its supply curve is an equilibrium one (8). The second model consists of the same equations apart from (8) where it has a sticky price Phillips curve like Frankel's, namely:

$$p_t - p_{t-1} = bx_{t-1} + \Delta \overline{m}_t \tag{15}$$

(We also assume in the spirit of disequilibrium models that speculators have full current information, and condition the expectations operator throughout on the basis of current information.) It turns out that the solution for x_t in this model is:

$$x_t = \mu_2 x_{t-1} + \frac{[\epsilon_t + \lambda u_t + (1 - \mu_1^{-1})(v_t - v_{t-1})]}{\mu_2(\lambda + \alpha)} \tag{16}$$

where μ_2 is the stable, μ_1 the unstable root of the characteristic equation:

$$\mu^2 - \{2 - \frac{\lambda\gamma - \delta}{\lambda + \alpha}\}\mu + 1 - \frac{\gamma[1 + \lambda] + \delta}{\lambda + \alpha} = 0 \tag{17}$$

Compare this to the solution for the equilibrium model:

$$x_t = x_{t-1} + \pi_0 q m_t^{ue} + q(\pi_1 - \pi_0) m_{t-1}^{ue} \tag{18}$$

This shows that it is not possible to distinguish between the equilibrium and disequilibrium models on the basis of the reduced-form (real) exchange rate equations alone; both are ARMA(1,0,1) time-series models (see Time Series Annex). It follows that the models can only be distinguished, if at all, on the basis of full structural estimation. This is another example of 'observational equivalence' (see chapter 15).

EMPIRICAL EVIDENCE ON MARKET EFFICIENCY

Our interest here is in the empirical evidence that testing for market efficiency sheds on the rational expectations hypothesis. In these tests, either part of the joint hypothesis may fail: the model of equilibrium expected returns or the RE hypothesis. But this is unavoidable in testing a hypothesis about expectations which are not directly observable.

Modelling of the equilibrium expected return is clearly crucial in empirical tests of market efficiency. As the examples above have illustrated asset prices or returns can have predictable patterns without necessarily violating the efficient markets hypothesis. The crucial element is that abnormal returns should not be systematically predictable.

Since a property of rational expectations is that any difference of outcome from the expected outcome is unforecastable from available information, we have that :

$$R_{it} = E_t R_{it} + v_{it} \tag{81}$$

so that v_{it} is independent of $E_t R_{it}$, the rational expectation. Substituting the determinants of $E_t R_{it}$from CAPM, for example, gives:

$$R_{it} = R_t + q_{it} + v_{it} \tag{82}$$

where q_{it} is the risk premium. If q_{it} were constant (82) can be estimated by ordinary least squares (with the coefficient on R_t constrained to unity), and the estimated error term, $\widehat{v_{it}}$, should be independent of all information available at the beginning of period t: not merely past $\widehat{v_{it}}$ (weak-form), but also all relevant data (such as money supply, inflation and growth). This is known as an orthogonality test. It is also possible to estimate (81) freely, in which case the coefficient on R_t should not be significantly different from unity, a further check on the joint hypothesis: the other tests apply as before. A further implication of (81) is that any trading rule, TR (a systematic rule for trading assets), which uses information at the start of t, including past $\widehat{v_{it}}$, to buy and sell asset i, intending to make profits because

$$E[R_{it} - E_t R_{it}] \mid TR > 0 \tag{83}$$

must fail under the efficiency hypothesis since by (81)

$$E[R_{it} - E_t R_{it}] = 0 \tag{84}$$

Since under the efficiency assumption any trading strategy has an expected abnormal return of zero it must do worse, given the increased transactions costs associated with an active rule compared with a trading strategy of buy and hold (do nothing). The returns to each rule differ by expected transactions costs.

An important class of models in which efficiency prevails (abnormal returns are unforecastable) is that of martingales. Formally if a variable Z_t is described by the stochastic process

$$E[Z_{t+1} \mid Z_t, Z_{t-1}, \ldots = Z_t \tag{85}$$

or

$$E[Z_{t+1} - Z_t \mid Z_t, Z_{t-1}, \ldots] = 0 \tag{86}$$

it is known as the martingale property.

The process

$$Z_{t+1} = Z_t + u_{t+1} \tag{87}$$

is therefore a martingale. The error term has the property that $E_t u_{t+1} = 0$. The error can exhibit structure such as time varying heteroskedasticity (e.g. ARCH effects – Time-Series Annex). If a constant term is added to (87) it is known as a submartingale. The terminology of random walk and martingale are often interchanged. In fact a random walk as conventionally defined is a stronger concept in that the error term is assumed to be independently and identically distributed (iid).

So the process

$$Z_{t+1} = Z_t + \alpha + u_{t+1} \tag{88}$$

where α is a constant and $E_t u_{t+1} = 0$, is a submartingale and a random walk if u_{t+1} is iid.

THE RATIONALE FOR MARKET INEFFICIENCY

Broadly the implicit mechanism involved for the market to be efficient in the sense of Fama is that if asset markets were not efficiently aggregating and processing information the disparity between fundamental values and market prices would present traders with profit opportunities. Rational speculators it is argued will, essentially instantaneously, drive asset prices back to their fundamental values.

The case for market inefficiency rests on either or both of the premisses that prices of assets move when there is no new information concerning fundamentals and that the action of speculators may not move asset prices towards their fundamental values.

Some empirical observations that are offered as consistent with these premisses are market crashes such as October 19th 1987 when world markets fell around 20 per cent without apparently any important news being evident which could account for the fall, or sustained rises in prices, known as bubbles, that are seemingly inexplicable in terms of market fundamentals.

Also it is observed that many trading decisions are based on past prices. Chartism, the extrapolation of past prices, is widely employed as the basis for trading rules. In addition, there is extensive use of stop-loss orders, whereby an asset is sold if its price falls by a pre-specified amount as well as the growth of dynamic hedging strategies such as portfolio insurance where investors buy (sell) into rising (falling) markets. Whilst none of these activities necessarily imply market inefficiency they raise the question as to whether informed rational speculators are arbitraging out the trading rules of any uninformed or irrational traders; if they are not, then inefficiency may be present.

The first theoretical model of inefficiency we examine is that of rational bubbles.

SPECULATIVE BUBBLES

History is replete with examples where asset prices have exhibited dramatic increases then falls which it is argued are not readily explained by movements in the 'fundamentals' of the asset such as the expected future dividend stream. One example is the South Sea bubble in the UK: in the 18th century the stock of a company which traded in the South Sea experienced exponential price increases before plummeting in value. Another is the tulip bulb episode in Holland in the late sixteenth century where (single) tulip bulbs were exchanged for land and gold before tulips ultimately became near worthless (though see Garber, 1989).

It is argued that these episodes represent speculative bubbles in which the anticipation of future capital gains leads to spiralling upward price movements before the bubble eventually collapses or pops and the price exhibits dramatic falls. Since the 1980s there has been a considerable amount of theoretical and empirical work on speculative bubbles. Our purpose in this section is to provide an introduction to this literature; our discussion is related to our earlier one in chapter 2 where we showed that rational expectations with expectations of future variables can have bubbles in their solution.

We assume for simplicity that investors are risk neutral so that via arbitrage expected returns are equal to those on a riskless asset with rate of return $\overline{R}$, assumed constant, so that $E_t R_{t+1} = \overline{R}$. Given these assumptions we obtain (31) above, which we reproduce for convenience:

$$P_t = \frac{1}{(1+\overline{R})} E_t P_{t+1} + \frac{1}{(1+\overline{R})} E_t D_{t+1} \tag{89}$$

Assuming rational expectations and solving this model forwards N periods as in 33 we obtain

$$P_t = E_t \left[\sum_{i=1}^{N} \frac{D_{t+i}}{(1+\bar{R})^i} \right] + \frac{E_t P_{t+N}}{(1+\overline{R})^i} \tag{90}$$

The second term in (90) is the discounted value of the stock price N periods in the future. In the absence of bubbles as we let N go to infinity we assume that this term goes to zero. If so, the current asset price is equal to the expected value of the stream of dividends into the indefinite future: this expression is the fundamental of the process, F_t.

The idea of speculative bubbles is that equation (90) is also consistent with rational expectations solutions other than the fundamental solution. If we try the solution

$$P_t = F_t + B_t \tag{91}$$

in (89) we find that as long as B_t follows the process

$$(1+\overline{R})B_t = E_t B_{t+1} \tag{92}$$

it is a valid mathematical solution to (89).

By substitution of (91) in (89) we obtain

$$P_t = F_t + B_t = \frac{1}{(1+\overline{R})} E_t B_{t+1} + \frac{1}{(1+\overline{R})} E_t F_{t+1} + \frac{1}{(1+\overline{R})} E_t D_{t+1}$$

(92) is consistent with this and the solution form for

$$F_t = \frac{1}{(1+\overline{R})} E_t F_{t+1} + \frac{1}{(1+\overline{R})} E_t D_{t+1}$$

is the same as (90) where $\frac{E_t F_{t+N}}{(1+\overline{R})^i}$ tends to zero as N tends to ∞. In other words if agents believe that the process B_t is driving asset prices then it will be a "rational" solution, a "self-fulfilling prophecy"; notice that it implies $E_t P_{t+N} = E_t F_{t+N} + E_t B_{t+N}$ which explodes endlessly, so that the bubble cannot be expected to burst ever.

As a consequence of the rational expectations assumption

$$B_{t+1} = E_t B_{t+1} + \epsilon_{t+1} \tag{93}$$

where ϵ_{t+1} is a random error.

Substitution of (92) into (93) gives

$$B_{t+1} = (1+\overline{R})B_t + \epsilon_{t+1} \tag{94}$$

(94) makes clear that the deterministic solution for B is an asymptotically explosive process. It is therefore important that there be no transversaility condition putting a limit on this process; such a condition was how we ruled out bubbles in chapter 2.

We can also write the solution for the bubble in the form (see Salge, 1997)

$$B_t = \frac{M_t}{\alpha^t} \tag{95}$$

where $\alpha = \frac{1}{(1+\bar{R})}$ and

$$E_t M_{t+1} = M_t \tag{96}$$

implying that M_t is a martingale process.

Leading (95) one period and taking expectations, noting that $\frac{1}{\alpha^t}$ is a deterministic process, we obtain

$$E_t B_{t+1} = \frac{E_t M_{t+1}}{\alpha^{t+1}} = \text{from (96)}\ \frac{M_t}{\alpha^{t+1}} = \frac{\alpha^t B_t}{\alpha^{t+1}} = \frac{B_t}{\alpha} \tag{97}$$

Consequently a bubble contains a martingale component and any process for M_t satisfying this condition is a valid rational bubble.

A general form of a stochastic martingale process is given by

$$M_t = \rho_t M_{t-1} + u_t v_t \tag{98}$$

where the random variable ρ_t, has conditional expectation that $E[\rho_{t+1} \mid I_t] = 1$. Other assumptions are that $E\{v_{t+i}\} = 0,\ i = 1 - n,\ ,\ E[\rho_t M_t \mid I_t] = 0,\ E[\rho_t v_t \mid I_t] = 0,\ E[\rho_t u_t \mid I_t] = 0,\ E[u_t M_t \mid I_t] = 0,\ E[u_t v_t \mid I_t] = 0,\ E[v_t M_t \mid I_t] = 0$.

These assumptions establish the independence of all stochastic variables in all leads and lags. No restricting assumptions are required concerning the nature of the random variable u_t.

Suppose $u_t = 1$; define a random variable h_t that is normally distributed with mean μ and variance σ_h^2. We can then exploit the property of conditional log normality and define ρ_t for any arbitrary constant λ as

$$\rho_t = e^{\lambda h_t - \left(\lambda\mu + \frac{\lambda^2\sigma_h^2}{2}\right)]} \tag{99}$$

because

$$Ee^{\lambda h_t} = Ee^{\lambda h_{t+1}} = e^{\lambda\mu + \frac{\lambda^2\sigma_h^2}{2}} \tag{100}$$

Taking expectations of (99) the condition $E\rho_{t+1} = 1$ is satisfied.

Consequently we can write the martingale process of (98) as:

$$M_t = e^{\lambda h_t - \left(\lambda\mu + \frac{\lambda^2\sigma_h^2}{2}\right)]} M_{t-1} + v_t \tag{101}$$

Substitution of (101) into (95) gives the implied bubble as:

$$B_t = e^{\lambda h_t - \left(\lambda\mu + \frac{\lambda^2\sigma_h^2}{2} + \ln\alpha\right)]} B_{t-1} + \epsilon_t \tag{102}$$

where $\epsilon_t = \frac{v_t}{\alpha^t}$ and $e^{-\log\alpha} = \frac{1}{\alpha}$.

($E_t\epsilon_{t+i} = 0$ for $i \geq 1$. Note substitution of M_t from (95) into (98) (with $u_t = 1$) gives $B_t = \alpha^{-1}\rho_t B_{t-1} + \frac{v_t}{\alpha^t}$; employing the defintion of ρ_t from (99) we have (102)).

Several different types of bubbles can be obtained exploiting the insight that rational bubbles include a martingale process. In fact any process that follows a martingale process can be included in the bubble.

For example suppose the fundamental can be described by a martingale process

$$F_t = F_{t-1} + \theta_t \tag{103}$$

where θ_t is a random variable.

In this case we can let M_t be:

$$M_t = F_t \text{ so that the bubble is } B_t = \frac{F_t}{\alpha^t} \tag{104}$$

For more general specifications of fundamentals the method is to substitute appropriate random variables for h_t. For example let us add a constant component to fundamentals so that they follow the process

$$F_t = F_{t-1} + \mu + \eta_t \tag{105}$$

where η_t is $N(0,\ \sigma_h^2)$. In order to find the bubble that corresponds to this process we inspect the general bubble formulation (102). We can substitute for the variable h_t in this formulation so long as the process we substitute in has a mean of μ and a variance σ_h^2, because for these parameter values we can obtain the martingale process (101). $F_t - F_{t-1}$ in (105) has a constant mean (μ) and variance σ_h^2 so we can substitute $F_t - F_{t-1}$ for h_t into the general bubble formulation (102) (with $\epsilon_t = 0$ assumed zero here for simplicity) to obtain

$$\frac{B_t}{B_{t-1}} = e^{\lambda(F_t - F_{t-1}) - \left(\lambda\mu + \frac{\lambda^2\sigma_h^2}{2} + \ln\alpha\right)]} = \frac{e^{\lambda F_t - \left(\lambda\mu + \frac{\lambda^2\sigma_h^2}{2} + \ln\alpha\right)t}}{e^{\lambda F_{t-1} - \left(\lambda\mu + \frac{\lambda^2\sigma_h^2}{2} + \ln\alpha\right)(t-1)}} \tag{106}$$

(106) implies that the bubble process in fundamentals corresponding to the fundamental process (105) is given by

$$B_t = e^{\lambda F_t - \left(\lambda\mu + \frac{\lambda^2\sigma_h^2}{2} + \ln\alpha\right)t]} = e^{\lambda F_t - \left(\lambda\mu + \frac{\lambda^2\sigma_h^2}{2}\right)t - \ln\alpha^t]} \tag{107}$$

If fundamentals follow the geometric process

$$\ln F_t - \ln F_{t-1} = \mu + \eta_t \tag{108}$$

where $\eta_t = N(0,\ \sigma_h^2)$, we obtain following the above procedure

$$\frac{B_t}{B_{t-1}} = e^{\lambda(\ln F_t - \ln F_{t-1}) - \left(\lambda\mu + \frac{\lambda^2\sigma_h^2}{2} + \ln\alpha\right)\Big]} = \frac{e^{\lambda \ln F_t - \left(\lambda\mu + \frac{\lambda^2\sigma_h^2}{2} + \ln\alpha\right)t}}{e^{\lambda \ln F_{t-1} - \left(\lambda\mu + \frac{\lambda^2\sigma_h^2}{2} + \ln\alpha\right)(t-1)}} \tag{109}$$

which implies

$$B_t = e^{\lambda \ln F_t - \left(\lambda\mu + \frac{\lambda^2\sigma_h^2}{2} + \ln\alpha\right)t} = F_t^\lambda e^{-\ \left(\lambda\mu + \frac{\lambda^2\sigma_h^2}{2}\right)t - \ln\alpha^t\Big]} \tag{110}$$

(note $e^{\lambda \ln F_t} = F_t^\lambda$). We observe that if $\lambda\mu + \frac{\lambda^2\sigma_h^2}{2} + \ln\alpha = 0$, then the bubble process is given by

$$B_t = F_t^\lambda \tag{111}$$

Alternatively if $\lambda = 0$

$$B_t = \frac{1}{\alpha^t} \tag{112}$$

When a bubble depends on its own value in the previous period it is called a Markovian bubble. When the bubble depends on fundamentals it is called an intrinsic bubble (Froot and Obstfeld, 1991). When the bubble depends on arbitrary processes it is called an extrinsic or extraneous bubble.The solution for extraneous bubbles follows the same procedure as for intrinsic bubbles. For instance if the extraneous process, S_t, follows a martingale process then the rational bubble is given by $B_t = \frac{S_t}{\alpha^t}$. Salge (1997) demonstrates how to solve for bubbles for the general ARMA specification of fundamentals or extraneous variables. Depending upon the specification of λ a variety of different bubble processes are feasible.

If bubbles were non-stochastic, $\epsilon_{t+1} = 0$, then the solution to (92) is simply

$$B_t = B_0(1 + \overline{R})^t \tag{113}$$

so that the solution for the price would simply embody a deterministic explosive component and would in principle be readily amenable to statistical tests.

Whilst the possibility of such deterministic bubbles have been investigated empirically for periods of hyperinflation before monetary reform (Flood and Garber, 1980), it would appear that bubbles of a deterministic form are not features of asset or other prices. As a consequence bubbles would not apear to be plausible empirically unless there is a significant probability that they will collapse after reaching high levels.

Blanchard (1979) and Blanchard and Watson (1982) proposed a probabilistic bubble that can embody this feature. Essentially there are two regimes which occur with constant probabilities q and $1-q$. In the first state (A) the bubble survives with probability q and continues to increase at an expected rate of $E_t B_{t+1}/A = \frac{(1+\overline{R})B_t}{q}$. In the second state (C), with probability $1-q$, the bubble collapses so that $E_t B_{t+1}/C = 0$.

Adding stochastic terms we have

$$B_{t+1} = \frac{(1+\overline{R})B_t}{q} + \epsilon_{t+1} \text{ with probability } q \text{ in state } A \tag{114}$$

and:

$$B_{t+1} = \epsilon_{t+1} \text{ with probability } (1-q) \text{ in state } C \tag{115}$$

where the error has the property that $E_t \epsilon_{t+1} = 0$ As a consequence we have

$$E_t B_{t+1} = q\left(\frac{(1+\overline{R})B_t}{q}\right) + (1-q)0 \tag{116}$$

We note from (116) that the bubble has the form of equation (92) and is therefore a valid rational expectations solution. In addition we observe that in state A the bubble grows at a faster rate on average $(\frac{1}{q})$ than the non-probabilistic bubble in order to compensate for the probability of collapse. Collapsing bubbles are consistent with the analysis employing martingales; we simply define the process

$$M_t = \frac{\rho_t}{\pi} M_{t-1} + u_t v_t \text{ with probability } \pi \tag{117}$$

and

$$M_t = u_t v_t \text{ with probability } 1-\pi \tag{118}$$

We can also derive the expected excess return, which is defined as the return on the asset which incorporates the bubble minus the rate of return on the riskless asset in regime A and C. Defining the expected excess return at the end of period one as $X_{t+1} = E_t R_{t+1} - \overline{R}$, then from (89)

$$X_{t+1} = \frac{E_t P_{t+1} + E_t D_{t+1}}{P_t} - (1+\overline{R}) \tag{119}$$

Taking expectations at time t of (91) at time $t+1$ we obtain

$$E_t P_{t+1} = E_t F_{t+1} + E_t B_{t+1} \tag{120}$$

where

$$E_tF_{t+1} = E_t\left[E_{t+1}\left\{\sum_{i=1}^{\infty}\frac{D_{t+i+1}}{(1+\overline{R})^i}\right\}\right] = E_t\left\{\sum_{i=1}^{\infty}\frac{D_{t+i+1}}{(1+\overline{R})^i}\right\} \tag{121}$$

now

$$E_tF_{t+1} + E_tD_{t+1} = E_t\sum_{i=1}^{\infty}\frac{D_{t+i+1}}{(1+\overline{R})^i} + E_tD_{t+1} = (1+\overline{R})F_t = (1+\overline{R})(P_t - B_t) \tag{122}$$

so substituting (122) and (120) into (119) we obtain

$$X_{t+1} = \frac{(1+\overline{R})(P_t - B_t) + E_tB_{t+1}}{P_t} - (1+\overline{R}) \tag{123}$$

In regime A we substitue for E_tB_{t+1} from (116) into (123) to obtain expected excess returns as

$$X_{t+1} = \frac{(1+\overline{R})B_t(1-q)}{qP_t} \tag{124}$$

In regime C we substitute for E_tB_{t+1} from (116) into (123) to obtain expected returns as

$$X_{t+1} = -\frac{(1+\overline{R})B_t}{P_t} \tag{125}$$

We observe from (124) and (125) that expected excess returns differ substantially in the two periods. However expected excess returns are zero across the two regimes. Rational bubbles do not create a predictable pattern in excess returns; rather they create volatility in prices.

Whilst the the above probabilistic bubble has the property of collapsing, Diba and Grossman (1988) show that the impossibility of negative rational bubbles in stock markets (because of the implication of a negative expected asset price in the future which violates limited liability) implies that a bubble once collapsed can never restart. Essentially if the bubble takes a zero value, then from (92) its expected value in the future is zero. Because negative values are ruled out for stock prices this implies that the average of the positive values must be zero, but this is a contradiction, so it can only be zero if it takes the value of zero in all future periods. This point also carries the implication that if a bubble exists today it must have always existed, i.e. since the moment trading began.

Evans (1991) and Van Norden (1996) have formulated processes for bubbles that meet this theoretical point. Van Norden allows for the possibility that the bubble is expected to collapse only partially in state C and that the probability of a bubble's continued growth falls as the bubble grows

Van Norden specifies that the probability of the bubble's continued growth is given by

$$q_t = q(B_t) \text{ with } \frac{dq(B_t)}{d \mid B_t \mid} < 0 \tag{126}$$

(the absolute value of the bubble to allow for negative bubbles in markets such as exchange rates.).

In regime C the bubble is expected to collapse only partially and is given by

$$E_t B_{t+1} = u(B_t) \text{ in state } C \text{ with probability } q_t \tag{127}$$

where $u(.)$ is a continuous and everywhere differentiable function such that $u(0) = 0$ and $1 \geq \frac{du(B_t)}{dB_t} \geq 0$.

In state A the bubble is expected to grow at rate

$$E_t B_{t+1} = \frac{(1+\overline{R})B_t}{q(B_t)} - \frac{[1-q(B_t)]u(B_t)}{q(B_t)} \text{ with probability } 1 - q_t \tag{128}$$

It is easy to verify that (128) and (127) imply equation (92). We can deduce from (128) that the expected value of the bubble in the surviving state is a decreasing function of the probability of survival $q(B_t)$. As a consequence, as with the Blanchard bubble, the greater the probability of collapse the larger is the expected gain on a surviving bubble in order to compensate the investor for the possibility of collapse.

Van Norden's specification of the bubble process is interesting in demonstrating how the probability of collapse can be readily endogenised, and also how the process can be modified so that the bubble is not necessarily zero in the collapsed state. Both these features could be relevant in empirical work on detecting bubbles.

Evans formulates a bubble that is always positive but nevertheless periodically collapses. The Evans bubble takes the form

$$B_{t+1} = (1+\overline{R})B_t u_{t+1} \text{ if } B_t \quad k \tag{129}$$

and

$$B_{t+1} = \quad \delta + \left. \frac{\theta_{t+1}(1+\overline{R})[B_t - (1+\overline{R})^{-1}\delta]}{q} \right] u_{t+1} \text{ if } B_t > k \tag{130}$$

where k and δ are positive parameters with $0 < \delta < (1+\overline{R})k$ and u_{t+1} is an exogenous independently and identically distributed (iid) positive random variable with $E_t u_{t+1} = 1$. θ_{t+1} is an exogenous i.id Bernoulli process(independent of u) which takes the value unity with probability q and zero with probability $1 - q$.

Taking expectations at t of (129) we observe that the bubble is equation (92) when it is in the regime where $B_t \quad k$. When $B_t > k$ the bubble has the expected value of

$$E_t B_{t+1} = \quad \delta + \frac{(1+\overline{R})[B_t - (1+\overline{R})^{-1}\delta]}{q}\Bigg] = \quad \frac{(1+\overline{R})B_t}{q} - \frac{\delta(1-q)}{q}\Bigg] \quad \text{with probability } q \tag{131}$$

and

$$E_t B_{t+1} = \delta \text{ with probability } 1 - q \tag{132}$$

so that when $B_t > k$

$$E_t B_{t+1} = q \quad \frac{(1+\overline{R})B_t}{q} - \frac{\delta(1-q)}{q}\Bigg] + (1-q)\delta = (1+\overline{R})B_t \tag{133}$$

Consequently the bubble satisfies condition (92).

The Evans bubble has the property that when $B_t \quad k$ it grows at mean rate $1+\overline{R}$. When $B_t > k$ the bubble 'erupts' and grows at a faster mean rate as long as the process continues. When the bubble collapses it falls to a mean value of δ and the bubble process begins again. Evans notes that by varying the parameters δ, k and q one can create bubbles where the frequency with which the bubble erupts, the average length of time before collapse and the scale of the bubble vary. An example of an Evans bubble is depicted in Figure 14.3.

An important feature of the Evans bubble is that standard empirical tests for bubbles based on unit root and cointegration methods (Time-Series Annex) may not detect bubbles when they are present. Evans simulated bubbles and applied unit root tests to the simulated bubbles. Even though bubbles are asymptotically explosive for $q \quad 0.75$ for more than 90% of the simulated bubbles of length 100 observations, statistical tests for unit roots rejected the hypothesis of a bubble in favour of a stable alternative.

More recent empirical work has endeavoured to apply alternative econometric approachs such as switching regime regression models to ascertain the presence of bubbles (Hamilton, 1994; Van Norden 1996; Van Norden and Vigfusson, 1998) given that the Evans-type model describes behaviour for different regimes. These statistical methods appear to offer greater promise of detecting bubbles. As yet however it is probably fair to say that the different empirical methods which have been applied to a

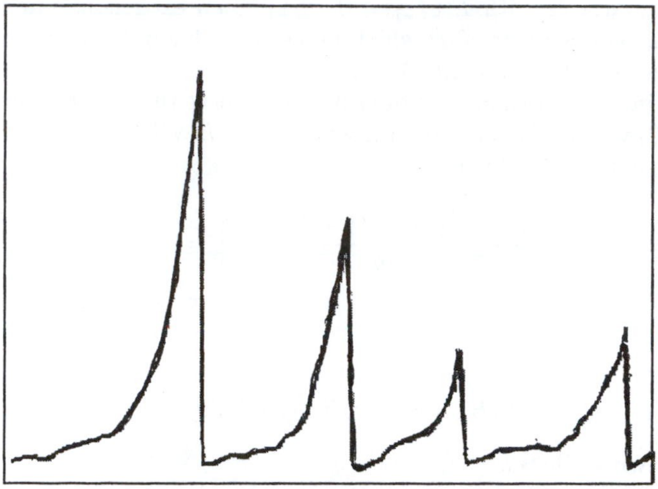

Figure 14.3: Example of an Evans Bubble

variety of different asset markets including stock and exchange markets have not generated any consistent evidence of speculative bubbles.

It should be noted that theoretical work by Tirole (1982, 1985) has demonstrated that bubbles cannot arise in certain models. For example in an overlapping generations model with an infinite number of finite-lived representative agents, Tirole shows that when the interest rate exceeds the growth rate in the economy (so that it is dynamically efficient) a bubble would ultimately violate some agents' budget constraints. It would appear that bubbles could only exist in economies which are dynamically inefficient if the model is of the representative-agent type and agents are rational. From this perspective Froot and Obstfeld (1991) suggest interpreting empirical tests for bubbles as tests of the rational expectations assumption.

We can put this another way. RE models are, generally, 'over-identified'. That is, everything in the reduced form is derived from structural relationships and more restrictions exist than reduced-form parameters; the reduced-form errors are combinations of the structural parameters and structural errors. Errors such as bubbles are not present in the structural model and hence should not appear in the reduced form.

Only fundamentals are included in it.

Should we write down a structural model in which some bubble variable is allowed to enter, then we must ensure that it satisfies both the transversality conditions on the model (including private and budget constraints as they tend to infinity) and the optimality conditions. For example, as we showed in chapter 2, deterministic explosive bubbles in prices will violate reasonable government limits on inflation and so will be ruled out from the start. In the Blanchard and Watson example reviewed above, of a stochastic bubble, at least one of the paths must have a positive probability of continuing indefinitely for the bubble even to begin. Is such a path consistent with such limits? Above we noted the objections of Tirole to bubbles in one context, and the caveats expressed by Obstfeld and Rogoff. In each case of a bubble we must ask whether theory as above permits it.

When we turn to empirical testing, we can note that the 'forward solution' of the model discussed in chapter 2 has the form of a bubble. One can for example write down a model of prices in which a large positive future shock (to the money supply, say) is expected with some probability; as the period approaches the price level rises until at the period it either jumps upwards if the shock occurs or collapses if it does not. Distinguishing this non-bubble solution from a supposed bubble clearly is difficult. Remember a bubble relates to what people in markets expect for the future; this could well relate to an expectation about a fundamental.

The difficulty with bubbles is therefore both theoretical and empirical. This critique of bubbles within rational expectations models does not of course extend to models where expectations are not rational; here, by construction, people may believe in curiosa – 'fads' and so forth. To such models we now turn.

Fads and Noise Traders

Shiller (1984), (1989) and (1997) has emphasised the importance of mass psychology in financial markets with the implication that investors may exhibit fashions or fads. A fad is a depature from fundamental values due to 'psychologically' induced changes in market sentiment. We first illustrate the implications following the model in Fama and French (1988) and Cutler, Poterba and Summers (1990, 1991).

Let

$$P_t = F_t + e_t \tag{134}$$

where P_t is the return or price of an asset, F_t is the fundamental value and e_t is a fad. Fundamentals are assumed to follow the process

$$F_t = F_{t-1} + h_t \tag{135}$$

The fad is described by the stationary process

$$e_t = \rho e_{t-1} + v_t \tag{136}$$

where ρ is a positive constant less than unity and v_t is a random error.

Cutler, Poterba and Summers (1991) consider the case where a proxy, F_t^*, is available to measure fundamentals, given that in applied work we typically do not measure the fundamentals with precision or are employing approximations to the theoretical model. Let

$$F_t = F_t^* + w_t \tag{137}$$

where w_t is the measurement error assumed to be random.

Differencing (134) and substituting from (135) and (136) we obtain the true reduced form for ΔP_t as

$$\Delta P_t = (\rho - 1)(P_{t-1} - F_{t-1}) + h_t + v_t \tag{138}$$

Consider the regression estimate of β in the relationship

$$\Delta P_t = \alpha + \beta(P_{t-1} - F_{t-1}^*) + \theta_t \tag{139}$$

The regression coefficient will have a probability limit of

$$\beta = \frac{(\rho - 1)Cov(P_{t-1} - F_{t-1}, P_{t-1} - F_{t-1}^*)}{var(P_{t-1} - F_{t-1}^*)} = \frac{(\rho - 1)Cov(e_{t-1}, e_{t-1} + w_{t-1})}{Var(e_{t-1} + w_{t-1})} = \frac{(\rho - 1)var(e)}{var(e) + var(w)} \tag{140}$$

The implication is that changes in asset prices will be predicted by lagged deviations of the price from its proxy fundamental (for which in their empirical work Cutler, Poterba and Summers (1991) employ the log of the real dividend). In addition prices or returns can be shown to exhibit a predictable pattern.

Of course predictable patterns in the difference between prices and fundamentals raises the issue of why rational speculators do not arbitrage the process. It is implicitly assumed that they face some sort of liquidity constraint preventing them from dominating the market. However, it is also possible that they do so arbitrage, so that the fad occurs but is then removed from the data next period. This would correspond to $\rho = 0$

in our example. In this case, prices could differ from their fundamental value so implying inefficiency, and yet the difference between the price and fundamentals could still be unpredictable. This distinction points to a caveat in the interpretation of efficiency given by Fama; Shiller makes the point that the absence of predictability does not necessarily imply market efficiency. Clearly the existence of systematic abnormal profits is sufficient to invalidate efficiency. However absence of predictable abnormal returns could be consistent with market inefficiency if prices were more volatile than was consistent with the volatility in the fundamental. Bubbles or some fad processes are consistent with this interpretation of inefficiency. Efficiency therefore requires the complete elimination of fads from the price process ($e_t = 0$); otherwise a trading rule operating on $P_t = F_t$ would make money (this is a particularly simple rule, viz. of current arbitrage).

Other models of market inefficiency assume the coexistence of heterogeneous traders. In these models there are smart traders, the rational speculators, as well as the noise traders. The noise trader trades on fads or charts or other extraneous information ('noise'). The key requirement of the models is that arbitrage activity by the smart traders is limited. This can be a consequence of the assumption of risk-averse rational speculators combined with a micro-structure rationale where for example arbitrageurs have limited capacity to borrow funds due to signalling problems (see e.g. Shleifer and Vishny, 1997).

The consequence is that arbitrage activity by the rational traders may not eliminate the influence of the noise traders from the outcome for returns or prices so that the market is inefficient in aggregate (see e.g. Figlewski, 1979).

Other specifications of this type of model have the informed traders as not holding rational expectations but rather forming their expectations on the basis of a relatively well-informed rule such as PPP deviations for exchange rates (section below) or price-dividend deviations for stock prices using say the Gordon (1962) model . If it is assumed that the proportion of the two types of agent in the market varies with the extent of the deviation of the asset price from its long run value, then these models can exhibit complex nonlinear dynamics of the asset price including chaotic outcomes (Time-Series Annex; and e.g. De Grauwe, Dewachter and Embrechts, 1993).

Some recent models of asset price determination investigate more formally the micro-structure determining asset prices. An important class of models consider the implications of assuming that traders do not behave competitively and take prices as given. The models are solved using the game-theoretic Bayesian Nash equilibrium concept where the strategies of other traders rather than prices are taken as given. These models allow analysis of strategic interactions in which traders take their price impact into account (see Brunnermeier, 1999, for a survey). In essence each trader recognises that large trades will move prices against him. The models incorporate features such as asymmetric information, noise traders, speculators, market-makers and explicit assumptions concerning the mechanism by which traders submit orders to trade. They produce many interesting insights.

When it is assumed that traders have short investment horizons, perhaps due to financial constraints which make arbitrage activities cheaper for short-term assets, herd behaviour can result (see e.g. Froot, Scharfstein and Stein, 1992). In addition strategic interaction can give rise to rational profit-maximising speculators, accentuating asset price volatility caused by noise traders as they strategically exploit feedback elements such as herding (see e.g. De Long, Shleifer, Summers and Waldman, 1991).

The models can also generate market crashes as in e.g. Romer (1993) where information is heterogeneous and investors are uncertain about the quality of information other investors have.

Although this literature is rich in insight and can provide a rationale for market inefficiency, it remains an empirical issue whether efficiency as defined by Fama is violated. We now turn to some empirical tests.

EMPIRICAL TESTS OF MARKET EFFICIENCY

There has been an enormous amount of empirical work which has examined the efficiency of asset markets including gambling markets (see e.g. Sauer, 1998; Thaler and Ziemba, 1987). Violations of the efficient markets hypothesis are typically referred to as anomalies. The anomalies reported may constitute evidence of abnormal returns or violations of the rational expectations assumption. Before considering some of this evidence it is important to note that the dangers of data-driven inference or data-snooping whilst always a consideration in applied analysis (see Leamer, 1978, for a discussion of pretest bias) needs to be given formal weight when interpreting some anomalies as demonstrated by Sullivan, Timmermann and White (1999, 2001). In the limited sample sizes typically encountered in studies, significant relationships or sytematic patterns are bound to occur if the data are analyzed with sufficient intensity. For example the orthogonality property of rational expectations will be rejected by the usual statistical criteria five percent of the time. Clearly if authors are searching in the universe of variables and significant rejections are reported it could appear that the hypothesis is invalid even though it is true.

An apparent rejection of the market efficiency hypothesis which is data-driven is the finding reported by numerous researchers that stock returns exhibit seasonal regularities (see Sullivan, Timmermann and White, 2001, for key references). Abnormal returns are related to day of the week, week of the month, month of the year, holidays etc. If these results have validity then the efficient markets hypothesis is in serious trouble given it is 'such a simple violation'.

The issue is one of 'data-snooping' — in other words, researchers cannot avoid being influenced by their sample of data. They 'find' rules that are in that set of data by repeated trials. This will occur even when some data is kept aside – because this data too is known about to some degree and trials on it may lead to respecification of the rule on the used data before a renewed trial. To control for this problem the researcher must not allow the data to influence his choice of rule. Thus all possible rules must be given an equal chance to work on the data; some of course will work well for particular samples even if they do not in general work at all. By doing this exercise for all rules for repeated samples one may calculate the probability of a rule 'doing well' in a given sample. Clearly for a rule to be considered significant it must do better than this. This exercise has been carried out by Sullivan, Timmermann and White (2001) for calendar effects.

They construct a universe of calendar trading rules, using permutational arguments that do not bias in favour or against particular calendar rules.They consider some 9500 calendar effects. They imagine that this set of calendar rules was not inspected by any one individual investor or researcher. Rather the search for calendar rules has operated sequentially across the investment community or researchers with the results of investors or researchers being reported through the survival of the 'fittest' calendar rules. Their findings are striking and important. They find that although many calendar rules generate abnormal returns that are highly significant when considered in isolation, once the dependencies operating across different calendar rules are allowed for, then the best calendar rule is no longer significant. In addition they consider a smaller number of 244 rules that remove any doubts that irrelevant rules are pooled with'genuine' rules in the 9500 experiment. Their results are the same. The apparent statistical significance of the best calendar effects is not robust to data-snooping effects.

Weak-form efficiency tests

Weak-form efficiency in the sense of Fama implies that the expected returns from a trading rule based on past prices should be less than those generated by a buy-and-hold strategy equal to the number of trades times the transactions costs. In fact according to Taylor and Allen (1992) and Brock, Lakonishok and LeBaron (1992) chartist or technical techniques are widely employed in asset markets as either a basis for published technical commentary or for direct use. The term technical analysis or chartism is given as a generic title for any trading rule based on the past history of prices or returns. Essentially more or less sophisticated rules are employed to extrapolate past changes in asset prices or returns. One common example is to employ two moving averages of past returns one based on a short horizon, say 1 to 10 days, and the other on a long moving average, say 150 to 500 days. When the short moving average rises above (or falls below) the long moving average this is a signal to buy (or sell). A variant of this procedure is to modify the rule by introduction of a band around the moving average to eliminate 'whiplash' signals when the two moving averages are close.

There is a plethora of empirical work that has investigated the efficacy of technical analysis — e.g. Alexander (1961); Fama and Blume (1966); Taylor and Allen (1992); Brock, Lakonishok and LeBaron (1992); Neely, Weller and Dittmar (1997); Sullivan, Timmermann and White (1999).

Whilst many rules developed by chartists have been reported to generate abnormal returns, and some theoretical analysis — e.g. Brown and Jennings (1989); Blume, Easley and O'Hara (1994) — demonstrates that technical analysis can have value particularly for small less widely-followed assets, the empirical results of Sullivan, Timmermann and White (1999) appear to be of importance in the interpretation of chartism. Following a similar methodolgy to the one outlined above they construct 7846 parameterizations of trading rules which are applied to the Dow Jones Industrial Average over the full period from 1897 to1986 as well as four subperiods. The period 1987-1996 is employed to evaluate the rules on a hold-out sample. Their idea is to develop a test statistic which evaluates the performance of a chartist rule relative to the full set of models that gave rise to the rule, so that the effect of data-snooping is explicitly allowed for. One important conclusion is that even though a particular trading rule is capable of producing superior performance of almost 10% during the sample period, which is significant at 4% level when considered in isolation, the fact that the trading rule is drawn from a wide universe of rules means that its effective data-snooping-adjusted probability value is 0.9, i.e. totally insignificant. They also find that the best-performing trading rule in sample is totally insignificant out of sample even at conventional statistical levels. Clearly chartist rules may exist which generate abnormal returns; however the analysis of Sullivan, Timmermann and White (1999) demonstrates that great care has to be taken in their interpretation.

Another issue concerning chartists or technical rules is that they can be interpreted as special cases of univariate time series of a linear or nonlinear form (Time-Series Annex). If there is predictability in past returns it would appear that employment of an explicit univariate model would in general dominate. Studies such as Diebold and Nason (1990), Lane, Peel and Raeburn (1996) are suggestive that nonlinear univariate models for modelling the conditional mean of a series provide improvement over linear models but do not appear to forecast better than linear models, with neither of them generating abnormal returns (though see Granger and Pesaran, 1999).The results of Hsieh (1991) who found that stock returns exhibit nonlinear structure but that this is parsimoniously captured by a model linear in mean but nonlinear in variance (Time-Series Annex) is probably the model that is currently thought of as most applicable to asset prices or returns. Clearly chartist methods may conceivably deal more parsimoniously with nonstationarities or regime changes than explicit nonlinear models though it is not altogether clear why this should be the case.

Overall it would appear that the market efficiency hypothesis has not as yet been invalidated at the weak-form level.

Semi-Strong Market Efficiency

Numerous empirical tests of semi-strong efficiency exist. Some of the work reporting anomalies would appear to be subject to the data-snooping caveat. Others are harder to explain. In the latter context we mention the empirical work that demonstrates that monthly or quarterly stock returns are predictable (e.g. Campbell, 1987; Fama and French, 1989; Pesaran and Timmermann, 1994, 1995, 2000). Consideration of the loglinear form of the present value model illustrates that if expectations of future dividend change are not too noisy then stock returns may have predictability in that variables that help predict future returns may exist. This would not invalidate market efficiency. The question is whether the predictability has economic value in the sense of generating abnormal returns. From this perspective standard measures of forecasting accuracy have modest information content, since they do not allow for transactions costs or map into the nature of the profit decision. For example a forecast that the market would rise by 12% when it rises by

5% is inferior from the perspective of a squared error measure of forecast accuracy to a forecast of 0%. Clearly a decision rule of the buy-sell type would value the forecast differently (see e.g. Pesaran, 1992; Granger and Pesaran, 1999). It is not clear as yet whether the predictability in asset returns generates abnormal returns particularly when the potential for changing risk is allowed for.

Strong-Form Market Efficiency

Insider trading in the major asset markets is subject to legal restrictions in a number of countries and has been illegal for a number of years. For instance in the US the Securities and Exchange Act of 1934 prohibits agents from trading securities while in possession of material inside information. Insiders are defined to include not only corporate insiders but also anyone who obtains material, non-public information from a corporate insider, or from the issuer, or who steals such information from another source. In subsequent years further acts were passed and in 1988 insider trading sanctions were further increased so that infringement can result in fines of up to one million dollars or five to ten years in jail. In the UK insider trading is a criminal offense and can result in up to two years in jail. As a consequence of this, indirect methods have to be employed to ascertain whether insiders can make abnormal returns on the basis of their private information. That insider trading does take place is *prima facie* supported by studies such as Keown and Pinkerton(1981) who found that on average 40-50% of the price gain experienced by a target firm's stock occurs before the actual takeover announcement.

Insiders who obey the law are in a number of countries, such as the US and UK, required to notify the stock exchanges of their 'routine trades' in the shares of their companies. This information is published reasonably quickly. A number of researchers have investigated whether this legal trading by corporate insiders can predict future stock market returns – e.g. Finnerty (1986), Friederich et al. (2000), Gregory et al. (1994), Pope et al. (1990), Seyhun (1986, 1992).These tests are semi-strong tests, since the information set underpinning the tests is public. The evidence is suggestive that excess returns can be obtained though the measurement of normal returns is an issue in some studies.

Jeng et al. (1999) examine the returns to corporate insiders themselves (based on legal trades) using a comprehensive sample of reported insider transactions from 1975 to1996. Their carefully-conducted study provides evidence of significant abnormal returns.

Meulbroek (1992) investigates the returns to illegal trades by insiders. Her sample consisted of individuals charged with insider trading during

1980-1989. Her data base included information on the charges brought, penalties incurred, profits earned, number of securities traded, type and source of the inside information. Among the defendants who traded, the median defendant transacted in one security and reaped \$17,628 in profit per security. By analysing security prices on the days insiders traded and did not prior to public announcements Meulbroeck could investigate the impact of insiders on stock price movements. She concluded that insider trading increases stock price accuracy by moving stock prices significantly. She found that the abnormal price movement on insider trading days is 40-50% of the subsequent price reaction to the public announcement of the inside information. It would appear therefore from the studies conducted so far that strong-form efficiency is not empirically supported.

The arguments for and against the legality of insider trading are discussed in e.g. Ausubel (1990), Benabou and Laroque (1992), Leland (1992), Khanna, Slezak, and Bradley (1994), Tighe and Michener (1994),

We now consider in more detail some tests for semi-strong market efficiency.

Variance Bounds Tests

An important test of the efficiency of present value models of asset prices was originally developed by LeRoy and Porter (1981) and Shiller (1979, 1981). This exploits the property of rational expectations that the variance of the outcome is greater than the variance of the rational expectation forecast.

For a variable Y_t

$$\mathrm{var}(Y_t) = \mathrm{var}(E_t Y_{t+i}) + \mathrm{var}(v) \tag{141}$$

where v_t is the forecast error. This follows since rational expectations implies that the covariance between the forecast and the forecast error is zero.

In models of asset prices rational expectations implies that the actual variance of an asset price, P_t, which is a weighted average of future expectations of fundamentals should be less than the variance of the asset price computed on the basis of the actual stochastic process of the fundamentals.

For simplicity we consider the model in level rather than log level form. The asset price has the value, as we have seen in e.g. (33), of:

$$P_t = E_t \left[\sum_{i=1}^{\infty} \frac{D_{t+i}}{(1+\overline{R})^i} \right] \tag{142}$$

where D_{t+i} are the fundamental returns and $1+\overline{R}$ is the constant discount rate.

Assuming rational expectations we can decompose the present value relationship into two components one of which is the perfect foresight path and the other the sequence of rational expectations prediction errors:

$$P_t = \sum_{i=1}^{\infty} \frac{D_{t+i}}{(1+\overline{R})^i} - \sum_{i=1}^{\infty} \frac{u_{t+i}}{(1+\overline{R})^i} \tag{143}$$

where the u_{t+i} are the forecast errors. Consequently

$$P_t^* = P_t + v_t \tag{144}$$

where

$$P_t^* = \sum_{i=1}^{\infty} \frac{D_{t+i}}{(1+\overline{R})^i} \text{ and } v_t = \sum_{i=1}^{\infty} \frac{u_{t+i}}{(1+\overline{R})^i}$$

From (144)

$$\text{var}(P_t^*) = \text{var}(P_t) + \text{var}(v_t) \tag{145}$$

Hence plainly var P_t var P_t^*.

The striking finding of the early literature was that stock prices appear to move too much to be consistent with subsequent changes in actual fundamentals. For example Shiller (1981, b) employing annual data on price and dividends from 1871 to1979 for the US stock market, so that the actual dividend stream is employed up to 1979 plus a proxy for 1980 to infinity (typically the actual last value of the asset price) to compute the variance in 1871, found that the actual asset price was some five times higher than the perfect foresight asset price. Leroy and Porter (1981) obtained similar results employing measures of earnings as fundamentals.

Two statistical problems with this analysis were pointed out by Flavin (1983), Kleidon (1986) and Marsh and Merton (1986). Computation of the sample variances in (144) involves use of the sample mean. In small samples Flavin and Kleidon demonstrate that use of the sample rather than population mean leads to a bias towards rejecting efficiency.

Marsh and Merton demonstrate that the variance bounds tests proposed by Shiller are not appropriate if the process generating the fundamentals are non stationary.

Mankiw, Romer and Shapiro (1985) develop a variance bounds test which is robust to these two points. Consider a naive forecast of the asset price, P_t^n

$$P_t^n = E_t^n \sum_{i=1}^{\infty} \frac{D_{t+i}}{(1+\overline{R})^i} \tag{146}$$

where E_t^n is the naive expectation of future fundamentals (say a constant growth of dividends model).

We can write

$$P_t^* - P_t^n = (P_t^* - P_t) + (P_t - P_t^n) \tag{147}$$

Taking the square of the left- and right-hand sides of (147) and taking unconditional expectations of t information

$$E(P_t^* - P_t^n)^2 = E(P_t^* - P_t)^2 + E(P_t - P_t^n)^2 \tag{148}$$

since by rational expectations $E(P_t^* - P_t)(P_t - P_t^n) = 0$ (i.e. the rational expectations forecast error, the first term in braces, is orthogonal to the second term)

Equation (141) implies that

$$E(P_t^* - P_t^n)^2 \geq E(P_t^* - P_t)^2 \tag{149}$$

and

$$E(P_t^* - P_t^n)^2 \geq E(P_t - P_t^n)^2 \tag{150}$$

The first expression states that the perfect foresight path is better forecast by the actual asset price than the naive forecast; the second expression states that the perfect foresight path fluctuates more around the naive path than does the actual price.

On the basis of tests that exploit these bounds Marsh and Merton also reject efficiency though the violation is smaller than in the original tests. In defense of the efficiency hypothesis we should note, as pointed out by various authors (e.g. LeRoy and LaCivita, 1981), that the models assume a constant discount rate or constant realized returns if the model is cast in loglinear form (see e.g. Campbell, Lo and Mackinlay, 1997), and the assumption that agents are risk neutral.

Empirical Tests: The Foreign Exchange Market

The foreign exchange market in particular has been looked at particularly exhaustively and is clearly of great interest for macroeconomics. We examine some of the empirical issues in detail in this section since many of the issues are relevant to other empirical work. A building block of many analyses is that covered interest arbitrage holds. Since this is an arbitrage condition, violation of it would be highly damaging to the efficient markets hypothesis. Numerous empirical studies have examined the covered condition. It appears that, once appropriate allowance is made for transactions costs and care is taken to ensure that data in empirical tests is sampled at the same moment in time, the condition is violated very infrequently (see e.g. Taylor, 1987, 1989). From the uncovered and covered arbitrage conditions we obtain that the logarithm of the forward exchange rate is equal to the market expectation of the logarithm of the future spot rate defined by the maturity date of the interest rate. In the case of a one period horizon we obtain

$$F_t^t = E_t S_{t+1} \tag{151}$$

Under the assumption of rational expectations we can rewrite (151) as

$$S_{t+1} = F_t^t + u_{t+1} \tag{152}$$

where u_{t+1} is the rational expectations forecast error so that $u_{t+1} = S_{t+1} - E_t S_{t+1}$.

Since S_{t+1}, and F_t^t are observable, early tests of the rationality of F_t^t were conducted by estimating the relationship

$$S_{t+1} = \alpha_0 + \alpha_1 F_t^t + \epsilon_{t+1} \tag{153}$$

and testing whether $\hat{\alpha}_0 = 0$, $\hat{\alpha}_1 = 1$ and the error term exhibited serial correlation.

These tests were supportive in general of the efficiency of the forward rate as a predictor. However it was realized subsequently that because the spot and forward rate appear to be nonstationary I(1) processes (Time-Series Annex), a coefficient of unity obtained in estimates of α_1 would be a weak test, even if appropriate standard errors were employed, since non-rational predictors which shared a common trend would exhibit this property.

Fama (1984) reported regression estimates for numerous currencies in the post-war floating period of the form

$$S_{t+1} - S_t = \gamma_0 + \gamma_1 (F_t^t - S_t) + \epsilon_{t+1} \tag{154}$$

Comparison of (152) and (154) shows that if the estimates of γ_1 and γ_0 are not significantly different from one and zero respectively then the forward rate is an efficient predictor.

In fact Fama obtained the striking result that the estimates of γ_1 were negative and significantly different from unity (or zero). Qualitatively the same results have been obtained for numerous different data sets and time periods.

For example using monthly data from 1978.01 to 1990.07 McCallum(1994) reports the following results for the Dollar/Pound

$$S_{t+1} = -0.0137 + 0.977 F_t \quad \overline{R}^2 = 0.96 \tag{155}$$

$$S_{t+1} - S_t = -0.0078 - 4.7403(F_t^t - S_t) \quad \overline{R}^2 = 0.111 \tag{156}$$

Whilst employing weekly data for the Dollar/Pound between December10th 1921–May 20th1925 we obtain

$$S_{t+4} = 0.121 + 0.920F_t \quad \overline{R}^2 = 0.86 \tag{157}$$

$$S_{t+4} - S_t = 0.0056 - 3.3166(F_t^t - S_t) \quad \overline{R}^2 = 0.043 \tag{158}$$

The coefficients on the forward premium are significantly different from unity in these regressions and also significantly less than zero. The negative coefficient implies that not only is the forward rate an inefficient predictor, it is also inferior to the spot rate as a predictor of the future spot rate. These results appear to imply that the foreign exchange market is inefficient. Whilst this may be the case, and directly observed survey data of exchange rate expectations support such an interpretation since they typically exhibit bias and inefficiency (see e.g. Frankel and Froot, 1987, and Froot and Frankel, 1989) a number of possible resolutions of this apparent anomaly have been suggested which are consistent with market efficiency. We might also note in passing that if the outcome was due to inefficient expectations it poses a major problem for economic analysis given the systematic nature of the bias of the forward premium over 70 or so years.

The first explanation of the anomalous finding was set out by Fama (1984): the existence of a variable risk premium.

A time-varying risk premium

If we relax the assumption that investors are risk averse then agents will require a risk premium for undertaking the uncovered position. A variety of alternative theoretical derivations of the risk premium have been proposed (see e.g. Bekaert, 1996; Hansen and Hodrick, (1983), Hodrick, 1989; Sibert, 1989). In what follows we use the Consumption CAPM model.

The ex-post nominal return, $(1 + R_t^s)$, to an uncovered domestic transaction, is

$$1 + R_t^s = \frac{(1 + R_t^f)s_{t+1}}{s_t} \tag{159}$$

where R_t^f is the risk-free nominal foreign interest rate and s_t is the exchange rate measured as domestic currency per unit of foreign currency. Covered interest arbitrage for the risk-free nominal domestic interest rate, $(1+R_t)$ is given by

$$1+R_t = \frac{(1+R_t^f)f_t}{s_t} \qquad (160)$$

where f_t is the forward exchange rate in levels. (Note that (68) is an approximation to (160) where $\log(1+R^f) \simeq R^f$, and $S = \ln s$)

Substitution out of the foreign interest rate from the covered condition and substitution in (159) gives

$$1+R_t^s = \frac{(1+R_t)s_{t+1}}{f_t} \qquad (161)$$

The real ex-post domestic return from an uncovered speculation $(1+\overline{R}_t^s)$ is given by

$$1+\overline{R}_t^s = \frac{(1+R_t)s_{t+1}P_t}{f_t P_{t+1}} = \frac{(1+R_t)s_{t+1}s_t P_t}{s_t f_t P_{t+1}} \qquad (162)$$

where P is the price level. The real *ex-post* domestic return from the risk-free nominal bond $(1+\overline{R}_t)$ is

$$1+\overline{R}_t = \frac{(1+R_t)P_t}{P_{t+1}} \qquad (163)$$

From the consumption CAPM

$$\frac{E_t\beta(1+\overline{R}_t^s)u'(c_{t+1})}{u'(c_t)} = \frac{E_t\beta(1+\overline{R}_t)u'(c_{t+1})}{u'(c_t)} \qquad (164)$$

Assuming conditional log normality and the form of utility function in (21) we can employ (164) and (162) to obtain

$$E_t S_{t+1} = F_t - 0.5\text{var}(\log\frac{s_{t+1}}{s_t}) + \text{cov}([\log s_{t+1}/s_t]\log P_{t+1}/P_t) + \delta\text{cov}([\log s_{t+1}/s_t]\log c_{t+1}/c_t) \qquad (165)$$

(note again: $F = \log f$, $S = \log s$).

The risk premium reflects the covariation between changes in the logarithm of the exchange rate and the logarithm of changes in consumption. It is interesting to note that if $\delta = 0$, so that the consumer is risk neutral there are still terms driving a wedge between the expected future spot rate and the forward rate. These terms occur by virtue of what is known as Jensen's inequality.

If

$$f_t = E_t s_{t+1} \qquad (166)$$

where we measure say in pounds to dollars we also require measuring in dollars to pounds that.

$$\frac{1}{f_t} = E_t \frac{1}{s_{t+1}} \tag{167}$$

However by Jensen's inequality

$$E_t \left(\frac{1}{s_{t+1}} \right) > \frac{1}{E_t s_{t+1}} \tag{168}$$

We cannot simultaneously have (166) and (167) holding which would appear to imply that one party can make expected nominal profits, known as Siegel's (1972) paradox. The resolution is that traders are interested in expected real profits. Given the assumption of lognormal distributions (165) shows the appropriate condition. The terms resulting from Jensen's inequality are generally presumed to be small but Sibert (1989) shows that this assumption may be inappropriate.

Addition of a risk premium to the uncovered arbitrage condition implies, in conjunction with the covered condition which remains unchanged (it is riskless), that

$$F_t = E_t S_{t+1} + p_t \tag{169}$$

where p_t is the 'risk premium' (inclusive of all the terms).

Subtracting the spot rate from both sides of (169) we obtain that

$$F_t - S_t = E_t S_{t+1} - S_t + p_t \tag{170}$$

Now consider the regressions

$$F_t - S_{t+1} = \alpha_1 + \beta_1 (F_t - S_t) + \epsilon_{1t+1} \tag{171}$$

and

$$S_{t+1} - S_t = \alpha_2 + \beta_2 (F_t - S_t) + \epsilon_{2t+1} \tag{172}$$

where the α and β are constants and the ϵ are the error terms.

The least squares estimates of β_1 and β_2 are given by

$$\beta_1 = \frac{\text{cov}(F_t - S_{t+1}, F_t - S_t)}{\text{var}(F_t - S_t)} = \frac{\sigma^2(p) + \text{cov}(p_t, E_t S_{t+1} - S_t)}{\sigma^2(p) + 2\text{cov}(p_t, E_t S_{t+1} - S_t) + \sigma^2(E_t S_{t+1} - S_t)} \tag{173}$$

and

$$\beta_2 = \frac{\text{cov}(S_{t+1} - S_t, F_t - S_t)}{\text{var}(F_t - S_t)} =$$

$$\frac{\sigma^2(E_tS_{t+1}-S_t)+\text{cov}(p_t,E_tS_{t+1}-S_t)}{\sigma^2(p)+2\text{cov}(p_t,E_tS_{t+1}-S_t)+\sigma^2(E_tS_{t+1}-S_t)} \quad (174)$$

(recall in the least squares regression $Y = \alpha + \beta X$, the estimate of $\beta = \frac{\text{cov}(Y,X)}{\text{var}(X)}$) and that under rational expectations cov(ϵ_{t+1}, any variable at t) $= 0$. Note also that $S_{t+1} - S_t = E_tS_{t+1} - S_t + \epsilon_{t+1}$, where ϵ_{t+1} is the rational expectations forecast error.

We note the regressions are mirror images of each other with the property that $\beta_1 + \beta_2 = 1$, $\alpha_1 + \alpha_2 = 0$ and $\epsilon_{1t+1} + \epsilon_{2t+1} = 0$.

We note from the numerator of (174) that if the estimate of β_2 is negative this is consistent with a time-varying risk premium if the covariation between expected changes in the spot rate and the risk premium is negative and greater than the variance of expected changes in the spot rate.

Because β_1 is positive this implies that the variance of the risk premium is greater than the covariation between the expected change in the spot rate and the risk premium. Together these two conditions also imply that the risk premium must have a variance greater than the variance of expected changes in the spot rate. Hodrick and Srivatava (1986) showed how a negative covariation between expected changes in the spot rate and the risk premium could be obtained in a properly formulated theoretical model. Consequently the negative coefficient obtained in the regressions of changes in spot on the forward premium could be consistent with rational expectations and a time varying risk premium. Unfortunately data which would allow direct proxying of the risk premium are not available at the frequencies required. Time series methods based on modelling the risk premium as a function of the variance of the spot rate or forecast errors have not provided much direct support for a variable risk premium, though the models of the risk premia are possibly poor approximations – see e.g. Baillie and Bollerslev (1990) and Domowitz and Hakkio (1985), Bollerslev and Hodrick (1996) Engel (1996). In addition the magnitude of the variance of the risk premia implied by the estimates of β_2 are regarded by some as perhaps implausibly high (though see Pagan, 1988). For example an estimate of β_2 of -4 implies that $\text{var}(p_t) > 5\text{var}(F_t - S_t)$ (note $\beta_2 = -4 = 1 - \frac{(\text{cov}(p_t,E_tS_{t+1}-S_t)+\sigma^2(p_t)}{\text{var}(F_t-S_t)}$ is a different way of writing the estimate of β_2).

A second potential explanation of the empirical findings is called the 'peso problem', to which we now turn.

Peso Problems

The expression 'peso problem' was probably first employed by Milton Friedman in his analysis of the behaviour of the Mexican currency, the peso, in the early 1970s. Although the Mexican exchange rate was fixed between April 1954 and August 1976 at 0.08 dollars per peso, Mexican interest rates were substantially above US interest rates. This finding presented an apparent puzzle, since rational expectations of a continuing fixed exchange rate regime would, given negligible risk premia, imply via uncovered interest arbitrage near equality of Mexican and US interest rates of similar type. Friedman rationalized the differential in terms of a market expectation of a devaluation of the peso. In fact in August 1976 these expectations were subsequently realized when the peso was allowed to float and fell some 46% in value. The peso problem thus refers to a situation where rational agents anticipate the possibility of future changes in the data-generating mechanism of economic variables.

To illustrate the nature of the peso problem suppose there are two possible economic regimes in which the variable y_t follows the process

$$y_t = \overline{y}_1 + \theta y_{t-1} + u_t \text{ in regime 1} \tag{175}$$

or

$$y_t = \overline{y}_2 + u_t \text{ in regime 2} \tag{176}$$

where $\overline{y}_1$, $\overline{y}_2$ and θ are constants and u_t is a random variable which is assumed to be the same, for simplicity, in each regime.

Consider the rational expectation of y_{t+1} formed on the basis of the information set Ω available at time t, $E(y_{t+1} \mid \Omega_t)$. We assume that rational agents do not know which regime will prevail in the next period; rather they have probabilities q_t that regime 1 will occur and $1-q_t$ that regime 2 will occur.

The rational expectation of y_{t+1} is then given by

$$E(y_{t+1} \mid \Omega_t) = q_t(\overline{y}_1 + \theta y_t) + (1 - q_t)\overline{y}_2 \tag{177}$$

The peso problem in its starkest form can be illustrated by assuming that only one of the regimes is ever observed in a sample of data. Consider the case where only regime 1 occurs. The rational expectations forecast error for this case is given by

$$\overline{y}_1 + \theta y_t + u_{t+1} - E(y_{t+1} \mid \Omega_t) = u_{t+1} + (1 - q_t)[\overline{y}_1 - \overline{y}_2] + (1 - q_t)\theta y_t \tag{178}$$

We observe from (178) that the *ex-post* forecast error in this case will exhibit bias and exhibit correlation with variables in the information set when expectations are formed (y_t). In fact if $\theta = 1$, in our example the forecast error will be non-stationary, a possibility pointed out by Evans and Lewis (1993, 1994).

It is also interesting to note what happens when a standard orthogonality or efficiency test for rational expections is run on data generated by this outcome, assuming q_t is constant: let the researcher estimate the relationship

$$y_{t+1} - E(y_{t+1} \mid \Omega_t) = \alpha + \beta(E(y_{t+1} \mid \Omega_t) - y_t) + \epsilon_{t+1} \tag{179}$$

where α and β are constants and ϵ_{t+1} is the error term.

The least squares estimate of $\widehat{\beta}$ =cov$(Y, X)/$var(X) where Y is the dependent variable and X the independent) is given by

$$\widehat{\beta} = \frac{-\theta(1-q)}{(1-\theta q)} \tag{180}$$

Consequently for $\theta > 0$ the regression estimate of β, which is negative, would imply that the rational expectation of y_{t+1} was an inferior predictor to the current level of y_t.

Non-occurrence of a regime (event) in a particular sample provides the extreme example of the peso problem. Such possiblities could occur when for instance there is a small probability of a change in regime. Such cases would not be amenable to differentiating empirically between rational expectations and an alternative unless the probability q and the alternative regimes could be described.

Evans (1996) has set out a general method of analysis of the peso problem some of which we now set out. We can define the rational expectations forecast error, e_{t+1}, as

$$e_{t+1} \equiv y_{t+1} - E(y_{t+1} \mid \Omega_t) \tag{181}$$

To examine how the properties of the forecast error are affected by the presence of discrete changes in regime Evans supposes that y_{t+1} can switch between two processes which are indicated by changes in a discrete-valued variable, $Z_t = \{0,\ 1\}$, so that Z_t only takes the value zero or unity. Let $y_{t+1}(z)$ denote realized returns in regime $Z_{t+1} = z$. The peso problem is to consider the behaviour of forecast errors, $y_{t+1} - E(y_{t+1} \mid \Omega_t)$. Evans does this by decomposing realized returns into the conditionally expected return in regime z, which is denoted $E(y_{t+1}(z) \mid \Omega_t)$ and a residual u_{t+1} (which for simplicity is assumed to be the same in both regimes).

The decomposition has the following form:

$$y_{t+1} = E(y_{t+1}(0) \mid \Omega_t) + \Delta E(y_{t+1} \mid \Omega_t) Z_{t+1} + u_{t+1} \tag{182}$$

where

$$\Delta E(y_{t+1} \mid \Omega_t) \equiv E(y_{t+1}(1) \mid \Omega_t) - E(y_{t+1}(0) \mid \Omega_t) \tag{183}$$

Substitution of (183) into (182) and setting Z_{t+1} as either one or zero informs us, as pointed out by Evans, that it will always be possible to decompose y_{t+1} in this way regardless of the process y_{t+1} follows in either regime or the precise specification of the information set Ω_t. Given the assumption of rational expectations $E(u_{t+1} \mid \Omega_t) = 0$, so that the error term u_{t+1} has the conventional rational expectations properties, Evans defines this error as the within-regime forecast error, since it represents the error when the $t+1$ regime is known.

When agents are unaware of the regime in $t+1$ their forecast errors will differ from the within-regime errors. Taking expectations of both sides of (182) on the basis of Ω_t information, we have from the properties of rational expectations that

$$E(y_{t+1} \mid \Omega_t) = E(y_{t+1}(0) \mid \Omega_t) + \Delta E(y_{t+1} \mid \Omega_t)E(Z_{t+1} \mid \Omega_t) \qquad (184)$$

where we note that the right-hand side now contains the expected regime in $t+1$.

Subtraction of (184) from (182) and substitution in (181) gives the *ex-post* forecast error as

$$e_{t+1} = u_{t+1} + \Delta E(y_{t+1} \mid \Omega_t)[Z_{t+1} - E(Z_{t+1} \mid \Omega_t)] \qquad (185)$$

We observe from (185) that when the regime at $t+1$ is known, so that $Z_{t+1} - E(Z_{t+1} \mid \Omega_t) = 0$, the forecast error is the standard within-regime error so that there is no peso problem. When the future regime is unknown the second term in (185) adds a component to the within-regime error (given that the within-regime forecasts differ so that $\Delta E(y_{t+1} \mid \Omega_t) \neq 0$).

Evans illustrates this point more clearly by supposing that in period $t+1$ regime 1 occurs. From (185) with $Z_{t+1} = 1$ we obtain that

$$e_{t+1}(1) = u_{t+1} + \Delta E(y_{t+1} \mid \Omega_t)[1 - E(Z_{t+1} \mid \Omega_t)] \qquad (186)$$

or

$$e_{t+1}(1) = u_{t+1} + \Delta E(y_{t+1} \mid \Omega_t)\,\Pr\{(Z_{t+1} = 0 \mid \Omega_t)\} \qquad (187)$$

where Pr denotes probability.

When the probability of regime 0 is non-zero the rational expectation error contains an additional component which is the difference between the within-regime forecasts multiplied by the probability that regime 0 occurs. As we illustrated with our example above when the within-regime forecasts differ this can generate an ex-post rational errors which may have a non-zero mean, so that they appear to be biased or serially correlated, and so inefficient. It is also apparent from (185) that the extent to which this issue will be important in empirical evaluations of forecasts will be dependent upon the frequency of regime shifts in the data sample. In the extreme case when only one regime occurs the errors will match those in (186). When there are a number of regime changes the forecast error will be a weighted average of $e_{t+1}(1)$ and $e_{t+1}(0)$ (defined anologously to (186)).The effect in this case on the properties of the forecast error will depend on the sample properties of the forecast error for regimes $Z_{t+1} - E(Z_{t+1} \mid \Omega_t)$. When the number of regime changes in the sample is representative of the underlying distribution of regime changes, from which the rational expectations of agents are generated, then the forecast error for regimes will exhibit a zero mean and the forecast errors will exhibit the standard rational expectations errors.

An interesting extension of the peso issue considered by Evans and referred to by Kaminsky (1993) as the generalised peso problem is when agents do not know which current regime they are in (for instance the central bank's preferences). Evans illustrates some implications by assuming that the degree of uncertainty of the regime is given by $\Pr(Z_t \mid \Omega_t)$. When the regime is known and there is no uncertainty $Z_t = z$ and $\Pr(Z_t \mid \Omega_t) = 1$. When $\Pr(Z_t \mid \Omega_t) \neq 1$ Evans discusses some implications in the following manner. First we employ the identity

$$\Pr(Z_{t+1} = 0) \equiv \Pr(Z_{t+1} = 0 \mid Z_t = 1) - \Pr(Z_{t+1} = 0 \mid Z_t = 1) \\ + \Pr(Z_{t+1} = 0) \quad (188)$$

where for simplicity we have dropped the notation for the information set Ω_t. (We read e.g. the second term of (188), $\Pr(Z_{t+1} = 0 \mid Z_t = 1)$, as follows: the probability of $Z_{t+1} = 0$ given $Z_t = 1$, all conditional on the information set Ω_t).

We substitute (188) into (187) to obtain

$$e_{t+1}(1) = u_{t+1} + \Delta E(y_{t+1}) \Pr(Z_{t+1} = 0 \mid Z_t = 1) - \\ \Pr(Z_{t+1} = 0 \mid Z_t = 1) + \Pr(Z_{t+1} = 0)] \quad (189)$$

or

$$e_{t+1}(1) = u_{t+1} + \Delta E(y_{t+1})\{\Pr(Z_{t+1} = 0 \mid Z_t = 1\} - \\ \Delta E(y_{t+1})[\Pr(Z_{t+1} = 0 \mid Z_t = 1) - \Pr(Z_{t+1} = 0)] \quad (190)$$

Now

$$[\Pr(Z_{t+1} = 0 \mid Z_t = 1) - \Pr(Z_{t+1} = 0)] \quad (191)$$

the last term in (190), is equal to

$$[\Pr(Z_{t+1} = 0 \mid Z_t = 1) - \Pr(Z_{t+1} = 0 \mid Z_t = 0)] \Pr(Z_t = 0) \quad (192)$$

since equating (191) and (192) and rearranging gives the definitional statement

$$\Pr(Z_{t+1}=0)=\Pr(Z_{t+1}=0\mid Z_t=1)[1-\Pr(Z_t=0)]+\Pr(Z_{t+1}=0\mid Z_t=0)[\Pr(Z_t=0)] \quad (193)$$

(note $1-\Pr(Z_t=0)=\Pr(Z_t=1)$).

Consequently the last term in (190) can be rewritten as

$$-\Delta E(y_{t+1})[\Pr(Z_{t+1}=0\mid Z_t=1)-\Pr(Z_{t+1}=0\mid Z_t=0)]\Pr(Z_t=0) \quad (194)$$

Recognizing that the first two terms on the right-hand side of (190) are the same as those in (187) we see that uncertainty about the current regime manifests itself in an additional term in the forecast error given by (194). We observe that this term will only be zero if the probability of regime 0 at time $t+1$ is independent of the current regime or of course that within-regime forecasts are equal. In addition we observe that changes in $\Pr(Z_t=0)$ (perhaps due to learning about the regime) will contribute to the structure of the error term.

Evans (1996) documents a number of other interesting implications of the peso problem. In the context of asset prices, where current values depend on expected values of fundamentals into the indefinite future, he demonstrates how news about future fundamentals can influence current prices through the normal channel of changed forecasts of future fundamentals as well as the additional channels of the difference in fundamentals in the different regimes as well as the dynamics of regime switching. In the context of empirical work he demonstrates how peso problems can contribute to the explanation of some of the puzzles found in asset markets, such as the bias of the forward premium. Bekaert, Hodrick and Marshall (2001) show how peso problems can contribute to an explanation of anomalies in the term structure of interest rate (see below).

The peso problem is that sample statistics are not representative of the population so that statistical inferences are potentially misleading. It is clearly of considerable importance in evaluating models of expectations.

Statistical Rationale

An alternative statistical rationale for the forward premium bias is suggested by Baillie and Bollerslev (1997). An empirical regularity in the exchange market is that the statistical properties of changes in the spot rate and the forward premium are markedly different. In monthly data the variance of changes in the spot rate is typically some 100 or so times greater than the variance of the forward premium. In addition whilst changes in the spot rate typically exhibit little evidence of serial correlation and can often be well approximated by martingales the forward premium typically displays very persistent slowly decaying autocorrelations which may be described as a fractional process – see e.g. Baillie and Bollerslev (1994), Byers and Peel (1996), also the Time-Series Annex). The statistical properties of changes in the spot rate and the forward premium imply that estimates of β_2 in small samples may be fragile. Baillie and Bollerslev show this is the case. They report estimates of β_2 in the Fama regression obtained from a rolling sample of data. Employing monthly data for the DM/dollar they consider 208 five-year rolling regression estimates for β_2 obtained by beginning in March 1973 and using a total of sixty observations through to February 1978. Then the next estimate was obtained by using data from April 1973 through to March 1978, until the final estimate was based on data from December 1990 through to November 1995. The estimates of β_2 display marked instability varying between -13 and 3.52. These findings suggest that for many sample sizes encountered in practice, the estimate of β_2 is likely to be uninformative about the true value of β_2.

They provide further support for this view by simulating data from a known structure which is calibrated to produce the stylized statistical properties exhibited by the spot and forward premiums. The expectation embodied in the forward premium is rational by construction. Their simulated models are found to generate results which are similar to those reported in the literature. In particular, the forward premium exhibits persistent autocorrelation and the estimates of β_2 are widely dispersed between negative and positive numbers.These empirical findings are of some interest since the statistical properties exhibited by the dependent and independent variables in the Fama regression are qualitatively similar to those exhibited in other tests of market efficiency such as bond rates (see below).

McCallum (1994) illustrates another important point that needs to be given consideration when testing market efficiency relationships. This is whether the relationship is invariant to government policy. To illustrate, McCallum assumes that the monetary authorities manage interest rates so as to smooth their movements while also resisting changes in exchange rates.

Defining $x_t = R_t - R_t^F$ he considers the policy rule

$$x_t = \lambda(S_t - S_{t-1}) + \sigma x_{t-1} + e_t \tag{195}$$

where λ, σ are constants and e_t is a random error.

Uncovered arbitrage is given by

$$x_t = E_t S_{t+1} - S_t + v_t \tag{196}$$

McCallum interprets v_t as measurement error though it could be interpreted as a risk premium. He assumes that

$$v_t = \rho v_{t-1} + u_t \tag{197}$$

where ρ is a constant and u_t is a random error. Assuming a solution for changes in the spot rate of the form

$$S_t - S_{t-1} = Ax_{t-1} + Bu_t + Ce_t \tag{198}$$

and equating coefficients we obtain the solution as

$$S_t - S_{t-1} = \frac{(\rho - \sigma)}{\lambda} x_{t-1} + \frac{u_t}{(\lambda + \sigma - \rho)} - \frac{e_t}{\lambda} \tag{199}$$

(note that $x_{t-1} = R_{t-1} - R^f_{t-1} = F_{t-1} - S_{t-1}$). The solution for x_t can also be obtained as

$$x_t = \rho x_{t-1} + \frac{\lambda u_t}{(\lambda + \sigma - \rho)} \tag{200}$$

The important point to note is that the coefficient on x_{t-1} ($= F_{t-1} - S_{t-1}$ via the covered arbitrage condition) in (199) contains the policy parameters λ and σ. If σ is close to unity and greater than ρ and λ is positive, then the coefficient can be negative. In addition, the forward premium will exhibit persistent serial correlation for ρ close to unity and if the variance of u_t is very small relative to the variance of e_t then changes in the spot rate will be closely approximated by a white noise error process even though the true process is a persistent ARMA(1, 1) process.

This concludes our discussion of tests of market efficiency in the exchange market. It has emphasised the considerable difficulties in determining from *ex-post* regression whether this market is efficient.

We next consider, more briefly, the implications of market efficiency for the behaviour of interest rates.

LONG-RUN INTEREST RATES UNDER MARKET EFFICIENCY

There are a great variety of bonds. Bonds are issued by private companies, local authorities and by the government. Naturally the probability of default can vary across bonds with different issuers. But government bonds are normally regarded by investors as free of default risk and it is the pricing of these types of bonds in an efficient market that we will consider here. Government bonds can be broadly categorized as being of two main types. The first type are bonds which pay a regular coupon, usually semi-annual, which is a fixed fraction of the face value of the bond up to the maturity date when the face value is also repaid. The other type are zero-coupon bonds, also called discount bonds which make one payment at the maturity date of the bond. Bonds are offered with a great variety of maturity dates, from short up to undated (consols in the UK). Bonds paying coupons can be interpreted as packages of zero-coupon bonds with one corresponding to each coupon payment and one corresponding to the repayment of the principal and coupon at the maturity date. For an individual trader, long-run bonds are substitutable for short-run bonds, since it is possible for him to hold a series of short bonds rather than a long bond over the same holding period, or conversely to hold a long bond for a short period and then sell it rather than hold a short bond to maturity.

More formally, assume initially that traders are completely certain of the future. Initially we consider pure discount bonds so that the return is simply the discount from par at which the bond is sold at the beginning of the period relative to the redeemed par price at the end of the period.

The price, P_{nt}, at time t of a bond which makes a payment of £1 at time $t+n$ is given by

$$P_{nt} = \frac{1}{(1+R_{nt})^n} \tag{201}$$

where R_{nt} is the bond's yield to maturity.

In a world of certainty the pure expectations hypothesis assumes that the the following condition must hold:

$$(1+R_{nt})^n = (1+R_{1t})(1+R_{1t+1})(1+R_{1t+2})\ldots(1+R_{1t+n-1}) \tag{202}$$

The left hand side of (202) is simply the rate of return on holding an n-period bond until maturity. The right side of (202) is the rate of return implied by holding a one-period bond for one period, then reinvesting the proceeds (principal plus interest) in a one-period bond for the next period and so on.

By taking logarithms and recalling that for small values of the fraction Z, $\ln(1+Z)$ can be approximated by Z, we can rewrite (202) as:

$$R_{nt} = \frac{1}{n}(R_{1t} + R_{1t+1} + R_{1t+2} + \ldots + R_{1t+n-1}) \tag{203}$$

In other words (203) informs us that long-run interest rates are simply averages of future interest rates over the time period to maturity. It tells us, for instance, that if short-run interest rates remain constant for the indefinite future, then long rates will be equal to short rates. Conversely, if future short rates are expected to fall, the current long rate will be below the short rate. The relationship is known as the expectations theory of the term structure of interest rates.

When we relax the assumption of perfect knowledge of the future and recognize that traders can observe the current long rate R_{nt} and the current one-period short rate R_{1t}, it follows if traders are risk neutral that:

$$R_{nt} = \frac{1}{n}[R_{1t} + E_t R_{1t+1} + E_t R_{1t+2} + \ldots E_t R_{1t+n-1}] \tag{204}$$

If traders are risk averse, then we must add a risk premium to the right-hand side of (204) but this does not affect the argument, provided it is constant.

If we consider a bond with a two-period maturity date then

$$R_{2t} = \frac{1}{2}[R_{1t} + E_t R_{1t+1}] \tag{205}$$

We can rewrite (205) as

$$E_t R_{1t+1} - R_{1t} = 2(R_{2t} - R_{1t}) \tag{206}$$

or assuming rational expectations that

$$R_{1t+1} - R_{1t} = 2(R_{2t} - R_{1t}) + v_{t+1} \tag{207}$$

where $v_{t+1}$is the expectations forecast error. Accordingly we observe that the expected change in yield on a one-period bond is related to twice the difference between the yield on a two-period bond and the yield on a one-period bond and that the actual change differs from this term by an expectational error. The expectations hypothesis implies testable implications such as this for bonds of different maturities. We now examine some of these implications further.

We first introduce the concept of the holding-period return, H_{nt+1}, which for simplicity we assume is one-period. This is the return from purchasing an n-period bond at time t and selling it at time $t+1$. At time $t+1$ the bond will become an $n-1$ period bond and will be sold for a price P_{n-1t+1} .

From (201)

$$1 + H_{nt+1} = \frac{P_{n-1t+1}}{P_{nt}} = \frac{(1 + R_{nt})^n}{(1 + R_{n-1t+1})^{n-1}} \tag{208}$$

The expectations hypothesis also implies that

$$R_{1t} = E_t[H_{nt+1}] \tag{209}$$

Equation (209) tells us that the yield on a one-period bond should equal, ignoring any risk premium, the expected holding-period return on an n-period bond held for one period. Taking logs of (208) and approximating as above, and then taking expectations, we can use (209) to eliminate the expected holding-period yield. Manipulation of the resultant gives:

$$E_t(R_{n-1t+1} - R_{nt}) = \frac{(R_{nt} - R_{1t})}{n-1} \tag{210}$$

Equation (210) informs us that when the spread (the difference in yield between the long-maturity and short-maturity bond) is positive, changes in yields on long-maturity bonds are expected to increase. Campbell, Lo and Mackinlay (1997) and others have tested (210) by estimating the equation

$$R_{n-1t+1} - R_{nt} = \alpha + \beta\frac{(R_{nt} - R_{1t})}{n-1} + \varepsilon_t \tag{211}$$

where ε_t is the forecast error.

The estimate of β should not differ from unity when equation (211) is estimated for discount bonds of different maturity dates. The results are not supportive of the expectations hypothesis. Estimates of β are often negative, particularly for bonds of long maturity dates.

A variety of explanations exist for this anomalous finding and they mimic the explanations for the anomolous empirical finding in the exchange market discussed above whereby the forward premium is negatively related to future changes in the spot rates. These are time-varying risk premia, peso problems, goverment policy rules and low statistical power of the regressions.

We can also write (204) in the form

$$R_{nt} - R_{1t} = \frac{1}{n}[R_{1t} + (E_tR_{1t+1} - R_{1t} + R_{1t}) + (E_tR_{1t+2} - R_{1t} + R_{1t}) + \ldots + (E_tR_{1t+n-1} - R_{1t} + R_{1t})] - R_{1t} \tag{212}$$

or

$$R_{nt} - R_{1t} = E_t\sum_{i=1}^{n}\frac{\Delta R_{1t+i-1}}{n} \tag{213}$$

Equation (213) informs us that the spread is a predictor of future changes in short run interest rates. This implication can also be empirically tested. One method is to replace the expected terms on the right hand side of (213) by their actual values and regress the resultant on the spread, employing an estimator that corrects for the overlapping expectational errors. The coefficient should not differ from unity. Campbell, Lo and Mackinlay (1997) report such estimates. Their results suggest a U-shaped pattern in the estimates for different maturities. For short maturities, the spread has a positive coefficient which is less than unity and declines initially, becoming insignificant with the maturity horizon. At longer horizons a significant positive coefficient is obtained sometimes greater than unity. It thus appears that the spread has ability to predict short-run interest rates changes for both relatively short and long horizons but not intermediate horizons. The empirical results can again be explained by reference to the arguments explaining previous anomalous findings above.

We now turn to analysis of coupon-paying bonds.

The yield to maturity, or long-run interest rate Y_t^n, on an n-period bond is determined by the fact that the price P_t^n of the bond is the present value of a coupon (C), assumed paid at the end of each period, and repayment of the principal (normalized here to unity) at the terminal date discounted by Y_t^n. We have that

$$P_t^n = \frac{C}{1+Y_t^n} + \frac{C}{(1+Y_t^n)^2} + \frac{C}{(1+Y_t^n)^3} + \ldots + \frac{C}{(1+Y_t^n)^n} + \frac{1}{(1+Y_t^n)^n} \tag{214}$$

Letting $u = \frac{1}{1+Y_t^n}$ we can multiply (214) by u to obtain

$$uP_t^n = Cu^2 + Cu^3 + Cu^4 + \ldots + Cu^{n+1} + u^{n+1} \tag{215}$$

Subtracting (215) from (214) we obtain

$$P_t^n(1-u) = Cu - Cu^{n+1} + u^n - u^{n+1} \tag{216}$$

Dividing (216) by $1-u$, noting that $P_t^n(1-u) = Cu(1-u^n) + u^n(1-u)$, and $\frac{u}{1-u} = \frac{1}{Y_t^n}$, rearranging after substitution back for u we obtain that

$$P_t^n = \frac{C}{Y_t^n} + \frac{Y_t^n - C}{Y_t^n(1+Y_t^n)^n} \tag{217}$$

If $Y_t^n = C$, $P_t^n = 1$, and conversely. Bonds with this characteristic, whose price today equals the principal paid at maturity are selling ‘at par’.

We also notice from (217) that for an undated security or perpetuity, $n = \infty$ and so $P_t = \frac{C}{Y_t}$, so that the price is the coupon divided by the very long-term interest rate, Y_t.

The one-period holding yield, H_t^n, on a n-period coupon-paying bond consists of both the yield in the holding period plus the capital gain or loss. This gives us

$$H_t^n = \frac{P_{t+1}^{n-1} - P_t^n + C}{P_t^n} \tag{218}$$

recalling again that an n-period bond at time t becomes an $n-1$ bond at time $t+1$.

We note from (218) that for a perpetuity, $n = \infty$,

$$H_t = Y_t - \frac{(Y_{t+1} - Y_t)}{Y_{t+1}} \tag{219}$$

Equating the expected holding-period yield from the perpetuity to the yield on a short-term coupon-paying bond we have that

$$Y_t^1 = Y_t - \frac{(Y_{t+1} - Y_t)}{Y_{t+1}} \tag{220}$$

If we take a first-order Taylor expansion of the last term on the right-hand side of (220) around $\overline{Y}$ we obtain

$$Y_t^1 = Y_t - 1 + 1 + \frac{(Y_t - \overline{Y})}{\overline{Y}} - \frac{\overline{Y}(Y_{t+1} - \overline{Y})}{\overline{Y}^2} \tag{221}$$

Rearranging (221) we obtain in expectational form

$$E_t Y_{t+1} - Y_t = \overline{Y}(Y_t - Y_t^1) \tag{222}$$

We observe that expected changes in the yield on the perpetuity are positively related to the spread between the yield on the perpetuity and the yield on the short maturity bond.

Equation (222) can also be solved forward to obtain the solution for Y_t as

$$Y_t = \frac{\overline{Y}}{1 + \overline{Y}} E_t \sum_{i=0}^{\infty} \frac{Y_{t+i}^1}{(1 + \overline{Y})^i} \tag{223}$$

so that the perpetuity is a weighted average of expected future short yields. Clearly (223) is a linear approximation to a nonlinear structural equation and its ability to approximate will naturally be dependent on interest rates not being too volatile so that the approximation remains reasonably accurate

In the more general case of coupon-paying bonds with an n-period horizon the derivation can proceed in a similar manner. We substitute for the price of the bond from (217) into the holding period yield (218). This gives us the rather messy relation

$$H_t^n = \frac{\left(C + \frac{C}{Y_{t+1}^{n-1}} + \frac{Y_{t+1}^{n-1} - C}{Y_{t+1}^{n-1}(1+Y_{t+1}^{n-1})^{n-1}}\right)}{\left(\frac{C}{Y_t^n} + \frac{Y_t^n - C}{Y_t^n(1+Y_t^n)^n}\right)} - 1 \tag{224}$$

(In Shiller, 1979, equation (224) is linearized around $Y_t^n = Y_{t+1}^{n-1} = \overline{Y} = C$.) This gives the relationship

$$H_t^n = \frac{Y_t^n - \gamma_n Y_{t+1}^{n-1}}{1 - \gamma_n} \tag{225}$$

where $\gamma_n = \{1 + \overline{Y}[1 - 1/(1+\overline{Y})^{n-1}]^{-1}\}^{-1}$

Equating (225) to a short yield, Y_t^1 (plus any constant risk premium) we can solve the resulting difference equation for Y_t^n, given the terminal condition that the price of the bond is 1 at $t+n$, as

$$Y_t^n = \frac{1-\gamma}{1-\gamma^n} E_t \sum_{i=0}^{\infty} \gamma^i Y_{t+i}^1 + \phi_n \tag{226}$$

where ϕ_n is any constant risk or liquidity premium. Equation (226) informs us that the n-period yield on a coupon-paying bond is a weighted average of the expected yields on the one-period bond.

Shiller exploits these properties to evaluate empirically whether long-run bond yields are too volatile to be consistent with rational expectations and the observed volatility in short rates (a test analogous to the variance bounds test for stock prices outlined above). His empirical findings are inconsistent with rational expectations. Again the results could be reconciled by appeal to the sort of issues raised above.

LEARNING AS AN ALTERNATIVE TO RATIONAL EXPECTATIONS:

The tests we have been examining all assume rational expectations. One possible cause of failure could therefore be that expectations are not rational but rather the result of a learning procedure — of which adaptive expectations is an approximation, as shown by Benjamin Friedman (1979).

We observed in the appendix to chapter 2 that if a series followed an ARIMA(0,1,1) process then an adaptive expectations scheme could in fact be a representation of the rational expectation. Earlier in this chapter we also found that a regressive expectations scheme could be rational in the Dornbusch overshooting model. In general of course these methods of expectations formation will not have the rational expectations property. They illustrate however that in any particular model structure, since the rational expectation solution can be written in terms of observable variables, there is a 'mechanistic' method of expectation formulation which will have the properties of rational expectations for the particular model structure. In this book we are primarily concerned with investigating the properties of models when it is assumed that agents' expectations, or the aggregate of agents' expectations, have the rational expectations property. Maintained assumptions of this approach are that agents know the true model, or act as though they did, and also assume that other agents also possess this information (see Townsend, 1978). In this approach econometricians will come across cases of 'adaptive' expectations which by chance represent the rational forecasting mechanism.

However there is an important literature that relaxes these assumptions and assumes that expectations follow a learning rule,which has the potential to converge to rational expectations (see e.g. Evans and Honkapohja, 1999, 2001, and Sargent, 1993). From this perspective the adaptive or regressive expectations schemes can be interpreted as simple learning rules which have converged on the rational expectations solution. A variety of learning rules, in general possibly more intelligent, have been studied. One such example is least-squares learning whereby agents employ least-squares regression to estimate the parameters of a model and employ the resulting model to forecast the variable of interest. This approach to learning models agents in the same way as economists who employ econometrics and statistical inference in deciding between competing models. Employing this approach also highlights another aspect of rational expectations that agents in the model are assumed to possess more information than the outside observer.

One motivation for studying learning rules is to ascertain whether they converge on rational expectations and how fast this process is. Answers to such questions may be relevant for some in deciding how plausible the rational expectations assumption is.

Whilst the implausibility of the assumption that agents know the true model may be sufficient justification for some for studying the implications of the learning assumption there are other properties of the rational expectations assumption that have been used to justify such an approach.

The first of these is the issue of 'non-uniqueness' (as set out in chapter 2). When the model exhibits more than one stationary solution methods that are not part of the formal model structure have to be employed to determine which solution is chosen by agents. The solution chosen by different learning rules has been widely studied. However, as we argued in chapter 2, 'non-uniqueness' should really be seen as the failure of a stability condition for the 'forward' root. The ultimate remedy is to find a specification which satisfies stability conditions that presumably hold in the real world.

The second justification is when a model has more than one equilibrium solution. For example, take the widely used model of hyperinflation which has been extensively studied in this context. If we assume a government prints money to finance a constant budget deficit, then

$$P_tG_t = M_t - M_{t-1} \tag{227}$$

where P_t is the price level, $G_t = \overline{G}$ is the constant real deficit, and M_t is the money stock.

Assume a demand function for money of the form

$$\frac{M_t}{P_t} = f(E_tp_{t+1}) \tag{228}$$

where $E_tp_{t+1} = E_t(\log(P_{t+1}/P_t)$ is the expected rate of inflation:

$$\frac{\partial \frac{M_t}{P_t}}{\partial E_tp_{t+1}} < 0 \tag{229}$$

and real output has been assumed constant.

Assuming money demand is equal to money supplied we can substitute (2) into (1) to obtain

$$\overline{G} = f(E_tp_{t+1}) - f(E_{t-1}p_t)e^{-p_t} \tag{230}$$

(since $\log\frac{P_t}{P_{t-1}} = p_t, \frac{P_t}{P_{t-1}} = e^{p_t}$)

Equation (3) has two equilibrium solutions if $\overline{G}$ is not too large (where $E_tp_{t+1} = E_{t-1}p_t = p_t = \overline{p}$). Intuitively if inflation is zero in equilibrium the authorities generate no receipts, whilst if inflation is infinite agents hold no money so receipts are also zero. Consequently the equilibrium surface $\overline{G} = g(\overline{p})$ exhibits two equilibria for $\overline{G} < \overline{G}_{\max}$. Assuming rational expectations the equilibrium exhibiting higher inflation is mathematically stable and the lower one unstable. These rankings are reversed assuming adaptive expectations. If the view is taken that mathematical stability is not the appropriate selection criteria in a rational expectations model then there is no mechanism, which is part of the formal model structure, to choose between the two equilibria. More generally a rational expectations models could exhibit multiple stable equilibria.

A third justification is structural change. Say a new government or a new central banker appears, it is natural to model agents as learning about the new regime. How 'wet' or 'dry' the new governor is and how the probabilities change as new information accrues seem best analyzed in a learning framework.

We will now briefly illustrate some examples of learning mechanisms. Evans and Honkapohja (1999) have divided the approaches into three groups and we follow their taxonomy.

Eductive approaches

In this literature researchers investigate whether the coordination of expectations on an rational expectations equilibrium can be attained by a mental process of reasoning. We illustrate with an example based on DeCanio(1979).

Suppose the demand and supply in a market are given by

$$q_t = a - bp_t + w_t \tag{231}$$

$$q_t = c + dE_{t-1}p_t + v_t \tag{232}$$

where p_t is the price level, w_t and v_t are random disturbances and a, b, c and d are constants.

The reduced form for prices in this system assuming demand is equal to supply is given by

$$p_t = \frac{a-c}{b} - \frac{d}{b}E_{t-1}p_t + \frac{w_t - v_t}{b} = A - BE_{t-1}p_t + u_t \tag{233}$$

where the definitions of A,B,u_t are obvious.

Suppose agents form their expectations initially in an arbitrary manner.The question is whether they can modify their behaviou r in such a way as to lead them closer to rational expectations, given by $\frac{A}{1+B}$. Suppose the initial, arbitrary expectation of all agents is given by

$$E^0_{t-1}p_t = p_{t-1} \tag{234}$$

From (232) given this expectation the actual evolution of prices will be given by

$$p_t = A - Bp_{t-1} + u_t \tag{235}$$

DeCanio assumes that after some passage of time agents realize (reason or deduce) that prices are evolving according to (234) and form the new expectation

$$E^1_{t-1}p_t = A - Bp_{t-1} \tag{236}$$

However this new expectation changes the evolution of the system to

$$p_t = A - B(A - Bp_{t-1}) + u_t = A - BA + B^2 p_{t-1} + u_t \tag{237}$$

Agents observing the new evolution of prices in the market agents revise expectations to

$$E^2_{t-1} p_t = A - BA + B^2 p_{t-1} \tag{238}$$

so that actual prices evolve as

$$p_t = A - B(A - BA + B^2 p_{t-1}) + u_t = A - BA + B^2 A - B^3 p_{t-1} + u_t \tag{239}$$

Continuing in this manner after n iterations we will have

$$E^n_{t-1} p_t = A - BA + B^2 A - B^3 A + - + AB^n + B^n p_{t-1} \tag{240}$$

If $|B| < 1$, for large n expectations will converge to the rational expectation

$$E^n_{t-1} p_t = \frac{A}{1+B} \tag{241}$$

since $\frac{1}{1+B} = 1 - B + B^2 - B^3 + - +$ for $|B| < 1$.

Clearly convergence to the rational expectation is not guaranteed even in the simple example if $|B| > 1$. When iterative expectations converge on the rational expectations solution the rational expectation is said to be iteratively E-stable. The iterative expectations of agents were assumed to be homogenous in the above example. When convergence occurs and the iterative expectations of agents are heterogeneous as in Guesnerie (1992) the rational expectations model is said to be strongly rational. Evans (1985, 1986) employ the iterative expectations method in models embodying multiple solutions, Peel and Chappell (1986) in a model embodying multiple equilibria and Bullard and Mitra (2000) in a model where agents learn about monetary policy rules.

Adaptive Approaches

Early on Benjamin Friedman (1979) argued that agents would learn from data via regression about the model and the policy regime. This, he pointed out, would produce expectations formation very similar to adaptive expectations without necessarily ever leading to rational expectations. Such statistical learning was subsequently examined to see whether it would converge on rational expectations. We consider the least-squares learning mechanism initially analyzed by Bray and Savin (1986) and Fourgeaud, Gourieroux and Pradel (1986), though we note that more complicated estimation procedures such as neural nets and genetic algorithms have been employed (see Sargent, 1993).

Suppose for simplicity that the reduced form for prices follows the process

$$p_t = A + BE_{t-1}p_t + Cz_{t-1} + u_t \tag{242}$$

From (241) the rational expectation is given by $E_{t-1}p_t = \frac{A+Cz_{t-1}}{1-B}$ so that prices evolve as

$$p_t = A + \frac{(AB+C)}{1-B}z_{t-1} + u_t = A + Gz_{t-1} + u_t \tag{243}$$

Suppose agents believe that prices follow the process given by (242) but are unaware of the values of the parameters A and G. In the least-squares approach to learning agents are assumed to run least-squares regressions of p_t on z_{t-1} and an intercept using previous data on the variables. Expectations are then generated from the estimated model. As more data becomes available the model is then reestimated, expectations formed and so on. Researchers have demonstrated that the conditions for convergence of recursive least-squares expectations can be weaker than those under iterative expectations. ($B < 1$ in this model as opposed to $|B| < 1$ with iterative expectations.)

In the case of least-squares learning where agents perceive the reduced form as

$$y_t = \beta' x_t + e_t \tag{244}$$

where β' is a vector of coefficients, x_t a vector of explanatory variables and e_t an error, the least-squares estimated coefficients are given by

$$\beta_t = \left(\sum_{i=0}^{t-1} x_i x_i'\right)^{-1} \left(\sum_{i=0}^{t-1} x_i y_i\right) \tag{245}$$

It can be demonstrated that the recursive least-squares estimates are generated as

$$\beta_t = \beta_{t-1} + \gamma_t R_t^{-1} x_{t-1}(y_{t-1} - \beta_{t-1}' x_{t-1}) \tag{246}$$

and

$$R_t = R_{t-1} + \gamma_t (x_{t-1}x_{t-1}' - R_{t-1}) \tag{247}$$

with $\gamma_t = \frac{1}{t}$. and where R_t is an estimate of the moment matrix for x_t. For suitable initial conditions $R_t = t^{-1} \sum_{i=0}^{t-1} x_i x_i'$.

We note that the term $\gamma_t = \frac{1}{t}$ is known as the 'gain'. It is important in determining the speed of convergence to the true parameter. Some intuition of the least-squares updating formulae can be obtained by considering the recursive least-squares estimate of the mean $Ez_t = \mu$. The least-squares estimate is the sample mean $\overline{z}_t = \frac{1}{t}\sum_{n=1}^{t} z_n$.

Subtracting the sample mean at $t-1$ from both sides of $\overline{z}_t$ and rearranging gives

$$\overline{z}_t = \overline{z}_{t-1} + \frac{1}{t}(z_t - \overline{z}_{t-1}) \tag{248}$$

since $t\overline{z}_t = \sum_{n=1}^{t} z_n = z_t + \sum_{n=1}^{t-1} z_n$ and $(t-1)\overline{z}_{t-1} = \sum_{n=1}^{t-1} z_n$ so that $t(\overline{z}_t - \overline{z}_{t-1}) = z_t + \sum_{n=1}^{t-1} z_n - t\overline{z}_{t-1}$
$= z_t + (t-1)\overline{z}_{t-1} - t\overline{z}_{t-1} = z_t - \overline{z}_{t-1}$.

Adaptive methods of learning have the same general type of structure which is given by

$$\theta_t = \theta_{t-1} + \lambda_t Q(t, \theta_{t-1}, X_t) \tag{249}$$

where θ_t is a vector of parameters, λ_t is the gain parameter equal to $\frac{1}{t}$ in the case of least-squares, Q is a function and X_t is the vector of variables in the structural model. We note that adaptive expectations is a special case of (248) where the gain parameter is constant..

The evolution of X_t will depend on θ_{t-1}, in the case of a linear system

$$X_t = A(\theta_{t-1})X_{t-1} + B(\theta_{t-1})W_t \tag{250}$$

where W_t is a vector of disturbance terms.

Marcet and Sargent (1989a,b), Evans and Honkapohja (1998) derive stability results for linear (and nonlinear) systems. Sargent (1999) assumes the US authorities used constant-gain least-squares learning about the Phillips Curve and maximised a social objective function to pick inflation; he argues this fits US post-war data, accounting for the 'great inflation' where rational expectations cannot.

Rational Learning

Rational learning has to be interpreted from a perspective that acknowledges the benefits and costs of more accurate forecasts for an agent as in Feige and Pierce (1976) or Evans and Ramsey (1992), so that rational expectations may not be attained unless calculation costs are zero. However the method most widely employed to model rational learning has been to employ Bayes' rule. Bayes' rule is the basic property of conditional probability and is a method of updating our belief or probability of event or hypothesis A given new evidence B. Specifically, our posterior belief $P(A/B)$ is calculated by multiplying our prior belief $P(A)$ by the likelihood $P(B/A)$ that B will occur if A is true. To see this we can rearrange the conditional probability formula to get:

$$P(A/B)P(B) = P(A,B) \tag{251}$$

where $P(A,B)$ is the joint probability of A and B.

By symmetry we also have

$$P(B/A)P(A) = P(A,B) \tag{252}$$

It follows from (250) and (251) that .

$$P(A/B) = \frac{P(B/A).P(A)}{P(B)} \tag{253}$$

Equation (252) is called Bayes' rule or Bayes' theorem. The formulation carries the implication that beliefs change by learning: agents come to know of a new fact and form their posterior belief by conditioning their prior belief on these facts.

An alternative form of Bayes' rule is given by

$$P(A/B) = \frac{P(B/A).P(A)}{\sum\limits_i P(B/A_i).P(A_i)} \tag{254}$$

since $P(B) = \sum\limits_i P(B/A_i).P(A_i)$ where A_i refers to the event space.

From (252) we observe that the data or new facts B only influence the posterior inference through the function or probability $P(B/A)$ which is called the likelihood function.

The ratio of the posterior probability evaluated at the two events A_1 and A_2 is called the posterior odds.

We have

$$\frac{P(A_1/B)}{P(A_2/B)} = \frac{P(A_1)P(B/A_1)/P(B)}{P(A_2)P(B/A_2)/P(B)} = \frac{P(A_1)P(B/A_1)}{P(A_2)P(B/A_2)} \tag{255}$$

In words, the posterior odds are equal to the prior odds multiplied by the likelihood ratio.

Bayes' rule has been widely employed to model learning in the economics literature — see e.g. Cyert and DeGroot (1974), Backus and Driffill (1985), Ellison and Valla (2000), Lewis (1998) Sill and Wrase (1999),

Townsend (1978). Types of problem analyzed employing Bayes'rule include learning about a new regime. We will give one example which is a slight modification of Lewis (1988). She demonstrates how beliefs that a policy process may have switched can induce apparent ex-post biased forecasts of exchange rates even after the switch has occurred. In addition, in her model, exchange rates may appear to contain a speculative bubble component since they will systematically deviate from the levels implied by observing fundamentals ex-post.

Assume the reduced form for the exchange rate (see chapter 14) is given by

$$s_t = m_t + \alpha(E_t s_{t+1} - s_t) \tag{256}$$

where s_t is the money supply at time t, s_t is the exchange rate and α is a positive constant.

Assume the money supply process is given by

$$m_t = \theta_0 + \varepsilon_t^0 \tag{257}$$

where θ_0 is a constant and ε_t^0 is a normally distributed random variable with mean zero and variance σ_0^2.

Suppose at a particular point in time, say $t = 0$, agents come to believe that the money supply process may have changed, due to an exogenous process such as a change in government or a statement by officials. The new process has for simplicity the same form as the old except with a different mean and variance:

$$m_t = \theta_1 + \varepsilon_t^1 \text{ for t} \geq 0 \tag{258}$$

It is assumed that $\theta_1 < \theta_0$ and $\theta_1 = 0$, so that the process can be interpreted as going from 'loose' to 'tight' money. Agents are not sure which money supply process is in operation. It is further assumed for simplicity that agents believe that if policy has changed it will not be changed back and they also know the parameters of the potential new process.

Solving (29) forward we obtain the solution

$$s_t = (1-\gamma)\sum_{i=0}^{\infty} \gamma^i E_t m_{t+i} \tag{259}$$

where $\gamma = \frac{1}{1+\alpha}$.

Expected money supply given the assumptions above is equal to

$$E_t m_{t+i} = \theta_0(1 - P_{1t}) \text{ for any } i > 0, t \geq 0 \tag{260}$$

where P_{1t} is agents' assessed probability at time t that the process changed at time 0.

Consequently the exchange rate is given by

$$s_t = (1-\gamma)m_t + \gamma(1-P_{1t})\theta_0 \tag{261}$$

(note $E_t s_{t+1} = \theta_0(1-P_{1t})$ from (30) and (31) since $\frac{1}{1-\gamma} = 1+\gamma^1+\gamma^2+ -+\gamma^\infty$ and $\frac{1}{1+\alpha} = 1-\gamma$)

To obtain the best estimate of P_{1t}, agents combine their prior beliefs about the probability together with their observations of money outcomes each period to update their posterior probabilities according to Bayes' Rule.

$$P_{1t} = \frac{P_{1t-1}f(I_t/\theta_1)}{P_{1t-1}f(I_t/\theta_1) + P_{0t-1}f(I_t/\theta_0)} \tag{262}$$

where P_{0t} is the probability of no change at $t=0$, $f(I_t/\theta_i)$ is the probability of observing the information set I_t given that m_t follows the ith process. The posterior probabilities of each process, the posterior odds ratio, is given by

$$\frac{P_{1t}}{P_{0t}} = \left.\frac{P_{1t-1}f(m_t/\theta_1)}{P_{0t-1}f(m_t/\theta_0)}\right] = \left.\frac{P_{1t-1}}{P_{0t-1}}\right]\left[\frac{(\frac{1}{\sigma_1})e^{(\frac{-m^2}{2\sigma_1^2})}}{(\frac{1}{\sigma_0})e^{(\frac{(m-\theta_0)^2}{2\sigma_0^2})}}\right] \tag{263}$$

The first term on the right-hand side of (262) shows that the change from $t-1$ to t in the relative conditional probabilities depends upon the observation of the current money supply at time t. For example for some observation of current money supply, say $\overline{m}$, the probability of being under either regime is equal, so that the posterior probabilities, $\frac{P_{1t}}{P_{0t}}$, are equal to the prior probabilities $\frac{P_{1t-1}}{P_{0t-1}}$. Observations of money supply different from $\overline{m}$ convey information about the regimes causing the probabilities to be revised. The last term on the right-hand side of (262) quantifies this information. For a normally distributed error the sampling distribution for a single scalar observation, m, from a normal distribution parameterized by a mean θ and a variance σ^2 is given by

$$P(m/\theta) = \frac{e^{-\frac{(m-\theta)^2}{2\sigma^2}}}{\sqrt{2\pi}\sigma} \tag{264}$$

Clearly the information accruing from an observation will depend on the particular distribution of the error term.

If for simplicity we assume that $\sigma_0 = \sigma_1 = \sigma$ then we can write (36) as

$$\ln(\frac{P_{1t}}{P_{0t}}) = \ln\frac{P_{1t-1}}{P_{0t-1}} + \ln\frac{f(m_t/\theta_1)}{f(m_t/\theta_0)} \tag{265}$$

so that for any realization of the money process m_k

$$\ln \frac{f(m_k/\theta_1)}{f(m_k/\theta_0)} = \left. \frac{(m_k - \theta_0)^2 - m_k^2}{2\sigma^2} \right] \tag{266}$$

Substituting (265) into (266) we obtain a linear difference equation that can be solved as

$$\ln(\frac{P_{1t}}{P_{0t}}) = \ln \frac{P_{1,0}}{P_{0,0}} + \sum_{k=1}^{t} \left. \frac{(m_k - \theta_0)^2 - m_k^2}{2\sigma^2} \right] \tag{267}$$

In equation (266) the evolution of probabilities is seen to depend on the actual observations of the process. When the money supply observed today is very negative agents will think it more likely that policy has changed and vice versa.

Taking expectations of (266), defining θ_i as the true θ gives

$$E\ln(\frac{P_{1t}}{P_{0t}}) = \ln \frac{P_{1,0}}{P_{0,0}} + t \left. \frac{(\theta_i - \theta_0)^2 - \theta_i^2}{2\sigma^2} \right] \tag{268}$$

$$= \ln \frac{P_{1,0}}{P_{0,0}} + t \left. \frac{\theta_0^2 - 2\theta_i\theta_0}{2\sigma^2} \right] \tag{269}$$

Equation (268) illustrates that the expected value of the 'true' process rises over time. For instance when policy has changed so $\theta_i = \theta_1 = 0$, from (268) we observe that the log probability increases to infinity because of the trend term $\frac{t\theta_0^2}{2\sigma^2}$ (or that P_{0t} goes to zero). When policy has not changed so that $\theta_i = \theta_o$ the reverse is true due to the trend term $\frac{-t\theta_0^2}{2\sigma^2}$. Consequently agents' assessed probabilities of a policy change are random variables determined by random observations of the money supply.

Given this analysis of the evolution of probabilities Lewis is able to investigate the effects on the exchange rate and forecast errors.Taking expectations at $t-1$ of (260) and subtracting from (260) we obtain the forecast errors corresponding to each potential process as:

$$s_t - E_{t-1}s_t = (1-\gamma)\varepsilon_t^0 + \theta_0(P_{1,t-1} - \gamma P_{1t}) \text{ if } \theta_i = \theta_0 \tag{270}$$

and

$$s_t - E_{t-1}s_t = (1-\gamma)\varepsilon_t^1 - \theta_0(P_{0,t-1} - \gamma P_{0t}) \text{ if } \theta_i = \theta_1 \tag{271}$$

(note $E_{t-1}P_{1t} = P_{1,t-1}, E_{t-1}P_{0t} = P_{0,t-1}$).

Equations (269) and (270) illustrate that whilst agents are learning, expectation errors will exhibit a systematic component and 'appear non-rational *ex-post*'.

Taking expectations of the forecast errors in (270) conditional upon a change in policy to θ_1 the expected evolution of the forecast errors, for a large number of m_k is given by

$$E(s_t - E_{t-1}s_t/\theta_1) = -\theta_0[E(P_{0,t-1}/\theta_1) - \gamma E(P_{0t}/\theta_1)] < 0 \qquad (272)$$

The inequality is negative since γ is less than one and $EP_{0t}/\theta_1 < E(P_{0,t-1}/\theta_1)$.

From (271) we observe that if agents do not fully realize that policy has changed the exchange will be expected to be weaker than subsequently occurs. Ex-post expectations will appear to be irrational.

Lewis' model nicely illustrates how learning about a regime change using Bayes' rule can mimic the outcomes of the Peso problem discussed earlier in this chapter.

CONCLUSIONS

In this chapter we have discussed some of the implications of the proposition that financial markets are efficient. As particular applications of the proposition we examined the behaviour of stocks, exchange rates and bond markets. The theoretical work on efficiency in asset markets is large and is expanding dramatically so that we have only been able to provide a flavour of the debate. Whilst the new generation of models which stress micro-structure arguments appear of great interest, our own view is that the empirical evidence for (approximate) semi-strong efficiency in the capital market is sufficiently powerful and convincing for it to be regarded as a 'stylized fact'. In fact it is now standard practice for macroeconomic model builders to simulate or forecast the impact of changes in government policy within models that assume capital market efficiency.

APPENDIX 14A1 – INCOMPLETE CURRENT INFORMATION

The purpose of this appendix is to show the manner in which the standard test of efficiency based on equation (81) of this chapter has to be modified if agents have an incomplete current information set. For analytical simplicity (though the argument is quite general), we assume the series y_t is the summation of two infinite moving average error processes in the two white noise errors, ϵ and z.

$$y_t = \overline{y} + \sum_{i=0}^{\infty} \pi_i \epsilon_{t-i} + \sum_{i=0}^{\infty} \delta_i z_{t-i} \tag{1}$$

where $\overline{y}$ is the mean of the series, and the π_i and δ_i are constant coefficients.

Consider the rational expectation of y_{t+1} formed at time t. If there is full current information at time t the expectation will be given by:

$$E_t y_{t+1} = \overline{y} + \sum_{i=0}^{\infty} \pi_i \epsilon_{t-i+1} + \sum_{i=0}^{\infty} \delta_i z_{t-1+i} \tag{2}$$

In this case, given the one-period forecast horizon, the ex-post forecast error will be given by a white noise error:

$$y_{t+1} - E_t y_{t+1} = \pi_0 \epsilon_{t+1} + \delta_0 z_{t+1} \tag{3}$$

Consequently the standard tests based on (81) are correct in these circumstances.

Suppose next that agents have incomplete current information at time t, and instead observe some current global information (for instance via asset markets), but other global information with a one-period lag. In particular we will assume for simplicity (though the argument is easily generalized) that there is one global indicator (say the interest rate) which is given the representation:

$$R_t = \overline{r} + \sum_{i=0}^{\infty} (d_i \epsilon_{t-i} + h_i z_{t-i}) \tag{4}$$

where $\overline{r}$ is the mean of the series and the d_i and h_i are constant coefficients.

In this incomplete current information case the one-period-ahead expectation of y_t is given by:

$$E_t y_{t+1} = \overline{y} + \pi_1 E_t \epsilon_t + \sum_{i=2}^{\infty} \pi_i \epsilon_{t-i+1} + \delta_1 E_t z_t + \sum_{i=2}^{\infty} \delta_i z_{t-i+1} \tag{5}$$

Consequently the forecast error is given by:

$$y_{t+1} - E_t y_{t+1} = \pi_0 \epsilon_{t+1} + \delta_0 z_{t+1} + \pi_1[\epsilon_t - E_t \epsilon_t] + \delta_1[z_t - E_t z_t] \quad (6)$$

Given current observation of the global indicator R_t, and using the usual signal extraction formulae (as discussed in chapter 3) we obtain:

$$E_t \epsilon_t = \frac{1}{d_o} \phi_\epsilon (d_0 \epsilon_t + h_0 z_t) \quad (7)$$

$$E_t z_t = \frac{1}{h_0} (1 - \phi_\epsilon)(d_0 \epsilon_t + h_0 z_t) \quad (8)$$

where

$$\phi_\epsilon = \frac{d_o^2 \sigma_\epsilon^2}{d_o^2 \sigma_\epsilon^2 + h_o^2 \sigma_z^2}$$

and σ_ϵ^2 and σ_z^2 are the variances of the two errors, ϵ and z respectively. Consequently the forecast error (K_{t+1}) is given by:

$$K_{t+1} = \pi_0 \epsilon_{t+1} + \delta_0 z_{t+1} + \pi_1 \left[(1 - \phi_\epsilon)\epsilon_t - \frac{h_o}{d_o} \phi_\epsilon z_t \right] + \delta_1 \left[\phi_\epsilon z_t - \frac{d_0}{h_o}(1 - \phi_\epsilon)\epsilon_t \right] \quad (9)$$

Serial Correlation of Forecast Errors

If we take expectations of two successive errors we find:

$$E(K_{t+1},\ K_t) = \left\{ \frac{\sigma_z^2 \sigma_\epsilon^2}{d_o^2 \sigma_\epsilon^2 + h_0^2 \sigma_z^2} \right\} [\pi_1 h_0 - d_1 d_0].[\pi_0 h_0 - \delta_0 d_0] \quad (10)$$

Consequently, in general, incomplete current information will give rise to a moving-average error process. This will not be the case if, first, we have implicitly full current information (for example, if there are as many global indicators in the economy as random shocks; see Karni, 1980), or if, secondly, we observe the current value of the variable to be forecast (it being itself a global indicator). In this latter case $\pi_0 = d_0$, $\delta_0 = h_0$ (also $\pi_1 = d_1$, $\delta_1 = h_1$) and the expected correlation in (10) is equal to zero.

It would appear from this result that standard tests of efficiency based on (81) will have the usual properties for asset prices in particular (which it can be assumed are observed currently), even under incomplete current information. However, the general point remains that variables not currently observed (i.e. the majority) will under incomplete information be inappropriately tested for efficiency by these methods. Furthermore, one needs to scrutinize carefully the assumption that the asset prices in question are contemporaneously observed. In very high frequency data (e.g. hourly) this will obviously not be so except for a few continuously-broadcast asset prices; it will also not be so in lower frequency data for averages of variables (e.g. the level of all short-term interest rates), which are often examined in these studies.

In general, in circumstances of incomplete current information the moving-average error in equation (9) will be given by $s + j - 1$, where s is the time horizon of the forecast and j is the longest lag on global information relevant for forecasting y_t. Clearly there may be some *a priori* doubt as to the magnitude of j, which may cause some problems in interpretation of tests based on (81). As a consequence of the moving-average error process, least squares estimates of (81) under incomplete current information will be inefficient but unbiased, since

$$E(K_{t+1},\ E(y_{t+1})) = 0 \tag{11}$$

and least squares estimates have the property of unbiasedness even in the presence of moving-average error processes. This situation is the same as that of overlapping information in the usually assumed case of full current information; overlapping information here occurs with $s > 1$, familiarly introducing a moving-average process with the same effects.

These results have potential implications for a number of empirical studies (see e.g. Holden and Peel, 1977; Turnovsky, 1970) in which an implicit assumption of full current information has been made when studying directly-observed consumer price expectations data which cannot readily be assumed to be part of the current information set. The point here is that price data are not currently observable on any reasonable assumptions. Consequently, the 'expectations errors' should be serially correlated, as indeed has often been found in these tests. It is possible that these survey data may well reveal rationality after all. For further implications of partial current information sets for the testing of efficiency, see Minford and Peel (1984).

APPENDIX 14A2 COMPOSITE MOVING-AVERAGE ERROR PROCESSES

Testing for the efficiency of relationships involving moving-average errors poses problems. We wish to form a moving-average error process from the composite error process

$$av_{t+1} + bv_t + cu_{t+1} + du_t \tag{1}$$

where v_{t+i} and $u_{t+i} (i = 1,\ 0)$ are serially uncorrelated random variables.

We define the new moving-average process

$$\phi_{t+1} + j\phi_t = av_{t+1} + bv_t + cu_{t+1} + du_t \tag{2}$$

where ϕ_{t+i} $(i = 1,\ 0)$ is a serially uncorrelated random variable.

The method is to equate the ratio of the variance to the covariance of the error processes on the left- and right-hand sides of (2) (where the variances and covariances of the left- and right-hand sides are equal by definition — a similar method is employed for higher-order composite processes).

We obtain that

$$\frac{(1 + j^2)\sigma_\phi^2}{j\sigma_\phi^2} = \frac{(a^2 + b^2)\sigma_v^2 + (c^2 + d^2)\sigma_u^2 + 2(bd + ac)\text{cov}(uv)}{ab\sigma_v^2 + cd\sigma_u^2 + (ad + bc)\text{cov}(uv)} \tag{3}$$

where σ_ϕ^2, σ_v^2, σ_u^2 are the variances of ϕ, v, u and $\text{cov}(uv)$ is the covariance between u and v.

Equation (3) is a quadratic equation in j (note σ_ϕ^2 cancels). The root of the equation which has modulus less than unity is chosen so that the process can be stationary. Clearly the magnitude of j will reflect relative magnitudes of variances and covariances. For example if $a = 1,\ b = -1,\ c = 1$ and $d = 0,\ \sigma_u^2 = \sigma_v^2$ and $cov(uv) = 0$ then $j = \frac{-3+5^{0.5}}{2}$.

Using the lag operator it is also useful to note that we can express ϕ_{t+1} as

$$\phi_{t+1} = \frac{[av_{t+1} + bv_t + cu_{t+1} + du_t]}{(1 + jL)} =$$
$$[av_{t+1} + bv_t + cu_{t+1} + du_t]\{1 - jL + j^2L^2 - j^3L^3 + \ldots] \tag{4}$$

From (4) we observe that ϕ_{t+1} can be expressed as an infinite sum of the past errors v and u. This is important in some tests of efficiency under rational expectations. Since the errors in the composite process are in principle any errors in the economy if a moving-average error process is estimated jointly with the other parameters of the model it will induce correlations between the regressors and the error term which will result in biased and inconsistent parameter estimates. For instance consider the two-period ahead rational expectations forecast error for the process,

$$y_t = \overline{y} + \sum_{i=0}^{\infty} \gamma_i u_{t-i} + \sum_{i=0}^{\infty} \delta_i v_{t-i} \tag{5}$$

We have that

$$y_t = E_{t-2} y_t + \gamma_0 u_t + \gamma_1 u_{t-1} + \delta_0 v_t + \delta_1 v_{t-1} \tag{6}$$

Although the error term is a moving-average process, in a test of efficiency it would be inappropriate to estimate jointly the parameters of the model and the moving-average process

$$y_t = \alpha_0 + \alpha_1 E_{t-2} y_t + \phi_t + j\phi_{t-1} \tag{7}$$

and test that $\hat{\alpha}_0 = 0$, $\hat{\alpha}_1 = 1$. As shown above the error term can be written as an infinite summation of previous errors. This is also a property of the forecast so that there will be correlation between the error and the explanatory variable. An appropriate procedure is to estimate (7) by least squares and employ standard errors which are modified to allow for the serial correlation in the error term (see e.g. Hansen and Hodrick, 1980).

It is also useful to note that an ARMA forecast of a variable, even assuming the underlying model is linear, is less efficient than a rational expectations forecast if the reduced form of a variable includes composite moving-average errors. Suppose for illustration a variable, y_t, is generated by the process

$$y_t = u_t - u_{t-1} + v_t \tag{8}$$

The rational one-period ahead forecast, $E_{t-1} y_t = -u_{t-1}$. Let the moving-average process for (8) be given by $y_t = \phi_t - j\phi_{t-1}$ $(j > 0)$ so that the one-period ARMA forecast is $E^a_{t-1} y_t = -j\phi_{t-1}$. The associated forecast errors are

$$y_t - E_{t-1} y_t = u_t + v_t \tag{9}$$

for the rational expectation and for the ARMA forecast

$$y_t - E^a_{t-1} y_t = \phi_t = \frac{u_t - u_{t-1} + v_t}{(1 - jL)} \tag{10}$$

Assuming for simplicity that $cov(uv)$ is zero the variance of the rational expectations forecast is

$$\sigma_u^2 + \sigma_v^2 \tag{11}$$

The ARMA forecast error can be written as

$$y_t - E^a_{t-1}y_t = u_t - (1-j)u_{t-1} - j(1-j)u_{t-2} - j^2(1-j)u_{t-3} + \dots \\ + v_t + jv_{t-1} + j^2 v_{t-2} + \dots \quad (12)$$

(Recall that $\frac{1}{(1-jL)} = 1 + jL + j^2L^2 + j^3L^3 + \dots$)

Although the ARMA forecast error appears serially correlated this is in fact not the case as substitution for j in terms of the variances of u and v, though messy, will demonstrate.

The variance of the ARMA forecast error is given by

$$\sigma_u^2 + \sigma_u^2(1-j)^2[1 + j^2 + j^4 + j^6 + \dots] + \\ \sigma_v^2\{1 + j^2 + j^4 + j^6 + \dots\} \quad (13)$$

which we can simplify as

$$\sigma_u^2 + \frac{(1-j)^2\sigma_u^2}{(1-j^2)} + \frac{\sigma_v^2}{(1-j^2)} \quad (14)$$

Because j is less than one the variance of the ARMA forecast is greater than the rational expectations forecast error. Essentially information is lost in forecasting the composite error process. In addition the innovation from the ARMA process, ϕ_t, though serially uncorrelated, will not necessarily be orthogonal to variables that are correlated with past u and v innovations, due to the implicit dependence of the ARMA innovation on these variables.

15

Interpreting the Evidence: The Problem of Observational Equivalence

As was shown in chapter 4, it is a key implication of an economy embodying a Sargent-Wallace supply curve, rational expectations and identical information sets of public and private agents that, from a stabilization perspective, output (or the unemployment rate) will be invariant to anticipated rates of monetary change. Only unanticipated changes in the money stock will have any impact on output. This appears to suggest an attractive test of such a New Classical model; whether it is anticipated or unanticipated changes in the money supply that affect output. Barro(1977) in a seminal paper attempted to determine empirically the relative impacts of unanticipated and actual rates of monetary change on the unemployment rate in the USA over the period 1946-73. Since his initial paper, he and others have carried out similar tests for a number of other countries, as well as repeating the US tests in different ways.

Barro's empirical procedure involved two stages. First, a policy reaction function was determined for the authorities. This involved explaining the actual rates of change of the money stock in terms of variables previously known to the authorities. The residuals, or unexplained part of monetary change, from this reaction function are interpreted as the unanticipated rate of monetary change.

Thus if the reaction function of the authorities is given by:

$$m_t = a_m X_{t-1} + u_{mt} \tag{1}$$

where m is the rate of monetary expansion, X is a vector of variables, a_m a vector of coefficients, u_{mt} is a random residual. Then

$$m_t - E_{t-1} m_t = u_{mt} \tag{2}$$

Having obtained estimates of the monetary innovations, Barro proceeds to use these innovations, current and lagged (along with other postulated determinants of the natural rate of unemployment such as a minimum wage variable and a measure of military conscription), to explain the rate of unemployment.

Barro's empirical results appear impressive. They suggest that the current and previous two years' monetary innovations are significant determinants of the rate of unemployment with the correct negative sign. Moreover, when Barro adds previous rates of change of the money supply to his unemployment equation, they are found not to be statistically significant.

The basic type of analysis conducted by Barro has been replicated by a large number of different authors for a number of different countries (see e.g. Barroand Rush, 1980; Leiderman, 1980; Attfield et al., 1981a, b; Mishkin, 1982). The results reported by all these authors except Mishkin seem to suggest that real variables, either unemployment or output, are responsive only to unanticipated rates of monetary change and not the actual rate. Consequently, it would appear from this empirical evidence that there is powerful support for the joint hypothesis of rational expectations and independence of unemployment or output from anticipated rates of monetary change.

Sargent (1976b) in an important paper, showed that this interpretation of the empirical evidence may be incorrect. Sargent demonstrated that the reduced form for output or unemployment in a Keynesian model, in which systematic monetary policy will influence the variance of output, may be statistically indistinguishable from that of a classical model in which only unanticipated movements in the money stock impact on output or unemployment. The Keynesian and New Classical models are said to be observationally equivalent in their reduced forms.

Sargent's main point can be made most simply by consideration of the following model. Suppose the 'true' reduced-form equations for an economy are given by the equations:

$$y_t = a_c X_{t-1} + b_c(m_t - E_{t-1}m_t) + u_{ct} \tag{3}$$

and the money supply reaction function is (1) above. Then $E_{t-1}m_t = a_m X_{t-1}$ and we can rewrite (3) as:

$$y_t = (a_c - b_c a_m)X_{t-1} + b_c m_t + u_{ct} \tag{4}$$

which has all the appearance of a Keynesian model.

Alternatively take a Keynesian model to be the true one:

$$y_t = a_k X_{t-1} + b_k m_t + u_{kt} \tag{5}$$

By adding and subtracting expected money supply we can change it into:

$$y_t = (a_k + b_k a_m)X_{t-1} + b_k(m_t - E_{t-1}m_t) + u_{kt} \tag{6}$$

an apparently New Classical model.

It is obvious from Sargent's analysis that 'unrestricted' single equation reduced forms for output have no information content, at least with respect to the manner in which changes in the money supply impact on an economy. A simple regression of output on the money supply simply cannot inform us of the true nature of the impact of monetary change on these variables.

The point that Sargent is making is that two quite different types of model, Keynesian and New Classical, have indistinguishable reduced forms for output in terms of either actual or unanticipated money stock. This does not imply that the models *in toto* are not distinguishable; clearly they are, on the basis of a variety of tests on structural coefficients and also on reduced-form equations for more variables than simply output. Therefore the point is a narrow but important one, related to this particular test carried out by economists (remember that there has been great interest in money-supply/output relationships ever since the debate over Friedman and Meiselman, 1965).[1]

In particular, it needs to be stressed, because there has been some confusion on the point, that Sargent's point is not about 'identification' as such. Both the Keynesian and New Classical models may be fully identified; that is, the parameters of each may be individually retrieved by estimation of the full model (i.e. subject to all its restrictions). However, there is a useful potential connection with the concept of identification. If two models can be 'nested' in a more general model (usually, a linear combination of the two), then, provided the coefficients of each model can be identfied in this general model, it is possible to test for their significance and accordingly that of each model. In this situation, if (and only if) the coefficients cannot be identified, the models will be 'observationally equivalent'.

Sargent's point has provoked a lively literature attempting to establish conditions under which a limited number of reduced forms can

[1] The analogous point also turns out to be applicable to reduced forms for the exchange rate (see chapter 14, Box 14.1) as a means of distinguishing 'equilibrium' from 'disequilibrium' open economy models. It will also often be applicable when a reduced form on any single variable is appealed to as a means of distinguishing equilibrium from disequilibrium models; appeals to the 'stylized facts' about any single variable have accordingly to be treated with the greatest caution.

distinguish between the two models. These attempts have centred on identification within such a general model, in this case one which nests two distinct reduced forms.

IDENTIFICATION

In order to discuss this issue more fully it is necessary first to set out the basic issues which arise in indentification of an economic system. (For a comprehensive outline the reader should consult a standard econometric text such as Johnston and DiNardo, 1997).

Suppose that the demand and supply for a commodity is given by:

$$q_t = a_{11}p_t + a_{12}y_t \quad \text{(demand)} \tag{7}$$

$$q_t = a_{21}p_t + a_{22}z_t \quad \text{(supply)} \tag{8}$$

where the as are constants, p is price, q quantity and y and z are exogenous variables which affect demand and supply respectively. Demand and supply are assumed to be equal. Random disturbances and constants are omitted from (7) and (8) for simplicity. The equations are treated here as structural or behavioural equations and the as as structural coefficients. The issue of identification is: given that these two equations are both operative, can each be confused with the other? To put it another way, is it possible to distinguish between each equation and a linear combination of the two equations together?

Form a linear combination of the two equations:

$$\mu q_t + (1-\mu)q_t = q_t = [\mu a_{11} + (1-\mu)a_{21}]p_t + \mu a_{12}y_t + (1-\mu)a_{22}z_t \tag{9}$$

Plainly the demand equation is different from it because it has no term in z_t; similarly the supply equation because it has no term in y_t. So if we fit these two equations to the data, we will get estimates of the four as. (We would still want to worry about the best way to estimate them, given simultaneous equation bias; but that is another matter — concerning the *technique* of estimation)

Now suppose instead that the supply equation was:

$$q_t = a_{21}p_t + a_{22}y_t \quad \text{(supply)} \tag{10}$$

Our linear combination of the two equations would then be:

$$q_t = [\mu a_{11} + (1-\mu)a_{21}]p_t + [\mu a_{12t} + (1-\mu)a_{22}]y_t \tag{11}$$

It is clear from inspection that now neither the demand nor the supply equation can be distinguished from this. When you estimate the demand equation you could be picking up the coefficients of the supply equation or the demand equation or any combination of the two; it is impossible to know what you have estimated across this set of possibilities. The same applies when you estimate the supply equation. Notice that it matters not what technique of estimation you use (TSLS, FIML, indirect via the reduced form); the point is you just do not know what you are picking up, however sophisticated your estimation method and however much data you have. We say that neither equation is identified.

Now suppose the supply equation was:

$$q_t = a_{21}p_t + a_{22}z_t + a_{23}y_t \tag{12}$$

Our linear combination would be:

$$q_t = [\mu a_{11} + (1-\mu)a_{21}]p_t + [\mu a_{12t} + (1-\mu)a_{22}]y_t + (1-\mu)a_{23}z_t \tag{13}$$

It is now clear that the demand equation is distinct from this (and so identified) while the supply equation is not (and so unidentified). What has enabled an equation, in this case the demand one, to be identified is a restriction it imposes; viz in this case the exclusion restriction on one variable.

In fact we can generalise this analysis to other restrictions, notably cross-equation restrictions on parameters. For example suppose that the coefficient $a_{11} = a_{21}$, then plainly we could always be sure to estimate a_{11}, whatever else we could not be sure of, since in the linear combination the coefficient on p_t would never be anything else. What this also illustrates is that even if equations are not identified, coefficients can be. In general we can look at which coeffcieints in a system of equations are identified.

Once we introduce this idea of restrictions of any sort, we can also find that a coefficient is 'over-identified' by which is meant that the restrictions can clash in estimating the coefficient. Suppose we go back to our original model where each equation was identified by excluding a variable. Now super-impose the cross-equation restriction that $a_{11} = a_{21}$; you can immediately see that estimating each equation will provide a separate, valid estimate of a_{11}. This coefficient is thus over-identified. This is not however a problem; on the contrary it is rather an *embarras de richesses,* since plainly having two ways of tying the coefficient down means there is twice as much information about it in the data. When one uses a simultaneous equation estimator, one chooses the value that gives the best fit for both equations taken together; this estimator thus makes use of all the information in the data to estimate the coefficient.

From this it can be seen that the more restrictions we can impose from our theory, the more over-identification of coefficients is achieved and the more information from any given set of data is brought to bear on the coefficients of the model.

IDENTIFICATION OF KEYNESIAN AND CLASSICAL REDUCED-FORM COEFFICIENTS

We now return to the problem raised by Sargent. Let us initially suppose that there are no lagged effects; the salient points can be made for this case. We know that a New Classical model can be written in the 'semi-reduced' form (semi because expectations have not been eliminated):

$$y_t = a_c X_{t-1} + b_c(m_t - E_{t-1}m_t) + u_{ct} \tag{14}$$

and that a Keynesian model will have a reduced form:

$$y_t = a_k X_{t-1} + b_k m_t + u_{kt} \tag{15}$$

where the us are the error terms which we can in practice ignore.

Now suppose that the rest of the model is a policy reaction function for the money supply:

$$m_t = a_m X_{t-1} + u_{mt} \tag{16}$$

where u_{mt} is a random error independent of u_{ct} and u_{kt} which again we can ignore. (Much of the discussion which follows is based on Buiter (1983), to which the reader is referred for further analysis.)

Sargent's point can now be expressed as the impossibility of identifying b_c and b_k in this model. As we saw above, since $E_{t-1}m_t = a_m X_{t-1}$, substituting into the New Classical model gives us

$$y_t = (a_c - b_c a_m)X_{t-1} + b_c m_t + u_{ct} \tag{17}$$

from which it is plain that the New Classical and Keynesian models are unidentified, in other words indistinguishable from each other and a linear combination of the two. Similarly, we also showed we could make the Keynesian one look New Classical by rewriting it:

$$y_t = (a_k + b_k a_m)X_{t-1} + b_k(m_t - E_{t-1}m_t) + u_{kt} \tag{18}$$

We can equivalently write down a linear combination, μ times New Classical and $1 - \mu$ times Keynesian; and check that indeed we cannot estimate the parameters in it, or infer the value of μ – as lack of identification plainly implies. This is a useful alternative way of approaching the problem. Combining the two equations yields a composite equation:

$$\begin{aligned} y_t = [\mu a_c + (1-\mu)a_k]X_{t-1} + \mu b_c(m_t - E_{t-1}m_t) + (1-\mu)b_k m_t \\ + [\mu u_{ct} + (1-\mu)u_{kt}] \\ = aX_{t-1} + b(m_t - E_{t-1}m_t) + cm_t + u_t \end{aligned} \quad (19)$$

In this we would like to be able to identify b and c; since we expect one or other to be zero, that would in turn identify μ. However, as we have seen, the substitution of $a_m X_{t-1}$ for $E_{t-1}m_t$ in the above shows that we will estimate

$$y_t = (a - ba_m)X_{t-1} + (b+c)m_t + u_t \quad (20)$$

enabling none of the coefficients, a, b or c, to be estimated, or by implication μ.

To identify the crucial $b_i (i = c,\ k)$ parameters, we must set one of the elements in a_i to zero (if X is a single variable, $a_i = 0$ is necessary); that is, at least one variable appearing in the monetary policy reaction function must not appear in the output equation. Suppose for instance, that our model is given by:

$$y_t = a_c X_{1t-1} + b_c(m_t - E_{t-1}m_t) + u_{ct} \quad (21)$$

$$y_t = a_k X_{1t-1} + b_k m_t + u_{kt} \quad (22)$$

$$m_t = a_{m1}X_{1t-1} + a_{m2}X_{2t-1} + u_{mt} \quad (23)$$

then the first two equations are distinct. We can substitute for $E_{t-1}m_t$ in the New Classical equation, for example, to get:

$$y_t = (a_c - b_c a_{m1})X_{1t-1} + b_c m_t - b_c a_{m2}X_{2t-1} + u_{ct} \quad (24)$$

which differs from the Keynesian one by the term in X_{2t-1}. In terms of our linear combination, we would have

$$y_t = (a - ba_{m1})X_{1t-1} + (b+c)m_t - ba_{m2}X_{2t-1} + u_t \quad (25)$$

Given that we know the $a_{mi}(i = 1,\ 2)$ from estimating the money supply equation, we can estimate b from the coefficient on X_{2t-1} and so c and a from the other two.

What this all amounts to is that the expectations term $E_{t-1}m_t$ implicitly contains in it other variables known at time $t-1$. If these variables also appear in the output equations then both these equations are indistinguishable because there is no way of telling the effect of expectations in the New Classical from the direct effect in both equations. But if the output equations exclude at least one of these variables that go to form expected money supply, they can be distinguished. Here an exclusion restriction achieves identification.

This, however, is hard to visualize in any model, because the reduced form of output will generally contain all the lagged exogenous variables of the model which are candidates for the money supply reaction function. Barro, in his work on the USA, assumes with this in mind that government expenditure enters the money supply function but not the output function. This is implausible, given that government expenditure appears in the GDP identity. It might be possible to develop the New Classical model to exclude all such lagged exogenous variables, on the grounds that output depends only on current shocks to supply and to money. Go back to our original model, for example, but exclude X_{t-1} from the New Classical:

$$y_t = b_c(m_t - E_{t-1}m_t) + u_{ct} \tag{26}$$

$$y_t = a_k X_{t-1} + b_k m_t + u_{kt} \tag{27}$$

$$m_t = a_m X_{t-1} + u_{mt} \tag{28}$$

We can now rewrite the New Classical as:

$$y_t = b_c m_t - b_c a_m X_{t-1} + u_{ct} \tag{29}$$

which can be distinguished from the Keynesian by a cross-equation restriction – viz. if the coefficient on X_{t-1} equals minus that on m_t times a_m, then the model is New Classical.

The difficulty with this is that the New Classical model supply curve also has the intertemporal substitution effect from real interest rates (and in open economy models the analogous effect from the real exchange rate); the real interest rate (or the real exchange rate) is affected by all the exogenous variables in the model. Those using this test must (and in practice do) assume that these effects are negligible. But by so doing they restrict 'New Classical' to a limited class of model within the broader New Classical type; furthermore, some (intertemporal or other) substitution is a necessary component of the New Classical supply curve, otherwise no Phillips curve is possible. We also saw that there is scope for fiscal stabilization through government spending and (when there are wealth effects of government bonds) also for monetary stabilization in models with these effects. If Barro and his disciples were to demonstrate that the limited New Classical model held, they would be undermining the foundations of the New Classical model.

There remains the issue of partial macro information and signal extraction. This issue is assumed away in Barro's testing framework: none of the current money supply shock is assumed to be inferred from current information such as local prices, interest rates and exchange rates.

Yet again such signal extraction is at the core of the New Classical supply curve, as set out for example in Lucas' 'islands' model (Lucas, 1972, 1973). If included, signal extraction implies that

$$E_t m_t = E_{t-1} m_t + (\phi_0 u_{mt} + \phi_1 u_{ct}) \quad (30)$$

where ϕ_0 and ϕ_1 are linear combinations of structural parameters and error variances.

It can be seen that if the New Classical model has the exclusion restriction in it (on real interest rates and real exchange rate effects), then it is still possible to distinguish the two models via the cross-equation restriction discussed above. Nevertheless, the policy implications are different if there is signal extraction: stabilization policy may become effective, as discussed in chapter 4. The policy aspects of the Barro tests must therefore be approached with caution (this has also been stressed by Buiter, 1983).

The effectiveness of the test proposed by Barro really boils down, therefore, to the acceptability of the exclusion restriction he must make to allow the test to discriminate. With the exclusion restriction, the 'New Classical' model appears to be vitally impoverished: but without it the test is no use.

Sargent has suggested that models such as (14) and (15), which are as they stand observationally equivalent, may be identified if a structural break is known to have occurred in the policy regime during the sample period. If the world is New Classical, then the output coefficient on X_{t-1}in the regression on m_t and X_{t-1} will be invariant to a change in the policy regime (when a_m changes). Consequently tests for stability of such an equation across the samples before and after the break will discriminate between Keynesian and New Classical models. Nevertheless, this is not helpful in general (when breaks in regime either do not occur or cannot be known to have occurred), and it has rarely been used.

This discussion can be extended to include lags. Write our linear combination (19) and money supply equation (16) in general lagged form as:

$$[1 - q(L)]y_t = a(L)X_t + [b_0 + b(L)](m_t - E_{t-1}m_t) + [c_0 + c(L)]m_t + u_t \quad (31)$$

$$[1 - r(L)]m_t = a_m(L)X_t + u_{mt} \tag{32}$$

where L is the lag operator and $a(L)$, for example, is a polynomial in L $(1,\ 2,\ldots)$. It is convenient to substitute the error, $\hat{u}_{mt}$, for $m_t - E_{t-1}m_t$ and $m_t = \widehat{r}(L)m_t + \hat{a}_m(L)X_t + \hat{u}_{mt}$. The hats show that we have estimates of these from (32).

So we rewrite (31) as:

$$[1 - q(L)]y_t = \{a(L) + [c_0 + c(L)]\,\hat{a}_m(L)\}\,X_t + [b_0 + b(L) + c_0 + c(L)]\hat{u}_{mt} + [c_0 + c(L)][\widehat{r}(L)]m_t + u_t \tag{33}$$

The b and c coefficients cannot be separately recovered. The cs will only be retrievable if at least one of the X_t variables is excluded from (31) as before in the no-lag case (for example if X_t is a single variable, then $a(L) = 0$ will suffice).

Another possibility for discrimination when there are lags has been pointed out by McCallum (1979). This is the special case where the classical model contains only the current monetary innovation as a determinant of output. This case corresponds to having $b(L) = 0$ in (31). In this case we retrieve $c(L)$ from the coefficients on lagged money supply; for the model to be New Classical, lagged money supply should not enter the output reduced form.

The exclusion of past monetary innovations from the output equations may well not be valid; it places absolute reliance on the absence of a moving-average process on the term $p_t - E_{t-1}p_t$ entering the Sargent–Wallace supply curve. Yet it only requires a one-period delay in one sector's observed response to such shocks to yield such a process; this surely cannot be ruled out, in view of decision and delivery lags.

This suggests a final problem: the difficulty of discriminating between a New Classical and a New Keynesian model with the Barro test, supposing that the Keynesian model can be rejected by it in some way. Barro's original test in fact included the current and lagged money innovation in the output equation, using normal data. Yet this is consistent with a simple overlapping contract model of the sort illustrated in chapter 4, where both the current and lagged money shock affected output. More complex models such as Taylor (1979) add serial correlation to such moving averages of shocks, so that these shocks became an ARMA process. This is not obviously distinguishable from the processes Barro assumes. Only if an assumption is made, as in McCallum, about the New Classical error process, can the two be distinguished. Yet as we have seen, the basis for such an assumption is questionable, even without confronting the well-known empirical difficulties of testing between different error processes.

CONCLUSIONS

The empirical evidence presented by Barro and others on the impact of unanticipated or actual money on real variables appears to give impressive support to the New Classical model, as set out in the Sargent–Wallace model of Chapter 2.

Unfortunately, ingenious as Barro's original idea was and little as one would wish to ignore any empirical evidence, there are difficulties in the interpretation of these tests: it is impossible to distinguish a New Classical from a Keynesian reduced form equation for output unless it is assumed that at least in the New Classical model output is unaffected by exogenous variables which affect the money supply. This is a difficult assumption for New Classical economists to make in view of the importance they attach to intertemporal substitution and/or other mechanisms which induce relative price effects in the output supply curve. Various suggestions have been made to modify these tests but ultimately none has been successful in restoring credibility to this mass of empirical work. It should also be noted that even if the tests show a 'New Classical' model, that does not imply policy ineffectiveness because: (a) New Classical models with signal extraction in general create policy effectiveness and cannot be distinguished from New Classical models without signal extraction; (b) a New Keynesian model with overlapping contracts cannot be distinguished by these tests from a 'New Classical' model. To test for the restrictions which together give the full New Classical properties, the reduced form test of Barro is therefore inadequate. We turn next to estimation of structural models and how they may provide tests of these restrictions.

16

Direct Tests of Rational Expectations

So far we have looked at two indirect ways of testing the rational expectations hypothesis: the test for market efficiency (a joint hypothesis of equilibrium expected returns and rational expectations) and the Barro reduced form test for whether any money surprises affect output (a joint hypothesis that the model has a 'Sargent–Wallace supply curve' and rational expectations). We now consider the two direct tests of the rational expectations hypothesis (REH): direct testing on whether surveys of expectations display the properties of rationality, and estimation of structural models with a test for the REH restriction.

SURVEY DATA

A number of surveys of industrialists and private consumers have been carried out over the years for inflation and for output. The best known are the Livingston series in the USA and Carlson and Parkin's (1975) interpretation of the Confederation of British Industry survey in the UK: another series which has been examined (Visco, 1984) is for Italy, the Mondo Economico magazine (with Confindustria) surveys of wholesale and retail prices.

These surveys have generally satisfied the unbiasedness property (a weak test of rationality since it is shared with most other expectations hypotheses, notably adaptive expectations) but not the efficiency property: that is, information available to the survey participants was not independent of the expectations errors. Some of them get close to efficiency: Holden et al. (1985, chapter 3) review a number of these survey studies. For example, Visco finds that, up to the 1973 oil crisis, the Italian survey inflation expectations were unbiased, serially uncorrelated and efficiently incorporated all available information; bias and inefficiency occur in the few sample years after the oil crisis but Visco argues that this reflected turbulence and learning.

There are two problems with tests based on surveys. First, are those surveyed the key participants in the markets? The REH asserts that the 'average participant has rational expectations': this is an 'as if' proposition which implies that the price should behave as if those active in the market have rational expectations. 'Those active in the market' means agents 'on the margin', to whom a decision whether to buy or sell matters at the time. We are all on many occasions not really interested in a particular market: for example, we are not most of the time buying a house, but when we are we become interested in being well-informed. It is clearly impossible for a survey to select those market participants who are at each time active in the market. To the extent that the survey does not, however, some of those who answer will not be well-informed and should not have rational expectations.

The second problem may be no less important: the veracity of participants' answers. The theory of revealed preference indicates that we should look at people's actions not their words to reveal their tastes or views. In answer to questions, either they may not wish to reveal their true tastes or views or they may not truly know them — not perhaps yet having gone through the decision process that would reveal it to themselves, or perhaps not even understanding their implicit views having done so (rather like a bicyclist who cannot explain how he has stayed upright).

For similar reasons, economists have paid little attention to surveys of whether firms maximize profits or consumers maximize utility. For example, Hall and Hitch (1939) and Wilson and Andrews (1951) found from questioning firms that they did not consider themselves to be setting prices in a manner consistent with profit maximization. Similarly, psychologists have found that some consumers are irrational (Akerlof and Yellen, 1987). Economists have preferred to use maximizing models in spite of this evidence because the models have performed well empirically. A possible reason for this is that most people take advice from experts (usually organised in an industry, such as the forecasting or investing industry) when decisions are important to them; the REH does not suggest that rationality is a trivial attribute, easily acquired in the ordinary course of life. Rather it is put forward as a benchmark which people strive to attain and devote some resources to when necessary.

This reveals that it is the empirical performance of a hypothesis — the capacity to predict (past or future) conditionally on exogenous inputs — that matters to economists, if it is also attractive theoretically (that is, it is logical, tractable and based on non-absurd assumptions about behaviour). The REH has obviously exercised considerable theoretical appeal, as argued earlier, indeed throughout this book implicitly in one way or another. It remains then to consider the last main predictive test: structural estimation subject to the REH.

STRUCTURAL MODELS WITH RATIONAL EXPECTATIONS

The natural way to test the REH is in the context of a macro model. Estimate the structural coefficients of the model subject to the REH. One may then test the restriction of the REH against less restrictive alternatives, such as adaptive expectations or ARMA time series: this can be done by a likelihood ratio test if FIML is used or by an F-test within single-equation estimation.

It will help to understand the estimation of a full structural model if we take a simple example. We consider first the question of identification. Write down an aggregate supply and demand model of the economy:

$$y_t = \alpha(p_t - E_{t-1}p_t) + \beta f_t + u_t^s \tag{1}$$

$$y_t = \phi(m_t - p_t) + \gamma(E_t p_{t+1} - p_t) + u_t^d \tag{2}$$

We assume that the goods market clears continuously. (1) is the supply curve, with surprise inflation and f representing the fundamental driving the natural rate of output; (2) is the demand curve, driven by real balances and expected inflation (proxying interest rates as in the Cagan equation used in chapter 2). We assume that the exogenous processes, monetary and real, follow random walks:

$$m_t = m_{t-1} + v_t \tag{3}$$

$$f_t = f_{t-1} + w_t \tag{4}$$

To check identification we proceed as in chapter 15 and substitute for the expectations to find what restrictions they place on the estimation of the coefficients in the demand and supply equations. If we equate (1) and (2), take expectations at $t-1$ and substitute for $E_{t-1}m_t = m_{t-1}$ and $E_{t-1}f_t = f_{t-1}$, we obtain:

$$\beta f_{t-1} = \phi m_{t-1} - \phi E_{t-1}p_t + \gamma E_{t-1}p_{t+1} - \gamma E_{t-1}p_t \tag{5}$$

This can be rearranged as:

$$E_{t-1}p_t = \frac{\phi m_{t-1} - \beta f_{t-1}}{(\phi+\gamma)(1 - \frac{\gamma}{\phi+\gamma}B^{-1})}$$

$$= \frac{1}{\phi+\gamma}\sum_{i=0}^{\infty}(\frac{\gamma}{\phi+\gamma})^i E_{t-1}(\phi m_{t-1+i} - \beta f_{t-1+i})$$

$$= m_{t-1} - \frac{\beta}{\phi} f_{t-1} \quad (6)$$

where B^{-1} is the expectations forward operator discussed in chapter 2. By implication,

$$E_t p_{t+1} = m_t - \frac{\beta}{\phi} f_t \quad (7)$$

Substituting for these into our demand and supply curves yields, respectively:

$$y_t = \alpha p_t - \alpha m_{t-1} - \frac{\alpha\beta}{\phi} f_{t-1} + \beta f_t + u_t^s \quad (8)$$

$$y_t = (\phi+\gamma)m_t - (\phi+\gamma)p_t - \frac{\gamma\beta}{\phi} f_t + u_t^d \quad (9)$$

We can see that equation (8) has an exclusion restriction (it excludes m_t — notice that though (9) appears to exclude f_{t-1}, since $f_t = f_{t-1} + w_t$ it includes it implicitly). But additionally there are restrictions across the parameters which we can summarise by saying that there are seven coefficients to be estimated for only four parameters. Each equation contains a set of restrictions across its coefficients that distinguishes it from the other and from a linear combination of the two. In short the model is heavily over identified, as a result of imposing the rational expectations constraint. (Under backward-looking expectations the model is identified by an exclusion restriction on each equation, provided the expectations terms do not smuggle the excluded variables in via the backward-looking formula). One can see from this example how demanding the model is of the data; that is to say, the parameters, though tightly constrained by the model's over-identifying restrictions, must still fit the data.

We now turn to estimation.This is not the place to describe fully the technical econometrics for estimating an RE model: this has already been done by others (e.g. Wallis, 1980; Wickens, 1982; McCallum, 1976) and the techniques are available in software packages. There are two methods: limited and full information. In limited information (LI), the expectations variables are replaced by proxies generated from a first stage regression on the full set or a subset of the model's predetermined variables. In full information (FI), the expectations variables are the estimated model's own predictions: a package to do this written by Fair and Parke (1989) is available, implementing Fair and Taylor's (1983) procedure. More recently a robust algorithm to compute the full information maximum likelihood estimates for a large model together with its bootstrap confidence limits has been developed by Minford and Webb (2002). The idea of this is to search over the parameter set in a simple grid-search-cum-hill-climbing procedure until the likelihood of the resulting structural errors is at a maximum. We now briefly describe this method.

Our models are in general nonlinear and so we represent them quite generally as

$$\begin{aligned} y_t &= f[y_t, (L)y_t, x_t, (L)x_t, y_t^e, (L)y_t^e; \pi] + u_t \quad t = 1, 2, ..., n \quad (10) \\ x_t &= A(L)x_t + \in_t \quad (11) \end{aligned}$$

y_t is the vector of G endogenous variables, x_t is that of the exogenous variables, assumed to follow linear univariate time-series processes. (L) is the lag series L, L^2, L^3, ..., L^k (where k is the maximum lag length). y_t^e is the vector of rational expectations projections of the model based on information at t (these include the 'natural rate' variables, which are the solution of the equilibrium relationships in the model; they are projections of expected equilibrium based on current information). π is the vector of parameters. u_t is the vector of structural equation errors; that is to say, the errors when the endogenous variables on the right-hand side are at their true values.

In our method we evaluate the likelihood of (10), to find the set of maximizing parameters. Disregarding expectations, u_t measures the fit of each equation, regardless of how the poorness of fit in one variable spills over into poorness of fit in the others; hence as a parameter varies, its effect on the fit of only the variables in the equations where it appears is maximized. One can think of this as like simultaneously running OLS on each equation if the errors are not cross-correlated.

However, this discussion omits expectations y_t^e which will reflect all the model parameters in principle. As a result poorness of model projection wlll spill over into equations containing expectations — that is all of them. Hence every parameter's effect on the fit of all equations via its effect on expectations will also be taken account of. Given the importance of expectations in the models we are dealing with here, this amounts to taking account of a high degree of simultaneity.

We assume that the errors in either case follow a multivariate normal distribution with expectation of zero and variance-covariance matrix of Σ; and that estimation has eliminated any autocorrelation. This implies that the likelihood is:

$$p(u_1, u_2, ..., u_n) = (2\pi)^{-nG/2}(\det \Sigma)^{-n/2} \exp\left(-\frac{1}{2}\sum_{t=1}^{n} u_t'\Sigma^{-1}u_t\right) \quad (12)$$

We evaluate this likelihood directly. That is to say, for each trial set of parameters $\widetilde{\pi}$ we obtain an implied set of u_t for which (12) yields the likelihood. This is maximized by the algorithm described above. In practice, replacing Σ by the estimated variance-covariance matrix of the errors, the first and last terms of this expression will be constants, so that the log likelihood becomes $-n/2 \ln \det \widehat{\Sigma}$ and hence we are minimizing the log of the determinant of the variance/covariance matrix of the $\hat{u}_t$. For example, where $G = 2$, we are minimizing $\ln(\widehat{\sigma}_1^2 \widehat{\sigma}_2^2 - \widehat{\sigma}_{12}^2)$. With disturbances uncorrelated across equations, this minimizes the log of the product of the sums of squared residuals or $\ln \widehat{\sigma}_1^2 + \ln \widehat{\sigma}_2^2$.

Because there is no analytic method for computing the confidence limits in the effectively-small samples we have, we must use bootstrapping. The bootstrap procedure takes the $\hat{u}_t$ generated by the maximum-likelihood parameter set, $\widehat{\pi}$. It then resamples these with replacement and inserts the sample with $\widehat{\pi}$ into (10) to generate the bootstrap samples of y_t. In order to preserve the correlation across the elements of $\widehat{u_t}$, we sample $\widehat{u_t}$ by t-th vector — that is, we draw the t vectors repeatedly in different orders $(t = 1, 2, ..., n)$.The x_t are held constant across bootstraps. Then the above estimation procedure is repeated on each bootstrap sample.

FIML estimation as above thus locates the set of parameters that generate maximum likelihood, taking account of the expectations they generate as well as their fit given any set of expectations. To find the expectations requires model solution (convergence) in every period of the sample: this is a very stringent requirement and experience with the Liverpool model of the UK shows that it is frequently not met for a macroeconomic model, even of limited size (as with the Liverpool one), with arbitrarily chosen parameters. Hence the one available programme for estimating such models by FIML, that of Fair and Parke (1989), can easily break down if the initiating parameters do not permit convergence; the algorithm, finding non-convergence, may be unable to locate a parameter set which does converge and the estimation does not get off the ground.

For this reason, it appears necessary to begin with LI estimation and model simulation to locate a promising initial set of parameters. Movement towards maximum likelihood can then be achieved by iteration, as follows: (1) generate expectations (and equilibrium values) from the initial set of coefficients and compute their likelihood; (2) holding expectations and equilibrium values constant, run a standard FIML programme to convergence to obtain a new set of coefficients; (3) repeat steps (1) and (2) until the likelihood in step (1) is maximized (for more detail see Minford and Webb, 2001). Confidence limits can then be found by bootstrapping this FIML procedure.

We do not yet know how much difference it makes, especially in small samples, to use FI rather than LI estimation. Asymptotically (i.e. in large samples), standard errors should fall in moving from single equation to FIML estimation (West, 1986), for example, computes the asymptotic reduction in standard error for a small model as typically a rather small 20 per cent). Work on the Liverpool model in Minford and Webb (2001) indicates much bigger reductions for major structural parameters in preliminary work.

When structural coefficient estimates have been obtained the REH restriction can then be tested. However, this has not been done at all widely. The reason is that for LI estimates the test has hardly any power: the less restricted expectations merely imply a different group of first-step regressors and the test involved is the weak one of chi-squared on choice of instruments. Most RE models have been estimated by LI.

FIML estimates can test the restriction with considerable power. But so far such tests are not available. It is possible that, just as the over-identifying restrictions imposed by rational expectations force parameter values into a narrow range to achieve compatibility with all the data, so relaxing them by adopting backward-looking expectations may achieve a closer fit to the data. The question would then be posed: should one accept better fit at the expense of less demanding theory? Much would depend then on whether the loss of theory damaged the stability of relationships. It is possible that models will give worse in-sample fit under RE than under backward-looking expectations but their consistency with theory may also yield better out-of-sample (forecasting) stability.

VECTOR AUTOREGRESSION ESTIMATION OF MACRO MODELS

An increasingly popular way of estimating models, following Sims's (e.g. 1992) rejection of orthodox structural models as having 'incredible' identifying assumptions, is the VAR. In Sims's and his disciples' original methodology, the idea was to abandon normal identification altogether and simply estimate the unrestricted 'joint final form' of the endogenous variables of a model (in stationary form), treating the exogenous variables as error processes to be combined with 'structural' errors. Each endogenous variable would then be a function of its own and other variables' lagged values, once one had substituted out for the current period interaction with other endogenous variables. 'VAR identification' would then consist of deciding on a recursive ordering of the endogenous variables in the current period — for example, output might respond first, then prices. Then one can label the errors as 'the output error' and by subtracting from the other error this error's effect one can identify in the price residual the pure 'price error'.

To clarify matters, let us apply it to our simple example. If we take equations (8) and (9), difference them and substitute out for the exogenous processes we obtain the following equations in stationary variables and errors:

$$\Delta y_t = \alpha \Delta p_t - \alpha v_{t-1} - \frac{\alpha\beta}{\phi} w_{t-1} + \beta w_t + u_t^s - u_{t-1}^s \quad (13)$$

$$\Delta y_t = (\phi + \gamma) v_t - (\phi + \gamma) \Delta p_t - \frac{\gamma\beta}{\phi} w_t + u_t^d - u_{t-1}^d \quad (14)$$

Notice that the errors are in fact a mixture of structural and exogenous process errors: call them respectively $\in_t^s$and $\in_t^d$. In order to create the VAR where moving-average processes are ruled out in favour of autoregression for convenience of estimation, we represent the error processes as autoregressive:

$$\frac{\in_t^s}{1 - \rho_s L}, \frac{\in_p^d}{1 - \rho_d L} \quad (15)$$

Multiplying through by lag operator terms and substituting out for the current interactions we obtain the joint final form as:

$$\Delta y_t = \partial_1 \Delta y_{t-1} + \partial_2 \Delta p_{t-1} + \eta_t^y \quad (16)$$

$$\Delta p_t = \partial_3 \Delta y_{t-1} + \partial_4 \Delta p_{t-1} + \eta_t^p \quad (17)$$

where

$$\begin{aligned}
\partial_1 &= (\rho_s[\phi + \gamma] + \alpha\rho_d)/D \\
\partial_2 &= -\alpha[\phi + \gamma](\rho_s - \rho_d)/D \\
\partial_3 &= -(\rho_s - \rho_d)/D \\
\partial_4 &= (\alpha\rho_s - \rho_d[\phi + \gamma])/D \\
D &= \alpha + \phi + \gamma \\
\eta_t^y &= (\in_t^s [\phi + \gamma] + \alpha \in_t^d)/D \\
\eta_t^p &= [- \in_t^s + \in_t^d]/D
\end{aligned}$$

It is plain that VAR identification is now difficult since the two errors are mixtures of the shocks to output and prices.

One identification scheme that has been widely used was proposed by Blanchard and Quah (1989). This is to assume that only supply shocks (which we will here identify with $\in_t^s$) have a long-run effect on output; or in other words demand shocks have no long-run effect. To make the situation as favourable as possible, assume that both errors are actually changes in (permanent) demand and supply shocks; thus $\in_t^s = \Delta S_t$, $\in_t^d = \Delta D_t$ where S_t, D_t are permanent supply and demand shocks respectively. Then it is easy to see that the necessary restriction to prevent D_t affecting output in the long run is that $\alpha = 0$. In this case the error η_t^y in the output equation of the VAR, (15), is identifiable as the innovation in the supply shock. One can then attempt to disentangle the effect of this shock (using correlation analysis or some prior estimate of $\phi + \gamma$) from the error in the price equation and so identify the demand shock.

Clearly the Blanchard-Quah assumption is entirely justified (and of course emerges from our simple model). The problem lies in applying it in practice to the mongrel errors we have in this model. Our 'supply shock' composite is as (13) reveals not really the change in a permanent supply shock at all, but a mixture of that (Δu_t^s) with innovations, current and lagged, in money and productivity. It is for this reason that when we apply the constraint in practice, we get the obviously wrong result here that $\alpha = 0$, when of course plainly it is non-zero; the reason is that our error includes the lagged effect of errors on expected prices. While in more complex models it may be possible to make a better case for the practical method of applying such an identifying restriction, this simple example shows the potential pitfalls.

It has by now been widely recognized that somehow VAR models must be constrained by restrictions of the structural model so that sensible identification can be achieved and yet sufficient freedom be allowed for the joint final form to fit the data flexibly. This half-way house has for example taken the form of imposing the long-run restrictions of all the theory (through a set of cointegrating relationships) but allowing the short-run dynamics to be entirely unconstrained (Motto and Wickens, 2000). This takes somewhat further the Blanchard–Quah approach. This of course still leaves short-run impacts unidentified except by arbitrary assumptions about the recursive ordering of variables.

The dilemma for VAR proponents is that the more structure is imposed the less the data is incorporated flexibly in the estimated coefficients; while identification requires some theoretical structure, which is hard to impose in the flexible joint final form of the VAR. The resulting estimates of the VAR are hard to interpret, apart from being routinely vulnerable to the Lucas critique.

CONCLUSIONS

The rational expectations hypothesis is a modelling assumption. It does not assert that everyone everywhere always have rational expectations any more than the marginal utility hypothesis asserts that all consumers everywhere maximize utility at all times. Therefore tests of the hypothesis through surveys are, though interesting, not persuasive, since they check what certain groups (say they) think rather than what their and others' behaviour is in the market. A modelling assumption can only ultimately be tested, as Friedman (1953) has stressed, by testing the goodness of fit of the model, with and without it. Such a test is still not widely practised as it requires full systems estimation of a macro model with all the RE restrictions imposed and this has proved difficult in practice; we discuss some recent work implementing a new algorithm and bootstrap method for this purpose. VAR analysis is widely used to describe the lead-lag relationships between endogenous variables and the shocks driving them; but identification is a serious problem for interpreting these models as evidence for any particular expectations process or indeed for structural coefficients generally. We conclude with the suggestion that the best hope for estimating and testing a modern macro model and rational expectations is to use full systems methods along the lines sketched out here.

17

Where are we going?

This book has reviewed a huge body of work. In this brief last chapter we look at only one issue but the central one of this subject: how are macroeconomists today tackling the modelling of the economy, how does it compare with what went before and in what directions is it leading?

When the first edition of this book was written twenty years ago models of the economy contained backward-looking expectations and were large systems of demand and supply equations of the IS/LM/Phillips curve type. We reviewed them in Chapter 1 of this edition. We argued then that they were misspecified, mainly because of the lack of rational expectations. We were, however, quite doubtful of how much benefit would be derived from jettisoning the demand/supply curve set-up as well as the expectations assumption; the Lucas Critique suggested these curves could shift under relevant regime change but the evidence was mixed on the seriousness of such shifts for practical policy evaluation. But we agreed that the representative-agent and real-business-cycle research programme was exciting and could yield eventual results.

Two decades on, two contrasting things have happened. On the one hand representative-agent models have been developed in great numbers with a wide variety of assumptions about constraints (on cash and liquidity needs, notably), utility functions and investment technology. On the other hand we have seen the return of models with nominal rigidities based on Phillips curves with overlapping wage contracts, completed by an IS curve and an interest-rate setting rule for monetary policy — similar in many respects to the neo-Keynesian-synthesis models of Chapter 1. This is a paradox indeed. Adherents of the latter (Clarida et al., 1999) have proclaimed that these models now dominate the field as vehicles for the 'new science of monetary policy'. Proponents of the former are quietly contemptuous of such claims, since such models are nothing if not rough and ready aggregations of decision rules which will shift with regime change; policy evaluation could not credibly be based on them.

To which the response of these latter-day neo-Keynesians has been that their models do 'fit the facts' in recognisable traditional ways: R^2, predictive performance and so on. In terms of fit the representative-agent models have proffered the mimicing of unconditional moments in the data by the models — as opposed to the conditional moments stressed in the traditional methods. This has been fairly unconvincing to the bulk of the profession; policy makers have generally ignored these models as a result.

There has been another problem with these models. Their complexity is by now overwhelming — in a way that used to be levelled as a severe criticism at the large neo-Keynesian models of Chapter 1 ('too many equations for anyone to understand the reasons for what is going on'). These models are extremely large and nonlinear, posing problems of solution and possible multiplicity of equilibria that have not been tackled; virtually all practitioners ignore them, find a steady state, linearize around it, and then use heavy-duty mathematics to establish theorems about how the economy will behave over the business cycle. Yet these claims lack credibility when the models have not themselves been solved and the existence and stability of the possible equilibria have not been established.

It is not surprising perhaps in these circumstances that central bankers and Treasury officials have turned gratefully back to the new-look IS/LM/Phillips curve models they were brought up on and have now been told it is respectable again to use. Yet when one considers this as a basis for serious monetary policy regime choice, one cannot but be dubious. We have spent much time in this book examining why such methods are vulnerable. Monetary regimes underpin the length of nominal contracts themselves, and their degree of indexation; we pointed out in Chapter 6 that the issue of whether central banks should target the level of prices or the money supply may well turn precisely on these features of the environment.

Meanwhile, more or less orthogonally to this modelling aimed at policy regime analysis, we have burgeoning statistical modelling centred on vector autoregression (VAR) where, as we argued in the last chapter, there is restricted scope for convincing identification of structural coefficients. Essentially therefore this is a black-box forecasting methodology with limited use in policy analysis. Even as a description of 'the stylized facts' of the effects of shocks such as a monetary contraction on output and prices, it is unconvincing; the reason being that identification of the shocks in these equations is imposed from some scheme whose choice is a subjective matter for the researcher.

What this all adds up to is that while macroeconomics has been an exciting subject to be in during the past twenty years, it has failed yet to converge on any consensus of how to model economies or how to evaluate policy. Yet in spite of this there has been an extraordinary convergence in the area of monetary policy among both macroeconomists and policy makers: on the proposition that monetary policy's key role is to control prices, regardless of the short-term unpleasantness of the task. This was most decidely not the case twenty years ago; then Keynesians asserted in the teeth of monetarist fury, that 'core' inflation was too costly to bring down by monetary and supportive fiscal policies and that instead incomes and price controls should be used. Such views today would be unthinkable.

This suggests in the end that we have seen substantial progress in macroeconomic thinking on the crucial issue of how inflation is determined; here the rational expectations revolution was the key factor with its emphasis on the potential speed with which an inflation equilibrium could change in the face of a serious change of policy. We still have much work to do on how the business cycle is determined and how that in turn interacts with monetary policy.

Time-series annex: an introduction to linear and nonlinear time series

The purpose in this Annex is to provide an introduction to some of the relatively recent developments in time series which are becomingly standard in empirical analysis in macroeconomics and finance. We will not be concerned with statistical tests in this chapter. The interested reader can consult the references provided for these tests and a more detailed and formal analysis of the material we cover.

LINEAR TIME-SERIES MODELS

ARMA Processes

In chapter 2 we introduced the Wold decomposition as a method — the Muth method — of solving linear rational expectations models. We found that all variables in a linear model can be described by such a decomposition. For a variable y_t it is given by

$$y_t = \bar{y} + \sum_{i=0}^{\infty} \beta_i u_{t-i} \tag{1}$$

where $\overline{y}$ is a deterministic component assumed at this stage to be a constant and β_i are constants; the u_{t-i} are random variables which have zero expected value and constant variance and are assumed at this stage to be normally distributed and independent of all past information. Such an error process is called Gaussian white noise..

It is assumed that y_t is a covariance-stationary process so that its properties are unaffected by a change of starting date. This results in the mean, variance and the (auto) covariances of the series being constant.

Thus for y_t to be stationary for all values of t,

$$E(y_t) = \overline{y} \tag{2}$$

$$\text{var}(y_t) = E(y_t - \overline{y})^2 = \sigma_y^2 < \infty \tag{3}$$

$$\text{cov}(y_t y_{t+s}) = \text{cov}(y_t y_{t-s}) = E(y_t - \overline{y})(y_{t+s} - \overline{y}) = E(y_t - \overline{y})(y_{t-s} - \overline{y}) = \gamma_s \tag{4}$$

where in (2) $\overline{y}$ is the constant mean, in (3) σ^2 is the constant variance and in (4) γ_s is the constant s-order covariance. Notice in particular that the covariance between y_t and y_{t+s} depends only on s, the lead or lag between the two y values, and it is a measure of whether they move together. Also, the covariance for lag zero is the variance, γ_0. Naturally a series may have to be transformed by extracting a trend or differencing to induce stationarity and we shall see below the transformation required to induce stationarity has important implications.

Equation (1) is known as a moving-average (MA) error process. The order of a moving-average process is given by the maximum lagged error term so that $y_t = 2 + u_t + 0.1u_{t-1} - 0.01u_{t-50}$ is a moving-average error process of order fifty, MA(50).

We can also write a linear process in terms of its own past values. For a variable x_t we have

$$x_t = \bar{x} + \sum_{i=1}^{\infty} \alpha_i x_{t-i} + \epsilon_t \tag{5}$$

where $\overline{x}$ is a deterministic component, i.e. contains no random elements, such as a constant and or trend, α_i are constants and ϵ_t is a random variable.

Equation (5) is known as an autoregressive process (AR process). The order of an autoregressive process is given by the maximum lagged x term so that $x_t = 0.95x_{t-1} + 0.01x_{t-2} + \epsilon_t$ is an autoregressive process of order two, AR(2).

Consider the MA(1) process

$$y_t = \overline{y} + u_t + \beta_1 u_{t-1} \tag{6}$$

where $|\ \beta_1\ | < 1$

Employing the lag operator, L, we can write (6) as

$$y_t = \overline{y} + (1 + \beta_1 L)u_t \quad \text{or} \quad \frac{y_t - \overline{y}}{(1 + \beta_1 L)} = u_t \tag{7}$$

Expanding the polynomial in the lag operator, $\frac{1}{1+\beta_1 L} = 1+(-\beta_1 L)+\beta_1^2 L^2 + \left(-\beta_1^3\right) L^3 + \ldots$ we find that

$$y_t = \frac{\overline{y}}{1+\beta_1} + \beta_1 y_{t-1} - \beta_1^2 y_{t-2} + \beta_1^3 y_{t-3} + \ldots + u_t \qquad (8)$$

So we observe that the MA(1) process can be written as an AR(∞). More generally, assuming the MA polynomial can be inverted, any MA process can be rewritten as an infinite AR process.

Consider next the AR(1) process $x_t = \overline{x} + \alpha_1 x_{t-1} + \epsilon_t$. Employing the lag operator and the same procedure as above we can write the AR(1) process as an MA(∞)

$$x_t = \frac{\overline{x}}{1-\alpha_1} + \epsilon_t + \alpha_1 \epsilon_{t-1} + \alpha_1^2 \epsilon_{t-1} + \alpha_1^3 \epsilon_{t-3} + \ldots \qquad (9)$$

For empirical purposes we can model a series as a finite mixture of autoregressive and moving average components. Such a process is known as an ARMA process and for a series y_t is written as

$$y_t = y_0 + \alpha_1 y_{t-1} + \alpha_2 y_{t-2} + \alpha_3 y_{t-3} + \ldots + \alpha_p y_{t-p} + u_t + \beta_1 u_{t-1} + \beta_2 u_{t-2} + \beta_3 u_{t-3} + \ldots + \beta_q u_{t-q} \qquad (10)$$

where y_0 is a constant.

Equation(10) has p autoregressive terms and q moving average terms and is known as an ARMA(p, q).

Consequently the process $y_t = 2 + 0.5 y_{t-1} + u_t + 0.1 u_{t-1} - 0.01 u_{t-2}$ is an ARMA(1, 2). This process can also be rewritten as either an ARMA(∞, 0) or as an ARMA(0, ∞).

Any variable in a linear model has an ARMA(p, q) representation[1][2]. Naturally the ARMA representations of a variable will in general change if the policy regime changes, hence ARMA representations of endogenous

---

[1] For instance in the model (all standard notation)
$m_t = p_t + y_t$
$m_t = \overline{m} + \rho p_{t-1} + u_t$
$y_t = \overline{y} + a(p_t - E_{t-1} p_t) + \lambda y_{t-1}$
Assuming rational expectations we can obtain ARMA reduced forms for each of the variables where y_t is an ARMA(1,0), p_t is an ARMA(2,1) and m_t is an ARMA(2,2). We leave this as an exercise for the reader.

[2] We should note that care has to be taken empirically not to over-parameterize a process. For instance the process $y_t = 0.75 y_{t-1} - 0.1 y_{t-2} + u_t - 0.75 u_{t-1} + 0.1 u_{t-2}$ can be simplified to $y_t = u_t$ (since $1 - 0.75L + 0.1L^2$ is a common polynomial for the AR and MA processes.) Simple macro models typically imply ARMA representations for variables which are much more complicated than parsimoniously estimated processes. The fact that roots cancel, or near cancel, is probably the reason.

variables are naturally subject to the Lucas critique. Given this point however ARMA processes can be readily estimated using many statistical packages and are often employed to model exogenous variables in macroeconomic models as well as representing the 'naive' forecast in forecast comparisons.They have also been suggested as proxies for modelling expectations, e.g. Feige and Pierce (1976).

We defined in (4) above the (auto)covariance function. It is frequently more convenient to employ autocorrelations rather than covariances since autocorrelations vary between −1 and 1. They are simply the correlations between y_t and y_{t+s}, and are defined by

$$\rho_s = \frac{\gamma_s}{\gamma_0} \tag{11}$$

As s is varied the values of ρ_s trace out the autocorrelation function (ACF). For a white noise series, u_t, since each value is uncorrelated with every other value, all the autocorrelations $E(u_t u_{t+s})$ are zero for all $s \neq 0$, and as the mean and variance are constants, the series is stationary.

More generally, in the regression framework the autocorrelations are given by the coefficient in the regression

$$y_t = \rho_s y_{t-s} + \epsilon_t \tag{12}$$

where ϵ_t is the error process.

Another important property of a series is its partial autocorrelation function (PACF). This is possibly best explained in the context of regression. Consider the regression of y_t on $y_{t-1}$and y_{t-2}.

$$y_t = \phi_{12} y_{t-1} + \phi_{22} y_{t-2} + \epsilon_t \tag{13}$$

where the symbol ϵ_t is used for convenience again to denote the error process though it differs from that in (12). The first subscript on ϕ indicates the lag of the variable concerned (1 for y_{t-1}) and the second the maximum order of the regression (2 in this example). The coefficient on y_{t-2} is the partial autocorrelation coefficient since it indicates the partial or extra effect of adding y_{t-2} to the equation when y_{t-1} is already there. In the case of (13) it is the partial autocorrelation coefficient (PAC) of order 2. The first order PAC is given by

$$y_t = \phi_{11} y_{t-1} + \epsilon_t \tag{14}$$

and from comparison with (12) for $s = 1$ we observe that $\phi_{11} = \rho_1$. More generally, the PAC of order p is ϕ_{pp} in

$$y_t = \phi_{1p} y_{t-1} + \phi_{2p} y_{t-2} + \ldots + \phi_{pp} y_{t-p} + \epsilon_t \tag{15}$$

The properties of the ACF and PACF are important guides to determining the generation process for a series. If a variable is stationary a sample of data for y can be regarded as a sample of n observations from the underlying probability distribution of y. This means that we can use the data to estimate these parameters.The estimates based on a sample of n observations $y_1, y_2, \cdots, y_n$ are

$$\hat{\overline{y}} = \frac{\sum y}{n} \tag{16}$$

$$\hat{\sigma}^2 = \frac{\sum (y_t - \hat{\overline{y}})^2}{n-1} \tag{17}$$

$$\hat{\gamma}_s = \frac{\sum (y_t - \hat{\overline{y}})((y_{t+s} - \hat{\overline{y}})}{n-s} \tag{18}$$

Theoretical Autocorrelations and Partial Autocorrelations

Consider the MA(1) process

$$y_t = \overline{y} + u_t + \beta u_{t-1} \tag{19}$$

where u_t is a random variable defined as in (1). The expectation of y_t is given by

$$E(y_t) = E(\overline{y} + u_t + \beta u_{t-1}) = \overline{y} + E(u_t) + \beta E(u_{t-1}) = \overline{y} \tag{20}$$

The variance of y_t is

$$\begin{aligned} E(y_t - \overline{y})^2 = E(u_t + \beta u_{t-1})^2 &= E(u_t^2 + 2\beta u_t u_{t-1} + \beta^2 u_{t-1}^2) \\ &= \sigma^2 + 0 + \beta^2\sigma^2 = (1+\beta^2)\sigma^2 \end{aligned} \tag{21}$$

where σ^2 is $E(u_t)^2$, the variance of u_t. The first autocovariance is

$$\begin{aligned} E(y_t - \overline{y})(y_{t-1} - \overline{y}) &= E(u_t + \beta u_{t-1})(u_{t-1} + \beta u_{t-2}) \\ &= E(u_t u_{t-1} + \beta u_t u_{t-2} + \beta u_{t-1}^2 + \beta^2 u_{t-1} u_{t-2}) = \beta\sigma^2 \end{aligned} \tag{22}$$

Higher autocovariances are all zero:

$$E(y_t - \overline{y})(y_{t-s} - \overline{y}) = E(u_t + \beta u_{t-1})(u_{t-s} + \beta u_{t-s-1}) = 0 \quad (s > 1) \tag{23}$$

From the definition of the autocorrelation (11)

$$\rho_1 = \frac{\gamma_1}{\gamma_0} = \frac{\beta\sigma^2}{(1+\beta^2)\sigma^2} = \frac{\beta}{(1+\beta^2)} \tag{24}$$

Higher autocorrelations are all zero.
For the qth order MA(q) process

$$y_t = \overline{y} + u_t + \beta_1 u_{t-1} + \beta_2 u_{t-2} + \ldots + \beta_q u_{t-q} \tag{25}$$

The mean of (25) is given by

$$Ey_t = \overline{y} + E(u_t) + \beta_1 E(u_{t-1}) + \beta_2 E(u_{t-2}) + - \ldots + \beta_q E(u_{t-q}) = \overline{y} \tag{26}$$

The variance of the MA(q) process is given by

$$\gamma_0 = E(y_t - \overline{y})^2 = E(u_t + \beta_1 u_{t-1} + \beta_2 u_{t-2} + \ldots + \beta_q u_{t-q})$$
$$(u_t + \beta_1 u_{t-1} + \beta_2 u_{t-2} + \ldots + \beta_q u_{t-q}) \tag{27}$$

since the us are uncorrelated so that $E(u_t u_{t-s}) = 0$ for $s > 1$

$$\gamma_0 = E(y_t - \overline{y})^2 = \sigma^2 + \beta_1^2\sigma^2 + \beta_2^2\sigma^2 + \ldots + \beta_q^2\sigma^2 =$$
$$(1 + \beta_1^2 + \beta_2^2 + \ldots + \beta_q^2)\sigma^2 \tag{28}$$

The autocovariances are given by

$$\gamma_s = E(y_t - \overline{y})(y_{t-s} - \overline{y}) = E(u_t + \beta_1 u_{t-1} + \beta_2 u_{t-2} + \ldots + \beta_q u_{t-q})$$
$$(u_{t-s} + \beta_1 u_{t-s-1} + \beta_2 u_{t-s-2} + \ldots + \beta_q u_{t-s-q}) \tag{29}$$

The cross terms all have expectation zero so (29) gives

$$\gamma_s = E(y_t - \overline{y})(y_{t-s} - \overline{y}) = E(\beta_s u_{t-s}^2 + \beta_{s+1}\beta_1 u_{t-s-1}^2$$
$$+ \beta_{s+2}\beta_2 u_{t-s-2}^2 + \ldots + \beta_q \beta_{q-s} u_{t-q}^2) \tag{30}$$

so that

$$\gamma_s = (\beta_s + \beta_{s+1}\beta_1 + \beta_{s+2}\beta_2 + \ldots + \beta_q\beta_{q-s})\sigma^2 \text{ for } s = 1, 2, \ldots, q \tag{31}$$

$\gamma_s = 0$ for $s > q$

For example, consider the MA(3) process, $y_t = \overline{y} + u_t + \beta_1 u_{t-1} + \beta_2 u_{t-2} + \beta_3 u_{t-3}$. In it:

$$\begin{aligned} \gamma_0 &= (1 + \beta_1^2 + \beta_2^2 + \beta_3^2)\sigma^2 \\ \gamma_1 &= (1 + \beta_1 + \beta_2\beta_1 + \beta_3\beta_2)\sigma^2 \end{aligned}$$

$$\begin{aligned}\gamma_2 &= (1+\beta_2+\beta_3\beta_1)\sigma^2\\ \gamma_3 &= (\beta_3)\sigma^2\\ \gamma_4 &= \gamma_5 = \ldots = 0\end{aligned}$$

so that

$$\begin{aligned}\rho_1 &= \frac{\gamma_1}{\gamma_0} = \frac{(1+\beta_1+\beta_2\beta_1+\beta_3\beta_2)}{(1+\beta_1^2+\beta_2^2+\beta_3^2)}\\ \rho_2 &= \frac{\gamma_2}{\gamma_0} = \frac{(1+\beta_2+\beta_3\beta_1)}{(1+\beta_1^2+\beta_2^2+\beta_3^2)}\\ \rho_3 &= \frac{\gamma_3}{\gamma_0} = \frac{(\beta_3)}{(1+\beta_1^2+\beta_2^2+\beta_3^2)}\\ \rho_4 &= \rho_5 = \ldots = 0\end{aligned}$$

Autoregressive Processes

Consider the AR(1) process

$$y_t = y_0 + \alpha_1 y_{t-1} + u_t \tag{32}$$

where u_t is a random white noise error process and $\mid \alpha_1 \mid < 1$.

Writing (32) as an infinite MA process we have

$$y_t = \frac{y_0}{1-\alpha} + u_t + \alpha_1 u_{t-1} + \alpha_1^2 u_{t-2} + \alpha_1^3 u_{t-3} + \ldots \tag{33}$$

Consequently the mean of (33) is

$$E(y_t) = E\left(\frac{y_0}{1-\alpha_1} + u_t + \alpha_1 u_{t-1} + \alpha_1^2 u_{t-2} + \alpha_1^3 u_{t-3} + \ldots\right) = \frac{y_0}{1-\alpha_1} = \overline{y} \tag{34}$$

The variance is given by

$$\gamma_0 = E(y_t - \overline{y})^2 = E(u_t + \alpha_1 u_{t-1} + \alpha_1^2 u_{t-2} + \alpha_1^3 u_{t-3} + \ldots)^2 \tag{35}$$

so that

$$\gamma_0 = E(y_t - \overline{y})^2 = E(1 + \alpha_1^2 + \alpha_1^4 + \alpha_1^6 + \ldots) \tag{36}$$

therefore since $\frac{1}{1-\alpha_1^2} = 1 + \alpha_1^2 + \alpha_1^4 + \alpha_1^6 + \ldots$

$$\gamma_0 = E(y_t - \overline{y})^2 = \frac{\sigma^2}{1-\alpha_1^2} \tag{37}$$

(37) illustrates why the condition $|\alpha_1| < 1$ is required for stationarity.

The sth autocovariance is given by

$$\gamma_s = E(y_t - \overline{y})(y_{t-s} - \overline{y}) = \\ E(u_t + \alpha_1 u_{t-1} + \alpha_1^2 u_{t-2} + \ldots + \alpha_1^s u_{t-s} + \alpha_1^{s+1} u_{t-s-1} \ldots) \\ (u_{t-s} + \alpha_1 u_{t-s-1} + \alpha_1^2 u_{t-s-2} + \alpha_1^3 u_{t-s-3} + \ldots) \quad (38)$$

so that

$$\gamma_s = E(y_t - \overline{y})(y_{t-s} - \overline{y}) = (\alpha_1^s + \alpha_1^{s+2} + \alpha_1^{s+4} + \ldots)\sigma^2 = \\ \alpha^s(1 + \alpha_1^2 + \alpha_1^4 + \ldots) \quad (39)$$

therefore

$\gamma_s = E(y_t - \overline{y})(y_{t-s} - \overline{y}) = \frac{\alpha_1^s \sigma^2}{1-\alpha_1^2}$

As a consequence the s-autocorrelation is given from (39) and (37) by

$$\rho_s = \frac{\gamma_s}{\gamma_0} = \frac{\frac{\alpha_1^s \sigma^2}{1-\alpha_1^2}}{\frac{\sigma^2}{1-\alpha_1^2}} = \alpha_1^s \quad (40)$$

Consequently the autocorrelation function follows a pattern of geometric decay.

Rather than employing the infinite moving-average representation to derive these properties we could have assumed that the process was stationary and proceeded directly as follows.

Taking expectations of (32)

$$E(y_t) = y_0 + \alpha_1 E(y_{t-1}) + E(u_t) \quad (41)$$

Letting $E(y_t) = \overline{y} = E(y_{t-1})$ we have

$$\overline{y} = y_0 + \alpha_1 \overline{y} + 0 \quad (42)$$

or

$$\overline{y} = \frac{y_0}{1 - \alpha_1} \quad (43)$$

Similarly the variance is obtained by substituting (42) into (32) to obtain

$$y_t = \overline{y}(1 - \alpha_1) + \alpha_1 y_{t-1} + u_t \quad (44)$$

or

$$y_t - \overline{y} = \alpha_1(y_{t-1} - \overline{y}) + u_t \tag{45}$$

If we square both sides of (45) and take expectations:

$$E(y_t - \overline{y})^2 = \alpha_1^2 E(y_{t-1} - \overline{y})^2 + 2\alpha_1 E((y_{t-1} - \overline{y})u_t) + Eu_t^2 \tag{46}$$

Since u_t is uncorrelated with y_{t-1} (which is a summation of shocks at $t-1$ and before from (33)), we obtain from (46) that

$$E(y_t - \overline{y})^2 = \alpha_1^2 E(y_{t-1} - \overline{y})^2 + \sigma^2 \tag{47}$$

The assumption of stationarity implies that

$$E(y_t - \overline{y})^2 = E(y_{t-1} - \overline{y})^2 = \gamma_0 \tag{48}$$

so that the variance of y_t is given by

$$\gamma_0 = E(y_t - \overline{y})^2 = \frac{\sigma^2}{1 - \alpha_1^2} \tag{49}$$

Also multiplying (45) by $y_{t-s} - \overline{y}$ and taking expectations we can obtain the autocovariance function

$$\gamma_s = E(y_t - \overline{y})(y_{t-s} - \overline{y}) = \alpha_1 E(y_{t-1} - \overline{y})(y_{t-s} - \overline{y}) + E(u_t)(y_{t-s} - \overline{y}) \tag{50}$$

The last term on the right-hand side of (50) has zero expectation and using the fact that $t - s = t - 1 - (s - 1)$ implies that the first term on the right-hand side of (50) is $E(y_{t-1} - \overline{y})(y_{t-1-(s-1)} - \overline{y})$ which is the $s - 1$ autocovariance of y_t. Consequently (50) simplifies to

$$\gamma_s = \alpha_1 \gamma_{s-1} \tag{51}$$

This difference equation has the solution

$$\gamma_s = \alpha_1^s \gamma_0 \tag{52}$$

(52) is the solution (40).

We next consider the AR(2) process

$$y_t = y_0 + \alpha_1 y_{t-1} + \alpha_2 y_{t-2} + u_t \tag{53}$$

Using the procedures above, so that we once again assume stationarity,

$$E(y_t) = y_0 + \alpha_1 E(y_{t-1}) + \alpha_2 E(y_{t-2}) + E(u_t) \tag{54}$$

and

$$E(y_t) = E(y_{t-1}) = E(y_{t-2}) = \overline{y} \tag{55}$$

so that

$$E(y_t) = \frac{y_0}{1-\alpha_1-\alpha_2} = \overline{y} \tag{56}$$

Rewriting (53) using (56) we obtain

$$y_t - \overline{y} = \alpha_1(y_{t-1} - \overline{y}) + \alpha_2(y_{t-2} - \overline{y}) + u_t \tag{57}$$

Following the procedure for the AR(1) case we multiply (57) by $y_{t-s} - \overline{y}$ and take expectations to obtain

$$\gamma_s = \alpha_1\gamma_{s-1} + \alpha_2\gamma_{s-2} \tag{58}$$

Consequently we observe that the autocovariances follow the same process as the the autoregressive process. Restrictions on α_1 and α_2 are required to ensure stationarity.

The autocorrelations are obtained by dividing (58) by γ_0. We obtain

$$\rho_s = \alpha_1\rho_{s-1} + \alpha_2\rho_{s-2} \tag{59}$$

For $s = 1$ we obtain

$$\rho_1 = \alpha_1\rho_0 + \alpha_2\rho_{-1} \tag{60}$$

ρ_{-1}, the autocorrelation one period ahead, is the same as ρ_1 by the assumption of stationarity and $\rho_0 = 1$ (the autocorrelation of a variable with itself), hence $\rho_1 = \alpha_1\rho_0 + \alpha_2\rho_1$ so that

$$\rho_1 = \frac{\alpha_1}{1-\alpha_2} \tag{61}$$

For $s = 2$,

$$\rho_2 = \alpha_1\rho_1 + \alpha_2 \tag{62}$$

To calculate the variance we multiply (57) through by $y_t - \overline{y}$ and take expectations to obtain

$$E(y_t - \overline{y})^2 = \alpha_1 E(y_t - \overline{y})(y_{t-1} - \overline{y}) + \alpha_2 E(y_t - \overline{y})(y_{t-2} - \overline{y}) + E(y_t - \overline{y})(u_t) \tag{63}$$

so that

$$\gamma_0 = \alpha_1\gamma_1 + \alpha_2\gamma_2 + \sigma^2 \tag{64}$$

where $\sigma^2 = E(y_t - \overline{y})(u_t)$ since $y_t = u_t +$ linear terms in lagged ys which are uncorrelated with u_t.

We write (64) using definitions of ρ_1 and ρ_2 in terms of γ_0, γ_1 as

$$\gamma_0 = \alpha_1 \rho_1 \gamma_0 + \alpha_2 \rho_2 \gamma_0 + \sigma^2 \tag{65}$$

Substituting from (61) and (62) into (65) we obtain

$$\gamma_0 = \alpha_1 \left(\frac{\alpha_1}{1-\alpha_2} \right) \gamma_0 + \alpha_2 \left(\alpha_1 \frac{\alpha_1}{1-\alpha_2} + \alpha_2 \right) \gamma_0 + \sigma^2 \tag{66}$$

which simplifies to

$$\gamma_0 (1 - \alpha_2 - \alpha_1^2 - \alpha_2 \alpha_1^2 - \alpha_2^2 + \alpha_2^3) = (1 - \alpha_2)\sigma^2$$

which can be rewritten as

$$\gamma_0 = E(y_t - \overline{y})^2 = \frac{\sigma^2 (1-\alpha_2)}{(1+\alpha_2)[(1-\alpha_2)^2 - \alpha_1^2]} \tag{67}$$

Pth Order Autoregressive Process and General ARMA Processes

The mean, variance and autocovariance function for the pth order AR(p) process can be obtained in a similar manner to the above though the mathematics is more difficult — see Hamilton (1994).

The key property is that the autocorrelations and autocovariances follow the same process as the AR(p) process, known as the Yule-Walker equations. Consequently the autocorrelations are given by

$$\rho_s = \alpha_1 \rho_{s-1} + \alpha_2 \rho_{s-2} + \alpha_3 \rho_{s-3} + \ldots \alpha_p \rho_{s-p} \tag{68}$$

The solution of this difference equation will give p roots if they are distinct. Consequently the autocorrelations can display a variety of patterns, dependent upon the signs of the roots and whether they are complex, but they will decay over time.

For the ARMA(p, q) process the autocorrelations will be given by the Yule-Walker conditions, i.e the pattern of coefficients governing the AR(p) component but only for $s>q$. Up to this point moving-average terms will induce more complicated patterns in the autocorrelations than the pure AR(p) process.

Finally in this section we illustrate diagrammatically the time-series behaviour of a few ARMA processes. In figures 18.1a-f we plot the realizations of a variety of processes. The random error term is drawn from a random number generator that has a normal distribution and is Gaussian white noise (see footnote 3 for the definition). The standard deviation of the error is 1. We set the initial values of y_0, y_1 at zero and simulated 1000 observations of each process. The realizations from observations 600–1000 are plotted in the figures. The ACF and PACF are also reported for the first ten lags of the processes. If the sample size (n) is large, the estimated individual autocorrelations and partial autocorrelations have a standard error of approximately $\frac{1}{\sqrt{n}}$ and their significance can be tested using a normal distribution ($\frac{1}{\sqrt{n}}$ is approximately 0.05 for our data sets). In figure 18.1a we plot the random variable. Each of the autocorrelations is not significantly different from zero as would be expected from theoretical considerations. Figure 18.1b plots an MA(1) process with coefficient −0.6 which appears somewhat more spiked than the white noise process.The ACF is significant at order 1, consistently with the theoretical result above. The PACF is significant at orders 1 and 2. If we recall that the MA(1) can be written as an AR(∞), the insignificance of coefficients in the PACF after order 2 informs us the series can be well approximated by an AR(2).

Figure 18.1c is a plot of an AR(1) process with coefficient 0.9. The plot exhibits an outcome that looks fairly cyclical. The ACF declines relatively slowly and the PACF has a significant coefficient at order one; the remaining coefficients are insignificant. As the AR(1) coefficient declines the waves become more choppy. This is illustrated in figure 18.1d with an AR coefficient of 0.5. For this case the ACF does not decline geometrically as theoretically predicted. This is the result of sampling error. The PACF exhibits one significant coefficient at order 1. In figures 18.1e and 1f we plot an ARMA(1, 1), with coefficients AR(0.9) MA(−0.25); and an AR(2), with coefficients 1.3 and −0.4, which are close to those found for some aggregate macro time series. The series exhibit similar cyclical behaviour though the amplitude is different. For the ARMA(1, 1) case the ACF declines slowly and the PACF is significant at order 1 and 2. For the AR(2) the ACF and PACF exhibit similar qualitative features.

In practice we look at the ACF and PACF which may be suggestive of the type of process to estimate. More generally we estimate models with smallish values of p and q and use diagnostic measures to choose between the models and to see if the model is in need of modification (see e.g. Hamilton (1994), Franses and Van Dijk (2000), Mills (1993).

NONLINEAR TIME SERIES MODELS:

Structural economic models are typically a mixture of linear and nonlinear structural equations. Budget constraints for instance are nonlinear

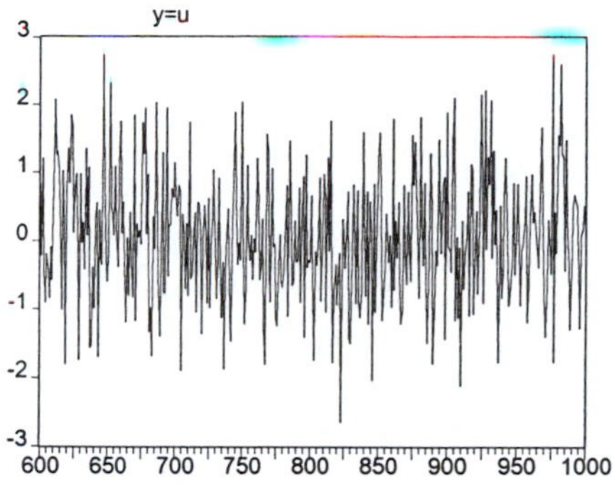

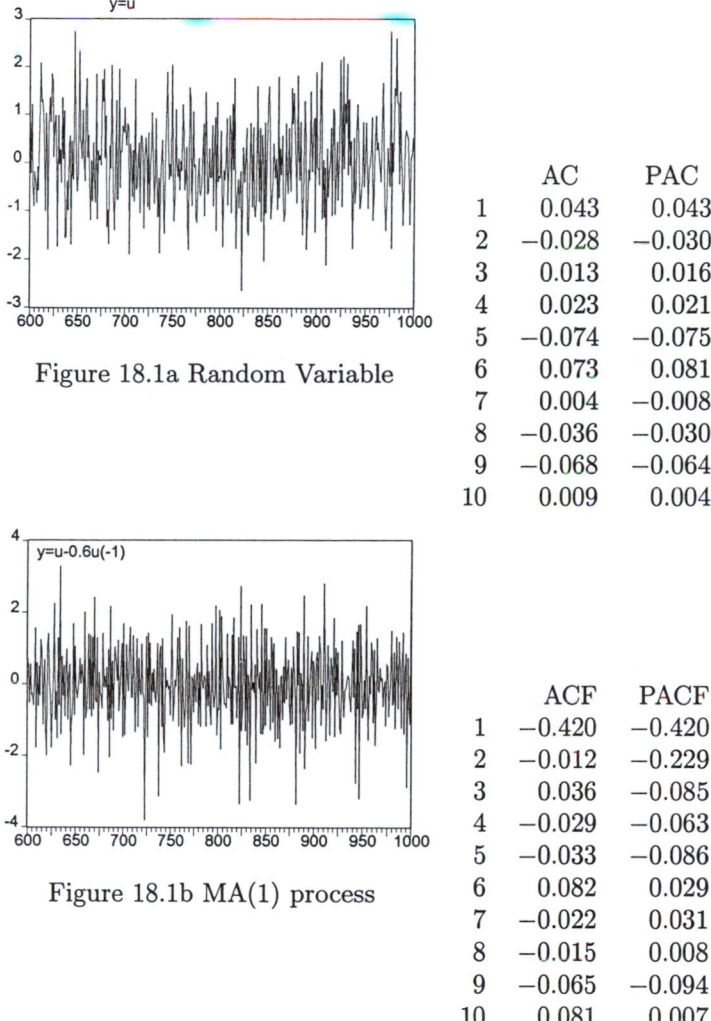

Figure 18.1a Random Variable

	AC	PAC
1	0.043	0.043
2	−0.028	−0.030
3	0.013	0.016
4	0.023	0.021
5	−0.074	−0.075
6	0.073	0.081
7	0.004	−0.008
8	−0.036	−0.030
9	−0.068	−0.064
10	0.009	0.004

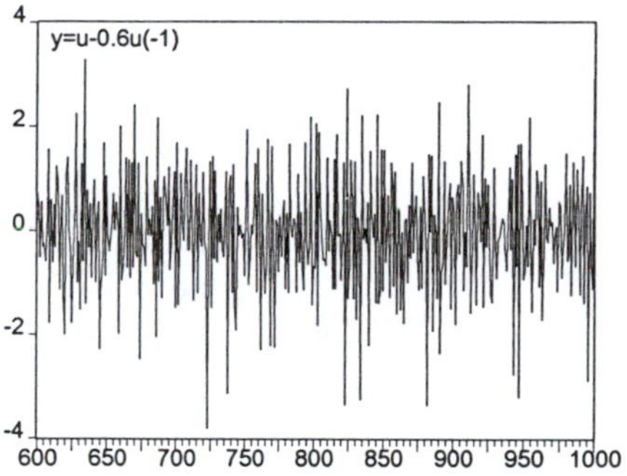

Figure 18.1b MA(1) process

	ACF	PACF
1	−0.420	−0.420
2	−0.012	−0.229
3	0.036	−0.085
4	−0.029	−0.063
5	−0.033	−0.086
6	0.082	0.029
7	−0.022	0.031
8	−0.015	0.008
9	−0.065	−0.094
10	0.081	0.007

Figure 18.1: Pth order autoregressive processes

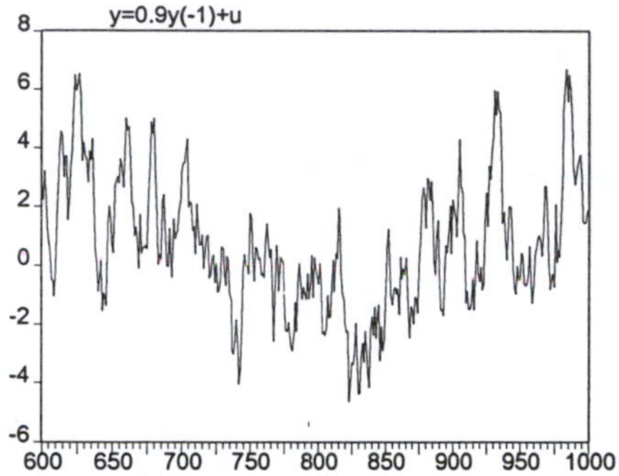

Figure 18.1c AR(1) process, $\rho = 0.9$

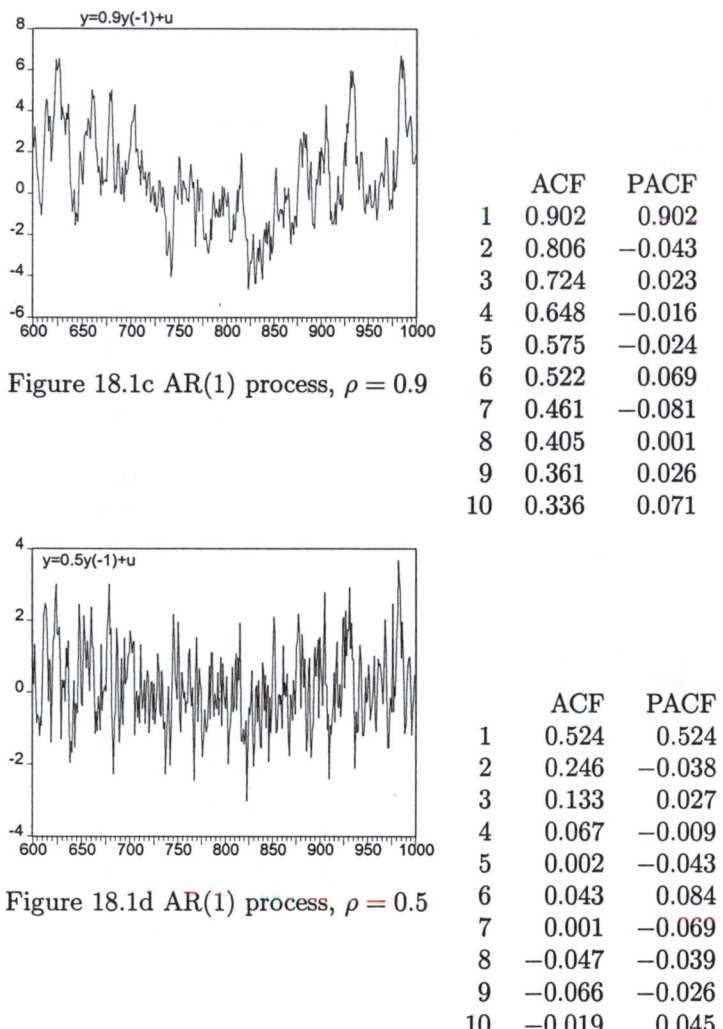

	ACF	PACF
1	0.902	0.902
2	0.806	−0.043
3	0.724	0.023
4	0.648	−0.016
5	0.575	−0.024
6	0.522	0.069
7	0.461	−0.081
8	0.405	0.001
9	0.361	0.026
10	0.336	0.071

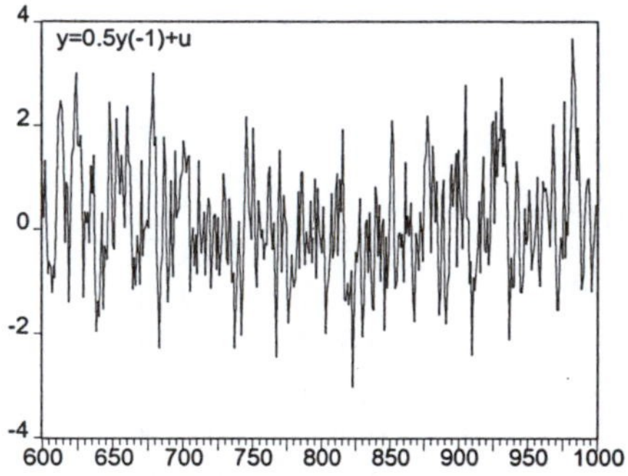

Figure 18.1d AR(1) process, $\rho = 0.5$

	ACF	PACF
1	0.524	0.524
2	0.246	−0.038
3	0.133	0.027
4	0.067	−0.009
5	0.002	−0.043
6	0.043	0.084
7	0.001	−0.069
8	−0.047	−0.039
9	−0.066	−0.026
10	−0.019	0.045

Figure 18.1: Pth order autoregressive processes (continued)

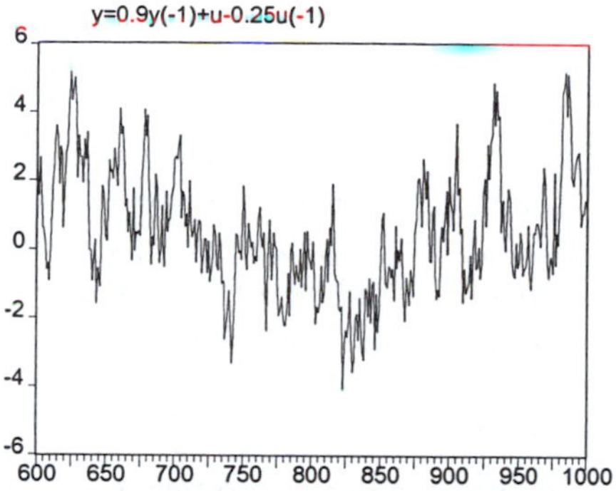

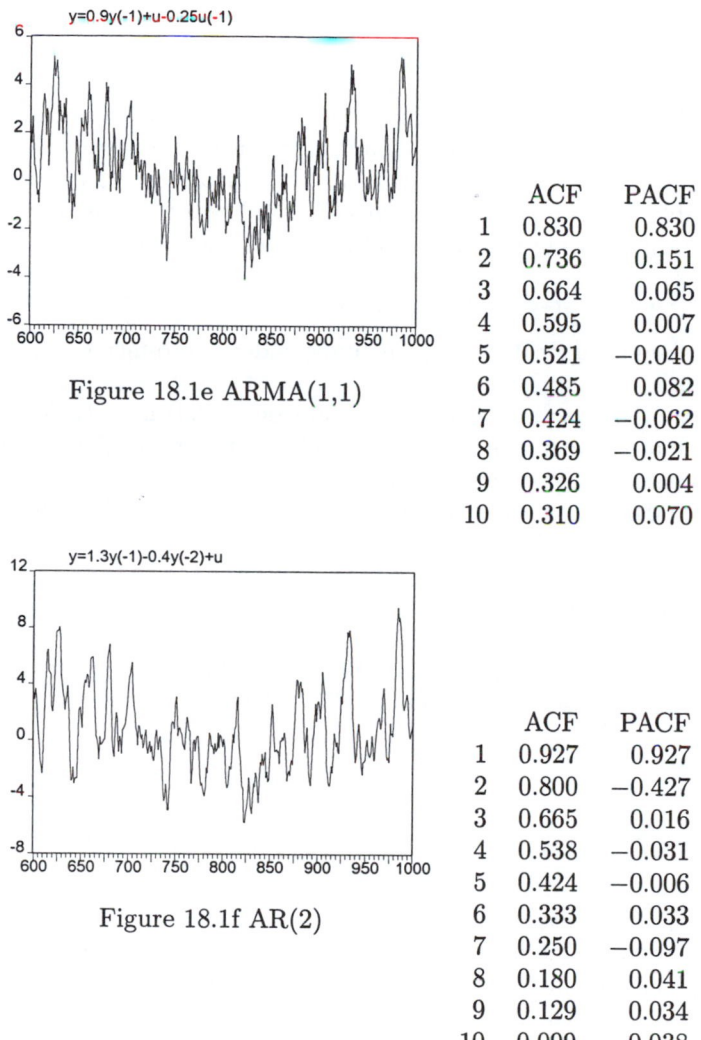

Figure 18.1e ARMA(1,1)

	ACF	PACF
1	0.830	0.830
2	0.736	0.151
3	0.664	0.065
4	0.595	0.007
5	0.521	−0.040
6	0.485	0.082
7	0.424	−0.062
8	0.369	−0.021
9	0.326	0.004
10	0.310	0.070

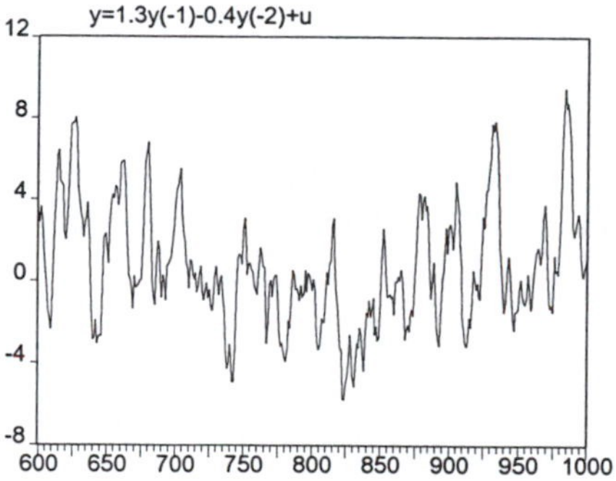

Figure 18.1f AR(2)

	ACF	PACF
1	0.927	0.927
2	0.800	−0.427
3	0.665	0.016
4	0.538	−0.031
5	0.424	−0.006
6	0.333	0.033
7	0.250	−0.097
8	0.180	0.041
9	0.129	0.034
10	0.099	0.038

Figure 18.1: *P*th order autoregressive processes (continued)

(in that they include the products of variables). In addition where fixed costs of adjustment are incurred agents may respond to shocks that drive them from equilibrium in a nonlinear manner, that is do nothing until it is worthwhile incurring the fixed cost. It would perhaps be surprising if the time-series behaviour of macroeconomic variables could, in general, be well approximated by ARMA processes. In recent years there has been a great deal of empirical work on this issue.

An infinite number of nonlinear models can be proposed. In order to make progress, various simplifying assumptions have to be made. Analogous to the ARMA(p, q) representation of a variable, we can assume that a variable can be explained in terms of a nonlinear function of finite number of past values of realizations of outcomes and shocks.

$$y_t = h(y_{t-1}, y_{t-2}, y_{t-3}, \dots, y_{t-p}, u_{t-1}, u_{t-2}, \dots, u_{t-q}) + u_t \tag{69}$$

where we assume again the u_{t-i} are independent zero-mean random variables.

Priestley (1988) expands the right-hand side of (69) as a Taylor series expansion to order one about an arbitrary but fixed time point. By further restrictions on this expansion, he obtains various 'classes' of nonlinear models.We consider the most frequently employed nonlinear models obtained from this procedure.

The Bilinear Model

Bilinear models were introduced into the statistical literature by Granger and Andersen (1978) and Subba-Rao (1981). The bilinear model is given by

$$y_t = \sum_{i=1}^{p} \alpha_i y_{t-i} + \sum_{i=1}^{q} \beta_i u_{t-i} + \sum_{i=1}^{m} \sum_{j=1}^{k} \theta_{ij} y_{t-i} u_{t-j} + u_t \tag{70}$$

where the α_i, β_i and θ_{ij} are constant.

We observe that the bilinear model has a linear ARMA component and is supplemented by terms which represent interactions between past noise and past ys, such as $y_{t-1}u_{t-2}$, $y_{t-3}u_{t-1}$.

A simple case of a bilinear model is the first-order model

$$y_t = y_0 + \alpha_1 y_{t-1} + u_t + \theta_{11} y_{t-1} u_{t-1} \tag{71}$$

In this model is y_t is stationary if $\alpha_1^2 + \theta_{11}^2 < 1$. The mean of the process is given by

$$Ey_t = \frac{y_0 + \theta_{11}\sigma^2}{1 - \alpha_1} \tag{72}$$

where σ^2 is the variance of u. Expressions for the variance and covariances are more complex to work out — see Priestley(1988).

Brockett (1976) demonstrates that the bilinear model can approximate a wide class of nonlinear relatioships to an arbitrary degree of accuracy over a finite time horizon. The bilinear model does not however capture certain types of cyclical behaviour such as limit cycles (see below). It does capture series which exhibit 'bursts' of large amplitude or spiking behaviour.

Some realizations of bilinear processes are shown in figures 18.2a-c. In each case u is normal with a mean of 0 and a standard deviation of 1. Initial values of lagged y were set at zero and the first 600 observations discarded. The ACF and PACF are reported to illustrate the (misleading) 'linear properties' of the series. Figure 18.2b taken from Priestley (1988) is particularly graphic, illustrating a 'burst of large amplitude'. y does not have constant values in the figure but the compression makes it appear so. The other figures illustrate the spiking effect that bilinear processes can produce. Bilinear processes have not been employed very much in economics. This is perhaps because the model is not obviously derivable from an economic model. Maravall (1983) and Peel and Speight (1998)) provide examples of its use in modelling economic data.

Threshold and Smooth Transition Threshold models

As demonstrated by a number of authors — e.g. Dumas (1992), Caballero and Engel (1992) — when agents face fixed adjustment or transactions costs adjustment to equilibrium will not be linear. Rather there will be a 'band of inertia' followed by action which will depend on the precise specification of adjustment or transactions costs. More generally we can think of variables behaving differently, so that some of their properties, such as mean and variance, differ in different regimes or states of the world, like slumps or booms.

One form which can be obtained from the Taylor approximation of (69) is a generalization of the linear AR model given by

$$y_t = y_0(s_t) + \alpha_1(s_t)y_{t-1} + \alpha_2(s_t)y_{t-2} + \ldots + \alpha_p(s_t)y_{t-p} + u_t \tag{73}$$

where $y_0(s_t)$, $\alpha_1(s_t)$, $\alpha_2(s_t), \ldots, \alpha_p(s_t)$ are functions of states or regimes.

Threshold models proposed by Tong (1990)) and their extensions, the smooth-transition threshold models, are one important class of such

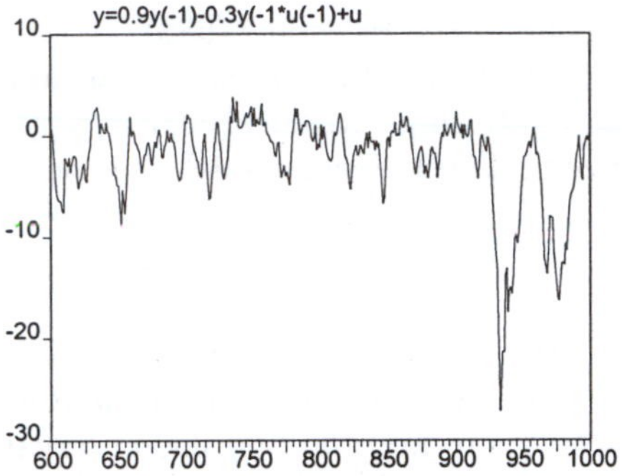

Figure 18.2a Realization of bilinear process

	AC	PAC
1	0.946	0.946
2	0.867	−0.264
3	0.787	0.009
4	0.705	−0.088
5	0.636	0.106
6	0.582	0.041
7	0.525	−0.111
8	0.468	−0.015
9	0.418	0.018
10	0.373	0.032

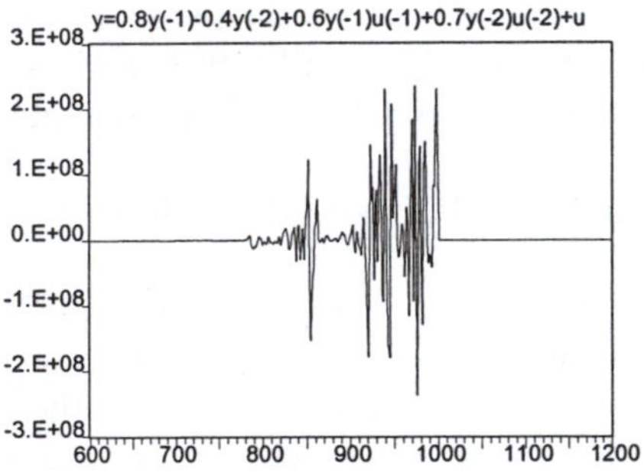

Figure 18.2b Realization of bilinear process

	AC	PAC
1	0.564	0.564
2	−0.110	−0.628
3	−0.306	0.359
4	−0.169	−0.350
5	−0.016	0.266
6	0.045	−0.253
7	−0.035	−0.031
8	−0.142	−0.016
9	−0.067	0.124
10	0.100	−0.107

Figure 18.2: Bilinear model

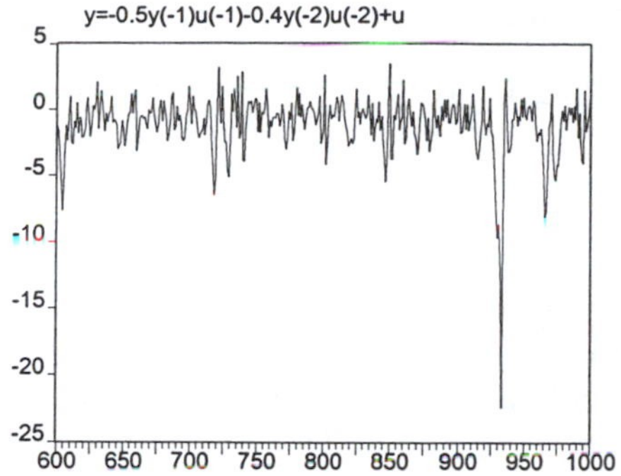

Figure 18.2c Realization of bilinear process

	AC	PAC
1	0.619	0.619
2	0.299	−0.137
3	0.171	0.075
4	0.137	0.041
5	0.094	−0.018
6	0.086	0.052
7	0.064	−0.019
8	0.048	0.013
9	0.018	−0.029
10	0.033	0.050

Figure 18.2: Bilinear model (continued)

models which have been extensively employed in economics and finance. In these models the state s is modelled as a function of observed variable(s), say x_t. The Threshold Autoregressive (TAR) model of Tong assumes that the state is determined by the value of x_t relative to a constant threshold value, λ. When the x_t is a previous value of y, so that $x_t = y_{t-d}$, where d is an integer greater than zero, the process was called by Tong a Self-Exciting TAR (SETAR) model.

One example of such a model is the three-regime SETAR model

$$y_t = \overline{y}_0 + \alpha_{01} y_{t-1} + u_{0t} \quad \text{if} \quad y_{t-1} < -\lambda$$

$$y_t = \overline{y}_1 + \alpha_{11} y_{t-1} + u_{1t} \quad \text{if} \quad -\lambda \le y_{t-1} \le \lambda \tag{74}$$

$$y_t = \overline{y}_2 + \alpha_{21} y_{t-1} + u_{2t} \quad \text{if} \quad y_{t-1} > \lambda$$

where the u are assumed at this stage to be Gaussian random variables.

If we interpret λ as a transaction cost and set the constants $\overline{y}_0$, $\overline{y}_1$, $\overline{y}_2$ to zero, and $\alpha_{01} = \alpha_{21} = 0$, $\alpha_{11} = 1$, $u_{0t} = u_{2t}$. We would obtain a TAR model which might represent the behaviour of an arbitraged variable. For instance suppose y_t was the deviation from covered interest arbitrage. We might suppose that within the transactions band the deviation is a random walk so that $y_t = y_{t-1} + u_{1t}$. Outside the transactions band arbitrage would make y_t a random variable, possibly with very low error variance.

Another example is the two-regime model

$$y_t = \overline{y}_0 + \alpha_{01} y_{t-1} + \alpha_{02} y_{t-2} + \alpha_{03} y_{t-3} + u_{0t} \text{ if } y_{t-2} \leq \lambda$$

$$y_t = \overline{y}_1 + \alpha_{11} y_{t-1} + u_{2t} \text{ if } y_{t-2} > \lambda \tag{75}$$

TAR models can exhibit many interesting properties. If we 'switch the noise off', i.e. put the random terms to zero and simulate the deterministic component of the model (called the skeleton by Tong), the resulting nonlinear difference equations can generate cyclical behaviour, including asymmetric cycles, that is cycles of different length, as well as chaos (see below). This is also a feature shared by an extension of the threshold models known as smooth transition models.

A smooth transition model has the form

$$y_t = \sum_{i=1}^{p} \alpha_i y_{t-i} + (1 - F_t) \left\{ \sum_{i=1}^{r} \delta_i y_{t-i} \right\} + u_t \tag{76}$$

where $\alpha_i$and $\delta_i$are constants, u_t is assumed at this time to be Gaussian and F_t is the continuous transition function, which is usually specified to be bounded between zero and unity.

Ozaki (1978) and Haggan and Ozaki (1981) introduced the exponential autoregressive model known more widely these days as the Exponential STAR (ESTAR) model.

ESTAR Model

In the ESTAR model

$$F_t = e^{-\gamma(y_{t-d} - \lambda)^2} \tag{77}$$

where d is the delay,. γ is a positive constant and λ is a constant.

The transition function for the ESTAR model is symmetric in deviations of y_{t-d} from λ. We observe from (76) that as F_t varies between zero and one we obtain an infinite number of different autoregressive processes each corresponding to a different state.

An interesting special case of the ESTAR which illustrates some of the possibilities is the model

$$y_t = y_{t-1} e^{-\gamma(y_{t-1})^2} + u_t \tag{78}$$

When the deviation y_{t-1} is large (78) will give approximately $y_t = u_t$. Conversely when y_{t-1} is small (78) will give approximately $y_t = y_{t-1} + u_t$ or $y_t - y_{t-1} = u_t$ so that y exhibits behaviour which varies from where y is approximately random to where changes in y are approximately random.

The deterministic component of (78) is plotted in Figure 18.4(a) with $y_t - y_{t-1}$ on the vertical axis and y_{t-1} on the horizontal axis. We observe the symmetric nature of the plot and the non-responsiveness of $y_t - y_{t-1}$ to y_{t-1} near zero, which is the equilibrium value in this model. This type of adjustment was employed by Michael, Nobay and Peel (1997) to model deviations of real exchange rates from equilibrium. It captures the idea that there is little response of real exchange rates to deviations from equilibrium when they are small but adjustment is proportionately faster the greater the deviation.

The ESTAR model also has the property, unlike the bilinear or threshold model that it can exhibit multiple equilibria. In fact (78) can exhibit up to three equilibrium values. This is readily shown by taking the special case

$$y_t = \alpha_1 y_{t-1} e^{-\gamma(y_{t-1})^2} + u_t \tag{79}$$

Ignoring the error term, the equilibrium of the deterministic component of (79) is given by

$$y_t = y_{t-1} = \overline{y} \tag{80}$$

Setting $y_t = y_{t-1} = \overline{y}$ in (79) we obtain the equilibrium solutions $\overline{y} = 0,\ \mp(\frac{\ln \alpha_1}{\gamma})$ so that for $0 < \alpha_1 < 1$ the model has three equilibria. Not surprisingly in the general case of the ESTAR model (76) the model can also exhibit one, two or three equilibria which can be non-zero and different. Their stability properties can also differ so that for instance the lowest of the three equilibria could be unstable in one model but stable in another (see Byers and Peel, 2000).

The ESTAR model can also capture cyclical behaviour. This is illustrated in figure 18.3 where we have plotted observations generated from ($y_1 = 0.1$, first 600 points discarded)

$$y_t = 4y_{t-1} e^{-0.1(y_{t-1})^2} \tag{81}$$

In some circumstances such as "arbitrage" the symmetric nature of adjustment in the ESTAR model may make it the preferred nonlinear model. However symmetric adjustment between regimes may not be a property of the data or theory. A model which allows for asymmetric adjustment but can also exhibit multiple equilibria and cyclical behaviour is the LSTAR model.

The LSTAR model

In the LSTAR model the transition function F_t in (76) is given the logistic form

$$F_t = \frac{1}{1 + e^{-\gamma(y_{t-d} - \lambda)}} \tag{82}$$

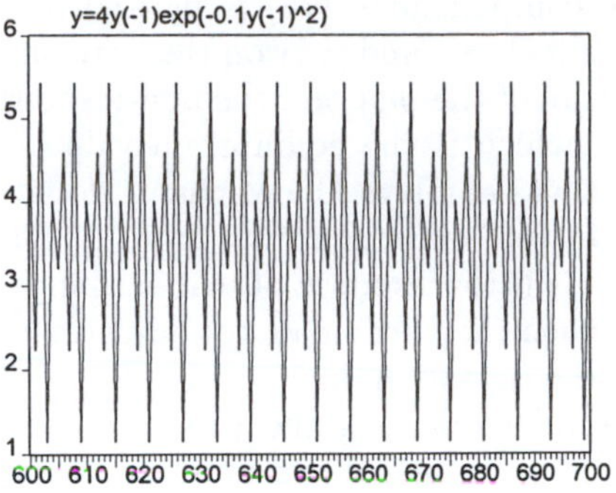

Figure 18.3: ESTAR cyclical model

where $\gamma > 0$.

Differences between the ESTAR and LSTAR transition forms are illustrated in figures 18.4a,b and 5a,b where $1 - F_t$ is plotted against y_{t-1} (the same figure would be obtained for y_{t-d}). In both cases as γ gets larger the transition between the two extreme regimes $F_t = 0$, $F_t = 1$, becomes quicker. Whilst the ESTAR transition is symmetric this is not the case for the LSTAR. We also notice that as γ gets larger in the case of the LSTAR the transition from $F_t = 0$ or 1 becomes almost instantaneous as y_{t-d} differs from λ (set at zero in the figures). Consequently the LSTAR can approximate a two-regime SE(TAR) threshold model unlike the ESTAR model.

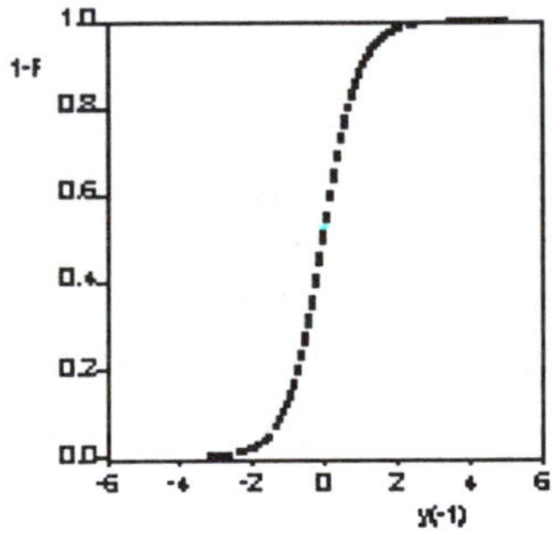

18.4a $\gamma = 2$

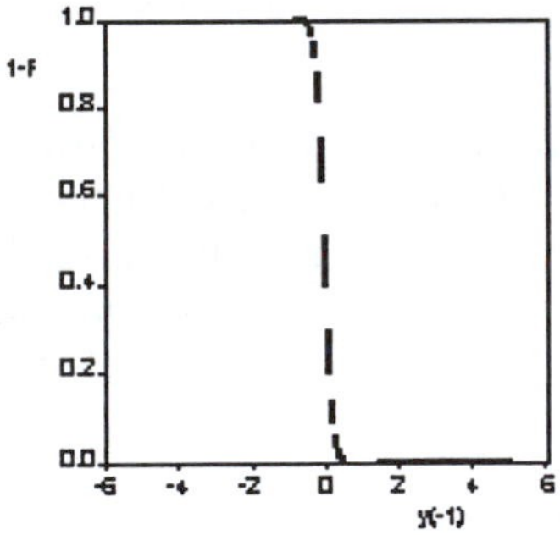

18.4b $\gamma = 10$

Figure 18.4: LSTAR transition

A further generalization of the transition function which can capture

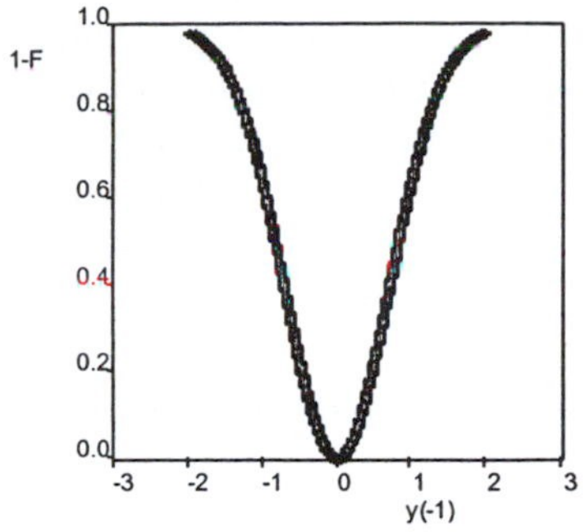

18.5a $\gamma = 1$

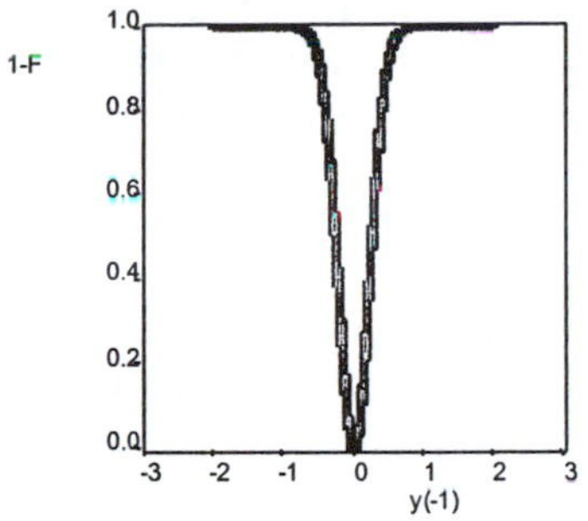

18.5b $\gamma = 10$

Figure 18.5: ESTAR transition

a four-regime SETAR model as a special case is the quadratic logistic function proposed by Jansen and Terasvirta(1996).

This takes the form

$$F_t = \frac{1}{1 + e^{-\gamma(y_{t-d}-\lambda_1)(y_{t-d}-\lambda_2)}} \tag{83}$$

where $\gamma > 0$ and $\lambda_1, \ \lambda_2$ are constants.

The quadratic logistic function is very flexible and can approximate as special cases both the ESTAR and LSTAR by choice of parameter. Figures 18.6a and b provide a couple of shapes.

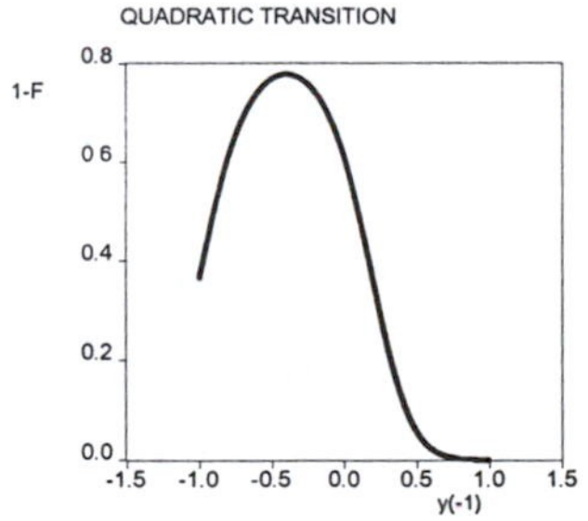

18.6a

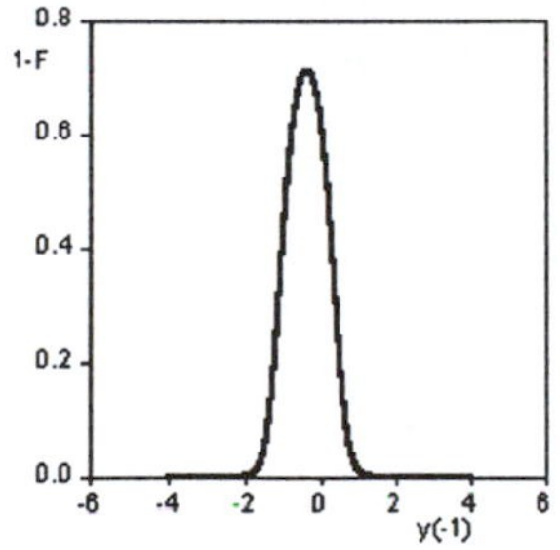

18.6b

Figure 18.6: Quadratic transition

The smooth-transition models have been extensively employed in the last few years to model both macroeconomic and financial data sets. They appear to provide a parsimonious fit to many economic time series.

In the specifications of the threshold and smooth-transition models outlined above we have illustrated by assuming that the transition state s was a function of past values of y, 'self-exciting models'. More generally of course the transition state can be a function of either past ys or other variables x depending on the theoretical model underpinning the analysis. For example the transition variable in the analysis of inflation might involve political variables if political parties were thought to have different policies. An alternative assumption is that the regime that occurs at time t cannot be observed since it is determined by an unobservable process which we can call s.

In the case of two regimes we postulate, as with the case of the threshold model of Tong that the outcome follows a different n-autoregressive process dependent upon the state of the world which we can call states, $s_t = 1$ and $s_t = 2$.

In order to give content to the model we need to specify the properties of the process generating s_t, the model most widely employed by economists is the Markov-Switching model developed by Hamilton (1989).

The MARKOV-switching Model

Suppose in both regimes the process follows an AR(2) process we have

$$y_t = \overline{y}_0 + \alpha_{01} y_{t-1} + \alpha_{02} y_{t-2} + u_t \text{ if } s_t = 1$$

$$y_t = \overline{y}_1 + \alpha_{11} y_{t-1} + \alpha_{22} y_{t-2} + u_t \text{ if } s_t = 2 \tag{84}$$

The process s_t is assumed to follow a first-order Markov process.

If we assume that the probability that s_t equals j (= 1 or 2 in our example) depends on the past only through the most recent value s_{t-1} (call it $i = 1$ or 2)

$$\text{prob}(s_t = j \mid s_{t-1} = i) = prob(s_t = j \mid s_{t-1} = i) = p_{ij} \tag{85}$$

Such a process is described as a Markov chain with transition probabilities $\{p_{ij}, j = 1, 2\}$. The transition probability p_{ij} is the probability that state i will be followed by state j.

Writing out in full we have

$$\text{prob}(s_t = 1 \mid s_{t-1} = 1) = p_{11},$$

$$\text{prob}(s_t = 2 \mid s_{t-1} = 1) = p_{12}, \tag{86}$$

$$\text{prob}(s_t = 1 \mid s_{t-1} = 2) = p_{21},$$

$$\text{prob}(s_t = 2 \mid s_{t-1} = 2) = p_{22},$$

Because probabilities sum to unity we must have that

$$p_{11} + p_{12} = 1 \tag{87}$$

and

$$p_{21} + p_{22} = 1 \tag{88}$$

Further properties of Markov chains and issues of estimation are set out in Hamilton (1994) and Timmermann (2000).

Markov-switching models are an appealing way of dealing with peso problems (as discussed in chapter 14). Naturally if the transition probabilities are specified as functions of observed variables, as by for instance Diebold (1994), the models have similarities to the smooth-transition models.

STATIONARITY VERSUS NONSTATIONARY VARIABLES

In the discussion so far we have assumed that the variable y is stationary. If a series is non-stationary then its mean, variance and covariances are changing, an important violation of these earlier models' assumptions. It will be clear from plotting many series that they exhibit a trend and hence are non-stationary. Plots of other series may be more problematic and it is clear we require formal tests to determine whether a variable is stationary and the appropriate test to render it stationary. Obvious filters to render a variable stationary are to remove the trend by regression so that the deviations around trend are stationary or to difference the series. In fact the method employed to remove trend has crucial differences as we now illustrate.

Consider removing a trend by regression of the variable on a time trend. We have

$$y_t = \alpha + \beta t + u_t \tag{89}$$

where α and β are the intercept and slope terms, t is the time trend and u_t is a random disturbance which we assume to be white noise but can be any stationary ARMA process. Here the non-stationary variable y is represented by what is known as a deterministic trend, that is, the trend itself is perfectly predictable and is non-stochastic. Of course the addition of the stationary variable u_t results in variation about the trend so that y is stochastic, but in the long run the only information we have about y_t is its mean $(\alpha + \beta t)$. Consequently, neither current nor past events alter long-term forecasts for this process. It is this feature which makes the trend deterministic. It also follows that the long-term forecast error will have finite variance and therefore, as pointed out by Nelson and Plosser (1982) uncertainty is bounded even in the indefinitely distant future.

An alternative approach to dealing with trends is to difference a series to make it stationary. A process that needs to be differenced to make it stationary is known as an integrated process. An integrated process is said to exhibit a stochastic trend.

When a series is integrated and one fits an ARMA process to the differenced series, the process for the 'raw data' is known as an ARIMA (p, d, q) where d is the number of times the series has to be differenced to make it stationary (0, 1, 2 etc., though it can take non-integer numbers — a so-called fractional process, see below): p is the order of the autoregressive component and q the order of the moving-average component.

While the effect is to model the general movement of the series, there is a crucial difference between the two methods. To illustrate this difference, suppose y_t is given by the nonstationary process:

$$y_t = \beta + y_{t-1} + u_t \tag{90}$$

where u is white noise and the variable $x_t = y_t - y_{t_{-1}} = \beta + u_t$ is stationary, so y_t is an ARIMA(0, 1, 0)

(90) can be written by repeated substitution as

$$y_t = y_0 + \beta t + u_t + u_{t-1} + u_{t-2} + u_{t-3} + \dots \tag{91}$$

where y_0 is some starting value in the past and the errors run back to this point. By comparison of (91) with (89) instead of α there is y_0, and instead of the single disturbance u there is the sum of t disturbances. This illustrates that the two types of non-stationary process, namely the deterministic trend and the integrated process, have broadly similar forms, in particular the time trend. However, (91) is crucially different from (89). In (89) α is a fixed parameter whilst in (91) it is given by a past historical event, the starting point. In (89) the deviations from the trend are stationary whilst in (91) the error variance increases without bound as time passes. Consequently, the long-term forecast of y_t from (91) will be influenced by the starting value and the variance of the forecast error will increase without bound as the forecast horizon lengthens. The economic importance of this distiction is crucial. If we model a variable as having a deterministic trend (being 'trend-stationary'), we have made the assumption that shocks have a temporary impact on the variable in question. If we assume that a variable is an integrated process and has to be differenced to make it stationary we are assuming that shocks have a permanent impact on the variable.

Given these rather different properties, it is important to know for any particular non-stationary series whether it is described by a deterministic trend or whether it is an integrated process described by a stochastic trend. Nelson and Kang (1984) investigate the implications of making the wrong choice. They show that if a variable described by the process (90) is regressed on time, the $\overline{R}^2$ value will approach one as the sample size increases. Also, if the series is detrended, the autocorrelation function is determined entirely by the sample size, exhibiting high positive autocorrelation at low lags and spurious cyclical patterns at long lags.

One area where these issues created much debate is whether real output is more appropriately described by a deterministic or integrated process (see Campbell and Mankiw, 1987). Currently, the available empirical evidence supports the view that many nonstationary economic time series appear to be generated by integrated processes (see Nelson and Plosser, 1982 and Phillips and Perron, 1988). Statistical tests to determine whether a non-stationary series is best described by a deterministic or integrated process have been developed by Dickey and Fuller (1981), Phillips and Perron (1988), Kwiatkowski et al. (1992).

Cointegration

In our discussion of non-stationary variables above we introduced the idea of an integrated series as being one which, after differencing, becomes stationary. If a stationary series is defined to be integrated of order zero, or $I(0)$, a series x_t, is said to be integrated of order d if it becomes stationary after differencing d times or

$$(1-L)^d x_t = y_t \tag{92}$$

where L is the lag operator and y_t is stationary. To reiterate, the reason stationarity is important is because it is one of the basic assumptions made in modelling and forecasting. If a series is not stationary, then its mean, variance and covariances are changing so that models which assume these are constants will be misleading. For example, the 'random walk' series y_t, given by $y_t = y_{t-1} + u_t$ where u_t is a random disturbance, has an infinite variance. Any estimated variance will be finite and so must be an underestimate of the true value. It is also easily seen that y_t, is $I(1)$, and we note that if we add another $I(0)$ variable to y_t the result will also be an $I(1)$ process.

These considerations are also important where relationships between different series are concerned. For example, Phillips (1987) has demonstrated that the standard t-tests in regression are not valid when the variables are non-stationary. More generally, Engle and Granger (1987) discuss the joint properties of integrated series. While the results apply for any number of series, we will limit consideration to just two. Suppose two series x_t, and y_t are both $I(d)$, then in general any linear combination of them will also be $I(d)$, there is no relationship between the variables so the regression error will have infinite variance, though as noted by Engle and Granger the $\overline{R}^2$ will often be rather high — a spurious fit. However, it sometimes occurs that a combination of two or more $I(d)$) variables is $I(d-b)$ where $b > 0$. More formally, if a new variable, ϵ_t, can be defined by

$$\epsilon_t = y_t - Ax_t \tag{93}$$

where ϵ_t is $I(d-b)$ then x_t and y_t are said to be cointegrated and A is called the constant of cointegration (or in the case of more than two variables the vector of constants) so that it becomes the cointegrating regression equation. So for example if real dividends are a non-stationary $I(1)$ variable then for stock markets to be efficient under standard assumptions we must find that the real stock price is an $I(1)$ process and also cointegrated with real dividends so that the residual from a regression of real stock prices on real dividends is an 1(0) variable.

We now consider some of the properties of cointegrated variables. First, including a constant in a cointegrating regression does not have any effect. Second, if two variables are cointegrated then the constant of cointegration is unique (though not for n variables) This can be shown by replacing A in (93) by a new constant k which equals $A + g$. This gives

$$\epsilon_t = y_t - kx_t = y_t - Ax_t - gx_t \tag{94}$$

If $y_t - Ax_t$ is stationary and x_t is $I(1)$ only if $g = 0$ can (93) and (94) be consistent. Third, it has been proved that cointegration in levels of variables implies cointegration in their logarithms, while cointegration in logarithms of variables does not imply cointegration in levels. This point suggests that unless there are strong theoretical reasons for choosing a particular functional form then some experimentation with non-linear transformations of the variables in the cointegrating relationship is desirable. Fourth, cointegration implies the two variables will not drift apart, since ϵ_t, which measures the gap between y and x, and can be regarded as the 'error', is stationary with a mean of zero. This results in one interpretation of

$$y_t - Ax_t = 0 \tag{95}$$

as the long-run or equilibrium relationship between x and y. However in the case where say x_t was a forecast of y_t which applies in some efficient market tests the long-run equilibrium interpretation is not valid (e.g. Campbell and Shiller, 1988a,b).

Fifth, Engle and Granger (1987) have proved that if x and y are both $I(1)$, have constant means and are cointegrated, then an 'error-correcting' data generating mechanism or error correction model (ECM) exists which takes the form

$$\Delta y_t = y_t - y_{t-1} = \rho_0 - \rho_1 \epsilon_{t-1} + lagged(\Delta y, \Delta x) + u_t \tag{96}$$

and

$$\Delta x_t = x_t - x_{t-1} = \rho_3 - \rho_4 \epsilon_{t-1} + lagged(\Delta y, \Delta x) + \eta_t \tag{97}$$

where ϵ_t is given by (93) above, and u_t and η_t are stationary error processes often taken to be white noise in practice though this is not required; also the errors could be correlated. In addition so that stability is ensured we require

$$| \rho_1 | + | \rho_4 | \neq 0 \tag{98}$$

This last condition ensures that ϵ_{t-1} occurs in at least one of the equations. The validity of (96) and (97) follows from x and y being $I(1)$, so their differences are $I(0)$ and each term is therefore $I(0)$. It is also the case that not only must cointegrated variables obey such a model, but the reverse is true: data generated by an ECM must also be cointegrated.

This result is of great importance because it links two previously separate areas: time-series models and ECMs. Error-correction models have been widely used in economics since Sargan (1964) and Davidson, Hendry, Srba and Yeo (1978). They require that the economic system has a well-defined equilibrium and that the speed of movement of variables towards the equilibrium will reflect the distance the system is away from that equilibrium. Consequently, (95), the cointegrating equation, reflects the specification of the equilibrium of the system. The absolute value of the cointegrating residual ϵ_{t-1} measures the distance from the equilibrium in the previous period.

These results have implications for modelling and forecasting since the order of integration of the dependent variable in a regression must be equal to a linear combination of the explanatory variables as a necessary condition for a meaningful relationship between the variables to exist. In other words for equations to have $I(0)$ errors, the variables must also be $I(0)$ or, if $I(1)$, they must be cointegrated. This illustrates the need to examine the degree of integration of each candidate variable in a proposed model prior to estimation.

In order to provide further insight into the above discussion we show how the ECM can be derived from the data-generating process for two variables employing a simple example from Engle and Granger (1987).

The data-generating process is given by

$$x_t + \beta y_t = u_t \tag{99}$$

$$x_t + \alpha y_t = \epsilon_t \tag{100}$$

where α, β are constants and the error processes u_t and ϵ_t are given by

$$u_t = u_{t-1} + v_{1t} \tag{101}$$

$$\epsilon_t = \rho\epsilon_{t-1} + v_{2t} \quad \text{with} \mid \rho \mid < 1 \tag{102}$$

ρ is a constant and v_{1t} and v_{2t} are error terms which have zero expected value and constant variances though quite feasibly non-zero covariance. Solving the pair of simultaneous equations for x_t and y_t from the above system with $\alpha \neq \beta$ gives

$$x_t = \frac{\alpha u_t}{(\alpha - \beta)} - \frac{\beta\epsilon_t}{(\alpha - \beta)} \tag{103}$$

$$y_t = \frac{-u_t}{(\alpha - \beta)} + \frac{\epsilon_t}{(\alpha - \beta)} \tag{104}$$

Since u_t is a non-stationary process (from (101) it is a random walk) we observe from (103) and (104) that x_t and y_t are integrated processes of order one, $I(1)$, since they depend on u_t and the stationary $I(0)$ error process ϵ_t. However from (100) we observe that the two variables are cointegrated since a linear combination of the two variables, with cointegrating vector (1, α) is stationary.

If we difference equation (99) and (100) and employ (101) and (102) we can obtain

$$\Delta x_t + \beta\Delta y_t = v_{1tt} \tag{105}$$

$$\begin{aligned} \Delta x_t + \alpha\Delta y_t = \Delta\epsilon_t = \epsilon_t - \epsilon_{t-1} &= \rho\epsilon_{t-1} + v_{2t} - \epsilon_{t-1} \\ &= v_{2t} - (1-\rho)\epsilon_{t-1} \end{aligned} \tag{106}$$

Solving for Δx_t and Δy_t from (105) and (106) we obtain the error-correction forms

$$\Delta y_t = \frac{v_{2t} - v_{1t}}{\alpha - \beta} - \frac{(1-\rho)\epsilon_{t-1}}{\alpha - \beta} \tag{107}$$

$$\Delta x_t = \frac{\alpha v_{1t} - \beta v_{2t}}{\alpha - \beta} + \frac{\beta(1-\rho)\epsilon_{t-1}}{\alpha - \beta} \tag{108}$$

If $\beta = 0$ in the above system so that x_t is an exogenous process we could write (107) and (108) in the equivalent form

$$\Delta y_t = \frac{v_{2t}}{\alpha}\frac{-\Delta x_t}{\alpha} - \frac{(1-\rho)\epsilon_{t-1}}{\alpha} \tag{109}$$

$$\Delta x_t = \frac{\alpha v_{1t}}{\alpha} \tag{110}$$

The form (107) might be estimated for purposes of explanation and the form (109) for forecasting.

As the error processes in (101) and(102) are made more complex we obtain the general form of linear error-correction mechanisms given by equations (96) and (97).

We observe here that Fama estimated an error-correction form in his tests of efficiency of the exchange market discussed in chapter 14. If the spot rate and forward rate are integrated processes then efficiency, assuming a stationary risk premium, implies they are cointegrated. Consequently in the regression

$$s_t = \delta_0 + \delta_1 f_t + \epsilon_t \tag{111}$$

where s_t is the spot rate and f_t the forward rate we would expect to find that the error ϵ_t is $I(0)$ regardless of the order of integration of s_t and f_t (though typically found to be $I(1)$ processes these could take higher values, for instance in times of hyperinflation if inflation is an I(1) process). Early tests of efficiency examined whether the estimate of δ_1 was significantly different from unity. It was then recognised that inefficient forms of expectation formation could be consistent with this property as long as expectation forecast errors were stationary. The equation Fama estimated for $I(1)$ data to test efficiency, namely

$$\Delta s_t = \gamma_0 + \gamma_1(f_{t-1} - s_{t-1}) + u_t \tag{112}$$

is a restricted form of ECM (restricted in the sense that he could have added further lagged changes in forward rates and spot rates and tested whether their coefficient values too were significantly different from zero).

Nonlinear Error Correction

While the above derivation of the ECM employed a linear system for ease of exposition there is nothing in statistical theory that prevents the ECM from having a nonlinear structure and indeed much economic theory suggests it should have. Consequently much recent research has investigated the efficacy of nonlinear error-correction forms — see e.g. Enders and Granger (1998); Peel and Taylor (2002).

These have generally employed some form of threshold or smooth-transition threshold structure since these are implied by transactions or arbitrage bands. So, for instance, we might suppose that adjustment to deviations from say purchasing power parity or equilibrium money demand is nonlinear due to transactions bands. Peel and Davidson (1998) also employ a Bilinear ECM where the economic rationale is less clear (it could be where adjustment speeds are directly related to the magnitudes of shocks in the system). A smooth-transtion ECM for an $I(1)$ variable, y_t, which is cointegrated with x_t would take the form

$$\Delta y_t = \gamma_0 + \sum_{i=1}^{n} \gamma_t \Delta y_{t-i} + \sum_{i=0}^{m} \lambda_i \Delta x_{t-i} + \delta \epsilon_{t-i} +$$
$$(1 - F_t)\left\{ \gamma_{10} + \sum_{i=1}^{o} \gamma_{1t} \Delta y_{t-i} + \sum_{i=0}^{p} \lambda_{1i} \Delta x_{t-i} + \delta_1 \epsilon_{t-j} \right\} \quad (113)$$

where the γ, λ, δ are constants and ϵ is the cointegration error. The lag on the cointegrating residual is often one but need not be. F_t is the transition function as in the various threshold models outlined above. The transition variable, s_t, in the transition function is an $I(0)$ variable, often the lagged cointegrating variable but not restricted to this variable.

Vector Autoregressive Models

If we consider equations (107) and (108) above we could write them in the equivalent form

$$y_t = \frac{v_{2t} - v_{1t}}{\alpha - \beta} - \frac{(1-\rho)}{\alpha - \beta} x_{t-1} + (1 - \frac{(1-\rho)\alpha}{\alpha - \beta}) y_{t-1} \quad (114)$$

$$x_t = \frac{\alpha v_{1t} - \beta v_{2t}}{\alpha - \beta} + (1 + \frac{\beta(1-\rho)}{\alpha - \beta}) x_{t-1} + \frac{\alpha\beta(1-\rho)}{\alpha - \beta} y_{t-1} \quad (115)$$

In this form the sytem would be known as a vector autoregressive model (VAR).

Sims (1980) as part of a critique of conventional model building in macroeconomics proposed the estimation of unrestricted reduced forms in which all the variables in a chosen system are treated as being endogenous for use in forecasting (and policy evaluation). The linear VAR has the form

$$y_{1t} = f(y_{1t-1}, y_{1t-2}, \ldots, y_{1t-p}, y_{2t-1}, \ldots, y_{2t-p}, \ldots, y_{kt-1}, \ldots, y_{kt-p})$$

$$y_{2t} = f(y_{1t-1}, y_{1t-2}, \cdots, y_{1t-p}, y_{2t-1}, \cdots, y_{2t-p}, \cdots, y_{kt-1}, \cdots, y_{kt-p}) \tag{116}$$

$$y_{kt} = f(y_{1t-1}, y_{1t-2}, \cdots, y_{1t-p}, y_{2t-1}, \cdots, y_{2t-p}, \cdots, y_{kt-1}, \cdots, y_{kt-p})$$

where there are k variables and the common lag length p. Notice that the right hand side variables are the same in each equation and do not include any current values. In these circumstances ordinary least squares is a suitable estimation method.

Clearly if we estimate a VAR we must determine the form in which variables should enter the VAR. Sometimes researchers employ first differences of variables since this makes them stationary. Clearly if variables in the system are cointegrated this would imply that information on the equilibrium of the system, the cointegrating residual, has not been employed so that the VAR is misspecified. A model estimated in levels would implicitly capture the cointegration restriction. Fuller discussion of VARs is found in, for example, Hamilton (1994).

Fractional Integration or Long Memory

So far we have assumed that the filter to make an integrated series stationary is an integer number, 1, 2, etc. However Granger and Joyeux (1980) and Hosking (1981) have introduced the idea of fractional integration.

The fractionally integrated time series model can be defined as

$$(1 - L)^d y_t = u_t \tag{117}$$

where u_t is a ARMA(p, q) process and d is a non-integer where $-1 < d < 1$.

Such a process is called an ARFIMA(p, d, q) process (see Diebold and Rudebusch, 1989).

The difference operator on the left-hand side of (117) can be expanded as a binomial expansion to give

$$(1 - L)^d = 1 + (-d)\,L + \frac{1}{2}d\,(d-1)\,L^2 + \left(-\frac{1}{6}d\,(d-1)\,(d-2)\right)L^3 + \frac{1}{24}d\,(d-1)\,(d-2)\,(d-3)\,L^4 + \ldots \tag{118}$$

We observe from (118) that y_t is a function of all past values of y.

For $0 < d < \frac{1}{2}$ the autocorrelation function, ACF, for y declines at a much slower hyperbolic rate towards zero than the ultimately exponential decay of a standard ARMA process. The hyperbolic decay of the memory of a fractionally integrated process enables ARFIMA processes to model dependence between observations at long range.

When $d > \frac{1}{2}$ the process is nonstationary. But at the same time, in contrast to the I(1) (or unit root) case, these processes exhibit eventual mean reversion.

The formula in (117) is also valid for $-1 < d < 0$, which can be thought of as the case obtained by the simple differencing of a fractionally integrated process.

Because fractional integrated series can be nonstationary there is a developing literature on fractional cointegration (see Davidson, 2000) and all the associated issues of spurious correlation.

A large number of authors have recently reported empirical results which suggest that a number of macroeconomic and financial time series exhibit autocorrelation functions that decay hyperbolically rather than geometrically and can be described by fractionally integrated ARFIMA (p,d,q) processes — e.g. Baillie et al. (1996); Ding, Granger and Engle (1993); Ding and Granger (1996).

The rationale for why economic time series should follow fractional processes is less clear. Granger (1980) provides an explanation whereby aggregation over heterogeneous micro agents who display different degrees of persistence can generate an aggregate series which displays the fractional property. This rationale was exploited by Byers, Davison and Peel (1997) in their analysis of political popularity. It is less clear that this rationale can explain the apparent fractional property of macroeconomic series. Recent work is suggestive that the apparent fractional property of some macroeconomic data may be a misleading linear property. Granger and Terasvirta (1999) and Byers and Peel (2000) show how nonlinear models can exhibit outcomes that appear fractional. For instance the LSTAR and ESTAR models can generate data which appears to have the long memory property. Also Engle and Smith (1998) and Granger and Hyung (1999) show how structural breaks or Markov-switching models can generate data which appears to have the d property. It seems clear that there will be a lot more research devoted to explanation and analysis of data with the d property.

TIME-VARYING VOLATILITY

In the univariate models considered above namely

$$y_t = f(y_{t-1}, y_{t-2}, \ldots) + u_t \tag{119}$$

we have assumed that the error had expectation zero and was white noise or a Gaussian white noise process.[3] Also that the error had constant variance both unconditionally, $E(u_t^2)$, and conditionally, $E(u_t^2 \mid \Omega_{t-1})$, so that $E(u_t^2) = E(u_t^2 \mid \Omega_{t-1}) = \sigma^2$ where σ^2 is the constant variance and Ω_{t-1} is the information set consisting of all relevant information up to and including time $t-1$.

It has been noted for a long time that the squared residuals from fitted ARIMA processes for many financial time series exhibited serial correlation e.g. Mandelbrot (1963a,b). The same finding was also discovered later for many macroeconomic time series (see e.g. Engle, 1982).

Such a finding could be evidence of mispecification of the mean function. For instance we fitted an AR(1) process to the bilinear process:

$$y_t = \alpha y_{t-1} + \beta y_{t-1}u_{t-1} + u_t \tag{120}$$

where $\alpha = 0.5$, $\beta = 0.4$ and u_t is Gaussian white noise, $N(0,\, 1)$. We obtained a first-order autocorrelation coefficient for the squared value of the residuals from a fitted AR(1) process of 0.28 in a sample of 400 (the first 600 observations were discarded). This value is significant.

However there are numerous models based for instance on diffusion of information flows in financial markets or pricing of risk in asset markets which provide a rationale for serially correlated squared residuals (see e.g. Bollerslev, Chou and Kroner(1992)). We should note of course that a

---

[3]Having discussed some nonlinear processes we can be clearer about this distinction. A process having the properties $E(u_t) = 0, E(u_t^2) = \sigma^2$ =constant, $E(u_{t-i}, u_{t-q}) = 0$ for $i \neq q$ is known as white noise. Consider now the example taken from Priestley (1988):

$$u_t = v_t + \beta v_{t-1}v_{t-2} \tag{a1}$$

where v_t is white noise but also independent of all past information. It follows that $E(u_t) = 0$ (since $\beta E(v_{t-1}v_{t-2}) = 0$), also $E(u_t^2) = \sigma_v^2$. The autocovariance function is given by

$$E(u_t u_{t+s}) = E\{v_t v_{t+s} + \beta v_{t-1}v_{t-2}v_{t+s} + \beta v_t v_{t+s-1}v_{t+s-2} + \beta^2 v_{t-1}v_{t-2}v_{t+s-1}v_{t+s-2}\} \tag{a2}$$

For all $s \neq 0$ each of the terms in (a2) has zero expectation so that u_t is an uncorrelated process. Consequently it is a white noise process. However because u_t has the nonlinear process specified in (a1) we can construct a forecast of u_{t+1} which is non-zero and given by $\hat{u}_{t+1} = \beta v_t v_{t-1}$. Consequently a stronger condition than assuming a white noise error is to assume the error is independent of all previous information (i.e linearly and non-linearly). Such a process is called an independent white noise process. When the variance of the error is also normally distributed the independent white noise process is called Gaussian white noise.

predictable pattern of the variance of asset prices would not imply market inefficiency. Rather the issue would be whether the econometricians' forecasts of variance are superior to those embodied in e.g. option prices.

Models of time-varying volatility relax the assumption that the conditional variance is constant. It is assumed that the conditional variance

$$E(u_t^2 \mid \Omega_{t-1}) = h_t \tag{121}$$

where h_t is some non-negative function.

Engle(1982) specified the process

$$u_t = z_t h_t^{0.5} \tag{122}$$

where z_t is independent and identically distributed with zero mean and unit variance. In early work it was also assumed that z was normally distributed, which we also assume, but this assumption can be relaxed.

From (122) and the properties of z, it follows that the distribution of u_t conditional on the information set is normal with mean zero and variance h_t. We can also derive that the unconditional variance of u_t is constant since

$$E(u_t^2) = E\{E(u_t^2 \mid \Omega_{t-1})) = E(u_t^2 \mid \Omega_{t-1}) = h_t \tag{123}$$

The distinguishing features of time varying volatility models is in the specification of how h_t evolves over time. Engle(1982) proposed AutoRegressive Conditionally Heteroscedastic (ARCH) models, where the conditional variance is a linear function of past squared errors. The ARCH model has the form

$$h_t = \gamma_0 + \gamma_1 u_{t-1}^2 + \gamma_2 u_{t-2}^2 + \dots \tag{124}$$

where the γ are nonzero constants to ensure h_t is positive. In a financial market setting the idea of (124) would be that turbulent periods of large u_t^2 are followed by further turbulence, so-called volatility clustering. For certain applications the assumption of long lags in the squared errors may be more parsimoniously captured by the form proposed by Bollerslev (1986) which is the Generalised ARCH or GARCH(p, q) process given by

$$h_t = \gamma_0 + \sum_{i=1}^{q} \beta_i u_{t-i}^2 + \sum_{i=1}^{p} \alpha_i h_{t-i} \tag{125}$$

The reader will have noticed the similarity of (124) to an MA process and (125) to an ARMA process. If we define $\theta_t \equiv u_t^2 - h_t = h_t(z_t^2 - 1)$, obtained by squaring (122), we can write for instance a GARCH(1, 1) process

$$h_t = \gamma_0 + \beta_1 u_{t-1}^2 + \alpha_1 h_{t-1} \tag{126}$$

equivalently as

$$u_t^2 = \gamma_0 + (\beta_1 + \alpha_1)u_{t-1}^2 + \theta_t - \alpha_1\theta_{t-1} \tag{127}$$

From (127) we observe that we can write the GARCH(1,1) process as an ARMA(1,1) process in the squared errors. Note also that $E(\theta_t \mid \Omega_{t-1}) = 0$. As with an ARMA(1,1) process we would require $\beta_1 + \alpha_1 < 1$ for stationarity in (127).

As nonlinear models in the conditional mean function discussed above were natural extensions of the ARMA processes so nonlinear models of time-varying volatility have been developed. Similarly mirroring extensions of the linear model there are integrated GARCH processes and fractionally integrated Garch processes (FIGARCH).These different models allow for asymmetric impacts of shocks on conditional volatility, long memory, hyperbolically declining impacts, etc. These methods have been extensively employed in univariate modelling of series in macroeconomics and finance and are well covered along with issues of estimation and statistical properties in Franses and van Dijk (2000).

Chaos

In the models discussed above it has been assumed that the models are stochastic. In the last decade or so there has been discussion of whether outcomes in economics, particularly asset markets and macroeconomics, might be the product of a chaotic process. A chaotic process is a deterministic process, so that the explanation of outcomes does not rely on shocks. Perhaps the best way to illustrate the idea is to consider the nonlinear difference equation

$$y_t = Ay_{t-1}(1 - y_{t-1}) \tag{128}$$

where A is a constant, $0 < A \leq 4$.

The deterministic nonlinear difference equation (128) has been termed the simplest nonlinear difference equation. It can be obtained as a reduced form from the more general second-order difference equation

$$Z_t = a + bZ_{t-1} + cZ_{t-2} \tag{129}$$

by letting[4] $Z_t = \lambda y_t + \gamma$.

[4] By substitution
$c\gamma^2 + (b-1)\gamma + a = 0$
$\lambda = -\frac{A}{c}$
$A = 2c\gamma + b$
and
$A^2 - 2A + 2b - b^2 + 4ac = 0$

In order to analyse the dynamic behaviour of equation (128) we first determine the points of equilibrium ($\overline{y}$) obtained where $y_t = y_{t-1} = \overline{y}$ in (128).We find by substitution that there are two equilibrium points given by

$$\overline{y} = 0, \text{ and } \overline{y} = \frac{(A-1)}{A} \tag{130}$$

The slope of the function is given by $\frac{dy_t}{dy_{t-1}}$. This is equal to

$$\frac{dy_t}{dy_{t-1}} = A - 2Ay_{t-1} \tag{131}$$

(131) implies that the graph of y_t against y_{t-1} has a maximum value at $y_{t-1} = \frac{1}{2}$.

In figure 18.7a we plot the the relationship between y_t and y_{t-1} — called the phase curve — in the range $0 \leq y_{t-1} \leq 1$ for three values of A. The graph is hill-shaped and known as a tent map. By changing the parameter A, we can adjust the height and steepness of the hill. It turns out that the 'tuning parameter' A is crucial for the dynamics of the system. The value of A is also sometimes called the 'knob setting'. In order to illustrate the dynamic behaviour of the system we can draw a 45° line to give the points where $y_t = y_{t-1} = \overline{y}$. Clearly the points of intersection of the graph of (128) and the 45° line are the equilibrium points given by (130). This is illustrated in figure 18.7b with $A = 2$. To show how the dynamics of the system evolve we start the system at the arbitary non-equilibrium initial value in the unit interval, $y_0 = 0.2$. This value generates a value of $y(1) = 0.32$ in the next time period (point B). We now wish to repeat the process, this time commencing from $y(1)$. To do this we move horizontally to point C on the 45° line. The point vertically below C is $y(1)$ on the horizontal axis, because the two coordinates of any point of the 45° line must be equal. From $y(1)$, we move directly to point D on the phase curve. Continuing in this fashion we will trace out the path of y. In this case the path converges to the equilibrium point K where $y = 0.5$.

In order that we converge on an equilibrium point it is necessary that the slope of the phase curve at the equilibrium point has modulus less than unity. (Note also that for any starting values of y_{t-1} which do not begin in the unit interval (i.e. between 0 and 1) the system tends to negative infinity).

The slope of the phase curve at the two equilibrium points is

$$\frac{dy_t}{dy_{t-1}} = A - 2Ay_{t-1} \tag{132}$$

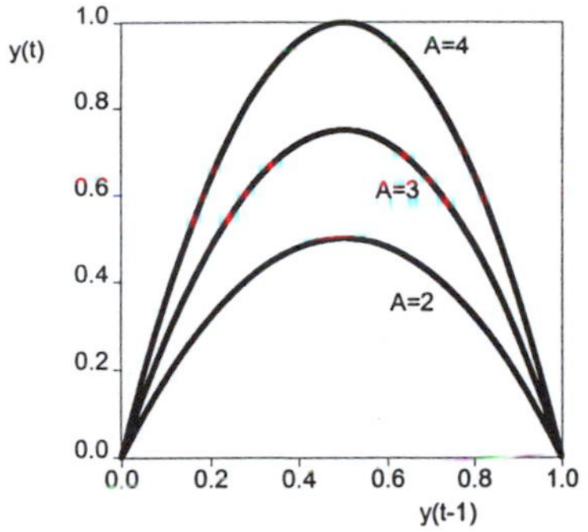

18.7a Phase curve

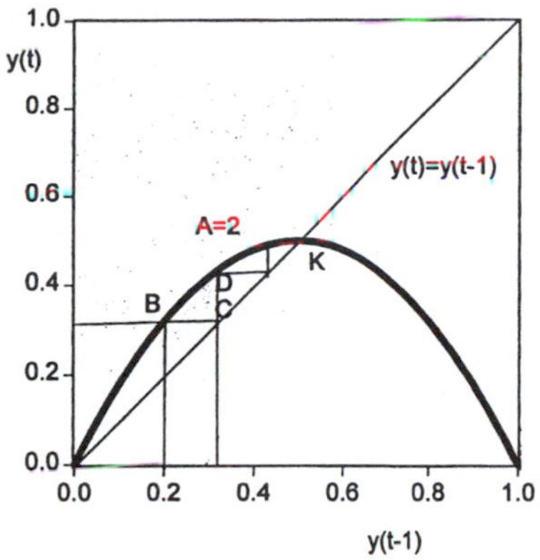

18.7b Phase curve, dynamic behaviour

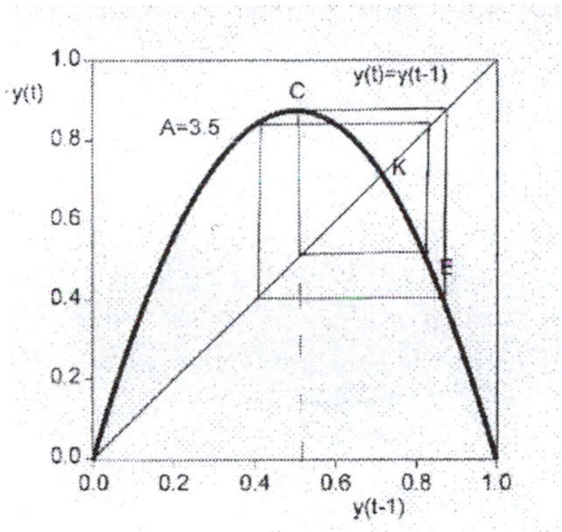

18.7c Phase curve, 4 period cycle

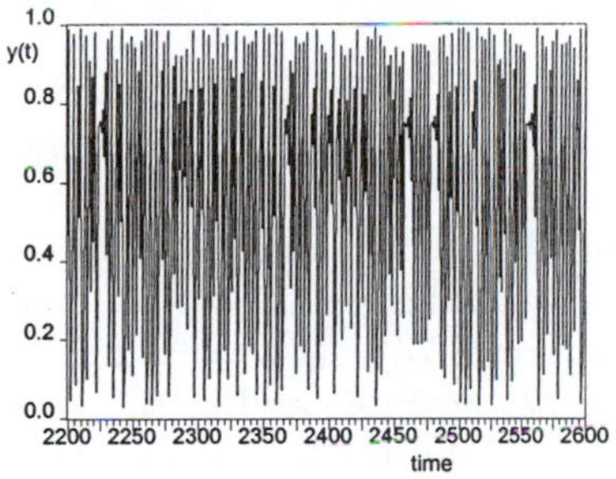

18.7d Segment of time-path

Figure 18.7: Phase curve

$$= A \text{ when } \overline{y} = 0 \tag{133}$$

and

$$= 2 - A \text{ when } \overline{y} = 1 - \frac{1}{A} \tag{134}$$

It follows that for $0 < A < 1$, the equilibrium point of the system is zero since (133) has slope less unity whilst (134) has slope greater than unity.

For the case $1 < A < 3$, we find that the equilibrium point, $1 - 1/A$, is stable or 'attracting', while that for $\overline{y}$ is 'repelling' or unstable. In other words, any deviation from zero causes the system to move further away, whilst any paths in the neighbourhood of $1 - 1/A$, converge on the equilibrium point. We note further that for $2 < A < 3$, dy_t/dy_{t-1} will be negative from (134), implying ultimately stable oscillations in the trajectory of y around the higher equilibrium point from any initial starting point apart from equilibrium.

When A is greater than or equal to 3, the slope at the higher equilibrium point becomes unstable. In the case of a linear equation if the slope is greater than one in absolute value the oscillations will be explosive (i.e. y_t will tend to infinity). However, with the hill-shaped phase curve, this cannot occur because, as the oscillations increase, the path will eventually 'expand into' the positively-sloping side of the hill and produce a value of y_{t+j} closer to the equilibrium point than some earlier point in the trajectory y_{t+j-k}. From this point the cyclical path will begin converging towards the equilibrium point. However, since the equilibrium point is unstable, convergence cannot occur so that the path will once again at some point begin to diverge. This is illustrated in figure 18.7c, with $A = 3.5$, where we note that starting from initial condition y_0, point C is closer to the equilibrium point ($K = 0.714$) than is point E.

As A is gradually increased between 3 and 4, a plethora of different dynamic paths of the system are exhibited. For A equal to or just greater than 3 the path converges on a stable two-period cycle. As A is gradually increased, the two-period limit cycle becomes unstable and exactly at this point a stable four-period cycle emerges (also illustrated in figure 18.7c). As we continue to increase A the four-period cycle itself becomes unstable and at this point is replaced by a stable eight-period cycle. As A is further increased the process continues until ultimately the path of y evolves into an infinite number of cycle lengths. Feigenbaum (1980) demonstrated that the interval of A over which a cycle is stable shrinks at a geometric rate. In particular, each interval is approximately 4.669 times smaller than the previous interval. He also showed that this property is universal for all functions that have 'hill-shaped' maps (for example, a sine wave). The period doublings as A increases are known as 'period doubling bifurcations'. At points of bifurcation the system under consideration changes discontinuously. This is one possible path to chaos. Although the cycles initially only have even periods it turns out that cycles with odd numbers of periods eventually begin to appear. Initially these will have very long periods, but in due course they are joined by cycles of shorter and shorter duration which encompass every positive odd integer .

As we continue to increase A we find that there are essentially an infinite number of initial values of A for which the time path of A never repeats itself. When a system starting from an initial value never repeats

Row	Value A	y_0	y_{10}	y_{23}	y_{72}
1	3.95000	0.3000	0.41538	0.45516	0.06589
2	3.95000	0.3001	0.38369	0.69396	0.09839
3	3.10000	0.3000	0.62339	0.75924	0.58104
4	3.10000	0.3001	0.62362	0.75918	0.58104
5	3.95001	0.3000	0.41471	0.24035	0.41117

Table 18.1: Path of y in equation (128)

itself it is said to exhibit aperiodic motion. Aperiodic motion does not imply that the observed patterns appear to have no structure. It is possible, for example, to distinguish patterns which look like cycles but which disappear after a number of periods. Systems exhibiting aperiodic motion can be thought of as chaotic.

The different types of dynamic behaviour which we observe as we vary A illustrates the notion of an attractor. An attractor in a linear system is a point, more generally a subspace, to which the system converges. The fixed-point equilibrium is defined as an attractor of period one. Limit cycles of whatever period are also types of equilibrium of a system, and are known as periodic attractors. When the system is in the chaotic region we have another type of attractor known as a strange attractor. The strange attractor is an attractor for all paths in its neighbourhood. Unlike limit cycles, trajectories within the strange attractor are not periodic, and no point is ever visited twice.

In figure 18.7d we plot a segment of the path for a value $A = 3.95$, which is within the chaotic region. We notice that y appears quite volatile but always remains within the 0-1 range. We also see that periods of relatively large cyclical oscillations can be followed by periods of relative stability (e.g. observations around 2340). Such abrupt qualitative changes in the path of y are characteristic of chaotic systems (and some non-linear stochastic equations, for instance the bilinear simulation of figure 18.2b).

Chaotic systems possess a number of other interesting properties. One is that the time path of y is highly sensitive to initial conditions (y_0 in our systems). Table 18.1 illustrates this property. In row 1 we set out, for a value of A of 3.95 (within the chaotic region), the values that X takes after 10, 23 and 72 from a starting value of 0.3. In row 2 we set the starting value of A at 0.3001. We observe that after ten periods to five decimal places the paths are close together, but after 23 periods the values are becoming different.

In fact, after 500 iterations the $\overline{R}^2$ correlation coefficient between the two series is close to zero at -0.02 and quickly approaches zero. In rows

3 and 4 we carry out a similar experiment with $A = 3.10$ (outside the chaotic region). Now the values of y remain close together and the R after 500 iterations is approximately 1.0. The sensitive dependence of the path of y on the initial conditions in a chaotic region of a model was termed the 'butterfly effect' by Lorenz (1963) in a reference to the possibility that if the weather system is chaotic, a butterfly flapping its wings may set off a sequence of meteorological events that result in tornadoes, the sensitivity of the system being such that minute changes in initial conditions give rise to outcomes which are dramatically different. We also note that since equation (128) is deterministic, the path of y is totally predictable if we know the exact initial condition. However, the sensitivity to initial conditions informs us that in all practical situations, where there will almost inevitably be errors in measurement and rounding errors in computation, it will almost certainly not be possible to make meaningful long-term forecasts

A second interesting feature of chaotic systems is that the time path exhibits sensitivity to small changes in parameter values. This is also illustrated in Table 18.1 where in row 5 we set out values of y at various points on the path for a value of A of 3.95001, and a starting value of 0.3. The value can be contrasted with those in row 1 where A has the value 3.95. The values soon become quite different.

A third feature of chaotic processes (shared by some other non-chaotic deterministic processes) is that the observed time paths appear to be random or those of a linear/non-linear system subject from time to time to 'very large' random shocks. Frank and Stengos (1988) illustrate the first possibility by considering the autocorrelation function of equation (128) for the first 1000 iterations with $y_0 = 0.3$ and $A = 4$. On the basis of the usual statistics, we would accept that the series is random. No doubt the fact that chaotic data can appear random may have motivated, in part, the applications to financial data, given that high frequency data changes in asset prices are well described by a white noise process.

It is certainly suprising to find the rich number of different paths that can be generated by the simple equation (128) including chaotic outcomes. The macroeconomy appears much more complex and the question that naturally arises is the potential applicability of chaos in macroeconomics. A number of statistical methods now exist which, given a sufficiently large number of observations, can determine whether an observed time series is chaotic or has the characteristics of a chaotic series (see, e.g.,Grassberger and Procaccia, 1983, Brock, Hsieh and LeBaron,1991). One of the tests is based upon the correlation dimension. If one formulates and estimates a model then the residuals should be independent of past information, i.e. unforecastable. The BDS test of Brock et al. (1996) is employed to test the null that the residuals have no remaining structure. Essentially if a series is random then plotting the residual against the lagged residual (say normalised to lie between zero and one) would fill the square with points. Similarly in three dimensions plotting the residual against the first and second lags would fill the cube. And so on into n dimensions. The test is based on examining whether the relevant space is filled. A chaotic process leaves an imprint. This is illustrated in figures 18.8a and b. Figure 18.8a is a scatter of 20,000 points of Gaussian white noise plotted against its lagged value. There is no relationship: the space will clearly be filled with enough observations. In figure 18.8b the scatter is the residuals from a fitted ESTAR process to 20,000 observations from the chaotic process $y_t = 3.97y_{t-1}(1 - y_{t-1}).(y_0 = 0.1)$. The ESTAR process which has two lags of y has a fitted $\overline{R}^2$ of 0.9998, a very high fit to the data, nevertheless we observe that the scatter of the residuals at t and $t-1$ has not filled the space but rather left a distinctive pattern.

Though wide use has been made of these test statistics, there is perhaps as yet no convincing empirical evidence of chaotic behaviour in the economic series examined to date (mostly asset prices or macroeconomic series) — though see De Grauwe, Dewachter and Embrechts (1993). However, a number of theoretical models generating chaos have been developed — e.g. Benhabib (1992), Dechert (1996), Grandmont (1986).

CONCLUSION

The purpose in this chapter has been to present a necessarily brief introduction to some of the time-series methods employed in macroeconomics. We have not discussed statistical tests which can be found in the text books cited. Also we have not discussed (amongst other omissions) neural nets or non-parametric methods. These are of interest but space precludes their discussion — see e.g. Franses and van Dijk (2000), Hardle (1990). One value of these methods is in presenting the theoretician with much more information about the nature of the 'stylized facts' the theoretical models have to explain.

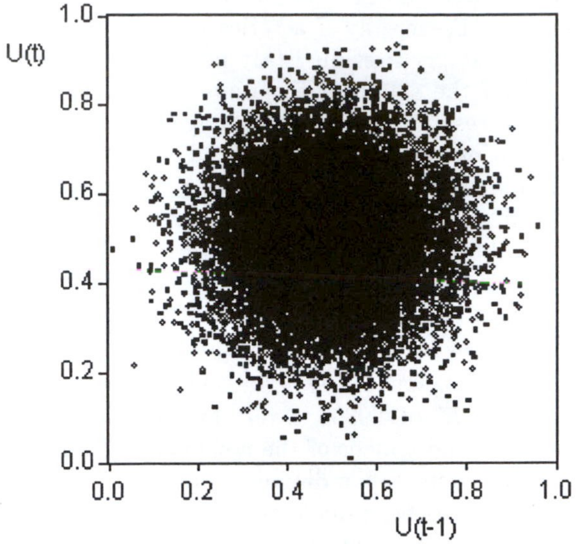

18.8a Scatter of Gaussian white noise (U)

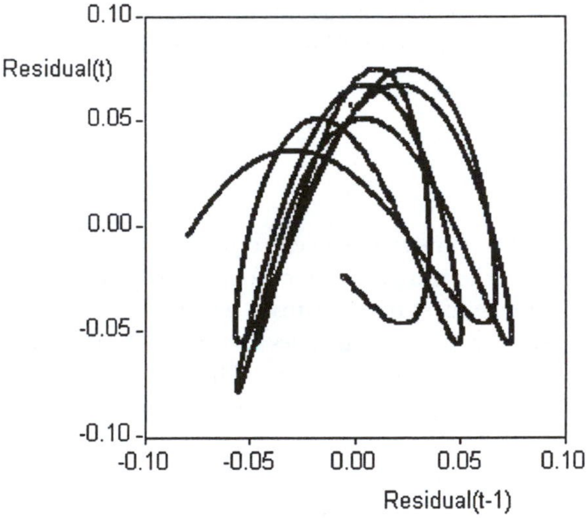

18.8b Scatter of residuals from ESTAR model fitted to chaotic data

Figure 18.8: Chaotic data and ESTAR transformation

Bibliography

Adams, D. (1978) 'The restaurant at the end of the universe', *A Hitchhiker's guide to the galaxy*, BBC Radio Series, also available (different versions) in Pan Books.

Adler, M. and Dumas, B. (1984) 'International portfolio choice and corporation finance', *Journal of Finance*, **39**, 935–84.

Aghion, P. and Howitt, P. (1992) 'A model of growth through creative destruction', *Econometrica*, **60**, 323–51.

Akerlof, G.A. and Yellen, J.L. (1987) 'Rational models of irrational behaviour', *American Economic Review*, **77**, 137–42.

Alesina, A. (1987) 'Macroeconomic policy in a two-party system as a repeated game', *Quarterly Journal of Economics*, **102**, 651–78

Alesina, A. (1989) 'Macroeconomics and politics', in S. Fisher (ed.), *NBER Macroeconomics Annual 1988*, Cambridge MA: MIT Press, 13–52.

Alesina, A. and Gatti, R. (1995) 'Independent Central Banks: Low Inflation at No Cost?' *American Economic Review, Papers and Proceedings*, 196–200.

Alesina, A. and Sachs, J. (1988) 'Political parties and the business cycle in the United States, 1948–1984', *Journal of Money, Credit and Banking*, **20**, 62–82.

Alesina, A. and Tabellini, G. (1989) 'External debt, capital flight and political risk', *Journal of International Economics*, **27**, 199–220.

Alesina, A. and Tabellini, G. (1990) 'A positive theory of fiscal deficits and government debt in a democracy', *Review of Economic Studies*, **57**, 403–14.

Alesina, A., Roubini, N. and Cohen, G. (1997) *Political Cycles and The Macroeconomy*, Cambridge, MA: MIT Press.

Alexander, S. (1961) 'Price Movements in Speculative Markets: trends or Random Walks', *Industrial Management Review*, **2**, 7–26.

Allen, D.E. (1985) *Introduction to the Theory of Finance*, Oxford: Basil Blackwell.

Anderson, P., Arrow, K. and Pines, D. (eds.) (1988) *The economy as an evolving complex system*, Redwood City, CA: Addison-Wesley.

Aoki, M. and Canzoneri, M. (1979) 'Reduced forms of rational expectations models', *Quarterly Journal of Economics*, **93**, 59–71.

Arrow, K.J. (1971) *Essays on the Theory of Risk Bearing*, Amsterdam: North-Holland.

Arrow, K.J. and Hahn, F.H. (1971) *General Competitive Analysis*, San Francisco: Holden Day. (reprinted, Amsterdam: North-Holland.)

Attfield, C.L.F., Demery, D. and Duck, N.W. (1981a) 'A quarterly model of unanticipated monetary growth, output and the price level in the UK 1963–78', *Journal of Monetary Economics*, **8**, 331–50.

Attfield, C.L.F., Demery, D. and Duck, N.W. (1981b) 'Unanticipated monetary growth, output and the price level', *European Economic Review*, **16**, 367–85.

Ausubel, L.M.(1990) 'Insider Trading in a Rational Expectations Economy', *American Economic Review*, **80**, 1022–41.

Backus, D. and Driffill, J. (1985a) 'Inflation and reputation', *American Economic Review*, **75**, 530–38.

Backus, D. and Driffill, J. (1985b) 'Rational Expectations and Policy Credibility Following a Change in Regime', *The Review of Economic Studies*, **52**, 211–21.

Baillie, R.T .and Bollerslev, T. (1990) 'A multivariate generalized ARCH approach to modelling risk premia in forward foreign exchange rate markets', *Journal of Intenational Money And Finance*, **9**, 309–24.

Baillie, R.T .and Bollerslev, T. (1994) 'The long memory of the forward premium', *Journal of International Money and Finance*, **13**, 309–24.

Baillie, R.T .and Bollerslev, T. (1997) 'The forward premium anomaly is not as bad as you think', Mimeo Michigan State University.

Baillie, R.T., Bollerslev, T. and Mikkelsen, H.-O. (1996) 'Fractionally integrated generalized autoregressive conditional heteroskedasticity', *Journal of Econometrics*, **74**, 3–30

Baillie, R.T., Chung, C.F. and Tieslau, M.A. (1996) 'Analysing inflation by the fractionally integrated ARFIMA-GARCH model', *Journal of Applied Econometrics*, **11**, 23–40.

Baillie, R.J., Lippens, R.E. and McMahon, P.C. (1983) 'Testing rational expectations and efficiency in the foreign exchange market', *Econometrica*, **51**, 553–63.

Baillie, R.J. and McMahon, P.C. (1989) *The foreign exchange market — theory and econometric evidence*, Cambridge: Cambridge University Press.

Balke, N.S. and Fomby, T.B. (1997) 'Threshold cointegration', *International Economic Review*, **38**, 627–46

Banerjee, A., Dolado, J., Galbraith, J.W. and Hendry, D.F. (1993)

Co-Integration, Error Correction and The Econometric Analysis Of Non-Stationary Data, Oxford: Oxford University Press

Barro, R.J. (1972) 'A theory of monopolistic price adjustment', *Review of Economic Studies*, **39**, 17–26.

Barro, R.J. (1974) 'Are government bonds net wealth?', *Journal of Political Economy*, **82**, 1095–117.

Barro, R.J. (1976) 'Rational expectations and the role of monetary policy', *Journal of Monetary Economics*, **2**, 1–33.

Barro, R.J. (1977) 'Unanticipated monetary growth and unemployment in the United States', *American Economic Review*, **67**, 101–15.

Barro, R.J. (1980) 'A capital market in an equilibrium business cycle model', *Econometrica*, **48**, 1393–417.

Barro, R.J. and Fischer, S. (1976) 'Recent developments in monetary theory', *Journal of Monetary Economics*, **2**, 133–67.

Barro, R.J. and Gordon, D. (1983) 'Rules, discretion and reputation in a model of monetary policy', *Journal of Monetary Economics*, **12**, 101–22.

Barro, R.J. and Rush, M. (1980) 'Unanticipated money and economic activity', in S. Fischer (ed.) *Rational Expectations and Economic Policy*, Chicago: University of Chicago Press.

Barro, R.J. and Sala-I-Martin, X. (1998) *Economic Growth*, Cambridge MA: MIT Press.

Bean, C., Layard, R. and Nickell S. (1986) 'The rise in unemployment: a multi-country study', Chapter 1 of Bean, Layard and Nickell (eds), *The Rise in Unemployment*, Oxford: Basil Blackwell.

Beaver, W.H. (1981) *Financial Accounting: An Accounting Revolution*, Englewood Cliffs, NJ: Prentice-Hall.

Beenstock, M. (1980) *A Neoclassical Analysis of Macroeconomic Policy*, Cambridge: Cambridge University Press.

Beetsma, R. and Jensen, H. (1998) 'Inflation targets and contracts with uncertain central banker preferences', *Journal of Money, Credit and Banking*, **30**, 384–403.

Begg, D.K.H. (1982) *The Rational Expectations Revolution in Macroeconomics — Theories and Evidence*, Oxford: Philip Allan.

Bekaert, G. (1996) 'The time variation of risk and return in foreign exchange markets', *Review of Financial Studies*, **9**, 427–70.

Bekaert, G., Hodrick, R. and Marshall, D. (2001) 'Peso problem explanations for term structure anomalies', *Journal of Monetary Economics*, **48**, 241–70.

Bell, S. and Beenstock, M. (1980) 'An application of rational expectations in the UK foreign exchange market', in D. Currie and W. Peters (eds) *Studies in Contemporary Economic Analysis*, **2**, London: Croom

Helm.

Benabou, R. and Laroque, G.(1992) 'Using privileged information to manipulate markets:insiders, gurus and credibility', *The Quarterly Journal Of Economics*, 921–58.

Benhabib, J. (ed.) (1992) *Cycles and Chaos in Economic Equilibrium*, Princeton NJ: Princeton University Press.

Bewley, T. (1980) 'The optimum quantity of money', in J.H. Kareken and N. Wallace (eds) *Models of Monetary Economies*, Minneapolis: Federal Reserve Bank of Minneapolis, pp.169–210.

Bilson, J.F.O. (1980) 'The rational expectations approach to the consumption function', *European Economic Review*, **13**, 273–99.

Black, S.A. (1973) *International Money Markets and Flexible Exchange Rates*, Studies in International Finance No. 32, Princeton NJ: International Finance Section, Princeton University.

Blanchard, O.J. (1979) 'Speculative Bubbles, Crashes, and Rational Expectations', *Economics Letters*, **3**, 387–9.

Blanchard, O.J. (1981) 'Output, the stock market and interest rates', *American Economic Review*, **71**, 132–43.

Blanchard, O.J. and Quah, D. (1989) 'The dynamic effects of aggregate demand and aggregate supply shocks', *American Economic Review*, **79(4)**, 655–673.

Blanchard, O. J. and Watson, M. (1982) 'Bubbles, Rational Expectations and Financial Markets', in P. Wachtel (ed.), *Crisis in the Economic and Financial Structure*, Lexington MA: Lexington Books, pp. 295–315.

Blanchard, O.J. and Wyplosz, C. (1981) 'An empirical structural model of aggregate demand', *Journal of Monetary Economics*, **7**, 1–28.

Blinder, A.S. (1994) 'Opening Statement of Alan S. Blinder at Confirmation Hearing Before the US Senate Committee on Banking, Housing, and Urban Affairs' (May), Mimeo, Federal Reserve Board

Blinder, A.S. and Solow, R.M. (1973) 'Does fiscal policy matter?' *Journal of Public Economics*, **2**, 319–37.

Blume, L., Easley, D. and O'Hara, M. (1994) 'Market statistics and technical analysis: the role of volume', *Journal of Finance*, **49**, 153–181.

Bollerslev, T., (1986) 'Generalized autoregressive conditional heteroscedasticity', *Journal of Econometrics*, **31**, 307–27

Bollerslev, T., Chou, R.Y. and Kroner, K.F. (1992) 'ARCH modeling in finance: a review of the theory and empirical evidence', *Journal of Econometrics*, **52**, 5–59

Bollerslev, T., Engle, R.F. and Nelson, D.B. (1994) 'ARCH models', in R.F. Engle and D.L. McFadden (eds.), *Handbook of Econometrics*, Amsterdam: Elsevier Science, pp. 2961–3038

Bollerslev, T., Engle, R.F. and Wooldridge, J.M. (1988). 'A capital asset pricing model with time varying covariances', *Journal of Political Economy*, **96**, 116–31

Borooah, V. and Van der Ploeg, R. (1982) 'British government popularity and economic performance. A comment', *Economic Journal*, **92**, 405–10.

Bos, C., Franses, P.H. and Ooms, M. (1999) 'Re-analyzing inflation rates: evidence of long memory and level shifts', *Empirical Economics*, **24**, 427–49

Box, G.E.P. and Jenkins, G.M. (1970) *Time Series Analysis: Forecasting and Control*, San Francisco: Holden-Day

Box, G.E.P., Jenkins, G.M. and Reinsel, G.C. (1994) *Time Series Analysis; Forecasting and Control*, 3rd edn., Englewood Cliffs, NJ: Prentice-Hall

Box-Steffensmeier, J. M. and Smith, R.M. (1996) 'The dynamics of aggregate partisanship', *American Political Science Review*, **90 (September)**, 567–80

Bray, M.M. and Savin, N.E. (1986) 'Rational Expectations Equilibria, Learning, and Model Selection', *Econometrica*, **54(5)**, 1129–60.

Briault, C.Haldane, A., and King, M. (1996) 'Independence and Accountability', in I. Kuroda (ed.), *Toward More Effective Monetary Policy*, Proceedings of the Seventh International Conference sponsored by the Bank of Japan's Institute for Monetary and Economic Studies, 26–27 October 1995, Basingstoke: Macmillan Press.

Brock, W., Dechert, W., Scheinkman, J. and LeBaron, B. (1996) 'A Test for Independence Based Upon the Correlation Dimension', *Econometric Reviews*, **15(3)**, 197–235.

Brock, W., Lakonishok, J. and LeBaron, B. (1992) 'Simple Technical Trading Rules sand the Stochastic Properties of Stock Returns', *Journal of Finance*, **47**, 1731–1764.

Brock, W.A. and Hommes, C. (1998) 'Heterogeneous beliefs and routes to chaos in a simple asset pricing model', *Journal of Economic Dynamics and Control*, **22**, 1235–74

Brock, W., Hsieh, D. and LeBaron, B. (1991) *Nonlinear dynamics, chaos, and instability — statistical theory and economic evidence*, Cambridge, MA: MIT Press.

Brockett, R.W. (1976) 'Volterra series and geometric control theory', *Automatica*, **12**, 167–176.

Brown, D.P.and Jennings, R.H. (1989) 'On Technical Analysis', *Review of Financial Studies*, **2**, 527–52.

Brown, S. Goetzmann, W. and Ross, S. 1995 'Survival' *Journal of Finance*, **50**, 853–73.

Brunner K., Cukierman, A. and Meltzer, A.H. (1980) 'Stagflation, persistent unemployment and the permanence of economic shocks', *Journal of Monetary Economics*, **6**, 467–92.

Brunner, K. and Meckling, W.H. (1977) 'The perception of man and the conception of government', *Journal of Money, Credit and Banking*, **9**, 70–85.

Brunnermeier, M.K. (1999) 'Prices and new information in financial markets, theoretical explanations for bubbles, crashes, technical analysis and herding', Mimeo, FMG Discussion Paper 270, London School of Economics.

Bruno, M. and Sachs, J.D. (1985) *The Economics of Worldwide Stagflation*, Oxford: Basil Blackwell..

Buiter, W.H. (1981) 'The superiority of contingent rules over fixed rules in models with rational expectations', *Economic Journal*, **91**, 647–70.

Buiter, W.H. (1983) 'Real effects of anticipated and unanticipated money: some problems of estimation and hypothesis testing', *Journal of Monetary Economics*, **11**, 207–24.

Buiter, W.H. (1999) 'The fallacy of the fiscal theory of the price level', CEPR discussion paper no. 2205, Centre for Economic Policy Research, London, August.

Buiter, W.H. and Miller, M. (1981) 'Monetary policy and international competitiveness: the problems of adjustment', *Oxford Economic Papers*, **33**, 143–75.

Buiter, W.H. and Tobin, J. (1979) 'Debt neutrality: a brief review of doctrine and evidence', in G. Von Furstenberg (ed.), *Social Security vs Private Saving in Post Industrial Societies*, New York: Ballinger.

Bullard, J. and Mitra, K. (2000) 'Learning about monetary policy rules', Mimeo, University of York.

Burda, M. (1988) 'Wait unemployment in Europe', *Economic Policy*, **7** (October), 391–416.

Byers, J.D., Davidson, J. and Peel, D.A. (1997) 'Modelling political popularity: an analysis of long-range dependence in opinion poll series', *Journal of the Royal Statistical Society Series A*, **160**, 471–490

Byers, J.D. and Peel, D.A. (1996) 'Long memory risk premia in exchange rates', *The Manchester School, 4, 421–38*

Byers, J.D., and Peel, D.A. (2000) 'Non-linear dynamics of inflation in high inflation economies', *The Manchester School*, **68**, 23–37.

Byers, J.D., Davidson, J. and Peel, D.A. (1999) 'The dynamics of aggregate political popularity: evidence from eight countries', *Electoral Studies, **19**, 49–62.*

Caballero, R.J., and Engel, R. (1992) 'Beyond The Partial Adjustment Model', *American Economic Review, Papers and Proceedings*, **82**,

360–64.

Cagan, P. (1956) 'The Monetary dynamics of hyperinflation', in M. Friedman (ed.) *Studies in the Quantity Theory of Money*, Chicago: University of Chicago Press.

Calvo, G.A. (1978) 'On the time inconsistency of optimal policy in a monetary economy', *Econometrica*, **46**, 1411–28.

Calvo, G. (1983) 'Staggered prices in a utility-maximizing framework', *Journal of Monetary Economics*, **12**, 383–98.

Campbell, J.Y. (1987) 'Stock Returns and The Term Structure', *Journal Of Financial Economics*, 373–99.

Campbell, J.Y. (1991) 'A Variance Decomposition for Stock Returns', *Economic Journal*, **101**, 157–79.

Campbell, J.Y. (1996) 'Consumption and the Stock Market: Interpreting International Evidence', National Bureau of Economic Research Working Paper 5610.

Campbell, J.Y. and Cochrane, J. H. (2000) 'Explaining the poor performance of consumption-based asset pricing models.' *Journal of Finance*, **55(6)**, 2863–78.

Campbell, J.Y., Lo, A.W. and Mackinlay, A.C. (1997) *The Econometrics of Financial Markets*, Princeton University Press, Princeton, New Jersey.

Campbell, J.Y. and Shiller, R. (1988a) 'The Dividend-Price Ratio and Expectations of Future Dividends and Discount Factors', *Review of Financial Studies*, **1**, 195–227.

Campbell, J.Y., and Shiller, R. (1988b) 'Stock prices, earnings and expected dividends', *Journal of Finance*, **43**, 661–676.

Canzoneri, M.B. (1980) 'Labour contracts and monetary policy', *Journal of Monetary Economics*, **6**, 241–55.

Canzoneri, M.B. (1983) 'Rational destabilizing speculation and exchange intervention policy', *Journal of Macroeconomics*, **5**, 75–90.

Carlson, J.A. and Parkin, M. (1975) 'Inflation expectations', *Economica*, **42**, 123–38.

Cass, D. and Shell, K. (eds) (1976) *The Hamiltonian Approach to Dynamic Economics*, Philadelphia: University of Pennsylvania Press.

Chappell, D. and Peel, D.A. (1979) 'On the political theory of the business cycle', *Economics Letters*, **2**, 327–32.

Cheung. Y.-W. and Diebold, F.X. (1994) 'On maximum likelihood estimation of the differencing parameter of fractionally integrated noise with unknown mean', *Journal of Econometrics*, **62**, 301–316

Chiang, A.C. (1984) *Fundamental Methods of Mathematical Economics*, 3rd edition, Irwin/McGraw-Hill.

Chow, G.C. (1975) *Analysis and Control of Dynamic Economic Systems*, New York: John Wiley.

Chow, G.C. (1980) 'Estimation of rational expectations models', *Journal of Economic Dynamics and Control*, **2**, 241–55.

Christiano, L., Eichenbaum, M. and Evans, C. (2002) 'Nominal rigidities and the dynamic effects of a shock to monetary policy', Mimeo, Northwestern University.

Chrystal, K.A. and Alt, J.E. (1981) 'Some problems in formulating and testing a politico-economic model of the United Kingdom', *Economic Journal*, **91**, 730–36.

Clarida, R., Gali, J. and Gertler, M. (1999) 'The science of monetary policy: a New Keynesian perspective', *Journal of Economic Literature*, **37(4)**, 1661–1707.

Cleaver, K. (1986) *The Crisis in Economics*, Unpublished Ph.D. thesis, University of Liverpool, Chapter 7.

Clower, R. (1965) 'The Keynesian counter-revolution: a theoretical appraisal', in F.H. Hahn and F.P.R. Brechling (eds) *The Theory of Interest Rates*, London: Macmillan.

Constantinides, G.M. (1990) 'Habit Formation:A Resolution of the Equity Premium Puzzle', *Journal of Political Economy*, **98**, 519–543.

Constantinides, G.M. and Duffie, D. (1996) 'Asset Pricing with Heterogeneous Consumers', *Journal of Political Economy*, **104**, 219–487.

Copeland, T.E. and Weston, J.F. (1988) *Financial Theory and Corporate Policy*, 3rd edn. Reading, MA: Addison-Wesley.

Cornell, B. (1977) 'Spot rates, forward rates and exchange market efficiency', *Journal of Financial Economics*, **5**, 55–65.

Crafts, N. (1997) *Britain's relative economic decline 1870–1995: a quantitative perspective*, London: The Social Market Foundation.

Crewe, I. (1988) 'Has the electorate become Thatcherite?' in R. Skidelsky (ed.), in *Thatcherism*, Oxford: Basil Blackwell, pp. 25–49.

Cukierman, A. (1992) *Central Bank Strategies, Credibility and Independence*, Cambridge, MA: MIT Press

Cukierman, A. and Meltzer, A. (1986a) 'A positive theory of discretionary policy, the cost of a democratic government, and the benefits of a constitution', *Economic Inquiry*, **24**, 367–88.

Cukierman, A. and Meltzer, A.H. (1986b) 'A theory of ambiguity, credibility, and inflation under discretion and asymmetric information', *Econometrica*, **54**, 1099–128.

Cutler, D.M., Poterba, J.M. and Summers, L.H. (1990) 'Speculative dynamics and the role of feedback traders', *American Economic Review*, **80**, 63–8.

Cutler, D.M., Poterba, J.M. and Summers, L.H. (1991), 'Speculative dynamics', *Review of Economic Studies*, **58**, 529–46.

Cyert, R.M and DeGroot, M.H. (1974) 'Rational expectations and bayesian analysis', *Journal of Political Economy*, **82**, 521–36.

Davidson, J.E.H. and Hendry, D.F., Srba, F. and Yeo, S. (1978) 'Econometric modelling of aggregate time series relationship between consumer's expenditure and income in the United Kingdom', *Economic Journal*, **88**, 661–92.

Davidson, J.E.H. and Hendry, D.F. (1981) 'Interpreting econometric evidence: the behaviour of consumers' expenditure in the UK', *European Economic Review*, **16**, 177–92.

Davis, J. and Minford, P. (1986) 'Germany and the European disease' (Symposium on unemployment in Europe, eds. J. Muysken and C. de Neubourg) *Recherches Economiques de Louvain*, **52**, 373–98.

De Grauwe, P and Dewachter, H.and Embrechts, M. (1997) *Exchange Rate Theory — Chaotic Models of Foreign Exchange Markets'*, Oxford: Blackwell..

De Long, J.B., Shleifer, A., Summers, L.H. and Waldman, R.J. (1991), 'Survival of noise traders in financial markets', *Journal of Finance*, **64**, 1–19.

DeCanio, S.J. (1979) 'Rational expectations and learning from experience', *Quarterly Journal of Economics*, **83**, 47–57

Dechert W. D. (ed.) (1996) *Chaos Theory in Economics — Methods, Models and Evidence*, Cheltenham: Edward Elgar.

Dechert W. E. and Hommes, C. (eds.) (2000) 'Complex nonlinear dynamics and computational methods', *Journal of economic dynamics and control*, **24**, 651–62.

Demery, D. (1984) 'Exchange rate dynamics — the Swiss/US case', *European Economic Review*, **24**, 151–59.

Denison, E.F. (1974) *Accounting for United States economic growth, 1929–1969*, Washington DC: Brookings Institution

Diba, B.T. and Grossman, H.L. (1988) 'The theory of rational bubbles in stock prices', *Economic Journal*, **98**, 746–57.

Dickey, D.A. and Fuller, W.A. (1981) 'Likelihood ratio tests for autoregressive time series with a unit root', *Econometrica*, **49**, 1057–72.

Dickinson, D.G., Driscoll, M.J. and Ford, J.L. (1982) 'Rational expectations, random parameters and the non-neutrality of money', *Economica*, **49**, 241–8.

Diebold, F.X. (1994) 'Regime Switching with Time-Varying Transition Probabilities', in C. Hargreaves (ed.), *Nonstationary Time Series Analysis and Cointegration*, (Advanced Texts in Econometrics, C.W.J. Granger and G. Mizon, eds.), 1994. Oxford: Oxford University Press, pp. 283–302.

Diebold, F.X. and Lopez, J.A. (1995) 'Modelling volatility dynamics', in K. Hoover (ed.), *Macroeconometrics — Developments, Tensions and Prospects*, Boston: Kluwer, pp. 427–72.

Diebold, F.X. and Mariano, R.S. (1995) 'Comparing predictive accuracy', *Journal of Business & Economic Statistics*, **13**, 253–63

Diebold, F.X.and Nason, J.A. (1990) 'Nonparametric exchange rate prediction', *Journal of International Economics*, **28**, 315–332.

Diebold, F.X. and Rudebusch, G.D. (1989) 'Long memory and persistence in aggregate output', *Journal of Monetary Economics*, **24**, 189–209.

Ding, Z. and Granger, C.W.J. (1996) 'Modelling volatility persistence of speculative returns: a new approach', *Journal of Econometrics*, **73**, 185–215

Ding, Z., Granger, C.W.J. and Engle, R.F. (1993) 'A long memory property of stock market returns and a new model', *Journal of Empirical Finance*, **1**, 83–106

Domowitz, I. and Hakkio, C.S. (1985) 'Conditional Variance and the Risk Premium in the Foreign Exchange Market', *Journal Of International Economics*, **18**, 47–66.

Dornbusch, R. (1976) 'Expectations and exchange rate dynamics', *Journal of Political Economy*, **84**, 1161–76.

Downs, A. (1957) *An Economic Theory of Democracy*, New York: Harper and Row.

Driskill, R.A. (1981) 'Exchange rate dynamics: an empirical investigation', *Journal of Political Economy*, **2**, 357–71.

Dueker, M.J. (1997) 'Markov switching in GARCH processes and mean-reverting stock-market volatility', *Journal of Business & Economic Statistics*, **15**, 26–34

Dumas, B. (1992) 'Dynamic equilibrium and the real exchange rate in a spatially separated world', *Review of Financial Studies*, **5**, 153–80

Dwyer, G.P., Locke, P. and Yu, W. (1996) 'Index arbitrage and nonlinear dynamics between the S&P 500 futures and cash', *Review of Financial Studies*, **9**, 301–32

Eitrheim, O. and Terasvirta, T. (1996) 'Testing the adequacy of smooth transition autoregressive models', *Journal of Econometrics*, **74**, 59–76

Ellison, M. and Valla, N. (2000) 'Learning, uncertainty and central bank activism in an economy with strategic interactions', Mimeo, European Central Bank, No.28.

Enders, W. and Granger, C.W.J. (1998) 'Unit-root tests and asymmetric adjustment with an example using the term structure of interest rates', *Journal of Business & Economic Statistics*, **16**, 304–11

Engel, C. (1996) 'The forward discount anomaly and the risk premium: a survey of recent evidence', *Journal of Empirical Finance*, **3**, 123–92.

Engle, R.F. (1982) 'Autoregressive conditional heteroscedasticity with estimates of the variance of United Kingdom inflation', *Econometrica*, **50**, 987–1007.

Engle, R.F. and Bollerslev, T. (1986) 'Modelling the persistence of conditional variances', *Econometric Reviews*, **5**, 1–50 (with discussion)

Engle, R.F. and Granger C.W.J (1987) 'Co-integration and error correction: representation, estimation and testing.' *Econometrica*, **55**, 251–76

Engle, R.F. and Smith, A.D. (1998) 'Stochastic Permanent Breaks', UCSD Economics Discussion Paper 98–03.

Epstein, L.G. and Zin, Stanley E. (1989) 'Substitution, risk aversion and the temporal behaviour of asset returns: a theoretical framework', *Econometrica*, **57**, 937–69.

Epstein, L.G. and Zin, Stanley E. (1991) 'Substitution, risk aversion and the temporal behaviour of asset returns', *Journal of Political Economy*, **99**, 263–87.

Erceg, C.J., Henderson, D.W., and Levin, A.T. (2000) 'Optimal monetary policy with staggered wage and price contracts', *Journal of Monetary Economics*, **46**, October, 281–313.

Evans, G. (1985) 'Expectational stability and the multiple equilibria problem in linear rational expectations models', *The Quarterly Journal of Economics*, **100**, 1217–33.

Evans, G. (1986) 'Selection criteria for models with non-uniqueness', *Journal of Monetary Economics*, **18**, 147–57 .

Evans, G.W. (1991) 'Pitfalls in testing for explosive bubbles in asset prices', *American Economic Review*, **81**, 922–30.

Evans, G. and Honkapohja, S. (1998) 'Economic dynamics with learning; new stability results', *Review of Economic Studies*, **65**, 23–44.

Evans, G and Honkapohja, S. (1999) 'Learning dynamics' Chapter 7 in J.Taylor and M.Woodford (eds), *Handbook of Macroeconomics*, North-Holland, 449–542.

Evans, G. and Honkapohja, S. (2001) *Learning and Expectations in Macroeconomics*, Princeton, NJ: Princeton University Press.

Evans, G.W. and Ramsey, G. (1992) 'Expectations calculation and currency collapse', *American Economic Review*, **82**, 207–24.

Evans, M.D.D. (1995) 'Peso problems: their theoretical and empirical implications', in G.S. Maddala and C.R. Rao (eds), *Handbook of Statistical Methods in Finance*, North-Holland.

Evans, M.D.D. and Lewis, K.K. (1993) 'Do risk premia explain it all? evidence from the term structure', *Journal of Monetary Economics*, **33**, 285–318.

Evans, M.D.D. and Lewis, K.K. (1993) 'Trends in Foreign Exchange and Eurocurrency Returns', *European Economic Review*, **37**, 1005–1019.

Fair, R.C. and Parke, W.R. (1989) *The Fair-Parke Program for the Estimation and Analysis of Nonlinear econometric Models*, Southborough, MA: Macro Inc.

Fair, R.C. and Taylor, J.B. (1983) 'Solution and maximum likelihood estimation of dynamic nonlinear rational expectations models', *Econometrica*, **51**, 1169–86.

Fama, E.F. (1970) 'Efficient capital markets: a review of theory and empirical work', *Journal of Finance*, **25**, 383–417.

Fama, E.F. (1975) 'Short term interest rates as predictors of inflation', *American Economic Review*, **65**, 269–82.

Fama, E.F. (1976) *Foundations of Finance*, Oxford: Basil Blackwell.

Fama, E.F. (1984) 'Forward and spot exchange rates', *Journal of Monetary Economics*, **14**, 319–338.

Fama, E.F. and Blume, M. (1970) 'Filter rules and stock market trading profits', *Journal of Business*, **39**, (special supplement, January), 226–41.

Fama, E.F. and French, K.R. (1988) 'Permanent and temporary components of stock prices', *Journal of Political Economy*, **96**, 246–73.

Fama, E.F. and French, K.R. (1989) 'Business conditions and expected returns on stock and bonds', *Journal of Financial Economics*, **25**, 23–49.

Feige, E.L. and Pierce, D.K. (1976) 'Economically rational expectations: are innovations in the rate of inflation independent of innovations in measures of monetary and fiscal policy', *Journal of Political Economy*, **84**, 499–552.

Feigenbaum, M.J. (1980) 'Universal behaviour in non-linear systems', *Los Alamos Science*, **1**, 4–27.

Feldstein, M. (1995) 'The effect of marginal tax rates on taxable income: a panel study of the 1986 Tax Reform Act', *Journal of Political Economy*, **103(3)**, 551–72.

Figlewski, S. (1978) 'Market efficiency in a market with heterogeneous information', *Journal of Political Economy*, **86**, 581–597.

Finnerty, J.E. (1976) 'Insiders and market efficiency', *Journal of Finance*, **31**, 1131–48.

Fischer, S. (1977a) 'Long term contracts, rational expectations and the optimum money supply rule', *Journal of Political Economy*, **85**, 191–205.

Fischer, S. (1977b) 'Long-term contracting, sticky prices, and monetary policy — a comment', *Journal of Monetary Economics*, **3**, 317–23.

Fischer, S. (ed.) (1980a) *Rational Expectations and Economic Policy*, Chicago: University of Chicago Press.

Fischer, S. (1980b) 'Dynamic inconsistency, cooperation and the benevolent dissembling government', *Journal of Economic Dynamics and Control*, **2**, 93–107.

Flavin, M. (1983) 'Excess volatility in the financial markets: a reassessment of the empirical evidence', *Journal of Political Economy*, **91**, 929–56.

Fleming, J.M. (1962) 'Domestic financial policies under fixed and under floating exchange rates', IMF Staff Papers, **9**, 369–79.

Flood, R.P. and Garber, P.M. (1980) 'Market fundamentals versus price-level bubbles: the first tests', *Journal of Political Economy*, **8**, 745–70.

Fourgeaud, C., Gourieroux, C. and Pradel, J. (1986) 'Learning procedures and convergence to rationality', *Econometrica*, **54**, 845–68.

Frankel, J.A. (1979) 'On the Mark: a theory of floating exchange rates based on real interest differentials', *American Economic Review*, **69**, 610–22.

Frankel, J.A. (1982) 'The mystery of the multiplying marks: a modification of the monetary model', *Review of Economics and Statistics*, **64**, 515–9.

Frankel, J.A.and Froot, K. (1987) 'Using survey data to test some standard propositions regarding exchange rate expectations', *American Economic Review*, **77**, 133–53.

Franses, P.H. and van Dijk, D. (2000) '*Nonlinear Time Series Models in Empirical Finance*, Cambridge: Cambridge University Press.

Frenkel, J. (1977) 'The forward exchange rate, expectations and the demand for money: the German hyperinflation', *American Economic Review*, **70**, 771–5.

Frenkel, J. (1981) 'Flexible exchange rates, prices and the role of the "news": lessons from the 1970s', *Journal of Political Economy*, **89**, 665–704.

Frenkel, J. and Levich, R. (1975) 'Covered interest arbitrage: unexploited profits?', *Journal of Political Economy*, **83**, 325–9.

Frey, B.S. and Schneider, F. (1978a) 'A politico-economic model of the United Kingdom', *Economic Journal*, **88**, 243–53.

Frey, B.S. and Schneider, F. (1978b) 'An empirical study of politico-economic interaction in the United States', *Review of Economics and Statistics*, **60**, 174–83.

Friederich, S. Gregory, A. Matatko, J. and Tonks, I. (2000) 'Stock

Price Patterns around Directors'Trades on the London Stock Exchange', Mimeo, University of Exeter

Friedman, B.M. (1978) 'Discussion of "After Keynesian macroeconomics" by R.E. Lucas and T.J. Sargent' in *After the Phillips Curve: Persistence of high Inflation and High Unemployment*, Boston: Federal Reserve Bank of Boston Conference Series, no. 19, pp. 73–80.

Friedman, B.M. (1979) 'Optimal expectations and the extreme information assumptions of rational expectations macromodels', *Journal of Monetary Economics*, **5(1)**, 23–41.

Friedman, B.M. (1979) 'Optimal expectations and the extreme information assumptions of rational expectations', *Journal of Monetary Economics*, **5(1)**, 23–42.

Friedman, M. (1953) 'The methodology of positive economics' in *Essays in Positive Economics*, Chicago: University of Chicago Press.

Friedman, M. (1957) *A Theory of the Consumption Function*, Princeton NJ: Princeton University Press.

Friedman, M. (1968) 'The role of monetary policy', *American Economic Review*, **58**, 1–17.

Friedman M. and Meiselman, D. (1963) 'The relative stability of monetary velocity and the investment multiplier in the US 1898–1958', in Commission on Money and Credit, *Stabilisation Policies*, Englewood Cliffs NJ: Prentice-Hall.

Froot, K.A. and Frankel, J.A. (1989) 'Forward discount bias: is it an exchange rate premium', *Quarterly Journal Of Economics*, **104**, 139–61.

Froot, K.A. and Obstfeld, M. (1991) 'Intrinsic bubbles: the case of stock prices', *American Economic Review*, **81**, 1189–214.

Froot, K.A., Scharfstein, D.S. and Stern, J.C. (1992) 'Herd on the street: informational inefficiencies in a market with short-term speculation', *Journal of Finance*, **47**, 1461–84.

Froot, K.A.and Thaler, R.H. (1990) 'Anomalies: foreign exchange', *Journal of Economic Perspectives*, **4**, 179–92.

Frydman, R. and Phelps, E.S. (1983) *Individual Forecasting and Aggregate Outcomes — 'Rational Expectations' Examined*, Cambridge: Cambridge University Press.

Gali, J., and Monacelli, T. (2002) 'Monetary policy and exchange rate volatility in a small open economy', Mimeo, Universitat Pompeu Fabra.

Garber, P. (1989) 'Tulipmania', *Journal of Political Economy*, **97**, 535–60.

Gartner, M. (1994) 'Democracy, elections and Macroeconomic Policy: Two Decades of Progress', *European Journal of Political Economy*, **10**, 85–109.

Gordon, M. (1962) *The Investment, Financing and Evaluation of the Corporation*, Homewood, Ill: Irwin.

Gourieroux, C., Laffont, J.J. and Montfort, A. (1982) 'Rational expectations in dynamic linear models — analysis of the solutions', *Econometrica*, **50**, 409–25.

Grandmont J. (ed.) (1986) *Nonlinear economic dynamics'*, New York: Academic Press.

Granger, C.W.J. (1980) 'Long memory relationships and the aggregation of dynamic models', *Journal of Econometrics*, **14**, 227–38

Granger, C.W.J. (1993) 'Strategies for modelling nonlinear time-series relationships', *Economic Record*, **69**, 233–8.

Granger, C.W.J. and Andersen, A. (1978) *An Introduction to Bilinear Time Series Models*, Gottingen: Vandenhoeck & Ruprecht.

Granger, C.W.J. and Hallman, J. (1991) 'Long memory series with attractors', *Oxford Bulletin of Economics and Statistics*, **53**, 11–26.

Granger, C.W.J. and Hyung, N. (1999) 'Occasional structural breaks and long memory', UCSD Economics Discussion Paper 99–14

Granger, C.W.J. and Joyeux, R. (1980) 'An introduction to long memory time series models and fractional differencing', *Journal of Time Series Analysis*, **1(1)**, 15–29.

Granger, C.W.J. and Lee, T.H. (1989) 'Investigation of production, sales and inventory relationships using multicointegration and non-symmetric error correction models', *Journal of Applied Econometrics*, **4**, S145–S159.

Granger, C.W. and Pesaran, M.H. (1999) 'Economic and statistical measures of forecast accuracy', Mimeo, University of Cambridge.

Granger, C.W.J. and Swanson, N.R. (1996) 'Future developments in the study of cointegrated variables', *Oxford Bulletin of Economics and Statistics*, **58**, 537–53.

Granger, C.W.J. and Terasvirta, T. (1993) *Modelling Nonlinear Economic Relationships*, Oxford: Oxford University Press.

Granger, C.W.J. and Terasvirta, T. (1999) 'A simple nonlinear time series model with misleading linear properties', *Economics Letters*, **62**, 161–5.

Granger, C.W.J., Terasvirta, T. and Anderson, H. (1993) 'Modeling non-linearity over the business cycle', in J.H. Stock and M.W. Watson (eds), *New Research on Business Bycles, Indicators and Forecasting*, Chicago: Chicago University Press, 311–25.

Grassberger, P. and Procaccia, I. (1983) 'Measuring the strangeness of strange attractors', *Physica*, 9D, 189–208.

Graybill, F.A. (1961) *An Introduction to Linear Stochastic Models, 1* , New York: McGraw-Hill.

Gregory, A.,Matatko, J. and Tonks, I. 1997, 'Detecting information from directors' trades: signal definition and variable size effects', *Journal of Business Finance and Accounting*, **24(3–4)**, 309–42.

Gregory, A., Matatko, J. Tonks, I. and .Purkis, R (1994), 'UK directors' trading: the impact of dealings in smaller firms', *Economic Journal*, **104**, 37–53.

Grossman, G. M. and Helpman, E. (1991) *Innovation and growth in the global economy*, MIT Press, Cambridge Mass.

Grossman, S.J. and Stiglitz, J.E. (1976) 'Information and competitive price systems', *American Economic Review*, **66**, 246–53.

Grossman, S.J. and Stiglitz, J.E. (1980) 'On the impossibility of informationally efficient markets', *American Economic Review*, **70**, 393–407.

Guesnerie, R. (1992) 'An Exploration of the eductive justification of the rational-expectations hypothesis', *American Economic Review*, **82**, 1254–78.

Gurley, J. and Shaw, E.S. (1960) *Money in a Theory of Finance*, Washington DC: Brookings Institution.

Hacche, G. and Townsend, J. (1981) 'Exchange rates and monetary policy: modelling sterling's effective exchange rate', *Oxford Economic Papers*, **33**, 201–47.

Haggan, V and Ozaki, T. (1981) 'Modelling nonlinear random vibration using an amplitude-dependent autoregressive time series model', *Biometrika*, **68**, 189–96.

Hall, R.E. (1978) 'Stochastic implications of the life cycle-permanent income hypothesis: theory and evidence', *Journal of Political Economy*, **86**, 971–88.

Hall, R.L. and Hitch, C.J. (1939) 'Price theory and business behaviour', *Oxford Economic Papers*, no. 2, May, 12–45. (Reprinted in Wilson and Andrews, 1951.)

Hamilton, J.D. (1989) 'A new approach to the economic analysis of nonstationary time series subject to changes in regime', *Econometrica*, **57**, 357–84.

Hamilton, J.D. (1994) *Time Series Analysis*, Princeton NJ: Princeton University Press.

Hansen, B.E. (1996) 'Inference when a nuisance parameter is not identified under the null hypothesis', *Econometrica*, **64**, 413–30.

Hansen, B.E. (1997) 'Inference in TAR models', *Studies in Nonlinear Dynamics and Econometrics*, **2**, 1–14.

Hansen, L.P and Hodrick, R.(1980) 'Forward Exchange Rates as Optimal Predictors of Future Spot Rates: An Econometric Analysis', *Journal of Political Economy*, **88**, 829–53.

Hansen, L.P and Hodrick, R. (1983) 'Risk Averse Speculation in the

Forward Foreign Exchange Market: An Econometric Analysis of Linear Models', in Jacob A. Frenkel, (ed.), *Exchange Rates and International Macroeconomics*, Chicago: University of Chicago Press, pp.113–142.

Hansen, L.P. and Sargent, T.J. (1980) 'Formulating and estimating dynamic linear rational expectations models', *Journal of Economic Dynamics and Control*, **2**, 7–46.

Hardle, W. (1990) *Applied Non-Prametric Regression*, Cambridge: Cambridge University Press.

Hart, O.D. (1983) 'Optimal labour contracts under asymmetric information: an introduction', *Review of Economic Studies*, **50**, 3–36.

Harte, C.P. (1986) 'Political economy and the new macroeconomics', Unpublished M.Phil. thesis, University of Liverpool, chapters 2 and 3.

Harte, C.P., Minford, A.P.L. and Peel, D.A. (1983) 'The political economy of government macroeconomic stabilisation policy', mimeo, University of Liverpool; also available as chapter 3 of Harte (1986).

Hartley, J.E., Hoover, K.D. and Salyer, K.D. (1998) *Real Business Cycles: a reader*, London and New York: Routledge.

Harvey, C.R. and Siddique, A. (2000) 'Conditional skewness in asset pricing tests', Journal of Finance, **55**, 1263–95.

Hayek, F.A. (1988) *The Fatal Conceit: the errors of Socialism*, London: Routledge.

Hellwig, M.F. (1982) 'Rational expectations equilibrium with conditioning on past prices. A mean variance example', *Journal of Economic Theory*, **26**, 279–312.

Henderson, D.W., and McKibbin, W.J. (1993) 'An assessment of some basic monetary-policy regime pairs: analytical and simulation results from simple multi-region macroeconomic models', in R.C. Bryant, P. Hooper and C.L. Mann (eds.), *Evaluating policy regimes — new research in empirical macroeconomics*, Washington DC: Brookings Institution.

Herrendorf, B. and Neumann, M.J.M. (1998) 'The political economy of inflation, labour market distortions and central bank independence', CEPR discussion paper 1969, Centre for Economic Policy Research, London.

Hibbs, D.A. Jr. (1978) 'Political parties and macroeconomic policy', *American Political Science Review*, **72**, 981–1007.

Hicks, J.R. (1939) *Value and Capital*, Oxford: Clarendon Press.

Hillier, B. and Malcomson, J. (1984) 'Dynamic inconsistency, rational expectations and optimal government policy', *Econometrica*, **52**, 1437–51.

Hodrick, R.J. (1989) 'Risk, uncertainty and exhange rates', *Journal of Monetary Economics*, **23**, 433–59.

Hodrick, R.J.and Srivastava, S. (1986) 'The covariation of risk premiums and expected future spot rates', *Journal of International Money and Finance*, **5**, 5–21.

Hoel, P.G. (1962) *Introduction to Mathematical Statistics*, 3rd edn. New York: John Wiley.

Holden, K. and Broomhead, A. (1990) 'An examination of vector autoregressive forecasts for the U.K. economy', *International Journal of Forecasting*, **6**, 11–23.

Holden, K. and Peel, D.A. (1977) 'An empirical investigation of inflationary expectations', *Oxford Bulletin of Economics and Statistics*, **39**, 291–9.

Holden, K., Peel, D.A. and Thompson, J.L. (1985) *Expectations — Theory and Evidence*, London: Macmillan.

Holly, S. and Zarrop, M.B. (1983) 'On optimality and time consistency when expectations are rational', *European Economic Review*, **20**, 23–40.

Holt, C.C., Modigliani, F., Muth, J.F. and Simon, H.A. (1960) *Planning Production, Inventories and Work Force*, Englewood Cliffs, NJ: Prentice-Hall.

Hosking, J.R.M. (1981) 'Fractional Differencing', *Biometrika*, **68**, 165–76.

Hsieh, D.A. (1991) 'Chaos and nonlinear dynamics: application to financial markets', *Journal Of Finance*, **46(5)**, 1839–76.

Hwang, S. and Satchell, S. (1997) 'Modelling emerging market risk premia using higher moments', Mimeo, University Of Cambridge.

Ikeda, S.and Shibata, A. (1992) 'Fundamentals-Dependent Bubbles in Stock Prices', *Journal of Monetary Economics*, **30**, 143–68

Jaffe, J. (1974) 'The effect of regulation changes on insider trading', *Bell Journal of Economics and Management Science'*, **5**, 93–121.

Jansen, E.S. and Terasvirta, T. (1996) 'Testing parameter constancy ansd super exogeneity in econometric equations', *Oxford Bulletin of Economics and Statistics*, **58**, 735–68.

Jeng, L.A. Metrick, A. and Zeckhauser, R.A.(1999) 'Estimating the returns to insider trading', Mimeo, Boston University.

John, K and Lang, L.H. (1991) 'Insider trading around dividend announcements: theory and evidence', *Journal Of Finance*, **46(4)**, 1361–89.

Johnson, H.G. (1968) 'Problems of efficiency in monetary management', *Journal of Political Economy*, **76**, 971–90.

Johnston, J. and DiNardo, J. (1997) *Econometric Methods*, 4th edition, New York: McGraw Hill.

Jordan J.S. and Radner, R. (1982) 'Rational expectations in microeconomic models, an overview', *Journal of Economic Theory*, **26**, 201–23.

Kabir, R., and T. Vermaelen, 1996, 'Insider Trading Restrictions and the Stock Market: Evidence from the Amsterdam Stock Exchange', *European Economic Review*, **40**, 1591–603.

Kalman, R.E. (1960) 'A new approach to linear filtering and prediction problems', Trans. ASME, *Journal of Basic Engineering*, Series D, **82**, 35–45.

Kaminsky, G. (1993) 'Is there a peso problem? Evidence from the dollar/pound exchange rate 1976–1987', *American Economic Review*, **3**, 450–72.

Karni, E. (1980) 'A note on Lucas's equilibrium model of the business cycle', *Journal of Political Economy*, **88**, 1231–8.

Kendall, M. G., and Stuart, A. (1961) *The Advanced Theory of Statistics*, **2**, New York: Hafner.

Keown, A.J. Pinkerton, J.M.(1981) 'Merger Announcements and Insider Trading Activity: An Empirical Investigation', *Journal of Finance*, **36(4)**, 855–69

Keynes, J.M. (1936) *The General Theory of Employment, Interest and Money*, London: Macmillan.

Keynes, J.M. (1939) 'Professor Tinbergen's method', *Economic Journal*, **49**, 558–68.

Khanna, N. Slezak, S.L. and Bradley, M.(1994) 'Insider trading, outside search, and resource allocation: why firms and society may disagree on insider trading restrictions' *The Review of Financial Studies*, **7**(3), 575–608.

King, M., and A. Roell, 1988, 'Insider Trading', *Economic Policy*, **7**, 163–93.

King, R.G. (1982) 'Monetary policy and the information content of prices', *Journal of Political Economy*, **90**, 247–79.

King, R.G. and Plosser, C.I. (1981) 'The behaviour of money, credit and prices in a real business cycle', Mimeo, University of Rochester.

Kiyotaki, N. and R. Wright (1989) 'On money as a medium of exchange' *Journal of Political Economy*, **97** (August), 927–54

Kiyotaki, N. and R. Wright (1991) 'A contribution to the pure theory of money', *Journal of Economic Theory*, **53**(2) (April), 215–35.

Kiyotaki, N. and R. Wright (1993) 'A search-theoretic approach to monetary economics', *American Economic Review*, **83** (March), 63–77.

Kleidon, A. (1986) 'Bias in Small Sample Tests of Stock Price Rationality', *Journal of Business*, **59**, 237–61.

Kochin, L.A. (1974) 'Are future taxes anticipated by consumers?', *Journal of Money Credit and Banking*, **6**, 385–94.

Kortian, T. (1995) 'Modern approaches to asset price formation: a survey of recent theoretical literature' Mimeo, International and Economic Research Department, Reserve Bank of Australia.

Koyck, L.M. (1954) *Distributed Lags and Investment Analysis*, Contributions to Economic Analysis no. 4, Amsterdam: North-Holland.

Kraus, A. and Litzenberger, R.H. (1976) 'Skewness Preference and the Valuation of Risk Assets', The Journal of Finance, **31**(4), 1085–100.

Krugman, P.R. (1978) 'Purchasing power parity and exchange rates: another look at the evidence', *Journal of International Economics*, **8**, 397–407.

Kuznetsov, Y. (1995) *Elements of applied bifurcation theory*, New York: Springer.

Kwiatkowski, D., Phillips, P.C.B., Schmidt, P. and Shin, Y. (1992) 'Testing the null hypothesis of stationarity against the alternative of a unit root', *Journal of Econometrics*, **54**, 159–78.

Kydland, F.E. and Prescott, E.C. (1977) 'Rules rather than discretion: the inconsistency of optimal plans', *Journal of Political Economy*, **85**, 473–91.

Kydland, F. and Prescott, E.C. (1982) 'Time to build and aggregate fluctuations', *Econometrica*, **50**, 1345–70.

Kyle, A., 1985, 'Continuous auctions and insider trading', *Econometrica*, **53**(4), 1315–35.

Laidler, D.E.W. (1982) *Monetarist Perspectives*, Oxford: Philip Allan.

Laidler, D. W., and Parkin, M.J. (1975) 'Inflation: a survey', *Economic Journal*, **85**, 741–809

Lal, D. (1998) *Unintended Consequences — the impact of factor endowments, culture and politics on long-run economic performance*, Cambridge MA: MIT Press.

Lancaster, T. (1979) 'Economic models for the duration of unemployement', *Econometrica*, **4**, 939–956.

Lane, J., Peel, D.A. and Raeburn, E. (1996) 'Some Empirical Evidence on the Time Series Properties of Four U.K. Asset Prices', *Economica*, **63**, 405–26.

Lawrence, C. (1983) 'Rational expectations, supply shocks and the stability of the inflation output trade-off: some time series evidence for the United Kingdom 1956–1977', *Journal of Monetary Economics*, **11**, 225–46.

Lawrence H. White (1999) *The Theory of Monetary Institutions*, Blackwell, Oxford.

Layard, R. and Nickell, S. (1985) 'The causes of British Unemployment', *National Institute Economic Review*, **111** (February), 62–85.

Layard, R., Nickell, S. and Jackman, R. (1991) *Unemployment — macroeconomic performance and the labour market*, Oxford: Oxford University Press.

Leamer, E. (1978) *Specification Searches*, New York: John Wiley and Sons Inc.

LeBaron, B. (1994) 'Chaos and Nonlinear Forecastability in Economics and Finance', *Philosophical Transactions of the Royal Society of London (A), **348**, 397–404.*

Leiderman, L. (1980) 'Macroeconomic testing of the rational expectations and structural neutrality hypothesis for the United States', *Journal of Monetary Economics*, **6**, 69–82.

Leland, H. 1992, 'Should Insider Trading Be Prohibited?', *Journal of Political Economy*, **100**(4), 859–87.

LeRoy, S.and LaCivita, C. (1981) 'Risk Aversion and the Dispersion of Asset Prices', *Journal of Business*, **54**, 535–47.

LeRoy, S.and Porter, R. (1981) 'The Present Value Relation: Tests Based on Variance Bounds', *Econometrica*, **49**, 555–77.

Levich, R.M. (1978) 'Further results on the efficiency of markets for foreign exchange', in *Managed Exchange Rate Flexibility: the Recent Experience*, Boston: Federal Bank of Boston Conference Series.

Levich, R.M. (1985) 'Empirical studies of exchange rates: price behaviour, rate determination and market efficiency', in R.W. Jones and P.B. Kenen (eds), *Handbook of International Economics*, **2**, Amsterdam: North-Holland, 979–1040.

Lewis, K.K. (1988) 'The persistence of the "peso problem" when policy is noisy', *Journal of International Money and Finance*, **7**, 5–21.

Lindsey, L.B. (1987a) 'Capital gains rates, realizations and revenues', in M. Feldstein (ed.), *The Effects of Taxation on Capital Accumulation*, for National Bereau of Economic Research, Chicago: Chicago University Press.

Lindsey, L.B. (1987b) 'Individual taxpayer response to tax cuts, 1982–4; with implications for the revenue maximising tax rates', *Journal of Public Economics*, **33**, 173–206.

Lipsey, R.G. (1960) 'The relation between unemployment and the rate of change of money wage rates in the united Kingdom 1862–1957: A further analysis', *Economica*, NS, **27**, 1–31.

Litterman, R.B. (1986) 'Forecasting with Bayesian vector autoregressions — five years' experience', *Journal of Business and Economic Statistics*, **4**, 25–38.

Lo, Andrew W. (1991) 'Long-term memory in stock market prices', *Econometrica, **59***(5), 1279–313

Long, J.B. and Plosser, C.I. (1983) 'Real business cycles', *Journal of*

Political Economy, **91**, 39–69.

Loughran, T., and J. Ritter, 2000, 'Uniformly Least Powerful Tests of Market Efficiency,' *Journal of Financial Economics*, **55**(3), 361–89.

Lucas, R.E. Jr (1972a) 'Econometric testing of the natural rate hypothesis', in O. Eckstein (ed.), *Econometrics of Price Determination Conference*, Washington, DC: Board of Governors, Federal Reserve System.

Lucas, R.E. Jr (1972b) 'Expectations and the neutrality of money', *Journal of Economic Theory*, **4**, 103–24.

Lucas, R.E. Jr (1973) 'Some international evidence on output-inflation trade-offs', *American Economic Review*, **68**, 326–34.

Lucas, R.E. Jr (1975) 'An equilibrium model of the business cycle', *Journal of Political Economy*, **83**, 1113–44.

Lucas, R.E. Jr (1976) 'Econometric policy evaluation : A critique', in K. Brunner and A.H. Meltzer (eds), *The Phillips Curve and Labour Markets*, Carnegie Rochester Conference Series on Public Policy No. 1, Supplement to the Journal of Monetary Economics.

Lucas, R.E. Jr (1978) 'Asset prices in an exchange economy', *Econometrica*, **46**, 1426–45.

Lucas, R.E. Jr (1980) 'Equilibrium in a pure currency economy', *Economic Inquiry*, **18**, 203–20.

Lucas, R.E. Jr (1988) 'On the mechanics of economic development', *Journal of Monetary Economics*, **22** (July), 3–42.

Lucas, R.E. Jr and Rapping, L.A. (1969) 'Real wages, employment and inflation', *Journal of Political Economy*, **77**, 721–54.

Lucas, R.E. Jr and Sargent, T.J. (1978) 'After Keynesian macroeconomics', in *After the Phillips Curve: Persistence of High Inflation and High Unemployment*, Minneapolis: Federal Reserve Bank of Minneapolis Quarterly Review, **3**(1).

Lucas, R.E. (Jr.) and Stokey, N.L. (1983) 'Optimal fiscal and monetary policy in an economy without capital', *Journal of Monetary Economics*, **12**, 55–93

Macdonald, R. (1988) *Floating Exchange Rates — Theories and Evidence*, London: Unwin Hyman.

Macrae, D.C. (1977) 'A political model of the business cycle', *Journal of Political Economy*, **85**, 239–63.

Mandelbrot, B. (1963a) 'New Methods in Statistical Economics', *Journal of Political Economy*, **71**, 421–40.

Mandelbrot, B. (1963b) 'The Variation of Certain Speculative Prices', *Journal of Business*, **40**, 394–419.

Mansfield, E. (1968) *The economics of technological change*, New York: W.W. Norton.

Maravall, A. (1983) 'An Application of Nonlinear Time Series Forecasting', *Journal of Business and Economic Statistics*, **3**, 350–5.

Marcet, A. and Sargent, T.J. (1989a) 'Convergence of Least-Squares Learning in Environments with Hidden State Variables and Private Information', *Journal of Political Economy*, **97**, 1306–322.

Marcet, A. and Sargent, T.J. (1989b) 'Convergence of Least-Squares Learning Mechanisms in Self-Referential Linear Stochastic Models', *Journal of Economic Theory*, **48**, 337–68.

Marini, G. (1985) 'Intertemporal substitution and the role of monetary policy', *Economic Journal*, **95**, 87–100.

Marini, G. (1986) 'Employment fluctuations and demand management', *Economica*, **53**, 209–18.

Markowitz, H. (1959) *Portfolio Selection: Efficient Diversification of Investment*, New York: John Wiley.

Marmol, F. (1998) 'Spurious regression theory with nonstationary fractionally integrated processes', *Journal of Econometrics*, **84**, 233–50

Marsh, T.and Merton, R. (1986) 'Dividend Variability and Variance Bounds Tests For The Rationality of Stock Market Prices', *American Economic Review*, **76**, 483–98.

Marshall, A. (1987) 'Minutes of evidence taken before the Royal Commission on Gold and Silver, Forty Third Day (19th Dec, 1887)', in *Final Report of the Royal Commission on Gold and Silver*, London: HMSO, pp.1–53.

Matthews, K.G.P., Blackman, S. and Minford, A.P.L. (1994a) 'An Algorithm for the Solution of Non-Linear Forward Rational Expectations Models with Current Partial Information', *Economic Modelling*, **11**(3), July, 351–358

Matthews, K.G.P., Blackman, S. and Minford, A.P.L. (1994b) 'The Quarterly Liverpool Model with Current Partial Information: An Exercise in Forecasting', *Journal of Forecasting*, **13**, 507–18.

Matthews, K.G.P. and Marwaha, S. (1981) 'Ratexp Mk 2', Mimeo, University of Liverpool.

McCallum, B.T. (1976) 'Rational expectations and the natural rate hypothesis: some consistent estimates', *Econometrica*, **44**, 43–52.

McCallum, B.T. (1978) 'Dating discounts and the robustness of the Lucas-Sargent proposition', *Journal of Monetary Economics*, **4**, 121–29.

McCallum, B.T. (1979) 'On the observational inequivalence of classical and Keynesian models', *Journal of Political Economy*, **87**, 395–402.

McCallum, B.T. (1983) 'On non-uniqueness in rational expectations models: An attempt at perspective', *Journal of Monetary Economics*, **11**, 139–68.

McCallum, B.T. (1984) 'Are bond-financed deficits inflationary? A Ricardian analysis', *Journal of Political Economy*, **92**, 123–35.

McCallum, B.T. (1994) 'A Reconsideration of the Uncovered Interest Parity Relationship', *Journal of Monetary Economics*, **33**, 105–32.

McCallum, B.T. (1995) 'Two fallacies concerning central bank independence', *American Economic Review*, **85**, 207–11.

McCallum, B.T. and Whittaker, J.K. (1979) 'The effectiveness of fiscal feedback rules and automatic stabilisers under rational expectations', *Journal of Monetary Economics*, **5**, 171–86.

McNees, S.K. (1986) 'Forecasting accuracy of alternative techniques: a comparison of U.S. macroeconomic forecasts', *Journal of Business and Economic Statistics*, **1**, 3–24.

Mehra, R.and Prescott, E.C. (1985) 'The Equity Premium:A Puzzle', *Journal of Monetary Economics*, **15**, 145–61.

Meiselman, D. (1962) *The Term Structure of Interest Rates*, Englewood Cliffs, NJ: Prentice-Hall.

Meltzer, A.H. and Richard, S.F. (1981) 'A rational theory of the size of government', *Journal of Political Economy*, **89**, 914–27.

Meltzer, A.H. and Richard, S.F. (1983) 'Tests of a rational theory of the size of government', *Public Choice*, **41**, 403–18.

Metzler, L.A. (1951) 'Wealth saving and the rate of interest', *Journal of Political Economy*, **59**, 93–116.

Menger, Carl (1892) 'On the origin of money', *Economic Journal*, **2**, 239–255.

Meulbroek, L., 1992, 'An Empirical Analysis of Illegal Insider Trading,' *Journal of Finance*, **47(5)**, 1661–99.

Michael, P., Nobay, A.R. and Peel, D.A. (1997) 'Transactions Costs and Nonlinear Adjustment in real exchange Rates: An Empirical Investigation', *Journal of Political Economy*, **105**, 862–79.

Mills, T.C. (1993) *The Econometric Modelling of Financial Time Series*, Cambridge: Cambridge University Press.

Minford, A.P.L (1978) *Substitution effects, speculation and Exchange Rate Stability*, Studies in International Economics no. 3, Amsterdam: North-Holland.

Minford, A.P.L. (1980) 'A rational expectations model of the United Kingdom under fixed and floating exchange rates', in K. Brunner and A.H. Meltzer (eds) *On the State of Macroeconomics*, Carnegie Rochester Conference Series on Public Policy, **12**, Supplement to the Journal of Monetary Economics.

Minford, A.P.L. (1981) 'The exchange rate and monetary policy', *Oxford Economic Papers*, **33 (supplement)**, 120–42.

Minford, A.P.L. (1983) 'Labour market equilibrium in an open economy', *Oxford Economic Papers*, **35 (supplement)**, 207–44.

Minford, A.P.L. (1986) 'Rational expectations and monetary policy', *Scottish Journal of Political Economy*, **33**, 317–33.

Minford, A.P.L. (1988) 'Interest rates and bond financed deficits in a Ricardian two-party democracy', *Weltwirtschaftliches Archiv*, **124**, 387–402.

Minford, A.P.L. (1995) 'Time-inconsistency, democracy and optimal contingent rules', *Oxford Economic Papers*, **47**, 195–210.

Minford, A.P.L. and Ashton, P. (1991) 'The poverty trap and the Laffer Curve — what can the GHS tell us?' *Oxford Economic Papers*, **43**, 245–79.

Minford, A.P.L., Perugini, F. and Srinivasan, N.K. (2002) 'Are interest-rate regressions evidence for a Taylor Rule?' *Economics Letters*, **76**, June 145–50.

Minford, A.P.L. and Brech, M. (1981) 'The wage equation and rational expectations', in D. Currie, A.R. Nobay and D.A. Peel (eds), *Macroeconomic Analysis*, London: Croom Helm.

Minford, A.P.L., Ashton, P.A., Davies, D.H., Peel, M.J. and Sprague, A. (1985) *Unemployment: Cause and Cure*, 2nd edn (1st edn, 1983, with Davies, Peel and Sprague. Oxford: Martin Robertson). Oxford: Basil Blackwell.

Minford, A.P.L. and Hilliard, G.W. (1977) 'The costs of variable inflation', in M.J. Artis and A. R. Nobay (eds), *Contemporary Economic Analysis*, **1**, London: Croom Helm.

Minford, A.P.L., Ioannidis, C.E. and Marwaha, S. (1983b) 'Dynamic predictive tests of a model under adaptive and rational expectations', *Economics Letters*, **11**, 115–21.

Minford, A.P.L., Brech, M. and Matthews, K.G.P., (1980) 'A rational expectations model of the UK under floating exchange rates', *European Economic Review*, **14**, 189–219.

Minford, A.P.L., Ioannidis, C.E. and Marwaha, S., (1983a) 'Rational expectations in a multilateral macro model', in P. de Grauwe and T. Peeters (eds), *Exchange Rates in Multi-Country Econometric Models*, London: Macmillan, 239–66.

Minford, A.P.L., Matthews, K.G.P. and Marwaha, S. (1979) 'Terminal conditions as a means of ensuring unique solutions for rational expectations models with forward expectations', *Economics Letters*, **4**, 117–20.

Minford, A.P.L., Matthews, K.G.P. and Rastogi, A. (1990) 'A quarterly version of the Liverpool model of the UK', working paper no. 90/06, Liverpool Research Group in Macroeconomics, University of Liverpool.

Minford, A.P.L. and Peel, D.A. (1979) 'The classical supply hypothesis and the observational equivalence of classical and Keynesian models', *Economics Letters*, **4**, 229–33.

Minford A.P.L. and Peel, D.A. (1980) 'The natural rate hypothesis and rational expectations — a critique of some recent developments', *Oxford Economic Papers*, 32, 71–81.

Minford, A.P.L. and Peel, D.A. (1981) 'On the role of monetary stabilisation policy under rational expectations', *Manchester School*, **69**, 39–50.

Minford, A.P.L. and Peel, D.A. (1982a) 'The political theory of the business cycle', *European Economic Review*, **17**, 253–70.

Minford, A.P.L. and Peel, D.A. (1982b) 'The Phillips curve and rational expectations', *Weltwirtschaftliches Archiv*, **118**, 456–78.

Minford, A.P.L. and Peel, D.A. (1983) 'Some implications of partial current information sets in macroeconomic models embodying rational expectations', *Manchester School*, **51**, 235–49.

Minford, A.P.L. and Peel, D.A. (1984) 'Testing for unbiasedness and efficiency under incomplete current information', *Bulletin of Economic Research*, **36**, 1–7.

Minford, A.P.L. and Webb, B.D. (2001) 'Estimating large-scale rational expectations models by FIML — a new algorithm with bootstrap confidence limits', Mimeo, Cardiff University.

Minford, A.P.L., Nowell, E. and Webb, B.D. (1999) 'Nominal contracts and monetary targets — drifting into indexation', CEPR discussion paper no. 2215, Centre for Economic Policy Research, London, revised August 2001, Mimeo Cardiff University, forthcoming *Economic Journal*.

Minford, A.P.L., Nowell, E., Meenagh, D., and Webb, B.D. (2001) 'Optimal monetary policy with endogenous contracts: is there a case for price-level targeting?' mimeo, Cardiff University.

Mishkin, F.S. (1978a) 'Efficient markets theory: implications for monetary policy', *Brookings Papers on Economic Activity*, **3**, 707–52.

Mishkin, F.S. (1978b) 'Simulation methodology in macroeconomics: An innovation technique', *Journal of Political Economy*, **87**, 816–36.

Mishkin, F.S. (1981) 'The real interest rates: an empirical investigation', in K. Brunner and A.H. Meltzer (eds), *The Costs and Consequences of Inflation*, Carnegie Rochester Conference Series on Public Policy **15**, Supplement to the Journal of Monetary Economics.

Mishkin, F.S. (1982) 'Does anticipated monetary policy matter: an empirical investigation', *Journal of Political Economy*, **99**, 22–51.

Mishkin, F.S.and Posen, A.S. (1997) 'Inflation targeting: lessons from four countries', National Bureau of Economic Research, Working Paper

6126.

Modigliani, F. and Grunberg, E. (1954) 'The predictability of social events', *Journal of Political Economy*, **62**, 465–78.

Modigliani, F. and Sutch R. (1966) 'Innovations in interest rate policy', *American Economic Review, Papers and Proceedings*, **56**, 178–97.

Motto, R., and Wickens, M.R. (2000) 'Estimating shocks and impulse response functions', Mimeo, University of York.

Mueller, D.C. (1979) *Public Choice. New York: Cambridge University Press.* , R.A. (1960) 'The monetary dynamics of international adjustment under fixed and flexible exchnage rates', *Quarterly Journal of Economics*, **74**, 227–57.

Mussa, M.H. (1979) 'Empirical regularities in the behaviour of exchange rates and theories of the foreign exchange market', *Carnegie Rochester Conference Series on Public Policy*, **11**, 9–57.

Mussa, M.H. (1981) 'Sticky individual prices and the dynamics of the general price level', *Carnegie Rochester Conference Series on Public Policy*, **15**, 261–96.

Muth, J.F. (1960) 'Optimal properties of exponentially weighted forecasts', *Journal of the American Statistical Association*, **55**, 299–306.

Muth, J.F. (1961) 'Rational expectations and the theory of price movements', *Econometrica*, **29**, 315–35.

Neely, C., Weller, P. and Dittmar, R. (1997) 'Is technical analysis in the foreign exchange market profitable? A genetic programming approach', Mimeo, Research Department, Federal Reserve Bank of St. Louis.

Nelson, C.R. and Plosser, C.I. (1982) 'Trends and random walks in macroeconomic time series: some evidence and implications', *Journal of Monetary Economics*, **10**, 139–62.

Nelson, C.R. and Schwert, G.W. (1977) 'Short-term interest rates as predictors of inflation: on testing the hypothesis that the real interest rate is constant', *American Economic Review*, **67**, 478–86.

Nerlove, M. (1958) 'Adaptive expectations and cobweb phenomena', *Quarterly Journal of Economics*, **72**, 227–40.

Nickell, S.J. (1979) 'The effect of unemployment and related benefits on the duration of unemployeemnet', *Economic Journal*, **89**, 39–49.

Nobay, A.R. and Peel, D.A. (2000) 'Optimal monetary policy in a model of asymmetric central bankers preference', Mimeo London School of Economics

Nolan, C. and Schaling, E. (1996) 'Monetary Policy Uncertainty and Central Bank Accountability', Bank Of England Working Paper, No.54, October.

Nordhaus, W.D. (1975) 'The political business cycle', *Review of Economic Studies*, **42**, 169–90.

North, D.C. (1981) *Structure and change in economic history*, New York: W.W. Norton.

Obstfeld, M., and Rogoff, K. (1996) *Foundations of International Macroeconomics*, Cambridge MA: MIT Press.

O'Connell, P.G.J. (1998) 'Market frictions and real Exchange rates', *Journal of International Money and Finance*, **17**, 71–95.

OECD (1996) *Economic Outlook*, OECD, Paris.

Olson, M. (1965) *The Logic of Collective Action*, Cambridge, MA: Harvard University Press.

Olson, M. (1982) *The Rise and Decline of Nations: Economic Growth, Stagflation, and Social Rigidities*, Newhaven, CT: Yale University Press.

Pagan, A.R. (1988) 'A Note on the Magnitude of Risk Premia', *Journal Of International Money and Finance*, **7**, 109–10.

Parente, S.L. and E.C. Prescott (1999) 'Monopoly rights: a barrier to riches', *American Economic Review*, **89** (December), 1216–33.

Parkin, J.M. (1978) 'A comparison of alternative techniques of monetary control under rational expectations', *Manchester School*, **46**, 252–87.

Parkin, M. (1986) 'The output inflation trade-off when prices are costly to change', *Journal of Political Economy*, **94**, 200–24.

Parkin, M. and Bade, R. (1988) *Modern Macroeconomics*, 2nd edn (1st edn 1982), Oxford: Philip Allan.

Patinkin, D. (1965) *Money, Interest and Prices*, 2nd edn, New York: Harper and Row.

Peel, D.A. (1981) 'Non-uniqueness and the role of the monetary authorities', *Economics Letters*, **4**, 117–20.

Peel, D.A. and Chappell, D. (1986) 'On Stylyzed Learning and Hyper-Inflations', *Metroeconomica*, **38**, 205–12.

Peel, D. and Davidson, J. (1998) 'A nonlinear error correction mechanism based on the bilinear model', *Economics Letters*, **58**(2), 165–70.

Peel, D.A. and Speight, A. (1997) 'Nonlinearities in East European Black Market Exchange Rates', *International Journal of Finance and Economics*, **2**, 39–57

Peel. D.A. and Speight, A.H. (1998) 'Modelling business cycle nonlinearity in conditional mean and conditional variance: some international evidence', *Economica*, **65**, 211–246

Peel. D.A. and Taylor, M.P. (2002) 'Covered interest rate arbitrage in the inter-war period and the Keynes-Einzig Conjecture', forthcoming, *Journal of Money, Credit and Banking, 34, 51–75.*

Persson, T. and Svensson, L. (1987) 'Checks and balances on the government budget', Mimeo, Institute of International Studies, Stockholm.

Persson, T.and Tabellini, G. (1990) *Macroeconomic Policy, Credibility and Politics*, New York: Harwood Academic Publishers.

Pesando, J.E. (1978) 'On the efficiency on the bond market: some Canadian evidence', *Journal of Political Economy*, **86**, 1057–76.

Pesaran, M.H. (1992) 'A Simple Nonparametric Test of Predictive Performance', *Journal of Business and Economic Statistics*, **10**, 461–65.

Pesaran, M.H. and Potter S. (eds.) (1992) 'Nonlinear Dynamics and Econometrics', *Journal of Applied Econometrics*, **1**, S1–S195.

Pesaran, M.H. and Timmermann, A. (1994) 'Forecasting Stock Return, An Examination of Stock Market Trading in the Presence of Transactions Costs', *Journal of Forecasting*, **13**, 330–65.

Pesaran, M.H.and Timmermann, A. (1995) 'The Robustness and Economic Significance of Predictability of Stock Returns', *Journal of Finance*, **50**, 1201–28.

Pesaran, M.H.and Timmermann, A. (2000) 'Recursive Modelling Approach to Predicting U.K. Stock Returns', *Economic Journal*, **110**, 159–191.

Phelps, E.S. (1970) 'The new microeconomics in employment and inflation theory', in E.S. Phelps et al. (eds) *Microeconomic Foundations of Employment and Inflation Theory*, New York: Norton, 1–27.

Phelps, E.S. and Taylor, J.B. (1977) 'The stabilizing powers of monetary policy under rational expectations', *Journal of Political Economy*, **85**, 163–90.

Phillips, A.W. (1958) 'The relation between unemployment and the rate of change in money wage rates in the UK, 1861–1957', *Economica*, **25**, 283–99.

Phillips, P.C.B. (1987) 'Time Series Regression with a Unit Root', *Econometrica*, **55**, 277–301.

Phillips, P.C.B. and Perron, P (1988) 'Testing for a Unit Root in Time Series Regression (with Pierre Perron), *Biometrika*, **75**, 335–346.

Pissarides, C. (1980) 'British Government Popularity and Economic Performance', *Economic Journal*, **90**, 569–81.

Poole, W. (l970) 'The optimal choice of monetary instrument in a simple stochastic macro model', *Quarterly Journal of Economics*, **84**, 197–221.

Pope, P., R. Morris, and D. Peel, 1990, 'Insider Trading: Some Evidence on Market Efficiency and Directors' Share Dealings in Great Britain', *Journal of Business Finance and Accounting*, **17**(3), 359–80.

Popper, K.R. (1945, 1966) *The Open Society and Its enemies*, London: Routledge and Kegan Paul, (5th edn 1966; 1st edn 1945).

Popper, K.R. (1988) 'The Open Society and Its Enemies revisited', *The Economist*, 23 April, 25–8.

Pratt, J.W. (1964) 'Risk aversion in the small and in the large', *Econometrica*, **32**, 122–36.

Priestley, M.B. (1988) *Non-linear and Non-Stationary Time Series Analysis*, Academic Press, Harcourt Brace Jovanovich.

Quah, D. (1993) 'Galton's Fallacy and Tests of the Convergence Hypothesis', *Scandinavian Journal of Economics*, December (reprinted in T.M. Andersen and K.O. Moene (eds.), *Endogenous Growth*, Blackwell, 1993.)

Ramsey, F.P. (1927) 'A contribution to the theory of taxation', *Economic Journal*, **37**, March.

Rietz, T. (1988) 'The Equity Premium Puzzle:A Solution?', *Journal of Monetary Economics*, **21**, 117–32.

Robinson, J.V. (1937) *Essays on the Theory of Employment*, London: Macmillan.

Rogoff, K. (1985) 'The optimal commitment to an intermediate monetary target', *Quarterly Journal of Economics*, **100**, 1169–89.

Rogoff, K. and Sibert, A. (1988) 'Equilibrium political business cycles', *Review of Economic Studies*, **55**, 1–16.

Romer, D. (1993) 'Rational Asset-Price Movements Without News', *American Economic Review*, **83**, 1112–30.

Romer, D.H and C.D. Romer (1997) 'Institutions for monetary stability', in Romer and Romer (eds) *Reducing Inflation: motivation and strategy*, Chicago: Chicago University Press for National Bureau of Economic Research.

Romer, D.H. (1996) *Advanced Macroeconomics*, 1st edn, Ney York: McGraw-Hill.

Romer, P.M. (1986) 'Increasing returns and long run growth', *Journal of Political Economy*, **94** (October), 1002–37.

Romer, P.M. (1990) 'Endogenous technological change', *Journal of Political Economy*, **98** (October) (part 2), S71–102.

Ross, S.A. (1976) 'The arbitrage theory of capital asset pricing', *Journal of Economic Theory*, **8**, 343–62.

Rotemberg, J. (1983) 'Aggregate consequences of fixed costs of changing prices', *American Economic Review*, **73**, 433–36.

Rotemberg, J. and M. Woodford (1998) 'Interest rate rules in a an estimated sticky price model', Mimeo, Princeton University.

Rotemberg, J. J., and Woodford, M. (1999) 'Interest-rate rules in an estimated sticky price model', in J.B. Taylor (ed) *Monetary Policy Rules*, NBER and Chicago University Press, 57–119.

Saidi, N.H. (1980) 'Fluctuating exchange rates and the international transmission of economic disturbances', *Journal of Money Credit and Banking*, **12**, 575–91.

Salge, M. (1997) Rational Bubbles : *Theoretical Basis, Economic Relevance, and Empirical Evidence With a Special Emphasis on the German Stock Market (Lecture Notes In)*, New York: Springer

Samuelson, P.A. (1958) 'An exact consumption-loan model of interest with or without the social contrivance of money', *Journal of Political Economy*, **66**, 467–82.

Sargan, J.D. (1964) 'Wages and Prices in the United Kingdom: A Study in Econometric Methodology', in Hart, P.E., Mills, G. and Whitaker, J.K. (eds), *Econometric Analysis for National Economic Planning*, **16 of Colston Papers**, London: Butterworth, pp.25–63.

Sargent, T.J. (1972) 'Rational expectations and the term structure of interest rates', *Journal of Money Credit and Banking*, **4**, 74–97.

Sargent, T.J. (1976a) 'A classical macroeconomic model of the United States', *Journal of Political Economy*, **84**, 207–38.

Sargent, T.J. (1976b) 'The observational equivalence of natural and unnatural rate theories of macroeconomics', *Journal of Political Economy*, **84**, 631–40.

Sargent, T.J. (1978) 'Estimation of dynamic labour demand schedules under rational expectations', *Journal of Political Economy*, **86**, 1009–44.

Sargent, T.J. (1979a) *Macroeconomic Theory*, New York: Academic Press.

Sargent, T.J. (1979b) 'A note on the maximum likelihood estimation of the rational expectations model of the term structure', *Journal of Monetary Economics*, **5**, 133–43.

Sargent, T.J. (1981) 'Interpreting economic time series', *Journal of Political Economy*, **89**, 213–48.

Sargent, T.J. (1987) *Dynamic Macroeconomic Theory*, New York: Academic Press.

Sargent, T, J. (1993) *Bounded Rationality in Macroeconomics*, Oxford: Clarendon Press.

Sargent, T.J. (1999) *The Conquest of American Inflation*, Princeton NJ: Princeton University Press.

Sargent, T.J. and Wallace, N. (1973) 'RAtional expectations and the dynamics of hyper inflation', *International Economic Review*, **14**, 328–358.

Sargent, T.J. and Wallace, N. (1975) 'Rational expectations, the optimal monetary instrument and the optimal money supply rule', *Journal of Political Economy*, **83**, 241–54.

Sargent, T.J. and Wallace, N. (1981) 'Some unpleasant monetary arithmetic', *Quarterly Review*, Federal Reserve Bank of Minneapolis, Fall, 1–17.

Sauer, R.D. (1998) 'The Economics of Wagering Markets', *Journal of Economic Literature*, **36**, 2021–64.

Schaling, E., Hoeberichts, M.and Eijffinger, S. (1998) 'Incentive Contracts for Central Bankers under Uncertainty: Walsh-Svensson non-Equivalence Revisited', *Center for Economic Research*, Tilburg.

Seater, J.J. (1982) 'Are future taxes discounted?', *Journal of Money*, Credit and Banking, **14**, 376–89.

Selgin, G. (1997) 'Network effects, adaptive learning, and the transition to fiat money', manuscript, University of Georgia.

Seyhun, H., 1986, 'Insiders' Profits, Costs of Trading and Market Efficiency', *Journal of Financial Economics*, **16**, 189–212.

Seyhun, N., 1992, 'Why Does Aggregate Insider Trading Predict Future Stock Returns?', *Quarterly Journal of Economics*, **107**, 1303–31.

Shackle, G.L.S. (1958) *Time in Economics*, Amsterdam: North-Holland.

Shiller, R. J. (1973) 'Rational expectations and the term structure of interest rates', *Journal of Money*, Credit and Banking, **3**, 856–60.

Shiller, R.J. (1978) 'Rational expectations and the dynamic structure of macroeconomic models — a critical review', *Journal of Monetary Economics*, **4**, 1–44.

Shiller, R.J. (1979) 'The volatility of long-term interest rates and expectations models of the term structure', *Journal of Political Economy*, **87**, 1190–219.

Shiller, R. (1981) 'Do stock prices move to much to be justified by subsequent changes in vividends?', *American Economic Review*, **71**, 421–36.

Shiller, R.J. (1981(b)) 'The Use of Volatility Measures in assessing Market Efficiency', *Journal of Finance*, **36**, 291–304.

Shiller, R.J. (1984) 'Stock Prices and Social Dynamics', *Brookings Papers on Economic Activity*, **2**, 457–98.

Shiller, R. (1989) *Market Volatility*, Cambride MA: MIT Press.

Shiller, R. (1997) 'Human Behaviour and the Efficiency of the Financial System' in J.B.Taylor and M.Woodford (eds), *Handbook of Macroeconomics*, Amsterdam: North-Holland.

Shleifer, A. and Vishny, R.W. (1997) 'The Limits of Arbitrage', *Journal of Finance*, **52**, 35–55.

Sibert, A. (1989) 'The Risk Premium in the Foreign Exchange Market', *Journal of Money Credit and Banking*, **21**, 49–65.

Siegel, J.J. (1972) 'Risk, Interest Rates and Forward Exchange', *Quarterly Journal of Economics*, **86**, 303–09.

Sill, K. and Wrase, J. (1999) 'Exchange Rates, Monetary Policy Regimes and Beliefs', Mimeo, Federal Reserve of Philadelphia, Paper no.99–6.

Sims, C.A. (1980) 'Macroeconomics and Reality', *Econometrica*, **48**, 1–48.

Sims, C.A. (1992) 'Interpreting the macroeconomic time-series facts: the effects of monetary policy', *European Economic Review*, **36**, 975–1000.

Sims, C.A. (1994) 'A simple model for the study of the price level and the interaction of monetary and fiscal policy', *Economic Theory*, **4**, 381–99.

Stern, R.M., Francis, J., and Schumacher, B. (1976) *Price Elasticities in International Trade: An Annotated Bibliography*, London: Macmillan.

St. Paul, G. (1996) 'Exploring the political economy of labour market institutions', *Economic Policy*, **23**, 265–300.

Subba-Rau, T. (1981) 'On the theory of Bilinear Models', *Journal of the Royal Statistical Society*, Series B, **43**, 244–55.

Sugden, R. (1986) *The Economics of Rights, Co-operation and Welfare*, Oxford: Basil Blackwell.

Sullivan, R., Timmermann, A.and White, H. (1998) 'Dangers of Data-Driven Inference: The Case of Caender Effects in Stock Returns', University of California, San Diego Discussion Paper 98–16.

Svensson, L. E.O. (1997) 'Optimal inflation targets, "conservative" central banks, and linear inflation contracts', *American Economic Review*, **87**, 98–114.

Tabellini, G. (1987) 'Reputational constraints on monetary policy: a comment', *Carnegie Rochester Conference Series on Public Policy*, **26**, 183–90.

Taylor, J.B. (1977) 'Conditions for unique solutions to macroeconomic models with rational expectations', *Econometrica*, **45**, 1377–85.

Taylor, J.B. (1979a) 'Estimation and control of a macroeconomic model with rational expectations', *Econometrica*, **47**, 1267–86.

Taylor, J.B. (1979b) 'Staggered wage setting in a macroeconomic model', *American Economic Review*, Papers and Proceedings, **69**, 108–13.

Taylor, J.B. (1980) 'Aggregate dynamics and staggered contracts', *Journal of Political Economy*, **88**, 1–23.

Taylor, J.B. (1999) 'The robustness and efficiency of monetary policy rules as guidelines for interest rate setting by the European central bank', *Journal of Monetary Economics*, **43**, June, Special issue: Monetary Policy Rules, 655–79.

Taylor, M.P. (1987) 'Covered interest parity: a high frequency, high-quality data study', *Economica*, **54**, 429–38.

Taylor, M.P. (1989) 'Covered Interest Arbitrage and Market Turbulence', *Economic Journal*, **99**, 376–91.

Taylor, M.P. and Allen, H. (1992) 'The Use of Technical Analysisin the Foreign Exchange Market', *Journal of International Money and Banking*, 11, 304–14.

Taylor, M.P. and Peel, D. (2000) 'Nonlinear Adjustment, Long-Run Equilibrium and Exchange Rate Fundamentals', *Journal of International Money and Finance*, **19**, 33–53

Taylor, M.P, Peel, D.A. and Sarno, L. (2001) 'Nonlinear Mean-Reversion in Real Exchange Rates: Towards a Solution to the Purchasing Power Parity Puzzles', CEPR Discussion Paper, DP2658, London: Centre for Economic Policy Research, Forthcoming *International Economic Review.*

Taylor, S.J. (1982) 'Test of the random walk hypothesis against a price trend', *Journal of Financial and Qualitative Analysis*, **17**, 31–61.

Thaler, R.H. and Ziemba, W.T. (1988) 'Anomalies-Parimutuel Betting Markets: Racetracks and Lotteries', *Journal of Economic Perspectives*, **2**, 161–74.

Tighe, C. and Michener, R.(1994) 'The Political Economy of Insider-Trading Laws', *American Economic Review Papers and Proceedings*, 164–69.

Tirole, J. (1985) 'Asset Bubbles and Overlapping Generations', *Econometrica*, **53**, 1071–100.

Tirole, J. (1982) 'On the Possibility of Speculation Under Rational Expectations', *Econometrica*, **50**, 1163–81.

Tong, H. (1990) *Non-Linear Time Series: A Dynamical Systems Approach*, Oxford: Oxford University Press.

Timmermann, A. (2000) 'Moments of Markov Switching Models', *Journal of Econometrics*, **96**, 75–111.

Tong, H. (1990) *Non-Linear Time Series: A Dynamical Sytems Approach*, Oxford: Oxford University Press.

Townsend, R.M. (1978) 'Market Anticipations, Rational Expectations, and Bayesian Analysis', *International Economic Review*, **19**, 481–94.

Townsend, R. (1980) 'Models of money with spatially separated agents', in J.H. Kareken and N. Wallace (eds), *Models of monetary economies*, Federal Reserve Bank of Minneapolis, 265–304.

Tsay, W.-J. and Chung, C.F. (1996) 'The spurious regression of fractionally integrated processes', Michigan State University, Economics Working Paper (revised, April 1996).

Tullock, G. (1976) *The Vote Motive*, Hobart Paper no. 9, London: Institute of Economic Affairs.

Tullock, G., Seldon, A.and Brady, G.L. (2000) *Government: whose obedient servant? A primer in public choice*, London: Institute of Economic Affairs.

Turnovsky, S.J. (1970) 'Empirical evidence on the formation of price expectations', *Journal of the American Statistical Association*, **65**, 1441–54.

Turnovsky, S.J. (1980) 'The choice of monetary instrument under alternative forms of price expectations', *Manchester School*, **48**, 39–63.

Turnovsky, S.J, (1983) 'The determination of spot and futures prices with storable commodities', *Econometrica*, **51(5)**, 1363-87.

van Dijk, (2000) *Smooth Transition Models: Extensions and Outlier Robust Inference*, Tinbergen Institute Research Series, Erasmus University Rotterdam.

van Norden, S. (1996) 'Regime Switching as a Test for Exchange Rate Bubbles', *Journal of Applied Econometrics*, **11**, 219–51.

van Norden, S. and Vigfusson, R. (1988) 'Avoiding the Pitfalls: Can Regime-Switching Tests Reliably Detect Bubbles', Bank Of Canada, discussion paper.

Vickers, J. (1986) 'Signalling in a model of moentary policy with incomplete information', *Oxford Economic Papers*, **38**, 443–55.

Visco, I. (1984) *Price Expectations in Rising Inflation*, Contributions to Economic Analysis, **152**, Amsterdam: North-Holland.

Wallace, Neil (1980) 'The overlapping generations model of fiat money', in J.H.Kareken and N.Wallace, (eds), *Models of Monetary Economies*, Federal Reserve Bank of Minneapolis, Minneapolis, 49–82.

Waller, C.J. (1989) 'Monetary policy games and central bank politics', *Journal of Money Credit and Banking*, **21**, 422–31.

Wallis, K.F. (1980) 'Econometric implications of the rational expectations hypothesis', *Econometrica*, **48**, 49–72.

Wallis, K.F., Andrews, M.J., Bell, D.N.F., Fisher, P.G. and Whitley, J.D. (1985) 'Comparative model properties — section 2.4: terminal conditions in rational expectations models', chapter 2 in K.F. Wallis (ed.) *Models of the UK Economy*, Oxford: Oxford University Press, 57–66.

Walsh, C.E. (1995) 'Optimal contracts for central banks', *American Economic Review*, **85**, 150–167.

Walters, A.A. (1971) 'Consistent expectations, distributed lags and the quantity theory', *Economic Journal*, **81**, 273–81.

Weiss, L. (1980) 'The role for active monetary policy in a rational expectations model', *Journal of Political Economy*, **88**, 221–33.

West, K, D. (1987) 'A Specification Test For Speculative Bubbles', *Quarterly Journal of Economics*, **102**, 553–80.

West, K.D. (1986) 'Full versus limited information estimation of a rational expectations model', *Journal of Econometrics*, **33**, 367–85.

Wickens, M.R. (1982) 'The efficient estimation of econometric models with rational expectations', *Review of Economic Studies*, **49**, 55–67.

Wicksell, K. (1907) 'The influence of the rate of interest on prices', *Economic Journal*, **17**, 213–20.

Wilson, T. and Andrews, P.W.S. eds. (1951) *Oxford Studies in the Price Mechanism*, Oxford: Clarendon Press.

Woodford, M. (1995) 'Price level determinacy without control of a monetary aggregate', *Carnegie Rochester Conference Series on Public Policy*, **43**, 1–46.

Woodford, M. (1998) 'Optimal monetary policy inertia', Mimeo, Princeton NJ: Princeton University.

Yadav, P.K., Pope, P.F. and Paudyal, K. (1994) 'Threshold autoregressive modelling in Finance: the price difference of equivalent assets', *Mathematical Finance*, **4**, 205–221.

Index